I0888856

THE ANNOTATED LUTHER

Volume 3
Church and Sacraments

Additional Praise for *Church and Sacraments*

"The editors and the publisher of this volume are to be commended for making more accessible these key texts from Luther. The notes and updated translations are welcome additions. What comes through these writings is Luther's insistence that God is at work in and through the sacraments, the community of faith, the ordinary creatures, and the events of this created world. Luther emphasizes God's grace and expresses confidence in God's incarnate activity. Key to understanding God, they are also important sources of hope and a basis for our calling in today's world."

—**Darrell Jodock** | Professor Emeritus,
Gustavus Adolphus College

THE ANNOTATED LUTHER

Volume 3
Church and Sacraments

VOLUME EDITOR
Paul W. Robinson

GENERAL EDITORS
Hans J. Hillerbrand
Kirsi I. Stjerna
Timothy J. Wengert

Fortress Press
Minneapolis

THE ANNOTATED LUTHER, Volume 3
Church and Sacraments

Copyright © 2016 Fortress Press. All rights reserved. Except for brief quotations in critical articles and reviews, no part of this book may be reproduced in any manner without prior written permission from the publisher. Visit http://www.augsburgfortress.org/copyrights/contact.asp or write to Permissions, Augsburg Fortress, Box 1209, Minneapolis, MN 55440.

Unless otherwise noted, Scripture quotations are from New Revised Standard Version Bible, copyright © 1989 by the Division of Education of the National Council of Churches of Christ in the United States of America.

Fortress Press Publication Staff: Scott Tunseth, Project Editor; Alicia Ehlers, Production Manager; Laurie Ingram, Cover Design; Esther Diley, Permissions.

Copyeditor: David Lott
Series Design and Typesetting: Ann Delgehausen, Trio Bookworks
Proofreader: Paul Kobelski

Library of Congress Cataloging-in-Publication Data is available

ISBN: 978-1-4514-6271-5
eISBN: 978-1-4514-6509-9

The paper used in this publication meets the minimum requirements of American National Standard for Information Sciences—Permanence of Paper for Printed Library Materials, ANSI Z329, 48-1984.

Manufactured in the U.S.A.

Contents

Series Introduction

Engaging the Essential Luther

Even after five hundred years Martin Luther continues to engage and challenge each new generation of scholars and believers alike. With 2017 marking the five-hundredth anniversary of Luther's *95 Theses*, Luther's theology and legacy are being explored around the world with new questions and methods and by diverse voices. His thought invites ongoing examination, his writings are a staple in classrooms and pulpits, and he speaks to an expanding assortment of conversation partners who use different languages and hale from different geographical and social contexts.

The six volumes of The Annotated Luther edition offer a flexible tool for the global reader of Luther, making many of his most important writings available in the *lingua franca* of our times as one way of facilitating interest in the Wittenberg reformer. They feature new introductions, annotations, revised translations, and textual notes, as well as visual enhancements (illustrations, art, photos, maps, and timelines). The Annotated Luther edition embodies Luther's own cherished principles of communication. Theological writing, like preaching, needs to reflect human beings' lived experience, benefits from up-to-date scholarship, and should be easily accessible to all. These volumes are designed to help teachers and students, pastors and laypersons, and other professionals in ministry understand the context in which the documents were written, recognize how the documents have shaped Protestant and Lutheran thinking, and interpret the meaning of these documents for faith and life today.

The Rationale for This Edition

For any reader of Luther, the sheer number of his works presents a challenge. Well over one hundred volumes comprise the scholarly edition of Luther's works, the so-called Weimar Ausgabe (WA), a publishing enterprise begun in 1883 and only completed in the twenty-first century. From 1955 to 1986, fifty-five volumes came to make up *Luther's Works* (American Edition) (LW), to which Concordia Publishing House, St. Louis, is adding still more. This English-language contribution to Luther studies, matched by similar translation projects for Erasmus of Rotterdam and John Calvin, provides a theological and historical gold mine for those interested in studying Luther's thought. But even these volumes are not always easy to use and are hardly portable. Electronic forms have increased availability, but preserving Luther in book form and providing readers with manageable selections are also important goals.

Moreover, since the publication of the WA and the first fifty-five volumes of the LW, research on the Reformation in general and on Martin Luther in particular has broken new ground and evolved, as has knowledge regarding the languages in which Luther wrote. Up-to-date information from a variety of sources is brought together in The Annotated Luther, building on the work done by previous generations of scholars. The language and phrasing of the translations have also been updated to reflect modern English usage. While the WA and, in a derivative way, LW remain the central source for Luther scholarship, the present critical and annotated English translation facilitates research internationally and invites a new generation of readers for whom Latin and German might prove an unsurpassable obstacle to accessing Luther. The WA provides the basic Luther texts (with some exceptions); the LW provides the basis for almost all translations.

Defining the "Essential Luther"

Deciding which works to include in this collection was not easy. Criteria included giving attention to Luther's initial key works; considering which publications had the most impact in his day and later; and taking account of Luther's own favorites, texts addressing specific issues of continued importance for today, and Luther's exegetical works. Taken as a whole, these works present the many sides of Luther, as reformer, pastor, biblical interpreter, and theologian. To serve today's readers and by using categories similar to those found in volumes 31–47 of Luther's works (published by Fortress Press), the volumes offer in the main a thematic rather than strictly chronological approach to Luther's writings. The volumes in the series include:

Volume 1: *The Roots of Reform* (Timothy J. Wengert, editor)
Volume 2: *Word and Faith* (Kirsi I. Stjerna, editor)
Volume 3: *Church and Sacraments* (Paul W. Robinson, editor)
Volume 4: *Pastoral Writings* (Mary Jane Haemig, editor)
Volume 5: *Christian Life in the World* (Hans J. Hillerbrand, editor)
Volume 6: *The Interpretation of Scripture* (Euan K. Cameron, editor)

The History of the Project

In 2011 Fortress Press convened an advisory board to explore the promise and parameters of a new English edition of Luther's essential works. Board members Denis Janz, Robert Kolb, Peter Matheson, Christine Helmer, and Kirsi Stjerna deliberated with

Fortress Press publisher Will Bergkamp to develop a concept and identify contributors. After a review with scholars in the field, college and seminary professors, and pastors, it was concluded that a single-language edition was more desirable than dual-language volumes.

In August 2012, Hans Hillerbrand, Kirsi Stjerna, and Timothy Wengert were appointed as general editors of the series with Scott Tunseth from Fortress Press as the project editor. The general editors were tasked with determining the contents of the volumes and developing the working principles of the series. They also helped with the identification and recruitment of additional volume editors, who in turn worked with the general editors to identify volume contributors. Mastery of the languages and unique knowledge of the subject matter were key factors in identifying contributors. Most contributors are North American scholars and native English speakers, but The Annotated Luther includes among its contributors a circle of international scholars. Likewise, the series is offered for a global network of teachers and students in seminary, university, and college classes, as well as pastors, lay teachers, and adult students in congregations seeking background and depth in Lutheran theology, biblical interpretation, and Reformation history.

Editorial Principles

The volume editors and contributors have, with few exceptions, used the translations of LW as the basis of their work, retranslating from the WA for the sake of clarity and contemporary usage. Where the LW translations have been substantively altered, explanatory notes have often been provided. More importantly, contributors have provided marginal notes to help readers understand theological and historical references. Introductions have been expanded and sharpened to reflect the very latest historical and theological research. In citing the Bible, care has been taken to reflect the German and Latin texts commonly used in the sixteenth century rather than modern editions, which often employ textual sources that were unavailable to Luther and his contemporaries.

Finally, all pieces in The Annotated Luther have been revised in the light of modern principles of inclusive language. This is not always an easy task with a historical author, but an intentional effort has been made to revise language throughout, with creativity and editorial liberties, to allow Luther's theology to speak free from unnecessary and unintended gender-exclusive language. This important principle provides an opportunity to translate accurately certain gender-neutral German and Latin expressions that Luther employed—for example, the Latin word *homo* and the German *Mensch* mean "human being," not simply "males." Using the words *man* and *men* to translate such terms would create an ambiguity not present in the original texts. The focus is on linguistic accuracy and Luther's intent. Regarding creedal formulations and trinitarian language, Luther's own expressions have been preserved, without entering the complex and important contemporary debates over language for God and the Trinity.

The 2017 anniversary of the publication of the *95 Theses* is providing an opportunity to assess the substance of Luther's role and influence in the Protestant Reformation. Revisiting Luther's essential writings not only allows reassessment of Luther's rationale and goals but also provides a new look at what Martin Luther was about and why new generations would still wish to engage him. We hope these six volumes offer a compelling invitation.

Hans J. Hillerbrand
Kirsi I. Stjerna
Timothy J. Wengert
General Editors

Abbreviations

ANF	Ante-Nicene Fathers
ASD	*Desiderii Erasmi Roterodami Opera omnia* (Amsterdam: North Holland, 1969–)
BC	*The Book of Concord*, ed. Robert Kolb and Timothy J. Wengert (Minneapolis: Fortress Press, 2000)
BCorr	*Correspondance de Martin Bucer*, Martini Buceri Opera omnia. Series 3, ed. Jean Rott et al. (Leiden: Brill, 1979–)
BDS	*Martin Bucers Deutsche Schriften*, Opera omnia. Series 1, ed. Robert Stupperich et al. (Gütersloh: Gütersloher Verlagshaus G. Mohn, 1960–)
CA	*The Augsburg Confession*
CCSL	*Corpus Christianorum Series Latina*
CH	*The Church History of Rufinus of Aquileia: Books 10 and 11*, trans. Philip R. Amidon (New York: Oxford University Press, 1997)
CIC	*Corpus Iuris Canonici*, ed. Emil Louis Richter and Emil Friedberg, 2 vols. (Graz: Akademische Druck- u. Verlagsanstalt, 1959)
CR	*Corpus Reformatorum*
CS	Schwenckfeld, Caspar. *Corpus Schwenckfeldianorum*, ed. Chester David Hartranft et al., 19 vols. (Leipzig: Breitkopf and Härtel, 1907–1961)
CSEL	*Corpus Scriptorum Ecclesiasticorum Latinorum*
DRTA. JR	*Deutsche Reichstagsakten unter Kaiser Karl V*, ed. Historische Kommission bei der Bayerischen Akademie der Wissenschaften (Gotha, 1893–).
ELW	*Evangelical Lutheran Worship* (Minneapolis: Augsburg Fortress, 2006).
GCS	*Die Griechischen Christlichen Schriftsteller der Ersten drei Jahrhunderte* (Berlin: Akademie Verlag, 1897–)
HZW	*Huldrych Zwingli: Writings*, ed. E. J. Furcha and H. Wayne Pipkin, 2 vols. (Allison Park, PA: Pickwick Publications, 1984)
LC	*The Large Catechism*
LSB	*Lutheran Service Book* (St. Louis: Concordia, 2006)
LW	*Luther's Works* [American edition], ed. Helmut Lehmann and Jaroslav Pelikan, 55 vols. (Philadelphia: Fortress Press/St. Louis: Concordia, 1955–1986).
LWZ	*The Latin Works and Correspondence of Huldreich Zwingli*, ed. Samuel Macauley Jackson, 3 vols. (New York, 1912; Philadelphia, 1922, 1929)
MLStA	*Martin Luther: Studienausgabe*, ed. Hans-Ulrich Delius, 6 vols (Berlin & Leipzig: Evangelische Verlagsanstalt, 1979–1999)
MPG	*Patrologiae cursus completus, series Graeca*, ed. Jacques-Paul Migne, 166 vols. (Paris, 1857–1866)
MPL	*Patrologiae cursus completus, series Latina*, ed. Jacques-Paul Migne, 217 vols. (Paris, 1844–64)
NPNF	*Nicene and Post-Nicene Fathers*, ed. Philip Schaaf and Henry Wace,

	series 1 [NPNF1], 14 vols.; and series 2 [NPNF2], 14 vols. (London: T&T Clark, 1886–1900)
ODCC	*The Oxford Dictionary of the Christian Church*, ed. F. L. Cross, 3d rev. ed., ed. E. A. Livingstone (Oxford: Oxford University Press, 2005)
OER	*Oxford Encyclopedia of the Reformation*, ed. Hans J. Hillerbrand, 4 vols. (New York: Oxford University Press, 1996)
STh	Thomas Aquinas, *Summa Theologica*
TAL	The Annotated Luther
W^2	*Dr. Martin Luthers sämmtliche Schriften*, ed. Johann Georg Walch, 23 vols. (St. Louis: Concordia, 1881–1910)
WA	*Luthers Werke: Kritische Gesamtausgabe* [*Schriften*], 73 vols. (Weimar: H. Böhlau, 1883–2009)
WA DB	*Luthers Werke: Kritische Gesamtausgabe: Deutsche Bibel*, 12 vols. (Weimar: H. Böhlau, 1906–1961)
WA Br	*Luthers Werke: Kritische Gesamtausgabe: Briefwechsel*, 18 vols. (Weimar: H. Böhlau, 1930–1985)
WA TR	*Luthers Werke: Kritische Gesamtausgabe: Tischreden*, 6 vols. (Weimar: H. Böhlau, 1912–1921)
Wander	*Deutsches Sprichwörter-Lexikon*, ed. K. F. Wander, 5 vols. (Darmstadt: Wissenschaftliche Buchgesellschaft, 1964)
WPBW	*Willibald Pirckheimers Briefwechsel*, ed. Emil Reicke et al., 7 vols. (Munich: Beck, 1940–2009)
Z	*Huldreich Zwinglis sämtliche Werke*, ed. Emil Egli et al., Corpus Reformatorum 88–108 (Leipzig/Zurich: Heinsius/TVZ, 1905–2013)

REFORMATION EUROPE
in the 16th century
Holy Roman Empire boundary
Provincial boundary
ATLANTIC OCEAN
SCOTLAND
Edinburgh
IRELAND
York
ENGLAND
London
North Sea
NORWAY
SWEDEN
Stockholm
DENMARK
Copenhagen
Baltic Sea
ESTONIA
LIVONIA
KURLAND
Königsberg
PRUSSIA
POMERANIA
Hamburg
BRANDENBURG
POLAND
Ghent
ARTOIS
NETHERLANDS
FLANDERS
HESSE
COLOGNE
SAXONY
LUXEMBOURG
SILESIA
BOHEMIA
Mainz
UPPER PALITANATE
LOWER PALITANATE
MORAVIA
BAVARIA
Paris
Nantes
Orleans
FRANCE
FRENCH COMTE
Augsburg
AUSTRIA
Vienna
IMPERIAL HUNGARY
Budapest
HUNGARY
SWISS CONFEDERATION
TYROL
CARINTHIA
CARNIOLA
BOURBON LANDS
SAVOY
Milan
Trent
Pavia
Venice
Mohacs
Valladolid
Toulouse
NAVARRE
Avignon
Genoa
VENETIAN REPUBLIC
PORTUGAL
SPAIN
Florence
PAPAL STATES
Madrid
Barcelona
Lisbon
CASTILE
Toledo
ARAGON
CORSICA (TO GENOA)
ITALY
OTTOMAN EMPIRE
BALERIC ISLANDS
Rome
Seville
SARDINIA (TO SPAIN)
Naples
NAPLES
Granada
GRANADA
Tangier
Mediterranean Sea
SICILY (TO SPAIN)
Algiers
Bizerte
Tunis
0
300 Miles
Lucidity Information Design, LLC

LUTHER'S GERMANY
Major political subdivisions
N
Baltic Sea
DENMARK
Wolgast
Hamburg
POMERANIA
Stettin
Bremen
Elbe
Amsterdam
NETHERLANDS
POLAND
Magdeburg
Wittenberg
Brussels
Cologne
Eisenach
Eisleben
Torgau
Leipzig
Marburg
Erfurt
Breslau
Oder
Schmalkalden
LUXEMBURG
Mansfeld
Prague
Worms
Nuremberg
Metz
Regansburg
Rhine
Strasbourg
Danube
Augsburg
FRANCE
AUSTRIA
Vienna
Zürich
Salzburg
SWISS CONFEDERATION
HUNGARY
Milan
Venice
VENETIAN DOMINION
0
200 Miles
Adriatic Sea
Florence

Introduction to Volume 3

PAUL W. ROBINSON

What does the gospel mean for the church, and what is the church? Martin Luther famously asserted, "God be praised, a seven-year-old child knows what the church is: holy believers and 'the little sheep who hear the voice of their shepherd.'"[a] True though that statement might be, it nevertheless belies the complexity and nuance of his body of work on the church and its sacraments. Having rejected a one-sided institutional understanding of church, Luther asserted the primacy of God's word—both the preached word and the sacramental word—in creating and sustaining believers and thus in forming and sustaining the church. The Spirit gathers this church around the oral proclamation of forgiveness in Christ, delivering that same forgiveness in baptism, absolution, and the Lord's Supper. Luther rejected other understandings, whether Rome's contention that it alone was the church and owned the sacraments or the teachings of other reformers that stripped the sacraments of both the Spirit's work and Christ's saving power and presence. Luther refused to tolerate a church built on human works, whether it was the pope's authority or the faith or works of individual believers. This is the thread that runs through all the texts in this volume:

a *The Smalcald Articles*, in BC, 324.

the church and sacraments belong to Christ, who founded and instituted them.

That is not to say that Luther's thinking on the church and sacraments did not develop over time in the course of his reforming activity. Although he began by defining his understanding of church and sacraments over against the teachings of Rome, he soon had to counter the claims of others attempting their own reforms, such as Ulrich Zwingli (1484–1531) and the Anabaptists. So, Luther found himself fighting these very different theological battles on multiple fronts and at the same time. The texts gathered here, which cover the period from 1520 to 1539, tell this story and highlight the theological themes Luther developed in the course of these controversies.

Luther came into his own as a reformer in 1520 when he published a series of remarkable treatises. Up until that point, he had defended his criticism of indulgences and in so doing had been forced into arguing about the limits of papal authority. When he debated Johann Eck (1486–1543) on that topic at Leipzig in 1519, Luther asserted that the papacy was a human institution and that even general councils could and had erred. He was left with the plain meaning of Scripture as the final authority for Christian faith and life. Furthermore, as he had already repeatedly stated, the central message of Scripture was the death and resurrection of Christ for the salvation of sinners as a pure gift received by faith. This understanding of the gospel contradicted the idea prevalent in Luther's day that the church existed to dispense the sacraments, which were themselves the source of grace (understood as a spiritual power) needed to perform the good works that were required for salvation. *The Babylonian Captivity of the Church*, one of the well-known 1520 treatises, is in essence a lengthy critique of this sacramental system. The treatise answered the question of what needed to be changed in the church so that the gospel could be proclaimed free of error, addition, and ambiguity. Most important, only those sacraments that Scripture clearly attests had been instituted by Christ should remain: baptism and the Lord's Supper. (Although in the first part of the treatise Luther also includes confession and absolution, by the end of the text he has subsumed this under baptism so that it no longer stands as a separate sacrament.) Even these sacraments, however, had been misunderstood and misrepresented, with the result that Luther's task included peeling away layers of tradition and theological speculation in order to restore their scriptural and gospel-centered practice.

The Babylonian Captivity proved remarkably influential and effectively raised the issue of precisely how the Roman church needed to be changed. One thing that desperately needed to be changed to reflect the new Evangelical teaching was the Mass. Luther had argued against transubstantiation and argued for the right of the laity to receive wine as well as bread when they communed. As important as these criticisms were, they were argued as much on the basis of ancient church tradition and a suspicion of Aristotelian ontology as anything else. His most piercing stroke, however, was to reject the idea that the Mass was a sacrifice offered to God on behalf of the living and the dead. He insisted instead that the bread and wine were Christ's body and blood given to Christians for the forgiveness of sins. The sacrament was entirely God's gracious doing, and the presider was no longer a priest who sacrificed but God's minister who served. The question raised in some readers' minds, however, was what this would mean for the communion liturgy, the service that the Lutheran reformers continued to call the Mass. What should an Evangelical Mass be?

In Wittenberg, members of the reform party there attempted to answer this question during Luther's enforced absence at the Wartburg castle following the Diet of Worms. The first laypersons, including Philip Melanchthon (1497–1560), received the wine in September 1521. Then, during Christmas of that year, Luther's university colleague Andreas Bodenstein from Karlstadt (1486–1541) celebrated Mass in German without wearing vestments, and he required all those attending to receive the wine and to take the bread in their hands. The perceived forced nature of this reform, among other things, led to Luther's return to Wittenberg, where he excoriated the leaders of reform for their legalism in a series of eight sermons known as the Invocavit sermons.[1] In these sermons, Luther also pointed a way forward by insisting on sufficient teaching and sensitivity to conscience when enacting reform. Luther put this approach into practice, not least when, after having proposed revisions in the Latin Mass in 1523, he authored the *German Mass*, which was published early in 1526. Written in response to numerous requests and a proliferation of German liturgies, Luther placed teaching of the basics of the Christian faith and an Evangelical approach to

1. See LW 51:67–100; TAL 4:7–45.

A scene depicting Luther's capture by friends, who carry him away to safety at the Wartburg castle, shown in upper left.

communion at the center of this liturgy. His concern for patient instruction—above all, of children—is apparent throughout his approach to the worship service.

Luther's concern for the common people and their faith also informed his reaction to those who differed from him in their understanding of the sacraments, that is, the Lord's Supper and baptism. As the Reformation movement expanded, differences arose among the Evangelicals themselves, and Luther found himself at odds with former colleagues like Karlstadt and other reformers like Zwingli over a host of issues that tended to coalesce around the question of the Lord's Supper. Although agreed in their opposition to Rome, they disagreed over how or whether Christ was present in this sacrament. Luther's contention that the body and blood of Christ were truly present with the bread and wine, even for unbelievers who might receive these elements, seemed too Romanizing to many. Yet for Luther, this question went to the heart of the gospel—Christ himself given for the forgiveness of sins. The bitter nature of the controversy is reflected in the sheer weight of treatises written on the subject and the number of reformers who engaged in the debate. This significant Reformation issue is here represented by the treatise *That These Words of Christ, "This Is My Body," etc., Still Stand Firm Against the Fanatics*. Written in 1527, Luther insisted that the New Testament accounts left no alternative to a literal interpretation of Christ's words instituting the supper. He dealt with his many opponents in broad categories rather than individually, since the sheer number of different arguments already made it almost impossible to address each one. This treatise was far from the last word on the subject, but it offers a clear presentation of the major points in the debate.

Central to the question of the Lord's Supper was whether God, in fact, worked through such outward ceremonies. Those who rejected such divine activity called into question the sacrament of baptism, and particularly the practice of infant baptism. Although questions about the baptism of infants arose from self appointed prophets who visited Wittenberg during Luther's absence in 1521, insistence on believer's baptism rather than infant baptism became the hallmark of a wide spectrum of groups known collectively as Anabaptists. Luther addressed the views of Anabaptists in the treatise *Concerning Rebaptism* in 1528. Once again, he responded out of his concern for faith and the gospel. For him, to insist that only adults who confessed their faith could be validly baptized, as the Anabaptists did, made faith uncertain and rooted the sacrament in human faith rather than in Christ's promise. In this way, faith became yet another good work with which to please God, and the gracious nature of God's gifts given in baptism was obscured, if not denied completely.

In 1539 Luther returned to the question of the nature of the church. Prompted by the pope's call for a general council, he penned *On the Councils and the Church*, a treatise that addressed both Rome's exclusive claim to the title *church* and the nature and authority of councils. In this treatise, Luther displayed his experience and wide reading as he marshaled citations from the church fathers and from histories of the councils to demonstrate the feebleness and fragility of his Roman opponents' arguments from tradition. He concluded that Rome was not alone in being the church and that councils had no authority in and of themselves but only as witnesses to the truth of the gospel. Building on a definition of the church's visible "signs" first proposed in 1521, he addressed the question of how the church might be identified in the world and provided both a list of marks of the church and the central claim that the gospel had to be at the very center of any claim to be the people of God.

Luther was not an easy or polite opponent, as these treatises demonstrate. Yet in every situation represented here, his passionate response was rooted in his radical understanding of the love of God in Christ Jesus and a fierce desire to make that gracious love real in the Christian assembly marked by word and sacraments and in the lives of believers.

This icon depicts Emperor Constantine (middle figure) accompanied by the bishops of the First Council of Nicaea (325). The figures are holding the Niceno-Constantinopolitan Creed of 381.

DE CAPTIVITATE
BABYLONICAE
ECCLESIAE,
Præludium Martini
Lutheri.

Vuittembergæ.

Title page of Luther's *The Babylonian Captivity of the Church* *[De Captivitate Babylonica Ecclesiae]*, published in Wittenberg by Melchior Lotter the Younger (1520).

The Babylonian Captivity of the Church

1520

ERIK H. HERRMANN

INTRODUCTION

At the end of his German treatise *Address to the Christian Nobility* (*An den christlichen Adel deutscher Nation*), Luther dropped a hint of what was coming next: "I know another little song about Rome and the Romanists. If their ears are itching to hear it, I will sing that one to them, too—and pitch it in the highest key!" This "little song" Luther would call a "prelude" on the captivity of the Roman church—or the *Babylonian Captivity of the Church*, published just a few months later in October of 1520. A polemical treatise, it was truly "pitched high," with Luther hiding little of his dissatisfaction with the prevalent sacramental practices sanctioned by Rome. Although he fully expected the work to elicit a cacophony of criticisms from his opponents, Luther's positive aim was to set forth a reconsideration of the sacramental Christian life that centered on the Word. His thesis is that the papacy had distorted the sacraments with its own traditions and regulations, transforming them into a system of control and coercion. The evangelical liberty of the sacramental promises had been replaced by a papal absolutism that, like a feudal lordship, claimed its own jurisdictional liberties and privileges over the totality of Christian life through a sacramental system that spanned birth to death. Yet Luther does not replace one tyranny for another; his argument for a return to the biblical understanding of the sacraments is moderated by a consideration of traditions and external practices in relation to their effects on the individual conscience and faith.

On the one hand, Luther's treatise is shaped by some of the specific arguments of his opponents. There are two treatises in particular to which Luther reacts. The first is by an Italian Dominican, Isidoro Isolani (c. 1480–1528), who wrote a tract calling for Luther's recantation, *Revocatio Martini Lutheri Augustiniani ad sanctam sedem* (1519). The second writing, appearing in July of 1520, was by the Leipzig theologian Augustinus Alveld (c. 1480–1535), who argued against Luther on the topic of communion in "both kinds." In some sense, the *Babylonian Captivity* serves as Luther's reply.

But Luther's ideas on the sacraments had been in development for some time before. His early personal struggles with penance and the Mass are well known and were the context for much of his *Anfechtungen*[1] and spiritual trials in the monastery. Likewise, his subsequent clarity on the teaching of justification and faith quickly reshaped his thinking on the sacramental life. By 1519, he had decided that only three of the seven sacraments could be defined as such on the basis of Scripture, publishing a series of sermons that year on the sacraments of penance, baptism, and the Lord's Supper.[a] In 1520, he wrote another, more extensive treatise on the Lord's Supper, a *Treatise on the New Testament*. In all of these works, the sacrament chiefly consists in the divine promise and the faith which grasps it. So it is in the *Babylonian Captivity*, where the correlative of faith and promise is the *leitmotif* that runs through the entire work.

As Luther discusses each of the sacraments, he exhibits a remarkable combination of detailed, penetrating biblical interpretation and pastoral sensitivity for the common person. In fact, it is precisely the perceived lack of attention to Scripture and to pastoral care that drives Luther's ire and polemic. Christians are being fleeced, coerced, and misled by those who should be guiding and caring for consciences. The errors of Rome are

1. *Anfechtung(en)* embraces several concepts and is not readily translated into a single English word. It can be simply understood as "temptation" or "trial" (Lat. *tentatio*) and is employed in this manner by Luther in his German translation of the Bible. But even these examples do not give a single picture on the nature of the temptation and from whence it comes. In some places *Anfechtung* is a struggle within—a conflict with flesh and spirit (e.g., Matt. 26:41); in other places the trial seems to come from the outside—from enemies and persecuters of the church (Luke 8:13 and James 1:12). In Luther's writings, he adds to the complexity of the term as he reflects both upon his own personal experiences of *Anfechtung* and the theological implications attached to them. At the basic level, they are experienced as a contradiction of God's love and protection, a perceived antagonism and hostility to the security of one's salvation. Satan's accusations, self-doubt and the weakness of the flesh, and God's wrath are all various aspects of this experience. Yet for Luther, such trials are ultimately to be received as a blessing from God, a tool of his fatherly love to refine faith and strengthen one's confidence in God's Word and promises. Thus, he describes *Anfechtung* as one of the necessary experiences for the making of a Christian theologian: "This is the touchstone which teaches you not only to know and understand, but also to experience how right, how true, how sweet, how lovely, how mighty, how comforting God's Word is, wisdom beyond all wisdom" (*Preface to the Wittenberg Edition of Luther's German Writings*, TAL 4:475–88).

a *The Sacrament of Penance* (LW 35:9–23; WA 2:714–23); *The Holy and Blessed Sacrament of Baptism* (LW 35:29–45; WA 2:727–37); *The Blessed Sacrament of the Holy and True Body of Christ and the Brotherhoods* (LW 35:49–73; WA 2:742–58). All are included in TAL 1.

intolerable because they are so injurious to faith. The most egregious for Luther was how the Eucharist was understood and practiced. Here he identifies three "captivities" of the Mass by which the papacy imprisons the Christian church: the reservation of the cup, the doctrine of transubstantiation, and the use of the Mass as a sacrifice and work to gain divine favor. In all three of these areas, Luther focuses on the pastoral implications of Rome's misuse and tyranny.

The *Babylonian Captivity* is written in Latin, attesting to the technical nature of the topic and to the education of Luther's audience. It is clear that he assumes for his reader at least a broad knowledge of Scholastic theology and, for his humanist readership, a facility with classical allusions which, relative to Luther's other writings, are not infrequent. The reception of the work was a mixed one. Georg Spalatin (1484–1545), the elector's secretary,[2] was worried about the effects the tone would have. Erasmus[3] believed (perhaps rightly) that the breach was now irreparable. Johannes Bugenhagen (1485–1558) was appalled upon his first reading, but upon closer study became convinced that Luther was in the right, and soon became Luther's trusted colleague, co-reformer, and friend. Henry VIII of England (1491–1547) even entered into the fray, writing his own refutation of Luther, a *Defense of the Seven Sacraments*, for which he received the title *Fidei defensor* from the pope. The papal bull[4] threatening Luther with excommunication was already on its way, so in some sense Luther hardly felt he could make matters worse. But in the end, the *Babylonian Captivity* had the effect of galvanizing both opponents and supporters. It became the central work for which Luther had to answer at the Diet of Worms in 1521.

Some of Luther's expressed positions—though provocative at the time—became less agreeable to his followers later on. In particular, Luther seemed ambivalent regarding the role of laws in civil affairs, suggesting that the gospel was a better guide for rulers. Luther himself deemed this position deficient when faced with the Peasants' War in 1525. Likewise, when discussing marriage, Luther was inclined to dismiss the manifold laws and regulations that had grown around the institution and rely only on biblical mandates and examples. This led to some of his more controversial remarks regarding the permissibility of bigamy. After the marital scandal of Philip of Hesse,[5] which ensued in part from following Luther's advice, these remarks were deemed

2. Spalatin served Elector Frederick III the Wise (b. 1463) from 1509 till Frederick's death in 1525.

3. Erasmus of Rotterdam (1466–1536) was a Dutch humanist whose works in moral philosophy and editions of the church fathers and the Greek New Testament made him famous throughout Europe.

4. Pope Leo X (1475–1521) issued the papal bull *Exsurge domine* calling for Luther's excommunication in 1520.

5. Philip I, landgrave of Hesse (1504–1567), was a supporter of the Reformation and used his political authority to encourage Protestantism in Hesse. Soon after he married Christine of Saxony in 1523, he engaged in an adulterous affair, and by 1526 was considering how to make bigamy permissible. Luther counseled Philip against this, advising Christians to avoid bigamous marriage, except in extreme circumstances.

A portrait of Philip I, Landgrave of Hesse, and his wife Christine of Saxony, painted by Jost V. Hoff.

unacceptable. When Luther's works were first collected and published in Jena and Wittenberg, the publishers excised these portions from Luther's treatise. These sections are indicated in the annotations of this edition.

THE BABYLONIAN CAPTIVITY OF THE CHURCH[6]

A PRELUDE OF MARTIN LUTHER ON THE BABYLONIAN CAPTIVITY OF THE CHURCH

Jesus

MARTIN LUTHER, AUGUSTINIAN, to his friend, Hermann Tulich,[7] greeting.

Whether I wish it or not, I am compelled to become more learned every day, with so many and such able masters eagerly driving me on and making me work. Some two years ago I wrote on indulgences, but in such a way that I now deeply regret having published that little book.[8] At that time I still clung with a mighty superstition to the tyranny of Rome, and so I held that indulgences should not be altogether rejected, seeing that they were approved by the common consent of so many. No wonder, for at the time it was only I rolling this boulder by myself.[9] Afterwards, thanks to Sylvester,[10] and aided by those friars who so strenuously defended indulgences, I saw that they were nothing but impostures of the Roman flatterers, by which they rob people of their money and their faith in God. Would that I could prevail upon the booksellers and persuade all who have read them to burn the whole of my booklets on indulgences,[b] and instead of all that I have written on this subject adopt this proposition: INDULGENCES ARE WICKED DEVICES OF THE FLATTERERS OF ROME.

b In addition to the *Ninety-Five Theses*, WA 1:233–38; LW 31:17–33; TAL 1:13–46, these include: *Explanations of the Ninety-Five Theses*, WA 1:525–628; *A Sermon on Indulgences and Grace*, WA 1:243–56; *The Freedom of the "Sermon on Papal Indulgences and Grace" of Doctor Martin Luther against the "Refutation," Being Completely Fabricated to Insult That Very Sermon*, WA 1:380–93.

6. The English translation for this edition is a revision of that which is found in vol. 36 of *Luther's Works* (Philadelphia: Muhlenberg Press, 1959), 3–126. The revisions are based on WA 6:497–573, and *Martin Luther: Studien Ausgabe*, vol. 2 (Leipzig: Evangelische Verlagsanstalt, 1982), 168–259. Annotations and footnotes are the work of the editors but are also informed by notes included in previous critical editions.

7. Hermann Tulich was born at Steinheim (c. 1488), near Paderborn, in Westphalia. He studied in Wittenberg in 1508 and in 1512 matriculated at the University of Leipzig where he was a proofreader in Melchior Lotter's printing house. He returned to Wittenberg in 1519 and received the doctorate in 1520 and became professor of poetry. He was a devoted supporter of Luther. Eventually he became rector of the Johanneum gymnasium at Lüneberg from 1532 until his death on 28 July 1540.

8. Luther apparently is referring to the *Explanations of the Ninety-Five Theses* (1518), WA 1:522f.; LW 31:83–252; but compare also *A Sermon on Indulgences and Grace* (1518), WA 1:243–56, written around the same time. There he noted that indulgences were not necessary, yet he deemed them permissible for "lazy Christians." See also TAL 1:57–66.

9. A reference to the Greek myth of Sisyphus rather than, as some have suggested, to the proverb from Erasmus's *Adagia* (2, 4, 40): *Saxum volutum non obducitur musco*—"a rolling stone gathers no moss."

10. Sylvester Prierias (i.e., Mazzolini), from Prierio in Piedmont (1456–1523), was a Dominican prior. As an official court theologian for Pope Leo X

Next, Eck and Emser and their fellow conspirators undertook to instruct me concerning the primacy of the pope.[11] Here too, not to prove ungrateful to such learned men, I acknowledge that I have profited much from their labors. For while I denied the divine authority of the papacy, I still admitted its human authority.[12] But after hearing and reading the super-subtle

Johann Eck (1486–1543)

(*magistri sacri palati*, "Master of the Sacred Palace"), Prierias was ordered to provide theological critique of Luther's *Ninety-Five Theses*. In 1518, Prierias wrote his *Dialogus de potestate papae* ("Dialogue on the Power of the Pope"), which set out a general critique of Luther's arguments against the theology behind indulgences. Like Luther's other opponents (the Dominicans Johann Tetzel [1475–1521] and Jacob van Hoogstraaten (c. 1460–1527), as well as Johann Eck), Prierias shifted the debate toward church authority rather than focusing solely on the question of indulgences.

11. Johann Eck (born Maier; 1486–1543), from the Swabian village of Eck, became professor at Ingolstadt in Bavaria in 1510. His opposition to Luther began with his criticism of the *Ninety-Five Theses* in his *Obelisci*, which led to heated exchanges with Luther and his colleague Andreas Bodenstein von Karlstadt (1486–1541) and culminated with the Leipzig Disputation in 1519. Hieronymus Emser (1477–1527), the secretary and chaplain of Duke George of Saxony (1471–1539), had been a humanist professor at Erfurt in the days that Luther attended. Emser published several works against Luther after the Leipzig debate. See David V. N. Bagchi, *Luther's Earliest Opponents: Catholic Controversialists, 1518–1525* (Minneapolis: Fortress Press, 1991).

12. Only a few months before, Luther expressed this opinion in his treatise *On the Papacy in Rome against the Most Celebrated Romanist in Leipzig*, LW 39:49–104. Cf. *Resolutio Lutheriana super propositione sua decima tertia de potestate papae* (1519), WA 2:180–240.

subtleties of these showoffs,[c] with which they so adroitly prop up their idol (for my mind is not altogether unteachable in these matters), I now know for certain that the papacy is the kingdom of Babylon and the power of Nimrod, the mighty hunter.[13] Once more, therefore, that all may turn out to my friends' advantage, I beg both the booksellers and my readers that after burning what I have published on this subject they hold to this proposition: The Papacy Is the Mighty Hunt of the Bishop of Rome. This is proved by the arguments of Eck, Emser, and the Leipzig lecturer on the Scriptures.[14]

[Communion in Both Kinds]

Now they are making a game of schooling me concerning communion in both kinds[15] and other weighty subjects: this is the task[d] lest I listen in vain to these self-serving teachers of mine.[16] A certain Italian friar of Cremona has written a "Recantation of Martin Luther before the Holy See," which is not that I revoke anything, as the words declare, but that he revokes me.[17] This is

c The original Latin here is *Trossulorum*, a reference to Roman knights who conquered the city of Trossulum in Etruria (central Italy) without the aid of foot soldiers (*Pliny* 32, 2; *Seneca*, ep. 87). Later the term was used in a derogatory sense of a conceited dandy.

d This phrase is perhaps a reference to Virgil's *Aeneid* 6, 129: ". . . *Hoc opus, hic labor est*" ("that is the work, that is the task"), wherein the Sibyl warns Aeneas that his desire to enter Hades is simple; it is *leaving* hell that is the difficult task.

13. A reference to Gen. 10:8-9: "Cush fathered Nimrod; he was the first on earth to be a mighty man. He was a mighty hunter before the Lord. Therefore it is said, 'Like Nimrod a mighty hunter before the Lord.'" Luther here voices the criticism that the pope was seeking power rather than being a good pastor. So he describes the pope as a "mighty hunter" and his use of authority as a "mighty hunt" rather than describing him as a shepherd tending the sheep.

14. Augustinus Alveld was a Franciscan professor at Leipzig who wrote a treatise against Luther in April of 1520, *Concerning the Apostolic See, Whether It Is a Divine Law or Not*, which sparked Luther's response *On the Papacy in Rome* (see n.8 above).

15. In June 1520, Alveld wrote a treatise against Luther on communion in both kinds, *Tractatus de communione sub utraque specie.* Luther already proposed restoring the cup to the laity in two earlier treatises: *The Blessed Sacrament of the Holy and True Body of Christ, and the Brotherhoods* (1519), LW 35:50; TAL 1:225-56; and *Treatise on the New Testament, That Is, the Holy Mass* (1520), LW 35:106-7.

16. The original Latin here is *Cratippos meos*, a reference to Cratippus of Pergamon (first century BCE), a philosopher who taught in Athens. Because he was an instructor of Cicero's son, Cratippus gained the famed orator's favor, thereby gaining Roman citizenship. The reference is consistent with Luther's opinion of his opponents as flatterers and sycophants.

17. Isidoro Isolani, a Dominican from Milan, published *Revocatio Martini Lutheri Augustiniani ad sanctam sedem* on 22 November 1519 in Cremona.

the kind of Latin the Italians are beginning to write nowadays.[18] Another friar, a German of Leipzig, that same lecturer, as you know, on the whole canon of Scripture[e] has written against me concerning the sacrament in both kinds and is about to perform, as I understand, still greater and more marvelous things. The Italian[f] was canny enough to conceal his name, fearing perhaps the fate of Cajetan[19] and Sylvester.[20] The man of Leipzig, on the other hand, as becomes a fierce and vigorous German, boasts on his ample title page of his name, his life, his sanctity, his learning, his office, his fame, his honor, almost his very clogs.[21] From him I shall doubtless learn a great deal, since he writes his dedicatory epistle to the Son of God himself: so familiar are these saints with Christ who reigns in heaven! Here it seems three magpies are addressing me, the first in good Latin, the second in better Greek, the third in the best Hebrew.[22] What do you think, my dear Hermann, I should do, but prick up my ears?[g] The matter is being dealt with at Leipzig by the "Observance" of the Holy Cross.[23]

18. A barb that would certainly delight his humanist readers.

19. Tomasso de Vio (Cardinal) Cajetan (1469–1534), vicar general of the Dominican order and influential Aquinas scholar, interviewed Luther at Augsburg in 1518 as papal legate in order to acquire a recantation. His three-day debate with Luther on indulgences, Aquinas, canon law, and church authority was recounted and critically reviewed by Luther in his published *Proceedings at Augsburg* (1518), LW 31:253–92; TAL 1:121–66.

20. Luther's response to Sylvester Prierias, *Ad dialogum Silvestri Prieratis de potestate papae responsio*, was published in 1518.

21. The title page of Alveld's treatise contained twenty-six lines. The "clogs" (*calopodia* = *calcipodium*) that Luther mentioned were the wooden-soled sandals worn by the Observant Franciscans.

22. Luther is referring to the unusual spelling, IHSVH, for Jesus that Alveld tries to justify by arguments which involve an admixture of the three languages.

23. Alveld belonged to the stricter part of the Franciscan order, known as the Observantines. Luther is playing on this word.

Cajetan (at the table, far left) and Luther (standing right) at Augsburg. Colored woodcut from Ludwig Rabus, *Historien der Heyligen Ausserwählten Gottes Zeugen* (Straßburg, 1557).

e I.e., Alveld.

f I.e., Isolani.

Fool that I was, I had hitherto thought that it would be a good thing if a general council were to decide that the sacrament should be administered to the laity in both kinds.[h] This view our more-than-learned friar would correct, declaring that neither Christ nor the apostles had either commanded or advised that both kinds be administered to the laity; it was therefore left to the judgment of the church what to do or not to do in this matter, and the church must be obeyed. These are his words.

You will perhaps ask, what madness has entered into the man, or against whom is he writing? For I have not condemned the use of one kind, but have left the decision about the use of both kinds to the judgment of the church. This is the very thing he attempts to assert, in order to attack me with this same argument. My answer is that this sort of argument is common to all who write against Luther: either they assert the very things they assail, or they set up a man of straw whom they may attack. This is the way of Sylvester and Eck and Emser, and of the men of Cologne and Louvain,[24] and if this friar had not been one of their kind, he would never have written against Luther.

This man turned out to be more fortunate than his fellows, however, for in his effort to prove that the use of both kinds was neither commanded nor advised, but left to the judgment of the church, he brings forward the Scriptures to prove that the use of one kind for the laity was ordained by the command of Christ.[i] So it is true, according to this new interpreter of the Scriptures, that the use of one kind was not commanded and at the same time was commanded by Christ! This novel kind of argument is, as you know, the one which these dialecticians[25] of Leipzig are especially fond of using. Does not Emser profess to speak fairly of me in his earlier book,[26] and then, after I had convicted him of the foulest envy and shameful lies, confess, when about to confute me in his later book,[j] that both were true, and that he has written in both a friendly and an unfriendly spirit? A fine fellow, indeed, as you know!

g "*Aures arrigam*," a common classical turn of phrase, cf. Terence, *Andria* 5, 4, 30; Virgil, *Aeneid* 1, 152; Erasmus, *Adagia* 3, 2, 56.

h See *The Blessed Sacrament of the Holy and True Body of Christ, and the Brotherhoods* (1519), LW 35:45–74; TAL 1:225–56. Cf. *Treatise on the New Testament, That Is, the Holy Mass* (1520), LW 35:106–7.

i See below where Luther details Alveld's interpretation of John 6.

j *A venatione Luteriana aegocerotis assertio* (1519).

24. In February of 1520, the theological faculties of Louvain and Cologne published a condemnation of Luther's doctrine based on his collected Latin writings as printed by the Basel printer Johann Froben in 1518.

25. A name derived from the discipline of dialectic, or logic, which was one of the three basic disciplines of medieval education, along with grammar and rhetoric.

26. Emser first published a report of the Leipzig debate between Luther and Eck with his interpretation of it, *De disputatione Lipsicensi, quantum ad Boemos obiter deflexa est* (1519).

But listen to our distinguished distinguisher of "kinds," to whom the decision of the church and the command of Christ are the same thing, and again the command of Christ and no command of Christ are the same thing. With such dexterity he proves that only one kind should be given to the laity, by the command of Christ, that is, by the decision of the church. He puts it in capital letters, thus: THE INFALLIBLE FOUNDATION. Then he treats John 6[:35, 41] with incredible wisdom, where Christ speaks of the bread of heaven and the bread of life, which is he himself. The most learned fellow not only refers these words to the Sacrament of the Altar, but because Christ says: "I am the living bread" [John 6:51] and not "I am the living cup," he actually concludes that we have in this passage the institution of the sacrament in only one kind for the laity. But here follow the words: "For my flesh is food indeed, and my blood is drink indeed" [John 6:55] and, "Unless you eat the flesh of the Son of Man and drink his blood" [John 6:53]. When it dawned upon the good friar that these words speak undeniably for both kinds and against one kind—presto! how happily and learnedly he slips out of the quandary by asserting that in these words Christ means to say only that whoever receives the sacrament in one kind receives therein both flesh and blood. This he lays down as his "infallible foundation" of a structure so worthy of the holy and heavenly "Observance."

I pray you now to learn along with me from this that in John 6 Christ commands the administration of the sacrament in one kind, yet in such a way that his commanding means leaving it to the decision of the church; and further that Christ is speaking in this same chapter only of the laity and not of the priests. For to the latter the living bread of heaven, that is the sacrament in one kind, does not belong, but perhaps the bread of death from hell! But what is to be done with the deacons and subdeacons,[27] who are neither laymen nor priests? According to this distinguished writer they ought to use neither the one kind nor both kinds! You see, my dear Tulich, what a novel and "Observant" method of treating Scripture this is.

But learn this too: In John 6 Christ is speaking of the Sacrament of the Altar, although he himself teaches us that he is speaking of faith in the incarnate Word, for he says: "This is the work of God, that you believe in him whom he has sent" [John 6:29]. But we'll have to give him credit: this Leipzig professor

27. Subdeacons and deacons are the fifth and sixth of the seven offices through which clergy advanced to the priesthood. Theologians debated whether these middle offices participated in the sacrament of Holy Orders until the Council of Trent decided that they did. For a discussion of the seven offices, see Martin Chemnitz, *Examination of the Council of Trent*, II:9:2 (St. Louis: Concordia, 1978).

of the Bible can prove anything he pleases from any passage of Scripture he pleases. For he is an Anaxagorian,[28] or rather an Aristotelian, theologian for whom nouns and verbs when interchanged mean the same thing and any thing.[29] Throughout the whole of his book he so fits together the testimony of the Scriptures that if he set out to prove that Christ is in the sacrament he would not hesitate to begin thus: "The lesson is from the book of the Revelation of St. John the Apostle." All his quotations are as apt as this one would be, and the wiseacre imagines he is adorning his drivel with the multitude of his quotations. The rest I will pass over, lest I smother you with the filth of this vile-smelling sewer.[k]

In conclusion, he brings forward 1 Cor. 11[:23], where Paul says that he received from the Lord and delivered to the Corinthians the use of both the bread and the cup. Here again our distinguisher of kinds, treating the Scriptures with his usual brilliance, teaches that Paul permitted, but did not deliver, the use of both kinds. Do you ask where he gets his proof? Out of his own head, as he did in the case of John 6. For it does not behoove this lecturer to give a reason for his assertions; he belongs to that order whose members prove and teach everything by their visions.[30] Accordingly we are here taught that in this passage the apostle did not write to the whole Corinthian congregation, but to the laity alone—and therefore gave no "permission" at all to the clergy, but deprived them of the sacrament altogether! Further, according to a new kind of grammar, "I have received from the Lord" means the same as "it is permitted by the Lord," and "I have delivered to you" is the same as "I have permitted to you." I pray you, mark this well. For by this method not only the church, but any worthless fellow, will be at liberty, according to this master, to turn all the universal commands, institutions, and ordinances of Christ and the apostles into mere "permission."

I perceive therefore that this man is driven by a messenger of Satan[l] and that he and his partners are seeking to make a name for themselves in the world through me, as men who are worthy to cross swords with Luther. But their hopes shall be dashed. In my contempt for them I shall never even mention their names, but content myself with this one reply to all their books. If they

k *Cloaca.*

l 2 Cor. 12:7.

28. Anaxagoras (c. 510–428 BCE) was a pre-Socratic philosopher charged with impiety for his novel interpretations of myths that he adapted to fit his naturalistic explanations of physical phenomena. Luther is using the comparison to highlight Alveld's forced interpretations of Scripture.

29. The philosophy of Aristotle (384–322 BCE) was an essential feature of Scholastic theology. Aristotle's categories, method, and scientific and ethical theories were often incorporated into the explanation of theological topics and the interpretation of Scripture. Such extensive and uncritical use of Aristotle in theology was quite controversial from the outset and a central point of Luther's early critique of Scholastic theology. Here Luther probably has in mind Aristotle's study of language, "On Interpretation," in his collection of logical treatises, the *Organon*.

30. Franciscans. St. Francis (c. 1182–1226) was known for his various visions, including the call to rebuild the ruined chapel of San Damiano that marked the beginning of his mendicant life and his vision at the end of his life on Mt. Verna which bestowed on him the *stigmata*, the five wounds of Christ.

are worthy of it, I pray that Christ in his mercy may bring them back to a sound mind. If they are not worthy, I pray that they may never leave off writing such books, and that the enemies of truth may never deserve to read any others. There is a true and popular saying:

> "This I know for certain—whenever I fight with filth,
> victor or vanquished, I am sure to be defiled."[31]

31. Luther used the common saying later in his edition of *Aesop's Fables* (1530). There he used it as the moral to the fable of the ass and the lion. See Carl P. E. Springer, *Luther's Aesop*, Early Modern Studies, vol. 8 (Kirksville, MO: Truman State University Press, 2011).

And since I see that they have an abundance of leisure and writing paper, I shall furnish them with ample matter to write about. For I shall keep ahead of them, so that while they are triumphantly celebrating a glorious victory over one of my heresies (as it seems to them), I shall meanwhile be devising a new one. I too am desirous of seeing these illustrious leaders in battle decorated with many honors. Therefore, while they murmur that I approve of communion in both kinds, and are most happily engrossed with this important and worthy subject, I shall go one step further and undertake to show that all who deny communion in both kinds to the laity are wicked men. To do this more conveniently I shall compose *a prelude on the captivity of the Roman church.* In due time, when the most learned papists have disposed of this book I shall offer more.

I take this course, lest any pious reader who may chance upon this book, should be offended by the filthy matter with which I deal and should justly complain that he finds nothing in it which cultivates or instructs his mind or which furnishes any food for learned reflection. For you know how impatient my friends are that I waste my time on the sordid fictions of these men. They say that the mere reading of them is ample confutation; they look for better things from me, which Satan seeks to hinder through these men. I have finally resolved to follow the advice of my friends and to leave to those hornets the business of wrangling and hurling invectives.

Of that Italian friar of Cremona[m] I shall say nothing. He is an unlearned man and a simpleton, who attempts with a few rhetorical passages to recall me to the Holy See, from which I am not as yet aware of having departed, nor has anyone proved that

m Isidoro Isolani; see n. 17, p. 15 above.

I have. His chief argument in those silly passages[n] is that I ought to be moved by my monastic vows and by the fact that the empire has been transferred to the Germans. Thus he does not seem to have wanted to write my "recantation" so much as the praise of the French people and the Roman pontiff.[32] Let him attest his allegiance in this little book, such as it is. He does not deserve to be harshly treated, for he seems to have been prompted by no malice; nor does he deserve to be learnedly refuted, since all his chatter is sheer ignorance and inexperience.

[Central Premise]

To begin with, I must deny that there are seven sacraments, and for the present maintain that there are but three: baptism, penance, and the bread.[33] All three have been subjected to a miserable captivity by the Roman curia, and the church has been robbed of all her liberty. Yet, if I were to speak according to the usage of the Scriptures, I should have only one single sacrament,[34] but with three sacramental signs, of which I shall treat more fully at the proper time.

[The Sacrament of the Lord's Supper]

Now concerning the sacrament of the bread first of all

I shall tell you now what progress I have made as a result of my studies on the administration of this sacrament. For at the time when I was publishing my treatise on the Eucharist,[35] I adhered to the common custom and did not concern myself at all with the question of whether the pope was right or wrong. But now that I have been challenged and attacked, no, forcibly thrust into this arena, I shall freely speak my mind, whether all the papists laugh or weep together.

In the first place the sixth chapter of John must be entirely excluded from this discussion, since it does not refer to the sacrament in a single syllable. Not only because the sacrament was not yet instituted, but even more because the passage itself and

n I.e., *Revocatio Martini Lutheri Augustiniani ad sanctam sedem*; cf. n. 15.

32. On Christmas day, 800, the Frankish ruler, Charlemagne (c. 747–814), was crowned by Pope Leo III as the "Emperor of the Romans" (*Imperator Romanorum*), and since that time Germanic kings claimed continuity with the ancient Roman Empire (*translatio imperii*), even though in the East the empire continued on with its own succession of emperors in Constantinople. More specifically, Luther is here referring to the most recent election of Charles V (1500–1558) in 1519 who, though only partly German, was certainly more so than Francis I of France, the pope's preferred candidate.

33. The common designation for the Lord's Supper, especially since the cup was withheld from the laity. By the end of the treatise Luther will conclude that there are only two sacraments; see p. 127.

34. 1 Tim. 3:16: "Without any doubt, the mystery of our religion is great: He was revealed in flesh, vindicated in spirit, seen by angels, proclaimed among Gentiles, believed in throughout the world, taken up in glory." In the Latin Bible, the word *mystery* is translated with *sacramentum*. See below, n. 210, p. 98. Cf. also thesis 18 of Luther's *Disputatio fide infusa et acquisita* ("Disputation Concerning Infused and Acquired Faith"), WA 6:85–86.

35. *The Blessed Sacrament of the Holy and True Body of Christ, and the Brotherhoods* (1519), LW 35:45–74; TAL 1:225–56.

the sentences following plainly show, as I have already stated, that Christ is speaking of faith in the incarnate Word. For he says: "My words are spirit and life" [John 6:63], which shows that he was speaking of a spiritual eating, by which he who eats has life; whereas the Jews understood him to mean a bodily eating and therefore disputed with him. But no eating can give life except that which is by faith, for that is truly a spiritual and living eating. As Augustine also says: "Why do you make ready your teeth and your stomach? Believe, and you have eaten."[36] For the sacramental eating does not give life, since many eat unworthily. Hence Christ cannot be understood in this passage to be speaking about the sacrament.

Some persons, to be sure, have misapplied these words in their teaching concerning the sacrament, as in the decretal *Dudum*[37] and many others. But it is one thing to misapply the Scriptures and another to understand them in their proper sense. Otherwise, if in this passage Christ were enjoining a sacramental eating, when he says: "Unless you eat my flesh and drink my blood, you have no life in you" [John 6:53], he would be condemning all infants, all the sick, and all those absent or in any way hindered from the sacramental eating, however strong their faith might be. Thus Augustine, in his *Contra Julianum*, Book II,[o] proves from Innocent[38] that even infants eat the flesh and drink the blood of Christ without the sacrament; that is, they partake of them through the faith of the church.[39] Let this then be accepted as proved: John 6 does not belong here. For this reason I have written elsewhere[p] that the Bohemians[40] cannot properly rely on this passage in support of the sacrament in both kinds.

Now there are two passages that do bear very clearly upon this matter: the Gospel narratives of the Lord's Supper and Paul in 1 Cor. 11[:23-25]. Let us examine these. Matt. [26:26-28], Mark [14:22-24], and Luke [22:19f.] agree that Christ gave the whole sacrament to all his disciples. That Paul delivered both kinds is so certain that no one has ever had the temerity to say otherwise. Add to this that Matt. [26:27] reports that Christ did not say of the bread, "eat of it, all of you," but of the cup, "drink of it, all of you." Mark [14:23] likewise does not say, "they all ate of it," but

o *Against Julian* II, 36; CSEL 85¹:183f.

p *Verklärung etlicher Artikel in einem Sermon vom heiligen Sakrament* (1520), WA 6:80.

36. Augustine (354–430), bishop of Hippo in North Africa, was the most influential church father in Western Christianity and remained particularly important for Luther. He is quoting from Augustine's *Sermo* 112, 5.

37. *Dudum* is the incorrect decretal. The correct reference is *Quum Marthae*, in the Decretals of Gregory IX (r. 1227–1241), lib. 3, tit. 41: *de celebratione missarum, et sacramento eucharistiae et divinis officiis*, CIC 2:636–39.

38. Pope Innocent I (d. 417).

39. Innocent's argument can be found in the letters of Augustine, *Ep.* 182, 5; CSEL 44:720.

40. Luther is referring to the followers of Jan Hus (1369–1415). After the condemnation and burning of Hus at the Council of Constance (1414–18), his successor, Jacobellus von Mies (c. 1372–1429), argued for the necessity of communion in both kinds—the bread and the cup—for salvation on the basis of John 6:54. The Bohemians were granted the use of the cup by the Council of Basel in 1433, but this was revoked by Pope Pius II (r. 1458–1464) in 1462.

"they all drank of it." Both attach the note of universality to the cup, not to the bread, as though the Spirit foresaw this schism, by which some would be forbidden to partake of the cup, which Christ desired should be common to all. How furiously, do you suppose, would they rave against us, if they had found the word "all" attached to the bread instead of to the cup? They would certainly leave us no loophole to escape. They would cry out and brand us as heretics and damn us as schismatics. But now, when the Scripture is on our side and against them, they will not allow themselves to be bound by any force of logic. Men of the most free will they are, even in the things that are God's; they change and change again, and throw everything into confusion.

But imagine me standing over against them and interrogating my lords, the papists. In the Lord's Supper, the whole sacrament, or communion in both kinds, is given either to the priests alone or else it is at the same time given to the laity. If it is given only to the priests (as they would have it),[41] then it is not right to give it to the laity in either kind. For it must not be given rashly to any to whom Christ did not give it when he instituted the sacrament. Otherwise, if we permit one institution of Christ to be changed, we make all of his laws invalid, and any man may make bold to say that he is not bound by any other law or institution of Christ. For a single exception, especially in the Scriptures, invalidates the whole.[q] But if it is given also to the laity, it inevitably follows that it ought not to be withheld from them in either form. And if any do withhold it from them when they ask for it they are acting impiously and contrary to the act, example, and institution of Christ.

41. Gabriel Biel's (c. 1420–1495) *Exposition of the Canon of the Mass* (Lect. 84), which Luther studied extensively, makes the argument that Christ's words, "do this in remembrance of me," were directed to the disciples and their successors, the priests. Thus the cup can be withheld from the laity in order to distinguish them from the clergy.

I acknowledge that I am conquered by this argument, which to me is irrefutable. I have neither read nor heard nor found anything to say against it. For here the word and example of Christ stand unshaken when he says, not by way of permission, but of command: "Drink of it, all of you" [Matt. 26:27]. For if all are to drink of it, and the words cannot be understood as addressed to the priests alone, then it is certainly an impious act to withhold the cup from the laymen when they desire it, even though an angel from heaven were to do it.[r] For when they say that the distribution of both kinds is left to the decision of the church,

q Perhaps a reference to James 2:10.

r Cf. Gal. 1:8.

they make this assertion without reason and put it forth without authority. It can be ignored just as readily as it can be proved. It is of no avail against an opponent who confronts us with the word and work of Christ; he must be refuted with the word of Christ, but this we[42] do not possess.

If, however, either kind may be withheld from the laity, then with equal right and reason a part of baptism or penance might also be taken away from them by this same authority of the church. Therefore, just as baptism and absolution must be administered in their entirety, so the sacrament of the bread must be given in its entirety to all laymen, if they desire it. I am much amazed, however, by their assertion that the priests may never receive only one kind in the Mass under pain of mortal sin; and that for no other reason except (as they unanimously say) that the two kinds constitute one complete sacrament, which may not be divided.[43] I ask them, therefore, to tell me why it is lawful to divide it in the case of the laity, and why they are the only ones to whom the entire sacrament is not given? Do they not acknowledge, by their own testimony, either that both kinds are to be given to the laity or that the sacrament is not valid when only one kind is given to them? How can it be that the sacrament in one kind is not complete in the case of the priests, yet in the case of the laity it is complete? Why do they flaunt the authority of the church and the power of the pope in my face? These do not annul the words of God and the testimony of the truth.

It follows, further, that if the church can withhold from the laity one kind, the wine, it can also withhold from them the other, the bread. It could therefore withhold the entire Sacrament of the Altar from the laity and completely annul Christ's institution as far as they are concerned. By what authority, I ask. If the church cannot withhold the bread, or both kinds, neither can it withhold the wine. This cannot possibly be disputed; for the church's power must be the same over either kind as it is over both kinds, and if it has no power over both kinds, it has none over either kind. I am curious to hear what the flatterers of Rome will have to say to this.

But what carries most weight with me, however, and is quite decisive for me is that Christ says: "This is my blood, which is poured out for you and for many for the forgiveness of sins."[44] Here you see very clearly that the blood is given to all those for whose sins it was poured out. But who will dare to say that it

42. Luther is speaking in the person of his opponents.

43. Thomas Aquinas (1225–1274), a Dominican theologian at the University of Paris, maintained that though there are several signs in the sacrament, namely, the bread and wine, this does not constitute two but only one complete sacrament. Both are necessary for the spiritual refreshment offered; *STh* III, q. 73, a. 2: "The bread and wine are materially several signs, yet formally and perfectively one, inasmuch as one refreshment is prepared therefrom." Regarding the communion of priests, in canon 5 of the Twelfth Council of Toledo (681 CE) it is required that the celebrating priest must receive both the body and blood of Christ. Likewise, there is a prohibition against dividing the sacrament in the twelfth-century *Decretum Gratiani*, pt. III, *de Consecratione*, d. 2, chap. 12: "Let them either receive the sacraments entire or be excluded from the entire sacraments, for a division of one and the same sacrament cannot be made without great sacrilege." Aquinas, aware of both, makes the same point in *STh* III, q. 82, a. 4.

44. The words of Christ in the *Canon of the Mass* harmonized the reading of Matt. 26:28, "poured out for many" (which is very possibly a reference to Isa. 53:12, "yet he bore the sin of many"), and Luke 22:20, "poured for you."

was not poured out for the laity? And do you not see whom he addresses when he gives the cup? Does he not give it to all? Does he not say that it is poured out for all? "For you" [Luke 22:20], he says—let this refer to the priests. "And for many" [Matt. 26:28], however, cannot possibly refer to the priests. Yet he says: "Drink of it, all of you" [Matt. 26:27]. I too could easily trifle here and with my words make a mockery of Christ's words, as my dear trifler[s] does. But those who rely on the Scriptures in opposing us must be refuted by the Scriptures.

This is what has prevented me from condemning the Bohemians,[t] who, whether they are wicked men or good, certainly have the word and act of Christ on their side, while we have neither, but only that inane remark of men: "The church has so ordained." It was not the church which ordained these things, but the tyrants of the churches, without the consent of the church, which is the people of God.

But now I ask, where is the necessity, where is the religious duty, where is the practical use of denying both kinds, that is, the visible sign, to the laity, when everyone concedes to them the grace of the sacrament without the sign?[u] If they concede the grace, which is the greater, why not the sign, which is the lesser? For in every sacrament the sign as such is incomparably less than the thing signified. What then, I ask, is to prevent them from conceding the lesser, when they concede the greater? Unless indeed, as it seems to me, it has come about by the permission of an angry God in order to give occasion for a schism in the church, to bring home to us how, having long ago lost the grace of the sacrament, we contend for the sign, which is the lesser, against that which is the most important and the chief thing; just as some men for the sake of ceremonies contend against love.[v] This monstrous perversion seems to date from the time

s Alveld, cf. n. 14, p. 15.

t See n. 40, p. 22.

u E.g., Augustine, *Sermo* 272; Peter Lombard, *Sentences* 4, d. 1, c. 2-4; Aquinas, *STh* III, q. 80, a. 1; Gabriel Biel, *Sentences* 4, d. 1, q.1, a.1, n. 1; Cf. *STh* III, q. 79, a. 4: "Two things may be considered in this sacrament, namely, the sacrament itself (*ipsum sacramentum*), and the reality of the sacrament (*res sacramenti*) . . . the reality of this sacrament is charity (*res autem huius sacramenti est caritas*)."

v Perhaps a reference to Matt. 15:1-9.

when we began to rage against Christian love for the sake of the riches of this world. Thus God would show us, by this terrible sign, how we esteem signs more than the things they signify. How preposterous it would be to admit that the faith of baptism is granted to the candidate for baptism, and yet to deny him the sign of this very faith, namely, the water!

Finally, Paul stands invincible and stops the mouth of everyone when he says in 1 Cor. 11[:23]: "For I received from the Lord what I also delivered to you." He does not say: "I permitted to you," as this friar[45] of ours lyingly asserts out of his own head. Nor is it true that Paul delivered both kinds on account of the contention among the Corinthians. In the first place, the text shows that their contention was not about the reception of both kinds, but about the contempt and envy between rich and poor. The text clearly states: "One is hungry and another is drunk, and you humiliate those who have nothing" [1 Cor. 11:21-22]. Moreover, Paul is not speaking of the time when he first delivered the sacrament to them, for he does not say "I receive from the Lord" and "I give to you," but "I received" and "I delivered"—namely, when he first began to preach among them, a long while before this contention. This shows that he delivered both kinds to them, for "delivered" means the same as "commanded," for elsewhere he uses the word in this sense.[46] Consequently there is nothing in the friar's fuming about permission; he has raked it together without Scripture, without reason, without sense. His opponents do not ask what he has dreamed, but what the Scriptures decree in the matter, and out of the Scriptures he cannot adduce one jot or tittle in support of his dreams, while they can produce mighty thunderbolts in support of their faith.

Rise up then, you popish flatterers, one and all! Get busy and defend yourselves against the charges of impiety, tyranny, and treason[w] against the gospel, and of the crime of slandering your brethren. You decry as heretics those who refuse to contravene such plain and powerful words of Scripture in order to acknowledge the mere dreams of your brains! If any are to be called heretics and schismatics, it is not the Bohemians or the Greeks,[47] for they take their stand upon the Gospels. It is you Romans who are the heretics and godless schismatics, for you presume upon

45. Luther is still dealing with Alveld's argument.

46. 1 Cor. 11:1 in the Vulgate reads, "but I praise you brothers that you remember me in everything and keep my *commandments* just as I *delivered* them to you" (*laudo autem vos fratres quod omnia mei memores estis et sicut tradidi vobis praecepta mea tenetis*).

47. That is, the Eastern Orthodox Church, which split from the Western church in 1054. In the Eastern Rite, both kinds in the sacrament are administered to the faithful with the eucharistic spoon.

w Or "lèse-majesté," from the Latin, *laesa maiestate*; literally, "having caused injury to the sovereignty," in this case of the gospel.

your figments alone against the clear Scriptures of God. Wash yourself of that, men!

But what could be more ridiculous and more worthy of this friar's brains than his saying that the Apostle wrote these words and gave this permission, not to the church universal, but to a particular church, that is, the Corinthian? Where does he get his proof? Out of one storehouse, his own impious head. If the church universal receives, reads, and follows this epistle as written for itself in all other respects, why should it not do the same with this portion also? If we admit that any epistle, or any part of any epistle, of Paul does not apply to the church universal, then the whole authority of Paul falls to the ground. Then the Corinthians will say that what he teaches about faith in the Epistle to the Romans does not apply to them. What greater blasphemy and madness can be imagined than this! God forbid that there should be one jot or tittle in all of Paul which the whole church universal is not bound to follow and keep! The fathers never held an opinion like this, not even down to these perilous times of which Paul was speaking when he foretold that there would be blasphemers and blind, insensate men.[x] This friar is one of them, perhaps even the chief.

However, suppose we grant the truth of this intolerable madness. If Paul gave his permission to a particular church, then, even from your own point of view, the Greeks and Bohemians are in the right, for they are particular churches. Hence it is sufficient that they do not act contrary to Paul, who at least gave permission. Moreover, Paul could not permit anything contrary to Christ's institution. Therefore, O Rome, I cast in your teeth, and in the teeth of all your flatterers, these sayings of Christ and Paul, on behalf of the Greeks and the Bohemians. I defy you to prove that you have been given any authority to change these things by as much as one hair, much less to accuse others of heresy because they disregard your arrogance. It is rather you who deserve to be charged with the crime of godlessness and despotism.

Concerning this point we may read Cyprian,[48] who alone is strong enough to refute all the Romanists. In the fifth book of his treatise *On the Lapsed,* he testifies that it was the widespread

48. Cyprian (c. 200–258) was bishop of Carthage during the Decian persecution (250–251). In dealing with the lapsed Christians who desired readmittance, Cyprian tried to steer a middle course between laxist and rigorist positions. The treatise *De lapsis* ("On the Lapsed") was written c. 251–252. Cyprian was martyred during the Valerian persecution on 14 September 258.

x 2 Tim. 3:1-9.

custom in that church [at Carthage] to administer both kinds to the laity, even to children, indeed, to give the body of the Lord into their hands. And of this he gives many examples. Among other things, he reproves some of the people as follows: "The sacrilegious man is angered at the priests because he does not immediately receive the body of the Lord with unclean hands, or drink the blood of the Lord with unclean lips." He is speaking here, you see, of irreverent laymen who desired to receive the body and the blood from the priests. Do you find anything to snarl at here, wretched flatterer? Will you say that this holy martyr, a doctor of the church endowed with the apostolic spirit, was a heretic, and that he used this permission in a particular church?

In the same place Cyprian narrates an incident that came under his own observation. He describes at length how a deacon was administering the cup to a little girl,[49] and when she drew away from him he poured the blood of the Lord into her mouth.[y] We read the same of St. Donatus, and how trivially does this wretched flatterer dispose of his broken chalice![50] "I read of a broken chalice," he says, "but I do not read that the blood was administered."[51] No wonder! He that finds what he pleases in the Holy Scriptures will also read what he pleases in the histories. But can the authority of the church be established, or the heretics be refuted, in this way?

But enough on this subject! I did not undertake this work for the purpose of answering one who is not worthy of a reply, but to bring the truth of the matter to light.

I conclude, then, that it is wicked and despotic to deny both kinds to the laity, and that this is not within the power of any angel, much less of any pope or council. Nor does the Council of Constance give me pause, for if its authority is valid, why not that of the Council of Basel as well, which decreed to the contrary that the Bohemians should be permitted to receive the sacrament in both kinds?[52] That decision was reached only after considerable discussion, as the extant records and documents of the Council show. And to this Council the ignorant flatterer refers in support of his dream; with such wisdom does he handle the whole matter.

49. The Latin, *infanti*, indicates a child under the age of seven.

50. Donatus (d. c. 372), not to be confused with the schismatic bishop of Carthage, was bishop of Arezzo. According to one legend, Donatus was celebrating the Eucharist with a glass chalice when, during a sudden attack by pagan intruders, the chalice was shattered. Miraculously, Donatus was able to reassemble the chalice immediately and even with a missing piece continue the celebration.

51. Alveld uses the story in his *Tractatus* to argue against the cup being administered to the laity.

52. The Council of Constance (1414–1418) adjudicated the case of Jan Hus and the Bohemian practice of communion in both kinds. The Council upheld the practice of withholding the cup and condemned Hus, burning him at the stake as a heretic. Alveld cited the decrees of the council in his *Tractatus*. On the other hand, the Council of Basel granted the Bohemians special privilege for the administration of the sacrament in both kinds in 1433.

y *De lapsis* 25; CSEL 31, 255. Augustine also mentions the story in a letter: *Ep.* 98,4; CSEL 34 II, 524–26.

[The First Captivity: Withholding the Cup]

In this polyptych (1320) by Pietro Lorenzetti (1280–1348), St. Donatus is pictured (far left) at the Church of Santa Maria della Pieve in Arezzo, Tuscany.

The first captivity of this sacrament, therefore, concerns its substance or completeness, which the tyranny of Rome has wrested from us. Not that those who use only one kind sin against Christ, for Christ did not command the use of either kind, but left it to the choice of each individual, when he said: "As often as you do this, do it in remembrance of me" [1 Cor. 11:25]. But they are the sinners, who forbid the giving of both kinds to those who wish to exercise this choice. The fault lies not with the laity, but with the priests. The sacrament does not belong to the priests, but to everyone. The priests are not lords but servants whose duty is to administer both kinds to those who desire them, as often as they desire them. If they wrest this right from the laity and deny it to them by force, they are tyrants; but the laity are without fault, whether they lack one kind or both kinds. In the meantime they must be preserved by their faith and by their desire for the complete sacrament.[53] These same servants are likewise bound to administer baptism and absolution to everyone who seeks them, because he has a right to them; but if they do not administer them, the seeker has the full merit of his faith, while they will be accused before Christ as wicked servants. Thus the holy fathers of old in the desert did not receive the sacrament in any form for many years at a time.[z]

Therefore I do not urge that both kinds be seized upon by force, as if we were bound to this form by a rigorous command, but I instruct men's consciences so that they may endure

53. Cf. Aquinas, *STh* III, q. 80, a.1: "the effect of the sacrament can be secured by every man if he receive it in desire, though not in reality. Consequently, just as some are baptized with the baptism of desire, through their desire of baptism, before being baptized in the baptism of water; so likewise some eat this sacrament spiritually ere they receive it sacramentally. Now this happens in two ways. First of all, from desire of receiving the sacrament itself, and thus are said to be baptized, and to eat spiritually, and not sacramentally,

z Cf. Luther's *A Treatise Concerning the Ban*, LW 39:3–22.

the Roman tyranny, knowing well that they have been forcibly deprived of their rightful share in the sacrament because of their own sin. This only do I desire—that no one should justify the tyranny of Rome, as if it were doing right in forbidding one kind to the laity. We ought rather to abhor it, withhold our consent, and endure it just as we should do if we were held captive by the Turk and not permitted to use either kind. This is what I meant by saying that it would be a good thing, in my opinion, if this captivity were ended by the decree of a general council,[a] our Christian liberty restored to us out of the hands of the Roman tyrant, and everyone left free to seek and receive this sacrament, just as we are free to receive baptism and penance. But now we are compelled by the same tyranny to receive the one kind year after year, so utterly lost is the liberty which Christ has given us. This is the due reward of our godless ingratitude.

[The Second Captivity: Transubstantiation]

The second captivity of this sacrament is less grievous as far as the conscience is concerned, yet the gravest of dangers threatens the person who would attack it, to say nothing of condemning it. Here I shall be called a Wycliffite[54] and a heretic by six hundred names. But what of it? Since the Roman bishop has ceased to be a bishop and has become a tyrant, I fear none of his decrees; for I know that it is not within his power, nor that of any general council, to make new articles of faith.[b]

Some time ago, when I was drinking in scholastic theology, the learned Cardinal of Cambrai[55] gave me food for thought in his comments on the fourth book of the *Sentences*.[56] He argues with great acumen that to hold that real bread and real wine, and not merely their accidents,[57] are present on the altar, would be much more probable and require fewer superfluous miracles—if only the church had not decreed otherwise. When I learned later

they who desire to receive these sacraments since they have been instituted. Secondly, by a figure: thus the Apostle says (1 Corinthians 10:2), that the fathers of old were 'baptized in the cloud and in the sea,' and that 'they did eat . . . spiritual food, and . . . drank . . . spiritual drink.' Nevertheless, sacramental eating is not without avail, because the actual receiving of the sacrament produces more fully the effect of the sacrament than does the desire thereof, as stated above of baptism."

54. John Wycliffe (c. 1331–1384), an English Scholastic theologian and philosopher at Oxford, was an early critic of the doctrine of transubstantiation. For this and a variety of other positions, Wycliffe was posthumously declared a heretic at the Council of Constance on 4 May 1415. Later, in 1428, his body was exhumed and burned.

55. Pierre d'Ailly (1350–1420), chancellor of the University of Paris and cardinal of Cambrai, was an influential Scholastic theologian in the Occamist tradition. Luther studied his *Questiones quarti libri sententiarum* in his early career as a student of theology in Erfurt.

56. The *Sentences* of Peter Lombard (c. 1096–1160) was the standard text for medieval Scholastic theology. Prominent theologians would often publish their own commentaries on Lombard's *Sentences*, which then became the focus of subsequent study and comment.

57. "Accident" refers to the property or quality of a thing that does not touch upon its essential nature or substance. This is an Aristotelian distinction that attained common usage in medieval

a See n. 52, p. 28.

b See Luther's *On the Councils and the Church* in this volume, pp. 317–443.

c The Latin saying is *inter sacrum et saxum*—literally, "between the sacred thing (i.e., sacrificial victim) and the stone knife." The meaning here is that when in such a position, hesitation due to uncertainty is extremely dangerous. Cf. Erasmus, *Adagia* 1, 1, 15.

what church it was that had decreed this, namely, the Thomistic[58]—that is, the Aristotelian church—I grew bolder, and having lingered "between knife and sacrifice,"[c] I at last found rest for my conscience in the above view, namely, that it is real bread and real wine, in which Christ's real flesh and real blood are present in no other way and to no less a degree than the others assert them to be under their accidents. I reached this conclusion because I saw that the opinions of the Thomists, whether approved by pope or by council,[59] remain only opinions, and would not become articles of faith even if an angel from heaven were to decree otherwise.[60] For what is asserted without the Scriptures or proven revelation may be held as an opinion, but need not be believed. But this opinion of Thomas hangs so completely in the air without support of Scripture or reason that it seems to me he knows neither his philosophy nor his logic. For Aristotle speaks of subject and accidents so very differently from St. Thomas that it seems to me this great man is to be pitied not only for attempting to draw his opinions in matters of faith from Aristotle, but also for attempting to base them upon a man whom he did not understand, thus building an unfortunate superstructure upon an unfortunate foundation.[61]

Image of John Wycliffe, English theologian, translator, and reformist, originally published in Bale's *Scriptor Majoris Britanniae* (1548).

theology; see for example Lombard, *Sentences* 4, d. 12, c. 1. In the doctrine of transubstantiation, the "accidents" of the bread and wine—i.e., their appearance, smell, and taste—are said to remain while the "substance" is miraculously changed into Christ's body and blood through consecration. Luther is probably referring to d'Ailly's comments in *Sentences* 4, qu. 6 J; however, see Leif Grane, "Luthers Kritik an Thomas von Aquin in 'De captivate Babylonica,'" *Zeitschrift für Kirchengeschichte* (1969): 3 n.7.

58. Thomas Aquinas (see n. 43 above) was known for his reliance on Aristotle in his attempt to demonstrate a synthesis between philosophy and theology. His articulation of the doctrine of transubstantiation came to be the most influential in the medieval church. See *STh* III, q. 75.

59. In 1215, the Fourth Lateran Council referred to the bread and wine as "transubstantiated" into the body and blood of Christ. Pope Innocent III presided over this council. An official decree on the doctrine of transubstantiation was not arrived at until the Council of Trent in 1551.

60. See Gal. 1:8: "But even if we or an angel from heaven should preach to you a gospel contrary to the one we preached to you, let him be accursed."

61. Aristotle did not conceive of accidental qualities existing apart from the substance; they are de facto a quality of a prior substance. Aquinas is aware of this difficulty; citing Aristotle, however, he appeals to divine providence and the power of God to dispense with this logical problem. Nonetheless, this is precisely the problem for Luther: Why insist on using Aristotle as an aid to theology if one must dispense with it precisely in the moment of theological difficulty?

Therefore I permit everyone to hold either of these opinions, as he or she chooses. My one concern at present is to remove all scruples of conscience, so that they need not fear being called heretics if they believe that real bread and real wine are present on the altar,[d] and that everyone may feel at liberty to ponder, hold, and believe either one view or the other without endangering one's salvation. However, I shall now set forth my own view.

In the first place, I do not intend to listen or attach the least importance to those who will cry out that this teaching of mine is Wycliffite, Hussite, heretical, and contrary to the decree of the church. No one will do this except those very persons whom I have convicted of manifold heresies in the matter of indulgences, freedom of the will and the grace of God, good works and sins, etc.[62] If Wycliffe was once a heretic, they are heretics ten times over; and it is a pleasure to be blamed and accused by heretics and perverse sophists, since to please them would be the height of impiety. Besides, the only way in which they can prove their opinions and disprove contrary ones is by saying: "That is Wycliffite, Hussite, heretical!" They carry this feeble argument always on the tip of their tongues, and they have nothing else. If you ask for scriptural proof, they say: "This is our opinion, and the church (that is, we ourselves) has decided thus." To such an extent these men, who are reprobate concerning the faith[63] and untrustworthy, have the effrontery to set their own fancies before us in the name of the church as articles of faith.

But there are good grounds for my view, and this above all—no violence is to be done to the words of God, whether by human or angel.[e] They are to be retained in their simplest meaning as far as possible. Unless the context manifestly compels it, they are not to be understood apart from their grammatical and proper

62. Some of Luther's most important writings on these topics since 1517: *Disputation Against Scholastic Theology* (1517); *[Ninety-Five Theses or] Disputation for Clarifying the Power of Indulgences* (1517); *A Sermon on Indulgences and Grace* (1518); *The Heidelberg Disputation* (1518); *Treatise on Good Works* (1520). See TAL, vol. 1.

63. See 2 Tim. 3:8: "As Jannes and Jambres opposed Moses, so these people, of corrupt mind and counterfeit faith [*reprobi circa fidem*], also oppose the truth."

64. Origen (c. 184–253) was a theologian who taught in the catechetical school in Alexandria. He was a prolific interpreter of the Scriptures and perhaps the most influential biblical commentator in the Western church. He helped shape principles for recognizing multiple spiritual meanings in the biblical text, commonly referred to as the allegorical approach to the Bible. While this approach was not without controversy, questions of orthodoxy focused primarily on Origen's theological speculation regarding the origin of the soul and the equality of the Son with the Father. He was posthumously condemned of heresy in the sixth century.

d The original of this part of the sentence is singular.

e Gal. 1:8.

sense, lest we give our adversaries occasion to make a mockery of all the Scriptures. Thus Origen was rightly repudiated long ago because, ignoring the grammatical sense, he turned the trees and everything else written concerning Paradise into allegories, from which one could have inferred that trees were not created by God.[64] Even so here, when the Evangelists plainly write that Christ took bread [Matt. 26:26; Mark 14:22; Luke 22:19] and blessed it, and when the Book of Acts and the Apostle Paul in turn call it bread [Acts 2:46; 20:7; 1 Cor. 10:16; 11:23, 26-28], we have to think of real bread and real wine, just as we do of a real cup (for even they do not say that the cup was transubstantiated). Since it is not necessary, therefore, to assume a transubstantiation effected by divine power, it must be regarded as a figment of the human mind, for it rests neither on the Scriptures nor on reason, as we shall see.

Therefore it is an absurd and unheard-of juggling with words to understand "bread" to mean "the form or accidents of bread," and "wine" to mean "the form or accidents of wine."[65] Why do they not also understand all other things to mean their "forms or accidents"? And even if this might be done with all other things, it would still not be right to enfeeble the words of God in this way, and by depriving them of their meaning to cause so much harm.

Moreover, the church kept the true faith for more than twelve hundred years, during which time the holy fathers never, at any time or place, mentioned this transubstantiation (an unnatural[f] word and a dream), until the pseudo philosophy of Aristotle began to make its inroads into the church in these last three hundred years.[66] During this time many things have been wrongly defined, as, for example, that the divine essence is neither begotten nor begets;[67] that the soul is the substantial form of the

f Portentoso. This word could also be translated "monstrous."

65. E.g., Aquinas, *STh* III, q. 75, a. 5: "It is evident to sense that all the accidents of the bread and wine remain after the consecration. And this is reasonably done by divine providence. . . . Christ's flesh and blood are set before us to be partaken of under the species of those things which are the more commonly used by men, namely, bread and wine." See also n. 74, p. 35 ["accident"].

66. The prominence of Aristotle in medieval theology came from several tributaries. The use of dialectic for resolving contradictory statements from various theological authorities became increasingly necessary during the Carolingian period. What was already known of Aristotle was prized for this endeavor as can be seen in such early theological logicians as Peter Abelard (1079–1142). In a relatively short period of time, however, a vast corpus of Aristotle's writings were discovered, coming into the Latin church via the Crusades, the reconquest of Muslim Spain, and various scholarly interactions in the Mediterranean provinces of Venice and Sicily. The result was a widespread effort to bring Aristotle's method and conclusions into conformation with theological doctrine in order to help clarify and defend Christian truth.

67. Lombard, *Sentences* 1, d. 5, c. 1: "In consensus with Catholic expounders, we say regarding this that neither did the Father generate a divine essence, nor did a divine essence generate the Son, nor did a divine essence generate an essence. And here by the term 'essence' we understand the divine nature, which is common to the three persons and is whole in each of them."

Aristotle portrayed in the 1493 *Nuremberg Chronicle* as a scholar of the fifteenth century.

human body.[68] These and like assertions are made without any reason or cause, as the Cardinal of Cambrai himself admits.[69]

Perhaps they will say that the danger of idolatry demands that the bread and wine should not be really present.[70] How ridiculous! The laymen have never become familiar with their subtle philosophy of substance and accidents, and could not grasp it if it were taught to them. Besides, there is the same danger in the accidents which remain and which they see, as in the case of the substance which they do not see. If they do not worship the accidents, but the Christ hidden under them, why should they worship the substance of the bread, which they do not see?

68. Aquinas, *STh* I, q. 76, a. 1: "Therefore this principle by which we primarily understand, whether it be called the intellect or the intellectual soul, is the form of the body. This is the demonstration used by Aristotle (*De anima* ii, 2)."

69. Pierre d'Ailly, *Sentences* 1, q. 5 E: "[The church] is not able to clearly conclude [these ideas on divine generation] from the canonical Scriptures. But if God wanted such truths [about divine generation] to be believed by catholics, then he himself would reveal [them] to the church and through [such a revelation] define [them]. Thus sometimes definitions of the church do not always proceed through obvious conclusions drawn from the Scriptures, but by a special revelation given to catholics."

70. Aquinas, *STh* III, q. 75, a. 2: "Some have held that the substance of the bread and wine remains in this sacrament after the consecration. But this opinion cannot stand . . . because it would be opposed to the veneration of this sacrament, if any substance were there, which could not be adored with adoration of *latria*."

And why could not Christ include his body in the substance of the bread just as well as in the accidents? In red-hot iron, for instance, the two substances, fire and iron, are so mingled that every part is both iron and fire.[71] Why is it not even more possible that the body of Christ be contained in every part of the substance of the bread?

What will they reply? Christ is believed to have been born from the inviolate womb of his mother.[72] Let them say here too that the flesh of the Virgin was meanwhile annihilated, or as they would more aptly say, transubstantiated, so that Christ, after being enfolded in its accidents, finally came forth through the accidents! The same thing will have to be said of the shut door[g] and of the closed mouth of the sepulcher,[h] through which he went in and out without disturbing them.

Out of this has arisen that Babel of a philosophy of a constant quantity distinct from the substance,[73] until it has come to such a pass that they themselves no longer know what are accidents and what is substance. For who has ever proved beyond the shadow of a doubt that heat, color, cold, light, weight, or shape are mere accidents? Finally, they have been driven to pretend that a new substance is created by God for those accidents on the altar, all on account of Aristotle, who says: "It is the nature of an accident to be in something,"[74] and endless other monstrosities. They would be rid of all these if they simply permitted real bread to be present. I rejoice greatly that the simple faith of this sacrament is still to be found, at least among the common people. For as they do not understand, neither do they dispute whether accidents are present without substance, but believe with a simple faith that Christ's body and blood are truly contained there, and leave to those who have nothing else to do the argument about what contains them.

But perhaps they will say: "Aristotle teaches that in an affirmative proposition subject and predicate must be identical," or (to quote the wild beast's own words in the sixth book of his *Metaphysics*): "An affirmative proposition requires the agreement

g John 10:19, 26.

h Matt. 28:2-6.

71. The analogy of fire and iron was not uncommon to describe a variety of consubstantial relationships in theology; for example, Origen when describing the possibility of the incarnation in *Concerning First Principles* 2, 6, 6: "the metal iron is capable of cold and heat. If, then, a mass of iron be kept constantly in the fire, receiving the heat through all its pores and veins, and the fire being continuous and the iron never removed from it."

72. The view that not only Christ's conception but also his birth occurred with his mother's virginity intact can already be found in the second-century *Protoevangelium of James*. Many others also speak of Mary as "ever-Virgin," including Origen, Hilary of Poitiers (c. 300–c. 368), Athanasius (c. 296–373), Epiphanius of Salamis (c. 310–403), Jerome (c. 347–420), Didymus the Blind (c. 313–398), and Augustine. Likewise, Luther would continue to use the title "the ever-Virgin Mary."

73. Because in the doctrine of transubstantiation the accidents of the bread and wine remain without the substance, one must now posit the accidental property of quantity purely in relation to other accidental properties. Accidental properties (e.g., quantity) without essential properties (e.g., substance) would be an absurdity according to the *Categories* of Aristotle.

74. Aristotle, *Metaphysics* 4, 30, 1: "'Accident' means that which attaches to something and can be truly predicated, but neither of necessity nor usually." See also Aquinas, *STh* I, q. 28, a. 2: "For the essence of an accident is to inhere [in something]."

of the subject and the predicate."[75] They interpret agreement to mean identity. Hence, when I say: "This is my body," the subject cannot be identical with the bread, but must be identical with the body of Christ.

What shall we say when Aristotle and these human doctrines are made to be the arbiters of such lofty and divine matters? Why do we not put aside such curiosity and cling simply to the words of Christ, willing to remain in ignorance of what takes place here and content that the real body of Christ is present by virtue of the words? Or is it necessary to comprehend the manner of the divine working in every detail?

But what do they say when Aristotle admits that all of the categories of accidents[76] are themselves a subject—although he grants that substance is the chief subject? Hence for him "this white," "this large," "this something" are all subjects, of which something is predicated.[77] If that is correct, I ask: If a "transubstantiation" must be assumed in order that Christ's body may not be identified with the bread, why not also a "transaccidentation," in order that the body of Christ may not be identified with the accidents?[78] For the same danger remains if one understands the subject to be "this white or this round is my body."[79] And for the same reason that a "transubstantiation" must be assumed, a "transaccidentation" must also be assumed, because of this identity of subject and predicate.

If, however, merely by an act of the intellect, you can do away with the accident, so that it will not be regarded as the subject when you say, "this is my body," why not with equal ease transcend the substance of the bread, if you do not want it to be regarded either as the subject, so that "this my body" is no less in the substance than in the accident? After all, this is a divine work performed by God's almighty power, which can operate just as much and just as well in the accident as it can in the substance.

Let us not dabble too much in philosophy, however. Does not Christ appear to have anticipated this curiosity admirably by saying of the wine, not *Hoc est sanguis meus*, but *Hic est sanguis meus*? [Mark 14:24]. He speaks even more clearly when he brings in the word "cup" and says: "This cup [*Hic calix*] is the new testament in my blood" [Luke 22:20; 1 Cor. 11:25].[80] Does it not seem as though he desired to keep us in a simple faith, sufficient for us to believe that his blood was in the cup? For my part, if I cannot fathom how the bread is the body of Christ, yet I will take my

75. It is not Aristotle's *Metaphysics* but his *Organon*; namely, the sixth book of *Concerning Interpretation* which contains this proposition.

76. Aristotle identifies nine categories of accidents: quantity, quality, relation, place, time, position, state, action, and affection.

77. Aristotle, *Metaphysics* 7, 3: "The word 'substance' is applied, if not in more senses, still at least in four ways; for the essence and the universal and the genus are thought to be the substance of each thing, and fourthly the subject. Now the subject is that of which everything else is predicated, while it is itself not predicated of anything else."

78. Luther is pointing out how relying simply on logical categories and the rules of philosophical language will not bring one nearer to Christian truth. By positing "transaccidentation," Luther shows how the requirements of logic can remain intact even while setting forth absurd theological statements.

79. That is, the accidental properties of the eucharistic host: white and round.

80. Luther is here appealing to the grammatical agreement between the demonstrative pronoun, *hic* ("this"), and *calix* ("cup"), which are both masculine. With the correlation of cup and blood with the demonstrative pronoun, Luther seems to be saying that the continued presence of the wine is indicated in the very words of Christ.

reason captive to the obedience of Christ,[i] and clinging simply to his words, firmly believe not only that the body of Christ is in the bread, but that the bread is the body of Christ. My warrant for this is the words which say: "He took bread, and when he had given thanks, he broke it and said, 'Take, eat, this (that is, this bread, which he had taken and broken) is my body'" [1 Cor. 11:23-24]. And Paul says: "The bread which we break, is it not a participation in the body of Christ?" [1 Cor. 10:16]. He does not say "in the bread there is," but "the bread itself is the participation in the body of Christ." What does it matter if philosophy cannot fathom this? The Holy Spirit is greater than Aristotle. Does philosophy fathom their transubstantiation? Why, they themselves admit that here all philosophy breaks down.[81] That the pronoun "this," in both Greek and Latin, is referred to "body" is due to the fact that in both of these languages the two words are of the same gender. In Hebrew, however, which has no neuter gender, "this" is referred to "bread," so that it would be proper to say *Hic* [bread] *est corpus meum*. Actually, the idiom of the language and common sense both prove that the subject ["this"] obviously points to the bread and not to the body, when he says: *Hoc est corpus meum—das ist meyn leyp*—that is, "This very bread here [*iste panis*] is my body."

Thus, what is true in regard to Christ is also true in regard to the sacrament. In order for the divine nature to dwell in him bodily [Col. 2:9], it is not necessary for the human nature to be transubstantiated and the divine nature contained under the accidents of the human nature. Both natures are simply there in their entirety, and it is truly said: "This man is God; this God is man." Even though philosophy cannot grasp this, faith grasps it nonetheless. And the authority of God's Word is greater than the capacity of our intellect to grasp it. In like manner, it is not necessary in the sacrament that the bread and wine be transubstantiated and that Christ be contained under their accidents in order that the real body and real blood may be present. But both remain there at the same time, and it is truly said: "This bread is my body; this wine is my blood," and vice versa. Thus I will understand it for the time being to the honor of the holy words of God, to which I will allow no violence to be done by

81. E.g., Gabriel Biel, *Sentences* 4, d. 11, q. 1, a. 3, dub. 6 N: "Because this cessation [of the substance of the bread] is supernatural and miraculous, one does not have a concept to impose from philosophy, but is able to speak about the cessation of the thing according to the whole."

i 2 Cor. 10:5.

petty human arguments, nor will I allow them to be twisted into meanings which are foreign to them. At the same time, I permit other men to follow the other opinion, which is laid down in the decree *Firmiter*,[82] only let them not press us to accept their opinions as articles of faith (as I have said above).

[The Third Captivity: The Mass as a Sacrifice]

The third captivity of this sacrament is by far the most wicked abuse of all, in consequence of which there is no opinion more generally held or more firmly believed in the church today than this, that the Mass is a good work and a sacrifice. And this abuse has brought an endless host of other abuses in its train, so that the faith of this sacrament has become utterly extinct and the holy sacrament has been turned into mere merchandise, a market, and a profit-making business. Hence participations,[83] brotherhoods,[84] intercessions, merits, anniversaries,[85] memorial days,[86] and similar goods are bought and sold, traded and bartered, in the church. On these the priests and monks depend for their entire livelihood.

I am attacking a difficult matter, an abuse perhaps impossible to uproot, since through century-long custom and the common consent of men it has become so firmly entrenched that it would be necessary to abolish most of the books now in vogue, and to alter almost the entire external form of the churches[87] and introduce, or rather reintroduce, totally different kinds of ceremonies. But my Christ lives, and we must be careful to give more heed to the Word of God than to all the thoughts of human beings and of angels. I will perform the duties of my office[88] and bring to light the facts in the case. As I have received the truth freely,[j] I will impart it without malice. For the rest let all look to their own salvation; I will do my part faithfully so that none may be able to cast on me the blame for their lack of faith and their ignorance of the truth when we appear before the judgment seat of Christ.[k]

In the first place, in order that we might safely and happily attain to a true and free knowledge of this sacrament, we must be particularly careful to put aside whatever has been added to

j Matt. 10:8.

k 2 Cor. 5:10.

82. Luther is referring to the first canon of the Fourth Lateran Council (1215), which uses the term *transubstantiation*: "His body and blood are truly contained in the sacrament of the altar under the forms of bread and wine, the bread and wine having been changed in substance (*transubstantiatis*), by God's power, into his body and blood, so that in order to achieve this mystery of unity we receive from God what he received from us." *Firmiter, Decretalium Gregorii IX, lib. I, tit I: de summa trinitate et fide catholica,* cap. 1, sec 3.

83. A "participation" was the notion that one could, without being present, obtain spiritual benefits from the saying of Masses. For example, such was possible with the regular Masses said in monasteries.

84. Confraternities that paid to have Masses said for them alongside other devotional practices for the purpose of gaining merit. The benefits accrued by one member through his devotion and attendance at Masses was then made available to all other members. See Luther's critique of this practice in his treatise *The Blessed Sacrament of the Holy and True Body of Christ, and the Brotherhoods* (1519), LW 35:45–74; TAL 1:225–56.

85. "Anniversaries" can refer to a year of daily Masses said on behalf of the soul of a deceased person or to Masses said every year on the anniversary of one's death.

86. Masses for the dead said on memorial days.

87. Medieval church architecture

its original simple institution by human zeal and devotion: such things as vestments, ornaments, chants, prayers, organs, candles, and the whole pageantry of outward things. We must turn our eyes and hearts simply to the institution of Christ and this alone,[89] and set nothing before us but the very word of Christ by which he instituted the sacrament, made it perfect, and committed it to us. For in that word, and in that word alone, reside the power, the nature, and the whole substance of the Mass. All the rest is the work of human beings, added to the word of Christ, and the Mass can be held and remain a Mass just as well without them. Now the words of Christ, in which he instituted this sacrament, are these:

"Now as they were eating, Jesus took bread, and blessed, and broke it, and gave it to his disciples and said, 'Take, eat; this is my body, which is given for you.' And he took a cup, and when he had given thanks he gave it to them, saying, 'Drink of it, all of you; for this cup is the new testament in my blood, which is poured out for you and for many for the forgiveness of sins. Do this in remembrance of me.'"[90]

Albrecht Dürer's woodcut illustration of the Lord's Supper (completed 1510).

facilitated these sacramental practices, from high altars for feast-day Masses to side altars and apsidiole chapels for private Masses, alcoves for the reservation and adoration of consecrated hosts, and screens dividing celebrants from the congregation.

88. As a sworn doctor of Holy Scripture (1512), Luther vowed to uphold the teachings of the Scripture and defend the faith from false doctrine.

89. Luther's examination of the biblical words of institution as the primary interpretation of the sacrament's meaning, benefit, and practice was first set forth a few months earlier in his *Treatise on the New Testament* (1520), LW 35:79-112.

90. Luther follows the canon of the Mass in conflating the various accounts of the words of institution from Matt. 26:26-28; Mark 14:22-24; Luke 22:19-20; and 1 Cor. 11:23-25, but excludes ornamental phrases in the canon not found explicitly in Scripture.

These words the Apostle also delivers and more fully expounds in 1 Cor. 11[:23-26]. On them we must rest; on them we must build as on a firm rock, if we would not be carried about with every wind of doctrine,[l] as we have till now been carried about by the wicked doctrines of men who reject the truth.[m] For in these words nothing is omitted that pertains to the completeness, the use, and the blessing of this sacrament; and nothing is included that is superfluous and not necessary for us to know. Whoever sets aside these words and meditates or teaches concerning the Mass will teach monstrous and wicked doctrines, as they have done who have made of the sacrament an *opus operatum*[91] and a sacrifice.

Let this stand, therefore, as our first and infallible proposition—the Mass or Sacrament of the Altar is Christ's testament, which he left behind him at his death to be distributed among his believers. For that is the meaning of his words, "This cup is the new testament in my blood" [Luke 22:20; 1 Cor. 11:25]. Let this truth stand, I say, as the immovable foundation on which we shall base all that we have to say. For, as you will see, we are going to overthrow all the godless opinions of men which have been imported into this most precious sacrament. Christ, who is the truth, truly says that this is the new testament in his blood, poured out for us. Not without reason do I dwell on this sentence; the matter is of no small moment, and must be most deeply impressed on our minds.

Thus, if we enquire what a testament is, we shall learn at the same time what the Mass is, what its right use and blessing, and what its wrong use.

A testament, as everyone knows, is a promise made by one about to die, in which he designates his bequest and appoints his heirs. A testament, therefore, involves first, the death of the testator, and second, the promise of an inheritance and the naming of the heir. Thus Paul discusses at length the nature of a testament in Rom. 4[:13f.], Gal. 3[:15-17] and 4[:1-7], and Heb. 9[:15-18].[92] We see the same thing clearly also in these words of Christ. Christ testifies concerning his death when he says: "This is my body, which is given, this is my blood, which is poured out" [Luke 22:19-20]. He names and designates the bequest when he

l Eph. 4:14.

m Titus 1:14.

91. The Scholastic notion of the sacrament as an *opus operatum* is the doctrine that the priestly act intrinsically offers grace without reference to the disposition or faith of the recipient. Luther first challenges this understanding of the sacrament's efficacy in his *Sermon on the Blessed Sacrament of the Holy and True Body and Blood of Christ* (1519), LW 35:45-74; TAL 1:225-56.

92. Luther still held the traditional view that Paul was the author of the epistle to the Hebrews. He would change his mind on this by the time of his 1522 translation of the New Testament so that his preface to the epistle reads: ". . . Hebrews is not an epistle of St. Paul, or any other apostle . . . who wrote it is not known, and will probably not be known for a while; it makes no difference." He was probably influenced by Erasmus, who first questioned the Pauline authorship in his annotations to the New Testament. Earlier that year, in a sermon on Heb. 1:1-4, Luther suggested that Apollos might be the actual author.

says "for the forgiveness of sins" [Matt. 26:28]. But he appoints the heirs when he says, "For you [Luke 22:19-20; 1 Cor. 11:24] and for many" [Matt. 26:28; Mark 14:24], that is, for those who accept and believe the promise of the testator. For here it is faith that makes us heirs, as we shall see.

You see, therefore, that what we call the Mass is a promise of the forgiveness of sins made to us by God, and such a promise as has been confirmed by the death of the Son of God. For the only difference between a promise and a testament is that the testament involves the death of the one who makes it. A testator is a promiser who is about to die, while a promiser (if I may put it thus) is a testator who is not about to die. This testament of Christ is foreshadowed in all the promises of God from the beginning of the world; indeed, whatever value those ancient promises possessed was altogether derived from this new promise that was to come in Christ. Hence the words "compact," "covenant," and "testament of the Lord"[93] occur so frequently in the Scriptures. These words signified that God would one day die. "For where there is a testament, the death of the testator must of necessity occur" (Heb. 9[:16]). Now God made a testament; therefore, it was necessary that God should die. But God could not die unless God became human. Thus the incarnation and the death of Christ are both comprehended most concisely in this one word, "testament."

From the above it will at once be seen what is the right and what is the wrong use of the Mass, and what is the worthy and what the unworthy preparation for it. If the Mass is a promise, as has been said, then access to it is to be gained, not with any works, or powers, or merits of one's own, but by faith alone. For where there is the word of the promising God, there must necessarily be the faith of the accepting person. It is plain, therefore, that the beginning of our salvation is a faith which clings to the word of the promising God, who, without any effort on our part, in free and unmerited mercy takes the initiative and offers us the word of his promise. "He sent forth his Word, and thus healed them," not: "He accepted our work, and thus healed us."[94] First of all there is God's Word. After it follows faith; after faith, love; then love does every good work, for it does no wrong; indeed, it is the fulfilling of the law.[95] In no other way can a person come to God or deal with God than through faith. That is to say, that the author of salvation is not human beings, by any works of their

93. The Latin for these three words are, respectively: *pactum, foedus, testamentum*. All three words are used interchangeably in the Latin Vulgate to translate the Hebrew *berith* in the Old Testament and the Greek *diathēkē* in the Septuagint or New Testament, rendered by most English translations as "covenant." E.g., Exod. 24:8: "Moses took the blood and dashed it on the people, and said, 'See the blood of the covenant [*sanguis foederis*] that the Lord has made with you in accordance with all these words'"; Gen. 9:8-9: "Then God said to Noah and to his sons with him, 'As for me, I am establishing my covenant [*pactum meum*] with you and your descendants after you . . .'"; Ps. 25:10: "All the paths of the Lord are steadfast love and faithfulness, for those who keep his covenant [*testamentum eius*] and his decrees."

94. Ps. 107:20. Luther inserted "thus" (*sic*) in his interpretation of the verse.

95. Rom. 13:10: "Love does no wrong to a neighbor; therefore love is the fulfilling of the law."

own,[n] but God, through his promise; and that all things depend on, and are upheld and preserved by, the word of his power,[96] through which he brought us forth, to be a kind of first fruits of his creatures.[97]

Thus, in order to raise up Adam after the fall, God gave him this promise when he said to the serpent: "I will put enmity between you and the woman, and between your seed and her seed; he shall bruise your head, and you shall bruise his heel" [Gen. 3:15]. In this word of promise Adam, together with his descendants, was carried as it were in God's bosom, and by faith in it he was preserved, waiting patiently for the woman who should bruise the serpent's head, as God had promised. And in that faith and expectation he died, not knowing when or who she would be, yet never doubting that she would come. For such a promise, being the truth of God, preserves even in hell[98] those who believe it and wait for it. After this came another promise, made to Noah—to last until the time of Abraham—when a bow was set in the clouds as a sign of the covenant,[o] by faith in which Noah and his descendants found God gracious. After that, he promised Abraham that all the nations should be blessed in his seed.[p] And this is Abraham's bosom,[q] into which his descendants have been received.[99] Then to Moses and the children of Israel,[r] especially to David,[s] he gave the plainest promise of Christ, and thereby at last made clear what the promise to the people of old really was.

And so it finally came to the most perfect promise of all, that of the new testament, in which, with plain words, life and salvation are freely promised, and actually granted to those who believe the promise. And he distinguishes this testament from the old one by a particular mark when he calls it the "new testament." For the old testament given through Moses was not a promise of forgiveness of sins or of eternal things, but of temporal things, namely, of the land of Canaan, by which no one was renewed in spirit to lay hold on the heavenly inheritance.

n The original here is singular.

o Gen. 9:12-17.

p Gen. 22:18.

q Luke 16:22.

r Deut. 18:18.

s 2 Sam. 7:12-16.

96. Heb. 1:3: "He is the radiance of the glory of God and the exact imprint of his nature, and he upholds the universe by the word of his power."

97. James 1:8: "Of his own will he brought us forth by the word of truth, that we should be a kind of firstfruits of his creatures."

98. Luther's reference to "hell" (*inferno*) here corresponds to the concept of *hades* or the Hebrew *Sheol* and the notion that, before Christ, the patriarchs remained imprisoned in this place of the dead until he would release them after his resurrection. Ephesians 4:7-10 and 1 Peter 3:19-20 were often interpreted as biblical allusions to this, and the view was relatively common in the early church. The medieval view was deeply influenced by the detailed account in the fourth-century apocryphal text *The Gospel of Nicodemus*. Dante (1265-1321) refers to this as the first circle of hell or "limbo." There the patriarchs of old were held until the "Mighty One," i.e., Christ, came and released them; cf. *Inferno*, Canto 4.52-63.

99. Hippolytus of Rome (170-235) referred to the place of the Old Testament righteous souls as the "Bosom of Abraham."

Wherefore also it was necessary that, as a figure of Christ, a dumb beast should be slain, in whose blood the same testament might be confirmed, as the blood corresponded to the testament and the sacrifice corresponded to the promise. But here Christ says "the new testament in my blood" [Luke 22:20; 1 Cor. 11:25], not somebody else's, but his own, by which grace is promised through the Spirit for the forgiveness of sins, that we may obtain the inheritance.

According to its substance, therefore, the Mass is nothing but the aforesaid words of Christ: "Take and eat, etc." [Matt. 26:26], as if he were saying: "Behold, O sinful and condemned human, out of the pure and unmerited love with which I love you, and by the will of the Father of mercies,[t] apart from any merit or desire of yours, I promise you in these words the forgiveness of all your sins and life everlasting. And that you may be absolutely certain of this irrevocable promise of mine, I shall give my body and pour out my blood, confirming this promise by my very death, and leaving you my body and blood as a sign and memorial of this same promise. As often as you partake of them, remember me, proclaim and praise my love and bounty toward you, and give thanks."

From this you will see that nothing else is needed for a worthy holding of Mass than a faith that relies confidently on this promise, believes Christ to be true in these words of his, and does not doubt that these infinite blessings have been bestowed upon it. Hard on this faith there follows, of itself, a most sweet stirring of the heart, whereby the human spirit is enlarged and enriched (that is love, given by the Holy Spirit through faith in Christ), so that a person is drawn to Christ, that gracious and bounteous testator, and made a thoroughly new and different person. Who would not shed tears of gladness, indeed, almost faint for joy in Christ, if he believed with unshaken faith that this inestimable promise of Christ belonged to him? How could he help but love so great a benefactor, who of his own accord offers, promises, and grants such great riches and this eternal inheritance to one who is unworthy and deserving of something far different?

Therefore it is our one and only misfortune that we have many Masses in the world, and yet none, or very few of us, recognize, consider, and receive these promises and riches that are

t 2 Cor. 1:3.

offered to us. Actually, during the Mass, we should do nothing with greater zeal (indeed, it demands all our zeal) than to set before our eyes, meditate upon, and ponder these words, these promises of Christ—for they truly constitute the Mass itself—in order to exercise, nourish, increase, and strengthen our faith in them by this daily remembrance. For this is what he commands, when he says: "Do this in remembrance of me" [Luke 22:19; 1 Cor. 11:24]. This should be done by the preachers of the gospel in order to impress this promise faithfully upon the people, to commend it to them, and to awaken their faith in it.

But how many are there today who know that the Mass is the promise of Christ? I will say nothing of those godless preachers of fables, who teach human ordinances instead of this great promise. And even if they teach these words of Christ, they do not teach them as a promise or testament, neither therefore as a means of obtaining faith.

What we deplore in this captivity is that nowadays they take every precaution that no layperson should hear these words of Christ, as if they were too sacred to be delivered to the common people. So mad are we priests that we arrogate to ourselves alone the so-called words of consecration, to be said secretly,[100] yet in such a way that they do not profit even us, for we too fail to regard them as promises or as a testament for the strengthening of the faith. Instead of believing them, we reverence them with I know not what superstitious and godless fancies. What else is Satan trying to do to us through this misfortune of ours but to let nothing of the Mass remain in the church, though he is meanwhile at work filling every corner of the globe with Masses, that is, with abuses and mockeries of God's testament—burdening the world more and more heavily with most grievous sins of idolatry, to its deeper condemnation?[101] For what more sinful idolatry can there be than to abuse God's promises with perverse opinions and to neglect or extinguish faith in them?

For God does not deal, nor has God ever dealt, with people otherwise than through a word of promise, as I have said. We in turn cannot deal with God otherwise than through faith in the Word of his promise. God does not desire works, nor has God need of them; rather we deal with other people and with ourselves on the basis of works. But God has need of this: that we consider God faithful in God's promises,[102] and patiently persist in this belief, and thus worship God with faith, hope, and love.

100. In the early Middle Ages, softly spoken prayers, called *secreta*, occurred before the canon of the Mass (see also n. 170 below) because the offertory psalm was being sung by the choir simultaneously. Later (probably around the eighth century), the canon of the Mass began also to be prayed quietly, after the singing of the Preface and *Sanctus*. The reason for this is probably a combination of priestly piety and a pastoral concern for profane usage by the common people. Cf. Durandus, *Rationale divinorum officiorum* 4, 35, 2. Luther attacked this practice of the *Stillmesse* in a later treatise, *The Abomination of the Secret Mass* (1525), LW 36:311–28.

101. Luther means here that nothing remains in the church of the Mass as it should be understood and celebrated, even as more and more Masses are celebrated in the wrong way and for the wrong purpose.

102. Heb. 10:23: "Let us hold fast to the confession of our hope without wavering, for he who has promised is faithful."

It is in this way that God obtains glory among us, since it is not of ourselves who run, but of God who shows mercy, promises, and gives, that we have and hold all good things.[103] Behold, this is that true worship and service of God which we ought to perform in the Mass. But if the words of promise are not delivered, what exercise of faith can there be? And without faith, who can have hope or love? Without faith, hope, and love, what service of God can there be? There is no doubt, therefore, that in our day all priests and monks, together with their bishops and all their superiors, are idolators, living in a most perilous state by reason of this ignorance, abuse, and mockery of the Mass, or sacrament, or promise of God.

For anyone can easily see that these two, promise and faith, must necessarily go together. For without the promise there is nothing to be believed; while without faith the promise is useless, since it is established and fulfilled through faith. From this everyone will readily gather that the Mass, since it is nothing but promise, can be approached and observed only in faith. Without this faith, whatever else is brought to it by way of prayers, preparations, works, signs, or gestures are incitements to impiety rather than exercises of piety. It usually happens that those who are thus prepared imagine themselves legitimately entitled to approach the altar, when in reality they are less prepared than at any other time or by any other work, by reason of the unbelief which they bring with them. How many celebrants you can see everywhere, every day, who imagine they—wretched men—have committed criminal offenses when they make some petty mistake, such as wearing the wrong vestment, or forgetting to wash their hands, or stumbling over their prayers! But the fact that they have no regard for or faith in the Mass itself, namely, the divine promise, causes them not the slightest qualms of conscience. O worthless religion of this age of ours, the most godless and thankless of all ages!

Hence the only worthy preparation and proper observance is faith, the faith by which we believe in the Mass, that is, in the divine promise. Those, therefore, who desire to approach the altar or receive the sacrament, let them beware lest they appear empty-handed before the face of the Lord God.[104] But they will be empty-handed unless they have faith in the Mass, or this new testament. By what godless work could they sin more grievously against the truth of God, than by this unbelief of theirs? By it,

103. Rom. 9:16: "So it depends not on human will or exertion, but on God who shows mercy."

104. Cf. Exod. 23:15: "You shall observe the festival of unleavened bread. . . . No one shall appear before me empty-handed"; Deut. 16:16: "Three times a year all your males shall appear before the LORD your God at the place that he will choose: at the festival of unleavened bread, at the festival of weeks, and at the festival of booths. They shall not appear before the LORD empty-handed."

as much as in their lies, they convict God of being a liar and a maker of empty promises.[105,u] The safest course, therefore, will be to go to the Mass in the same spirit in which you would go to hear any other promise of God, that is, prepared not to do or contribute much yourself, but to believe and accept all that is promised you there, or proclaimed as promises through the ministry of the priest. If you do not come in this spirit, beware of attending at all, for you will surely be going to your judgment.[106]

I was right then in saying that the whole power of the Mass consists in the words of Christ, in which he testifies that forgiveness of sins is bestowed on all those who believe that his body is given and his blood poured out for them. This is why nothing is more important for those who go to hear Mass than to ponder these words diligently and in full faith. Unless they do this, all else that they do is in vain. This is surely true, that to every promise of his, God usually adds some sign as a memorial or remembrance of the promise, so that thereby we may serve him the more diligently and he may admonish us the more effectually.[107] Thus, when he promised Noah that he would not again destroy the world by a flood, he added his bow in the clouds, to show that he would be mindful of his covenant [Gen. 9:8-17]. And after promising Abraham the inheritance in his seed, he gave him circumcision as a mark of his justification by faith [Gen. 17:3-11]. Thus he granted to Gideon the dry and the wet fleece to confirm his promise of victory over the Midianites [Judg. 6:36-40]. And through Isaiah he offered to Ahaz a sign that he would conquer the king of Syria and Samaria, to confirm in him his faith in the promise [Isa. 7:10-17]. And we read of many such signs of the promises of God in the Scriptures.

So in the Mass also, the foremost promise of all, he adds as a memorial sign of such a great promise his own body and his own blood in the bread and wine, when he says: "Do this in remembrance of me" [Luke 22:19; 1 Cor. 11:24-25]. And so in baptism, to the words of promise he adds the sign of immersion in water. We may learn from this that in every promise of God two things are presented to us, the word and the sign, so that we are to understand the word to be the testament, but the sign to be the sacrament. Thus, in the Mass, the word of Christ is the testament, and the bread and wine are the sacrament. And as

u The original of these sentences is singular.

105. This definition of unbelief can be found consistently through the earliest writings of Luther, especially as it touches on Rom. 3:4 and its citation of Pss. 116:11 and 51:4, "Although everyone is a liar, let God be proved true, as it is written, 'So that you may be justified in your words, and prevail in your judging.'"

106. Perhaps a reference to the consequences of unworthy eating that Paul mentions in 1 Cor. 11:29.

107. Luther gives many of the same examples in his earlier *Treatise on the New Testament* (1520), LW 35:86.

there is greater power in the word than in the sign, so there is greater power in the testament than in the sacrament; for a man can have and use the word or testament apart from the sign or sacrament. "Believe," says Augustine, "and you have eaten."[v] But what does one believe, other than the word of the one who promises? Therefore I can hold Mass every day, indeed, every hour, for I can set the words of Christ before me and with them feed and strengthen my faith as often as I choose. This is a truly spiritual eating and drinking.[108]

Here you may see what great things our theologians of the *Sentences*[109] have produced in this matter. In the first place, not one of them treats of that which is first and foremost, namely, the testament and the word of promise. And thus they make us forget faith and the whole power of the Mass. In addition, they discuss exclusively the second part of the Mass, namely, the sign or sacrament; yet in such a way that here too they do not teach faith, but their preparations and *opera operata*,[w] participations[x] and fruits of the Mass.[110] They come then to the profundities, babble of transubstantiation, and endless other metaphysical trivialities, destroy the proper understanding and use of both sacrament and testament together with faith as such, and cause Christ's people to forget their God—as the prophet says, days without number [Jer. 2:32]. Let the others tabulate the various benefits of hearing Mass; you just apply your mind to this, that you may say and believe with the prophet that God has here prepared a table before you in the presence of your enemies [Ps. 23:5], at which your faith may feed and grow fat. But your faith is fed only with the word of divine promise, for "One does not live by bread alone, but by every word that proceeds from the mouth of God" [Deut. 8:3; Matt. 4:4]. Hence, in the Mass you must pay closest heed above all to the word of promise, as to a most lavish banquet—your utterly green pastures and sacred still waters [Ps. 23:2]—in order that you might esteem this word above everything else, trust in it supremely, and cling to it most firmly, even through death and all sins. If you do this, you will obtain not merely those tiny drops and crumbs of "fruits of the

108. For a Scholastic understanding of spiritual eating in the sacrament, cf. Aquinas, *STh* III, q. 80, a. 2: "there are two ways of eating spiritually. First, . . . the angels eat Christ spiritually inasmuch as they are united with Him in the enjoyment of perfect charity, and in clear vision. . . . In another way one may eat Christ spiritually, . . . as a man believes in Christ, while desiring to receive this sacrament."

109. That is, commentators on the *Sentences* of Peter Lombard. See n. 56, p. 30.

110. "Fruits of the Mass" (*fructus missae*) has to do with the character and extent of benefits received in the celebration of the Mass, especially the relationship between the infinite benefits procured by Christ and present *ex opere operato* and the limited benefits correlative to the intensity of the devotion of those who participate.

v Cf. Augustine, *Sermo* 112, 5.

w See n. 91, p. 40.

x See n. 83, p. 38.

Mass" which some have superstitiously invented, but the very fountainhead of life, namely, that faith in the Word out of which every good thing flows, as is said in John 4:[111] "He who believes in me, 'Out of his heart shall flow rivers of living water.'" And again, "Whoever drinks of the water that I shall give him, it will become in him a spring of water welling up to eternal life" [John 4:14].

Now there are two things that are constantly assailing us, so that we fail to gather the fruits of the Mass. The first is that we are sinners, and unworthy of such great things because of our utter worthlessness. The second is that, even if we were worthy, these things are so high that our timid nature does not dare to aspire to them or hope for them. For who would not simply stand awe-struck before the forgiveness of sins and life everlasting rather than seek after them, once he had weighed properly the magnitude of the blessings which come through them, namely, to have God as father, to be God's child and heir of all God's goods! Against this twofold timidness of ours we must lay hold on the word of Christ, and fix our gaze much more steadfastly on it than on these thoughts of our own weakness. For "great are the works of the Lord, studied by all who have pleasure in them" [Ps. 111:2], who is able to give "more abundantly than all that we ask or think" [Eph. 3:20]. If they did not surpass our worthiness, our grasp, and all our thoughts, they would not be divine. Thus Christ also encourages us when he says: "Fear not, little flock, for it is your Father's good pleasure to give you the kingdom" [Luke 12:32]. For it is just this incomprehensible overflowing of God's goodness, showered upon us through Christ, that moves us above all to love God most ardently in return, to be drawn to God with fullest confidence, and, despising all else, be ready to suffer all things for God. Wherefore this sacrament is rightly called "a fountain of love."[112]

Let us take an illustration of this from human experience.[113] If a very rich lord were to bequeath a thousand gold coins[114] to a beggar or to an unworthy and wicked servant, it is certain that he would boldly claim and accept them without regard to his unworthiness and the greatness of the bequest. And if anyone should seek to oppose him on the grounds of his unworthiness and the large amount of the legacy, what do you suppose the man would say? He would likely say: "What is that to you? What I accept, I accept not on my merits or by any right that I may personally have to it. I know that I am receiving more than

111. John 7:38. Luther was looking ahead to the next verse cited from John 4.

112. While the phrase "fount of love" (*fons dilectionis*) is more commonly applied to the Blessed Virgin Mary in the Middle Ages, love is clearly the central benefit of the sacrament according to Scholastic theology, yet in such a way that love is infused in the recipient as a virtue meriting divine favor. See, for example, Lombard, *Sentences* 4, d. 12, c. 6: "For this Sacrament was instituted for two reasons: for the increase of virtue, namely love, and as medicine for our daily infirmity."

113. Luther used the following illustration in his earlier *Treatise on the New Testament* (1520), LW 35:89f.

114. *Guldens,* gold coins of the time, perhaps of the Holy Roman Empire.

a worthless one like me deserves; indeed, I have deserved the very opposite. But I claim what I claim by the right of a bequest and of another's goodness. If to Christ it was not an unworthy thing to bequeath so great a sum to an unworthy person, why should I refuse to accept it because of my unworthiness? Indeed, it is for this very reason that I cherish all the more his unmerited gift—because I am unworthy!" With that same thought all people[y] ought to fortify their consciences against all qualms and scruples, so that they may lay hold on the promise of Christ with unwavering faith, and take the greatest care to approach the sacrament not trusting in confession, prayer, and preparation, but rather, despairing of all these, with firm confidence in Christ who gives the promise. For, as we have said often enough, the word of promise must reign alone here in pure faith; such faith is the one and only sufficient preparation.

Hence we see how great is God's wrath with us, in that God has permitted godless teachers to conceal the words of this testament from us, and thereby to extinguish this same faith, as far as they could. It is already easy to see what is the inevitable result of this extinguishing of the faith, namely, the most godless superstition of works. For where faith dies and the word of faith is silent, there works and the prescribing of works immediately crowd into their place. By them we have been carried away out of our own land, as into a Babylonian captivity, and despoiled of all our precious possessions. This has been the fate of the Mass; it has been converted by the teaching of godless people into a good work. They themselves call it an *opus operatum*,[z] and by it they presume themselves to be all-powerful with God. Next they proceed to the very height of madness, and after inventing the lie that the Mass is effective simply by virtue of the act having been performed, they add another one to the effect that the Mass is none the less profitable to others even if it is harmful to some wicked priest who may be celebrating it.[115] On such a foundation of sand they base their applications, participations, brotherhoods, anniversaries,[a] and numberless other lucrative and profitable schemes of that kind.

y This sentence is singular in the original.

z See n. 91, p. 40.

a See n. 82, 83, and 85, p. 38.

115. Cf. Aquinas, *STh* III, q. 82, a. 6: "By reason of the power of the Holy Spirit, who communicates to each one the blessings of Christ's members on account of their being united in charity, the private blessing in the Mass of a good priest is fruitful to others. But the private evil of one man cannot hurt another, except the latter, in some way, consent." Luther refers here to the prayers of the Mass as an offering to God and not to the sacrament itself, which is God's work regardless of the worthiness of the priest. See below, p. 59.

These fraudulent disguises are so powerful, so numerous, and so firmly entrenched that you can scarcely prevail against them unless you exercise unremitting care and bear well in mind what the Mass is and what has been said above. You have seen that the Mass is nothing else than the divine promise or testament of Christ, sealed with the sacrament of his body and blood. If that is true, you will understand that it cannot possibly be in any way a work; nobody can possibly do any thing in it, neither can it be dealt with in any other way than by faith alone. However, faith is not a work, but the lord and life of all works.[b] Who in the world is so foolish as to regard a promise received by him, or a testament given to him, as a good work, which he renders to the testator by his acceptance of it? What heir will imagine that he is doing his departed father a kindness by accepting the terms of the will and the inheritance it bequeaths to him? What godless audacity is it, therefore, when we who are to receive the testament of God come as those who would perform a good work for God! This ignorance of the testament, this captivity of so great a sacrament—are they not too sad for tears? When we ought to be grateful for benefits received, we come arrogantly to give that which we ought to take. With unheard-of perversity we mock the mercy of the giver by giving as a work the thing we receive as a gift, so that the testator, instead of being a dispenser of his own goods, becomes the recipient of ours. Woe to such sacrilege!

Who has ever been so mad as to regard baptism as a good work, or what candidate for baptism has believed that he was performing a work which he might offer to God on behalf of himself and communicate to others? If, then, there is no good work that can be communicated to others in this one sacrament and testament, neither will there be any in the Mass, since it too is nothing else than a testament and sacrament. Hence it is a manifest and wicked error to offer or apply the Mass for sins, for satisfactions, for the dead, or for any needs whatsoever of one's own or of others.[116] You will readily see the obvious truth of this if you firmly hold that the Mass is a divine promise, which can benefit no one, be applied to no one, intercede for no one, and be communicated to no one, except only to one who believes with a

116. Luther is speaking against the so-called votive Mass, a Mass said with an intention other than the usual celebration of the day's divine office—often as an intercession for the sake of some need, e.g., the sick, the dead, the penitent, etc. It was a common practice throughout the Middle Ages, and became increasingly common due to the acceptance of money in exchange for such a Mass.

b On the relationship between faith and works, see Luther's *Treatise on Good Works* (1520), LW 44:15–114; TAL 1:257–368.

faith of one's own. Who can receive or apply, in behalf of another, the promise of God, which demands the personal faith of each one individually? Can I give to another the promise of God, even if that person does not believe? Can I believe for another, or cause another to believe? But this is what must happen if I am able to apply and communicate the Mass to others; for there are but two things in the Mass, the divine promise and the human faith, the latter accepting what the former promises. But if it is true that I can do this, then I can also hear and believe the gospel for another, I can be baptized for another, I can be absolved from sins for another, I can also partake of the Sacrament of the Altar for another, and—to go through the list of their sacraments also—I can marry a wife for another, get ordained for another, be confirmed for another, and receive extreme unction for another!

In short, why did not Abraham believe for all the Jews? Why was faith in the promise made to Abraham demanded of every individual Jew?[c]

Therefore, let this irrefutable truth stand fast: Where there is a divine promise, there everyone must stand on his own feet; his own personal faith is demanded, he will give an account for himself and bear his own load;[d] as it is said in the last chapter of Mark [16:16]: "He who believes and is baptized will be saved; but he who does not believe will be condemned." Even so each one can derive personal benefit from the Mass only by one's own personal faith. It is absolutely impossible to commune on behalf of anyone else. Just as the priest is unable to administer the sacrament to anyone on behalf of another, but administers the same sacrament to each one individually by himself. For in consecrating and administering, the priests are our servants. Through them we are not offering a good work or communicating something in an active sense. Rather, we are receiving through them the promises and the sign; we are being communicated unto in the passive sense. This is the view that has persisted with respect to the laity right up to the present day, for of them it is said not that they do something good but that they receive it. But the priests have strayed into godless ways; out of the sacrament and testament of God, which ought to be a good gift received, they

c Cf. Gen. 12:1f.; 15:5f.

d Gal. 6:5.

have made for themselves a good deed performed, which they then give to others and offer up to God.

But you will say: What is this? Will you not overturn the practice and teaching of all the churches and monasteries, by virtue of which they have flourished all these centuries? For the Mass is the foundation of their anniversaries, intercessions, applications, communications, etc., that is to say, of their fat income. I answer: This is the very thing that has constrained me to write of the captivity of the church.[117] For it is in this manner that the sacred testament of God has been forced into the service of a most impious traffic. It has come through the opinions and ordinances of wicked men, who, passing over the Word of God, have dished up to us the thoughts of their own hearts and led the whole world astray. What do I care about the number and influence of those who are in this error? The truth is mightier than all of them. If you are able to refute Christ, who teaches that the Mass is a testament and a sacrament, then I will admit that they are in the right. Or, if you can bring yourself to say that that man is doing a good work who receives the benefit of the testament, or to that end uses this sacrament of promise, then I will gladly condemn my teachings. But since you can do neither, why do you hesitate to turn your back on the multitude who go after evil? Why do you hesitate to give God the glory and to confess God's truth—that all priests today are perversely mistaken who regard the Mass as a work by which they may relieve their own needs and those of others, whether dead or alive? I am uttering unheard of and startling things, but if you will consider what the Mass is, you will realize that I have spoken the truth. The fault lies with our false sense of security, which blinds us to the wrath of God that is raging against us.

I am ready to admit, however, that the prayers which we pour out before God when we are gathered together to partake of the Mass are good works or benefits, which we impart, apply, and communicate to one another, and which we offer for one another.[118] Thus James [5:16] teaches us to pray for one another that we may be healed, and Paul in 1 Tim. 2[:1-2] commands "that supplications, prayers, and intercessions be made for all men, for kings and all who are in high positions." Now these are not the Mass, but works of the Mass—if the prayers of heart and lips may be called works—for they flow from the faith that is kindled or increased in the sacrament. For the Mass, or the

117. The transposition of the divine generosity and promise of the sacrament into a human work, the justification of this practice by human opinion and tradition rather than the Scriptures, and the consequent enlargement of papal power and riches are, for Luther, the fundamental abuses of the church. Much of his early theological critique can be summarized here: (1) the gospel is not to be turned into a law; (2) the word of God is the final theological authority, not human opinion; and (3) the church should shepherd the flock with practices and doctrine that strengthen faith in Christ, not fleece the sheep for its own gain.

118. In his early writings (e.g., *First Lectures on the Psalms*, 1513–1515), Luther can talk about the Mass as a sacrifice but limits the language to sacrifices of praise and thanksgiving (*sacrificium confessionis . . . laudis*). In his 1520 *Treatise on the New Testament*, Luther further develops this line of interpretation for the eucharistic sacrifice: "To be sure

promise of God, is not fulfilled by praying, but only by believing. However, as believers we pray and perform every good work. But what priest offers up the sacrifice in this sense, that he believes he is offering up only the prayers? They all imagine that they are offering up Christ himself to God the Father as an all-sufficient sacrifice, and performing a good work for all those whom they intend to benefit, for they put their trust in the work which the Mass accomplishes, and they do not ascribe this work to prayer. In this way the error has gradually grown, until they have come to ascribe to the sacrament what belongs to the prayers, and to offer to God what should be received as a benefit.

We must therefore sharply distinguish the testament and sacrament itself from the prayers that we offer at the same time. Not only this, but we must also bear in mind that the prayers avail utterly nothing, either to him who offers them or to those for whom they are offered, unless the testament is first received in faith, so that it will be faith that offers the prayers; for faith alone is heard, as James teaches in his first chapter.[119] There is therefore a great difference between prayer and the Mass. Prayer may be extended to as many persons as one desires, while the Mass is received only by the persons who believe for themselves, and only to the extent that they believe. It cannot be given either to God or to human beings. Rather it is God alone who through the ministration of the priest gives it to people, and people receive it by faith alone without any works or merits. Nor would anyone dare to be so foolish as to assert that a ragged beggar does a good work when he comes to receive a gift from a rich man. But the Mass (as I have said) is the gift of the divine promise, proffered to all people by the hand of the priest.

It is certain, therefore, that the Mass is not a work which may be communicated to others, but the object of faith (as has been said), for the strengthening and nourishing of each one's own faith.

Now there is yet a second stumbling block that must be removed, and this is much greater and the most dangerous of all. It is the common belief that the Mass is a sacrifice, which is offered to God. Even the words of the canon[120] seem to imply this, when they speak of "these gifts, these presents, these holy sacrifices," and further on "this offering." Prayer is also made, in so many words, "that the sacrifice may be accepted even as the sacrifice of Abel," etc. Hence Christ is termed "the sacrifice

this sacrifice of prayer, praise, and thanksgiving, and of ourselves as well, we are not to present before God in our own person. But we are to lay it upon Christ and let him present it for us as St. Paul teaches in Hebrews 13:15, 'Let us continually offer up a sacrifice of praise to God, that is, the fruit of lips that confess him and praise him,' and all this 'through Christ.' For this is why he is also a priest. . . . From these words we learn that we do not offer Christ as a sacrifice, but that Christ offers us. And in this way it is permissible, yea profitable, to call the Mass a sacrifice . . ." (LW 35:98–99).

119. James 1:5-8: "If any of you is lacking in wisdom, ask God, who gives to all generously and ungrudgingly, and it will be given you. But ask in faith, never doubting, for the one who doubts is like a wave of the sea, driven and tossed by the wind; for the doubter, being double-minded and unstable in every way, must not expect to receive anything from the Lord."

120. The canon of the Mass consisted of a series of prayers and collects that included the words of institution for the consecration of the bread and wine. In other words, the entire form of the liturgy around the consecration puts the celebration of the sacrament into the context of a priestly sacrifice and work spoken on behalf of the people, even as other prayers are such.

of the altar." Added to these are the sayings of the holy fathers, the great number of examples, and the widespread practice uniformly observed throughout the world.

Over against all these things, firmly entrenched as they are, we must resolutely set the words and example of Christ. For unless we firmly hold that the Mass is the promise or testament of Christ, as the words clearly say, we shall lose the whole gospel and all its comfort. Let us permit nothing to prevail against these words—even though an angel from heaven should teach otherwise [Gal. 1:8]—for they contain nothing about a work or a sacrifice. Moreover, we also have the example of Christ on our side. When he instituted this sacrament and established this testament at the Last Supper, Christ did not offer himself to God the Father, nor did he perform a good work on behalf of others, but, sitting at the table, he set this same testament before each one and proffered to him the sign. Now, the more closely our Mass resembles that first Mass of all, which Christ performed at the Last Supper, the more Christian it will be. But Christ's Mass was most simple, without any display of vestments, gestures, chants, or other ceremonies, so that if it had been necessary to offer the Mass as a sacrifice, then Christ's institution of it was not complete.

Not that anyone should revile the church universal for embellishing and amplifying the Mass with many additional rites and ceremonies. But what we contend for is this: No one should be deceived by the glamor of the ceremonies and entangled in the multitude of pompous forms, and thus lose the simplicity of the Mass itself, and indeed practice a sort of transubstantiation by losing sight of the simple "substance" of the Mass and clinging to the manifold "accidents" of outward pomp.[121] For whatever has been added to the word and example of Christ is an "accident" of the Mass, and ought to be regarded just as we regard the so-called monstrances[122] and corporal cloths[123] in which the host itself is contained.

Therefore, just as distributing a testament or accepting a promise differs diametrically from offering a sacrifice, so it is a contradiction in terms to call the Mass a sacrifice, for the former is something that we receive and the latter is something that we give. The same thing cannot be received and offered at the same time, nor can it be both given and accepted by the same person, any more than our prayer can be the same thing as that which

121. Luther's ironic use of the Scholastic language of transubstantiation is to illustrate that the papal Mass has focused on incidentals and ignored the essence or chief aspect of the sacrament.

122. The monstrance (from the Latin, *monstrare*, "to show") is a vessel designed to display the consecrated host for the veneration of the faithful, especially in the context of a liturgical procession like that of Palm Sunday or Corpus Christi. The practice of displaying and processing the consecrated host grew quickly out of the practice of the elevation of the host for the purpose of adoration. The elevation was introduced into the eucharistic liturgy in Paris in the thirteenth century, probably as a response to those who argued that the host was not the body of Christ until the wine was also consecrated. Evidence for the use of a monstrance can be identified from the fourteenth century.

123. Also called a "pall" (Lat. *palla*), which at the time was the cloth upon which the chalice and host rested. The corporal cloth was then often kept with the consecrated host.

In this sixteenth-century design for a monstrance by Daniel Hopfer (c. 1470–1535) the host is to be displayed in the center supported by angels. The twelve disciples occupy the niches above.

our prayer obtains, or the act of praying be the same thing as the act of receiving that for which we pray.

What shall we say then of the canon of the Mass and the patristic authorities? First of all, I would answer: If there were nothing at all to be said against them, it would be safer to reject them all than admit that the Mass is a work or a sacrifice, lest we deny the word of Christ and destroy faith together with the Mass. Nevertheless, in order to retain them, we shall say that we are instructed by the Apostle in 1 Cor. 11 that it was customary for Christ's believers, when they came together for Mass, to bring with them food and drink.[124] These they called "collections," and they distributed them among all who were in want, after the example of the apostles in Acts 4.[125] From this store was taken the portion of the bread and wine that was consecrated in

124. 1 Cor. 11:21, 33-34: "For when the time comes to eat, each of you goes ahead with your own supper, and one goes hungry and another becomes drunk. . . . So then, my brothers and sisters, when you come together to eat, wait for one another. If you are hungry, eat at home, so that when you come together, it will not be for your condemnation."

125. Acts 4:34-35: "There was not a needy person among them, for as many as owned lands or houses sold them and brought the proceeds of what was sold. They laid it at the apostles' feet, and it was distributed to each as any had need."

the sacrament.[126] And since all this store was consecrated by the word and prayer,[127] by being "lifted up" according to the Hebrew rite of which we read in Moses,[128] the words and rite of this lifting up or offering have come down to us, although the custom of bringing along and collecting that which was offered or lifted up has long since fallen into disuse.[129] Thus, in Isa. 37 Hezekiah commanded Isaiah to lift up his prayer in the sight of God for the remnant.[130] In the Psalms we read: "Lift up your hands to the holy place" [Ps. 134:2]. And again: "To you I will lift up my hands" [Ps. 63:4]. And in 1 Tim. 2[:8]: "In every place lifting holy hands." For this reason the words "sacrifice" and "offering" must be taken to refer not to the sacrament and testament, but to the collections themselves.[131] From this source also the word *collect* has come down to us for the prayers said in the Mass.

The same thing happens when the priest elevates the bread and the cup immediately after consecrating them. By this he does not show that he is offering anything to God, for he does not say a single word here about a victim or an offering. But this elevation is either a survival of that Hebrew rite of lifting up what was received with thanksgiving and returned to God, or else it is an admonition to us to provoke us to faith in this testament which the priest has set forth and exhibited in the words of Christ, so that now he also shows us the sign of the testament. Thus the oblation[132] of the bread properly accompanies the demonstrative "this" in the words, "this is my body," and by the sign the priest addresses us gathered about him; and in a like manner the oblation of the cup properly accompanies the demonstrative "this" in the words, "this cup is the new testament, etc." For it is faith that the priest ought to awaken in us by this act of elevation.[133] And would to God that as he elevates the sign, or sacrament, openly before our eyes, he might also sound in our ears the word, or testament, in a loud, clear voice, and in the language of the people,[134] whatever it may be, in order that faith may be the more effectively awakened. For why may Mass be said in Greek and Latin and Hebrew, but not in German or any other language?[e]

Therefore, let the priests who offer the sacrifice of the Mass in these corrupt and most perilous times take heed, first, that they do not refer to the sacrament the words of the greater and lesser canon,[135] together with the collects, because they smack

e See on p. 130 an image of the cover of Luther's *Deutsche Messe.*

126. See, for example, Hippolytus, *The Apostolic Tradition*, chs. 5–6, where it speaks about the bringing of oil, olives, milk, and cheese in addition to the bread and wine that is consecrated.

127. 1 Tim. 4:4-5: "For everything created by God is good, and nothing is to be rejected, provided it is received with thanksgiving; for it is sanctified by God's word and by prayer."

128. Lev. 8:27: "He placed all these on the palms of Aaron and on the palms of his sons, and raised them as an elevation offering before the LORD."

129. Luther supposes that the history of the elevation of the host is connected to the language of the Old Testament offering, giving the origin of the practice the benefit of the doubt. However, see n. 133 below.

130. Isa. 37:4: "It may be that the LORD your God heard the words of the Rabshakeh, whom his master the king of Assyria has sent to mock the living God, and will rebuke the words that the LORD your God has heard; therefore lift up your prayer for the remnant that is left."

131. Philip Melanchthon (1497–1560) sets forth an argument similar to Luther's in the *Apology of the Augsburg Confession*, XXIV, BC, 258–277.

132. Referring to a holy presentation made to God. Here, the offering of bread and wine.

133. This is an example of Luther's conservative approach to reform. While he distinguishes sharply between the essence of the sacrament as it centers on the words of Christ from the ceremonies and prayers that surround this, Luther is still willing to retain

too strongly of sacrifice. They should refer them instead to the bread and the wine to be consecrated, or to their own prayers. For the bread and wine are offered beforehand for blessing in order that they may be sanctified by the word and by prayer,[f] but after they have been blessed and consecrated they are no longer offered, but received as a gift from God. And in this rite let the priest bear in mind that the gospel is to be set above all canons and collects devised by men, and that the gospel does not sanction the idea that the Mass is a sacrifice, as has been shown.

Further, when a priest celebrates public Mass, he should determine to do nothing else than to commune himself and others by means of the Mass. At the same time, however, he may offer prayers for himself and others, but he must beware lest he presume to offer the Mass. But let him that holds private Masses determine to commune himself.[136] The private Mass does not differ in the least from the ordinary communion which any person receives at the hand of the priest, and has no greater effect. The difference is in the prayers, and in the fact that the priest consecrates the elements for himself and administers them to himself. As far as the blessing of the Mass and sacrament is concerned we are all equals, whether we are priests or lay.

If a priest is requested by others to celebrate so-called votive Masses,[g] let him beware of accepting a fee for the Mass, or of presuming to offer any votive sacrifice. Rather, he should take pains to refer all this to the prayers which he offers for the dead or the living, saying to himself: "Lo, I will go and receive the sacrament for myself alone, and while doing so I will pray for this one and that one." Thus he will receive his fee for the prayers, not for the Mass, and can buy food and clothing with it.[137] Let him not be disturbed because all the world holds and practices the contrary. You have the utmost certainty of the gospel, and by relying on it, you may well disregard the belief and opinions of others. But if you disregard me and insist upon offering the Mass and not the prayers alone, remember that I have faithfully warned you, and that I will be without blame on the day of judgment; you will have to bear your sin alone.[h] I have said what I was bound to say to you as brother to brother for your salvation; yours will be

f 1 Tim. 4:5.

g See n. 116, p. 50.

h Cf. Ezek. 3:19; 33:9.

traditional rites as long as they support the original biblical intention of the sacrament, namely, to awaken faith in the gospel.

134. Luther's pastoral desire to have the Mass in the vernacular is realized in his later efforts at liturgical reform, especially in his *Deutsche Messe und Ordnung des Gottesdiensts—The German Mass and Order of Service* (1526), LW 53:51–90; also pp. 131–61 in this volume. He also reformed the Latin Mass along the lines indicated here so that the benefit of sacrament as testament rather than sacrifice is clear; see his *Formula missae et communionis pro ecclesia Vuittembergensi* (*An Order of Mass and Communion for the Church at Wittenberg*) (1523), LW 53:15–40.

135. The offering until the conclusion of the communion distribution was considered the "canon" of the Mass. However, a distinction was made between the prayers following the prefatory dialogue (e.g., *Sursum corda*), and then the prayers leading to consecration that followed the *Sanctus*, the former being the "lesser canon" (*canon minor*) and the latter, the "greater canon" (*canon maior*).

136. The private Mass (*missa privata*) was just as it sounds, a Mass celebrated by a priest without a congregation. Luther's concern here is that someone actually commune to make it clear that the Mass is not intended only as a sacrifice. He would later reject the practice altogether; see *The Misuse of the Mass* (1521), LW 36:127–230.

137. Again, Luther is quite conservative in his approach. Focusing solely on preserving the gracious character of the sacrament, Luther allows prayers for the dead and even the fees exacted to continue as long as they are distinguished from the Mass itself.

the gain if you observe it, yours the loss if you neglect it. And if some should even condemn what I have said, I will reply in the words of Paul: "But evil men and impostors will go on from bad to worse, deceiving and being deceived" [2 Tim 3:13].

From the above everyone will readily understand the often quoted saying of Gregory:[138] "A Mass celebrated by a wicked priest is not to be considered of less effect than one celebrated by a good priest. Neither would a Mass of St. Peter have been better than that of Judas the traitor, if they had offered the sacrifice of the Mass."[139] This saying has served many as a cloak to cover their godless doings, and because of it they have invented the distinction between the *opus operatum* and the *opus operantis*, so as to be free to lead wicked lives themselves and yet benefit others.[140] Gregory speaks the truth, only they misunderstand his words. For it is true beyond a question that the testament or sacrament is given and received through the ministration of wicked priests no less completely than through the ministration of the most saintly. For who has any doubt that the gospel is preached by the ungodly? Now the Mass is part of the gospel; indeed, it is the sum and substance of it. For what is the whole gospel but the good tidings of the forgiveness of sins? Whatever can be said about forgiveness of sins and the mercy of God in the broadest and richest sense is all briefly comprehended in the word of this testament. For this reason popular sermons ought to be nothing else than expositions of the Mass, or explanations of the divine promise of this testament; this would be to teach the faith and truly to edify the church. But in our day the expounders of the Mass make mockery and jest with allegorical explanations of human ceremonies.

Therefore, just as a wicked priest may baptize, that is, apply the word of promise and the sign of water to the candidate for baptism, so he may also set forth the promise of this sacrament and administer it to those who partake, and even partake himself, as did Judas the traitor at the supper of the Lord.[i] It still remains the same sacrament and testament, which works its own work in the believer but an "alien work" in the unbeliever.[141] But when it comes to offering a sacrifice the case is quite different. For not the Mass but the prayers are offered to God, and therefore it is as plain as day that the offerings of a wicked priest avail

i Matt. 26:23-25.

138. Gregory I, "the Great" (b. 540), was pope from 590 to 604.

139. This precise quotation from Gregory cannot be identified, but the idea that the efficacy of the Mass is not dependent on the piety of the priest is prominent since Augustine's writings against the Donatists. Cf. *Augsburg Confession*, VII, BC, 42–43.

140. While the Scholastic distinction of *opus operatum* and *opus operantis* may have been used to excuse wicked behavior, the original intention of the distinction was to differentiate between the efficacy of the sacrifices of the Old Testament and that of the New. Since the sacrifices proscribed in the Mosiac law were merely signs pointing ahead to the death of Christ, their power to impart grace was not intrinsic but dependent on the faith and disposition of those performing the sacrifice (*opus operantis*). On the other hand, since the Eucharist was not a sign but the true sacrificial blood of Christ, its efficacy was intrinsic regardless of the faith or piety of the celebrant or recipient (*opus operatum*). See Artur Michael Landgraf, "Die Gnadenökonomie des Alten Bundes nach der Lehre der Frühscholastik," "Die Wirkungen der Beschneidung," and "Beiträge der Frühscholastik zur Terminologie der allgemeinen Sakramentenlehre," in *Dogmengeschichte der Frühscholastik*, 3/1 (Regensburg: Friedrich Pustet, 1954), 19–168.

nothing, but, as Gregory says again: When an unworthy person is sent as the intercessor, the heart of the judge is only turned to greater disfavor.[142] Therefore these two things—Mass and prayer, sacrament and work, testament and sacrifice—must not be confused; for the one comes from God to us through the ministration of the priest and demands our faith, the other proceeds from our faith to God through the priest and demands his hearing. The former descends, the latter ascends. The former, therefore, does not necessarily require a worthy and godly minister, but the latter does indeed require such a one, for "God does not listen to sinners" [John 9:31]. He knows how to do good through evil people, but he does not accept the work of any evil person; as he showed in the case of Cain,[143] and as is said in Prov. 15[:8]: "The sacrifice of the wicked is an abomination to the LORD," and in Rom. 14[:23]: "Whatever does not proceed from faith is sin."

But let us bring this first part to an end, though I am ready to go on with the argument if an opponent should arise. From all that has been said we conclude that the Mass was provided only for those who have a sad, afflicted, disturbed, perplexed, and erring conscience, and that they alone commune worthily. For, since the word of divine promise in this sacrament sets forth the forgiveness of sins, let all draw near fearlessly, whoever they may be, who are troubled by their sins, whether by remorse or by temptation. For this testament of Christ is the one remedy against sins, past, present, and future, if you but cling to it with unwavering faith and believe that what the words of the testament declare is freely granted to you. But if you do not believe this, you will never, anywhere, by any works or efforts of your own, be able to find peace of conscience. For faith alone means peace of conscience, while unbelief means only distress of conscience.

The Sacrament of Baptism

Blessed be God and the Father of our Lord Jesus Christ, who according to the riches of his mercy [Eph. 1:3, 7] has preserved in his church this sacrament at least, untouched and untainted by human ordinances, and has made it free to all nations and classes of people, and has not permitted it to be oppressed by the filth and great impiety of greed and superstitions. For he desired

141. The distinction of God's "alien" and "proper" work (*opus alienum—opus proprium*), derived from Isa. 28:21 ("For the LORD will rise up . . . to work his work—alien is his work"), can be found already in Luther's sermons in 1516 (e.g., WA 1:111–14). There he can speak of God's work as double (*duplex*) so that the gospel according to its proper function and intention is forgiveness and grace. Yet unbelief necessarily places one under its judgment, so that the gospel effects the opposite of its intended purpose, i.e., an alien work. Later Luther finds it clearer to correlate the language of alien and proper work with the distinction of law and gospel.

142. Gregory the Great, *Regula pastoralis* 1, 10: "For we all know well that, when one who is in disfavor is sent to intercede with an incensed person, the mind of the latter is provoked to greater severity." Cf. Gabriel Biel, *Canonis misse expositio*, lect. 27 C.

143. Gen. 4:5: "but for Cain and his offering he had no regard. So Cain was very angry, and his countenance fell."

Infant baptism as depicted in *Catechismus* by Johannes Brenz (1499–1570).

that by it little children, who were incapable of greed and superstition, might be initiated and sanctified in the simple faith of his Word; even today baptism has its chief blessing for them. But if the intention had been to give this sacrament to adults and older people, I do not believe that it could possibly have retained its power and its glory against the tyranny of greed and superstition which has overthrown all things divine among us. Here too the wisdom of the flesh would doubtless have devised its preparations and dignities, its reservations, restrictions, and other like snares for catching money, until water brought as high a price as parchment[144] does now.

But Satan, though he could not quench the power of baptism in little children, nevertheless succeeded in quenching it in all adults, so that now there are scarcely any who call to mind their own baptism, and still fewer who glory in it; so many other ways have been discovered for remitting sins and getting to heaven. The source of these false opinions is that dangerous saying of St. Jerome—either unhappily phrased or wrongly interpreted—in which he terms penance "the second plank after shipwreck," as if baptism were not penance.[145] Hence, when people have fallen into sin, they despair of the "first plank," which is the ship, as if it had gone under, and begin to put all their trust and faith in the second plank, which is penance.[146] This has given rise to those endless burdens of vows, religious orders, works, satisfactions, pilgrimages, indulgences, and monastic sects,[147] and from them in turn has arisen that flood of books, questions, opinions, and man-made ordinances which the whole world cannot contain. Thus the church of God is incomparably worse off under this tyranny than the synagogue or any other nation under heaven ever was.

It was the duty of the pontiffs to remove all these evils and to put forth every effort to recall Christians to the purity of baptism, so that they might understand what it means to be Christians and what Christians ought to do. But instead of this, their only work today is to lead the people as far astray as possible from their baptism, to immerse all people in the flood of their tyranny, and to cause the people of Christ (as the prophet says) to forget him days without number.[148] How unregenerate are all who bear the name of pontiff today! For they neither know nor do what is becoming to pontiffs, but they are ignorant of what they ought to know and do. They fulfill what Isa. 56[:10, 11] says:

144. I.e., letters of indulgence.

145. Jerome's quote, from *Ep.* 130, 9, "Let us know nothing of penitence, lest the thought of it lead us into sin. It is a plank for those who have had the misfortune to be shipwrecked," echoes the earlier saying of Tertullian (c. 155–240) in his treatise *De poenitentia*: "That repentance, O sinner, like myself . . . do you so hasten to, so embrace, as a shipwrecked man the protection of some plank. This will draw you forth when sunk in the waves of sins, and will bear you forward into the port of the divine clemency." See also Lombard, *Sentences* 4, d. 14, c. 1: "As Jerome says, it is 'the second plank after shipwreck,' because, if anyone has corrupted by sin the clothing of innocence which he received at baptism, he may repair it by the remedy of penance. . . . Those who have fallen after baptism can

"His watchmen are blind, they are all without knowledge; the shepherds also have no understanding; they have all turned to their own way, each to his own gain, etc."

[The First Part of Baptism: The Divine Promise]

Now, the first thing to be considered about baptism is the divine promise, which says: "The one who believes and is baptized will be saved" [Mark 16:16]. This promise must be set far above all the glitter of works, vows, religious orders, and whatever else human beings have introduced, for on it all our salvation depends. But we must so consider it as to exercise our faith in it, and have no doubt whatever that, once we have been baptized, we are saved. For unless faith is present or is conferred in baptism, baptism will profit us nothing; indeed, it will become a hindrance to us, not only at the moment when it is received, but throughout the rest of our lives. That kind of unbelief accuses God's promise of being a lie, and this is the greatest of all sins.[j] If we set ourselves to this exercise of faith, we shall at once perceive how difficult it is to believe this promise of God. For our human weakness, conscious of its sins, finds nothing more difficult to believe than that it is saved or will be saved; and yet, unless it does believe this, it cannot be saved, because it does not believe the truth of God that promises salvation.

This message should have been impressed upon the people untiringly, and this promise should have been dinned into their ears without ceasing. Their baptism should have been called to their minds again and again, and their faith constantly awakened and nourished. For just as the truth of this divine promise, once pronounced over us, continues until death, so our faith in it ought never to cease, but to be nourished and strengthened until death by the continual remembrance of this promise made to us in baptism. Therefore, when we rise from our sins or repent, we are merely returning to the power and the faith of baptism from which we fell, and finding our way back to the promise then made to us, which we deserted when we sinned. For the truth of the promise once made remains steadfast, always ready to receive us back with open arms when we return. And this, if I mistake not, is what they mean when they say, though obscurely,

j See n. 105, p. 46.

be renewed by penance, but not by baptism; it is lawful for someone to repent several times, but not to be baptized several times."

146. This notion of penance as an emergency rescue stems from questions regarding the possibility and consequences of postbaptismal sin. A rigorist position is demonstrable throughout the early church, possibly already reflected in Heb. 6:4f., but definitively set forth by the second-century Christian text, *Shepherd of Hermes*. The angel in the *Shepherd* admits that though one who is baptized should live a life of purity (Mandate IV, 1:8-9; 2:1; 3:1), God has mercifully introduced a single means of restoration. "'But I tell you,' said he, 'after that great and holy calling, if a man be tempted by the devil and sin, he has *one repentance*, but if he sin and repent repeatedly it is unprofitable for such a man, for scarcely shall he live'" (Mandate IV, 3:4-6). Incidentally, Luther's question over the apostolic authorship of Hebrews focuses especially on Heb. 6:4f.

147. The loss of baptism as the rhythm and shape of the daily Christian forgiveness has, according to Luther, left a vacuum that was then filled by every effort to bring security and satisfaction. This list represents many of the false *Geistlichkeiten* that Luther wished to abolish or reform, i.e., spiritual/devotional practices common throughout the Middle Ages to deal with postbaptismal sin.

148. Jer. 2:32: "Can a girl forget her ornaments, or a bride her attire? Yet my people have forgotten me, days without number."

that baptism is the first sacrament and the foundation of all the others, without which none of the others can be received.[149]

It will therefore be no small gain to penitents to remember above all their baptism, and, confidently calling to mind the divine promise which they have forsaken, acknowledge that promise before their Lord, rejoicing that they are still within the fortress of salvation because they have been baptized, and abhorring their wicked ingratitude in falling away from its faith and truth. Their hearts will find wonderful comfort and will be encouraged to hope for mercy when they consider that the promise which God made to them, which cannot possibly lie, is still unbroken and unchanged, and indeed, cannot be changed by sins, as Paul says (2 Tim. 2[:13]): "If we are faithless, he remains faithful—for he cannot deny himself." This truth of God, I say, will sustain them, so that if all else should fail, this truth, if they believe in it, will not fail them. In it the penitents have a shield against all assaults of the scornful enemy, an answer to the sins that disturb their conscience, an antidote for the dread of death and judgment, and a comfort in every temptation—namely, this one truth—when they say: "God is faithful in his promises, and I received his sign in baptism. If God is for me, who is against me?"[k,l]

The children of Israel, whenever they turned to repentance, remembered above all their exodus from Egypt, and remembering turned back to God who had brought them out. Moses impressed this memory and this protection upon them many times, and David afterwards did the same.[m] How much more ought we to remember our exodus from Egypt, and by this remembrance turn back to him who led us through the washing of regeneration,[n] remembrance of which is commended to us for this very reason! This can be done most fittingly in the sacrament of bread and wine. Indeed, in former times these three sacraments—penance, baptism, and the bread—were all celebrated at the same service, and each one supplemented the other. We

149. Lombard, *Sentences* 4, d. 2, c. 2: "Now let us examine the sacrament of baptism, which is the first among the sacraments of the new grace." Also Pope Eugene IV (1383–1447) issued a bull at the Council of Florence (1439), *Exultate Deo*: "Holy baptism, which is the gateway to the spiritual life, holds the first place among all the sacraments; through it we are made members of Christ and of the body of the Church." Cf. also Biel, *Sentences* 4, d. 2, q. 1, a. 1, n. 1 A: "just as faith is the first and foundation of the rest of the virtues, so baptism is the chief of sacraments and their doorway."

k Rom. 8:31.

l The original text of this paragraph is singular.

m Cf. Deut. 5:15; 6:12, 21; 8:14; Pss. 78:12f.; 80:8; 106:7f.; Jer. 2:5f.; Dan. 9:15.

n Titus 3:5.

also read of a certain holy virgin who in every time of temptation made baptism her sole defense, saying simply, "I am a Christian"; and immediately the enemy recognized the power of baptism and of her faith, which clung to the truth of a promising God, and fled from her.[150]

Thus you see how rich a Christian is, that is, one who has been baptized! Even if those who have been baptized would, they could not lose their salvation, however much they sinned, unless they refused to believe. For no sin can condemn them save unbelief alone.[o] All other sins, so long as the faith in God's promise made in baptism returns or remains, are immediately blotted out through that same faith, or rather through the truth of God, because he cannot deny himself if you confess him and faithfully cling to him in his promise. But as for contrition, confession of sins, and satisfaction,[151] along with all those carefully devised human exercises: if you rely on them and neglect this truth of God, they will suddenly fail you and leave you more wretched than before. For whatever is done without faith in God's truth is vanity of vanities and vexation of spirit.[p]

You will likewise see how perilous, indeed, how false it is to suppose that penance is "the second plank after shipwreck," and how pernicious an error it is to believe that the power of baptism is broken, and the ship dashed to pieces, because of sin.[q] The ship remains one, solid, and invincible; it will never be broken up into separate "planks." In it are carried all those who are brought to the harbor of salvation, for it is the truth of God giving us its promise in the sacraments. Of course, it often happens that many rashly leap overboard into the sea and perish; these are those who abandon faith in the promise and plunge into sin. But the ship itself remains intact and holds its course unimpaired. If anyone is able somehow by grace to return to the ship, it is not on any plank, but in the solid ship itself that that person is carried to life. Such a person is the one who returns through faith to the abiding and enduring promise of God. Therefore Peter, in 1 Pet. 1, rebukes those who sin, because they have forgotten that

150. St. Blandina was martyred in 177 CE in Lyon under the reign of Marcus Aurelius (121–180). The account of her death comes from a letter reproduced by Eusebius (c. 265–c. 340) in his *Church History*; see *Hist. Eccl.* 5, 1, 19.

151. On these three parts of sacramental penance see Lombard, *Sentences* 4, d. 16, c. 1: "In the performance of penance, three things are to be considered, namely compunction of heart, confession of the mouth, satisfaction in deed. . . . Just as we offend God in three ways, namely by heart, mouth, hand, so also let us make satisfaction in three ways."

o The original text of this section is singular.

p Eccles. 1:2f.

q See n. 145, p. 60.

they were cleansed from their old sins, and he clearly rebukes their wicked unbelief and their ingratitude for the baptism they had received.[152]

What is the good, then, of writing so much about baptism and yet not teaching this faith in the promise? All the sacraments were instituted to nourish faith. Yet these godless men pass over it so completely as even to assert that a Christian dare not be certain of the forgiveness of sins or the grace of the sacraments.[153] With such wicked teaching they delude the world, and not only take captive, but altogether destroy, the sacrament of baptism, in which the chief glory of our conscience consists. Meanwhile they madly rage against the miserable souls of human beings with their contritions, anxious confessions, circumstances,[154] satisfactions, works, and endless other such absurdities. Therefore read with great caution the "Master of the *Sentences*" in his fourth book;[r] better yet, despise him with all his commentators, who at their best write only of the "matter" and "form" of the sacraments;[155] that is, they treat of the dead and death-dealing letter[156] of the sacraments, but leave untouched the spirit, life, and use, that is, the truth of the divine promise and our faith.

Beware, therefore, that the external pomp of works and the deceits of man-made ordinances do not deceive you, lest you wrong the divine truth and your faith. If you would be saved, you must begin with the faith of the sacraments, without any works whatever. The works will follow faith, but do not think too lightly of faith, for it is the most excellent and difficult of all works. Through it alone you will be saved, even if you should be compelled to do without any other works. For faith is a work of God, not of man, as Paul teaches.[157] The other works he works

r Peter Lombard. Book 4 of the *Sentences* is dedicated to questions "On the Doctrine of Signs" (*De Doctrina Signorum*), i.e., the sacraments; see n. 56, p. 30 and n. 149, p. 62.

152. Probably a reference to 2 Pet. 1:5-9, "For this very reason, you must make every effort to support your faith with goodness, and goodness with knowledge, and knowledge with self-control, and self-control with endurance, and endurance with godliness, and godliness with mutual affection, and mutual affection with love. For if these things are yours and are increasing among you, they keep you from being ineffective and unfruitful in the knowledge of our Lord Jesus Christ. For anyone who lacks these things is short-sighted and blind, and is forgetful of the cleansing of past sins."

153. Aquinas, *STh* I-II, q. 112, a. 5: ". . . man cannot judge with certainty whether he has grace." However, see the posthumous supplement *STh* III Suppl., q. 10, a. 4. For a helpful discussion of the difference between Luther and Aquinas on the certainty of salvation, see Otto H. Pesch, "Existential and Sapiential Theology—the Theological Confrontation between Luther and Thomas Aquinas," in Jared Wicks, S.J., ed., *Catholic Scholars Dialogue with Luther* (Chicago: Loyola University Press, 1970), 61–81.

154. In the effort to confess the entirety of one's sins, the penitent must also divulge the circumstances, that is, the related conditions that accompany the action, so that the priest may determine the nature of the sin committed and degree of guilt. Circumstances may turn a venial sin into a mortal sin.

155. The early Scholastic use of the terms *matter* and *form* was more general than the technical use in Aristotle. The "matter" of the sacrament is the elements of the sign (e.g., baptism = water) and the "form" is the words used in its sacramental use (e.g., baptism =

through us and with our help, but this one alone he works in us and without our help.

From this we can clearly see that in baptizing there is a difference between the human minister and God the author. For the man baptizes, and yet does not baptize. He baptizes in that he performs the work of immersing the person to be baptized; he does not baptize, because in so doing he acts not on his own authority but in God's stead. Hence we ought to receive baptism at human hands just as if Christ himself, indeed, God himself, were baptizing us with his own hands. For it is not man's baptism, but Christ's and God's baptism, which we receive by the hand of a man, just as everything else that we have through the hand of somebody else is God's alone. Therefore beware of making any distinction in baptism by ascribing the outward part to man and the inward part to God. Ascribe both to God alone, and look upon the person administering it as simply the vicarious instrument of God, by which the Lord sitting in heaven thrusts you under the water with his own hands, and promises you forgiveness of your sins, speaking to you upon earth with a human voice by the mouth of his minister.

This the words themselves indicate, when the minister says: "I baptize you in the name of the Father, and of the Son, and of the Holy Ghost. Amen," and not: "I baptize you in my own name." It is as though he said: "What I do, I do not by my own authority, but in the name and stead of God, so that you should regard it just as if our Lord himself had done it in a visible manner. The doer and the minister are different persons, but the work of both is the same work, or rather, it is the work of the doer alone, through my ministry." For I hold that "in the name of"[158] refers to the person of the doer, so that the name of the Lord is not only to be uttered and invoked while the work is being done; but the work itself is to be done as something not one's own—in the name and stead of another. In this sense Christ says in Matt. 24[:5], "Many will come in my name," and Rom. 1[:5] says, "Through whom we have received grace and apostleship to bring about obedience for his name among all the nations."

This view I heartily endorse, for there is great comfort and a mighty aid to faith in the knowledge that one has been baptized, not by man, but by the Triune God himself, through a man acting among us in his name. This will put an end to that idle dispute about the "form" of baptism, as they term the words which

"I baptize you in the name . . . ," etc.). See, for example, Lombard, *Sentences* 4, d. 3, c. 2: "On the Form of Baptism: But what is that word, at whose addition to the element the sacrament is brought about?—Truth teaches it to you, who, laying down the form of this sacrament, said to the disciples: 'Go, teach all nations, baptizing them in the name . . .'"; Thomas Aquinas, adopted the earlier terminology but began interpreting it in a more precise Aristotelian manner, e.g., *STh* III, q. 60, a. 7: "As stated above, in the sacraments the words are as the form, and sensible things are as the matter. Now in all things composed of matter and form, the determining principle is on the part of the form, which is as it were the end and terminus of the matter. Consequently, for the being of a thing the need of a determinate form is prior to the need of determinate matter: for determinate matter is needed that it may be adapted to the determinate form. Since, therefore, in the sacraments determinate sensible things are required, which are as the sacramental matter, much more is there need in them of a determinate form of words."

156. 2 Cor. 3:6: "for the letter kills, but the Spirit gives life." Luther can use the language of this text to indicate the external and superficial versus the inner and essential, or he can use it in the Augustinian sense of the law versus grace.

157. Eph. 2:8: "For by grace you have been saved through faith, and this is not your own doing; it is the gift of God."

158. The Latin *in nomine* can certainly have the meaning "by the authority of"; however, the Greek of Matthew 28 from which the baptismal formula is

are used. The Greeks say: "May the servant of Christ be baptized," while the Latins say: "I baptize."[159] Others again, adhering rigidly to their pedantry, condemn the use of the words, "I baptize you in the name of Jesus Christ,"[160] although it is certain the apostles used this formula in baptizing, as we read in the Acts of the Apostles;[s] they would allow no other form to be valid than this: "I baptize you in the name of the Father, and of the Son, and of the Holy Ghost. Amen." But their contention is in vain, for they bring no proof, but merely assert their own dreams. Baptism truly saves in whatever way it is administered, if only it is administered not in the name of man, but in the name of the Lord. Indeed, I have no doubt that if anyone receives baptism in the name of the Lord, even if the wicked minister should not give it in the name of the Lord, he would yet be truly baptized in the name of the Lord. For the power of baptism depends not so much on the faith or use of the one who confers it as on the faith or use of the one who receives it. We have an example of this in the story of a certain actor who was baptized in jest.[161] These and similar perplexing disputes and questions are raised for us by those who ascribe nothing to faith and everything to works and rituals, whereas we owe everything to faith alone and nothing to rituals. Faith makes us free in spirit from all those doubts and mere opinions.

[The Second Part of Baptism: The Sign]

The second part of baptism is the sign, or sacrament, which is that immersion in water from which it derives its name, for the Greek *baptizō* means "I immerse," and *baptisma* means "immersion." For, as has been said, along with the divine promises signs have also been given to picture that which the words signify, or as they now say, that which the sacrament "effectively signifies." We shall see how much truth there is in this.

A great majority have supposed that there is some hidden spiritual power in the word and water, which works the grace of God in the soul of the recipient.[162] Others deny this and hold that there is no power in the sacraments, but that grace is given by God alone, who according to his covenant is present in the

s E.g., Acts 2:38; 8:16; 10:48; 19:5.

derived—*eis to onoma*—may also have the sense of "into the name." In this case, the meaning would be similar to Rom. 6:3, "baptized into Christ . . . into his death."

159. See the bull *Exultate Deo* (1439), from the Council of Florence: "The form is: 'I baptize you in the name of the Father and of the Son and of the Holy Spirit.' But we do not deny that true baptism is conferred by the following words: 'May this servant of Christ be baptized in the name of the Father and of the Son and of the Holy Spirit'; or, 'This person is baptized by my hands in the name of the Father and of the Son and of the Holy Spirit.' Since the Holy Trinity is the principle cause from which baptism has its power and the minister is the instrumental cause who exteriorly bestows the sacrament, the sacrament is conferred if the action is performed by the minister with the invocation of the Holy Trinity."

160. Alexander of Hales (1185–1245) denied the validity of a baptism performed "in the name of Jesus"; however, see Lombard, *Sentences* 4, d. 3, c. 3: "the apostles baptized in the name of Christ. But in this name [i.e., of Christ], as Ambrose explains, the whole Trinity is understood."

161. St. Genesius was a popular legendary saint, supposedly martyred under Emperor Diocletian (245–311). According to the legend, Genesius received a mock baptism on stage in ridicule of Christianity, but the effect was his sudden conversion.

162. Representatives of this view include Hugh of St. Victor (c. 1096–1141), *On the Sacraments of the Christian Faith* 1, 1, 1: "a sacrament, through its being sanctified, contains an invisible grace"; and Aquinas, *STh* III, q. 62, a. 4: "there

sacraments which he has instituted.[163] Yet all are agreed that the sacraments are "effective signs" of grace, and they reach this conclusion by this one argument: if the sacraments of the New Law were mere signs, there would be no apparent reason why they should surpass those of the Old Law.[164] Hence they have been driven to attribute such great powers to the sacraments of the New Law that they think the sacraments benefit even those who are in mortal sin; neither faith nor grace are required—it is sufficient that no obstacle be set in the way, that is, no actual intention to sin again.[165]

Such views, however, must be carefully avoided and shunned, because they are godless and infidel, contrary to faith and inconsistent with the nature of the sacraments. For it is an error to hold that the sacraments of the New Law differ from those of the Old Law in the effectiveness of their signs. For in this respect they are the same. The same God who now saves us by baptism and the bread saved Abel by his sacrifice,[t] Noah by the rainbow,[u] Abraham by circumcision,[v] and all the others by their respective signs. So far as the signs are concerned, there is no difference between a sacrament of the Old Law and one of the New, provided that by the Old Law you mean that which God did among the patriarchs and other fathers in the days of the Law. But those signs which were given to the patriarchs and fathers must be clearly distinguished from the legal symbols which Moses instituted in his law, such as the priestly usages concerning vestments, vessels, foods, houses, and the like. For these are vastly different, not only from the sacraments of the New Law, but also from those signs which God occasionally gave to the fathers living under the law, such as the sign of Gideon's fleece,[w] Manoah's sacrifice,[x] or that which Isaiah offered to Ahaz in Isa. 7.[y] In each of these alike some promise was given which required faith in God.

t Gen. 4:4.
u Gen. 6:13-22.
v Gen. 17:10f.
w Judg. 6:36-40.
x Judg. 13:16-23.
y Isa. 7:10-16.

is nothing to hinder an instrumental spiritual power from being in a body; in so far as a body can be moved by a particular spiritual substance so as to produce a particular spiritual effect . . . it is in this way that a spiritual power is in the sacraments, inasmuch as they are ordained by God unto the production of a spiritual effect."

163. Aquinas, though in disagreement, correctly describes this alternate position held by theologians such as Bonaventure (1221–1274) and Duns Scotus (c. 1266–1308), in *STh* III, q. 62, a. 4: "Those who hold that the sacraments do not cause grace save by a certain coincidence, deny the sacraments any power that is itself productive of the sacramental effect, and hold that the Divine power assists the sacraments and produces their effect." See also Gabriel Biel, *Sentences* 4, d. 1, q. 1, a. 1, c. 1, in which the sacraments are not effective intrinsically (*ex natura rei*) but because of the will and covenant of God (*ex voluntate Dei*).

164. Cf. Lombard, *Sentences* 4, d. 1, 3: "Observances of the Old Law are better called signs than sacraments. For those things which were instituted only for the sake of signifying are merely signs, and not sacraments; such were the carnal sacrifices and the ceremonial observances of the Old Law, which could never justify those who offered them." Aquinas, *STh* III, q. 62, a. 6: "it is therefore clear that the sacraments of the New Law do reasonably derive the power of justification from Christ's Passion, which is the cause of man's righteousness; whereas the sacraments of the Old Law did not."

165. The Scholastic doctrine that the sacraments of the New Testament intrinsically confer grace (*ex opere operato*) was conditioned by the absence of any spiritual obstacle. For example, if one receives the sacrament under false pretenses, the substance of the sacrament would still be received but the grace would not benefit the recipient (cf. Lombard, *Sentences* 4, d. 4, c. 2; Aquinas, *STh* III, q. 69, a. 9). Gabriel Biel identifies a mortal sin as an obstacle, *Sentences* 4, d. 1, q. 3, n. 2 B: "unless one impedes by an obstacle of mortal sin, grace is conferred."

The difference, then, between the legal symbols and the new and old signs is that the legal symbols do not have attached to them any word of promise requiring faith. Hence they are not signs of justification, for they are not sacraments of the faith that alone justifies, but only sacraments of works. Their whole power and nature consisted in works, not in faith. Those who performed them fulfilled them, even if they did it without faith. But our signs or sacraments, as well as those of the fathers, have attached to them a word of promise which requires faith, and they cannot be fulfilled by any other work. Hence they are signs or sacraments of justification, for they are sacraments of justifying faith and not of works. Their whole efficacy, therefore, consists in faith itself, not in the doing of a work. Those who believe them, fulfill them, even if they should not do a single work. This is the origin of the saying: "Not the sacrament, but the faith of the sacrament, justifies." Thus circumcision did not justify Abraham and his seed, and yet the Apostle calls it the seal of the righteousness by faith,[z] because faith in the promise, to which circumcision was added, justified him and fulfilled what the circumcision signified. For faith was the spiritual circumcision of the foreskin of the heart,[a] which was symbolized by the literal circumcision of the flesh. In the same way it was obviously not Abel's sacrifice that justified him, but it was his faith[b] by which he offered himself wholly to God, and this was symbolized by the outward sacrifice.

Thus it is not baptism that justifies or benefits anyone, but it is faith in that word of promise to which baptism is added. This faith justifies, and fulfills that which baptism signifies. For faith is the submersion of the old person and the emerging of the new.[c] Therefore the new sacraments cannot differ from the old sacraments, for both alike have the divine promises and the same spirit of faith, although they do differ vastly from the old symbols—on account of the word of promise, which is the sole effective means of distinguishing them. Even so, today, the outward show of vestments, holy places, foods, and all the endless

z Rom. 4:11.

a Deut. 10:16; Jer. 4:4.

b Heb. 11:4.

c Cf. Eph. 4:22-24; Col. 3:9-10.

ceremonies doubtless symbolize excellent things to be fulfilled in the spirit, yet, because there is no word of divine promise attached to these things, they can in no way be compared with the signs of baptism and the bread. Neither do they justify, nor benefit one in any way, since they are fulfilled in their very observance, even in their observance apart from faith. For while they are taking place, or being performed, they are being fulfilled, as the Apostle says of them in Col. 2[:22]: "Which all perish as they are used, according to human precepts and doctrines." The sacraments, on the contrary, are not fulfilled when they are taking place, but when they are being believed.

It cannot be true, therefore, that there is contained in the sacraments a power efficacious for justification, or that they are "effective signs" of grace. All such things are said to the detriment of faith, and out of ignorance of the divine promise. Unless you should call them "effective" in the sense that they certainly and effectively impart grace where faith is unmistakably present. But it is not in this sense that efficacy is now ascribed to them; as witness the fact that they are said to benefit all people, even the wicked and unbelieving, provided they do not set an obstacle in the way[d]—as if such unbelief were not in itself the most obstinate and hostile of all obstacles to grace. To such an extent have they exerted themselves to turn the sacrament into a command and faith into a work. For if the sacrament confers grace on me because I receive it, then indeed I receive grace by virtue of my work, and not by faith; and I gain not the promise in the sacrament but only the sign instituted and commanded by God. Thus you see clearly how completely the sacraments have been misunderstood by the theologians of the *Sentences*.[e] In their discussions of the sacraments they have taken no account either of faith or of promise. They cling only to the sign and the use of the sign, and draw us away from faith to the work, away from the word to the sign. Thus, as I have said, they have not only taken the sacraments captive, but have completely destroyed them, as far as they were able.

d See n. 165, pp. 67–68.

e See n. 56, p. 30.

Therefore let us open our eyes and learn to pay heed more to the word than to the sign, more to faith than to the work or use of the sign. We know that wherever there is a divine promise, there faith is required, and that these two are so necessary to each other that neither can be effective apart from the other. For it is not possible to believe unless there is a promise, and the promise is not established unless it is believed. But where these two meet, they give a real and most certain efficacy to the sacraments. Hence, to seek the efficacy of the sacrament apart from the promise and apart from the faith is to labor in vain and to find condemnation. Thus Christ says: "The one who believes and is baptized will be saved; but the one who does not believe will be condemned" [Mark 16:16]. He shows us in this word that faith is such a necessary part of the sacrament that it can save even without the sacrament, and for this reason he did not add: "The one who does not believe, and is not baptized."

[Baptism Signifies Death and Resurrection]

Baptism, then, signifies two things—death and resurrection,[f] that is, full and complete justification. When the minister immerses the child in the water it signifies death, and when he draws it forth again it signifies life. Thus Paul expounds it in Rom. 6[:4]: "Therefore we have been buried with [Christ] by baptism into death, so that just as Christ was raised from the dead by the glory of the Father, so we too might walk in newness of life." This death and resurrection we call the new creation, regeneration, and spiritual birth.[g] This should not be understood only allegorically as the death of sin and the life of grace, as many understand it, but as actual death and resurrection. For baptism is not a false sign. Neither does sin completely die, nor grace completely rise, until the sinful body that we carry about in this life is destroyed, as the Apostle says in the same passage.[166] For as long as we are in the flesh, the desires of the flesh stir and are stirred. For this reason, as soon as we begin to believe, we also begin to die to this world and live to God in the life to come; so

166. Rom. 6:6-7: "We know that our old self was crucified with him so that the body of sin might be destroyed, and we might no longer be enslaved to sin. For whoever has died is freed from sin."

f Cf. *The Holy Sacrament of Baptism* (1519), LW 35:30f.

g Cf. 2 Cor. 5:17; Titus 3:5; John 3:6.

that faith is truly a death and a resurrection, that is, it is that spiritual baptism into which we are submerged and from which we rise.

It is therefore indeed correct to say that baptism is a washing away of sins, but the expression is too mild and weak to bring out the full significance of baptism, which is rather a symbol of death and resurrection. For this reason, I would have those who are to be baptized completely immersed in the water, as the word says and as the mystery indicates.[h] Not because I deem this necessary, but because it would be well to give to a thing so perfect and complete a sign that is also complete and perfect. And this is doubtless the way in which it was instituted by Christ. The sinner does not so much need to be washed as he needs to die, in order to be wholly renewed and made another creature, and to be conformed to the death and resurrection of Christ, with whom he dies and rises again through baptism.[i] Although you may say that when Christ died and rose again he was washed clean of mortality, that is a less forceful way of putting it than if you said that he was completely changed and renewed. Similarly it is far more forceful to say that baptism signifies that we die in every way and rise to eternal life, than to say that it signifies merely that we are washed clean of sins.

Here again you see that the sacrament of baptism, even with respect to its sign, is not a matter of the moment, but something permanent. Although the ceremony itself is soon over the thing it signifies continues until we die, yes, even until we rise on the last day. For as long as we live we are continually doing that which baptism signifies, that is, we die and rise again. We die, not only mentally and spiritually by renouncing the sins and vanities of this world, but in very truth we begin to leave this bodily life and to lay hold on the life to come, so that there is, as they say, a "real" and bodily passing out of this world unto the Father.

We must therefore beware of those who have reduced the power of baptism to such small and slender dimensions that, while they say that by it grace is indeed poured in, they maintain that afterwards it is poured out again through sin, and

h Cf. *The Holy Sacrament of Baptism* (1519), LW 35:30f.

i Cf. Rom. 6:8.

that then one must reach heaven by another way, as if baptism had now become entirely useless.[j] Do not hold such a view, but understand that this is the significance of baptism, that through it you die and live again. Therefore, whether by penance or by any other way, you can only return to the power of your baptism, and do again that which you were baptized to do and which your baptism signified. Baptism never becomes useless, unless you despair and refuse to return to its salvation. You may indeed wander away from the sign for a time, but the sign is not therefore useless. Thus, you have been once baptized in the sacrament, but you need continually to be baptized by faith, continually to die and continually to live. Baptism swallowed up your whole body and gave it forth again; in the same way that which baptism signifies should swallow up your whole life, body and soul, and give it forth again at the last day, clad in the robe of glory and immortality. We are therefore never without the sign of baptism nor without the thing it signifies. Indeed, we need continually to be baptized more and more, until we fulfill the sign perfectly at the last day.

You will understand, therefore, that whatever we do in this life which mortifies the flesh or quickens the spirit has to do with our baptism. The sooner we depart this life, the more speedily we fulfill our baptism;[k] and the more cruelly we suffer, the more successfully do we conform to our baptism. Hence the church was at its best at the time when martyrs were being put to death every day and accounted as sheep for the slaughter,[l] for then the power of baptism reigned supreme in the church, whereas today we have lost sight of this power amid the multitude of human works and doctrines. For our whole life should be baptism, and the fulfilling of the sign or sacrament of baptism, since we have been set free from all else and given over to baptism alone, that is, to death and resurrection.

This glorious liberty of ours and this understanding of baptism have been taken captive in our day, and to whom can we give the blame except the Roman pontiff with his despotism? More than all others, as chief shepherd it was his first duty to proclaim this doctrine and defend this liberty, as Paul says in 1 Cor. 4[:1]:

j See n. 146, p. 61.

k Cf. *The Holy Sacrament of Baptism* (1519), LW 35:30f.

l Ps. 44:22; Rom. 8:36.

"This is how one should regard us, as servants of Christ and stewards of the mysteries, or sacraments, of God." Instead he seeks only to oppress us with his decrees and laws, and to ensnare us as captives to his tyrannical power. By what right, I ask you, does the pope impose his laws upon us (to say nothing of his wicked and damnable neglect to teach us these mysteries)? Who gave him power to deprive us of this liberty of ours, granted to us in baptism? One thing only, as I have said, has been enjoined upon us to do all the days of our lives—to be baptized, that is, to be put to death and to live again through faith in Christ. This and this alone should have been taught, especially by the chief shepherd. But now faith is passed over in silence, and the church is smothered with endless laws concerning works and ceremonies; the power and understanding of baptism are set aside, and faith in Christ is obstructed.

Therefore I say: Neither pope nor bishop nor any other person has the right to impose a single syllable of law upon Christians without their[m] consent; if anyone does, it is done in the spirit of tyranny. Therefore the prayers, fasts, donations, and whatever else the pope ordains and demands in all of his decrees, as numerous as they are iniquitous, he demands and ordains without any right whatever; and he sins against the liberty of the church whenever he attempts any such thing. Hence it has come to pass that the churchmen of our day are such vigorous guardians of "ecclesiastical liberty"—that is, of wood and stone, of lands and rents[167] (for to such an extent has "ecclesiastical" today come to mean the same as "spiritual"!). Yet with such verbal fictions they not only take captive the true liberty of the church; they utterly destroy it, even worse than the Turk, and in opposition to the word of the Apostle: "Do not become slaves of men" [1 Cor. 7:23]. For to be subjected to their statutes and tyrannical laws is indeed to become slaves of men.

This impious and desperate tyranny is fostered by the pope's disciples, who here twist and pervert that saying of Christ: "He who hears you hears me" [Luke 10:16]. With puffed cheeks they inflate this saying to a great size in support of their own ordinances. Though Christ spoke this word to the apostles when they

167. The word *liberty* (Lat. *libertas*) gained a new meaning and usage in the Middle Ages, especially in the context of feudal society. Whereas Christian liberty was expressed as freedom from the bondage of sin and death in order to be a servant of Christ (e.g., Rom. 6.6f.; Gal. 5:1; 1 Cor. 7:22f.), liberty in the feudal system indicated one's possession of power and jurisdiction—usually over property—without external coercion or limits. Thus, granting a liberty was to grant a privilege. Clergy already began receiving such liberties in the age of Constantine, but as the church participated in the emerging feudal system as a landowner, the notion of "ecclesiastical liberty" had more to do with political and economic jurisdiction than liberty in a spiritual or theological sense. Luther is exploiting this irony in his comments here. Luther would set forth a very different sense of "freedom" in his subsequent treatise, *The Freedom of the Christian* (1520). For more on "liberty" in the Middle Ages and its impact on the church, see Gerd Tellenbach, *Church, State and Christian Society at the Time of the Investiture Controversy* (Oxford: Oxford University Press, 1938).

m Singular in the original.

went forth to preach the gospel, and though it should apply only to the gospel, they pass over the gospel and apply it only to their fables. For he says in John 10[:27, 5]: "My sheep hear my voice, but the voice of a stranger they do not hear." He left us the gospel so that the pontiffs might sound the voice of Christ. Instead they sound their own voices, and yet hope to be heard. Moreover, the Apostle says that he was not sent to baptize, but to preach the gospel.[n] Therefore, no one is obliged to obey the ordinances of the pope, or required to listen to him, except when he teaches the gospel and Christ. And the pope should teach nothing but faith without any restrictions. But since Christ says, "He who hears you [plural] hears me" [Luke 10:16], why does not the pope also hear others? Christ does not say to Peter alone, "He who hears you" [singular]. In short, where there is true faith, there the word of faith must of necessity be also. Why then does not an unbelieving pope now and then hear a believing servant of his, who has the word of faith? Blindness, sheer blindness, reigns among the pontiffs.

Others, even more shameless, arrogantly ascribe to the pope the power to make laws, on the basis of Matt. 16[:19], "Whatever you bind, etc.," although Christ in this passage treats of binding and loosing sins, not of taking the whole church captive and oppressing it with laws. So this tyranny treats everything with its own lying words and violently twists and perverts the words of God. I admit indeed that Christians ought to bear this accursed tyranny just as they would bear any other violence of this world, according to Christ's word: "If any one strikes you on the right cheek, turn to him the other also" [Matt. 5:39]. But this is my complaint: that the godless pontiffs boastfully claim to do this by right, that they pretend to be seeking the church's welfare with this Babylon of theirs, and that they foist this fiction upon all people. For if they did these things and we suffered their violence, both sides being well aware that it was godlessness and tyranny, then we might easily number it among those things that contribute to the mortifying of this life and the fulfilling of our baptism, and might with a good conscience glory in the inflicted injury. But now they seek to deprive us of this consciousness of

n 1 Cor. 1:17.

our liberty, and would have us believe that what they do is well done, and must not be censured or complained of as wrongdoing. Being wolves, they masquerade as shepherds, and being Antichrists, they wish to be honored as Christ.

I lift my voice simply on behalf of liberty and conscience, and I confidently cry: No law, whether of men or of angels, may rightfully be imposed upon Christians without their consent, for we are free of all laws. And if any laws are imposed upon us, we must bear them in such a way as to preserve that sense of freedom which knows and affirms with certainty that an injustice is being done to it, even though it glories in bearing this injustice—so taking care neither to justify the tyrant nor to murmur against his tyranny. "Now who is there to harm you," says Peter, "if you are zealous for what is right?" [1 Pet. 3:13]. "All things work together for good to them that are the elect" [Rom. 8:28].

Nevertheless, since but few know this glory of baptism and the blessedness of Christian liberty, and cannot know them because of the tyranny of the pope, I for one will disengage myself, and keep my conscience free by bringing this charge against the pope and all his papists: Unless they will abolish their laws and ordinances, and restore to Christ's churches their liberty and have it taught among them, they are guilty of all the souls that perish under this miserable captivity, and the papacy is truly the kingdom of Babylon and of the very Antichrist.[168] For who is "the man of sin" and "the son of perdition" [2 Thess. 2:3] but he who with his doctrines and his laws increases the sins and perdition of souls in the church, while sitting in the church as if he were God?[169] All this the papal tyranny has fulfilled, and more than fulfilled, these many centuries. It has extinguished faith, obscured the sacraments and oppressed the gospel; but its own laws, which are not only impious and sacrilegious, but even barbarous and foolish, it has decreed and multiplied without end.

Behold, then, our miserable captivity. "How lonely sits the city that was full of people! How like a widow has she become, she that was great among the nations! She that was a princess among the cities has become a vassal. She has none to comfort her; all her friends have dealt treacherously with her, etc." [Lam. 1:1-2]. There are so many ordinances, so many rites, so many sects,[170] so many vows, so many exertions, and so many works in which Christians are engaged today, that they lose sight of their baptism. Because of this swarm of locusts, palmerworms, and

168. Calling the pope the Antichrist was not uncommon rhetoric, especially since the Western Schism (1378–1417). However, Luther's designation is more than rhetoric. He first privately floated the idea in a letter to a friend, Wenceslas Link (1482–1547), after his encounter with the papal legate, Cardinal Cajetan, in 1518, WA Br 1:270. With the threat of excommunication and no indication that the papacy would change its course, Luther finally put the epithet in print in his 1520 treatise against Augustinus von Alveld (see n. 14, p. 15), *On the Papacy in Rome, Against the Most Celebrated Romanist in Leipzig*, LW 39:49–104. For a helpful overview on the question, see Robert Rosin, "The Papacy in Perspective: Luther's Reform and Rome," in *Concordia Journal* 29 (October 2003): 407–26.

169. 2 Thess. 2:3-4: "Let no one deceive you in any way; for that day will not come unless the rebellion comes first and the lawless one is revealed, the one destined for destruction. He opposes and exalts himself above every so-called god or object of worship, so that he takes his seat in the temple of God, declaring himself to be God."

170. "Sects" here is taken to mean the various rival monastic orders and divisions within Scholastic theology.

cankerworms,[o] no one is able to remember that he is baptized, or what blessings baptism has brought him. We should be even as little children, when they are newly baptized, who engage in no efforts or works, but are free in every way, secure and saved solely through the glory of their baptism. For we are indeed little children, continually baptized anew in Christ.

In contradiction to what has been said, some might cite the baptism of infants who do not comprehend the promise of God and cannot have the faith of baptism; so that therefore either faith is not necessary or else infant baptism is without effect. Here I say what all say: Infants are aided by the faith of others, namely, those who bring them for baptism.[171] For the Word of God is powerful enough, when uttered, to change even a godless heart, which is no less unresponsive and helpless than any infant. So through the prayer of the believing church which presents it, a prayer to which all things are possible,[p] the infant is changed, cleansed, and renewed by the pouring in of faith [*fide infusa*].[172] Nor should I doubt that even a godless adult could be changed, in any of the sacraments, if the same church prayed for and presented him, as we read of the paralytic in the Gospel, who was healed through the faith of others.[q] I should be ready to admit that in this sense the sacraments of the New Law are efficacious in conferring grace, not only to those who do not,

o Cf. Joel 1:4.

p Cf. Mark 9:23.

q Cf. Mark 2:3-12.

171. Cf. Augustine, *Against Two Letters of the Pelagians*, I, 40: "in the Church of the Savior, infants believe by means of other people, even as they have derived those sins which are remitted them in baptism from other people"; Lombard, *Sentences* 4, d. 4, c. 2: "remission is not given in baptism to children without someone else's faith, since they are unable to have their own"; Aquinas, *STh* III, d. 68, a. 9: "Just as a child, when he is being baptized, believes not by himself but by others, so is he examined not by himself but through others, and these in answer confess the Church's faith in the child's stead, who is aggregated to this faith by the sacrament of faith."

172. Luther's point is somewhat different from the traditional understanding of the *fides aliena*, i.e., grace given through the faith of another. The faith of the church or of the sponsors does not stand in as proxy for the child's faith; rather, it is faith that acts in prayer and thus intercedes on behalf of the child. As an answer to this prayer, God grants the child the personal faith necessary to receive baptism. Luther would make the same point later when advising one on how to comfort a mother of a stillborn or miscarriage: "God accomplishes much through the faith and longing of another, even a stranger, even though there is still no personal faith. But this is given through the channel of another's intercession, as in the Gospel Christ raised the widow's son at Nain because of the prayers of his mother apart from the faith of the son" (LW 43:250).

Luther's use of the term *fides infusa* ("the pouring in of faith") is also different from the Scholastic usage which, following Aristotelian ethics, approximates the gift of the theological virtues (faith, hope, and love) to the

but even to those who do most obstinately present an obstacle.[173] What obstacle cannot be removed by the faith of the church and the prayer of faith? Do we not believe that Stephen converted Paul the Apostle by this power?[174] But then the sacraments do what they do not by their own power, but by the power of faith, without which they do nothing at all, as I have said.

The question remains whether an unborn infant, with only a hand or a foot projecting from the womb, can be baptized. Here I will confess my ignorance and make no hasty decision. I am not sure whether the reason they give is sufficient—that in any part of the body whatsoever the entire soul resides. For it is not the soul but the body that is externally baptized with water. But neither do I share the view of those who insist that he who is not yet born cannot be born again (even though it has considerable force).[175] I leave these things to the teaching of the Spirit, and "meanwhile allow everyone to enjoy his own opinion" [Rom. 14:5].

[Religious Vows Versus Baptism]

One thing I will add—and I wish that I could persuade everyone to do it—namely, that all vows should be completely abolished and avoided, whether of religious orders, or about pilgrimages or about any works whatsoever, that we may remain in that which is

acquisition of other virtues, namely, through the acquiring of a habit (*habitus*). But Luther is only stressing that faith is a divine gift with this phrase. Luther's critical engagement with the Scholastic teaching occurs also in 1520: *Disputatio de fide infusa et acquisita*, WA 6:85f. See also Reinhard Schwarz, *Fides, spes und caritas beim jungen Luther: unter besonderer Berücksichtigung der mittelalterlichen Tradition* (Berlin: Walter de Gruyter, 1962). The question of the possibility of faith in an infant is taken up by Luther more thoroughly in his treatise *Concerning Rebaptism: A Letter to Two Pastors* (1528), LW 40:225-62.

173. For the notion of setting an "obstacle" against the reception of grace, see n. 165, pp. 67-68.

174. Acts 7:58—8:1: "Then they dragged him out of the city and began to stone him; and the witnesses laid their coats at the feet of a young man named Saul. While they were stoning Stephen, he prayed, 'Lord Jesus, receive my spirit.' Then he knelt down and cried out in a loud voice, 'Lord, do not hold this sin against them.' When he had said this, he died. And Saul approved of their killing him." Augustine makes this point in a sermon on the birthday of St. Stephen, *Sermo* 382, 4, 4. "For if the martyr Stephen did not pray as he did, the church would not have Paul today."

175. Augustine held this opinion; cf. *Ep.* 187, 9: "No one can be reborn before being born." This opinion was carried on into much of the Scholastic tradition, for example, Lombard, *Sentences* 4, d. 6, c. 3. Aquinas holds an interesting middle position, *STh* III, q. 68, a. 11: "If, however, the head, wherein the senses are rooted, appear first, it should be baptized, in cases of danger: nor should it be baptized

supremely religious and most rich in works—the freedom of baptism.[176] It is impossible to say how much that most widespread delusion of vows detracts from baptism and obscures the knowledge of Christian liberty, to say nothing now of the unspeakable and infinite peril of souls which that mania for making vows and that ill-advised rashness daily increase. O most godless pontiffs and unregenerate pastors, who slumber on unheeding and indulge in your evil lusts, without pity for this most dreadful and perilous "ruin of Joseph"! [Amos 6:4-6].

Vows should either be abolished by a general edict, especially those taken for life, and all people recalled to the vows of baptism, or else everyone should be diligently warned not to take a vow rashly. No one should be encouraged to do so; indeed, permission should be given only with difficulty and reluctance. For we have vowed enough in baptism, more than we can ever fulfill; if we give ourselves to the keeping of this one vow, we shall have all we can do. But now we traverse sea and land to make many proselytes;[r] we fill the world with priests, monks, and nuns, and imprison them all in lifelong vows. You will find those who argue and decree that a work done in fulfillment of a vow ranks higher than one done without a vow, and in heaven is to be rewarded above others with I know not what great rewards. Blind and godless Pharisees, who measure righteousness and holiness by the greatness, number, or other quality of the works! But God measures them by faith alone, and with him there is no difference among works, except insofar as there is a difference in faith.

With such bombast wicked men by their inventions puff up human opinion and human works, in order to lure on the unthinking Masses who are almost always led by the glitter of works to make shipwreck of their faith, to forget their baptism, and to injure their Christian liberty. For a vow is a kind of law or requirement. When vows are multiplied, laws and works are necessarily multiplied, and when these are multiplied, faith is extinguished and the liberty of baptism is taken captive. Others, not content with these wicked allurements, assert in addition that entrance into a religious order is like a new baptism, which may afterward be repeated as often as the purpose to live

r Matt. 23:15.

again, if perfect birth should ensue. And seemingly the same should be done in cases of danger no matter what part of the body appears first. But as none of the exterior parts of the body belong to its integrity in the same degree as the head, some hold that since the matter is doubtful, whenever any other part of the body has been baptized, the child, when perfect birth has taken place, should be baptized with the form: 'If you are not baptized, I baptize you,' etc."

176. Luther's concern is with the view that religious and monastic vows have set up a spiritual standard above and beyond the sacrament of baptism. In the late-medieval context, members of the monastic life and, by derivation, the clerical office, were regarded as belonging to a higher spiritual class than ordinary lay Christians. After martyrdom, monasticism was long regarded as the religious ideal of Christianity. In an attempt to embody the sacrificial, radical tenets in the Gospels, the monastic distinguished himself from the ordinary Christian by his vows of poverty, chastity, and obedience. The Ten Commandments were important, but "if you would be perfect," said the Lord, "sell all you have, give it to the poor, and come follow me." Pursuing the path the "perfect" those who took up monastic vows could even regard them as a kind of second baptism. But in Luther's earlier treatise, *The Address to the Christian Nobility* (1520), he argued that all ordinary Christians were truly spiritual and religious. Only faith made one spiritual, and the life of the laity was a true religious sacrifice and worship when lived out from that faith. Likewise the priesthood—it was not ordination but baptism that made one priests (1 Pet. 2:9). See TAL 1:382.

the monastic life is renewed. Thus these votaries have appropriated to themselves all righteousness, salvation, and glory, and left to those who are merely baptized nothing to compare with them. Now the Roman pontiff, that fountain and source of all superstitions, confirms, approves, and adorns this mode of life with high-sounding bulls[177] and dispensations, while no one deems baptism worthy of even a thought. And with such glittering pomp, as I have said, they drive the pliable people of Christ into the "Clashing Rocks,"[178] so that in their ingratitude toward baptism they presume to achieve greater things by their works than others achieve by their faith.

This fresco, painted by Fra Angelico (c. 1395–1455), shows a monk with Roman tonsure, in which the top of the head is shaved as a sign of religious devotion.

177. A "bull" (*bulla*) is an official papal decree. The name is derived from the seal on the document that guaranteed its authenticity.

178. The Latin has *Symplegades*—the name of the rocks at the Bosphorus, the entrance to the Black Sea, which, according to the Greek myth of Jason and the Argonauts, would leave their moorings and crush all who attempted to pass through. The sense here is that monastic vows are put forth as a greater sense of security than mere faith, but like the Symplegades they are deceptively dangerous.

Therefore, God again is "perverse with the crooked" [Ps. 18:26], and to punish the makers of vows for their ingratitude and pride, God brings it about that they break their vows, or keep them only with prodigious labor, and remain sunk in them, never knowing the grace of faith and of baptism; that they continue in their hypocrisy to the end, since their spirit is not approved of God; and that at last they become a laughingstock to the whole world, ever pursuing righteousness and never attaining righteousness, so that they fulfill the word of Isa. 2[:8]: "Their land is filled with idols."

I am indeed far from forbidding or discouraging anyone who may desire to vow something privately and of his own free choice; for I would not altogether despise and condemn vows. But I would most strongly advise against setting up and sanctioning the making of vows as a public mode of life. It is enough that every one should have the private right to take a vow at his own peril; but to commend the vowing of vows as a public mode of life—this I hold to be most pernicious to the church and to simple souls. First, because it runs directly counter to the Christian life, for a vow is a kind of ceremonial law and a human ordinance or presumption, from which the church has been set free through baptism; for a Christian is subject to no law but the law of God. Second, because there is no instance in Scripture of such a vow, especially of lifelong chastity, obedience, or poverty.[179] But whatever is without warrant of Scripture is most hazardous and should by no means be urged upon anyone, much less established as a common and public mode of life, even if it be permitted to somebody who wishes to make the venture at his own peril. For certain works are wrought by the Spirit in a few people, but they must not be made an example or a mode of life for all.

Moreover, I greatly fear that these votive modes of life of the religious orders belong to those things which the Apostle foretold: "They will be teaching lies in hypocrisy, forbidding marriage, and enjoining abstinence from foods which God created to be received with thanksgiving" [1 Tim. 4:2-3]. Let no one retort by pointing to SS. Bernard, Francis, Dominic,[180] and others, who founded or fostered monastic orders. Terrible and marvelous is God in his counsels toward the sons of men. He could keep Daniel, Hananiah, Azariah, and Mishael holy at the court of the king of Babylon (that is, in the midst of godlessness);[s] why could God not sanctify those men also in their perilous mode of living

179. The common threefold vow of the monastic life.

180. Bernard of Clairvaux (1090–1153) was the leading figure of the Cistercian reforms and established 163 monasteries throughout Europe. Francis of Assisi (1182–1226) founded the *Ordo Fratrum Minorum* (Order of Little Brothers), dedicated to a life of absolute poverty in order to live in conformity with Christ and his apostles. Dominic de Guzman (c. 1170–1221) was a Spanish priest who founded the *Ordo Praedicatorum* (Order of Preachers), also known as the Dominicans. A mendicant order like the Franciscans, the Dominicans were originally dedicated to the evangelization and combating heresy.

or guide them by the special operation of his Spirit, yet without desiring it to be an example to others? Besides, it is certain that none of them was saved through his vows and his religious[181] life; they were saved through faith alone, by which all people are saved, and to which that showy subservience to vows is more diametrically opposed than anything else.

181. The designation "religious" is technical, referring to those having formally taken monastic vows.

But everyone may hold his or her[t] own view on this. I will return to my argument. Speaking now in behalf of the church's liberty and the glory of baptism, I feel myself in duty bound to set forth publicly the counsel I have learned under the Spirit's guidance. I therefore counsel those in high places in the churches, first of all, to abolish all those vows and religious orders, or at least not to approve and extol them. If they will not do this, then I counsel all men who would be assured of their salvation to abstain from all vows, above all from the major and lifelong vows. I give this counsel especially to teenagers and young people. This I do, first, because this manner of life has no witness or warrant in the Scriptures, as I have said, but is puffed up solely by the bulls (and they truly are "bulls"[182]) of human popes. Second, because it greatly tends to hypocrisy, by reason of its outward show and unusual character, which engender conceit and a contempt of the common Christian life. And if there were no other reason for abolishing these vows, this one would be reason enough, namely, that through them faith and baptism are slighted and works are exalted, which cannot be done without harmful results. For in the religious orders there is scarcely one in many thousands who is not more concerned about his works than about faith, and on the basis of this madness, they claim superiority over each other, as being "stricter" or "laxer," as they call it.[183]

182. The wordplay is on *bulla*, which can also mean "bubble."

183. Monastic orders had a history of debates regarding the proper interpretation of their particular rule. Often this led to divisions within their order with stricter "observants" separating from the more lax. The most famous conflict was among the Franciscans after the death of their founder, with the stricter "Spiritualists" set in opposition to the "Conventuals." Luther himself belonged to the stricter observant branch of the Augustinians.

Therefore I advise no one to enter any religious order or the priesthood; indeed, I advise everyone against it—unless he is forearmed with this knowledge and understands that the works of monks and priests, however holy and arduous they may be, do not differ one whit in the sight of God from the works of the rustic laborer in the field or the woman going about her household tasks, but that all works are measured before God by faith alone, as Jer. 5[:3] says: "O Lord, do not your eyes look for faith?"

s Cf. Dan. 1:6-21.

t Feminine added.

and Sir. 32[:23]: "In all your works believe with faith in thy heart, for this is to keep the commandments of God." Indeed, the menial housework of a manservant or maidservant is often more acceptable to God than all the fastings and other works of a monk or priest, because the monk or priest lacks faith. Since, therefore, vows nowadays seem to tend only to the glorification of works and to pride, it is to be feared that there is nowhere less of faith and of the church than among the priests, monks, and bishops. These men are in truth heathen or hypocrites. They imagine themselves to be the church, or the heart of the church, the "spiritual" estate and the leaders of the church, when they are everything else but that. This is indeed "the people of the captivity," among whom all things freely given to us in baptism are held captive, while the few poor "people of the earth" who are left behind,[184] such as the married folk, appear vile in their eyes.

From what has been said we recognize two glaring errors of the Roman pontiff.

In the first place, he grants dispensation from vows,[185] and does it as if he alone of all Christians possessed this authority; so great is the temerity and audacity of wicked men. If it is possible to grant a dispensation from a vow, then any brother may grant one to his neighbor, or even to himself. But if one's neighbor cannot grant a dispensation, neither has the pope any right to do so. For where does he get this authority? From the power of the keys? But the keys belong to all, and avail only for sins, Matthew 18.[186] Now they themselves claim that vows are "of divine right." Why then does the pope deceive and destroy the poor souls of people by granting dispensations in matters of divine right, in which no dispensations can be granted? In the section, "Of vows and their redemption,"[187] he babbles indeed of having the power to change vows, just as in the law the firstborn of an ass was changed for a sheep[188] as if the firstborn of an ass, and the vow he commands to be offered everywhere and always, were one and the same thing; or as if when the Lord decrees in the law that a sheep shall be changed for an ass, the pope, a mere man, may straightway claim the same power, not in his own law, but in God's! It was not a pope, but an ass changed for a pope, that made this decretal;[189] it is so egregiously senseless and godless.

The second error is this: The pope decrees, on the other hand, that a marriage is dissolved if one party enters a monastery without the consent of the other, provided that the marriage has not

184. Luther is referring to the Babylonian exile in the Old Testament. When King Nebuchadnezzar initiated the first deportation, he led out the upper class and aristocracy of the nation. These are the "people of captivity"—an expression taken from the Latin title to Psalm 65 (*populo transmigrationis*). Those left behind—the common folk—are the "people of the earth" (*populi terrae*); 2 Kgs. 24:14, "He carried away all Jerusalem, . . . no one remained, except the poorest people of the land."

185. E.g., Aquinas, *STh* II-II, q. 88, a. 10: "if it be decided absolutely that a particular vow is not to be observed, this is called a 'dispensation' from that vow; but if some other obligation be imposed in lieu of that which was to have been observed, the vow is said to be 'commuted.' Hence it is less to commute a vow than to dispense from a vow: both, however, are in the power of the Church."

186. Matt. 18:15-18: "If another member of the church sins against you, go and point out the fault when the two of you are alone. If the member listens to you, you have regained that one. But if you are not listened to, take one or two others along with you, so that every word may be confirmed by the evidence of two or three witnesses. If the member refuses to listen to them, tell it to the church; and if the offender refuses to listen even to the church, let such a one be to you as a Gentile and a tax collector. Truly I tell you, whatever you bind on earth will be bound in heaven, and whatever you loose on earth will be loosed in heaven."

187. Luther is referring to canon law, *Decretalium Gregorii IX,* lib. 3, tit. 34, *de*

yet been consummated.[190] Now I ask you, what devil puts such monstrous things into the pope's mind? God commands people to keep faith and not break their word to one another, and again, to do good with that which is their own, for God hates "robbery with a burnt offering," as is spoken by the mouth of Isaiah.[191] But spouses[u] are bound by the marriage contract to keep faith with one another, and they are not for themselves alone. They cannot break this faith by any right, and whatever they do with themselves alone is robbery, if it is done without the other's consent. Why does not those who are burdened with debt follow this same rule and obtain admission into a religious order, so as to be released from their debts and be free to break their word? O blind, blind people! Which is greater, the fidelity commanded by God or a vow devised and chosen by human beings? Are you a shepherd of souls, O pope? And you who teach these things, are you doctors of sacred theology? Why then do you teach them? No doubt because you have decked out your vow as a better work than marriage; you do not exalt faith, which alone exalts all things, but works, which are nothing in the sight of God, or which are all alike as far as merit is concerned.

I am sure, therefore, that neither human beings nor angels can grant a dispensation from vows, if they are proper vows. But I am not fully clear in my own mind whether all the things that people vow nowadays come under the head of vows. For instance, it is simply foolish and stupid for parents to dedicate their children, before birth or in infancy, to the "religious life," or to perpetual chastity;[192] indeed, it is certain that this can by no means be termed a vow. It seems to be a kind of mockery of God for them to vow things which are not at all in their power. As to the triple vow[193] of the monastic orders, the longer I consider it, the less I comprehend it, and I wonder where the custom of exacting this vow arose. Still less do I understand at what age vows may be taken in order to be legal and valid. I am pleased to find unanimous agreement that vows taken before the age of puberty are not valid.[194] Nevertheless, they deceive many young children who are ignorant both of their age and of what they are vowing. They do not observe the age of puberty in receiving such children; but the children, after making their profession, are held captive and

u This sentence and what follows were singular in the original.

voto et voti redemptione, c. 7 (hereafter *Decr. Greg. IX*).

188. Cf. Exod. 13:13: "But every firstborn donkey you shall redeem with a sheep; if you do not redeem it, you must break its neck."

189. "Decretal" refers to papal and conciliar decrees that made up most of church law. In the broadest sense, the decretals include all official letters of the pope in which a specific decision or decree is contained. More specifically, the term refers to various collections of such decrees.

190. *Decr. Greg. IX*, lib. 3, tit. 32, *de conversione coniugatorum*, c. 2: "before the marriage is consummated one of the spouses can enter a religious order, even if the other is unwilling."

191. Isa. 61:8: "For I the LORD love justice, I hate robbery and wrongdoing [*or* with a burnt offering]."

192. The child dedicated to the religious life by his parents is called an "oblate." Provisions for this practice were already present in the Rule of Benedict of Nursia (c. 480–571): "let parents draw up the petition which we have mentioned above; and at the oblation let them wrap the petition and the boy's hand in the altar cloth and so offer him [to God]." Rabanus Maurus (780–856) wrote a treatise on the practice, *De oblatione puerorum*, arguing on the basis of biblical precedent with the redemption of the firstborn, the dedication of the Levites, and the vow of Hannah to give Samuel.

193. Poverty, chastity, and obedience.

194. According to canon law the earliest one can take a vow is age fourteen for boys and twelve for girls;

Decr. Greg. IX, lib. 3, tit. 31, *de regularibus et transeuntibus ad religionem*, c. 8.

consumed by a troubled conscience as though they had afterward given their consent. As if a vow which was invalid could finally become valid with the passing of the years!

It seems absurd to me that the effective date of a legitimate vow should be predetermined for others by people who cannot predetermine it for themselves. Nor do I see why a vow taken at eighteen years of age should be valid, but not one taken at ten or twelve years. It will not do to say that at eighteen a man feels his carnal desires. What if he scarcely feels them at twenty or thirty, or feels them more keenly at thirty than at twenty? Why not also set a certain age limit for the vows of poverty and obedience? But what age will you set, by which a man should feel his greed and pride, when even the most spiritual persons hardly become aware of these emotions? Therefore, no vow will ever become binding and valid until we have become spiritual, and no longer have any need of vows. You see that these are uncertain and most perilous matters, and it would therefore be a wholesome counsel to keep such lofty modes of living free of vows, and leave them to the Spirit alone as they were of old, and never in any way to change them into a mode of life which is perpetually binding.

However, let this be sufficient for the present concerning baptism and its liberty. In due time I shall perhaps discuss vows at greater length,[195] and truly there is an urgent need for this.

195. Luther would, in fact, dedicate an entire treatise to this topic in 1521 while at the Wartburg, namely, *On Monastic Vows*, LW 44:243–400.

The Sacrament of Penance

In the third place, we are to discuss the sacrament of penance. On this subject I have already given no little offense to many people by the treatises and disputations already published, in which I have amply set forth my views.[v] These I must now briefly repeat in order to unmask the tyranny that is rampant here no less than in the sacrament of the bread. For, because these two

v The *Ninety-Five Theses against Indulgences* (1517), LW 31:25–33; TAL 1:13–46; *Ein Sermon von Ablaß und Gnade* (*A Sermon on Indulgences and Grace* [1517]), WA 1:239–46; TAL 1:57–66; *The Sacrament of Penance* (1519), LW 35:3–22; TAL 1:181–202; *Explanations of the Ninety-Five Theses* (1518), LW 31:83–252; *A Discussion on How Confession Should Be Made* (1520), LW 39:23–47.

sacraments furnish opportunity for gain and profit, the greed of the shepherds has raged in them with incredible zeal against the flock of Christ, although, as we have just seen in our discussion of vows, baptism too has sadly declined among adults and become the servant of greed.

In this woodcut by Albrecht Dürer (1471–1528), a man, perhaps King David, is depicted doing penance (1510).

The first and chief abuse of this sacrament is that they have completely abolished it. Not a vestige of the sacrament remains. For this sacrament, like the other two, consists in the word of divine promise and our faith, and they have undermined both of them. For they have adapted to their own tyranny the word of promise which Christ speaks in Matt. 16[:19] and 18[:18]: "Whatever you bind, etc.," and in the last chapter of John [20:23]: "If you forgive the sins of any, they are forgiven, etc." By these words the faith of penitents is aroused for obtaining the forgiveness of sins. But in all their writing, teaching, and preaching, their sole concern has been, not to teach what is promised to Christians in these words, or what they ought to believe, and what great consolation they might find in them, but only through force and violence to extend their own tyranny far, wide, and deep. It has finally come to such a pass that some of them have begun to command the very angels in heaven,[196] and to boast in incredible, mad wickedness that in these words they have obtained the right to rule in heaven and earth, and possess the power to bind even in heaven. Thus they say nothing of faith which is the salvation of the people, but babble only of the despotic power of the pontiffs, whereas Christ says nothing at all of power, but speaks only of faith.

196. The reference here is to a spurious bull of Pope Clement VI, *Ad memoriam*, promulgated during the Jubilee year of 1350. Many pilgrims traveling to Rome died from the plague that was widespread throughout Europe, and the bull responds by saying, "We command the angels of paradise that their souls be taken directly to the bliss of paradise, as being fully absolved from purgatory." Luther seems to be referring to this event again in his *Defense and Explanation of All the Articles* (1521), LW 32:74–75: "This is what happened in the days of John Hus. In those days the pope commanded the angels in heaven to lead to heaven the souls of those pilgrims who died on the way to Rome. John Hus objected to this horrible blasphemy and more than diabolic presumption. This protest cost him his life, but he at least caused the pope to change his tune and embarrassed by this sacrilege, to refrain from such proclamation."

For Christ has not ordained authorities or powers or lordships in his church, but ministries, as we learn from the Apostle, who says: "This is how one should regard us, as ministers of Christ and stewards of the mysteries of God" [1 Cor. 4:1]. Just as, when he said: "He who believes and is baptized will be saved" [Mark 16:16], he was calling forth the faith of those who were to be baptized, so that by this word of promise a person might be certain of salvation if baptized in faith. There was no conferring of any power there, but only the instituting of the ministry of those who baptize. Similarly, here where he says, "Whatever you bind, etc." [Matt. 16:19; 18:18], he is calling forth the faith of the penitent, so that by this word of promise we[w] might be certain that if we are absolved in faith, we are truly absolved in heaven. Here there is no mention at all of power, but only of the ministry of the one who absolves. One cannot but wonder what happened to these blind and overbearing men that they did not arrogate to themselves a despotic power from the promise of baptism; or, if they did not do it there, why they presumed to do it from the promise of penance? For in both there is a like ministry, a similar promise, and the same kind of sacrament. It cannot be denied: if baptism does not belong to Peter alone, then it is a wicked usurpation of power to claim the power of the keys for the pope alone.

Again, when Christ says: "Take, this is my body, which is given for you. This is the cup in my blood, etc." [1 Cor. 11:24-25], he is calling forth the faith of those who eat, so that when their conscience has been strengthened by these words they might be certain through faith that they receive the forgiveness of sins when they have eaten. Here too, nothing is said of power, but only of the ministry.

So the promise of baptism remains to some extent, at least for infants; but the promise of the bread and the cup has been destroyed and made subservient to greed, faith has become a work, and the testament has become a sacrifice. The promise of penance, however, has been transformed into the most oppressive despotism, being used to establish a sovereignty which is more than merely temporal.

Not content with these things, *this Babylon of ours has so completely extinguished faith* that it insolently *denies its necessity in this*

w The singular pronoun is replaced with the plural in this sentence.

sacrament. Indeed, with the wickedness of Antichrist it brands it as heresy for anyone to assert that faith is necessary.[x] What more could this tyranny do than it has done? Truly, "by the waters of Babylon we sit down and weep, when we remember thee, O Zion. On the willows there we hang up our lyres" [Ps. 137:1-2]. May the Lord curse the barren willows of those streams! Amen.

Now that promise and faith have been thus blotted out and overthrown, let us see what they have put in their place. *They have divided penance into three parts—contrition, confession, and satisfaction;*[y] but in such a way that they have removed whatever was good in each of them, and have established in each of them their caprice and tyranny.

[Contrition]

In the first place, they teach that contrition takes precedence over, and is far superior to, faith in the promise, as if contrition were not a work of faith, but a merit; indeed, they do not mention faith at all. They stick so closely to works and to those passages of Scripture where we read of many who obtained pardon by reason of their contrition and humility of heart; but they take no account of the faith which effected this contrition and sorrow of heart, as is written of the men of Nineveh in Jon. 3[:5]: "And the people of Nineveh believed God; they proclaimed a fast, etc." Others again, more bold and wicked, have invented a so-called attrition, which is converted into contrition by the power of the keys, of which they know nothing.[197] This attrition they grant to the wicked and unbelieving, and thus abolish contrition altogether. O the intolerable wrath of God, that such things should be taught in the church of Christ! Thus, with both faith and its work destroyed, we go on secure in the doctrines and opinions of men, or rather we perish in them. A contrite heart is a precious thing, but it is found only where there is an ardent faith in the promises and threats of God. Such faith, intent on the immutable truth of God, makes the conscience

197. "Attrition" is imperfect contrition, i.e., sorrow for sin for reasons less than altruistic, such as fear of punishment or love of reward. True or perfect contrition is sorrow for sin out of love for God. It is related to the traditional distinction of two kinds of "fear of God" (*timor Dei*), i.e., servile fear and filial fear. In late medieval theology, attrition was connected to the distinction of congruent merit (*meritum de congruo*—merit inadequate vis-à-vis its reward) and condign merit (*meritum de condigno*—merit intrinsically "worth" its reward). Though attrition did not fulfill the full requirements of contrition in the sacrament of penance, through the priest, God would mercifully consider it sufficient to merit grace (*meritum de congruo*), since God will not deny grace to those who do what is in them (*facere quod in se est*).

x Cf. Luther's dispute with Cajetan on the role of faith, *The Proceedings at Augsburg*, LW 31:271; also TAL 1:141–42.

y See n. 151, p. 63.

tremble, terrifies it and bruises it; and afterwards, when it is contrite, raises it up, consoles it, and preserves it. Thus the truth of God's threat is the cause of contrition, and the truth of his promise the cause of consolation, if it is believed. By such faith a man "merits" the forgiveness of sins. Therefore faith should be taught and aroused before all else. Once faith is obtained, contrition and consolation will follow inevitably of themselves.

Therefore, although there is some truth in their teaching that contrition is to be attained by the enumeration and contemplation (as they call it) of their sins,[198] yet their teaching is perilous and perverse so long as they do not teach first of all the beginnings and causes of contrition—the immutable truth of God's threat and promise which calls forth faith—so that men may learn to pay more heed to the truth of God, by which they are cast down and lifted up, than to the multitude of their sins. If their sins are regarded apart from the truth of God, they will excite afresh and increase the desire for sin rather than lead to contrition. I will say nothing now of the insurmountable task which they have imposed upon us, namely, that we are to frame a contrition for every sin. That is impossible. We can know only the smaller part of our sins; and even our good works are found to be sins, according to Ps. 143[:2]: "Enter not into judgment with your servant; for no one living is righteous before you." It is enough if we lament the sins which distress our conscience at the present moment, as well as those which we can readily call to mind. Whoever is in this frame of mind is without doubt ready to grieve and fear for all his sins, and will grieve and fear whenever they are brought to his knowledge in the future.

Beware, then, of putting your trust in your own contrition and of ascribing the forgiveness of sins to your own remorse. God does not look on you with favor because of that, but because of the faith by which you have believed God's threats and promises, and which has effected such sorrow within you. Thus we owe whatever good there may be in our penance, not to our scrupulous enumeration of sins, but to the truth of God and to our faith. All other things are the works and fruits which follow of their own accord. They do not make a person good, but are done by the one who is already made good through faith in the truth of God. Even so, "smoke goes up in his wrath; because he is angry he shakes the mountains and sets them on fire," as it is said in Ps. 18[:8, 7]). First comes the terror of this threatening, which sets

198. Cf. Aquinas, *STh* III Suppl., q. 9, a. 2: "In prescribing medicine for the body, the physician should know not only the disease for which he is prescribing, but also the general constitution of the sick person, since one disease is aggravated by the addition of another, and a medicine which would be adapted to one disease, would be harmful to another. The same is to be said in regard to sins, . . . hence it is necessary for confession that man confess all the sins that he calls to mind, and if he fails to do this, it is not a confession, but a pretense of confession."

the wicked on fire; then faith, accepting this, sends up smoke-clouds of contrition, etc.

But the trouble is not so much that contrition has been exposed to tyranny and avarice, as that it has been given over completely to wickedness and pestilent teaching. It is confession and satisfaction that have become the chief workshops of greed and power.

[Confession]

Let us first take up *confession*. There is no doubt that confession of sins is necessary and commanded of God, in Matt. 3[:6]: "They were baptized by John in the River Jordan, confessing their sins," and in 1 John 1[:9-10]: "If we confess our sins, he is faithful and just, and will forgive our sins. If we say we have not sinned, we make him a liar, and his word is not in us." If the saints may not deny their sin, how much more ought those who are guilty of great and public sins to make confession! But the institution of confession is proved most effectively of all by Matt. 18,[199] where Christ teaches that those[z] who sin should be told of their faults, brought before the church, accused, and if they will not hear, be excommunicated. They "hear" if they heed the rebuke and acknowledge and confess their sins.

As to the current practice of private confession, I am heartily in favor of it, even though it cannot be proved from the Scriptures. It is useful, even necessary, and I would not have it abolished. Indeed, I rejoice that it exists in the church of Christ, for it is a cure without equal for distressed consciences. For when we have laid bare our conscience to another Christian and privately made known to the evil that lurked within, we receive from that person's lips the word of comfort [as if] spoken by God. And, if we accept this in faith, we find peace in the mercy of God speaking to us through our brother or sister. There is just one thing about it that I abominate, and that is the fact that this kind of confession has been subjected to the despotism and extortion of the pontiffs. They reserve to themselves even the secret sins,[200] and command that they be made known to confessors named by them, only to trouble the consciences of people. They merely

z Plural substituted for singular in this and the next sentence.

199. Matt. 18:15-17: "If another member of the church sins against you, go and point out the fault when the two of you are alone. If the member listens to you, you have regained that one. But if you are not listened to, take one or two others along with you, so that every word may be confirmed by the evidence of two or three witnesses. If the member refuses to listen to them, tell it to the church; and if the offender refuses to listen even to the church, let such a one be to you as a Gentile and a tax collector."

200. The notion of "reserved cases" in which the pope claimed exclusive jurisdiction to grant remission and satisfaction (*casus papales*) developed gradually as bishops would refer certain grave transgressions to the Holy See, for example, violence done to clerics and the burning of church buildings being the most common early on. Official lists of cases reserved for the pope were enumerated in the bull *In coena domini*, which was published annually against heretics since 1364. This list, however, grew with papal discretion and continued to be a contentious conflict of jurisdiction over the bishops who had claimed the right to absolve a similar list of "secret" (*casus occultus*) as well as "public" sins. In 1414, the Council of Constance tried, though unsuccessfully, to curtail these cases and leave them at the discretion of the bishop. Even the Council of Trent in 1563 would try to limit papal cases only to certain public sins, leaving the secret sins in the hands of the bishops (*Sess.* 24, *de Reform*, c. 8 and c. 20), but this, too, was often overturned by the publication of *Coena domini*.

play the pontiff, while they utterly despise the true duties of pontiffs, which are to preach the gospel and to care for the poor. Indeed, the godless despots leave the great sins to the common priests, and reserve to themselves only those sins which are of less consequence, such as those ridiculous and fictitious things in the bull *Coena domini*. To make the wickedness of their error even more apparent, they not only fail to reserve, but actually teach and approve things which are against the service of God, against faith and the chief commandments—such as their running about on pilgrimages, the perverse worship of the saints, the lying saints' legends, the various ways of trusting in works and ceremonies and practicing them. Yet in all of these faith in God is extinguished and idolatry fostered, as we see in our day. As a result we have the same kind of priests today as Jeroboam ordained of old in Dan and Beersheba, ministers of the golden calves,[a] men who are ignorant of the law of God, of faith, and of whatever pertains to the feeding of Christ's sheep. They inculcate in the people nothing but their own inventions with fear and violence.

Although I urge that this outrage of reserved cases should be borne patiently, even as Christ bids us bear all human tyranny, and teaches us that we should obey these extortioners; nevertheless, I deny that they have the right to make such reservations, and I do not believe that they can bring one jot or tittle of proof that they have it. But I am going to prove the contrary. In the first place, Christ speaks in Matt. 18 of public sins and says that if our brother hears us, when we tell him his fault, we have saved the soul of our brother, and that he is to be brought before the church only if he refuses to hear us, so that his sin can be corrected among brethren.[b] How much more will it be true of secret sins, that they are forgiven if one brother freely makes confession to another? So it is not necessary to tell it to the church, that is, as these babblers interpret it, to the prelate or priest. On this matter we have further authority from Christ, where he says in the same chapter: "Whatever you bind on earth shall be bound in heaven, and whatever you loose on earth shall be loosed in heaven" [Matt. 18:18]. For this is said to each and every Christian. Again, he says in the same place: "Again I say to you, if two

a 1 Kgs. 12:26-32.

b Matt. 18:15-17.

of you agree on earth about anything they ask, it will be done for them by my father in heaven" [Matt. 18:19]. Now, the one who lays secret sins before another believer and craves pardon, certainly agrees with this brother or sister on earth, in the truth which is Christ. Of this Christ says even more clearly, confirming his preceding words: "For truly, I say to you, where two or three are gathered in my name, there am I in the midst of them" [Matt. 18:20].

Hence, I have no doubt but that we are absolved from our secret sins when we have made confession, privately before any brother or sister, either of our own accord or after being rebuked, and have sought pardon and amended our ways, no matter how much the violence of the pontiffs may rage against it. For Christ has given to every one of his believers the power to absolve even open sins. Add yet this little point: If any reservation of secret sins were valid, so that one could not be saved unless they were forgiven, then one's salvation would be prevented most of all by those aforementioned good works and idolatries that are taught by the popes nowadays. But if these most grievous sins do not prevent one's salvation, how foolish it is to reserve those lighter sins! In truth, it is the foolishness and blindness of the shepherds that produce these monstrous things in the church. Therefore I would admonish those princes of Babylon and bishops of Beth-aven[201] to refrain from reserving any cases whatsoever. Let them, moreover, permit all brothers and sisters most freely to hear the confession of secret sins, so that the sinner may make his sins known to whomever he will and seek pardon and comfort, that is, the word of Christ, by the mouth of his neighbor. For with these presumptions of theirs they only ensnare the consciences of the weak without necessity, establish their wicked despotism, and fatten their avarice on the sins and ruin of their brethren. Thus they stain their hands with the blood of souls; sons are devoured by their parents. Ephraim devours Judah, and Syria Israel, with an open mouth, as Isaiah says.[202]

To these evils they have added the "circumstances,"[c] and also the mothers, daughters, sisters, sisters-in-law, branches and fruits of sins; since these most astute and idle men have worked out, if you please, a kind of family tree of relationships and

c See n. 154, p. 64.

201. Hos. 4:15; 10:5. "Beth-aven" was the new name given to Bethel by the prophet in response to Israel's idolatry. Rather than "house of God," it was "house of nothingness."

202. Isa. 9:20-22: "They gorged on the right, but still were hungry, and they devoured on the left, but were not satisfied; they devoured the flesh of their own kindred; Manasseh devoured Ephraim, and Ephraim Manasseh, and together they were against Judah. For all this his anger has not turned away; his hand is stretched out still."

affinities even among sins—so prolific is wickedness coupled with ignorance. For this conception, whatever rogue may be its author, has become a public law, like many others. Thus do the shepherds keep watch over the church of Christ: whatever new work or superstition those most stupid devotees may have dreamed of, they immediately drag to the light of day, deck out with indulgences, and fortify with bulls. So far are they from suppressing such things and preserving for God's people true faith and liberty. For what has our liberty to do with the tyranny of Babylon?

My advice would be to ignore all "circumstances" whatsoever. With Christians there is only one circumstance—that a fellow Christian[d] has sinned. For there is no person to be compared with a fellow Christian. And the observance of places, times, days, persons, and all other rank superstition only magnifies the things that are nothing, to the injury of the things which are everything; as if anything could be of greater weight or importance than the glory of Christian fellowship! Thus they bind us to places, days, and persons, so that the name of [Christian] "brother" [or "sister"] loses its value, and we serve in bondage instead of being free—we, to whom all days, places, persons, and all external things are one and the same.

[Satisfaction]

How unworthily they have dealt with *satisfaction,* I have abundantly shown in the controversies concerning indulgences.[e] They have grossly abused it, to the ruin of Christians in body and soul. To begin with, they have taught it in such a manner that the people have never had the slightest understanding what satisfaction really is, namely, the renewal of one's life. Then, they so continually harp on it and emphasize its necessity, that they leave no room for faith in Christ. With these scruples they torture poor consciences to death; and one runs to Rome, one to this place, another to that; this one to Chartreuse,[203] that one to some other place; one scourges himself with rods, another mortifies his body with fasts and vigils; and all cry with the same

203. The founding cloister of the Carthusian order, founded by Bruno of Cologne (1030–1101) in 1084.

d *Brother* in the German.

e Cf. *A Sermon on Indulgence and Grace* (1518), WA 1:243–46; TAL 1:56–65; *Resolutiones* (1518), concl. 5., WA 1:538,1–35.

mad zeal: "Lo, here is Christ! Lo, there!" believing that the kingdom of Christ, which is within us, will come with observation.[204]

This image by an unknown artist depicts flagellants doing penance.

For these monstrous things we are indebted to you, O Roman See, and to your murderous laws and ceremonies, with which you have corrupted all humankind, so that they believe they can with works make satisfaction for sin to God, when God can be satisfied only by the faith of a contrite heart! Not only do you keep this faith silent with this uproar of yours, but you even oppress it, only so that your insatiable bloodsucker may have those to whom it may say, "Give, give!" [Prov. 30:15] and may traffic in sins.

Some have gone even further and have constructed those instruments for driving souls to despair, their decrees that the penitents must rehearse all sins anew for which they neglected to make the imposed satisfaction. What would they not venture to do, these men who were born for the sole purpose of carrying all things into a tenfold captivity?

Moreover, how many, I ask, are possessed with the notion that they are in a saved state and are making satisfaction for their sins, if they only mumble over, word for word, the prayers imposed by the priest, even though meanwhile they never give a thought to the amending of their way of life! They believe that their life is changed in the one moment of contrition and confession, and there remains only to make satisfaction for their past sins. How should they know better if they have not been taught otherwise? No thought is given here to the mortifying of the flesh, no value is attached to the example of Christ, who, when he absolved the woman caught in adultery, said: "Go, and do not sin again" [John 8:11], thereby laying upon her the cross, that is, the mortifying of her flesh. This perverse error is greatly encouraged by the fact that we absolve sinners before the satisfaction has

204. Cf. Luke 17:20f.: "The kingdom of God is not coming with things that can be observed; nor will they say, 'Look, here it is!' or 'There it is!' For, in fact, the kingdom of God is among you." Luther's wordplay is on "observation" (*observantia*), which can also refer to the monastic observants; see n. 183, p. 81.

been completed, so that they are more concerned about completing the satisfaction, which is a lasting thing, than they are about contrition, which they suppose to be over and done with when they have made confession. Absolution ought rather to follow on the completion of satisfaction, as it did in the early church, with the result that, after completing the work, penitents gave themselves with much greater diligence to faith and the living of a new life.

But this must suffice in repetition of what I have said more fully in connection with indulgences, and *in general this must suffice for the present concerning the three sacraments*, which have been treated, and yet not treated, in so many harmful books on the *Sentences*[f] and on the laws. It remains to attempt some discussion of the other "sacraments" also, lest I seem to have rejected them without cause.

205. Confirmation was seen in connection with the gift of the Holy Spirit through apostolic laying on of hands (e.g., Acts 8:15f.) in the context of baptism. Alternatively, the sacrament has also been called chrism, especially in the Eastern church; in reference to the anointing of the Spirit it also was accompanied by the anointing of oil. Because of its origination with the apostles, confirmation was, like ordination, a sacramental act performed by the bishop. Cf., for example, Aquinas, *STh* III, q. 72, a. 11: "the conferring of this sacrament is reserved to bishops, who possess supreme power in the Church: just as in the primitive Church, the fullness of the Holy Ghost was given by the apostles, in whose place the bishops stand (Acts 8). Hence Pope Urban I (r. 222–230) says: "All the faithful should, after baptism, receive the Holy Ghost by the imposition of the bishop's hand, that they may become perfect Christians."

Confirmation

It is amazing that it should have entered the minds of these men to make a sacrament of confirmation out of the laying on of hands. We read that Christ touched the little children in that way,[g] and that by it the apostles imparted the Holy Spirit,[h] ordained presbyters,[i] and cured the sick;[j] as the Apostle writes to Timothy: "Do not be hasty in the laying on of hands" [1 Tim. 5:22]. Why have they not also made a "confirmation" out of the sacrament of the bread? For it is written in Acts 9[:19]: "And he took food and was strengthened," and in Ps. 104[:15]: "And bread to strengthen man's heart." Confirmation would thus include three sacraments—the bread, ordination, and confirmation itself. But if everything the apostles did is a sacrament, why have they not rather made preaching a sacrament?

f See n. 56, p. 30.
g Mark 10:16.
h Acts 8:17; 19:6.
i Acts 6:6.
j Mark 16:18.

I do not say this because I condemn the seven sacraments, but because I deny that they can be proved from the Scriptures. Would that there were in the church such a laying on of hands as there was in apostolic times, whether we chose to call it confirmation or healing! But there is nothing left of it now but what we ourselves have invented to adorn the office of bishops,[205] that they may not be entirely without work in the church. For after they relinquished to their inferiors those arduous sacraments together with the Word as being beneath their attention (since whatever the divine majesty has instituted they seem to need to despise!) it was no more than right that we should discover something easy and not too burdensome for such delicate and great heroes to do, and should by no means entrust it to the lower clergy as something common, for whatever human wisdom has decreed must be held in honor among all! Therefore, as the priests are, so let their ministry and duty be. For a bishop who does not preach the gospel or practice the cure of souls—what is he but an idol in the world [1 Cor. 8:4], who has nothing but the name and appearance of a bishop?

Ein Sermon von dem heiligen hoch= wirdigen Sacrament der Tauffe doc toris Martini Luther Augustiner.

A woodcut of the seven sacraments of the Roman Catholic Church adorns the title page of this sermon on baptism (Leipzig, 1520) by Luther. The scene depicting the sacrament of confirmation is the center image on the left.

But *instead of this we seek sacraments that have been divinely instituted, and among these we see no reason for numbering confirmation.* For to constitute a sacrament there must be above all things else a word of divine promise, by which faith may be exercised. But we read nowhere that Christ ever gave a promise concerning confirmation, although he laid hands on many and included the laying on of hands among the signs in the last chapter of Mark [16:18]:

"They will lay their hands on the sick; and they will recover." Yet no one has applied this to a sacrament, for that is not possible.

For this reason it is sufficient to regard confirmation as a certain churchly rite or sacramental ceremony, similar to other ceremonies, such as the blessing of water and the like. For if every other creature is sanctified by the Word and by prayer,[k] why should not we much rather be sanctified by the same means? Still, these things cannot be called sacraments of faith, because they have no divine promise connected with them, neither do they save; but the sacraments do save those who believe the divine promise.

Marriage

[Marriage Is Not a Sacrament]

Not only is marriage regarded as a sacrament without the least warrant of Scripture,[206] but the very ordinances that extol it as a sacrament have turned it into a farce. Let us look into this a little.

We have said that in every sacrament there is a word of divine promise, to be believed by whoever receives the sign, and that the sign alone cannot be a sacrament. Nowhere do we read that the man who marries a wife receives any grace of God. There is not even a divinely instituted sign in marriage, nor do we read anywhere that marriage was instituted by God to be a sign of anything. To be sure, whatever takes place in a visible manner can be understood as a figure or allegory of something invisible. But figures or allegories are not sacraments, in the sense in which we use the term.

Furthermore, since marriage has existed from the beginning of the world and is still found among unbelievers, there is no reason why it should be called a sacrament of the New Law[207] and of the church alone. The marriages of the ancients were no less sacred than are ours, nor are those of unbelievers less true marriages than those of believers, and yet they are not regarded as sacraments. Besides, even among believers there are married folk who are wicked and worse than any heathen; why should marriage be called a sacrament in their case and not among

k 1 Tim. 4:4-5.

206. The Scripture most often cited in connected with marriage is Eph. 5:22-32, especially "the two will become one flesh. This is a great mystery . . . [Lat. *sacramentum*]." The sacramental character of marriage is articulated in the tradition in a variety of sources, though what constitutes a sacrament varied. For example, Augustine, in his work *On the Good of Marriage* (401), c. 32, notes the following: "Among all nations and all people the good that is secured by marriage consists in the offspring and in the chastity of married fidelity; but, in the case of God's people, it consists moreover in the holiness of the sacrament, by reason of which it is forbidden, even after a separation has taken place, to marry another as long as the first partner lives . . . just as priests are ordained to draw together a Christian community, and even though no such community be formed, the sacrament of orders still abides in those ordained, or just as the sacrament of the Lord, once it is conferred, abides even in one who is dismissed from his office on account of guilt, although in such a one it abides unto judgment." Peter Lombard lists marriage as one of the seven sacraments, noting that it offers only a remedy against sin rather than any helping grace, *Sentences* 4, d. 2, c. 1. In 1139, the Second Lateran Council assigned marriage along with the Eucharist and baptism as priestly acts, and at the Council of Verona, in 1184, marriage was designated as a sacrament.

207. "New Law" (*nova lex*) is a traditional designation for the gospel and the New Testament, set in contrast to the "Old Law" (*vetus lex*), i.e., the law of Moses.

A marriage ceremony presided over by a priest, depicted in a 1522 publication.

the heathen? Or are we going to talk the same sort of nonsense about baptism and the church and say that marriage is a sacrament only in the church, just as some make the mad claim that temporal power exists only in the church? That is childish and foolish talk, by which we expose our ignorance and foolhardiness to the ridicule of unbelievers.

But they will say, "The Apostle says in Eph. 5[:31-32], 'The two shall become one. This is a great sacrament.' Surely you are not going to contradict so plain a statement of the Apostle!" I reply: This argument like the others betrays great shallowness and a careless and thoughtless reading of Scripture. Nowhere in all of the Holy Scriptures is this word *sacramentum* employed in the sense in which we use the term; it has an entirely different meaning. For wherever it occurs it denotes not the sign of a sacred thing,[208] but the sacred, secret, hidden thing itself.[209]

208. Cf. Augustine, *The City of God* 10, 5: "a sacrament, that is, a sacred sign"; Lombard, *Sentences* 4, d. 1, c. 2: "A sacrament is a sign of a sacred thing"; Aquinas, *STh* III, q. 60, a. 3: "a sacrament properly speaking is that which is ordained to signify our sanctification. In which three things may be considered; viz. the very cause of our sanctification, which is Christ's passion; the form of our sanctification, which is grace and the virtues; and the ultimate end of our sanctification, which is eternal life. And all these are signified by the sacraments."

209. Cf. Aquinas, *STh* III, q. 60, a. 1: "a thing may be called a 'sacrament,' either from having a certain hidden sanctity, and in this sense a sacrament is a 'sacred secret'; or from having some relationship to this sanctity, which relationship may be that of a cause, or of a sign or of any other relation. But now we are speaking of sacraments in a special sense, as implying the habitude of sign: and in this way a sacrament is a kind of sign."

Thus Paul writes in 1 Cor. 4[:1]: "This is how one should regard us, as servants of Christ and stewards of the 'mysteries' of God," that is, the sacraments. For where we have the word *sacramentum* the Greek original has *mysterion*, which the translator sometimes translates and sometimes retains in its Greek form.[210] Thus our verse in the Greek reads: "They two shall become one. This is a great mystery." This explains how they came to understand a sacrament of the New Law here, a thing they would never have done if they had read *mysterium*, as it is in the Greek.

Thus Christ himself is called a "sacrament" in 1 Tim. 3[:16]: "Great indeed, is the sacrament (that is, the mystery): He was manifested in the flesh, vindicated in the Spirit, seen by angels, preached among the nations, believed on in the world, taken up in glory." Why have they not drawn out of this passage an eighth sacrament of the New Law, since they have the clear authority of Paul? But if they restrained themselves here, where they had a most excellent opportunity to invent new sacraments, why are they so unrestrained in the other passage? Plainly, it was their ignorance of both words and things that betrayed them. They clung to the mere sound of the words, indeed, to their own fancies. For, having once arbitrarily taken the word *sacramentum* to mean a sign, they immediately, without thought or scruple, made a "sign" of it every time they came upon it in the Holy Scriptures. Such new meanings of words, human customs, and other things they have dragged into the Holy Scriptures. They have transformed the Scriptures according to their own dreams, making anything out of any passage whatsoever. Thus they continually chatter nonsense about the terms: good work, evil work, sin, grace, righteousness, virtue, and almost all the fundamental words and things.[211] For they employ them all after their own arbitrary judgment, learned from the writings of men, to the detriment of both the truth of God and of our salvation.

Therefore, sacrament, or mystery, in Paul is that wisdom of the Spirit, hidden in a mystery, as he says in 1 Cor. 2, which is Christ, who for this very reason is not known to the rulers of this world, wherefore they also crucified him,[212] and for them he remains to this day folly, an offense, a stumbling stone,[213] and a sign that is spoken against.[214] The preachers he calls stewards of these mysteries[215] because they preach Christ, the power and the wisdom of God,[l] yet in such a way that, unless you believe, you cannot understand it. Therefore, a sacrament is a mystery, or

210. The common Latin translation of "mystery" (Gk.: *mysterion*) in the Vulgate Bible is *sacramentum*, though there are instances in which it retains a Latinized form of the original, i.e., *mysterium*.

211. In his Romans lectures (1515–16), Luther began to realize certain incompatibilities with the way the Scholastic tradition used and defined theological words and the manner in which Paul used them. Repeatedly he noted that there was a stark contrast between the way in which the apostle speaks (*modus loquendi apostoli*) and the way the Scholastics talked (*modus loquendi philosophiae . . . Aristoteli*). Exasperated, he famously wrote in his notes, "O pig-theologians . . . O ignorance of sin! O ignorance of God! O ignorance of the law!" In his 1522 translation of the New Testament, he included in his preface to Romans a list of biblical vocabulary that had been misinterpreted by the Scholastics, providing his own definitions for such key words as *law, sin, grace, faith, righteousness, flesh*, and *spirit*. See Leif Grane, *Modus Loquendi Theologicus: Luthers Kampf um die Erneuerung der Theologie 1515–1518*, Acta Theologica Danica, vol. 12 (Leiden: Brill, 1975).

212. 1 Cor. 2:7-8: "But we speak God's wisdom, secret and hidden, which God decreed before the ages for our glory. None of the rulers of this age understood this; for if they had, they would not have crucified the Lord of glory."

213. 1 Cor. 1:22-24: "For Jews demand signs and Greeks desire wisdom, but we proclaim Christ crucified, a stumbling block to Jews and foolishness to Gentiles, but to those who are the called, both Jews and Greeks, Christ the

secret thing, which is set forth in words, but received by the faith of the heart. Such a sacrament is spoken of in the passage before us: "The two shall become one. This is a great sacrament,"[m] which they understand as spoken of marriage,[216] whereas Paul himself wrote these words as applying to Christ and the church, and clearly explained them himself by saying: "I take it to mean Christ and the church" [Eph. 5:32]. See how well Paul and these men agree! Paul says he is proclaiming a great sacrament in Christ and the church, but they proclaim it in terms of man and a woman! If such liberty in the interpretation of the sacred Scriptures is permitted, it is small wonder that one finds here anything one pleases, even a hundred sacraments.

Christ and the church are, therefore, a mystery, that is, a great and secret thing which can and ought to be represented in terms of marriage as a kind of outward allegory. But marriage ought not for that reason to be called a sacrament. The heavens are a type of the apostles, as Ps. 19 declares; the sun is a type of Christ; the waters, of the peoples; but that does not make those things sacraments, for in every case there are lacking both the divine institution and the divine promise, which constitute a sacrament.[217] Hence Paul, in Ephesians 5, following his own mind, applies to Christ these words of Genesis 2 about marriage;[n] or else, following the general view, he teaches that the spiritual marriage of Christ is also contained therein, when he says: "As Christ cherishes the church, because we are members of his body, of his flesh and his bones. 'For this reason a man shall leave his father and mother and be joined to his wife, and the two shall become one.' This is a great sacrament, and I take it to mean Christ and the church." You see, he would have the whole passage apply to Christ, and is at pains to admonish the reader to understand that the sacrament is in Christ and the church, not in marriage.[o]

l 1 Cor. 1:24.

m Eph. 5:31-32.

n Gen. 2:24.

o At this point comes a paragraph that clearly breaks the flow of thought, though it is not clear how this might fit under Luther's treatment of penance earlier. It seems to have been an accidental

power of God and the wisdom of God." Cf. Rom. 9:32-33.

214. Luke 2:34: "Then Simeon blessed them and said to his mother Mary, 'This child is destined for the falling and the rising of many in Israel, and to be a sign that will be opposed.'"

215. 1 Cor. 4:1: "Think of us in this way, as servants of Christ and stewards of God's mysteries."

216. Lombard, *Sentences* 4, d. 26, c. 6: "since marriage is a sacrament, it is both a sacred sign and the sign of a sacred thing, namely of joining of Christ and the Church, as the Apostle says. . . . For just as there is between the partners to a marriage a joining according to the consent of souls and the intermingling of bodies, so the Church joins herself to Christ by will and nature." Aquinas, *STh* III Suppl., q. 42, a. 1.

217. Ps. 19:2-5: "The heavens are telling the glory of God; and the firmament proclaims his handiwork. . . . In the heavens he has set a tent for the sun, which comes out like a bridegroom from his wedding canopy." Luther's interpretation, which reflects the traditional allegorical interpretation of this Psalm in the history of exegesis, is first set forth in his lectures on the Psalms in 1513: "*the heavens tell*, [i.e.] the apostles and evangelists . . . *and the firmament proclaims*, [i.e.] the apostolic church . . . full of stars, i.e., the saints. . . . *for the sun*, in Christ . . . *he sets*, God . . . *his tabernacle*, his church" (WA 55/I:160; emphasis mine).

Granted that marriage is a figure of Christ and the church; yet it is not a divinely instituted sacrament, but invented by those in the church who are carried away by their ignorance of both the word and the thing. This ignorance, when it does not conflict with the faith, is to be borne in charity, just as many other human practices due to weakness and ignorance are borne in the church, so long as they do not conflict with the faith and the Holy Scriptures. But we are now arguing for the certainty and purity of faith and the Scriptures. We expose our faith to ridicule if we affirm that a certain thing is contained in the sacred Scriptures and in the articles of our faith, only to be refuted and shown that it is not contained in them; being found ignorant of our own affairs, we become a stumbling block to our opponents and to the weak. But most of all we should guard against impairing the authority of the Holy Scriptures. For those things which have been delivered to us by God in the sacred Scriptures must be sharply distinguished from those that have been invented by men in the church, no matter how eminent they may be for saintliness and scholarship.

So far concerning marriage itself.

insertion by the printer. The paragraph is reproduced here as a note for reference.

> I admit, of course, that the sacrament of penance existed in the Old Law, and even from the beginning of the world. But the new promise of penance and the gift of the keys are peculiar to the New Law. Just as we now have baptism instead of circumcision, so we have the keys instead of sacrifices and other signs of penance. We said above that the same God at various times gave different promises and diverse signs for the remission of sins and the salvation of men; nevertheless, all received the same. Thus it is said in 2 Cor. 4[:13], "Since we have the same spirit of faith, we too believe, and so we speak." And in 1 Cor. 10, "Our fathers all ate the same supernatural food and drank the same supernatural drink. For they drank from the supernatural Rock which followed them, and the Rock was Christ." Thus also in Heb. 11, "They all died, not having received what was promised, since God had foreseen something better for us, that apart from us they should not be made perfect." For Christ himself is, yesterday and today and forever the head of his church, from the beginning even to the end of the world. Therefore there are diverse signs, but the faith of all is the same. Indeed, without faith it is impossible to please God, yet by it Abel did please him.

p Cf. Gen. 10:8f. See n. 13, p. 15.

[Canonical Impediments to Marriage]

But what shall we say concerning the wicked laws of men by which this divinely ordained way of life has been ensnared and tossed to and fro? Good God! It is dreadful to contemplate the audacity of the Roman despots, who both dissolve and compel marriages as they please. I ask you, has humankind been handed over to the caprice of these men for them to mock them and in every way abuse them and make of them whatever they please, for the sake of filthy lucre?

There is circulating far and wide and enjoying a great reputation a book whose contents have been confusedly poured together out of all the dregs and filth of human ordinances. Its title is "The Angelic *Summa*,"[218] although it ought rather to be "The More than Devilish *Summa*." Among endless other monstrosities, which are supposed to instruct the confessors, whereas they most mischievously confuse them, there are enumerated in this book eighteen impediments to marriage. If you will examine these with the just and unprejudiced eye of faith, you will see that they belong to those things which the Apostle foretold: "There shall be those that give heed to the spirits of demons, speaking lies in hypocrisy, forbidding to marry" [1 Tim. 4:1-3]. What is "forbidding to marry" if it is not this—to invent all those hindrances and set those snares, in order to prevent people from marrying, or, if they are married to annul their marriage? Who gave this power to men? Granted that they were holy men and impelled by godly zeal, why should another's holiness disturb my liberty? Why should another's zeal take me captive? Let whoever will be a saint and a zealot, and to his heart's content, only let him not bring harm upon another, and let him not rob me of my liberty!

Yet I am glad that those shameful laws have at last reached their full measure of glory, which is this: that the Romanists of our day have through them become merchants. What is it that they sell? Vulvas and penises—merchandise indeed most worthy of such merchants, grown altogether filthy and obscene through greed and godlessness. For there is no impediment nowadays that may not be legalized through the intercession of mammon. These laws of men seem to have sprung into existence for the sole purpose of serving those greedy men and rapacious Nimrods[p] as snares for taking money and as nets for catching souls, and in

218. A fifteenth-century handbook on casuistry, the *Summa de casibus conscientiae* was popularly named after its author, Angelo Carletti di Chiviasso (1411–1495), and often used by priests as a guide to hearing confession. In the section on "Matrimony," the book listed eighteen impediments to marriage.

order that "abomination" might stand in "the holy place" [Matt. 24:15], the church of God, and openly sell to people the privy parts of both sexes, or (as the Scriptures say) "shame and nakedness,"[q] of which they had previously robbed them by means of their laws. O worthy trade for our pontiffs to ply, instead of the ministry of the gospel, which in their greed and pride they despise, being given up to a reprobate mind[r] with utter shame and infamy.

But what shall I say or do? If I enter into details, the treatise will grow beyond all bounds. Everything is in such dire confusion that one does not know where to begin, how far to go, and where to leave off. This I do know, that no state is governed successfully by means of laws. If rulers are wise, they[s] will govern better by a natural sense of justice than by laws. If they are not wise, they will foster nothing but evil through legislation, since they will not know what use to make of the laws nor how to adapt them to the case at hand. Therefore, in civil affairs more stress should be laid on putting good and wise leaders in office than on making laws; for such leaders will themselves be the very best of laws, and will judge every variety of ease with a lively sense of equity. And if there is knowledge of the divine law combined with natural wisdom, then written laws will be entirely superfluous and harmful. Above all, love needs no laws whatever.[219]

Nevertheless, I will say and do what I can. I ask and urge all priests and friars when they encounter any impediment to marriage from which the pope can grant dispensation but which is not stated in the Scriptures, by all means to confirm[220] all marriages that may have been contracted in any way[221] contrary to the ecclesiastical or pontifical laws. But let them arm themselves with the divine law which says: "What God has joined together, let no man put asunder" [Matt. 19:6]. For the joining together of a man and a woman is of divine law and is binding, however much it may conflict with the laws of men; the laws of men must give way before it without any hesitation. For if a man leaves father and mother and cleaves to his wife,[t] how much more will he tread underfoot the silly and wicked laws of men, in order to

q Cf. Lev. 18:6-18.

r Rom. 1:28.

s The male singular pronoun is replaced by the plural in this sentence.

t Matt. 19:5.

219. Luther's outspoken judgments about human institutions in this paragraph and elsewhere were evidently perceived as too radical and unreasonable. In the first editions of Luther's collected works, both the Wittenberg and Jena editions, this paragraph is entirely deleted.

220. Namely, by officiating the marriage ceremony.

221. Marriages were "contracted" by betrothal and most often arranged by parents. The secret engagement of young people without parental consent presented a problem at this time because marriage was often used to advance the family's fortunes. Many medieval theologians concluded that consent between two people constituted a valid marriage. Luther disagreed, but also encouraged both parents and children to deal with each other in a loving way. See *That Parents Should Neither Compel nor Hinder Marriage* . . . (1524), LW 45:385-93. Also, for apparently the same reasons as the previous paragraph, "in any way" (*quoquo modo*) is deleted from the Wittenberg and Jena editions of Luther's works.

cleave to his wife! And if pope, bishop, or official[222] should annul any marriage because it was contracted contrary to the laws of men, he is Antichrist, he does violence to nature, and is guilty of treason against the Divine Majesty, because this word stands: "What God has joined together, let no man put asunder" [Matt. 19:6].

Besides this, no human being had the right to frame such laws, and Christ has granted to Christians a liberty which is above all human laws, especially where a law of God conflicts with them. Thus it is said in Mark 2[:28]: "The Son of man is lord even of the Sabbath," and "Humankind was not made for the Sabbath, but the Sabbath for humankind" [Mark 2:27]. Moreover, such laws were condemned beforehand by Paul when he foretold that there would be those who forbid marriage.[223] Here, therefore, those inflexible impediments derived from affinity,[u] by spiritual or legal relationship, and from blood relationship must give way, so far as the Scriptures permit, in which the second degree of consanguinity alone is prohibited. Thus it is written in Lev. 18[:6-18], where there are twelve persons a man is prohibited from marrying: his mother, stepmother, full sister, half-sister by either parent, granddaughter, father's or mother's sister, daughter-in-law, brother's wife, wife's sister, stepdaughter, and his uncle's wife. Here only the first degree of affinity and the second degree of consanguinity are forbidden; yet not without exception, as will appear on closer examination, for the brother's or sister's daughter—the niece—is not included in the prohibition, although she is in the second degree.[224] Therefore, if a marriage has been contracted outside of these degrees, which are the only ones that have been prohibited by God's appointment, it should by no means be annulled on account of human laws. For marriage itself, being a divine institution, is incomparably superior to any laws, so that marriage should not be annulled for the sake of the law, rather the laws should be broken for the sake of marriage.

In the same way that nonsense about compaternities, commaternities, confraternities, consororities, and confilieties[225] must be completely abolished in the contracting of marriage.

u The Wittenberg and Jena editions delete this section from here to the end of the paragraph. See n. 219, p. 102.

222. The judge in the episcopal court.

223. 1 Tim. 4:1-3: "Now the Spirit expressly says that in later times some will renounce the faith by paying attention to deceitful spirits and teachings of demons, through the hypocrisy of liars whose consciences are seared with a hot iron. They forbid marriage and demand abstinence from foods, which God created to be received with thanksgiving by those who believe and know the truth."

224. The word *consanguinity* refers to kinship ties, while *affinity* refers to those who are related by marriage.

225. Relationships arising from sponsorship at baptism or through legal adoption.

What was it but superstition that invented this "spiritual affinity"? If one who baptized is not permitted to marry her whom he has baptized or stood sponsor for, what right has any Christian man to marry a Christian woman? Is the relationship that grows out of the external rite or sign of the sacrament more intimate than that which grows out of the blessing of the sacrament itself? Is not a Christian man the brother of a Christian woman, and is she not his sister? Is not a baptized man the spiritual brother of a baptized woman? How foolish we are! If a man instructs his wife in the gospel and in faith in Christ, does he not truly become her father in Christ? And is it not lawful for her to remain his wife? Would not Paul have had the right to marry a girl from among the Corinthians, of whom he boasts that he became their father in Christ?[v] See then, how Christian liberty has been suppressed through the blindness of human superstition.

There is even less in the "legal affinity," and yet they have set it above the divine right of marriage.[w] Nor would I agree to that impediment which they call "disparity of religion,"[x] which forbids one to marry an unbaptized person, either simply, or on condition that she be converted to the faith. Who made this prohibition? God or human beings? Who gave human beings the power to prohibit such a marriage? Indeed, the spirits that speak lies in hypocrisy, as Paul says.[y] Of them it must be said: "Godless men have told me fables which do not conform to your law" [Ps. 119:85].[226] The heathen Patricius married the Christian Monica, mother of St. Augustine;[z] why should that not be permitted today? The same stupid, or rather, wicked severity is seen in the "impediment of crime," as when a man has married a woman with whom he previously had committed adultery, or when he plotted to bring about the death of a woman's husband in order to be able to wed the widow.[a] I ask you, whence comes this cruelty of person toward person, which even God never demanded?

226. Luther is quoting the Latin Vulgate version of this psalm (118 in the Vulgate), which does not conform to modern English translations.

v 1 Cor. 4:15.

w The first sentence is also missing from the Wittenberg and Jena editions; see n. 219, p. 102.

x Cf. Aquinas, *STh* III Suppl., q. 59, "On the Disparity of Worship as an Impediment to Marriage."

y 1 Tim. 4:2.

z Cf. Augustine, *Confessions* 9, 9, 19.

a Cf. *Decr. Greg. IX*, lib. 4, tit. 7.

Do they pretend not to know that Bathsheba, the wife of Uriah, was wed by David, a most saintly man, after the double crime of adultery and murder?[b] If the divine law did this, what are these despotic men doing to their fellow servants?

They[c] also recognize what they call "the impediment of a tie," that is, when a man is bound to another woman by betrothal. Here they conclude that, if he has had sexual relations with a second woman, his engagement to the first becomes null and void. This I do not understand at all. I hold that he who has betrothed himself to one woman no longer belongs to himself. Because of this fact, by the prohibition of the divine law, he belongs to the first with whom he has not had intercourse, even though he has had intercourse with the second. For it was not in his power to give the latter what was no longer his own; he has deceived her and actually committed adultery. But they regard the matter differently because they pay more heed to the carnal union than to the divine command, according to which the man, having made a promise to the first woman, should keep it always. For whoever would give anything must give of that which is his own. And God forbids us to transgress and wrong a brother or sister in any matter.[d] This must be observed over and above all human ordinances.. Therefore I believe that such a man cannot with a good conscience live in marriage with a second woman, and this impediment should be completely reversed. For if a monastic vow makes a man no longer his own, why does not a pledge of mutual faithfulness do the same? After all, faithfulness is one of the precepts and fruits of the Spirit, in Gal. 5:[22], while a monastic vow is of human invention. And if a wife may claim her husband back, despite the fact that he has taken a monastic vow, why may not an engaged woman claim back her betrothed, even though he has intercourse with another? But we have said above that he who has promised to marry a girl may not take a monastic vow, but is in duty bound to marry her because he is in duty bound to keep faith with her; and this faith he may not break for any human ordinance, because it is commanded

b 2 Sam. 11:1-27.

c This entire paragraph is missing from the Wittenberg and Jena editions; see n. 219, p. 102.

d 1 Thess. 4:6.

by God. Much more should the man here keep faith with his first betrothed, since he could not promise marriage to a second except with a lying heart; and therefore did not really promise it, but deceived her, his neighbor, against God's command. Therefore, the "impediment of error"[227] enters in here, by which his marriage to the second woman is rendered null and void.

The "impediment of ordination" is also the mere invention of men, especially since they prate that it annuls even a marriage already contracted.[228] They constantly exalt their own ordinances above the commands of God. I do not indeed sit in judgment on the present state of the priestly order, but I observe that Paul charges a bishop to be the husband of one wife.[e] Hence, no marriage of deacon, priest, bishop, or any other order can be annulled, although it is true that Paul knew nothing of this species of priests and of the orders we have today. Perish then those cursed human ordinances which have crept into the church only to multiply perils, sins, and evils! There exists, therefore, between a priest and his wife a true and indissoluble marriage, approved by the divine commandment. But what if wicked men in sheer despotism prohibit or annul it? So be it! Let it be wrong among men; it is nevertheless right before God, whose command must take precedence if it conflicts with the commands of men.[f]

An[g] equally lying invention is that "impediment of public decency," by which contracted marriages are annulled. I am incensed at that foolhardy wickedness which is so ready to put asunder what God has joined together that one may well recognize Antichrist in it, for it opposes all that Christ has done and taught. What earthly reason is there for holding that no relative of a deceased fiancé, even to the fourth degree of consanguinity, may marry his fiancée? That is not a judgment of public decency, but ignorance of public decency. Why was not this judgment of public decency found among the people of Israel, who were endowed with the best laws, the laws of God? On the contrary, the next of kin was even compelled by the law of God to marry the widow of his relative.[229] Must the people of Christian lib-

e 1 Tim. 3:2.

f Acts 5:29.

g The following two paragraphs are not in the Wittenberg and Jena editions; see n. 219, p. 102.

227. Luther sarcastically pits one impediment against the other. Normally, the "impediment of error" has to do with mistaken identity. See Aquinas, *STh* III Suppl., q. 51, a. 2: "Wherefore error, in order to void marriage, must needs be about the essentials of marriage. Now marriage includes two things, namely the two persons who are joined together, and the mutual power over one another wherein marriage consists. The first of these is removed by error concerning the person, the second by error regarding the condition, since a slave cannot freely give power over his body to another, without his master's consent. For this reason these two errors, and no others, are an impediment to matrimony."

228. Cf. Aquinas, *STh* III Suppl., q. 53, a. 3: "Hence among the Greeks and other Eastern peoples a sacred order is an impediment to the contracting of matrimony but it does not forbid the use of marriage already contracted. . . . But in the Western Church it is an impediment both to marriage and to the use of marriage."

229. Cf. Deut. 25:5: "When brothers reside together, and one of them dies and has no son, the wife of the deceased shall not be married outside the family to a stranger. Her husband's brother shall go in to her, taking her in marriage, and performing the duty of a husband's brother to her."

erty be burdened with more severe laws than the people of legal bondage?[230]

But, to make an end of these—figments rather than impediments—I will say that so far there seem to me to be no impediments that may justly annul a contracted marriage except these: sexual impotence, ignorance of a previously contracted marriage, and a vow of chastity. Still, concerning this latter vow, I am to this day so far from certain that I do not know at what age such a vow is to be regarded as binding, as I also said above in discussing the sacrament of baptism. Thus you may learn, from this one question of marriage, how wretchedly and desperately all the activities of the church have been confused, hindered, ensnared, and subjected to danger through pestilent, ignorant, and wicked ordinances of men, so that there is no hope of betterment unless we abolish at one stroke all the laws of all men, and having restored the gospel of liberty we follow it in judging and regulating all things. Amen.

[Impotence]

We must therefore speak of sexual impotence, in order that we may the more readily advise the souls that are laboring in peril. But first I wish to state that what I have said about impediments is intended to apply after a marriage has been contracted. I mean to say that no marriage should be annulled by any such impediment. But as to marriages which are yet to be contracted, I would briefly repeat what I have said above. If there is the stress of youthful passion or some other necessity for which the pope grants dispensation, then any brother may also grant a dispensation to another or even to himself, and following that counsel snatch his wife out of the power of tyrannical laws as best he can. For with what right am I deprived of my liberty by somebody else's superstition and ignorance? If the pope grants a dispensation for money, why should not I, for my soul's salvation, grant a dispensation to myself or to my brother? Does the pope set up laws? Let him set them up for himself, and keep hands off my liberty, or I will take it by stealth!

Now[h] let us discuss the matter of impotence.

h The next two paragraphs were left out of the Wittenberg and Jena editions; see n. 231, p. 109.

230. The "people of legal bondage" (*populum servitutis legalis*) is certainly a pejorative phrase regarding Israel in the Old Testament, but the language is shaped by Pauline usage, especially Galatians 4, rather than another kind of anti-Jewish sentiment.

Consider the following case: A woman, wed to an impotent man, is unable to prove her husband's impotence in court, or perhaps she is unwilling to do so with the Mass of evidence and all the notoriety which the law demands; yet she is desirous of having children or is unable to remain continent. Now suppose I had counseled her to procure a divorce from her husband in order to marry another, satisfied that her own and her husband's conscience and their experience were ample testimony of his impotence; but the husband refused his consent to this. Then I would further counsel her, with the consent of the man (who is not really her husband, but only a dweller under the same roof with her), to have intercourse with another, say her husband's brother, but to keep this marriage secret and to ascribe the children to the so-called putative father. The question is: Is such a woman saved and in a saved state? I answer: Certainly, because in this case an error, ignorance of the man's impotence, impedes the marriage; and the tyranny of the laws permits no divorce. But the woman is free through the divine law, and cannot be compelled to remain continent. Therefore the man ought to concede her right, and give up to somebody else the wife who is his only in outward appearance.

Moreover, if the man will not give his consent, or agree to this separation—rather than allow the woman to burn with desire[i] or to commit adultery—I would counsel her to contract a marriage with another and flee to a distant unknown place. What other counsel can be given to one constantly struggling with the dangers of natural emotions? Now I know that some are troubled by the fact that the children of this secret marriage are not the rightful heirs of their putative father. But if it was done with the consent of the husband, then the children will be the rightful heirs. If, however, it was done without his knowledge or against his will, then let unbiased Christian reason, or better, charity, decide which one of the two has done the greater injury to the other. The wife alienates the inheritance, but the husband has deceived his wife and is defrauding her completely of her body and her life. Is not the sin of a man who wastes his wife's body and life a greater sin than that of the woman who merely alienates the temporal goods of her husband? Let him,

i 1 Cor. 7:9.

therefore, agree to a divorce, or else be satisfied with heirs not his own, for by his own fault he deceived an innocent girl and defrauded her both of life and of the full use of her body, besides giving her an almost irresistible cause for committing adultery. Let both be weighed in the same scales. Certainly, by every right, fraud should recoil on the fraudulent, and whoever has done an injury must make it good. What is the difference between such a husband and the man who holds another man's wife captive together with her husband? Is not such a tyrant compelled to support wife and children and husband, or else to set them free? Why should not the same hold true here? Therefore I maintain that the man should be compelled either to submit to a divorce or to support the other man's child as his heir. Doubtless this would be the judgment of charity. In that case, the impotent man, who is not really the husband, should support the heir of his wife in the same spirit in which he would at great expense wait on his wife if she fell sick or suffered some other ill; for it is by his fault and not by his wife's that she suffers this ill. This I have set forth to the best of my ability, for the strengthening of anxious consciences, because my desire is to bring my afflicted brothers and sisters in this captivity what little comfort I can.[231]

[Divorce]

As to divorce, it is still a question for debate whether it is allowable.[j] For my part I so greatly detest divorce that I should prefer bigamy to it;[232] but whether it is allowable, I do not venture to decide. Christ himself, the Chief Shepherd, says in Matt. 5[:32]: "Every one who divorces his wife, except on the ground of unchastity, makes her an adulteress; and whoever marries a divorced woman commits adultery." Christ, then, permits divorce, but only on the ground of unchastity. The pope must, therefore, be in error whenever he grants a divorce for any other cause; and no one should feel safe who has obtained a dispensation by this temerity (not authority) of the pope. Yet it is still a greater wonder to me, why they compel a man to remain unmarried after being separated from his wife by divorce, and why they will not permit him to remarry.[k] For if Christ permits divorce

j Cf. *Decr. Greg. IX*, lib. 5, tit. 19, *de divortiis*.

k Cf. *Decr. Greg. IX*, lib. 4, tit. 19, *de divortiis*, c. 2.

231. The advice given here was clearly found to be difficult by Luther's followers who removed it from the edition in his collected works. Still, several factors ought to be considered when judging the two preceding paragraphs: (1) Couched in the language of the scholars only, this Latin treatise was not intended for popular consumption but rather as a guide for bewildered and confused priests, who were called upon in the confessional to give practical advice and spiritual comfort to troubled souls. (2) The impediment of impotency was, even according to Roman church law, sufficient ground for declaring a marriage null and void. (3) But the legal process of securing an annulment demanded such an involved procedure for establishing proof that it was equally unpleasant for both parties. (4) Then, as now, divorce under any circumstances was absolutely forbidden by Roman church law. (5) As an alternate to an impossible legal solution, Luther's suggestion of a secret marriage was not without precedent; common law in parts of Westphalia and Lower Saxony, for example, prescribed that a man who could not perform his conjugal duty was required to seek satisfaction for his wife through a neighbor.

232. Luther famously gave this advice later to King Henry VIII of England and Landgrave Philip of Hesse, regarding it to be the lesser of two evils insofar as it was not without divinely sanctioned precedent in the Old Testament. This phrase, "that I should prefer bigamy to it," was deleted from the Wittenberg and Jena editions; see n. 231.

on the ground of unchastity and compels no one to remain unmarried, and if Paul would rather have us marry than burn with desire,[l] then he certainly seems to permit a man to marry another woman in the place of the one who has been put away. I wish that this subject were fully discussed and made clear and decided, so that counsel might be given in the infinite perils of those who, without any fault of their own, are nowadays compelled to remain unmarried; that is, those whose wives or husbands have run away and deserted them, to come back perhaps after ten years, perhaps never! This matter troubles and distresses me, for there are daily cases, whether by the special malice of Satan or because of our neglect of the Word of God.

I, indeed, who alone against all cannot establish any rule in this matter, would yet greatly desire at least the passage in 1 Cor. 7[:15] to be applied here: "But if the unbelieving partner desires to separate, let it be so; in such a case the brother or sister is not bound." Here the Apostle gives permission to put away the unbeliever who departs and to set the believing spouse free to marry again. Why should not the same hold true when a believer—that is, a believer in name, but in truth as much an unbeliever as the one Paul speaks of—deserts his wife, especially if he intends never to return. I certainly can see no difference between the two. But I believe that if in the Apostle's day an unbelieving deserter had returned and had become a believer or had promised to live again with his believing wife, it would not have been permitted, but he too would have been given the right to marry again. Nevertheless, in these matters I decide nothing (as I have said), although there is nothing that I would rather see decided, since nothing at present more grievously perplexes me, and many others with me. I would have nothing decided here on the mere authority of the pope and the bishops; but if two learned and good men agreed in the name of Christ[m] and published their opinion in the spirit of Christ, I should prefer their judgment even to such councils as are assembled nowadays, famous only for numbers and authority, not for scholarship and saintliness. Therefore I hang up my lyre[233] on this matter until a better man confers with me about it.

233. An allusion to Luther's remarks at the beginning of the treatise that he is writing a "prelude." Cf. Ps. 137:1-2: "By the rivers of Babylon—there we sat down and there we wept when we remembered Zion. On the willows there we hung up our lyres."

l 1 Cor. 7:9.

m Cf. Matt. 18:19-20.

Ordination

Of this sacrament the church of Christ knows nothing; it is an invention of the church of the pope. Not only is there nowhere any promise of grace attached to it, but there is not a single word said about it in the whole New Testament. Now it is ridiculous to put forth as a sacrament of God something that cannot be proved to have been instituted by God. I do not hold that this rite, which has been observed for so many centuries, should be condemned; but in sacred things I am opposed to the invention of human fictions. And it is not right to give out as divinely instituted what was not divinely instituted, lest we become a laughingstock to our opponents. We ought to see that every article of faith of which we boast is certain, pure, and based on clear passages of Scripture. But we are utterly unable to do that in the case of the sacrament under consideration.

This 1561 engraving illustrates one aspect of ordination to the priesthood: the laying on of hands. The bishop stands and lays his hands on the head of each person being ordained. The ordainee kneels and carries a chasuble, a priestly vestment, over one arm.

The church has no power to make new divine promises of grace, as some prate, who hold that what is decreed by the church is of no less authority than what is decreed by God, since the church is under the guidance of the Holy Spirit.[234] For the church was born by the word of promise through faith, and by this same word is nourished and preserved. That is to say, it is the promises of God that make the church, and not the church that makes the promise of God. For the Word of God is incomparably superior to the church, and in this Word the church, being a creature, has nothing to decree, ordain, or make, but only to be decreed, ordained, and made. For who begets his own parent? Who first brings forth his own maker?

This one thing indeed the church can do: It can distinguish the Word of God from the words of men; as Augustine confesses that he believed the gospel because he was moved by the authority of the church which proclaimed that this is the

234. Cf. John 14:16-17, 26: "And I will ask the Father, and he will give you another Advocate, to be with you forever. This is the Spirit of truth. But the Advocate, the Holy Spirit, whom the Father will send in my name, will teach you everything, and remind you of all that I have said to you"; John 16:13: "When the Spirit of truth comes, he will guide you into all the truth."

gospel.[235] Not that the church is therefore above the gospel; if that were true, the church would also be above God, in whom we believe, because it is the church that proclaims God is God. But, as Augustine says elsewhere,[236] the truth itself lays hold on the soul and thus renders it able to judge most certainly of all things; however, the soul is not able to judge the truth, but is compelled to say with unerring certainty that this is the truth. For example, our mind declares with unerring certainty that three and seven are ten; and yet it cannot give a reason why this is true, although it cannot deny that it is true. It is clearly taken captive by the truth; and, rather than judging the truth, it is itself judged by it. There is such a mind also in the church, when under the enlightenment of the Spirit she judges and approves doctrines; she is unable to prove it, and yet is most certain of having it. For as among philosophers no one judges the general concepts, but all are judged by them, so it is among us with the mind of the Spirit, who judges all things and is judged by no one, as the Apostle says.[237] But we will discuss this another time.

Let this then stand fast: The church can give no promises of grace; that is the work of God alone. Therefore she cannot institute a sacrament. But even if she could, it still would not necessarily follow that ordination is a sacrament. For who knows which is the church that has the Spirit? For when such decisions are made there are usually only a few bishops or scholars present; and it is possible that these may not be really of the church. All may err, as councils have repeatedly erred, particularly the Council of Constance,[n] which erred most wickedly of all. Only that which has the approval of the church universal, and not of the Roman church alone, rests on a trustworthy foundation. I therefore admit that ordination is a certain churchly rite, on a par with many others introduced by the church fathers, such as the consecration of vessels, houses, vestments, water, salt, candles, herbs, wine, and the like.[238] No one calls any of these a sacrament, nor is there in them any promise. In the same manner, to anoint a man's hands with oil, or to shave his head and the like is not to administer a sacrament, since no promise is attached to them; they are simply being prepared for a certain office, like a vessel or an instrument.

n See n. 52, p. 28.

235. Augustine, *Against the Epistle of Manichaeus Called "Fundamental"* 5, 6: "I should not believe the gospel except as moved by the authority of the church catholic."

236. Augustine, *On the Trinity* 9, 6, 10: "the judgment of truth from above is still strong and clear, and rests firmly upon the utterly indestructible rules of its own right; and if it is covered as it were by cloudiness of corporeal images, yet is not wrapped up and confounded in them."

237. Cf. 1 Cor. 2:11-13: "For what human being knows what is truly human except the human spirit that is within? So also no one comprehends what is truly God's except the Spirit of God. Now we have received not the spirit of the world, but the Spirit that is from God, so that we may understand the gifts bestowed on us by God. And we speak of these things in words not taught by human wisdom but taught by the Spirit, interpreting spiritual things to those who are spiritual."

238. Salt was used in connection with the rite of baptism, given to catechumens in the early church to signify purification, wisdom, and the promise of immortality; cf. Augustine, *Confessions* 1, 11. Candles were blessed especially for their use in Candelmas, the Feast of the Purification of Mary. Herbs, fruits, and flowers were often blessed at the beginning of the harvest season in connection with the Feast of the Assumption of Mary.

But you will say: "What do you do with Dionysius, who in his *Ecclesiastical Hierarchy* enumerates six sacraments, among which he also includes ordination?"[239] I answer: I am well aware that this is the one writer of antiquity who is cited in support of the seven sacraments, although he omits marriage and so has only six. But we read nothing at all about these "sacraments" in the rest of the fathers; nor do they ever regard them as sacraments when they speak of these things. For the invention of sacraments is of recent date.[240] Indeed, to speak more boldly, it greatly displeases me to assign such importance to this Dionysius, whoever he may have been, for he shows hardly any signs of solid learning. I would ask, by what authority and with what arguments does he prove his hodge-podge about the angels in his *Celestial Hierarchy*—a book over which many curious and superstitious spirits have cudgeled their brains? If one were to read and judge without prejudice, is not everything in it his own fancy and very much like a dream? But in his *Theology,* which is rightly called *Mystical,* of which certain very ignorant theologians make so much, he is downright dangerous, for he is more of a Platonist than a Christian. So if I had my way, no believing soul would give the least attention to these books. So far, indeed, from learning Christ in them, you will lose even what you already know of him. I speak from experience. Let us rather hear Paul, that we may learn Jesus Christ and him crucified.[o] He is the way, the life, and the truth;[p] he is the ladder[q] by which we come to the Father, as he says: "No one comes to the Father, but by me."[r]

Similarly, in the *Ecclesiastical Hierarchy,* what does this Dionysius do but describe certain churchly rites, and amuse himself with allegories without proving anything? Just as has been done in our time by the author of the book entitled *Rationale divinorum.*[241] Such allegorical studies are for idle people. Do you think I should find it difficult to amuse myself with allegories about anything in creation? Did not Bonaventura by allegory draw the liberal arts into theology?[242] And Gerson even converted the smaller Donatus into a mystical theologian.[243] It would not be

o 1 Cor. 2:2.

p John 14:6.

q Cf. Gen. 28:12; John 1:51.

r John 14:6.

239. Dionysius the Areopagite (a pseudonymous author from the sixth century) wrote several influential writings marked by a strong neo-Platonic structure. The *Ecclesiastical Hierarchy* lists as sacraments baptism, the Eucharist, unction, priestly ordination, monastic ordination, and burial.

240. A number of sacraments were listed in early Scholasticism with Peter Lombard's numbering of seven in his *Sentences* (4, d. 2, c. 1) winning general acceptance. These were not made official church doctrine until the bull *Exultate Deo* at the Council of Florence in 1439.

241. Guillaume Durandus (c. 1230–1296), bishop of Mende, wrote an explanation of the rites, ceremonies, and vestments used in the Mass: *Rationale divinorum officiorum* (i.e., "Explanation for the Divine Offices").

242. Like Aquinas, Bonaventure of Bagnoregio (1221–1274) sought to bring correlation and harmony between theological and philosophical knowledge. However, his *Opusculum de reductione artium ad theologiam* (*Little Work on the Restoration of the Arts to Theology*) takes a different approach than Aquinas, seeing the arts and sciences echoing in theology through types and figures.

243. Jean Gerson (1363–1429) was chancellor of the University of Paris. In addition to his influence in ecclesiastical affairs, Gerson also wrote several popular devotional and pastoral works. Luther is referring to his allegory of the *Ars minor*, a Latin grammar written by the fourth-century Roman grammarian, Aelius Donatus (flourished mid-fourth century).

244. Nine statements of Origen were condemned as heretical after his death by an edict of Emperor Justinian I (c. 483–565) and published by the Council of Constantinople in 553; see n. 64, p. 32.

245. The "indelible character" (*character indelibilis*) as a special mark or seal left on the soul after receiving three of the seven sacraments: baptism, confirmation, and ordination. Because the soul has been impressed with this mark, the sacrament cannot be repeated. After ordination a priest, therefore, can never be a layman again. The notion was first officially set forth by the Council of Florence in 1439, "Among these sacraments there are three—baptism, confirmation, and orders—which indelibly impress upon the soul a character, i.e. a certain spiritual mark which distinguishes them from the rest."

difficult for me to compose a better hierarchy than that of Dionysius; for he knew nothing of pope, cardinals, and archbishops, and put the bishop at the top. Who has so weak a mind as not to be able to launch into allegories? I would not have a theologian devote himself to allegories until he has exhausted the legitimate and simple meaning of the Scripture; otherwise his theology will bring him into danger, as Origen discovered.[244]

Therefore a thing does not need to be a sacrament simply because Dionysius so describes it. Otherwise, why not also make a sacrament of the funeral processions, which he describes in his book, and which continue to this day? There will then be as many sacraments as there have been rites and ceremonies multiplied in the church. Standing on so unsteady a foundation, they have nevertheless invented "characters" which they attribute to this sacrament of theirs and which are indelibly impressed on those who are ordained.[245] Whence do such ideas come, I ask? By what authority, with what arguments, are they established? We do not object to their being free to invent, say, and assert whatever they please; but we also insist on our liberty, that they shall not arrogate to themselves the right to turn their opinions into articles of faith, as they have hitherto presumed to do. It is enough that we accommodate ourselves to their rites and ceremonies for the sake of peace; but we refuse to be bound by such things as if they were necessary to salvation, which they are not. Let them lay aside their despotic demand, and we shall yield free obedience to their wishes, in order that we may live in peace with one another. It is a shameful and wicked slavery for a Christian, who is free, to be subject to any but heavenly and divine ordinances.

We come now to their strongest argument. It is this: Christ said at the Last Supper: "Do this in remembrance of me."[s] "Look," they say, "here Christ ordained the apostles to the priesthood." From this passage they also concluded, among other things, that both kinds are to be administered to the priest alone. In fact, they have drawn out of this passage whatever they pleased, as men who would arrogate to themselves the liberty to prove anything whatever from any words of Christ. But is that interpreting the words of God? I ask you: Is it? Christ gives us no promise here, but only commands that this be done in remembrance of

s Luke 22:19; 1 Cor. 11:24-25.

him. Why do they not conclude that he also ordained priests when he laid upon them the office of the Word and baptism, and said: "Go into all the world and preach the gospel to the whole creation, baptizing them in the name, etc."[t] For it is the proper duty of priests to preach and to baptize. Or, since it is nowadays the chief, and (as they say) indispensable duty of priests to read the canonical hours,[246] why have they not discovered the sacrament of ordination in those passages in which Christ commanded them to pray, as he did in many places—particularly in the garden, that they might not enter into temptation?[u] But perhaps they will evade this argument by saying that it is not commanded to pray; it is enough to read the canonical hours. Then it follows that this priestly work can be proved nowhere in the Scriptures, and thus their praying priesthood is not of God; as, indeed, it is not.

But which of the ancient fathers claimed that in this passage priests were ordained? Where does this new interpretation come from? I will tell you. They have sought by this means to set up a seedbed of implacable discord, by which clergy and laypersons should be separated from each other farther than heaven from earth, to the incredible injury of the grace of baptism and to the confusion of our fellowship in the gospel. Here, indeed, are the roots of that detestable tyranny of the clergy over the laity.[247] Trusting in the external anointing by which their hands are consecrated, in the tonsure and in vestments, they not only exalt themselves above the rest of the lay Christians, who are only anointed with the Holy Spirit, but regard them almost as dogs and unworthy to be included with themselves in the church. Hence they are bold to demand, to exact, to threaten, to urge, to oppress, as much as they please. In short, the sacrament of ordination has been and still is an admirable device for establishing all the horrible things that have been done hitherto in the church, and are yet to be done. Here Christian brotherhood has perished, here shepherds have been turned into wolves, servants into tyrants, churchmen into worse than worldlings.

If they were forced to grant that all of us that have been baptized are equally priests, as indeed we are, and that only the

t Mark 16:15; Matt. 28:19.

u Matt. 26:41.

246. The canonical hours are the seven daily prayer offices part of the early monastic tradition. Inspired in part by the words of Ps. 119:164, "Seven times a day I praise you for your righteous laws," they are respectively: matins (including nocturns and lauds), prime, tierce, sext, nones, vespers, and compline.

247. Cf. Luther's earlier treatise *The Address to the Christian Nobility* (1520), in which he identifies this spiritual division between the laity and the priesthood as one of the "Roman walls" that the papacy has erected to protect itself from being reformed. It is in this place that Luther introduces the notion that the priesthood in the New Testament has been given to all people through baptism and that ordination only signifies an office that exercises publicly the spiritual authority that all Christians possess. Luther's most thorough articulation of this spiritual priesthood of the baptized was set forth in his subsequent treatise against Hieronymus Emser (see n. 11, p. 14.) *Answer to the Hyperchristian, Hyperspiritual and Hyperlearned Book by Goat Emser in Leipzig* (1521), LW 39:137–224.

ministry was committed to them, yet with our common consent, they would then know that they have no right to rule over us except insofar as we freely concede it. For thus it is written in 1 Pet. 2[:9]: "You are a chosen race, a royal priesthood, and a priestly royalty." Therefore we are all priests, as many of us as are Christians. But the priests, as we call them, are ministers chosen from among us. All that they do is done in our name; the priesthood is nothing but a ministry. This we learn from 1 Cor. 4[:1]: "This is how one should regard us, as servants of Christ and stewards of the mysteries of God."

From this it follows that whoever does not preach the Word, though he was called by the church to do this very thing, is no priest at all, and that the sacrament of ordination can be nothing else than a certain rite by which the church chooses its preachers. For this is the way a priest is defined in Mal. 2[:7]: "The lips of a priest should guard knowledge, and people should seek instruction from his mouth, for he is the messenger of the Lord of hosts." You may be certain, then, that whoever is not a messenger of the Lord of hosts, or whoever is called to do anything else than such messenger service—if I may so term it[248]—is in no sense a priest; as Hos. 4[:6] says: "Because you have rejected knowledge, I reject you from being a priest to me." They are also called shepherds[v] because they are to shepherd, that is, to teach. Therefore, those who are ordained only to read the canonical hours and to offer Masses are indeed papal priests, but not Christian priests, because they not only do not preach, but they are not even called to preach. Indeed, it comes to this, that a priesthood of that sort is a different estate altogether from the office of preaching. Thus they are hour-reading and Mass-saying priests—sort of living idols called priests—really such priests as Jeroboam ordained, in Beth-aven, taken from the lowest dregs of the people, and not of Levi's tribe.[w]

See how far the glory of the church has departed! The whole earth is filled with priests, bishops, cardinals, and clergy; yet not one of them preaches so far as his official duty is concerned, unless he is called to do so by a different call over and above his sacramental ordination. Every one thinks he is doing full justice to his ordination by mumbling the vain repetitions of his

248. Luther is playing with the broader and narrower meanings of *angelus domini* in Malachi 2, i.e., messenger and angel.

v Lat. *pastores.*

w 1 Kgs. 12:31.

prescribed prayers and by celebrating Masses. Moreover, he never really prays when he repeats those hours; or if he does pray, he prays them for himself. And he offers his Mass as if it were a sacrifice, which is the height of perversity because the Mass consists in the use made of the sacrament. It is clear, therefore, that the ordination, which, as a sacrament, makes clergymen of this sort of men, is in truth nothing but a mere fiction, devised by men who understand nothing about the church, the priesthood, the ministry of the Word, or the sacraments. Thus, as the "sacrament" is, so are the priests it makes. To such errors and such blindness has been added a still worse captivity: in order to separate themselves still farther from other Christians, whom they deem profane, they have emasculated themselves, like the Galli, who were the priests of Cybele,[249] and they have taken upon themselves the burden of a spurious celibacy.

To satisfy this hypocrisy and the working of this error it was not enough that bigamy should be prohibited, that is, the having of two wives at one time, as it was forbidden in the law (and as is the accepted meaning of the term); but they have called it bigamy if a man marries two virgins, one after the other, or if he marries one widow.[250] Indeed, so holy is the holiness of this most holy sacrament that no man can become a priest if he has married a virgin and his wife is still living.[x] And—here we reach the very summit of sanctity—a man is even prevented from entering the priesthood if he has married a woman who was not a virgin, though he did so in ignorance or by unfortunate mischance.[251] But if one has defiled six hundred harlots, or violated countless matrons and virgins, or even kept many Ganymedes,[252] that would be no impediment to his becoming bishop or cardinal or pope. Moreover, the Apostle's word "husband of one wife" [1 Tim. 3:2] must now be interpreted to mean "the prelate of one church," and this has given rise to the "incompatible benefices."[253] At the same time the pope, that munificent dispenser, may join to one man three, twenty, or a hundred wives, that is, churches, if he is bribed with money or power, that is, "moved by godly charity and constrained by the care of the churches."[y]

O pontiffs worthy of this venerable sacrament of ordination! O princes, not of the catholic churches, but of the synagogues of

x Cf. *Decr. Greg. IX*, lib. 1, tit. 21, *de bigamis non ordinandis*, c. 3.

y 2 Cor. 11:28.

249. Galli (sg. Gallus) was the name for the eunuch priests who served Cybele, the ancient Phrygian goddess of nature whose worship became part of the cultic practices in the Roman Empire.

250. Aquinas, *STh* III Suppl., q. 66, a. 1: "By the sacrament of order a man is appointed to the ministry of the sacraments; and he who has to administer the sacraments to others must suffer from no defect in the sacraments. . . . the perfect signification of the sacrament requires the husband to have only one wife, and the wife to have but one husband; and consequently bigamy, which does away with this, causes irregularity. And there are four kinds of bigamy: the first is when a man has several lawful wives successively; the second is when a man has several wives at once, one in law, the other in fact; the third, when he has several successively, one in law, the other in fact; the fourth, when a man marries a widow."

251. Aquinas, *STh* III Suppl., q. 66, a. 3: "Gregory says, 'We command thee never to make unlawful ordinations, nor to admit to holy orders a bigamist, or one who has married a woman that is not a virgin, or one who is unlettered, or one who is deformed in his limbs, or bound to do penance or to perform some civil duty, or who is in any state of subjection.'"

252. In Greek mythology, Ganymede was the youthful consort of Zeus.

253. Benefices, rents, and profits derived from lands endowed to the church (see the earlier note on the church and feudal system, p. 73) in exchange for spiritual services were part of the livelihood for bishops. Laws were originally enacted that prevented bishops from holding more than one benefice, but the distinction between "compatible" and "incompatible" benefices was used to justify plurality in a variety of cases, as sanctioned by the pope. This distinction was used toward widespread abuse and was part of the reforms taken up by the Council of Trent.

Satan[z] and of darkness itself! I would cry out with Isaiah, "You scoffers, who rule this people in Jerusalem";[a] and with Amos 6[:1], "Woe to those who are at ease in Zion, and to those who feel secure on the mountain of Samaria, the notable men of the first of the nations, that go in with state into the house of Israel, etc.!" O the disgrace that these monstrous priests bring upon the church of God! Where are there any bishops or priests who even know the gospel, not to speak of preaching it? Why then do they boast of being priests? Why do they desire to be regarded as holier and better and mightier than other Christians, who are merely laymen? To read the hours—what unlearned men, or (as the Apostle says) men speaking with tongues[b] cannot do that? But to pray the hours—that belongs to monks, hermits, and men in private life, even though they are laymen. The duty of a priest is to preach, and if he does not preach he is as much a priest as a picture of a man is a man. Does ordaining such babbling priests make one a bishop? Or blessing churches and bells? Or confirming children? Certainly not. Any deacon or layman could do as much. It is the ministry of the Word that makes the priest and the bishop.

Therefore my advice is: Begone, all of you that would live in safety; flee, young men, and do not enter upon this holy estate, unless you are determined to preach the gospel, and can believe that you are made not one whit better than the laity through this "sacrament" of ordination! For to read the hours is nothing, and to offer Mass is to receive the sacrament. What then is there left to you that every layperson does not have? Tonsure and vestments? A sorry priest, indeed, who consists of tonsure and vestments! Or the oil poured on your fingers? But every Christian is anointed and sanctified both in body and soul with the oil of the Holy Spirit. In ancient times every Christian handled the sacrament with his hands as often as the priests do now. But today our superstition counts it a great crime if the laity touch either the bare chalice or the corporal;[254] not even a nun who is a pure virgin would be permitted to wash the palls and the sacred linens of the altar. O God! See how far the sacrosanct sanctity of this "sacrament" of ordination has gone! I expect the time will

254. The "corporal" is the altar cloth upon which the consecrated bread and wine are placed.

z Rev. 2:9.

a Isa. 28:14

b Cf. 1 Cor. 14:23.

come when the laity will not be permitted to touch the altar—except when they offer their money. I almost burst with indignation when I contemplate the wicked tyrannies of these brazen men, who with their farcical and childish fancies mock and overthrow the liberty and glory of the Christian religion.

Let all, therefore, who know themselves to be Christian, be assured of this, that we are all equally priests, that is to say, we have the same power in respect to the Word and the sacraments. However, no one may make use of this power except by the consent of the community or by the call of a superior. (For what is the common property of all, no individual may arrogate to himself, unless he is called.) And therefore this "sacrament" of ordination, if it is anything at all, is nothing else than a certain rite whereby one is called to the ministry of the church. Furthermore, the priesthood is properly nothing but the ministry of the Word—the Word, I say; not the law, but the gospel. And the diaconate is the ministry, not of reading the Gospel or the Epistle, as is the present practice, but of distributing the church's aid to the poor, so that the priests may be relieved of the burden of temporal matters and may give themselves more freely to prayer and the Word. For this was the purpose of the institution of the diaconate, as we read in Acts 5.[255] Whoever, therefore, does not know or preach the gospel is not only no priest or bishop, but he is a kind of pest to the church, who under the false title of priest or bishop, or dressed in sheep's clothing, actually does violence to the gospel and plays the wolf[256] in the church.

Therefore, unless these priests and bishops, with whom the church abounds today, work out their salvation[c] in some other way; unless they realize that they are not priests or bishops, and bemoan the fact that they bear the name of an office whose duties they either do not know or cannot fulfill, and thus with prayers and tears lament their wretched hypocritical life—unless they do this, they are truly the people of eternal perdition, and the words of Isa. 5[:13f.] are fulfilled in them: "Therefore my people go into exile for want of knowledge; their nobles are dying of hunger, and their multitude is parched with thirst. Therefore, Hell has enlarged its appetite and opened its mouth beyond measure, and the nobility of Jerusalem and her multitude go down, her throng

255. Luther is referring to the setting apart of Stephen and six others to distribute food to the poor and widows in Acts 6:1-4.

256. Cf. Matt. 7:15: "Beware of false prophets, who come to you in sheep's clothing but inwardly are ravenous wolves."

c Cf. Phil. 2:12.

and he who exults in her." What a dreadful word for our age, in which Christians are swallowed up in so deep an abyss!

According to what the Scriptures teach us, what we call the priesthood is a ministry. So I cannot understand at all why one who has once been made a priest cannot again become a layperson;[257] for the sole difference between him and a layperson is his ministry. But to depose a man from the priesthood is by no means impossible, because even now it is the usual penalty imposed upon guilty priests. They are either suspended temporarily, or permanently deprived of their office. For that fiction of an "indelible character" has long since become a laughingstock. I admit that the pope imparts this "character," but Christ knows nothing of it; and a priest who is consecrated with it becomes the lifelong servant and captive, not of Christ, but of the pope, as is the case nowadays. Moreover, unless I am greatly mistaken, if this sacrament and this fiction ever fall to the ground, the papacy with its "characters" will scarcely survive. Then our joyous liberty will be restored to us; we shall realize that we are all equal by every right. Having cast off the yoke of tyranny, we shall know that the one who is a Christian has Christ; and that the one who has Christ has all things that are Christ's, and can do all things.[d] Of this I will write more,[258] and more vigorously, as soon as I perceive that the above has displeased my friends the papists.

The Sacrament of Extreme Unction

To this rite of anointing the sick the theologians of our day have made two additions that are worthy of them: first, they call it a sacrament, and second, they make it the last sacrament. So it is now the sacrament of extreme unction, which is to be administered only to those who are at the point of death. Since they are such subtle dialectitians,[e] perhaps they have done this in order to relate it to the first unction of baptism and the two subsequent ones of confirmation and ordination.[259] But here they are able to cast in my teeth that, in the case of this sacrament, there are on the authority of the apostle James both promise

d Cf. Phil. 4:13.

e See n. 25, p. 17.

257. Because of the notion of indelible character; see n. 245, p. 114.

258. Luther takes this up in his subsequent treatise, *The Freedom of the Christian* (1520), LW 31:327–77; TAL 1:466–538.

259. Cf. Lombard, *Sentences* 4, d. 23, c. 2: "And there are three kinds of anointing. For there is an anointing which is done with chrism [i.e., confirmation], which is called the principal anointing . . . there is also another anointing by which catechumens and neophytes are anointed on the breast and between the shoulders at the reception of baptism. But there is a third anointing which is called the oil of the sick."

and sign, which, as I have maintained all along, do constitute a sacrament. For the apostle says [Jas. 5:14-15]: "Are any among you sick? They should call for the elders of the church and have them pray over them, anointing them with oil in the name of the Lord. The prayer of faith will save the sick, and the Lord will raise them up; and anyone who has committed sins will be forgiven." There, they say, you have the promise of the forgiveness of sins and the sign of the oil.

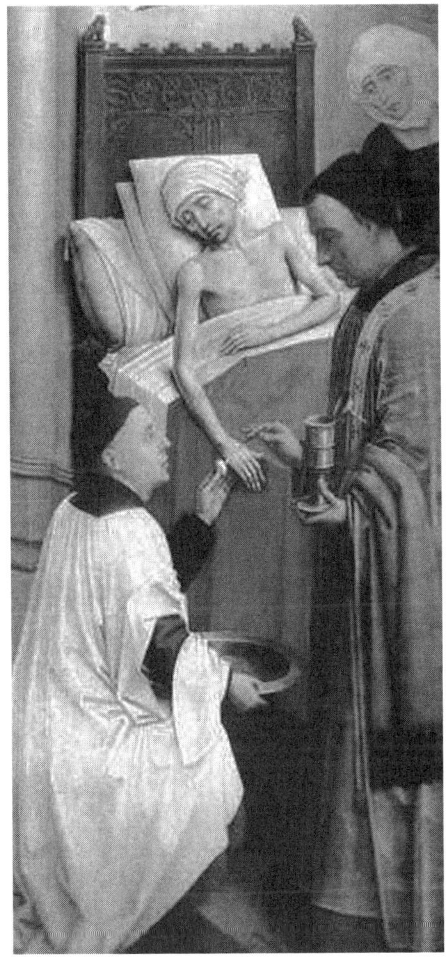

This detail of the *Seven Sacraments* altarpiece by artist Roger van der Weyden (c. 1400–1464) shows the sacrament of extreme unction.

But I say: If ever folly has been uttered, it has been uttered especially on this subject: I will say nothing of the fact that many assert with much probability that this epistle is not by James the apostle, and that it is not worthy of an apostolic spirit;[260] although, whoever was its author, it has come to be regarded as authoritative. But even if the apostle James did write it, I still would say, that no apostle has the right on his own authority to institute a sacrament, that is, to give a divine promise with a sign attached. For this belongs to Christ alone. Thus Paul says that he received from the Lord the sacrament of the Eucharist,[f] and that he was not sent to baptize, but to preach the gospel.[g] And nowhere do we read in the gospel about the sacrament of extreme unction. But let us also pass over the point. Let us examine the words of the apostle, or whoever was the author of the epistle, and we shall see at once how little heed these multipliers of sacraments have given to them.

In the first place, if they believe the apostle's words to be true and binding, by what right do they change and contradict them? Why do they make an extreme and a special kind of unction out

f 1 Cor. 11:23.

g 1 Cor. 1:17.

260. The apostolicity and authorship of the epistle of James were long debated in the church. For example, Jerome regarded the text as pseudonymous, and Eusebius, in his *Church History*, numbers it among the New Testament texts whose authority had been contested, i.e., *antilegomena*. In Luther's day, Erasmus questioned its authorship, and Luther's Wittenberg colleague Andreas von Karlstadt published a treatise (*De canonicis scripturis*

of that which the apostle wished to be general?[261] For the apostle did not desire it to be an extreme unction or administered only to the dying, but he says expressly: "Is any one sick?" He does not say: "Is any one dying?" I do not care what learned discussions Dionysius has on this point in his *Ecclesiastical Hierarchy*.[262] The apostle's words are clear enough, on which he as well as they rely; but they do not follow them. It is evident, therefore, that they have arbitrarily and without any authority made a sacrament and an extreme unction out of the words of the apostle which they have wrongly interpreted. And this works to the detriment of all other sick persons, whom they have deprived on their own authority of the benefit of the unction that the apostle enjoined.

But this is even a finer point: The apostle's promise expressly declares: "The prayer of faith will save the sick, and the Lord will raise them up, etc."[h] See, the apostle in this passage commands us to anoint and to pray, in order that the sick may be healed and raised up; that is, that they may not die, and that it may not be an extreme unction. This is proved also by the prayers that are used even to this day during the anointing, because the prayers are for the recovery of the sick.[263] But they say, on the contrary, that the unction must be administered to none but the dying;[264] that is, that they may not be healed and raised up. If it were not so serious a matter, who could help laughing at this beautiful, apt, and sensible exposition of the apostle's words? Is not the folly of the sophists here shown in its true colors? Because here, as in so many other places, it affirms what the Scriptures deny, and denies what the Scriptures affirm. Why should we not give thanks to these excellent masters of ours? Surely I spoke the truth when I said that they never uttered greater folly than on this subject.

Furthermore, if this unction is a sacrament, it must necessarily be (as they say)[i] an "effective sign" of that which it signifies and promises. Now it promises health and recovery to the sick, as the words plainly say: "The prayer of faith will save the sick, and the Lord will raise them up."[j] But who does not see that this promise is seldom, if ever, fulfilled? Scarcely one in a thousand is

libellus) only a few months earlier that gave a detailed treatment of the question of James's authority and place in the canon.

261. Lombard takes up the question of a more general repetition of the sacrament of unction in *Sentences* 4, d. 23, c. 4.

262. For example, the Supplement to Aquinas's *Summa* discusses the fact that the *Ecclesiastical Hierarchy* does not mention extreme unction as one of the sacraments; *STh* III Suppl., q. 29, a. 1.

263. The concluding prayer of the rite of extreme unction, used since the eighth century, included the following: "In your mercy restore him inwardly and outwardly to full health, so that, having recovered through the help of your mercy, he may return to his former duties."

264. E.g., *Exultate Deo*, from the Council of Florence (1439), "this sacrament ought not to be given except to the sick of whom death is feared."

h James 5:15.

i See nn. 163 and 164, p. 67.

j James 5:15.

restored to health, and when one is restored nobody believes that it came about through the sacrament, but through the working of nature or of medicine. Indeed to the sacrament they ascribe the opposite effect. What shall we say then? Either the apostle lies in making this promise or else this unction is no sacrament. For the sacramental promise is certain; but this promise fails in the majority of cases. Indeed—and here again we recognize the shrewdness and foresight of these theologians—for this very reason they would have it to be extreme unction, that the promise should not stand; in other words, that the sacrament should be no sacrament. For if it is extreme unction, it does not heal, but gives way to the disease; but if it heals, it cannot be extreme unction. Thus, by the interpretation of these masters, James is shown to have contradicted himself, and to have instituted a sacrament in order not to institute one; for they must have an extreme unction just to make untrue what the apostle intends, namely, the healing of the sick by it. If this is not madness, I ask you what is?

The word of the apostle in 1 Tim. 1[:7] describes these people: "Desiring to be teachers of the law, without understanding either what they are saying or the things about which they make assertions." Thus they read and follow everything uncritically. With the same carelessness they have also found auricular confession in the apostle's words: "Confess your sins to one another."[k] But they do not observe the command of the apostle, that the elders of the church be called, and prayer be made for the sick.[l] Scarcely one insignificant priest is sent nowadays, although the apostle would have many present, not because of the unction, but because of the prayer. That is why he says: "The prayer of faith will save the sick man, etc."[m] I have my doubts, however, whether he would have us understand "priests" when he says "presbyters," that is, "elders." For one who is an elder is not necessarily a priest or a minister. We may suspect that the apostle desired the older, graver men in the church to visit the sick, to perform a work of mercy, and pray in faith and thus heal him. Yet, it cannot be denied that the churches were once ruled by older persons,

k James 5:16.

l James 5:14.

m James 5:15.

chosen for this purpose without these ordinations and consecrations, solely on account of their age and long experience.

Therefore I take it that this unction is the same as that practiced by the apostles, of whom it is written in Mark 6[:13]: "They anointed with oil many that were sick and healed them." It was a rite of the early church, by which they worked miracles on the sick, and which has long since ceased. In the same way Christ, in the last chapter of Mark, gave to believers the power to pick up serpents, lay hands on the sick, etc.[n] It is a wonder that they have not made sacraments of those words also, for they have the same power and promise as these words of James. Therefore this extreme—which is to say fictitious—unction is not a sacrament, but a counsel of James, which anyone who will may follow; and it is derived from Mark 6[:13], as I have said. I do not believe that it was a counsel given to all sick persons, for the church's infirmity is her glory and death is gain;[o] but it was given only to such as might bear their sickness impatiently and with little faith, those whom the Lord allowed to remain in order that miracles and the power of faith might be manifest in them.

James made careful and diligent provision in this case by attaching the promise of healing and the forgiveness of sins not to the unction, but to the prayer of faith. For he says: "And the prayer of faith will save the sick, and the Lord will raise them up; and if anyone has committed sins, they will be forgiven."[p] A sacrament does not demand prayer and faith on the part of the minister, since even a wicked person may baptize and consecrate without prayer; a sacrament depends solely on the promise and institution of God, and requires faith on the part of the recipient. But where is the prayer of faith in our present use of extreme unction? Who prays over the sick one in such faith as not to doubt that he will recover? Such a prayer of faith James here describes, of which he said at the beginning of his epistle: "But ask in faith, with no doubting."[q] And Christ says of it: "Whatever you ask in prayer, believe that you receive it, and you will."[r]

There is no doubt at all that, even if today such a prayer were made over a sick person, that is, made in full faith by older,

n Mark 16:18.

o Cf. Phil. 1:21.

p James 5:15.

q James 1:6.

graver, and saintly men, as many as we wished would be healed. For what could not faith do? But we neglect this faith that the authority of the apostle demands above all else. Further, by "presbyters"—that is, men preeminent by reason of their age and faith—we understand the common herd of priests. Moreover, we turn the daily or temporally unrestricted unction into an extreme unction. And finally, we do not obtain the result promised by the apostle, namely, the healing of the sick, but we render the promise ineffective by doing the very opposite. And yet we boast that our sacrament, or rather figment, is established and proved by this saying of the apostle, which is diametrically opposed to it.[265] O what theologians!

Now I do not condemn this our "sacrament" of extreme unction, but I firmly deny that it is what the apostle James prescribes; for his unction agrees with ours neither in form, use, power, nor purpose. Nevertheless, we shall number it among those "sacraments" which we have instituted, such as the blessing and sprinkling of salt and water. For we cannot deny that any creature whatsoever may be consecrated by the Word and by prayer, as the apostle Paul teaches us.[s] We do not deny, therefore, that forgiveness and peace are granted through extreme unction; not because it is a sacrament divinely instituted, but because he who receives it believes that these blessings are granted to him. For the faith of the recipient does not err, however much the minister may err. For one who baptizes or absolves in jest,[266] that is, one who does not absolve so far as the minister is concerned, nevertheless does truly baptize and absolve if the person to be baptized or absolved believes. How much more will one who administers extreme unction confer peace, even though he does not really confer peace so far as his ministry is concerned, since there is no sacrament there! The faith of the one anointed receives even that which the minister either could not give or did not intend to give. It is sufficient for the one anointed to hear and believe the Word. For whatever we believe we shall receive, that we really do receive, no matter what the minister may or may not do, or whether he dissembles or jests. The saying of Christ holds good: "All things are possible to him who believes,"[t] and again: "Be it done for you

r Mark 11:24.

s 1 Tim. 4:4-5.

t Mark 9:32.

265. Luther uses a Greek proverbial expression here, *dis dia pason*, which signifies a great difference. In music, it was the greatest span in a given scale. Cf. Erasmus, *Adagia* 1, 2, 63.

266. On the Scholastic debate over this question, see, for example, Lombard, *Sentences* 4, d. 6, c. 5, "Concerning One Who Is Immersed in Jest." See also n. 161, p. 66.

as you have believed."[u] But in treating the sacraments our sophists say nothing at all of this faith, but only babble with all their might about the virtues of the sacraments themselves.[v] They will "listen to anybody and can never arrive at a knowledge of the truth."[w]

Still it was a good thing that this unction was made the extreme or "last" unction, for thanks to that, it has been abused and distorted least of all the sacraments by tyranny and greed. This one last mercy, to be sure, has been left to the dying—they may be anointed without charge, even without confession and communion.[267] If it had remained a practice of daily occurrence, especially if it had cured the sick, even without taking away sins, how many worlds, do you think, would not the pontiffs have under their control today? For through the one sacrament of penance and the power of the keys, as well as through the sacrament of ordination, they have become such mighty emperors and princes. But now it is a fortunate thing that they despise the prayer of faith, and therefore do not heal any sick, and that they have made for themselves, out of an ancient ceremony, a brand-new sacrament.

267. Luther is speaking of what was regarded as a widespread abuse of the sacrament, in which confession and communion were absent from the administration of extreme unction.

Let this now suffice for these four sacraments. I know how it will displease those who believe that the number and use of the sacraments are to be learned not from the sacred Scriptures, but from the Roman See. As if the Roman See had given these "sacraments" and had not rather received them from the lecture halls of the universities, to which it is unquestionably indebted for whatever it has. The papal despotism would not have attained its present position, had it not taken over so many things from the universities. For there was scarcely another of the celebrated bishoprics that had so few learned pontiffs as Rome. Only by violence, intrigue, and superstition has she till now prevailed over the rest. For the men who occupied the See a thousand years ago differed so vastly from those who have since come into power, that one is compelled to refuse the name of Roman pontiff to one group or the other.

u Matt. 8:13.

v Cf., for example, Aquinas, *STh* III, q. 69, a. 6.

w 2 Tim. 3:7.

[Other Sacraments]

There are still a few other things which it might seem possible to regard as sacraments; namely, all those things to which a divine promise has been given, such as prayer, the Word, and the cross. For Christ has promised, in many places, that those who pray should be heard; especially in Luke 11,[x] where by many parables he invites us to pray. Of the Word he says: "Blessed are those who hear the Word of God and keep it."[y] And who can count all the times God promises aid and glory to those who are afflicted, suffer, and are cast down? Indeed, who can recount all the promises of God? Why, the whole Scripture is concerned with provoking us to faith; now driving us with commands and threats, now drawing us with promises and consolations. In fact, everything in Scripture is either a command or a promise. The commands humble the proud with their demands; the promises exalt the humble with their forgiveness.

Nevertheless, it has seemed proper to restrict the name of sacrament to those promises which have signs attached to them. The remainder, not being bound to signs, are bare promises. Hence there are, strictly speaking, but two sacraments in the church of God—baptism and the bread.[z] For only in these two do we find both the divinely instituted sign and the promise of forgiveness of sins. The sacrament of penance, which I added to these two, lacks the divinely instituted visible sign, and is, as I have said, nothing but a way and a return to baptism. Nor can the scholastics say that their definition fits penance, for they too ascribe to the true sacrament a visible sign, which is to impress upon the senses the form of that which it effects invisibly.[a] But penance or absolution has no such sign. Therefore they are compelled by their own definition either to admit that penance is not a sacrament and thus to reduce their number, or else to bring forth another definition of a sacrament.

Baptism, however, which we have applied to the whole of life, will truly be a sufficient substitute for all the sacraments that we might need as long as we live. And the bread is truly the

x Luke 11:5-13.

y Luke 11:28.

z Cf. Luther's earlier remarks in which he initially proposes three sacraments; see p. 62, above.

a Cf. Lombard, *Sentences* 4, d. 1, c. 2.

sacrament of the dying and departing; for in it we commemorate the passing of Christ out of this world, that we may imitate him. Thus we may apportion these two sacraments as follows: baptism may be allotted to the beginning and the entire course of life, while the bread belongs to the end and to death. And the Christian should use them both as long as he is in this mortal frame, until, fully baptized and strengthened, he passes out of this world, and is born into the new eternal life, to eat with Christ in the kingdom of his Father, as he promised at the Last Supper, when he said: "Truly, I say to you, I shall not drink again of this fruit of the vine until it is fulfilled in the kingdom of God."[b] Thus he clearly seems to have instituted the sacrament of the bread with a view to our entrance into the life to come. For then, when the purpose of both sacraments is fulfilled, baptism and bread will cease.

[Conclusion]

Herewith I conclude this prelude, and freely and gladly offer it to all pious souls who desire to know the genuine sense of the Scriptures and the proper use of the sacraments. For it is a gift of no mean importance, to know the gifts that are given to us, as it is said in 1 Cor. 2[:12], and what use we ought to make of them. For if we are instructed with this judgment of the spirit, we shall not mistakenly rely on those things which are wrong. These two things our theologians never taught us; indeed, they seem to have taken pains to hide them from us. If I have not taught them, I certainly managed not to conceal them, and have given occasion to others to think out something better. It has at least been my endeavor to set them both forth. Nevertheless, "not all can do all things."[268] To the godless, on the other hand, and those who in obstinate tyranny force on us their own teachings instead of God's, I confidently and freely oppose these pages. I shall be completely indifferent to their senseless fury. Yet I wish even them a right understanding. And I do not despise their efforts; I only distinguish them from what is sound and truly Christian.

268. Luther is quoting Virgil, *Eclogues* 8, 63.

b Cf. Matt. 26:29; Mark 14:25; Luke 22:18.

I hear a rumor that new bulls[c] and papal maledictions are being prepared against me, in which I am urged to recant or be declared a heretic.[269] If that is true, I desire this little book to be part of the recantation that I shall make; so that the arrogant despots might not complain of having acted in vain. The remainder I will publish very soon;[270] please Christ, it will be such as the Roman See has never seen or heard before. I shall give ample proof of my obedience. In the name of our Lord Jesus Christ. Amen.

"Why doth that impious Herod fear
When told that Christ the King is near?
He takes not earthly realms away,
Who gives the realms that ne'er decay."[271]

269. The bull *Exsurge domine*, issued on 15 June 1520, gave Luther and his followers sixty days to recant before they would be declared of heresy. On 10 December, sixty days later, Luther and his colleagues invited the students of Wittenberg to a burning of papal and Scholastic books. There Luther publicly burned *Exsurge domine*. On 3 January 1521, the pope issued the bull *Decet Romanum pontificem*, formally excommunicating Luther.

270. On 29 November 1520, Luther published *Assertion of All the Articles Wrongly Condemned in the Roman Bull*. His treatise *On the Freedom of the Christian* was also published in the same month, with an accompanying letter to Pope Leo X (see LW 31:327–77; TAL 1:466–538).

271. The eighth stanza of Coelius Sedulius's *A solis ortus cardine* (fifth century). Luther would later translate stanzas 8, 9, 11, and 13 as an Epiphany hymn, *Was fürchtst du Feind, Herodes, sehr.*

c See n. 179, p. 79.

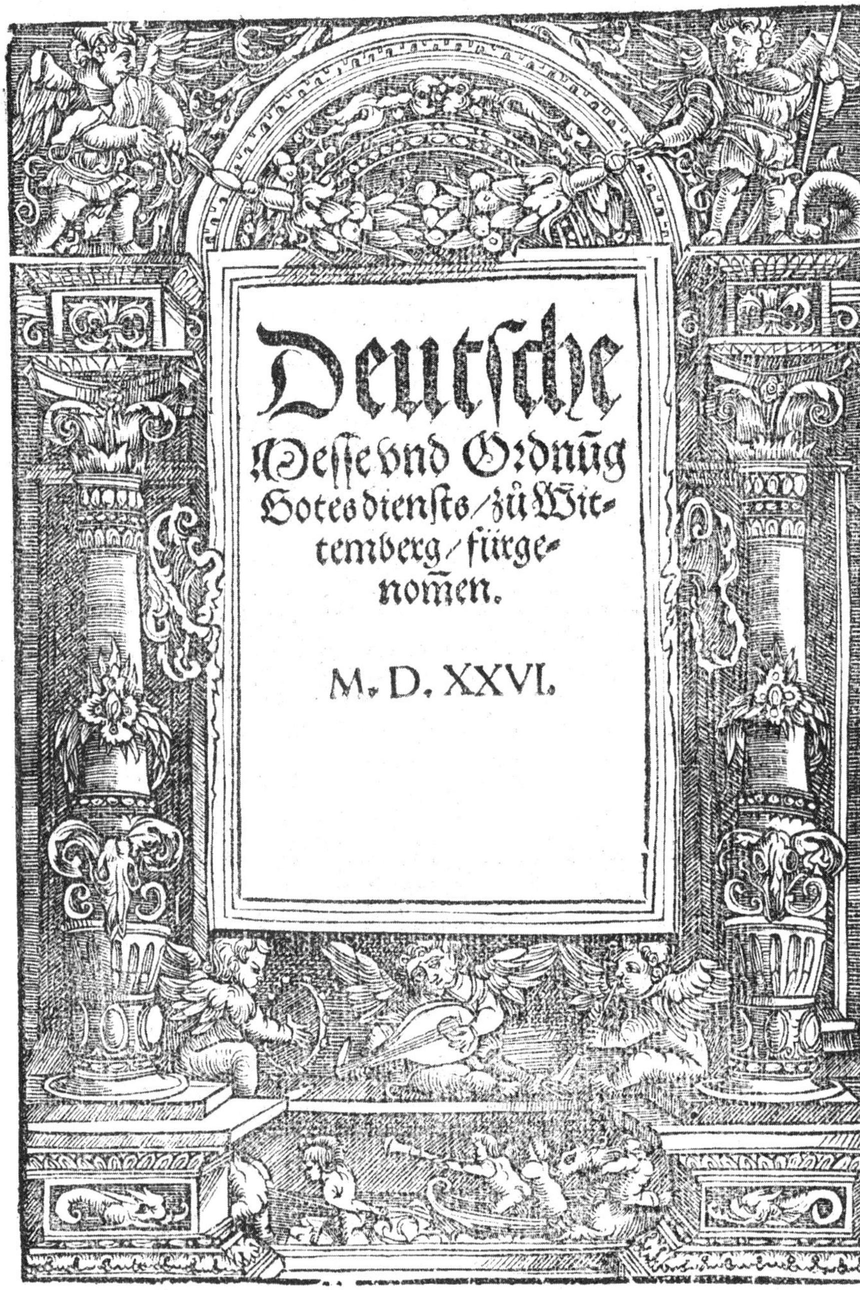

Deutsche
Messe vnd Ordnūg
Gotes diensts/ zů Wit-
temberg/ fürge-
nomēn.

M. D. XXVI.

The title page of the 1526 printing
of Martin Luther's *The German Mass and Order of the Liturgy*.

The German Mass and Order of the Liturgy

1526

DIRK G. LANGE

INTRODUCTION

Prior to the publication of the German Mass[1] in 1526, several Evangelical orders for the liturgy had been produced in various German cities and lands.[2] Already in 1521–22, the radical reformers in Wittenberg under Andreas Bodenstein von Karlstadt's (1486–1541) leadership were forcing a form of worship practices: requiring communion in two kinds (reception of both bread and wine), dismissing fasting and confessing, and beginning to remove images from the churches. The city, its churches, and university were in upheaval. Luther secretly left the Wartburg in 1522, returned to Wittenberg, and began preaching the Invocavit Sermons[3] that restored peace and order to the city. Recognizing that the people were not ready for such radical reforms, Luther restored communion in one kind. In his treatise *An Order of Mass and Communion for the Church at Wittenberg*, he expressed concern for the weak in faith, "who cannot suddenly exchange an old and accustomed order of worship for a new and unusual one . . ."[a] Luther's primary concern was that the gospel be proclaimed for the people, in their context, and

a LW 53:19.

1. The word *Mass* comes from Latin and was maintained by Luther for most of his life. Today, various expressions are used—for example, worship or liturgy or service. In the Preface, the most common designation that Luther employs is *Gottesdienst*. This German word does not translate well into English. It suggests service to God or God's service to us. It has often been translated as worship. Considering Luther's emphasis on the importance of an order or pattern—not for its own sake but for the sake of proclamation—liturgy is the more accurate translation. The concept of worship denotes the believer's stance or disposition toward God in any given moment, both public and private. Christian liturgy refers to the public practice of an assembly gathered around word and sacrament (font, book, and meal). In this translation, the words *liturgy* and *worship* will both be employed depending on the context.

2. In Nuremberg, for example, Andreas Osiander (1498–1552) had introduced a new baptismal rite and was continually revising the order of the liturgy throughout the second half of the 1520s. The Nuremberg Church Order received its final form in 1533. See Dr. jur. Emil Sehling, ed., *Die evangelischen Kirchenordnungen des XVI. Jahrhunderts, Bayern: Franken* (Tübingen: J. C. B. Mohr [Paul Siebeck], 1961). Other church orders appeared in Basel and Pforzheim (1522) and in Reutlingen, Wertheim, Königsberg, and Strasbourg (1524). Thomas Müntzer (c. 1489–1525) had also produced an order of the liturgy, including morning and evening prayer with newly composed plainchant, in 1523.

3. The eight *Invocavit Sermons* were preached in Wittenberg, March 1522 (LW 51:67–100; TAL 4:7–45).

that liturgical practice always embody that proclamation, even if it meant instituting reforms slowly.

Nonetheless, a plethora of liturgical orders appeared in the German lands. In many cases, these early Reformation liturgies were of poor quality. Luther was under increasing pressure to bring some order and direction.

When Luther begins to write about worship and compose an order for the liturgy, he does so very cautiously. He hesitates to add yet another liturgy into the mix. On the one hand, he is aware that a liturgy published under his authorship might quickly impose itself as normative. On the other hand, he is deeply concerned that Christian freedom is being abused and that the various liturgies are merely the result of personal taste or ambition.

Eventually, Luther cedes to the pressure and composes the German Mass. However, he prefaces it with many qualifications on how to approach and use what he has written and composed. In his hesitancy and reservation, Luther demonstrates a Gospel-like attention to his context and community and their need. For him, the liturgy is a form of proclamation and one that can have a lasting spiritual impact on the lives of people.

Liturgy: A Theology

Luther's introductory warning about the order he just composed is surprising: "Do not make it a rigid law or bind or entangle anyone's conscience"[b] with it. An order of liturgy is not an eternal law to be imposed in the same way in every place for everyone. This imposition is all too familiar, as if one era's translation and renewal could be forever applicable. Some will romanticize the pattern of the early church's worship; others will romanticize Luther's German Mass (oblivious to Luther's warning!). Unfortunately, when one order is established as law, the evangelical purpose of the liturgy is destroyed.

Luther's warning, however, does not stop him from composing an order for worship. The composition and the warning need to be continually held in juxtaposition. Clearly, Luther lifts up the historical pattern as the church has practiced it, that is, a

b See p. 138 below.

pattern centered in word and sacrament. The translation of word and sacrament into new contexts is what becomes the essential task of the theologian.

The questions or criteria for translation may be the following: Do these practices proclaim the gospel, the paschal mystery? Does this liturgical pattern and its practice immerse people into the life, death, and resurrection of Jesus Christ? Luther insists throughout the German Mass that the order of liturgy forms a community through the proclamation of the word. And "word" is here understood to be not only the word preached but also the word distributed, the visible (tangible) word. At the center of worship is word and sacrament.

In his effort to bring back word and sacrament in their evangelical character, Luther does not eliminate ritual, but reforms it. He takes the old, in this case the Mass, and makes it speak the gospel for the present moment. This reforming activity underlines another warning Luther notes in these pages. He had observed, in his day, that there were many attempts at eliminating ritual as well as many attempts at implementing totally new worship services. Luther is dealing with a similar situation to one we know today (with some nuances). There are those who defend traditional worship and those who desire contemporary worship! Luther finds himself on both sides of the equation depending on the circumstance and context. He responds to this tension wisely, not judgmentally, with attention to what is essential. "Some, he writes, have the best intentions, but others have no more than an itch to produce something novel so that they might shine before people as leading lights, rather than being ordinary teachers."[c] An order of liturgy cannot simply be a personal creation, as novel or attractive or entertaining as it may be. A liturgical order is both rooted in a tradition and innovative in its translation of the gospel, which, for Luther, doesn't preclude newness.

Luther struggles with this task of translation. In his preface, he describes his attempt to adapt the liturgical pattern in three different circumstances. The first order that he produced, the *Formula Missae* (1523), was primarily a simplified version of the Latin Mass. The primary and significant change made in the

c See p. 138 below.

Formula Missae was the elimination of the offertory prayers and the prayers of the canon that were said after the *Sanctus* and the inclusion of the words of institution[4] within the Preface[5] before the *Sanctus*.[d]

4. "In the night in which he was betrayed, our Lord Jesus took bread, etc."

5. Or Initial Thanksgiving: "It is indeed right, our duty and our joy, that we should at all times and in all places . . ."

Two years later (1525), Luther begins composing the German Mass. Though it is a simplification of the *Formula Missae*, the German Mass still maintains the key elements of the liturgical order. This is particularly true for the celebration of the sacrament of Holy Communion. In a significant phrase, just before introducing the words of institution,[e] Luther writes, "Darnach folget das ampt und dermunge . . . ," which I have translated as "The liturgy of Holy Communion and the consecration follows."[f] After the exhortation comes the liturgy of Holy Communion, which includes, of course, the consecration. Luther frames the consecration within a liturgy proper to the sacrament. This mini-pattern or order is known from the *Formula Missae* and dates back to the early church. It includes the *Sursum Corda* ("Lift up your hearts"), the Preface ("It is indeed our duty . . ."), the *Sanctus*, and the Our Father. The words of institution do not stand on their own but belong to an entire action.[6] Luther maintains the structure of this liturgy (or sacrifice) of praise within the entire liturgy of the Mass. The liturgy of the sacrament lifts up the hearts and feeds and strengthens faith.

6. See a later reflection on the "entire action" rule in the *Solid Declaration*, Article VII: "Holy Supper," BC, 607.

Luther never meant for the German Mass to replace the *Formula Missae*. He notes that, depending on the situation, the Latin Mass should continue to be used as is and not be abrogated or changed. Finally, he suggests the possibility of a third order of the liturgy. This third order would be for those who "seriously want to be Christian."[g]

It is unclear what Luther specifically envisioned with such an order that would perhaps be intended for a small house church. He does, however, insist that there still would be a form of liturgy in word and sacrament, although the instructions

d Frank C. Senn, *Christian Liturgy: Catholic and Evangelical* (Minneapolis: Fortress Press, 1997), 277.

e See p. 137 below on the musical significance of the words of institution in *The German Mass*.

f See p. 156 and n. 64.

g See p. 141 below.

and regulations for that liturgy might be significantly reduced. Unfortunately, Luther adds that he knows of no such people and is therefore not going to spend time outlining such a service! Did he think that such a liturgical order might be possible one day? Luther was aware that in the reform of any worship practice, the weak in faith need to be considered. This consideration was already evident in the aborted Wittenberg reforms of 1522 (see above). Luther includes himself in this consideration of the weak in faith when he writes that orders of the liturgy are for us "so that they may make Christians out of us."[h] Luther appears to be acknowledging his own weakness and confessing his own need for an established order of the liturgy.

The liturgy makes Christians out of us! Worship and catechism go hand in hand. But this does not mean that the liturgy is simply teaching the Bible. Liturgy, as has already been stated, is proclamation in word and sacrament, that is, in words and rites,[7] gestures, and deeds that shape and train and draw a community into a gospel pattern for life. This catechizing into a gospel pattern also happens through daily prayer—morning and evening prayer—that Luther also discusses in these pages.

7. Later, in the *Apology of the Augsburg Confession* (1531), Article XIII, Philip Melanchthon (1497–1560) would write, "The word and the rite have the same effect," BC, 219–20.

Liturgy and Music[i]

Music played an important part in the Mass and in daily, communal prayer. First of all, music carried the voice, making it more audible. Second, music brought people together as a community in thanksgiving and in lament.

In these pages, Luther places strong emphasis on music as an instrument of proclamation. Greatly concerned that people were not participating in worship, Luther expresses his desire for new hymns and chants in German, plus more German translations that matched text and music better. He worked with leading artists of his day[8] and called on more musicians to take up this task.

8. Notably Conrad Rupsch (1475–1530) and Johann Walter (1496–1570), who both came to Wittenberg in 1525 to work with Luther on the German Mass.

h See p. 139 below.

i For a detailed study of Luther's liturgical music, see Robin A. Leaver, *Luther's Liturgical Music: Principles and Implications*, Lutheran Quarterly Books (Grand Rapids: Eerdmans, 2007).

Two pages from Luther's *The German Mass and Order of the Liturgy* showing rules for chanting the Gospel reading and a portion of a particular reading from the Gospel of John.

In the *Preface to the Wittenberg Hymnal* (1524), Luther states that the hymns have been composed for the young,

> . . . who should at any rate be trained in music and other fine arts—something to wean them away from love ballads and carnal songs and to teach them something of value in their place, thus combining the good with the pleasing, as is proper for youth. Nor am I of the opinion that the gospel should destroy and blight all the arts, as some of the pseudo-religious claim. But I would like to see all the arts, especially music, used in the service of [God] who gave and made them.[j]

[j] LW 53:316.

The music in the German Mass serves this task of training, teaching, and preaching. It could be argued that the whole Reformation impulse is summarized in Luther's use of music in the German Mass. In order for the gathered people to understand that the sacrament of Holy Communion was not a sacrifice but gospel—that is, gift—for them ("for you," plural), Luther composes the words of institution in the same tone as the Gospel, which has just been sung. The presider, facing the people, showing the bread and the wine, sings this Gospel proclamation or mini-sermon. This simple use of music is perhaps one of the most brilliant strokes of the Reformation and highlights again the importance of gesture, ritual, and art in proclaiming the Gospel. Another example is found in the *Sanctus*, a paraphrase of Isaiah 6, and also composed by Luther. It powerfully unites the voices of the community with the angelic hosts in singing the praise of Jesus Christ, truly present in the sacrament.

The music, both chants and hymns, provided here render Luther's chant with updated text and contemporary musical notation. The full text of the psalm and of some of the scriptural texts have not been provided, but a model is given to demonstrate how the music functions in "singing/reading" the text, in chanting the prayers, and in congregational song.

Conclusion

The liturgy is an exercise of Christian freedom, which does not mean that it can simply be a personal, inspired project or be the result of an "anything goes" mentality. In the service of Christian freedom, an order of liturgy glorifies God and seeks the good of the neighbor.[k]

Luther's primary concern in his reform of the liturgy was placing the gospel back in the center. The liturgy is not about "me" and my personal likes and dislikes. Rather, it is immersing a community into that gospel reality: God creating, exercising, and molding faith in the believer and in the community for a service of love to the neighbor. At the heart of the liturgy is this attempt to translate and proclaim, through word and sacrament, the Christ event—the life, death, and resurrection of Jesus

k See pp. 138–39 below.

Christ—in every context. "The central things of Christian worship . . . welcome us to the full truth about ourselves and the world: sorrow and hope, hunger and food, loneliness and community, sin and forgiveness, death and life. God in Christ comes amidst these things, full of mercy."[l]

The first completely German service in Wittenberg was held on 29 October 1525. On Christmas Day of the same year it was definitively introduced and appeared in print early in 1526.[9]

9. The text of the original Wittenberg printing is found in WA 19:72–119.

THE GERMAN MASS AND ORDER OF THE LITURGY[10,m]

10. The first edition was printed in Wittenberg, 1526, by Michael Lotther. An original print is to be found in the Herzog August Bibliothek in Wolfenbüttel, Germany. This translation is a significant revision of the translation found in LW 53 by Augustinius Steimle and Ulrich S. Leupold. It is based on the first printing of *Deudsche Messe und ordnung Gottis diensts* found in WA 19:72–113.

Martin Luther's Preface

BEFORE ANYTHING ELSE, I would kindly request, also for God's sake, that all those who see this order of service or desire to follow it: do not make it a rigid law or bind or entangle anyone's conscience, but use it in Christian liberty as long, when, where, and how you find it to be practical and useful. For this is being published not as though we meant to lord it over anyone else, or to legislate for people, but because of the widespread demand for German Masses and liturgies and the general dissatisfaction and offense that has been caused by the great variety of new Masses, for everyone makes their own.[11] Some have the best intentions, but others have no more than an itch to produce something novel so that they might shine before people as leading lights, rather than being ordinary teachers. As is the way with Christian liberty, most use it for their own

11. Luther may be referring to liturgical services produced in various cities that had adopted the Evangelical reforms, such as Nuremberg. He found these services often lacking in musical quality. Luther had great concern that the German translation of chant and song be faithful to German syntax and vocabulary. He was opposed to the

l Gordon Lathrop, *Central Things: Worship in Word and Sacrament* (Minneapolis: Fortress Press, 2005), 33.

m See n. 1, pp. 131–32 for an explanation of the use of the word *liturgy*.

advantage and pleasure and not for the glory of God and the good of the neighbor. But while the exercise of this freedom is up to everyone's conscience and must not be cramped or forbidden, nevertheless, we must make sure that freedom shall be and remain a servant of love and of our neighbor.

practice of simply "fitting" a German text to an existing Latin melody, thereby losing both the integrity of the language and the music.

Where the people are perplexed and offended by these differences in practice, we are certainly bound to restrict our freedom and seek, if possible, to help them improve rather than to offend them by what we do or leave undone. Seeing then that this external order, while it cannot affect our conscience before God yet can serve the neighbor, we should seek in love, as St. Paul teaches,[12] to be of one mind and, as far as possible, observe the same ways and practices, just as all Christians have the same baptism and the same sacrament[n] and no individual has received a special one[o] from God.

12. Rom. 15:5-6; 1 Cor. 1:10; Phil. 2:2. In the original print, Luther did not always cite chapter and verse. Scriptural citations were added by the Weimar edition (WA) or by the English translation found in *Luther's Works* (LW).

That is not to say that those who already have good orders, or by the grace of God could make better ones, should discard theirs and adopt ours. For I do not propose that all of Germany should uniformly follow our Wittenberg order. It has never been the case that the chapters, monasteries, and parishes were alike in every rite. But it would be well if the service in every principality would be held in the same manner and if the order observed in a given city would also be followed by the surrounding towns and villages. Whether those in other principalities hold the same order or add to it ought to be a matter of free choice, and adding to the order or adopting another should not be subject to punishment. In short, we prepare such orders not for those who are already Christians; for they do not need them. We do not live for the orders but they live for us[13] who are not yet Christians so that they may make Christians out of us. Those who are already Christians have their worship in the spirit.

13. Possibly a reference to Mark 2:27: "Then Jesus said to them, 'The sabbath was made for humankind, and not humankind for the sabbath.'"

But such orders are needed for those who are still becoming Christians or need to be strengthened. Just as Christians[p] do not need baptism, the Word, and the sacrament as Christians—for all things are theirs—but as sinners. They are essential especially for the immature and the young who must be trained and

n Sacrament of the Altar, or Holy Communion.

o I.e., sacrament.

p The original was singular in this sentence.

disciplined in the Scripture and God's word daily so that they may become familiar with the Bible, grounded, well versed, and skilled in it, ready to advocate for their faith and in due time to teach others and to increase the kingdom of Christ. For this, one must read, sing, preach, write, and compose. And if it would help matters along, I would have all the bells pealing, and all the organs playing, and have everything ring that can make a sound. For this is the damnable thing about the papal services: they have made laws, works, and merits out of the orders and in this way suppressed faith. They did not use them to train the youth and common people in the Scriptures and in the word of God, but became so engrossed in them as to regard them as inherently useful and necessary for salvation. That is the devil. The elders did not institute or order them to that intent.

[Three Liturgical Orders][q]

Now there are three kinds of liturgies or Mass. The first is the one in Latin that we published earlier under the title *Formula Missae*.[r] It is not now my intention to abrogate or to change this service. And just as we have observed it up until now, so it remains free for us to continue using it when or where we are pleased to do so or the situation moves us to use it. For under no circumstance would I want to discontinue the service in the Latin language, because young people are my primary concern. And if I could bring it to pass, and Greek and Hebrew were as familiar to us as the Latin and had as many fine melodies and songs, we would hold Mass, sing, and read on successive Sundays in all four languages, German, Latin, Greek, and Hebrew. I do not at all agree with those who cling to one language and despise all others. I would rather train the young and not so young[s] who could also be witnesses to Christ in foreign lands and be able to converse with the people there. It shouldn't happen to us as it did to the Waldenses in Bohemia,[14] who have so ensconced their faith in their own language that they cannot speak plainly and clearly to anyone, unless people first learn their language. The Holy Spirit

q This heading in brackets and others below have been added to the text.

r 1523. See LW 53:15–40; WA 12:205–220.

s German: *jugent und leute*, literally, the "young and people."

14. The origin of the Waldensian movement is disputed, but historians have often claimed it was founded in the late twelfth century in Lyon by Valdes (Peter Waldo) [d.c. 1218]. It spread to northern Italy. The Bohemian Brethren was a movement that emerged after the martyrdom of Jan Hus (1369–1415) at the Council of Constance. They received episcopal ordination through the Waldenses and therefore were also labeled "Waldenses" by their opponents.

did not act like that in the beginning. The Spirit did not wait until all the world came to Jerusalem and studied Hebrew, but gave manifold tongues for the office of the ministry, so that the apostles could preach wherever they might go. I prefer to follow this example. It is also reasonable that young people should be trained in many languages; for who knows how God may use them in times to come? Our schools were founded for this purpose.[15]

The second is the *German Mass and Order of the Liturgy*, with which we are now concerned. It should be arranged for the sake of the simple laypeople. We must let these two orders[t] be used publicly in the churches for all the people, among whom are many who do not believe or are not yet Christian. Most of them stand around and gape, hoping to see something new, just as if we were holding a service among the Turks[16] or among the nonbelievers in a public square or out in a field. This is then not yet a well-ordered and confident congregation, in which Christians are ruled according to the proclamation of the Gospel; rather it is one where people are publicly drawn to faith and to Christianity.

The third kind of service should be a truly Evangelical order and should not happen publicly on the town square for all sorts of people. But those who seriously want to be Christians and who profess the gospel with hand and mouth should sign-in with their names and meet alone in a house to pray, to read, to baptize, to receive the sacrament, and to do other Christian works. According to this order, those who do not lead Christian lives could be known, reproved, corrected, excluded, or excommunicated, according to the rule of Christ, Matt. 18[:15-17]. Here one could also solicit gifts[17] to be willingly given and distributed to the poor, according to St. Paul's example (2 Corinthians 9). Here would be no need of elaborate or excessive singing. Here one could practice a brief and beautiful order for baptism and the sacrament and center everything on the Word, prayer, and love. Here one could have a good, short catechism on the Creed, the Ten Commandments, and the Lord's Prayer.[18]

Basically, if one had the kind of people and persons who seriously wanted to be Christians, the regulations and practices would soon be ready. But as yet I neither can nor desire to begin such a congregation or assembly or to make rules for it. For I

t *Formula Missae* and *Deutsche Messe*.

15. The first level of education in the Middle Ages focused almost entirely on learning Latin, which was the language used in higher education. Luther amends this tradition in a humanist vein by adding Greek and Hebrew. A Latin service in Wittenberg had the additional function of serving the university community. Many students came to Wittenberg from other parts of Europe and would have had only the Latin language in common with the other students and their teachers.

16. The growing power of the "Turks," Luther's shorthand for the Ottoman Empire and people of Muslim faith, was of deep concern to Europe in the 1520s.

17. Since no "work" merited salvation, the practice of almsgiving could serve its original intent, that is, to assist those in need to surmount the poverty in which they were trapped. A common chest was established in Wittenberg to help relieve the social distress of poverty. Luther's concern was not only the elimination of poverty but also the prevention of poverty.

18. *Vater unser.* Here and throughout Luther refers to the prayer by its first words, "Our Father," as was common in his day.

have not yet the people or persons for it, nor do I see many who want it. But if I should be requested to do it and could not refuse with a good conscience, I should gladly do my part and help as best I can. In the meanwhile the two above-mentioned orders of service must suffice. Besides preaching, I shall help to encourage such public liturgy for the people, to train young people and to call and attract others to faith, until they are Christians who earnestly understand the word and join together and conduct themselves as Christians. This kind of liturgy is necessary so that no sect arises from public worship as if I simply devised this service out of my own head.[19] For we Germans are a rough, rude, and reckless people, with whom it is hard to do anything, except in cases of dire need.

[Liturgy and Catechism]

Onward then in the name of God! First, the German service needs a down-to-earth, plain, simple, and good catechism. Catechism means the instruction in which the non-believers, who want to be Christians, are taught and guided in what they should believe, know, do, and leave undone, according to Christian faith. This is why candidates were called catechumens[20] when they had been admitted for instruction and learned the Creed before their baptism. I cannot present this instruction or catechization better or more plainly than has been done from the beginning of Christendom and retained until now, that is, in these three parts, the Ten Commandments, the Creed, and the Lord's Prayer. These three parts contain plainly and succinctly everything that a Christian needs to know. As long as there is no ideal congregation,[u] this instruction must be given from the pulpit at stated times or daily as may be needed, and repeated or read aloud evenings and mornings in the homes for the children and servants in order to make[21] them Christians. Nor should they only learn to say the words by rote. But they should be questioned point by point and respond with what each part means and how they understand it. If everything cannot be covered at once, let one point be taken up today and another tomorrow. If

u In reference to the "ideal" community described on pp. 137–38.

19. An order of liturgy is not simply to fulfill a personal need or plan or idea but must always serve the gospel.

20. Luther uses the Greek term *catechumenos*. One of the most detailed examples of the practice Luther describes is recorded in the sermons of Cyril of Jerusalem (c. 313–386), in particular the *Procatechesis* (c. 348). For an introduction, see Edward Yarnold, S.J., *The Awe-Inspiring Rites of Initiation*, 2d ed. (Collegeville, MN: Liturgical, 1994).

21. Luther's assertion that Christians are "made" is not surprising. In baptism, we have been justified (forgiven) once and for all. In this life, we are always saint and sinner. We are always growing deeper into the experience of righteousness. "For we perceive that a person who is justified is not yet a righteous person, but is in the very movement or journey toward righteousness." *The Disputation Concerning Justification*, LW 34:152.

A variant of Martin Luther's hymn "Jesus Christus, unser Heiland, der von uns den Gotteszorn wandt," as published in a Wittenberg hymnal (c. 1525–1550).

parents and guardians will not take the trouble to do this, either on their own or through others, there never will be a catechism, unless an ideal community be established as stated above.

Here is how they should be questioned:

What do you pray?

Answer: The Lord's Prayer.

What is it, when you say: Our Father in Heaven?

Answer: That God is not an earthly, but a heavenly Father who would make us rich and blessed in heaven.

What is: Hallowed be your name?

Answer: That we should honor God's name and keep it from being profaned.

How do we profane or dishonor God's name?

Answer: When we, who should be God's children, live evil lives and teach and believe what is wrong.

And so on, what is meant by the kingdom of God, how it comes, what is meant by the will of God, by daily bread, etc., etc.

And also in the Creed: what do you believe?

Answer: I believe in God the Father . . . to the end.

And so on from point to point, as time permits, one or two items at a time. For instance:

What does it mean to believe in God the Father Almighty?

Answer: It means to trust in God with all your heart and confidently to expect all grace, favor, help, and comfort from God, now and forever.

What does it mean to believe in Jesus Christ his Son?

Answer: It means to believe with the heart that we would all be eternally lost if Christ had not died for us, etc.

Likewise in the Ten Commandments, one must ask: What is meant by the First, the Second, the Third, and the other commandments? One may take these questions from our *Little Prayer Book*[22] where the three parts are briefly explained, or make others, until the heart may grasp the whole sum of Christian truth under two parts or, as it were, in two pouches. namely, faith and love. Faith's pouch has two pockets. In one pocket is the part that believes that we are all corrupt, sinners, and under condemnation through the sin of Adam—Rom. 5[:12] and Psalm 51[:5]). In the other is the part of faith that trusts that through Jesus Christ we are all redeemed from this corruption, sin, and condemnation—Rom. 5[:15-21] and John 3[:16-18]. Love's pouch also has two pockets. In the one is the piece that we should serve and do good to everyone, even as Christ has done for us, Romans 13. In the other is the piece that we should gladly endure and suffer all kinds of evil.

22. Luther had not yet written his *Large Catechism* or *Small Catechism*. His *Betbüchlein*, or *Little Prayer Book*, is found in LW 43:3–45. It contains a brief commentary on the Ten Commandments, the Creed, and the Lord's Prayer and was first published in 1522 (WA 10/II:376–501). See also TAL 4:159–200.

When children begin to understand this they[v] should be encouraged to bring home verses of Scripture from the sermon and to repeat them at mealtime for the parents, even as they formerly used to recite their Latin. And then these verses should be put into the pouches and pockets, just as pennies and silver or gold coins[23] are put into a purse. For instance, let faith's purse be for the gold coins, and in the first pocket belongs Rom. 5[:12, 18], "through the sin of one, all are sinners and condemned."[24] Also this one: Ps. 51[:5],[w] "Indeed, I was born guilty, a sinner when my mother conceived me." These are two Rhenish gold coins for the first pocket. Into the other pocket put the Hungarian gold coin,[25] for example, this text, Romans 5,[x] "[Jesus] was handed over to death for our trespasses and was raised for our justification." Again John 3,[y] "Behold, the Lamb of God, who takes away the sin of the world!" These would be two good Hungarian gold coins for the [second] pocket.

Love's purse is the purse for silver. In the first pocket belong the texts concerning well doing, such as Galatians 4,[z] "Serve one another in love";[26] and Matt. 25[:40], "as you did it to one of the least of these who are members of my family, you did it to me." These would be two silver coins for the first pocket. In the other pocket belongs this verse: Matt. 5[:11], "Blessed are you when people . . . persecute you . . . on my account"; and Heb. 12[:6], "for the Lord disciplines those whom he loves, and chastises every child whom he accepts." These are two big silver coins[27] for the second pocket.

And let none think that they are too wise for such child's play. Christ, to draw people, had to become human himself. If we wish to reach children, we must become children with them. Would to God that such child's play was widely practiced. In a short time we would have a great treasure of Christian people whose souls would be so enriched by Scripture and in the knowledge of God that of their own accord they would add more pockets, just as the *Loci Communes*,[28] and comprehend all Scripture in them.

v The original here is singular.

w The original text has Psalm 1 here.

x Luther cites Rom. 4:25 (not ch. 5).

y Luther cites John 1:29 (not ch. 3).

z Luther cites Gal. 5:13 (not ch. 4).

23. "*Grossen [Groschen] und gulden*" were, respectively, silver and gold coins. A penny was made of copper.

24. Luther freely elides Rom. 5:12 and 5:18: "just as sin came into the world through one man, and death came through sin . . ." and "Therefore just as one man's trespass led to condemnation for all."

25. The Rhenish *gulden* was the more common gold coin in Germany. It was also used for trade throughout the Holy Roman Empire. Of equal or even more value was the Hungarian gold coin, though perhaps less widespread in its use.

26. Gal. 5:13b: "through love become slaves to one another."

27. *Schreckenberger*: named for a mountain in the Erzgebirge mining region, this was a large silver coin minted in the late fifteenth century until the later sixteenth century. It was known as the "big *groschen*."

28. Philip Melanchthon wrote the *Loci Communes* (1521). Luther, who highly praised this work, refers here to the structure of the book, namely, that it derived theological topics (*loci*) from Scripture itself rather than resorting to those categories imposed by philosophy.

Otherwise, people can go to church daily and come away the same as they went. For they think they need only listen in the moment, without any thought of learning or remembering anything. Many listen to sermons for three or four years and do not retain enough to give a single answer concerning their faith (as I experience daily). Enough has been written in books, yes, but it has not yet been driven home to the hearts.

Concerning the Liturgy[a]

Since the preaching and teaching of God's Word is the most important part of the liturgy we have arranged for sermons and readings as follows: For the holy day or Sunday we retain the customary Epistles and Gospels and have three sermons. At five or six o'clock in the morning a few psalms are chanted for Morning Prayer.[29] A sermon follows on the Epistle of the day, chiefly for the sake of the servants so that they too may be cared for and hear God's Word, since they cannot be present at other sermons. After this an antiphon[30] and alternately the *Te Deum*[31] or the *Benedictus*,[32] with the Lord's Prayer, collects,[33] and *Benedicamus Domino*.[34] At the Mass, at eight or nine o'clock, the sermon is on the Gospel for the day. At Evening Prayer[35] in the afternoon, the sermon before the *Magnificat*[36] takes up the Old Testament chapter by chapter. For the Epistles and Gospels we have retained the customary pattern according to the church year,[37] because we do not find anything especially reprehensible in this use. And the present situation in Wittenberg is such that many are here who must learn to preach in places where this manner of dividing up the Gospels and Epistles is still being observed and may continue in force.[38] Since in this matter we can be of service to others without loss to ourselves, we leave it, but have no objection to others who take up the complete books of the evangelists.[39] This we think provides sufficient preaching and teaching for the laypeople. For those who desire more, they will find enough on other days.

Namely, on Monday and Tuesday mornings we have a German lesson on the Ten Commandments, the Creed, Lord's

a See n. 1, pp. 131–32.

29. Matins.

30. An antiphon (literally the opposite voice) is a short sung text that responds to or brackets another text, such as a psalm.

31. The *Te Deum* ("We Praise You, O God") is an ancient hymn of the church dating back to the late fifth century. It was a popular hymn in the Middle Ages and one of Luther's favorite hymns. He continued using it, being the first to translate it into German. See LW 53:171–75.

32. The *Benedictus* or the Song of Zechariah (Luke 1:67-79) is also traditionally sung at morning prayer.

33. Collects are short, succinct prayers at the beginning of the liturgy. They "collect" in prayer form the main theme for the day from the appointed Scripture. Today, they are often called the "prayer of the day." They follow a simple pattern: addressing God, acknowledging God's action in the past, beseeching God to act again now, and doxology.

34. In the Middle Ages, some Masses

Prayer, baptism, and sacrament, so that these two days preserve and deepen the understanding of the catechism. On Wednesday morning [there is] again a German reading, for which the evangelist Matthew has been appointed so that the day shall be his very own, seeing that he is an excellent evangelist for the congregation to learn, with the good sermon of Christ on the Mount,[40] which strongly urges the exercise of love and good works. But the evangelist John, who so powerfully teaches faith, has his own day too, on Saturday afternoon at Evening Prayer. So two of the evangelists have their own days for instruction. Thursday and Friday mornings have the weekday lessons from the Epistles[41] and the rest of the New Testament[42] assigned to them. Thus enough readings and sermons have been appointed to give the Word of God free course among us, not to mention the university lectures for scholars.

This is what we do to train the schoolboys[43] in the Bible. Every day of the week they chant a few psalms in Latin before the lesson, as has been customary at Morning Prayer up until now. For as we stated above, we want to keep the youth well versed in the Latin Bible. After the psalms, two or three boys in turn read a chapter from the Latin New Testament, depending on the length. Another one then reads the same chapter in German to familiarize them with it and for the benefit of any laity who might be present and listening. Then they proceed with an antiphon to the German reading as mentioned above. After the reading the whole congregation sings a German hymn, the Lord's Prayer is said silently, and the pastor or chaplain[44] reads a collect and closes with the *Benedicamus Domino* as usual.

Likewise at Evening Prayer they sing a few of the vesper psalms in Latin with an antiphon, as has been the case, followed by a hymn if one is available. Again two or three boys in turn then read a chapter from the Latin Old Testament or half a one, depending on length. Another one reads the same chapter in German. The *Magnificat* follows in Latin with an antiphon or hymn, the Lord's Prayer[b] said silently, and the collects with the *Benedicamus*. This is the daily service throughout the week in cities where there are schools.

b *Eyn vater unser.*

and all other services ended with the presider saying, "*Benedicamus Domino* [Let us bless the Lord]." The congregation responded, "*Deo gratias* [Thanks be to God]."

35. Vespers.

36. The *Magnificat* or Song of Mary (Luke 1:46-55) is sung at evening prayer.

37. The lectionary is a pattern of Scripture readings divided up throughout a year or several years. The liturgical or church year reconfigures time according to Gospel proclamation (Advent, Christmas, Epiphany, Lent, Holy Week, Easter, Pentecost, etc.).

38. Luther refers here to university students from outside of Electoral Saxony.

39. The entire four Gospels: Matthew, Mark, Luke, and John. Preaching on an entire book, particularly one of the Gospels, rather than the lectionary readings, had become a hallmark of the Reformation in other regions, for example, in Zwingli's Zurich.

40. The Beatitudes: Matthew 5 and 6.

41. The Pauline and other general Epistles.

42. The Acts of the Apostles, Revelation, and maybe even the Gospels.

43. Although Luther had advocated for education for girls already in 1524, normally only boys attended school. See *To the Councilmen of All Cities in Germany, That They Establish and Maintain Christian Schools*, LW 45:339–78; also TAL 5, forthcoming.

44. The *Capplan* (or *Kaplan*) was an ordained person who assisted the pastor. They were often in charge of special care ministries.

45. The liturgy of word and sacrament.

46. The high altar was traditionally placed against the east wall of the sanctuary. The priest would celebrate the Mass with his back turned toward the people.

On Sunday for the Laity

Here we retain the vestments, altar, and candles until they are used up or we are pleased to make a change. But we do not oppose anyone who would do otherwise. However, in the true Mass[45] of authentic Christians, the altar should not remain where it is,[46] and the priest should always face the people as Christ doubtlessly did in the Last Supper. But let that wait for its own time.

To begin the service we sing a hymn or a German Psalm in the First Tone as follows:

[Psalm 34][c]

c This is an abbreviated version of Psalm 34. In the WA and LW versions, the entire psalm is set to music.

Then follows the Kyrie eleison in the same tone, three times instead of nine,[47] as follows:

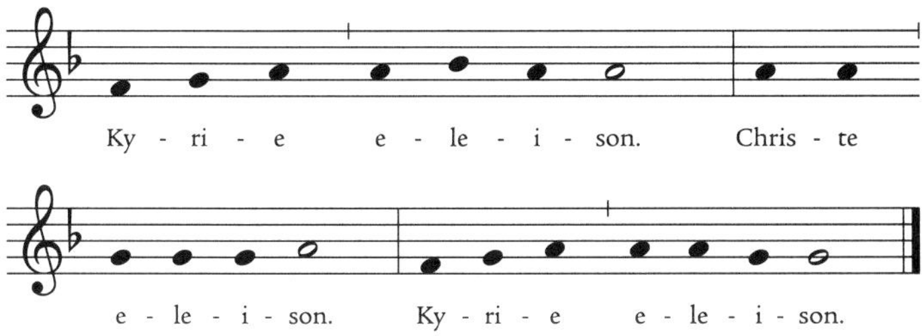

After which the priest reads a collect in monotone on *F (fa-ut)*[48] as follows:

> Almighty God, protector of all who trust in you, without whose grace no one is able to do anything, or to stand before you: Grant us richly your mercy, that by your holy inspiration we may think what is right and by your power perform the same; for the sake of Jesus Christ our Lord. Amen.

There follows the Epistle in the Eighth Tone, and let the one reciting remain on the same pitch as the collect. The rules for it are these:[49]

Period is the end of a sentence.
Colon is a part of a sentence.
Comma is a subdivision within the colon.

Rules for This Chant

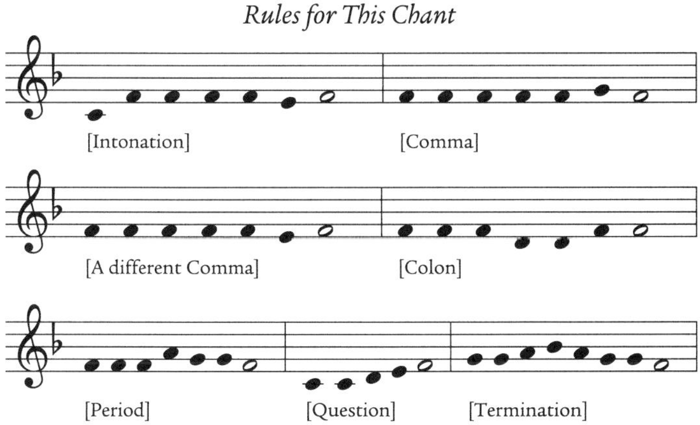

47. In the Middle Ages, the *Kyrie* might be sung three times or nine times depending on the amount of time it took the procession to reach the altar.

48. *F-fa-ut*: in the medieval system of attributing specific syllables to notes, the F-fa-ut (sometimes written *Ffaut*) stands for the F on the second highest line of the bass clef.

49. Luther writes this sentence and the following rules in Latin.

50. 1 Cor. 4:1-5. Luther reverts to German for the Epistle. This is an abbreviated version of Luther's original using NRSV Bible text.

Example: 1 Corinthians 4:1-5[50]

He should read the Epistle facing the people, but the collect facing the altar.

After the Epistle a German hymn, either "Now Let Us Pray to the Holy Spirit"[51] or any other, is sung with the whole choir.

Then he reads the Gospel in the Fifth Tone, again facing the people.[52]

The rules for this chant are as follows:[53]

51. "Now to the Holy Spirit Let Us Pray," LW 53:263–64. See also ELW 743; LSB 768.

52. For the Gospel reading, Luther followed the pattern of singing the Passion narrative in which different voices were given specific ranges and patterns. Usually three parts were designated: narrator, Christ, and any other role in the Gospel.

53. Luther writes this sentence and the following rules again in Latin.

Voice of the Evangelist

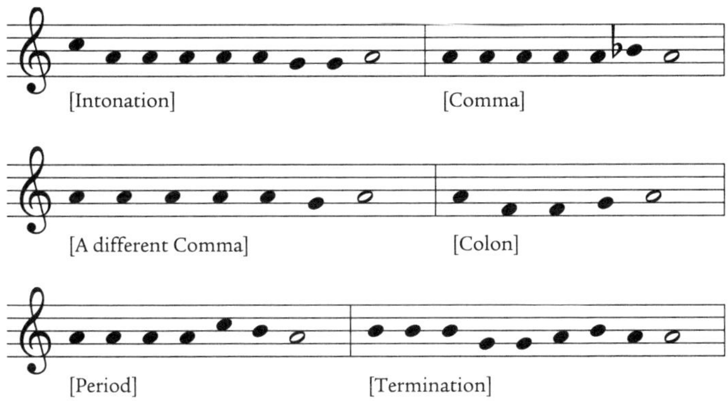

Voice of Persons

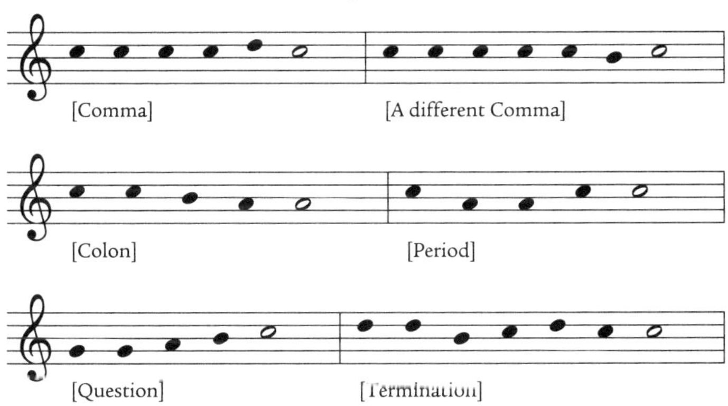

The Voice of Christ

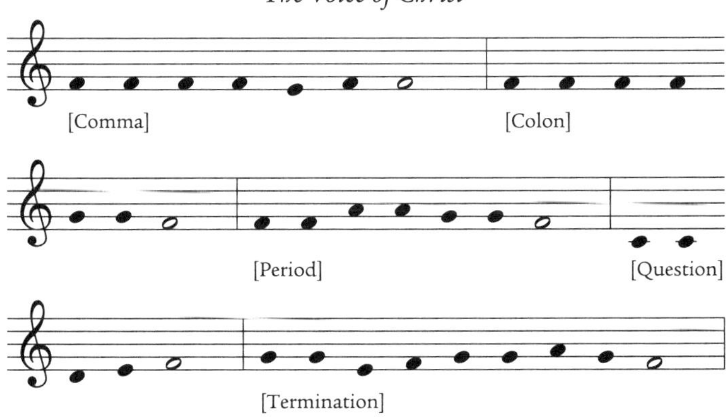

Example: John 1:19-28

The Gospel for the Fourth Sunday in Advent would be chanted as follows:[54]

54. John 1:19-28. After this sentence, Luther reverts back to German.

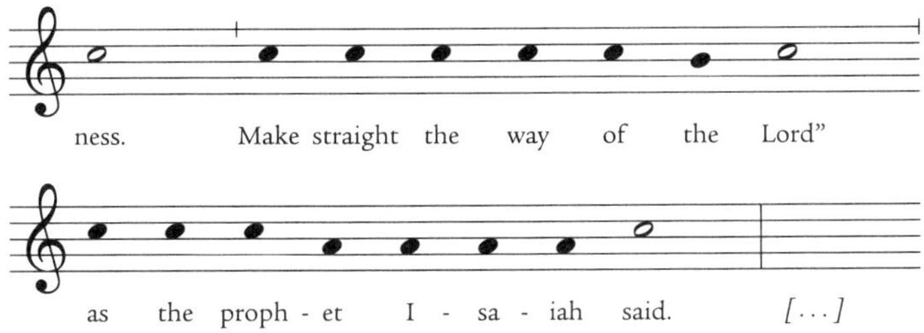

After the Gospel the whole congregation sings the Creed in German: “In One True God We All Believe.”[55]

Then comes the sermon on the Gospel for the Sunday or festival day. And I think that if we had the German postil[56] for the entire year, it would be best to appoint the sermon for the day to be read entirely or in part out of the book—not alone for the benefit of those preachers who can do nothing better,[57] but also for the purpose of preventing the rise of enthusiasts and sects.[58] If we observe the homilies read at Morning Prayer, we note a usage similar to this.[59] For unless there is a spiritual understanding and the Spirit itself speaks through the preachers (whom I do not wish hereby to restrict, for the Spirit teaches better how to preach than all the postils and homilies), we will ultimately reach the point where everyone will preach his own ideas, and instead of the Gospel and its exposition we will again have sermons about fables.[60] This is one of the reasons we retain the Epistles and Gospels as they are given in the postils—there are so few gifted preachers who are able to give a powerful and practical exposition of a whole evangelist or some other book of the Bible.

A public paraphrase of the Lord’s Prayer shall follow the sermon[61] and an admonition for those who want to share in the Sacrament,[62] in this or a better fashion:

> Beloved Friends in Christ: Since we are here assembled in the name of the Lord to receive his Holy Testament, I admonish you first of all to lift up your hearts to God to pray with me the Lord’s Prayer, as Christ our Lord has taught us and graciously promised to hear us.

55. “We All Believe in One True God.” See ELW 411; LSB 954.

56. A postil was a biblical commentary on particular texts in the lectionary, much like today’s websites or printed series for sermon preparation, though Luther’s postils resembled longer sermons on a biblical text than commentaries. Luther’s most famous postils are the Church Postil (1527) and House Postil (1542). The Church Postils have been newly published in LW 75, 76, and 77.

57. It was not an uncommon practice to advise those priests who were poor preachers to read good sermons from the pulpit! This counsel dates back to Augustine, if not earlier.

58. As the Reformation took hold, Luther contended with radical reformers who wished to abolish, among other things, all liturgical practices, including the sacraments. They argued that only inner inspiration through the Holy Spirit was required to know God. Luther often labeled these movements “enthusiasts” or “sects,” sometimes also “fanatics.” Luther suggests here that the postils might be one way to keep preachers on topic.

59. Excerpts from the church fathers were read at morning prayer.

60. *Blaw endten*—literally, “blue ducks”—was an expression in Luther’s time for an obviously untrue fable but that nonetheless was constantly repeated. Grimm’s famous dictionary of the German language uses this particular sentence from the German Mass to illustrate its usage.

61. *Eyne offentliche paraphrasis des vater unsers*. Luther later abandoned this paraphrase of the Lord’s Prayer, finding it not particularly effective.

62. The Lord’s Supper.

That God, our Father in heaven, may look with mercy on us, God's needy children on earth, and grant us grace so that God's holy name be hallowed among us and all the world through the pure and righteous teaching of God's Word and the fervent love of our lives. And that God would graciously turn away from us all false doctrine and evil living through which God's precious name is being blasphemed and profaned.

That God's kingdom may come to us and spread; that all transgressors and those who are blinded and bound in the devil's kingdom be brought to know Jesus Christ his Son by faith, and that the number of Christians may be increased.

That we may be strengthened by God's Spirit to do and to surrender[d] to God's will, both in life and in death, in good and in evil things, and always to break, sacrifice, and slay our own wills.

That God would also give us our daily bread, preserve us from greed and selfish cares,[e] and help us to trust that God will provide for all our needs.

That God would forgive our debts as we forgive our debtors so that our hearts may rest and rejoice in a good conscience before God, and that no sin may ever fright or alarm us.

That God would not lead us into temptation but help us by his Spirit to subdue the flesh, to despise the world and its ways, and to overcome the devil with all his wiles.

And lastly, that God would deliver us from all evil, both of body and soul, now and forever.

All those who truly desire these things will say from their hearts: Amen, trusting without any doubt that it is a Yes answered in heaven as Christ has promised [Mark

d Literally, "to suffer his will."

e Literally, "cares of the belly."

11:24]: "whatever you ask for in prayer, believe that you have received it, and it will be yours." Amen.

Secondly, I admonish you in Christ that you discern the Testament of Christ in true faith and, above all, take to heart the words in which Christ imparts to us his body and his blood for the remission of our sins. That you remember and give thanks for Christ's boundless love which he proved to us when he redeemed us from God's wrath, sin, death, and hell by his own blood and that you externally receive the bread and wine, that is, his body and blood, as the pledge and guarantee of this. Then, in his name and according to his command, let us receive and act upon the Word of the Testament.

Whether such paraphrase and admonition should be read in the pulpit immediately after the sermon or at the altar, I leave to everyone's judgment. It seems that in ancient times this was done from the pulpit, so that it is still the custom to read general prayers or to repeat the Lord's Prayer in the pulpit. But the admonition itself has since become a public confession. In this way, however, the Lord's Prayer together with a short exposition would be current among the people, and the Lord would be remembered, even as he commanded at the Last Supper.

I would, however, like to ask that this paraphrase or admonition follow a prescribed wording or be formulated[63] in a definite manner for the sake of ordinary people. We cannot have it done one way today, and tomorrow another different way, letting everybody parade their talents and confuse the people so that they can neither learn nor retain anything. What matters most is the teaching and guiding of the people. That is why we must limit our freedom and keep to one form of paraphrase or admonition, particularly in a given church or congregation, if, for the sake of freedom, the congregation does not wish to use another.

63. Luther writes this phrase in Latin as well, "*conceptis seu prescriptis verbis*." Luther sometimes reverts to Latin when he is employing technical phrases, whether theological or liturgical. In this sentence, he might be thinking about the rubrics that need to be written to guide this admonition.

The liturgy of Holy Communion and consecration[64] follow in this tune:

64. *Dermunge* (or *Dirmung*) designates the consecration. It comes from the Latin *terminare* (in its meaning of "to produce or accomplish"). The word appears to refer specifically to the recitation of the words of institution. The significant word in this sentence, however, is *Amt*, previously translated as "office" (LW 53:80). It would seem that the consecration or the recitation of the words of institution occurs alongside other liturgical components (the Dialogue and Preface, for example). The passage has therefore been translated by "the liturgy of Holy Communion." See introductory notes.

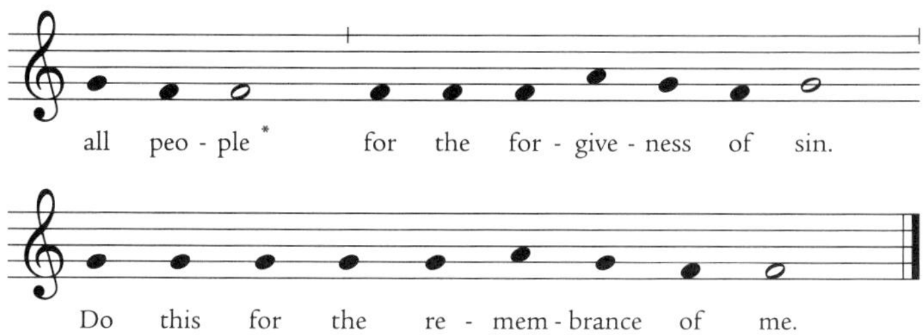

* The phrase "for all people" replaces the "for many" that was in LW version. Neither phrase appeared in Luther's original text.

It seems to me that it would accord with the Lord's Supper to administer the sacrament immediately after the consecration of the bread, before the cup is blessed, for both Luke and Paul say: He took the cup after supper, etc. [Luke 22:20; 1 Cor. 11:25]. Meanwhile, the German *Sanctus*[65] or the hymn, "Let God Be Blest,"[66] or the hymn of Jan Hus, "Jesus Christ, Our God and Savior,"[67] could be sung. Then shall the cup be blessed and administered, while the remainder of these hymns are sung, or the German *Agnus Dei*.[68] And that this happens in a decent and orderly manner, not men and women together, but the women after the men; they should also stand[69] apart from each other in separate places. What should be done about private confession, I have written elsewhere, and my opinion can be found in the *Little Prayer Book*.[70]

We do not want to abolish the elevation,[71] but retain it because it goes well with the German *Sanctus* and signifies that Christ has commanded us to remember him. For just as the sacrament is bodily elevated, yet Christ's body and blood are not seen in it, so he is also remembered and elevated by the word of the sermon as well as confessed and adored in the reception of the sacrament. In all this, Christ is apprehended only by faith. For we cannot see

65. German *Sanctus*, or "Holy, Holy, Holy," is a hymn that Luther wrote based on Isaiah 6 and Isaiah's encounter with God in the temple, "Isaiah in a Vision Did of Old." See ELW 868; LSB 960.

66. "O Lord, We Praise You," LW 53:252–54. See also ELW 499; LSB 617.

67. This hymn first appeared in the Wittenberg hymnal of 1524. See LW 53:249–51.

68. *Agnus Dei*, or "Lamb of God," which is often sung today as the distribution of Holy Communion begins.

69. Note that people stood during the service. Pews did not yet exist.

70. Throughout his life, Luther advocated for the private confession of sins though he always recognized Christian freedom in this matter. Private confession was to be freed of the burden of "works," that is, the enumeration of sins was not to be the source of comfort (because no one could be sure that they have confessed each and every sin) but, rather, God's word of forgiveness unconditionally given. In the *Personal [Little] Prayer Book* (LW 43:3–45; TAL 4:159–200, forthcoming), Luther simplifies the medieval catalogue of sins used to prepare for confession and replaces it with the Ten Commandments. The Ten Commandments serve as a guide to confession and to the good fruits of repentance. See also *Apology of the Augsburg Confession*, Article XII: "Repentence," in BC, 217. See also the *Augsburg Confession*, Article XXV (BC, 73ff.); and Luther's *Smalcald Articles*, "Concerning Confession" (BC, 321; TAL 2:458–59).

71. Luther understood the elevation to be simply showing or presenting the elements to the people to remind them of Christ's passion. It was not an offering to God (*Against the Heavenly Prophets in the Matter*

how Christ gives his body and blood for us and even now daily shows and offers it before God assuring us of grace.[72]

The German Sanctus[f]

f See n. 65.

of Images and Sacraments, LW 40:137; see also TAL 2:96). Luther, however, did not want to impose the practice. (In the medieval liturgy, the priest would raise or "elevate" the elements during the words of institution while the choir sang the *Sanctus*.) In Wittenberg, Johannes Bugenhagen (1485–1558) did away with the elevation and Luther did not object. In Luther's opinion, the presider was to remain free: "Yes, it's of little consequence to us. We don't care if it's abolished or not, provided the abuse—that is, the adoration—is not there. Some churches have seen that we have dropped the elevation [in Wittenberg] and have imitated us. We are pleased with that" (*Table Talk*, LW 54:462).

72. The primary focal point of the medieval liturgy of the Mass was divine sacrifice. The priest showed and offered Christ as a sacrifice to God. The priest was able to do this because of the power of his ordination, and his action in the Mass was considered meritorious in and of itself. By way of contrast, Luther makes the point that Christ is the great high priest showing and offering himself to the Father on behalf of all people, and all that is left for Christians to do, the presider included, is to receive his gifts.

The collect follows with the benediction:

We give thanks to you, Almighty God, that you have refreshed us with your salutary gift; and we beseech your mercy to strengthen us through the same in faith toward you, and in fervent love among us all; for the sake of Jesus Christ our Lord. Amen.

The Lord bless you and keep you.
The Lord's face shine on you and be gracious to you.
The Lord look upon you with favor and give you peace.

Exercise or Practice for the Intoning[73]

For those who would like to become more experienced and skillful in singing the colons, commas, and other pauses, I give another example.[g] Someone else may choose another.

This is what I have to say concerning the daily liturgy and instruction in the Word of God, which serves primarily to train the young and challenge the uneducated. For those who itch for new things will soon be bored and tired with it all, as they were with the Latin service. There was singing and reading in the churches every day, and yet the churches remained deserted and empty. Already they do the same in the German service. Therefore, it is best to plan the liturgy in the interest of the young and those of the uneducated who may happen to come. With the others neither law nor order, neither scolding nor coaxing, will help. Allow them to leave those things in the liturgy alone which they refuse to do willingly and gladly. God is not pleased with unwilling services; they are futile and vain.

But on the festivals, such as Christmas, Easter, Pentecost, St. Michael's, Purification,[74] and the like, we must continue to use Latin until we have enough German songs. This work is only beginning; therefore, not everything that is required is ready. At least one knows how to approach a common pattern in order that counsel and measure may be found for the many various orders.

Lent, Palm Sunday, and Holy Week are to be retained, not to force anyone to fast, but to preserve the Passion story and the Gospels appointed for that season. This, however, does not include the Lenten veil,[75] throwing of palms, veiling of pictures, and whatever other superstitious practices there might be; neither does it include chanting the four Passions, nor preaching on the Passion for eight hours on Good Friday. Holy Week should be like any other week except that the Passion history should be explained every day for an hour throughout the week or on as many days as may be desirable, and that the sacrament should be given to everyone who desires it. For among Christians everything in worship should center in the Word and sacrament.

g At this point in the translated text of LW 53 an additional sample of an Epistle setting and an additional sample of a Gospel setting are included. They have not been included in this edition but can be found in LW53:84-89.

73. For an unexplainable reason, the exercises presented at the end of the German Mass do not correspond to the earlier examples.

74. The Feast of the Presentation of Our Lord in the Temple, also known as the Purification of Our Lady (2 February). In the old liturgical calendar, it closes the Christmas cycle.

75. The *Hungertuch*, or "Lenten Veil," was a large fabric hung in front of the choir and sanctuary area of a church, separating the assembly optically from the altar. It often depicted the crucifix, though in its revival in modern practice, the fabric or cloth tells the whole story of Jesus through images.

In short, this or any other order is to be used in such a way that whenever it becomes an abuse, it will be immediately abolished and replaced by another, even as King Hezekiah put away and destroyed the brazen serpent because the children of Israel made an abuse of it, even though God had commanded it be made [2 Kgs. 18:4]. For the orders should serve the advancement[76] of faith and love and not to the detriment of faith. When they no longer do this, they are invalid, dead and gone, just as a good coin, when counterfeited, is canceled and changed because of the abuse, or as new shoes when they become old and uncomfortable are no longer worn, but thrown away, and new ones bought. An order is an external thing. No matter how good it is, it can be abused. Then it is no longer an order, but a disorder. Therefore, no order is valid in itself—as the papal orders were held to be until now. But the life, value, power, and virtue of any order is in its proper use.[77] Otherwise it is utterly worthless and good for nothing. God's Spirit and grace be with us all. Amen.

Martin Luther

76. The German *fordderung* (modern German: *Forderung*) literally means "challenge." Luther suggests that the order of liturgy should "challenge" faith and love to deepen and grow.

77. For Luther, the "proper use" was always for the proclamation of the gospel.

The title page of *Das diese wort Christi (Das ist mein leib, etce) noch fest stehen widder die Schwermgeister (That These Words of Christ [This Is My Body etc.] Still Stand Firm Against the Fanatics)* published in Wittenberg by Michael Lotther (1527). The treatise was reprinted seven times in 1527.

That These Words of Christ, "This Is My Body," etc., Still Stand Firm Against the Fanatics

1527

AMY NELSON BURNETT

INTRODUCTION

The Evangelical movement was united in its opposition to the Roman church, but by the mid-1520s it was fragmenting as disagreements in theology and practice emerged. None of these disagreements would be more important for the development of Protestantism than the eucharistic controversy that began in the fall of 1524. Underlying that controversy was the question of how Evangelicals defined heresy. Catholics denounced Luther and his followers as heretics from the beginning of the Reformation, but the Evangelicals insisted that their teachings were based on the word of God and so could not be heretical. Evangelicals agreed with their Catholic opponents, however, that rejection of the trinitarian and christological positions formulated by the church councils of the fourth and fifth centuries was heretical. The status of other doctrines was not so clear, and Evangelicals would divide over the question of Christ's bodily presence in the consecrated elements of the Eucharist. Was belief in that presence an essential part of the Christian faith whose rejection was heresy, or was it an error introduced by the medieval church?

In the ninth century and again in the eleventh century, debates over the Eucharist resulted in the church's emphasis on the presence of Christ's body and blood in the consecrated elements. The

Fourth Lateran Council of 1215 made this position official when it declared that Christ's body and blood were "truly contained in the sacrament of the altar under the species of bread and wine, the bread being transubstantiated into the body, the wine into the blood by divine power." Transubstantiation was understood in Aristotelian terms as the conversion of the substance of bread and wine into Christ's body and blood, although the outward appearance or "accidents" remained unchanged.[a] Late-medieval preachers emphasized the presence of Christ's body and blood in the consecrated host and encouraged devotional practices that reinforced this belief. Those who questioned that presence were condemned and burned at the stake as heretics.

In *On the Babylonian Captivity of the Church*[b] Luther argued that the church had no right to require acceptance of a particular Scholastic formulation, but he did not question the belief that the consecrated elements were Christ's true body and blood. Others were more radical than Luther, although fear of persecution kept them from voicing their views publicly. One who would be particularly influential was the Dutch jurist Cornelius Hoen, whose *Most Christian Letter* circulated in manuscript through the early 1520s. Hoen marshaled arguments taken from various sources, including popular heresy, to argue against Christ's bodily presence in the elements of bread and wine, and he suggested that Christ's words, "This is my body," should be understood as "This signifies my body."[1]

Luther's colleague in the Wittenberg theology faculty, Andreas Bodenstein von Karlstadt (1486–1541), was the first reformer to reject Christ's bodily presence in print. In the fall of 1524 Karlstadt published several pamphlets in which he asserted that Scripture did not teach that the bread and wine became Christ's body and blood. Luther responded to these pamphlets with a major work published in two parts, *Against the Heavenly Prophets*.[c] Karlstadt published a quasi-retraction of his views in

1. Cornelius Hoen (d. 1524) was arrested by the Inquisition in 1522 but released in the fall of 1524 and died a few months later. See Bart Jan Spruyt, *Cornelius Henrici Hoen (Honius) and His Epistle on the Eucharist (1525)*, Studies in Medieval and Reformation Traditions 119 (Leiden: Brill, 2006), 73–84; this work includes a critical edition of the Latin pamphlet and its contemporary German translation, 226–51. There is a partial English translation in Heiko A. Oberman, *Forerunners of the Reformation: The Shape of Late Medieval Thought Illustrated by Key Documents* (Philadelphia: Fortress Press, 1981), 268–78. Luther had read Hoen's pamphlet by 1523, for he rejected the equation of "is" with "signifies" in *The Adoration of the Sacrament*, LW 36:279–84.

a James F. McCue, "The Doctrine of Transubstantiation from Berengar through Trent: The Point at Issue," *Harvard Theological Review* 61 (1968): 385–430.

b See pp. 9–129 in this volume; also LW 36:3–136.

c LW 40:79–223; TAL 2:39–126. See Amy Nelson Burnett, *Karlstadt and the Origins of the Eucharistic Controversy: A Study in the Circulation of Ideas*, Oxford Studies in Reformation Theology (New York: Oxford University Press, 2011), 54–76.

the fall of 1525 and withdrew from the public debate, but by that time Hoen's pamphlet had been published and other works rejecting Christ's bodily presence were circulating. Luther condemned their authors as "sacramentarians" because they argued that the bread and wine were only signs and did not contain Christ's true body and blood.[2]

2. The term comes from the definition of *sacramentum* as a "sign of a sacred thing."

The sacramentarians may have disagreed about how they understood the Lord's Supper, but they were united in rejecting Christ's bodily presence in the consecrated elements, and in the first phase of the controversy, that was the only issue that mattered. Luther and his followers understood Christ's words, "This is my body," literally, and believed that the church had taught Christ's bodily presence since its foundation and rejection of that presence was therefore heretical. The sacramentarians, however, regarded the bodily presence as a medieval invention that enhanced the tyranny of the clergy and encouraged popular superstition and even idolatry, since it led to worship of bread, and they vigorously rejected the charge of heresy.

A portrait of Ulrich Zwingli by Hans Asper (1499–1571).

The reformers of Zurich, Basel, and Strasbourg became the most outspoken defenders of a sacramentarian position. In the spring and summer of 1525 Ulrich Zwingli (1484–1531) published three works in Latin that were quickly translated into German: a *Letter to Matthias Alber on the Lord's Supper*,[d] *Subsidiary Essay or Crown of the Work on the Eucharist*,[e] and *Commentary on True*

d Zwingli, *Ad Matthaeum Alberum de Caena Dominica Epistola*, Z 3:335–54; Ger. trans., *Epistel oder sendbrieff von des Herren nachtmal* (Zurich: Hager, 1525); English trans., HZW 2:131–45.

e Zwingli, *Subsidium sive Coronis de Eucharistia*, Z 4:440–504; Ger. trans., *Nachhüt von dem Nachtmal oder der Dancksagung Christi* (Zurich: Froschauer, 1525); Eng. trans., HZW 2:194–231.

and False Religion, a section of which was devoted to the Lord's Supper.[f] His counterpart in Basel, Johannes Oecolampadius (1482–1531), published an even more important work, *On the Genuine Exposition of the Lord's Words, "This Is My Body," According to the Oldest Authorities*,[g] that cited many of the church fathers to argue that the early church did not believe the elements became Christ's body and blood. From Strasbourg, Martin Bucer (1491–1551) sent copies of Oecolampadius's book and defended its arguments to Johannes Brenz (1499–1570) in Schwäbisch Hall and to others throughout southern Germany.

The new view of the Lord's Supper did not go unchallenged. Johannes Bugenhagen (1485–1558), Luther's colleague and pastor, published an *Open Letter Against the New Error on the Sacrament* aimed at Karlstadt and Zwingli.[h] Hoping to prevent further public debate, the Strasbourgers sent Gregor Casel (d. 1528) to Wittenberg with letters asking the Wittenbergers to consider the harm to the Evangelical movement caused by dissension within its ranks, and so to refrain from further public attacks.[i] Luther rebuffed their overtures, however, and the public debate only grew more heated over the next few months. The Nuremberg patrician Willibald Pirckheimer (1470–1530) published a *Response to Johannes Oecolampadius on the True Flesh of Christ and His True Blood*,[j] while the Nördlingen reformer Theobald Billican (d. 1554) wrote a *Letter on the Words of the Lord's Supper and the Vari-*

f Zwingli, *De vera et falsa religione commentarius*, Z 3:773–820; Ger. trans., *Von dem Nachtmal Christi/vidergedechtnus/oder dancksagung Huldrychen Zuinglis meinung* (Zurich: Froschauer, 1525); Eng. trans., Zwingli, *Commentary on True and False Religion*, ed. Samuel Macauley Jackson (Durham, NC: Labyrinth Press, 1981), 197–253.

g *Ioannis Oecolampadii de genvina verborum domini, hoc est corpus meum, iuxta uetustissimos authores, expositione liber* (Strasbourg: Knobloch, 1525); the treatise would have an even broader influence through the German translation by Ludwig Hätzer, *Vom Sacrament der Dancksagung. Von dem waren nateurlichen verstand der worten Christi: DAS IST MEIN LEIB nach der gar alten Lerern erklärung* (Zurich: Froschauer, 1526).

h Bugenhagen, *Contra novvm errorem, de sacramento corporis et sangvinis domini nostri Iesv Christi epistola Ioannis Bvgenhagii Pomerani* (Wittenberg: Lotter, 1525); Ger. trans., W[2] 20:500–506.

i The correspondence can be found in WA Br 3:585–87, 599–607; BCorr 2:46–48, 55–59, 71–78; BDS 3:421–30.

j Pirckheimer, *De vera Christi carne et vero eius sanguine ad Ioannem Oecolampadium responsio*, WPBW 6:80–85, 435–502.

ety of Opinions, which was published, with an approving response, by his Augsburg colleague Urbanus Rhegius (1489–1541).[k] Johannes Brenz wrote both a refutation of Oecolampadius's book in the name of his fellow Swabian pastors, the *Syngramma on the Words of the Lord's Supper*,[l] and a *Letter on the Lord's Words,*

Portrait of Willibald Pirckheimer engraved by Albrecht Dürer (1524).

A seventeenth-century engraving of Johannes Brenz.

k Billican, *De verbis coenae dominicae et opinionum uarietate. Theobaldi Billicani ad Vrbanum Regium epistola. Responsio Vrbani Regij ad eundem* (Augsburg: Ruff, 1526); Ger. trans., W² 17:1547–70.

l Brenz, *Syngramma clarissimorum qui Halae Suevorum convenerunt virorum super verbis cenae dominicae ad Johannem Oecolampadium*, in Johannes Brenz, *Werke. Eine Studienausgabe* (Tübingen: Mohr, 1970-86), 1/1:234–78.

"This Is My Body,"[m] addressed to Bucer. These works in turn produced rebuttals from the Swiss reformers[3] and from Bucer[n] in the spring of 1526. Although Oecolampadius and Bucer still wrote in Latin, Zwingli switched to German in order to give a *Clear Instruction on the Christ's Supper for the Sake of the Simple.*[o] The debate broadened further as radicals influenced by Karlstadt began to publish pamphlets attacking Christ's bodily presence.

Luther watched the growing controversy with concern. He believed that he had effectively countered the arguments of the sacramentarians in *Against the Heavenly Prophets*, but he provided a preface for the German translation of the *Syngramma* by the Eisleben schoolmaster Johann Agricola (1494–1566).[4] Oecolampadius responded to this attack on his *Genuine Exposition* in the summer of 1526 with his first German treatise, *Reasonable Answer to Martin Luther's Instruction Concerning the Sacrament.*[p]

At about the same time, Luther became aware that Bucer had inserted his own views of the Lord's Supper into his German version of Bugenhagen's Psalms commentary and in his annotations and prefaces to his Latin translation of Luther's postil. Zwingli's colleague Leo Jud (1482–1542) had also published a pamphlet, under the pseudonym of Ludwig Leopoldus, claiming that Erasmus, Luther, and Zwingli all agreed concerning the Lord's Supper.[q] Luther saw these publications as deliberate attempts to make readers think the Wittenbergers agreed with the sacramentarians. Although Luther's Wittenberg friends had

3. Zwingli wrote responses to Bugenhagen, Z 4:558–76 (Ger. trans., W² 20:506–21); and to Billican and Rhegius, Z 4:893–941. Oecolampadius combined his responses to the *Syngramma* and to Billican in one lengthy treatise, *Apologetica de dignitate Evcharistiae Sermones duo. Ad Theobaldvm Billicanvm quinam in uerbis Caenae alienum sensum inferant. Ad Ecclesiastas Svevos Antisyngramma* (Zurich: Froschauer, 1526), and published separately *Ad Billibaldum Pyrkaimerum de re Eucharistiae responsio* (Zurich: Froschauer, 1526).

4. This translation was published as the *Well-Founded and Sure Conclusion of Certain Preachers in Swabia Concerning the Words of the Supper . . . Written to Johann Oecolampadius*; Luther's preface is in LW 59:156–61. An earlier translation of the *Syngramma*, with a different title, had been published in Augsburg; a later translation with yet another title would be published, also with a preface by Luther, a few months later in Wittenberg.

m Brenz, *Epistola de verbis domini: Hoc est corpus meum*, BDS 2:39–45.

n *Apologia Martini Buceri qua fidei suae atque doctrinae, circa Christi coenam . . . rationem simpliciter reddit* (Strasbourg: Herwagen, 1526); abridged English trans. as "The Eucharist: The 1526 Apology," in *Common Places of Martin Bucer*, trans. and ed. D. F. Wright (Appleford, England: Sutton Courtenay Press, 1972), 313–53.

o Zwingli, *Eine klare Unterrichtung vom Nachtmahl Christi*, Z 4:773-862; English trans. as "On the Lord's Supper," in *Zwingli and Bullinger*, trans. and ed. G. W. Bromiley, Library of Christian Classics 24 (Philadelphia: Westminster, 1953), 185–238.

p Oecolampadius, *Billiche Antwortt auff D. Martin Luthers bericht des sacraments halb* (Augsburg: Steiner, 1526); the work also contained a German rebuttal of the *Syngramma*. There is a critical edition of the first part, addressed to Luther, in Adolf Laube et al., *Flugschriften vom Bauernkrieg zum Täuferreich (1526–1535)*, 2 vols. (Berlin: Akademie Verlag, 1992), 1:137–55; the entire treatise is in W² 20:582–635.

q Jud (Leopoldus), *Des hochgelehrten Erasmi von Rotterdam und Doktor Luthers Meinung vom Nachtmal Jesu Christi* (Zurich: Froschauer, 1526).

published his three Holy Week sermons on the Lord's Supper in the fall of 1526 as a way of making the reformer's position better known,[r] Luther resolved to enter the public debate himself with a treatise intended to respond to all of the sacramentarians.

Luther began work on *That These Words of Christ, "This Is My Body," etc., Still Stand Firm Against the Fanatics* at the beginning of 1527. The rather cumbersome title summarized the heart of his argument: Christ's words, "This is my body," must be understood literally, despite all efforts by the sacramentarians to interpret them differently. In accordance with the precepts of classical rhetoric, he first asserted his own position and then refuted the position of his opponents.[s] Rather than responding to individual pamphlets, Luther grouped his opponents' arguments under three main headings: that Christ had ascended into heaven and his body was seated at the right hand of the Father, as the creeds said, and so could not be in the consecrated elements of the supper; that Christ's statement, "The flesh is of no use" (John 6:63), meant that the carnal eating of his body was useless; and that the church fathers had not taught that Christ was bodily present in the elements. These arguments had been made most strongly by Oecolampadius in his Latin treatises, especially his *Genuine Exposition*, and had been repeated by other sacramentarians, including Zwingli. Luther also repeated arguments that other Evangelicals had advanced in their pamphlets against the sacramentarians. His discussion of the church fathers was especially indebted to Pirckheimer's two *Responses* to Oecolampadius, the second of which was published while Luther was writing his treatise.[t]

r *The Sacrament of the Body and Blood of Christ—Against the Fanatics*, LW 36:335–61.

s Amy Nelson Burnett, "Rhetoric and Refutation in Luther's *That These Words Still Stand Firm*," *Lutheran Quarterly* 29 (2015): 284–303.

t Pirckheimer, *Bilibaldi Birckheimheri de vera Christi carne & vero eius sanguine, ad Ioan. Oecolampadium responsio*, WPBW 6:80–85, 435–502; idem, *Responsio secunda de vera Christi carne et vero eius sanguine adversum convicia Joannis, qui sibi Oecolampadii nomen indidit*, WPBW 6:247–52 and 7:511–88; Amy Nelson Burnett, "'According to the Oldest Authorities': The Use of the Church Fathers in the Early Eucharistic Controversy," in Anne Marie Johnson and John A. Maxfield, eds., *The Reformation as Christianization: Essays on Scott Hendrix's Christianization Thesis*, Spätmittelalter, Humanismus, Reformation 66 (Tübingen: Mohr Siebeck, 2012), 373–95.

Luther finished his treatise in time for the spring book fair in Frankfurt. Zwingli also wrote two treatises on the Lord's Supper, available at the book fair, his *Friendly Exegesis* in Latin and his *Friendly Admonition Concerning Luther's Sermon* in German.[u] Both he and Oecolampadius would quickly pen rejoinders to Luther's *That These Words Stand Firm*,[v] and in response Luther would write his final *Confession Concerning Christ's Supper*.[5] With these treatises the positions of the two sides were clear. Despite later negotiations and elaboration of positions on both sides, the division within the Evangelical movement would never be mended.

5. LW 37:161–372. Zwingli and Oecolampadius published a joint response, *Über D. Martin Luthers Buch, Bekenntnis genannt, zwei Antworten*. Z 6/2:1–248 contains only Zwingli's contribution; Oecolampadius's contribution is in W² 20:1,378–1,472.

THAT THESE WORDS OF CHRIST, "THIS IS MY BODY," ETC., STILL STAND FIRM AGAINST THE FANATICS[6]

6. The critical edition of *That These Words Stand Firm* in WA 23:38–320 includes the texts of both the first printed edition and the manuscript that was the basis for that edition. This translation is based on the printed text, since that was the version that reached a public audience. It follows but updates the translation by Robert Fischer in LW 37:3–150. The notes in WA and LW provided a starting point for my own annotations, but I have added to and corrected them in order to draw attention to Luther's interaction with works concerning the Lord's Supper by his opponents and supporters.

[The Devil and Heresy][w]

THAT PROVERB WE USE IS VERY TRUE, which says that the devil is master of a thousand arts! He proves this powerfully in all those things through which he rules his world: in physical, outward tricks, guile, sins, wickedness, murder, destruction, etc. But especially and beyond all measure he demonstrates this in spiritual, inward matters that concern the glory of God and conscience. How he

u Zwingli, *Amica Exegesis*, Z 5:548–758; idem, *Freundlich Verglimpfung über die Predigt Luthers*, Z 5:771–94.

v Zwingli, *Das diese Worte, "Das ist mein Leib" etc. ewiglich den alten Sinn haben warden*, Z 5:805–977; Oecolampadius, *Daß der Mißverstand . . . nit bestehn mag. Die ander billich antwort* (Basel: Cratander, 1527).

w Headings in brackets were added throughout to guide the reader and were not in the original manuscript.

can slither, squirm, twist, and turn in all directions, and hinder and thwart us on all sides, that no one may be saved and remain in the Christian truth. Let us consider the history of Christianity (I won't mention the ancient fathers and the Jews) as an example. In the beginning of the gospel, when God's Word was preached by the apostles purely and clearly, and no human commandments but only Holy Scripture was set forth, it seemed as if there would never be any trouble, since Holy Scripture was the empress among the Christians.

But what could the devil not do? He finally permitted Scripture to be the sole authority, and allowed no pharisaical, Jewish commandments or laws concerning works to prevail any longer. But he also had some of his followers in the Christians' schools, through whom he stealthily snuck and crept into Holy Scripture.[7] Once he was inside and was sure of his position, he burst out on all sides, creating a real brawl over Scripture and producing many sects, heresies, and factions among Christians. Since every faction claimed Scripture for itself and interpreted it according to its own understanding, the result was that Scripture began to lose its worth, and eventually even acquired the reputation of being a heretics' book and the source of all heresy, since all heretics seek the aid of Scripture. Thus the devil was able to wrest from the Christians their weapons, armor, and fortress (i.e., Scripture), so that it not only became feeble and ineffective against him, but it even had to fight against the Christians themselves. He got Christians to become suspicious of it, as if it were plain poison against which they had to defend themselves. Tell me, wasn't that a clever scheme of the devil?

Once Scripture had become like a broken net and no one would be restrained by it, but everyone poked a hole in it wherever they stuck their snouts, and followed their own opinions, interpreting and twisting Scripture any way they pleased, the Christians knew no other way to cope with these problems than to call many councils.[8] In these they issued many outward laws and ordinances alongside Scripture, in order to keep the common people together in the face of these divisions. From this undertaking (though they meant well) arose the saying that Scripture was not sufficient, that we also needed the laws and interpretations of councils and the fathers, and that the Holy Spirit did not reveal everything to the apostles but reserved certain things for the fathers. Out of this finally developed the papacy, in which

7. Luther is thinking especially of the heresies of the fourth and fifth centuries, but his discussion also reflects his attitude toward Andreas Bodenstein von Karlstadt, his colleague on the Wittenberg theology faculty, who had worked closely with him at the beginning of the Reformation but whose disagreements with Luther became apparent by the spring of 1522.

8. The Councils of Nicaea (325) and Constantinople (381) concerned the Arian heresy; the Councils of Ephesus (431) and Chalcedon (451) concerned christological heresies.

there is no authority but human commandments and glosses[9] according to the "chamber of the holy father's heart."[10]

When the devil saw this he jeered and thought, "Now I have won! Scripture lies prostrate, the fortress is destroyed, the weapons are beaten down. In their place they now weave walls of straw and make weapons of hay, i.e., they intend now to array themselves against me with human commandments. Now it becomes serious: what shall I do? I won't fight against this but will help them build in confidence, so that they remain nicely united and gather enough straw and hay.[x] It serves me well that they do not dispute over Scripture and neglect the Word, but that on this very point they are at peace and believe what the councils and the fathers say. But within this peace and unity I will stir up other controversies and quarrels, so that the pope will contend against emperor and kings, bishops against princes and lords, scholars against scholars, clerics against clerics, and everyone against the other, for the sake of temporal honor, possessions, and pleasure, yet leaving untouched their unity of belief in the holy fathers.[11] The fools! What can they expect to accomplish with quarrels over Scripture and the things of God they do not understand? It is better for them to quarrel over honor, kingdoms, principalities, property, pleasure, and bodily needs, which they do understand, and meanwhile remain pious Christians united in the glossed faith of the fathers, i.e., a flimsy faith."[y]

This is the way the attack went on the fathers: because they thought they should have Scripture without quarreling and dissension, this became the cause of turning wholly and completely away from Scripture to pure human drivel. Then, of course, there was necessarily an end to dissension and contention over Scripture, which is a divine quarrel in which God contends with the devil, as St. Paul says in Ephesians 6[:12], "We have to contend not against flesh and blood, but against spiritual wickedness in the air." But in place of this, there has broken out human dissension over honor and goods on earth, yet there remain a united blindness, a lack of understanding of Scripture, and a loss of the true Christian faith, i.e., a united obedience to the glosses of the fathers and to the holy see at Rome. Isn't this also a piece of devil-

x An allusion to 1 Cor. 3:12-13.

y An untranslatable pun in German, where the words for "gloss" and "flimsy" rhyme.

9. A gloss was the explanation of a word or passage printed in the margin of a book.

10. A decree of Boniface VIII (b. c. 1235; pope from 1294 to 1303) incorporated into canon law stated that the Roman pontiff has all laws "in the chamber of his heart"; *Sexti Decretalium*, lib. I, tit. II, cap. 1, CIC 2:937.

11. Beginning with the Investiture Controversy in the eleventh century, much of medieval history is marked by struggles between popes and rulers for both control of appointment to high church office and secular control of the Italian peninsula. Within the Holy Roman Empire there were struggles over control of the church between bishops and territorial rulers, religious orders competed with each other for adherents, and parish clergy and friars fought over the rights and income associated with providing pastoral care.

ish craftiness? No matter what play we make, he is a master and an expert at the game.

Now in our day, because we saw that Scripture was utterly neglected[z] and that the devil made us captives and fools with the mere straw and hay of human commands, we have tried by God's grace to aid the situation. With immense and bitter effort indeed we have brought Scripture to the fore again and dismissed human commands, freed ourselves and escaped the devil, although he stubbornly resisted and still resists. But although he had to let us go, he does not forget his tricks and has secretly sown his seeds among us[a] so that they may take hold of our teachings and words. This is done not to aid and assist us in fostering Scripture, but, while we were leading the fight against human drivel, they would attack us from behind, incite rebellion, and raise an uproar against us so that, caught between two enemies, we would more easily be destroyed.[12] This is what I call throwing quicksilver into the pool![13]

He does not leave the matter there, though, but begins most quickly with the sacraments, although on this topic he has already torn at least ten holes and ways of escape in Scripture. I have never read of a more shameful heresy, which from the outset has so many heads, so many factions and dissensions among itself, although they are united on the main point, the persecution of Christ.[14] But he will keep on and attack still other articles of faith, as he already declares with flashing eyes that baptism, original sin, and Christ are nothing.[15] Once more there will arise a brawl over the Scriptures, and such dissension and so many factions that we may well say with St. Paul, "The mystery of lawlessness is already at work" [2 Thess. 2:7], just as he also saw that many more factions would arise after him.

If the world lasts much longer, people will do as the ancients did on account of this dissension, and again seek human schemes and issue laws and commands to keep the people in the unity of the faith. Their success will be the same as it was in the past. In short, the devil is too clever and too mighty for us. He resists and hinders us at every point. When we wish to deal with Scripture, he creates so much dissension and quarreling over it that we become tired and too weak to trust Scripture and must

z Lit., "lay under the bench."

a Matt. 13:25.

12. The two enemies are the Catholics and those in the Evangelical movement who went beyond Luther by advocating a reform of society according to God's law. Luther blamed the latter for the Peasants' War of 1525.

13. It was a common German belief that casting mercury into a well would destroy its ability to hold water.

14. Luther made this point already in early 1526 when he wrote to the church of Reutlingen that his opponents could not agree on how to interpret Christ's statement, "This is my body," WA 19:121–23.

15. Both Zwingli, *Commentary*, 184–87, and Oecolampadius, *Billiche Antwortt*, W^2 20:612, saw baptism only as an external sign. Luther regarded Zwingli's assertion that righteous pagans could be saved as denial of original sin. Zwingli, "Declaration Regarding Original Sin," in Ulrich Zwingli, *On Providence and Other Essays*, The Latin Works and the Correspondence of Huldreich Zwingli 2 (Durham: Labyrinth Press, 1983), 12–13.

forever be scuffling and wrestling with him. If we wish to stand upon human councils and counsels, we lose Scripture entirely and remain in the devil's possession, body and soul.[b] He is and is called Satan, i.e., an adversary.[16] He must be an adversary and cause misfortune; he cannot do otherwise. Moreover, he is the prince and god of this world,[c] so that he has sufficient power to do so. Since he is able and determined to do all this, we should not think that we will have peace from him. He takes no vacation and he does not sleep. Choose, then, whether you would rather wrestle with the devil or else belong to him. If you consent to be his, you will receive his guarantee to leave you in peace with Scripture. If you refuse to be his, then grab him by the hair! He won't fail you but will create such dissension and factions over Scripture that you will not know where Scripture, faith, Christ, and you yourself stand. [. . .][d]

It is precisely the same devil who now assails us through the fanatics[17] by blaspheming the holy and venerable sacrament of our Lord Jesus Christ, out of which they would like to make mere bread and wine as a symbol or memorial sign of Christians, as they dream or fancy. They allege that the Lord's body and blood are not present, even though the plain, clear words stand right there: "Eat, this is my body," and those words still stand firm and invulnerable against them. Now, I dealt with this subject carefully in my attack against Karlstadt,[18] in such a way that anyone who did not take pleasure in erring could find guidance against this specter of the devil.[e] But my dear fanatics despise me so haughtily that they do not consider me worthy of a careful answer. It is enough for them to look at my book and turn up their noses at it and say, "It lacks Spirit." How does it help if I write at length? They scorn it, and if they just babble a few words about it, without touching a single argument correctly, they consider it refuted. They rest their case only on writing many books and soiling much paper.

16. The Hebrew word *Satan* means "adversary"; cf. 1 Pet. 5:8.

17. *Schwärmer*, a term derived from the swarming of bees, which Luther used against all those who claimed the inspiration of the Holy Spirit prior to or apart from Scripture. He first used the term against Thomas Müntzer (c. 1489–1525) and the Zwickau prophets, three men who came to Wittenberg at the turn of 1521–22 claiming to have visions from God. By 1524 he had extended the term to include Karlstadt and all those who rejected Christ's bodily presence in the bread and wine. "Fanatic" is the conventional translation of *Schwärmer*, although the word has lost the sense that it had in the seventeenth century of one who acts as if possessed or mad.

18. In a series of pamphlets published in the fall of 1524, Karlstadt was the first to claim in print that the bread and wine remained simply bread and wine in the Lord's Supper. Luther responded to these pamphlets in *Against the Heavenly Prophets*, published in two parts at the turn of 1524–25.

b Lit., "with skin and hair."

c John 12:31.

d Here and elsewhere in the treatise, bracketed ellipses denote that a portion of the treatise has been omitted. Here, a portion of LW 37:17–18.

e *Against the Heavenly Prophets*, Part II, LW 40:144–223; TAL 2:39–126.

One of the reasons I have hesitated until now to write further against them is that I have sensed such arrogance and contempt beneath their celebrated humility. Secondly, their fanaticism is such sheer, empty prattle that it amazes me how these fine, erudite people ever got entangled with it. They proceed, moreover, with such a timid, despairing conscience that it appears to me they wish the beer were back again in the keg. Had they not started the affair, I believe, they would now leave well enough alone. I see in this affair nothing but the wrath of God, who gives the devil free rein to produce crude, clumsy errors and thick darkness to punish our shameful ingratitude for having scorned the holy gospel and held it as worthless, "so that," as St. Paul says, "we believe what is false, because we have not accepted the love of truth" [2 Thess. 2:10-11]. This fanaticism, moreover, lacks nothing but being new. For we Germans are the kind of fellows who pounce upon anything new and cling to it like fools, and whoever restrains us only makes us more crazy for it; but if no one restrains us, we will soon on our own become fed up and bored with it, and soon chase after something else that is new. Thus the devil has the advantage that no teaching or dream, however crazy, can arise but he can find disciples for it, and the crazier it is, the faster they come.

A portrait of Andreas Bodenstein von Karlstadt (c. 1541).

But "God's word alone endures forever" [Isa. 40:8]; errors always spring up by its side and pass away again. For this reason I am not worried that this fanaticism will last long. It is much too crude and impudent, and it does not attack obscure or uncertain Scripture, but instead clear, plain Scripture, as we shall hear. So I shall once more set myself against the devil and his fanatics, not for their sake, but for the sake of the weak and simple. For I have no hope that the teachers of a heresy or fanaticism will be converted. Indeed, if that were possible, so much has already been written that they would have been converted. It has never been reported that the originator of false doctrine was converted. For this sin is too great, because it blasphemes God's Word and sins against the Holy Spirit.[f] Therefore God lets it become hardened, with the result, according to the word of Isa. 6[:9-10], "With seeing eyes you shall not see and with hearing ears you shall not hear, for this people's heart is hardened."

Christ did not convert any high priests, but their disciples were indeed converted—Nicodemus, Joseph, Paul, and the like.[g] The ancient prophets did not convert any false prophets. Paul, too, was not able to convert false apostles, but he laid down the teaching: "When one has been admonished two or three times, let that person be avoided and dismissed as perverted" [Titus 3:10]. So too the holy teachers have never converted an arch-heretic; not because they had not sufficiently opposed and confuted all the heretics' errors with the truth, but their hearts were obsessed with their own fancies, and they fared the same as those who look through a colored glass: place before them whatever color you will, they see no other color than that of their glass. The fault is not that you have placed the wrong color before them but that their glass has a different color, as the same passage in Isa. [6:9] also puts it, "You shall see," he says, "and yet not see." What is this but to say: It will appear before your eyes quite clearly enough for you to see, and others will see it, but you will not. This is the reason, says John 12[:40], that one cannot convert such people. The proffered truth does not do it. God must take away the colored glass; this we cannot do.

Even if I too cannot convert any arch-fanatic, yet I shall leave nothing undone, God willing, to place the truth clearly and plainly before their eyes and win away some of their disciples, or at least to strengthen the simple and weak and protect them from the fanatics' poison. Even if I do not succeed in this (may God protect me from this!), at any rate I will have testified and confessed before God and all the world that I have nothing to do with these blasphemers of the sacrament and fanatics, and that I never had or ever will, God willing; and I shall wash my hands of all the blood of those souls whom they steal, murder, and seduce from Christ with their poison. I am innocent of it and have done my part. On my own account, of course, I do not need to write against them, but their own writings are my strength.

f Mark 3:29.

g John 3:1-2; 19:38-39; Acts 9:1-9.

When I read these they fill me with strength and joy, because I see that though the devil rages so bitterly against God's Word, yet God permits him no more than to spew out feeble, stale, rotten obscenities, so that I must say, "You would like to, but you cannot!" So to spite the devil again, I shall on this occasion take up only the single saying of Christ, "This is my body," and show how the fanatics have mutilated it up to the present time. Most especially, since they are so slippery and fickle, twisting and turning in a thousand secret corners, I would plead with them in God's name to take their stand on this one passage and to give me a real answer. The other passages I shall save for another time.[19]

[Response to Calls for Tolerance]

I would like to ask them in a friendly way not to become angry when I condemn their doctrine and ascribe it to the devil. I cannot do otherwise or call it anything other than I believe in my heart. Since they regard us as un-Christian and as those whom the Spirit of God has forsaken,[20] they really ought to be tolerant too, in accordance with their spirit and boasts, and demonstrate in deeds this tolerance with which they spatter so many books full. For there is no end or limit of boasting in their writings what holy martyrs they are, how much they suffer, how meek and forbearing they are, how they seek only the glory of Christ.[21] Yet they are always crying and complaining meanwhile how the ministers of Christ are vilified and how the common people are offended by this.[22] And they wish that we should simply praise them, saying, "you are pure spirit, pure spirit; you teach pure truth, pure truth!" Then they would be tolerant. In addition, we godless and intolerant un-Christians must put up with having these holy and moderate teachers revile us as idolaters and having our God called the baked God, the edible and drinkable God, the bread-God, the wine-God, and ourselves called God-forsaken Christians and such names.[23] This altogether venomous, devilish abuse and slander exceeds all bounds (for a person would rather be upbraided for being full of devils than have a baked God). Yet we must not be praised for our tolerance or moderation in putting up with this, for our ministers of Christ are not vilified or our people offended by it. We must call it pure praise and reform, joy and gladness, when they revile us! But if

19. By this Luther excludes discussion of the communion of bread and cup (1 Cor. 10:16-17), the words concerning the cup (Matt. 26:28; Mark 14:24; Luke 22:20; and 1 Cor. 11:25), and the explanation of unworthy eating (1 Cor. 11:27-29), all of which were used by both sides to justify their position.

20. Oecolampadius claimed that God's Spirit had forsaken Luther; *Billiche Antwortt*, W^2 20:584, 599.

21. Bucer defended the reputations of Zwingli and Oecolampadius in his *Apologia*; cf. the abridged translation in *Common Places*, 316–17. He did the same in the instructions to Gregor Casel, who was sent to Wittenberg in the fall of 1525 in the hope of forestalling further public controversy over the Lord's Supper, BDS 3:425–26. Zwingli also boasted of his moderation and reserve in "On the Lord's Supper," *Zwingli and Bullinger*, 237.

22. Bucer emphasized the offense to the simple folk caused by the eucharistic controversy in his instructions for Casel, BDS 3:422.

23. In their Latin treatises, the Swiss reformers equated adoration of the consecrated bread with idolatry, and they called flesh-eaters or cannibals those who believed they ate Christ's physical body in the elements; Zwingli, *Commentary*, 216, 223, 249–50; Oecolampadius, *Genvina expositione*, fol. B4v, K6v. Oecolampadius referred to the *impanated body* in *Genvina expositione*, fol. C6v, G8v. The German translations of these treatises encouraged more radical authors such as the pseudonymous "Conrad Ryss zu Ofen" to use even more offensive terms, such as "bready Lord God," *Antwort dem Hochgeleerten Doctor Johann Bugenhage*, fol. B2r, C2v. In a letter to Johann

Bugenhagen (1485–1558) of 8 Oct. 1525, Guillaume Farel (1485–1565) also mocked belief in an "edible God," in A.-L. Herminjard, ed., *Correspondance des Réformateurs dans les pays de langue française* (Geneva: H. Georg, 1866–97), 1:394.

one only looks sideways at them or displeases them—oh, that is hindering the glory of Christ, defaming Christ's ministers, offending the whole world; there you have suffering, there you have tolerance, there you have all the martyrs' crowns in a single heap! And even when they are not chided openly, they torture a casually written word and wring from it a complaint over their suffering, dragging the subject in by the ears, as Oecolampadius does against Pirckheimer of Nuremberg,[24] in order that they may boast of their tolerance.[25] A person simply dare not speak with them without their raising a howl and complaint, doubtless because of their great tolerance and holiness.

Since we un-Christians and intolerant heathens, I say, must put up with such horrible slander and shameful vilification from them, they, as the holy Christians, in turn should put up with something too, even though they are unwilling to put up with as much as we. For they have to remember that in our conscience and faith we take God's Word just as seriously as they do in their faith, since we too wish to be saved and come to God. We too hope that we shall do as much as they in this matter, and more than they. Thus St. Paul says, "We are not contending against flesh and blood" [Eph. 6:12]. Therefore I do not fix my attention as much upon them, as upon him who speaks through them—the devil, I mean—just as they regard me as full of devils. Yet we are glad to be garbage and scum[h] so they may rule, if only we remain free to confess our faith and to shun and condemn what is not of our faith. Now then, let us proceed to the subject at hand.

In the first place, we begin at the point where they write, produce books, and admonish that these subjects ought not be the occasion for rending Christian unity, love, and peace. It is a minor matter, say they, and an insignificant quarrel, for the sake of which Christian love should not be obstructed. They chide us for being so stubborn and obstinate about it and for creating disunity.[26] Now, see here, my dear friend, what should I say? We are in the same situation as the sheep that came to the watering place to drink with the wolf. The wolf went upstream, the sheep downstream to the water. Then the wolf chided the sheep for making the water muddy. The sheep said, "How can I be making it muddy for you? You are upstream, and you are making

24. Willibald Pirckheimer belonged to one of Nuremberg's leading families and had a distinguished political career serving his home city. He was also a highly respected humanist known for his translations of classical Greek texts into Latin. He published a refutation of Oecolampadius's *Genvina expositione* in 1526, beginning a published exchange that resulted in five treatises by the two men over the next two years. See also the introduction, above, p. 166.

25. Oecolampadius complained that Pirckheimer had defamed his character in *Ad Pyrkaimerum responsio*, a3r-a7r.

26. This was the view especially of the Strasbourg reformers Martin Bucer and Wolfgang Capito (1478–1541), both in their published pamphlets and in their contacts with Luther; see n. 21, p.177.

h 1 Cor. 4:13.

it muddy for me." In short, the sheep was forced to admit that he had made the water muddy for the wolf.[27] So too with my fanatics: they have kindled this fire, as they themselves with all lordliness boast as a blessing, and now they would like to shove off the blame for disunity upon us. Who ordered Dr. Karlstadt to start it?[28] Who ordered Zwingli and Oecolampadius to write?[29] Haven't they done it on their own accord? We would have been, and would still be, glad for peace, yet they were unwilling; now the blame is ours, of course!

I earnestly wish, however, that even if these fanatics refuse to fear God, they would at least feel a little abashed before the people and not write such shameless lies. They say there should be peace, but they themselves do not cease to increase strife, as everyone sees and hears; and the more it continues the more they rejoice. Again, they say it is a minor matter, yet there is no topic that they so diligently promote and cultivate and espouse; all other topics lie dormant. Here they become martyrs and saints. Anyone who does not share their fanaticism is no Christian and can accomplish nothing in Scripture and in matters of the spirit. It is a great and magnificent skill when anyone can say, "Bread and wine!" With this skill the Holy Spirit alone now operates! In reality what is going on here is simply that on top of everything the damnable devil is mocking us through them, as if to say, "I intend to cause all kinds of mischief and dissension in deeds, and then to wipe my mouth and say in words, 'I seek and desire love and unity!'"—as the Psalter also says, "They speak peace with their neighbors, while mischief is in their hearts" [Ps. 28:3].

Well, since they are so completely wicked as to mock the whole world, I shall add a Lutheran warning and say: Cursed be such love and unity in the abyss of hell, because such unity not only divides the Christian church wretchedly, but in true devilish fashion even mocks it and pokes fun at it for its wretchedness. Now I do not mean to interpret it so harshly as to hold that they do this out of malice. But I think they are blinded by Satan, and perhaps they have developed a conscience that bites them, saying, "Truly we have caused a great offense and kindled a great fire,

A detail of the thirteenth-century Fontana Maggiore, in Perugia, Italy, sculpted after 1275 by Nicola Pisano and Giovanni Pisano. The detail shows Aesop's fables "The Wolf and the Crane" and "The Wolf and the Lamb."

27. This is one of Aesop's fables that Luther included in the collection he published in 1530, WA 50:441.

28. At a meeting in Jena in August 1524, Luther gave Karlstadt a golden *gulden* as a token that Karlstadt would be allowed to print his pamphlets against Luther.

29. Although he dissociated himself from Karlstadt's understanding of "This is my body," Zwingli defended Karlstadt's position in his *Letter to Matthias Alber* and in his *Commentary on True and False Religion*, both published in March 1525. His *Subsidiary Essay* was published in the late summer of 1525, as was Oecolampadius's *Genvina expositione*.

now we must paste and putty up the affair with words, and claim indulgence because it is not an important matter. And even if we lose the argument, let us declare in advance that we have not lost anything important, but have committed only a minor offense, and as we say of singers when they make a mistake, 'They only slipped a little.'"[i]

No, dear sirs, none of this peace and love for me! If I were to strangle someone's father and mother, wife and child, and try to choke him too, and then say, "Keep the peace, dear friend, we wish to love one another; the matter is not so important that we should be divided over it!" what should he say to me? O how he should love me! Thus the fanatics strangle Christ my Lord, and God the Father in his words, and my mother the church[j] too, along with my brethren. Moreover, they would have me dead too, and then they would say I should be at peace, for they would like to cultivate love in their relations with me. But I intend to expose the fanatics here and everyone may see what kind of spirit is in them, so that their adherents may realize who it is they believe and follow.

It is perfectly clear, of course, that we are at odds concerning the words of Christ in the Supper. And it is well known on both sides that these are Christ's or God's words. That is one thing. So we say, on our part, that according to the words, Christ's true body and blood are present when he says, "Take, eat; this is my body." If our belief and teaching go wrong here, tell us, what are we doing? We are lying to God, and proclaiming that he did not say this but said the opposite. Then we are assuredly blasphemers and liars against the Holy Spirit, betrayers of Christ, and murderers and seducers of the world. Our opponents say that mere bread and wine are present, not the body and blood of the Lord. If they believe and teach wrongly here, then they blaspheme God and are giving the lie to the Holy Spirit, betray Christ, and seduce the world. One side must be of the devil, and God's enemy. There is no middle ground.

i Lit., "they have only made a piglet," a colloquialism for making a small error.

j *Christenheit*, a term Luther uses throughout the treatise as synonymous with the church; cf. Rom. 5:14; Eph. 5:32.

Now let every faithful Christian see whether this is a minor matter, as they say, or whether God's Word is to be trifled with. Here you have the fanatics and their spirit. I have often said that no ungodly person can have a high regard for God's Word. These fanatics demonstrate forthrightly that they regard the words and works of Christ as nothing but human prattle, like the opinions of academic hairsplitters, which ought fairly to yield to love and unity. But a faithful Christian knows clearly that God's Word concerns God's glory, the Spirit, Christ, grace, everlasting life, death, sin, and all things. These, however, are not minor matters. You see, this is how they seek God's glory, as they boast everywhere.

Neither does it help them to assert that at all other points they have a high and noble regard for God's words and the entire gospel, except in this matter. My friend, God's Word is God's Word; this point does not require much haggling! When one blasphemes and calls God a liar with a single word, or says it is a minor matter if God is blasphemed or called a liar, one blasphemes the entire God and makes light of all blasphemy. There is only one God, who will not be divided, praised in one place and reprimanded in another, glorified in one word and scorned in another. The Jews believe the Old Testament, but because they do not believe Christ, it does them no good. You see, the circumcision of Abraham [Gen. 17:10ff.] is now an old dead thing and no longer necessary or useful. But if I were to say that God did not command it in its time, it would do me no good even if I believed the gospel. So St. James asserts, "Whoever offends in one point is guilty in all respects" [James 2:10]. He possibly heard the apostles say that all the words of God must be believed or none, although he applies their interpretation to the works of the law.

Why is it any wonder, then, if fickle fanatics juggle and play the clown with the words of the Supper according to their fancy, since at this point they are convicted of belittling God's words and concerns, and making them secondary to human love? Just as if God must yield to human beings, and let the authority of his Word depend on whether people are at one or at odds over it. How can one believe that these fanatics teach rightly and well, when they are clearly found to be entertaining such devilish ideas and advising things which make for the despising, blaspheming, and disgrace of God and our eternal death and destruction, and who yet think they have acted well and presented a salutary Christian teaching?

But we poor sinners, who are altogether devoid of Spirit, have this to say out of the holy gospel against these holy Christians, "Whoever loves father and mother, wife and child, house and home, or even his own soul more than me is not worthy of me" [Matt. 10:37].[30] And again, "I have not come to bring peace on earth, but a sword" [Matt. 10:34]. And Paul, "What agreement does Christ have with Belial?" [2 Cor. 6:15]. If we are to practice Christian unity with them and extend Christian love to them, we must also love and be satisfied with, or at least tolerate, their doctrine and behavior. Let anyone do that if he wishes—not I. For Christian unity consists in the Spirit, when we are of one faith, one mind, one heart, Eph. 4[:3ff.]. We will, however, gladly do this: in civil matters we will be one with them—that is, we will maintain outward, temporal peace. But in spiritual matters, as long as we have breath, we intend to shun, condemn, and censure them, as idolaters, corrupters of God's Word, blasphemers, and liars; and meanwhile, to endure from them, as from enemies, their persecution and schism as far and as long as God endures them; and to pray for them, and admonish them to stop. But to acquiesce in, keep silence over, or approve their blaspheming, this we shall not and cannot do.

I have exposed all these things in order to show how the devil can disguise himself under false humility, peace, and tolerance, for the warning of all who do not humble themselves from the heart, that they should beware both of the devil and of themselves. For God will not be either deceived or mocked [Gal. 6:7]. God would rather take an ass and condemn great prophets through her mouth, as he did Balaam [Num. 22:28ff.]. Therefore, to these fanatics and spirits who offer us such a peace, we may well say as Christ said to his betrayer, Judas, in the garden, "O Judas, would you betray the Son of man with a kiss?" [Luke 22:48]. Yes indeed, a Judas's peace and a traitor's kiss it is when they would be friendly to us and get us to the point of watching in silence while they ravage with fire and sword,[31] by which they bring so many souls into the everlasting fire of hell, all the while wishing it to be regarded as a minor matter and of no consequence. God warns us against these spirits by allowing them to come into the open and betray themselves and reveal how they traffic in lies and falsehoods. And if they are not shocked or

30. Luther's text here approaches a paraphrase of Matt. 10:37-39 rather than a quotation of a single verse. Matt. 10:37 reads: "Whoever loves father or mother more than me is not worthy of me; and whoever loves son or daughter more than me is not worthy of me."

31. The revolts known collectively as the Peasants' War broke out in the spring of 1525, at about the same time that the eucharistic controversy began. Willibald Pirckheimer had explicitly connected the two in his *Responsio to Oecolampadius*, WPBW 6:437.

warned by stratagem, then let them go; they want to be lost! The Holy Spirit offers no such stratagems through his poor sinners as the devil does here through his saints.

[Consideration of Christ's Words: Defense of Literal Understanding]

Now, to come to grips with the subject, let us take up the saying of Christ, which Matthew and Mark record: "He took bread, and gave thanks, and broke it, and gave it to his disciples and said, 'Take, eat; this is my body which is given for you.'"[32] As I have said, I wish at this time to take up this saying alone, in defiance of the devil and all his spirits, in order to prove that this single text is strong and mighty enough to stand against all their rotten, empty prattle. The other texts can be addressed at another time. Now, here stands the text, stating clearly and lucidly that Christ gives his body to eat when he distributes the bread. On this we take our stand, and we also believe and teach that in the Supper we eat and take to ourselves Christ's body truly and physically. But how this takes place or how he is in the bread, we do not know and are not meant to know. We should believe God's Word without setting bounds or measure to it. The bread we see with our eyes, but we hear with our ears that Christ's body is present.

32. As he did in the German Mass (LW 53:81), Luther combines "Take, eat; this is my body," from Matt. 26:26, with "This is my body, which is given for you," from Luke 22:19.

This woodcut, attributed to Lucas Cranach the Elder, depicts Evangelical communion in both kinds, with the Bohemian reformer Jan Hus distributing the bread and Luther giving the wine.

Against this saying they have up to now brought forth nothing in their many writings that even seems plausible, let alone is a solid argument. I let them boast and show off and even boldly swear by God's judgment and wrath how sure of the matter they are and how they have grasped the truth. But these are just words, with which they would dearly love to conceal and cover over their uncertain conscience so that no one may notice how their heart shakes and quakes within like a reed swayed by the wind [Matt. 11:7], because of the great uncertainty of their fancies and delusions. I too dare take an oath that this saying of Christ, "This is my body," sticks in their hearts like an everlasting splinter from which they can never be free, except by being so completely callous as to feel nothing any longer, Eph. 4[:18f.].[33] I know, of course, what bad consciences do when they begin to make themselves aprons from fig leaves to try and hide themselves.[34] Since they misinterpret God's Word and follow their own fancy, it is easy also to judge their heart by Scripture, which teaches us that the wicked have no rest: "Their hearts are like a wave of the sea, which cannot rest," Isa. 57[:20].[k]

This is clearly proved by the anxious tone of their writings. Here they boast, there they complain; here they beg for peace, there they crave instruction; here they shy away from offense, there they seek the glory of Christ.[35] There is so much of this unnecessary mending and patching that they seldom get around to the subject, and write precious little about it. And when they have to come to it, they tread as lightly as if they were actually walking on eggs, and afterward slip away as if the devil were after them, fearful that they may break their neck with every letter. When they have safely escaped, they wipe away their sweat and anxiety, and thank God for the truth; and there follows so great a teaching and praise of the spiritual eating of the body of Christ and of his remembrance—over which no one contends with them; we knew about these things just as well as they, and before them—that it is clear they do not know what they are saying, or how they should go about bamboozling the people.[36] My friend, a sure conscience, which is certain about the matter, does not hem and haw so; it speaks out distinctly and boldly, since it is altogether confident. Therefore, let no one believe their swearing and boasting. They are assuredly lying.

But listen, I ask you, how they remove our interpretation from this saying of Christ and bring in their own. They say, "The word 'is' must mean the same as the word 'signifies,'" as Zwingli writes;[l] and the expression "my body" must mean the same as the expression "sign of my body,"[37] as Oecolampadius writes.[m] So Christ's word and meaning according to Zwingli's text would read, "Take, eat; this signifies my body," or according to Oecolampadius's text, "Take and eat; this is a sign of my body." Ah,

k Luther adds "their hearts" to the text from Isaiah.

l Zwingli, *Letter to Alber*, HZW 2:138–39; in Latin, *significat*; in German, *bedeutet*.

m Oecolampadius, *Genvina expositione*, fol. B8r.

33. "They are darkened in their understanding, alienated from the life of God because of their ignorance and hardness of heart," Eph. 4:18.

34. As Adam and Eve had done in the garden, Gen. 3:7.

35. Classical rhetoric taught that an oration should begin with a *captatio benevolentiae*, an effort to win the goodwill of the audience. This rhetorical technique had an important function in the treatises of Zwingli and Oecolampadius, which tried to persuade readers to accept a position long condemned by the church as heretical. Luther, however, interprets the use of this technique as a mark of their uncertainty.

36. Luther may have been thinking especially of Zwingli's *Letter to Alber*. The first half of this pamphlet is a discussion of the spiritual eating of Christ's flesh based on John 6, and Zwingli devotes only two pages to his explanation of "This is my body."

37. Oecolampadius used "figure" (*figura*/*Gestalt*) rather than "sign" (*Zeichen*), the word Luther uses here. This is a subtle but significant difference, because people or objects in the Old Testament, such as the Passover lamb, could be understood as "figuring" or foreshadowing Christ.

they are so certain about this meaning and they stand so firm in their hearts—like a reed that the wind blows to and fro, as has been pointed out. Then at once they boast that we have no passage from Scripture which says that Christ's body is in the Supper. Next they humble themselves again, would like to be instructed, and offer to follow if we can prove with Scripture that Christ's body is present.

This certainly is an extraordinary situation! It is just as if I denied that God had created the heavens and the earth, and asserted with Aristotle and Pliny[38] and other heathens that the world existed from eternity,[n] but someone came and held Moses under my nose, Gen. 1[:1], "In the beginning God created the heavens and the earth." I would then try to make the text read: "God" now should mean the same as "cuckoo,"[39] "created" the same as "ate," and "the heavens and the earth" the same as "the warbler, feathers and all." The word of Moses[40] thus would read according to Luther's text, "In the beginning the cuckoo ate the warbler, feathers and all," and could not possibly mean, "In the beginning God created the heavens and the earth." What a marvelous art this would be—one with which rascals are quite familiar! Or, if I denied that the Son of God had become man, and someone confronted me with John 1[:14], "The Word became flesh," suppose I were to say: Let "Word" mean "crooked staff" and "flesh" mean "a mallet," and thus the text must now read, "The crooked staff became a mallet." And if my conscience tried to reproach me, saying, "You take a good deal of liberty with your interpretation, Sir Martin, but—but—" etc., I would press until I became red in the face, and say, "Keep quiet, you traitor with your 'but,' so that the people won't notice that I have such a bad conscience!" Then I would boast and clap my hands, saying, "The Christians have no Scripture which proves that God's Word became flesh." But I would then humble myself a little, offer gladly to be instructed, if they would show me with the Scripture that I have just finished twisting around. Ah, what a rumpus I would stir up among Jews and Christians, in the New and the Old Testaments, if such brazenness were allowed me!

If you ask, "What devil would allow you to do such a thing?" the answer is, "What devil other than the one who allows Zwingli and Oecolampadius to do it? I wouldn't know anyone else,

n Aristotle, *On the Heavens* I.3; Pliny, *Natural History* II.1.

38. The scientific works of Aristotle (384–322 BCE) were part of the regular university curriculum. The encyclopedic *Natural History* of the Roman soldier and author Pliny the Elder (23–79) was a major source of scientific ideas through the Middle Ages.

39. "Cuckoo" was used in the sixteenth century as a euphemism for the devil; Jakob Grimm et al., *Deutsches Wörterbuch* (Leipzig: Hirzel, 1854–1960), 11:2526.

40. Luther refers to the traditional understanding that Moses authored Genesis and the other four books of the Pentateuch.

either!" Whoever read in Scripture that "body" means the same as "sign of the body," and "is" means the same as "signifies"? Indeed, what language in all the world has ever expressed itself so? It is only the arrogance and frivolous wickedness of the very devil, who mocks us through such fanatics in these important matters. He wants to be shown with Scripture—provided that he first eliminates the Scripture or twists it to his own fancy. Just as if I were to rob a man of his weapons with crafty words and gave him in exchange sham weapons made of paper, exactly like his own, and then defiantly challenged him to strike me with them or defend himself against me. Now this would be a valiant hero! He would be spit upon and pelted out of the village with dung, if he were really in earnest, or it would be a good joke at carnival time, if he were jesting. This is just the way these fanatics treat us also. They wish first of all to change the natural words and meanings of Scripture into their own words and meanings; then they boast that we do not have Scripture, in order that the devil may have his joke on us, or rather, may surely strangle us as defenseless. Against all this, however, just one word serves exceedingly well: No! So they stand like butter in the sun.[41]

41. That is, in an impossible position.

Here let the judge between us be not only Christians but also heathens, Turks,[42] Tartars,[43] Jews, idolaters, and the whole world: whose responsibility is it to prove his text? Should it be the Luther who asserts that Moses says, "In the beginning the cuckoo ate the warbler," or the one who asserts that Moses says, "In the beginning God created the heavens and the earth"? I hope the decision would be that Luther ought to prove his text, since in no language does "God" mean the same as "cuckoo." Well, that Luther creeps away to the cross,[o] grieved that he cannot prove that "God" means "cuckoo." For anyone who ventures to interpret words in Scripture any other way than what they say is obligated to prove this from the text of the same passage or by an article of faith.[p] But who will enable the fanatics to prove that "body" is the equivalent of "sign of the body," and "is" the equivalent of "signifies"? No one has brought them to this point yet. They rant and rave, "Where is your Scripture? Where is your Scripture?" and press us to prove that the gospel says, "This is my body," though the whole world reads it and must read it. That

42. Luther frequently uses the word *Turk* to refer to all Muslims.

43. The Tatars (or Tartars) joined forces with the Mongols in the thirteenth century, and Europeans used the word *Tartar* to refer to the Mongols in general.

o A German idiom that expresses humiliation.

p *Artickel des glaubens* is ambiguous and can also mean an article of the [Apostles'] Creed.

it also says, however, "This signifies my body" or "This is a sign of my body"—O that is so sure that they defy God's judgment over it, even though no one ever has or can read this in the gospel.

God knows, with these crude illustrations I do not wish to offend Zwingli, and especially not Oecolampadius, to whom God has given many gifts beyond so many others.[44] Indeed, I am heartily sorry for the man. I aim such words not at them but only upon the arrogant, mocking devil who has so deceived and misled them, and again I yield my pleasure in this to the glory of God, and I mock him again for these clumsy follies of his. [. . .][q]

A sixteenth-century portrait of Johannes Oecolampadius by Hans Asper.

I write these things in order that our people may have answers for the fanatics when they ask so mockingly where it is written in Scripture that "bread" is Christ's body, and stupidly act as if they have never read it. Should one ask them in return where it is written in Scripture that "body" means "sign of the body"? It is up the chimney, that's where! That is where their Bible is!

The sum of all this is that we have on our side the clear, distinct Scripture that reads, "Take, eat; this is my body," and it is not necessary, nor can we be pressed, to go beyond this Scripture text—though we could do so abundantly. On the contrary, they should produce Scripture that reads, "This signifies my body," or, "This is a sign of my body." [. . .][r]

Therefore we beg the fanatics not to demand from us a proof of this text, "This is my body." This is something they might ask seven-year-old boys who are learning to spell these words in school, because the Bible is available in Greek, Latin, and German. But what they ought to have done was to show us a

q Text omitted (see LW 37:33).

r Text omitted (see LW 37:33).

44. Oecolampadius had a reputation for learned piety in the early 1520s. He had a doctorate in theology, was involved with Erasmus's editorial projects, and had translated the writings of several Greek church fathers into Latin. He wrote some of the earliest humanist pamphlets favoring Luther and was better known than Zwingli outside of Switzerland at the time the eucharistic controversy began.

Bible in which was written, "This is a sign of my body." If they could not do this, they should obediently bridle their mouths and lower their pens for a while, until they can produce such a Bible or prove with good reasons that this text should be made to read this way. Meanwhile they should keep still and not boast, "Where is your Scripture? Where is your Scripture?" unless they scream these words to themselves—as they ought—and not to us. For they are acting against their own conscience. [. . .][s]

Title page of Zwingli's *Subsidiary Essay*, printed in Zurich by Christoph Froschauer (1525). The image of the Last Supper reflects Zwingli's emphasis on the Lord's Supper as a remembrance of Christ's passion and death.

[Consideration of Christ's Words: Rejection of Figurative Meaning]

It is certain that Zwingli and Oecolampadius agree in their understanding of the text, even though their words differ. For Zwingli's expression, "This signifies my body," is exactly the same as Oecolampadius's, "This is a sign of my body."[t] The German language and all other languages concede that it is the same to say, "laughing signifies joy," and "laughing is a sign of joy." There is no question or doubt that "to signify" and "to be a sign" are the same thing. But since the point at issue here is whether the word "is" necessarily means the same in Scripture as the word "signifies," Zwingli is obliged to prove this from Scripture. If he does not do this, his argument is mere dung. Similarly, Oecolampadius is obligated to prove from Scripture that the word "body" necessarily means the same as the word "sign of the body." If he doesn't, he too is dung, and our text remains firm as a rock—"This is my body."

s Text omitted (see LW 37:34).

t Oecolampadius stated this in *Genvina expositione*, fol. B8r.

Indeed, to show how far they miss the truth: not only are they obligated to prove from Scripture that "body" is the same as "sign of the body," and that "to be" is the same as "to signify," but one thing more: even though they should produce such an example in one passage of Scripture (which, however, is impossible), they are still obligated to prove that it is necessarily so here in the Supper as well, that "body" is "sign of the body."[45] It would not help them at all, even if the entire Scripture showed nothing but mere signs of the body in other passages, if they did not show it also at this passage on the Supper. Our present quarrel is not primarily whether somewhere in Scripture "body" means "sign of the body," but whether in this text of the Supper it has this meaning. Consciences want to be certain and sure on this point. Therefore, even if you proved, for example, that in Moses[46] "body" is the same as "sign of the body,"[47] consciences are not satisfied but just mumble and say, "Yes, my friend, but who knows whether it therefore means the same in the Supper, too?" We must be assured of this also through God's Word; otherwise the words remain firm for us and hold us captive with the clear, distinct text, "This is my body."

Oh, how the devil's pants stink here! How keenly he senses that he is under this obligation, and how reluctant he is to carry it out! For we demand both of these things, and we challenge him in both. For this reason, too, the fanatics shrink from this obligation more than any devil has ever shrunk from the cross. Moreover, it is too much to hope that they will stand still and look you in the eye or hear what they are asked. All they do is flee and storm out. No one will attack this subject. Our pastor Johannes Bugenhagen once challenged Zwingli in writing to prove that in the Supper "to be" meant the same as "to signify."[u] But when he ought to have answered him, Zwingli sang instead a ditty about his great sufferings, and tried to show whether it meant this in other passages of Scripture, but found none. He did not dare to touch the question of whether it must mean this in the Supper.[v] He would have been a fool if he had tried, and he wouldn't listen to advice.

45. Luther made this argument already in 1523, in *The Adoration of the Sacrament*, LW 36:281.

46. I.e., in the Pentateuch, the first five books of the Old Testament traditionally attributed to Moses.

47. In his *Subsidiary Essay*, Zwingli used Exod. 12:11b, "It is the Lord's Passover," as an example where "is" means "signifies," HZW 2:210–14.

u Bugenhagen, *Contra novvm errorem*; contemporary German translation in W² 20:500–501.

v Zwingli, *Ad Bvgenhagii epistolam responsio*, Z 4:558–76.

This is the way he proves his "signifying"[w]: St. Paul says in 1 Cor. 10[:4], "The rock was Christ," i.e., the rock signifies Christ; therefore, the same should apply here also: "This is my body" means, "This signifies my body." Again, Moses, in Exod. 12[:11], "Eat the lamb in haste, for it is the Lord's Passover," i.e., it signifies the Lord's Passover; therefore, here too, "This is my body" equally must mean, "This signifies my body."[x]

I ask Zwingli now: St. Paul doesn't say, "The rock signifies Christ," but, "The rock was Christ." How then can you prove with this that there is such signifying in the Supper, which is not even in Paul? Through him you try to prove your point, but just as you dreamed it up in the Supper, so you imagine it in Paul also. Similarly, Moses does not say, "Eat in haste, it signifies the Lord's Passover," but, "Eat in haste, it is the Lord's Passover." Thus Zwingli is obliged to prove his signifying in Paul and Moses just as much as in the Supper, for it is not obvious in any of these places. Boys in school are taught that such an argument is called "begging the question,"[48] or "proving the uncertain by the uncertain," but these exalted spirits have not learned this yet. What will Zwingli say on these threadbare subjects? He cannot admit his error, of course, for that would be disgraceful. He would much rather say that he is full of the Spirit and must suffer many things, and keep up his boasting until we are ready to believe that this signifying occurs in Paul and Moses even if no one sees it there.

48. Luther uses the technical Latin term *petitio principii*, which means to include the point to be proven in the initial premise of the argument.

Now, let me assume that it were true that such signifying occurs in Paul and Moses, and we obligingly believed him, what does he accomplish? But let us see how masterfully he draws his conclusion. Paul says, "The rock was Christ," i.e., the rock signifies Christ; therefore, when Christ says, "This is my body," it must also be the same as, "This signifies my body." My friend, let us also draw some conclusions according to this wonderful method. All right, I shall prove, using the Zwinglian method, that Sarah, the holy mother of the Jews, remained a virgin, as follows: Luke writes that Mary remained a virgin,[49] therefore Sarah also must have remained a virgin. Isn't this fine syllogiz-

49. Luke 1:34ff. Luther interprets this to mean that Mary remained a virgin before, during, and after Jesus' birth.

w *Deuteley*, a word Luther coins from *bedeuten* (to signify) to indicate a false interpretation.

x Zwingli, *Subsidiary Essay*, HZW 2:210–14; *Ad Bvgenhagii epistolam responsio*, Z 4:559-61.

ing and well proven? Again, I shall prove that Pilate is an apostle of Christ, as follows: The evangelist Matthew [10:2] writes that Peter is Christ's apostle, therefore this Pilate must also be Christ's apostle. And so on; whatever I please shall and must be deduced as an article of faith by such a method. "Yes," you say, "but this is not valid; you must prove in each particular instance, that Sarah is a virgin and Pilate an apostle." Why? If Zwingli does not need to prove that this signifying occurs in the Supper, as long as it occurs in a single passage in Paul or Moses, it is enough. Children in school know that "no deduction can be drawn from pure particulars and even less from negatives."[y] But for these spirits of ours, it is the highest skill to make such arguments from particulars and without Scripture into such sacred articles of faith.

We must realize, of course, that this is sheer, arrogant mockery on the part of the devil, who in great self-confidence plays the fool with us and monkeys around with this rotten signifying and clown's play. How else, without the influence of Satan, could such learned men be so blind and boast so highly of their empty dreams, and advertise them in the world as the strongest of all grounds of faith? No, it is not human to have such gross, thick darkness. So Zwingli lies in the ash heap with his signifying, just as Dr. Karlstadt before him fell with his *touto*.[50] For Zwingli can prove neither point, i.e., that there is any signifying in any single passage of Scripture, much less that it must be in the Supper. He does not prove either point, though he is obligated to prove both.

The signifying is quickly taken away from him in Paul and Moses, because Paul says, "They drank from the spiritual rock, and the Rock was Christ" [1 Cor. 10:4]. Here St. Paul himself shows that he speaks of a spiritual rock. Now the spiritual rock does not signify Christ; the rock was Christ himself among the Jews, just as our rock now does not signify but is nothing else but Christ. The preachers in Swabia[51] have convincingly shown this, as I did against Dr. Karlstadt even before them.[z] But these lofty spirits disregard our writings, skip through them and fuss over them a little, and we have an adequate reply. Similarly, when Moses says, "Eat in haste, it is the Lord's Passover" [Exod. 12:11],

y Luther uses the Latin: *partibus ex puris sequitur nil atque negatis*.

z *Syngramma*, in Brenz, *Werke* 1/1:247–48. Luther did not address 1 Cor. 10:4 in *Against the Heavenly Prophets*, but he did discuss it in *Adoration of the Sacrament*, LW 36:280–81.

50. Karlstadt proposed that the antecedent of "this" (in Greek, *touto*) was Christ's body, so that Christ's statement should be understood as "This [body] is my body which is given for you," *The Eucharistic Pamphlets of Andreas Bodenstein von Karlstadt*, trans. and ed. Amy Nelson Burnett (Kirksville: Truman State University Press, 2011), 146–47, 171–75. Luther mocked Karlstadt's exegesis in *Against the Heavenly Prophets*, LW 40:162–70; TAL 2:111–22.

51. Johannes Brenz wrote the *Syngramma* in the name of his fellow preachers in Swabia as a refutation of Oecolampadius's *Genvina expositione*. In addition to the Latin original, there were three different German translations of the *Syngramma* published in 1526, two of them done in Wittenberg and provided with prefaces by Luther, LW 59:156–62.

Zwingli cannot prove that "Passover" signifies the paschal lamb. The rejoinder is quickly made, "Eat in haste, it is the Lord's Passover" means, as we say in German, "Eat meat, it is Sunday; drink water, it is Friday." In this instance no one will force me to admit that meat signifies Sunday or water signifies Friday. So also here, "Eat in haste, for it is the Lord's Passover," i.e., this is the day when the Lord went from Egypt.

There is no proof of signifying, either, in all the other passages that they quote. For example, where Christ says, "I am the true vine" [John 15:1], he speaks of the true spiritual vine, which he also *was*, not which *signifies* him. How should it read: "I signify the true vine," or, "I am signified by the true vine"? Who then is the true vine, apart from any signifying? Again, "I am the shepherd" [John 10:11], "I am the door" [John 10:7], "I am the resurrection and the life" [John 11:25], and all the others. All these sayings expressed and are understood in terms of being, not of signifying. They will never convincingly show any signifying there; it is sheer imagination and their own ideas. Moreover, as I have said, even if they discovered any examples of signifying, still they cannot prove thereby that it is so in the Supper, and all the toil and care they have expended is merely lost effort. They give me this much credit, however, that in the case of Karlstadt I demolished his *touto*, and that his was not a sound argument. But if I were to judge between Karlstadt and Zwingli, I would say that Dr. Karlstadt's *touto* served this error better than Zwingli's signifying which, however, has absolutely nothing in it that can disguise the error, because it tries to prove its case purely by unknown, uncertain, and particular propositions—which to every rational mind is ludicrous and should be mocked.

Dr. Oecolampadius would also like to help out this same signifying. When the preachers in Swabia struck it down with a powerful treatise,[a] so that he himself could not deny that Paul speaks of the spiritual rock and there is no signifying here, he still did not honor the truth but grumbled a little against it and said that Paul in this expression was visualizing and thinking of the physical rock that signified Christ[b]—as if we were asking here what Paul was visualizing or thinking of, instead of whether there is any signifying in Paul's words. We know very well that

a I.e., the *Syngramma*.

b Oecolampadius, *Apologetica*, fol. L2v-L3v; *Billiche Antwortt*, W^2 20:610.

the corporeal rock signifies Christ, and hence Christ is in name and reality a spiritual rock. They need to teach us not this point, but rather whether there is any signifying in Paul's words, as Zwingli dreams. Here they remain silent and nimbly rush past the question; and true to their manner, they let us ask about God and answer us about their cuckoo and then boast that no one is producing any Scripture against them. Indeed, if it is acceptable that one does not have to respond to the Scripture cited but may jabber about something else instead, then no one is producing any Scripture against them, even if a world full of Scripture were brought up against them!

Now Dr. Oecolampadius also ought to prove his "sign of the body" from Scripture. Our Scripture states, "Take, eat; this is my body"; it doesn't say, "This is a sign of my body." It is also impossible for him to produce one passage of Scripture where "body" is the same as "sign of the body," not to mention that he should prove it in the case of the Supper. Indeed, as far as proof is concerned, he lies as deep in the ash heap as Karlstadt and Zwingli. Yet they refuse to do God the honor of admitting that this is true, but boast that no Scripture is brought up against them. However, if they were not such frivolous despisers of Scripture, one clear saying from Scripture would move them as profoundly as if the whole world were full of Scripture—which it actually is. For as I see it, every single passage makes the world too narrow. They flutter past, however, and think, "This is only a man's word." Small wonder that no Scripture compels them!

Nachhůt von dem Nachtmal oder der Dancksagung Christi/durch Huldrychen Zwinglin in Latin beschriben/vnd durch Georgen Binder vertütschet.

Christus Matthei xj. Kumend zů mir alle die arbeytend vnd beladen sind/vnd ich wil üch rüw geben.

STADT BIBLIOTHEK IN ZURICH.

Title page of the German translation of Zwingli's *Subsidiary Essay*, both of which were printed by Christoph Froschauer (1525). The image of Passover visually demonstrates the parallel Zwingli drew between "this is my body" and "this is the Lord's Passover."

Even if Oecolampadius holds the opinion that it is mere bread and wine, he still cannot on that account conclude with certainty that "body" necessarily means "sign of the body." That is, his argument is not convincing, since one may well interpret the word "body" in other ways than as "sign of the body," and his interpretation can be neither certain nor unambiguous as it should in order to be convincing. There are many other people who share his opinion yet accept neither the signifying nor the sign-making.[52] Karlstadt lets "body" remain body, and bases his position on the *touto*. Others torture the text thus: "Take and eat; my body, given for you, is this," viz., a spiritual food.[53] These also let "body" be body, and yet are one in faith with him. Others crucify the sacred words thus: "Take and eat; that which is given for you is my body."[54] So many factions and heads does this single sect have already, though they agree on the main point,[55] but the Holy Spirit must be in all of them, as they are always boasting everywhere. And he must show this with proofs and arguments that are not only at variance, but even self-contradictory and not in agreement with himself. But he clearly testifies thereby that one errs as much as the other, since none of them holds the Scripture as it reads, and no one can prove that it is to be understood in any other way than as it reads. [. . .][c]

How gladly would [Oecolampadius] let the matter rest if "body" might be called "sign of the body," although he could not prove that it should and must be so called, as he is obligated to do. But he cannot; God has stepped in and prevented him. It must stand as his own dream, and be labeled Oecolampadius's silly sign-making and foolery. A faithful Christian, however, who listens to our fanaticism and hears how we play dice with the sacred words of Christ, each according to his own fancy, would surely say, "Oh, you are rascals, the whole lot of you, treating God's Word as jokes and foolery; I shall hold to the simple text."

[Opponents' Arguments: Against the Claim That Scriptures Are Contradictory]

Perhaps they will reproach me, however, for consigning Oecolampadius's sign-making so utterly to the devil, and claim that even if he cannot prove the word "sign of the body" from Scripture, yet there are plenty of Scripture passages that force the conclusion that it must be mere bread and wine there. Answer: Where are these passages then? They say, "The Scriptures contradict

c Text omitted (see LW 37:41–45).

52. Luther distinguishes between Zwingli's "signifying" (*deuteley*) and Oecolampadius's "sign-making" (*zeicheley*).

53. This was the view of the Silesian nobleman Caspar Schwenckfeld (1489–1561) and his friend Valentin Crautwald (c. 1465–1545), a canon at the Liegnitz cathedral. Schwenckfeld visited Wittenberg in December 1525 and discussed his understanding of "This is my body" with Luther and Bugenhagen; CS 2:235–82; cf. Amy Nelson Burnett, *Karlstadt and the Origins of the Eucharistic Controversy: A Study in the Circulation of Ideas* (New York: Oxford University Press, 2011), 129–34.

54. This interpretation was contained in *Antwort dem Hochgeleerten Doctor Johann Bugenhage*, published under the pseudonym of Conrad Ryss zu Ofen. Ryss's identity has been debated, but his position was very close to that of Karlstadt; Burnett, *Karlstadt*, 125–27.

55. Luther emphasized this in his preface to the first Wittenberg translation of the *Syngramma*, LW 59:156–58; see also n. 4, p. 168. In return, the Swiss reformers pointed to the disunity of their opponents, Zwingli, *Responsio ad Billicani*, Z 4:901–92; Oecolampadius, *Billiche Antwortt*, W[2] 20:591.

themselves, and no one can reconcile them unless one believes that mere bread and wine are present in the Supper." Answer: What Scripture? They say, "Oh, where the article of the Creed asserts that Christ ascended to heaven and sits on the right hand of God in his glory.[d] Again, eating flesh is of no avail, John 6[:63], 'The flesh is of no avail.'[e] If, then, flesh and blood are in the Supper, Christ could not be sitting at the right hand of God in his glory, and he would be giving us something to eat which is of no use for salvation. Therefore a uniform interpretation of Scripture must instruct us and make of Christ's body a 'sign of the body,' and this must be the text in the Supper."

Who would have expected such lofty wisdom from the fanatics? Here you see the best single argument that they have. Suppose now that I ask them whether they have something from Scripture and can prove that these two scriptural passages are contradictory: that Christ is seated in heaven and that his body is in the Supper; or again, that the flesh is of no avail and that Christ's body is eaten in the Supper; and, where all this is supposed to be written. They will answer me, "You must hold us dear along with Scripture; you must believe us. We are certain of it without Scripture, and more certain than if Scripture said it."

I reply: How is this? [They say,] "Oh, you fool, open your eyes! Don't you see that heaven, where Christ is seated in his glory, is high above, and the earth where his Supper is observed is here, far below? How can a body be seated so high in glory and at the same time be here below, allowing itself to be profaned and taken by hands, mouth, and belly, as if it were a fried sausage? Would this be consistent with the majesty of God and the glory of heaven? Ah, this is more than certain!"[56]

Thank you, good gentlemen! I did not know that with regard to the articles of faith it was entirely unnecessary to inquire into God's Word, but only to open our physical eyes and judge according to them, by the standards of reason, what is to be believed. Now I understand what is meant by "faith is the conviction of things not seen" [Heb. 11:1].[f] In the new interpretation of these

56. This is a very general and polemical paraphrase of Oecolampadius's argument in several works: *Genvina expositione*, fol. E3v; *Apologetica*, fol. C4v-C5r; *Ad Pyrkaimerum responsio*, fol. h4v-h5r. Karlstadt also mocked the belief that impure priests could bring Christ's body into the bread, *Pamphlets*, 200–201.

d *Zwingli and Bullinger*, 212–15; Oecolampadius, *Billiche Antwortt*, W[2] 20:591, 600–604.

e Zwingli, *Letter to Alber*, HZW 2:134–36; see also his *Commentary*, 208–10.

f Luther quotes the verse in Latin: *fides est non apparentium*.

spirits it means: "Faith must believe no more and no farther than one's eyes and fingers point out to him and the reason can measure."[57] Now anyone who asks too many questions becomes unwelcome, but I must ask some more, that I may become still more clever. How do we become certain, good gentlemen, that a body may not through the power of God be at the same time in heaven and in the Supper, since the power of God has neither measure nor number, and does things which no mind can comprehend but must simply be believed? He says, "This is my body"; how then shall I calm my heart and convince it that God has neither the means nor the power to do what his Word says? And perhaps, even if a body is not now visibly present at several places, he may well have ways and know how he might render a body present invisibly—indeed, even visibly—in many places at the same time. If he could do this, would you not have deceived us woefully by saying "No" before you knew for sure? Do you have proof from Scripture that says God is not omnipotent in this matter?

57. A polemical reference to Zwingli's explanation of Heb. 11:1, *Subsidiary Essay*, HZW 2:214–18.

Friend, don't confuse us with Scripture; it is not the fanatics' practice to rely upon Scripture.[58] [They say,] "But you ought to produce Scripture that God does and can do such things." All right, here is my Scripture: What God says, he can do, Romans 4[:21], and with God no word is impossible, Luke 1[:37]. Since then he says here, "This is my body," he truly can and does do this. Now you in turn must prove that he does not and cannot do this. For that is your sovereign argument with which you would dislodge these words. [. . .][g]

58. Luther implies that the fanatics value both reason and the direct inspiration of the Spirit more highly than Scripture.

There lies the celebrated argument, now, that they gabble about the most, above all others, and on which they rely and insist most stubbornly, when they say that the two Scripture passages are contradictory: Christ is seated in heaven, and his body is in the Supper, though they do not prove it. But they do prove clearly that these two passages and their reason are contradictory. It would not have been necessary to prove this, though; I could have told them just as well. For what you say—that Scripture is contradictory—is not valid. Who asks what you say? I would laud and honor them, however, if they would prove their assertion with Scripture or in some other way. But they must

g Text omitted (see LW 37:47–48).

leave this undone, in order that this text may remain firm, "This is my body."

If we establish that Oecolampadius can neither prove this assertion of his nor indicate how Scripture is contradictory with regard to God—which, to be sure, he can never do—then the whole argument has been won and we have established everything. For if it turns out that for us the words remain, "This is my body," i.e., that Christ's body is present in the Supper, then the saying in John 6[:63], "The flesh is of no avail," will harmonize perfectly well. Miracles aplenty will then take place, the sacraments will not be mere symbols,[59] and their whole swarm,[h] which is so big, will scatter and fly away like dust before the wind. For Christ's body and blood must not be left as useless and insignificant things—of this I am sure.

59. In his paraphrases on the Gospels, Erasmus used the word *symbolon* with regard to the Eucharist, but after the outbreak of the eucharistic controversy he denied that by it he meant an empty symbol, John B. Payne, *Erasmus: His Theology of the Sacraments* (Richmond, Va.: John Knox Press, 1970), 136–38. The Swiss and South Germans followed Erasmus in referring to the Lord's Supper or its elements as symbols, Zwingli, *Letter to Alber*, HZW 2:139; Oecolampadius, *Ad Pyrkaimerum responsio*, fol. c5v-c6r; Bucer, *Common Places*, 317–23.

However, if we should judge the articles of our faith and Scripture according to our reason and our eyes, as Oecolampadius does here,[i] then indeed every point in Scripture is in opposition to the other. For the text that Mary is a virgin and mother [Luke 1:27, 31] is opposed to the texts, "Be fruitful and multiply" and "I will make for man a helper fit for him" [Gen. 1:28; 2:18]. If for that reason I should deny that she was a virgin, and exclaim, "Scripture is contradictory," someone would fairly answer me, "Yes, for you and your reason it is contradictory; but how is it contradictory before God? Tell me that!" So I would be in the same position as Oecolampadius is here.

Again, that Christ is God is contrary to the text "God created man" [Gen. 1:27]. Go on now and say, "He is not God, because divinity and humanity are more opposed to each other than heaven and earth; and the person, Christ, cannot be at the same time in the Godhead and in humanity." Let your reason be that these texts are contradictory. Then someone will answer you, "Yes, you say so, and in your eyes they are contradictory, but show me that they are also contradictory in God's sight!"

So too, Oecolampadius says that it is a contradiction that Christ's body is both in heaven and in the Supper, and so it is in his eyes.[j] Yes, but no one asked him to teach us his fables and

h *Geschwürm*, a pun on *Schwärmer*, translated here as fanatics.

i Oecolampadius, *Ad Pyrkaimerum responsio*, fol. c6v-c8r.

j Oecolampadius, *Billiche Antwortt*, W^2 20:601–2.

what appears to him to be thus and so, but what God says and how it is in God's eyes. There he lies helpless, yet he must and should do so, if he wishes to make his teaching certain and sure. Here let them answer; here let us see how they will crack their heads. But they do not do it. They will grumble something foolish and pipe a different tune, so that no one notices how they are being forced into a tight spot.

Compare them now, these fanatics and corrupters of the Scriptures. Karlstadt produced his *touto*, which turned out to be untenable. Then Zwingli came and tried to improve the matter with his signifying, which was even less tenable. Next comes Oecolampadius with his "sign of the body," as the best idea of all, and it proves least tenable of all. So his argument runs: "I, Oecolampadius, say that Scripture on this point is contradictory." Now isn't this a fine, delicate basis of faith, when a person can say, "Although God's Word stands there and says, 'This is my body,' nevertheless because I cannot comprehend or believe it, and it appears to me to contradict Scripture, it is therefore not true and must have another meaning, regardless of how clearly God's Word stands there." This is Oecolampadius's spirit and his celebrated truth, that human fancy and unbelief shall prevail over God's Word and form the basis of our faith. Who could not do the same thing in all other articles of faith as well? How profoundly can Satan mislead such people? Hence this argument of Oecolampadius is overthrown with a single word: NO! These texts are not contradictory; one may say so and imagine so, but not prove it. Thus all his fancy arguments lie in the filth. [. . .][k]

If they had first considered and seen to it that they spoke nothing but God's words, as St. Peter teaches [1 Pet. 4:11], and had left their own fables and assumptions at home, they would not have created so much misfortune. This saying, "Scripture is not self-contradictory," would not have misled Oecolampadius, for it is grounded in God's Word that God does not lie nor does his Word deceive. But this addition to his word, "I, Oecolampadius, say that Scripture here is contradictory," brings him into such toil and sweat that he denies, twists, reinterprets, and tortures the Word of God any way he pleases. Lord God, how easily such a horrible downfall takes place, and still we are sure and fearless on this slippery path!

k Text omitted (see LW 37:50).

But I shall more clearly touch on and describe their real argument that moves them to such an error, and I shall stake my body and soul, which I would not gladly lose, that I shall not fail in my purpose. Poor sinner that I am, I too know a little about the Spirit, and a great deal about the old rogue who rages in us—I mean, the flesh. This one factor moves them above all others: that according to reason it is altogether absurd to believe that we should bodily eat and drink Christ's body and blood in the Supper. And I know for certain that if they should win, their ultimate exultation would be, "Yes, I was perfectly sure that it could not be right: it just never made sense to me that Christ's body and blood should be treated in this way,"[60] as they are now whispering secretly among themselves, and as the foolish masses are prattling openly. But they would like to conceal this, for they are ashamed to admit it. They know very well that it is worthless talk, but they are pleased to see the foolish masses blurt it out, and they say and write nothing against it. It is shameful, however, that they have not enough decency and honesty to confess openly what they really wish in their hearts and what they would like to have and see and hear but allege instead that Scripture compels them—which they know is not true, for they seize Scripture with guile and malice in order to adorn themselves before the people, and under the guise of Scripture they spread their poison among the people.

Although they conceal all this with great diligence, still the old rogue peeks out and exposes himself to view clearly enough. Zwingli as much as confesses that he never believed it his whole life long, and I have no doubt that he believes nothing at all. Indeed, what is more, he places himself upon the judgment seat and judges the heart and spirit of all people, declaring that no one has ever believed this.[l] If this is not too rash, it certainly is rash enough, and besides, it is not true, as I know only too well. Now from this confession it is to be observed that he does not draw this notion from Scripture, which he discovered only long afterward, as his book *Subsidiary Essay*, in particular, and others prove. Long before he ever found that treatise he had these beliefs, and only now does he run and hunt up Scripture and force it to suit his notion.[61] Before Dr. Karlstadt started writing, he too said a long time ago to a certain person, "My friend, you

60. Peter the layman, one of the figures in Karlstadt's *Dialogue on the Misuse of the Sacrament*, expressed this view, in *Pamphlets*, 175.

61. In the fall of 1525, Zwingli stated that he had long believed "this is my body" should be understood figuratively, but he had not understood that "is" should be understood as "signified" until he read the *Most Christian Letter* of Cornelis Hoen; *Ad Bvgenhagii epistolam responsio*, Z 4:560.

l Zwingli, *Letter to Alber*, HZW 2:142; *Subsidiary Essay*, HZW 2:195, 213.

will not persuade me that God is in the bread and wine." So, by the power of God, they are caught off guard.

In the same way when Oecolampadius skips over the Scripture confronting him, God help us, how gaily he leaps and dances with his notion, asking: "What benefit comes from it? Why didn't the disciples worship the bread? Why does Scripture indicate no miracle here? How does it help if Christ is invisibly present? Why must Christians believe such a difficult thing? What sense does it make that the King of glory permits such wicked fellows to trifle with him?"[m] In particular, however, it is his blasphemous words that portray his heart best, when he calls our God a baked God, a bread-God, a meat-God, and many, many other names.[62] Who can possibly fail to understand now what they think in their hearts? If Scripture moved them, they would surely have done with such obscenities and deal with Scripture.

62. Oecolampadius defended these terms in *Billiche Antwortt*, W² 20:588–9, in response to Luther's condemnation of them in the preface to the first Wittenberg translation of the *Syngramma*, LW 59:157; see also n. 23, p. 177.

This is the rancor and hatred of natural reason, which wants nothing to do with this article and therefore spits and vomits against it, and then tries to wrap itself in Scripture so that it may avoid being recognized. Not a single article of faith would remain if I followed the rancor of reason. I too could use this spitting and vomiting against it, so that the blasphemers do not think that such spitting is simply an art of the Holy Spirit. I can say of God: What benefit is it that he is man? Why must one believe such a difficult thing? Why don't the apostles worship him in the Supper? What sense does it make that this Divine Majesty permits himself to be crucified by wicked fellows? Oh, what a meat-God! Oh, what a bloody God! Oh, what a dead God! And so forth.

With this rancor, however, my dear fanatics prepare the way for the virtual denial of Christ, God, and everything, as they have already, in part, made a start at believing nothing at all. They follow the fancy of reason, which they expect to lead them aright. But this mockery only serves the purpose of stirring up the foolish masses, who do not trouble themselves with Scripture. They themselves know perfectly well that all their heathenish vomiting proves nothing against this article, or if it disproves this one, it also disproves all articles. For God's Word is always folly to

m Oecolampadius, *Genvina expositione*, fol. B1r-v, D5r; *Apologetica*, fol. C4v-5r, D8v; *Ad Pyrkaimerum responsio*, fol. D1r, e5r; *Billiche Antwortt*, W² 20:604, 607–8.

reason, 1 Cor. 1[:18]. Therefore they would have kept silent about all this if they were really in earnest about Scripture and did not have hearts full of sheer rancor and unbelief which had to spill out of their mouths. More on this subject later.

Again, when Oecolampadius in his first book plays nasty tricks and defames the sayings of the fathers, he must confess that he has not derived his notion from the fathers' writings,[63] for they speak so mightily that they very frequently extort the admission from him, "This appears to be against us."[n] My friend, what else is this than to say, "The fathers express themselves strongly in this way; I cannot derive my argument from their writings but must work hard to twist their nose around to my sense"? But anyone who must work so hard to twist and force these sayings around to his position confesses that they yield not his position but rather the very opposite, and he is importing and reading his own thoughts into them. What advantage his nose-twisting of the fathers brings him, however, we shall see later.

The amazing thing, meanwhile, is that of all the fathers, as many as you can name, not one has ever spoken about the sacrament as these fanatics do. None of them uses such an expression as, "It is simply bread and wine," or, "Christ's body and blood are not present." Yet since this subject is so frequently discussed by them, it is impossible that they should not at some time have let slip such an expression as, "It is simply bread," or, "Not that the body of Christ is corporeally present," or the like, since they are greatly concerned not to mislead the people; actually, they simply proceed to speak as if no one doubted that Christ's body and blood are present. Certainly among so many fathers and so many writings a negative argument should have turned up at least once, as happens in other articles; but actually they all stand uniformly and consistently on the affirmative side. Our fanatics, however, can speak of virtually nothing but the negative. In short: Oecolampadius has derived his view neither from the Scriptures nor from the fathers, but he sweats and toils to import it into both.

This should be quite enough to answer the fanatics. For since we prove and establish that the saying of Christ, "This is

63. A central argument of Oecolampadius's *Genvina expositione* was that the church fathers did not believe Christ's body was physically present in the sacrament. In some of his discussions of patristic citations he argued that the passage did not mean what it seemed to say.

n *Hoc apparet contra nos esse.* Oecolampadius, *Genvina expositione,* fol. F5r, F8r, G3v.

my body," still stands firm, and that their best arguments are worthless, and bare and devoid of all proof, then surely all the other texts concerning Christ's Supper also stand firm. For I have taken up the least and simplest of them, just to challenge the impotent, unsound, feeble prattle of the fanatics. So I treated this subject not without care also in my book *Against the Heavenly Prophets*, and up to now no fanatic has refuted that book for me.[o] I maintain, however, that they scorn it and do not read it, or if they do read it, they curl their lips and pass it by, on account of their great humility and fullness of all wisdom and holiness.

However, in order to strengthen our people, I shall go on and show that the fanatics' reasons and arguments are worthless, and shall prove to the point of superfluity that it is contrary neither to Scripture nor to the articles of faith for Christ's body to be at the same time in heaven and in the Supper. I shall do this even though I do not owe it to the fanatics; rather, they are obligated to prove that it is contrary to Scripture, and they cannot do it, as said above. If I have proven this, however, then the words, "This is my body," should be allowed to stand and remain just as they read. That I should show visibly with eyes and finger that Christ's body is at the same time in heaven and at table, as the fanatics ask of us, of course I cannot do.[64] He who is unwilling to believe the words of God need not demand anything further from me. So I do enough if I prove that it is not contrary to God's Word, but consistent with Scripture.

64. Oecolampadius challenged his readers to prove from Scripture that a body could be in more than one place, *Billiche Antwortt*, W² 20:603.

[Christ's Ascension: Definition and Location of God's Right Hand]

In the first place, we take up the article that Christ sits at the right hand of God, which the fanatics maintain does not allow that Christ's body can also be in the Supper. Now if we ask how they interpret God's "right hand" where Christ sits, I suppose they will dream up for us, as one does for children, an imaginary heaven in which a golden throne stands, and Christ sits beside the Father in a cowl and golden crown, the way artists paint it. For if they did not have such childish, fleshly ideas of the right hand of God, they surely would not allow the idea of Christ's

o LW 40:144–223; TAL 2:39–126.

bodily presence in the Supper to vex them so or castigate themselves so with the saying of Augustine (whom in other respects they do not believe at all, nor anyone else), "Christ must be bodily in one place, but his truth is everywhere."[65]

65. Oecolampadius cited this passage, familiar from both Peter Lombard's *Sentences* IV, dist. 10, c.1 (MPL 192:859–60) and from canon law (CIC 1:1330), in *Genvina expositione*, fol. C6v.

A rendering of the Trinity depicting Christ seated beside God, with the dove as Holy Spirit. From an illustrated Bible published by Jean Crespin (1527).

From these childish ideas it must follow further that they also bind God to one place in heaven, on the same golden throne, since apart from Christ there is no God, and where Christ is there is the Godhead in all its fullness, as Paul says, "In him the whole Godhead dwells bodily" [Col. 2:9], and John 6 [14:9f.], "Have I been with you so long, and yet you do not know me, Philip? The one who has seen me has seen the Father. Do you not believe that the Father is in me and I am in the Father?" From this it follows still further that we and all creatures also sit on the same throne of God—perhaps as the lice and fleas in his cowl—since Paul says, Acts 17[:28], "We are his offspring, and in him we live and move and have our being."

We ask them further: Where is the Scripture that forces the right hand of God into one place? They say: "God help us, don't we produce texts enough? Are you blind? Don't you see how our books are full of passages from Scripture?" Indeed, I see very well that you are worthless spouters, that you produce an enormous amount of prattle where it is not necessary, as for example about spiritual eating, Christ's sitting in heaven, remembrance of him in the Supper, and the like, about which no one is questioning you. This is your cuckoo letting himself be heard; here you are full of Scripture. But where it is necessary you pass by, dumb as a clod, indulging in the dream that all of Scripture is in harmony with your notion. As Solomon says in Ecclesiastes 5[:3], it is the way of the world that "what lies on one's mind, one dreams about"—one can't get it out of one's mind. And Virgil, "Lovers fashion dreams of their own."[p]

Why do you not ponder and learn first whether or not Scripture says that God's right hand is a specific place, because Scripture speaks quite abundantly of the right hand of God? But you erect such a great and risky fanaticism upon your empty dream and then boast that you produce much Scripture; and because you enjoy joining in this dance so much, it seems to you that heaven is full of fiddles. As they say, the person who likes to dance is easy to pipe to.[66] Thus, since it pleases you that Christ is in heaven and not in the Supper, you let St. Augustine's saying persuade you so easily to affirm that God's right hand is a place in heaven—you who otherwise are so stubborn, clever, and inflexible about the sayings of all the fathers that, even if all of them together unanimously constrain you to a "Yes," you will still make a "No" out of it. Yet you think no one should notice why you produce a great deal of Scripture on unnecessary topics, while on the necessary topics you produce not a tittle but only your own dreams.

66. Luther alludes to two popular proverbs: "Heaven isn't full of fiddles," and "It's easy to pipe for those who want to dance"; Wander, 2:646; 3:1260.

Scripture teaches us, however, that the right hand of God is not a specific place in which a body must or may be, such as on a golden throne, but that it is the almighty power of God, which at one and the same time can be nowhere and yet must be everywhere. It cannot be at any one place, I say. For if it were at some specific place, it would have to be there in a perceptible and circumscribed manner, as everything which is at one place must be at that place circumscribed and determinate, so that it cannot meanwhile be at any other place. But the power of God cannot

p *Qui amant, sibi somnia fingunt.* Virgil, *Eclogues* 8.108, in Virgil, *Eclogues, Georgics, Aeneid I-VI*, trans. H. Rushton Fairclaugh, rev. ed., Loeb Classical Library 63 (Cambridge: Harvard University Press, 1999), 82–83.

be so circumscribed and determined, for it is immeasurable and cannot be grasped with the senses, beyond and above all that is or may be.

On the other hand, it must be present in its essence at all places,[67] even in the tiniest tree leaf. The reason is this: It is God who creates, effects, and preserves all things through God's almighty power and right hand, as our Creed confesses. For God dispatches no officials or angels when God creates or preserves something, but all this is the work of God's divine power itself. If God is to create or preserve it, however, God must be present and must make and preserve creation both in its innermost and outermost aspects. Therefore, indeed, God must be present in every single creature in its innermost and outermost being, on all sides, through and through, below and above, before and behind, so that nothing can be more truly present and within all creatures than God and God's power. For it is God who makes the skin and the bones; it is God who makes the hair on the skin and the marrow in the bones; it is God who makes every bit of the hair, and every bit of the marrow. Indeed, God must make everything, both the parts and the whole. Surely, then, God's hand which makes all this must be present; that cannot be lacking.

At this point the passage of Isa. 66[:2], alluding to Genesis 1, undeniably applies: "Has not my hand made all these things?" [. . .][q] Isaiah 66[:1], "Heaven is my throne and the earth is my footstool." God does not say, "A part of heaven is my throne, a part of or place on the earth is my footstool," but, "Whatever and wherever heaven is, there is my throne, whether heaven is beneath, above, or beside the earth. And whatever and wherever earth is, whether at the bottom of the sea, in the grave of the dead, or at the middle of the earth, there is my footstool." Come and tell me now, where are God's head, arm, breast, body, if with God's feet the earth is filled and with God's legs heaven is filled? Widely, widely God reaches out and beyond the world, above heaven and earth.

What can Isaiah intend with this saying but, as St. Hilary[68] also says on this subject,[r] that God's essence is present everywhere, in and through the whole creation in all its parts and in

q Luther also quotes Ps. 139:7-10; Acts 5:31; Ps. 118:15-16; Acts 17:27-28; Rom. 11:36; and Jer. 23:23-24. Text omitted (see LW 37:58).

r Hilary, *On the Trinity* I.6 (MPL 10:29; NPNF2, 9:41–42).

67. *Wesentlich und gegenwartig.* The German word *wesentlich* was used for two concepts in Aristotelian philosophy: essence (that which is) and substance (that which gives it its fundamental characteristics).

68. Hilary (c. 300–c. 368) was bishop of Poitiers in the province of Gaul (France) and an outspoken opponent of the Arians. His opposition to the Arian emperor resulted in exile to Asia Minor. His treatise *On the Trinity,* written while in exile, was the first significant defense in Latin of the Nicene position.

all places, and so the world is full of God who fills it all, yet God is not circumscribed or enclosed by it, but is at the same time beyond and above the whole creation? All this is an infinitely incomprehensible thing, yet this is an article of our faith, clearly and powerfully attested in Scripture. In comparison with this it is a trivial matter that Christ's body and blood are at the same time in heaven and in the Supper. And if the fanatics began to approach this point with their reason and their eyes, they would quickly fall headlong and say that it is nothing and (as it is the great virtue of the ungodly to say), "There is no God," Psalm 14[:1].

For how can reason tolerate it that the Divine Majesty is so small as to be present in essence in a kernel, on a kernel, above a kernel, throughout a kernel, inside and outside—and, even though it is one single Majesty, can nevertheless be completely and entirely present in every individual thing, countless in number though they be? For God certainly makes every single kernel in particular, in all its parts, on the inside and throughout, so God's power must be present there throughout, in and on the kernel. But now, God's power is one and simple and is not divided, as if God made the husk of the kernel by hand and the pith of the kernel with God's feet. Thus the entire divine power must be present throughout, in and on the kernel. For God alone makes it all. On the other hand, the same Majesty is so great that neither this world nor even a thousand worlds could surround it and say, "See, there it is!"

Here, now, let the fanatics answer me. Bodies, of course, can be compared with other bodies; they may fit together, as for example bread is a body, wine is a body, Christ's flesh is a body. Here one body may be in another, as I can be in the open air, and in a garment or a house, as money can be in a purse, or wine in a cask or jug. But here, where we are dealing not with body but spirit—indeed, who knows what this is that we call God? God is beyond body, beyond spirit, beyond everything one can say or hear or think: how at one and the same time can such a being be completely and entirely present in every single body, every created thing and being everywhere, and on the other hand, must and can be outside of, beyond, and above all created things and beings, as our Creed and Scripture testify to both truths about God? Here reason must simply conclude: "Oh, surely this is utter nonsense and can be nothing but nonsense." Now if God has found the way whereby God's own divine nature can be wholly and entirely in all creatures and in every single individual being, more deeply, more inwardly, more present than the creature is to itself, and yet on the other hand may and can be circumscribed nowhere and in no being, so that God actually circumscribes all things and is in all, but no one being circumscribes God and is in God—should not this same God also know some way whereby God's body could be wholly and completely present in many places at the same time, and yet none of these places could be where God is? Ah, we miserable children of men, who judge God and God's doings according to our own imagination, and think of God as a cobbler or a day laborer!

"Yes," they say, "of course we believe that God's power is everywhere. But it is not necessary on that account for his divine essence or his right hand to be everywhere." Answer: I believe also, of course, that at the bottom of your hearts you believe nothing either about God or about God's power. I am certain, moreover, that you will, of course, leap over all these irrefutable Scripture passages which I am adducing and expounding here, and that you will curl your lips and say, "Humph! He speaks of kernels and tree leaves, but he produces no Scripture." For this is what you are accustomed to do. And then you jabber something about your tolerance or babble about irrelevant matters, and that must serve as Scripture. We know, however, that God's power, arm, hand, essence, face, Spirit, wisdom, etc., are all one thing; for apart from the creation there is nothing but the one simple Deity itself. And thus, if before the creation of the universe there doubtless existed the power and hand of God, God's essence itself, then it did not become something else after the creation of the universe. Indeed, God makes and does nothing except through God's Word, Gen. 1[:3, 6, 9], John 1[:3, 10], i.e., God's power. And this power is not an ax, hatchet, saw, or file with which God works, but is truly God. Then if God's power and Spirit are present everywhere and in all things to the innermost and outermost degree, through and through, as it must be if God is to make and preserve all things everywhere, then God's divine right hand, essence, and majesty must also be everywhere. God must surely be present if God makes and preserves them.

For good measure I shall also prove this with an example and story from Scripture. It is our belief, of course, as Scripture teaches us, that our Lord Jesus Christ is in essence and by nature true God, and "in him the fullness of the Godhead dwells bodily," as St. Paul says in Col. 2[:9]. Thus, apart from Christ there is simply no God or Divinity at all, as he himself also says in John 16 [14:9f.], "Philip, he who has seen me has seen the Father. Do you not believe that the Father is in me and I am in him?" All right, Christ walks on earth, and the entire Godhead is in him in essence and person on earth. Now tell me: How can it be true at one and the same time that God is entirely present, in essence and person, in Christ on earth in his mother's womb, yes, in the crib, in the temple, in the wilderness, in cities, in houses, in gardens, in fields, on the cross, in the grave, etc., yet nonetheless also in heaven in the Father's bosom? If this is true and undeniably consistent with the faith that the Godhead itself is in essence and person present in Christ on earth in so many places, and yet at the same time in heaven with the Father, it follows that he is everywhere at the same time, and in essence and person fills heaven and earth and everything with his own nature and majesty, in accordance with Scripture, Jer. 22 [23:23 f.], "I fill heaven and earth, and am a God near at hand," and Ps. 139[:7], "Where can I flee from your presence?"

Moreover, when Christ, the Son of God, was to be conceived in his mother's womb and become man, he certainly had to be already present in essence and person in the Virgin's womb, and had to assume humanity there. For the Godhead is immutable in itself and cannot pass from one place to another as created things do. Therefore he did not climb down from heaven as on a ladder or descend as by a rope, but was already in the Virgin's womb in essence and person, as he was also in all other places, everywhere, according to the nature, character, and power of divinity. If he is in a certain place, then, such as the Virgin's womb, in his essence and in his own person, and at the same time present with his Father, as our Creed requires, he is certainly also present everywhere in this way. For there can be no reason why he should be able to be in the Virgin's womb and not also be present everywhere.

Yet in Christ there is something different, higher, and greater than in all other created things. For in him God not only is present in his essence as in all others, but also dwells bodily in him in such a way that one person is man and God. Although I can say of all created things, "There is God, or God is in it," I cannot say, "This is God himself." But of Christ the Creed[69] asserts not

69. The Nicene Creed asserts that Christ is "God from God, light from light, true God from true God."

only that God is in him but that Christ is God himself. Anyone who kills a man may be called a murderer of a being who belongs to God and in whom God is present, but one who kills Christ has killed God's Son—indeed, God and the Lord of glory himself. Now, that God not only is in him but also dwells in him in such a way that God and man are one person—this is the mighty work and wonder of God, which makes all reason foolish, and which faith alone must hold to; otherwise all is lost. [. . .][s]

It has been shown convincingly enough by now that the right hand of God is not a particular place where Christ's body is seated, as the fanatics dream, but is the very power of God. For God's right hand, of course, cannot be a created thing but must be something above and apart from all created things, for there is no one and nothing other than God who is everywhere in all things. Therefore this also must be true, that God's right hand is everywhere in all things, as we have heard. I truly believe that we do not bypass Scripture here like the fanatics, or discuss things other than those that pertain to the subject, but that we have firmly established and concluded from the clear and correct ground of Scripture and the articles of the Creed that the right hand of God is everywhere. They, however—the fanatics—lose the point and fail to maintain their position when they say it is a particular place, supporting their carnal ideas from Augustine.

[Christ's Ascension: Ubiquity of Christ's Body]

Now let us come to grips with them. They admit that Christ is at the right hand of God, and thereby claim to have won the point that he is not in the Supper. This is indeed the fearful sword of the giant Goliath of which they boast.[t] But what if we should take this same sword away from you and lop off your head with it, and prove that Christ's body must be present in the Supper using the same text with which you want to prove that it must not be there—wouldn't you then regard this as a true deed of David? Very well then: Take notice and listen to us. Christ's body is at the right hand of God; that is granted. The right hand of

s Text omitted (see LW 37:63).

t Cf. 1 Sam. 17:4, 41-51.

God, however, is everywhere, as you must grant from our previous demonstration. Therefore it surely is present also in the bread and wine at table. Now where the right hand of God is, there Christ's body and blood must be, for the right hand of God is not divisible into many parts but a single, simple entity. So too, the article of the Creed does not say that Christ is at one part of the right hand of God, such as a little finger or fingernail, but it says simply, "at the right hand of God," that wherever and whatever God's right hand is in reality and in name, there is Christ, the Son of man.

This is also the intention of Christ wherever he confesses in the gospel that all things have been delivered to him by the Father [Luke 10:22] and all things put under his feet, Psalm 8[:6]. That is, he is at the right hand of God, which means nothing other than that even as a man he is over all things, has all things under him, and rules over all. Therefore he must also be near at hand, in and about all things, and have all things in his hands. For nothing is delivered to him or put under his feet according to his divinity, since he himself first made all things and preserves them. But to sit at God's right hand is the same as to rule and have power over all things. If he is to have power and rule, surely he must also be present there in his essence through the right hand of God, which is everywhere.

Now what is the result? Just this: even if Christ had never spoken or set forth these words at the Supper, "This is my body," still the words "Christ sits at the right hand of God" would require that his body and blood may be there as well as at all other places, and that although there need be no transubstantiation or conversion of the bread into his body,[70] it can well be present nonetheless, just as the right hand of God does not need to be converted into all things even though it is surely present and in them. How this takes place, however, is not for us to know; we are to believe it, since Scripture and the articles of the Creed[u] so irrefutably confirm it.

We poor sinners, indeed, are not so mad as to believe that Christ's body is in the bread in a crude visible manner, like bread in a basket or wine in a cup, as the fanatics charge us with, to

70. Transubstantiation was the teaching that the substance of the bread and wine were converted into Christ's body and blood when the priest spoke the words, "This is my body," although the outward appearance (the "accidents") of bread and wine remained unchanged. In *Babylonian Captivity*, Luther rejected not the doctrine of transubstantiation per se but, rather, the requirement that one believe transubstantiation as the explanation for how Christ's body is present. He argued that Aristotle should not be used as the basis for theological speculation.

u Cf. n. *p*, p. 186.

amuse themselves with our madness.[v] But we believe simply that his body is present, as his words say and indicate: "This is my body." When the fathers and we occasionally say, "Christ's body is in the bread," we do so quite simply because by our faith we wish to confess that Christ's body is present. Otherwise we may well allow it to be said, "he is in the bread, he is the bread, he is where the bread is," or whatever you wish.[71] We do not wish to argue over words, just so the meaning is retained that it is not mere bread that we eat in Christ's Supper, but the body of Christ.

Moreover, the fanatics should consider that God has more ways by which to have one object in another than this crude mode that they set forth, as wine is in a barrel, bread in a box, or money in a pocket.[72] "Levi was in the loins of Abraham," says the writer to the Hebrews [7:10], as Scripture describes all children as in their fathers' loins or from their loins. Again, all colors and lights and everything that one sees are said to "be in their eyes," so that even heaven and earth may be in one's eye. Again, everything that stands before a mirror is in it. Again, trees and all fruits are in the kernel or seed. Again, all things are in our hearts, even God, which indeed is a greater wonder than all others. Who will doubt, then, that God has many more modes, which God does not tell us about, where one thing is in another, or two things are present at the same time in one place?

But it is just as great a miracle that many bodies are in one place as that one body is in many places. He who can bring about the one can bring about the other also. Now we have clear Scripture that Christ came to his disciples through the locked door, and out of his grave, even through the sealed stone. Whether he entered through the window or the door, his body and that through which his body passed must have been simultaneously in one place, both intact and unchanged. The evangelist says not that they saw him enter, but, "He appeared or stood in their midst" [Luke 24:36], which sounds as if he had been there already, hidden, and now revealed himself, as he also did to Mary Magdalene at the grave [John 20:14], and with all to whom he appeared. And in Acts 8 [7:55f.] he appeared to St. Stephen in the town hall standing at the right hand of God. And in Acts

71. Karlstadt criticized the traditional wording, that the body of Christ was "in and under the form of bread and wine"; *Pamphlets*, 144–46. Karlstadt's argument was taken up by others, e.g., Oecolampadius, *Genvina expositione*, fol. C3r.

72. Medieval theologians had discussed various modes of presence by which two things could be in the same place simultaneously. Luther's view was influenced by William of Ockham's discussion of "diffinitive presence," Hartmut Hilgenfeld, *Mittelalterlich-traditionelle Elemente in Luthers Abendmahlsschriften*, Studien zur Dogmengeschichte und systematischen Theologie 29 (Zurich: Theologischer Verlag, 1971), 183–97; Hermann Sasse, *This Is My Body: Luther's Contention for the Real Presence in the Sacrament of the Altar* (Minneapolis: Augsburg, 1959), 124–28.

v Oecolampadius, *Genvina expositione*, fol. Avr, E7r; *Ad Pyrkaimerum responsio*, fol. d1r.

22[:17f.] he appeared to St. Paul in the temple. Again, in Matt. 17[:5] the Father appeared in the clouds upon Mt. Tabor, and in Luke 3[:22], too, the Father came in his voice and the Holy Spirit in the form of a dove. These and similar appearances that were granted to the prophets, apostles, and saints many, many times, show indeed that both God and Christ are not far away but near, and it is only a matter of revealing themselves, since they do not move up and down or back and forth, for God is immutable, and Christ also sits at the right hand of God and does not move hither and yon.

So too, Christ says in John 3[:13], "No one has ascended into heaven but he who descended from heaven, the Son of man who is in heaven," whereby he shows indeed that his body is at the same time in heaven and on earth, yes, even at the ends of the earth. For by his glorification he did not become another person, but before as well as after was present everywhere. Yet Oecolampadius imagines he has won a great point over Willibald Pirkheimer of Nuremberg, claiming he does not know how great a sin it is for Pirkheimer to interpret this text as referring to the humanity of Christ.[73] If I were Pirkheimer, however, I would send Oecolampadius some spectacles and ask him to count the letters. Perhaps this would help to keep them from stepping so lightly over the texts of Scripture and substituting for them their own dreams in the books they have scribbled for us.

But what is the meaning of "Son of man—descended—ascended"? He speaks so clearly about the Son of man as the one who descended and ascended. Now of course it is certain that Christ did not descend or ascend according to his divinity, but according to his humanity. If Oecolampadius indeed wished to boast so haughtily, he should first prove that this text refers to Christ according to his divinity, and teach the meaning of "to descend" and "to ascend," and expound the text carefully and cogently. But that is not necessary for us fanatics. It is enough if we rave like fanatics, and this will instantly be called pure Scripture. However, since many teachers have expounded the descent from heaven, I shall forgo such an explanation until I hear my fanatics express themselves. I cannot write everything all at once.

By this kind of talk perhaps I shall now attract other fanatics who would like to trip me up, arguing: "If Christ's body is everywhere, ah, then I shall eat and drink him in all the taverns, from all kinds of bowls, glasses, and jugs! Then there is no difference

73. Pirckheimer cited John 3:13 to argue that Christ's glorified body could be in more than one place, WPBW 6:477–78. Oecolampadius criticized Pirckheimer's interpretation, arguing that it was an essential characteristic of a body to be in only one place, *Ad Pyrkaimerum responsio*, fol. f6v-f7v.

between my table and the Lord's table. Oh, how we will gobble him up!"[74] Such shameful pigs are we dreadful Germans for the most part that we have neither restraint nor reason, and if we hear something about God we pay as much attention as if it were a buffoon's fairy tale. Just now a story against the sacrament is circulating among the masses who have been misled by the teaching of the fanatics, that it would be better to die than to write a sermon among them. For they quickly run about when they hear that it is nothing, and they want to do a mess on it and wipe their behinds with it. The civil government ought to punish such blasphemers. It is an offense against the law and an act of insolence, since they know nothing about what they are saying but speak blasphemy anyway. God knows, I write about such difficult matters with great reluctance, for it is destined to reach such dogs and pigs.[75] But what am I to do about it? The fanatics must bear the responsibility for pushing me to it.

Late medieval German depictions of the ascension focused on Christ's absence and the disciples' reaction, as in this engraving by Albrecht Dürer (c. 1511).

Listen now, you pig, dog, or fanatic, whatever kind of unreasonable ass you are: Even if Christ's body is everywhere, you do not therefore immediately gobble or swill or grasp him; nor do I talk with you about such things in this manner, either; go back to your pigpen and your filth. I said above that the right hand of God is everywhere, but at the same time nowhere and imperceptible, above and apart from all creatures. There is a difference between God being present and your grasping God, who is free and unbound wherever God is, and does not have to stand there like a rogue set in a pillory or neck irons.

See, the bright rays of the sun are so near you that they pierce into your eyes or your skin so that you feel it, yet you are unable to grasp them and put them into a box, even if you should grope after it forever. Prevent them from shining in through the window—this you can do, but grope and grasp them you cannot. So too with Christ: although he is everywhere present, he does

74. Karlstadt argued that the Lord's Supper was bread and wine eaten in remembrance of Christ, *Pamphlets*, 215. Anabaptists and other radicals adopted this idea and met together to break and share bread in private homes, which led Luther and others to accuse them of reducing the Lord's Supper to a common meal.

75. An allusion to Matt. 7:6, "Do not give what is holy to dogs; and do not throw your pearls before swine, or they will trample them under foot and turn and maul you."

not permit himself to be so caught and grasped; he can easily shell himself, so that you get the shell but not the kernel. Why? Because it is one thing if God is present, and another if God is present for you. God is there for you when God adds the Word and binds himself, saying, "Here you shall find me."[76] Now when you have the Word, you can grasp and have God with certainty and say, "Here I have you, as you have said." Just as I say of the right hand of God: although this is everywhere, as we may not deny, still because it is also nowhere, as has been said, you can actually grasp it nowhere, unless for your benefit it binds itself to you and summons you to a definite place. This God's right hand does, however, when it enters into the humanity of Christ and dwells there. There you surely find it. Otherwise you will run back and forth throughout all creation, groping here and groping there yet never finding, even though it is actually there; for it is not there for you.

76. Luther's description of a hidden God who cannot be grasped by reason but who chose to reveal himself through God's Word reflects his nominalist training, with its distinction between God's wholly free absolute power and God's ordained power by which God binds himself to a specific order and way of acting. Heiko A. Oberman, "'Via Antiqua' and 'Via Moderna': Late Medieval Prolegomena to Early Reformation Thought," *Journal of the History of Ideas* 48 (1987): 23–40.

So too, since Christ's humanity is at the right hand of God, and also is in all and above all things according to the nature of the divine right hand, you will not gobble or swill him like the cabbage and soup on your table, unless he wills it. He also now exceeds any grasp, and you will not catch him by groping about, even though he is in your bread, unless he binds himself to you and summons you to a particular table through his Word, and he himself points out the bread to you, through his Word, bidding you to eat him. This he does in the Supper, saying, "This is my body," as if to say, "At home you may eat bread also, where I am indeed sufficiently near at hand too; but this is the true *touto*,[w] the 'This is my body': when you eat this, you eat my body, and nowhere else. Why? Because I wish to attach myself here with my Word, in order that you may not have to buzz about,[x] trying to seek me in all the places where I am. This would be too much for you, and you would also be too puny to grasp me in these places without my Word."

O how very few there are even among the most learned who have ever pondered this article concerning Christ so profoundly, or have ever believed what is so utterly incomprehensible, that God should be man and man should be God! But there stands the Scripture, and faith holds it to be certain truth. If it is true,

w See n. 50, p. 191.

x *Schwermen*, the root word for *Schwermer* or "fanatics."

then, we have here overthrown one of the fanatics' best arguments—namely, that for Christ's body to be at the same time in heaven and in the Supper is not a contradiction, but consistent with Scripture and the Creed. And it is grounded actually in the first article, where we say, "I believe in God the Father almighty, maker of heaven and earth."[77] Precisely this article shields and sustains our interpretation of the Supper, as we have heard. Not that I wished hereby to measure and span God's power with measuring rods, as the fanatics do, as if he had not many other ways than I have demonstrated by which to maintain a body in many places—for I believe God's words, that God can do more than all the angels may conceive—but I have indicated one of these modes, to stop the fanatics' mouths and vindicate our faith.

They go as far as to boast that their opinion is the certain truth—"most certain, most certain truth" it must be called.[y] They therefore truly are obligated to prove that Christ's body may not be in heaven and the Supper, and that such articles are contradictory, and that the right hand of God is a specific place. For if their boast is true, that they have the truth with certainty, they must also be certain that the right hand of God is a special place, and still more certain that a body may not be in heaven and the Supper, and that such articles are contradictory. I challenge them, however, to make good their boast with proof, as they should and ought. If they do it, I shall recant and join their side; but against this I am fortified. I warn them, however, to produce clearer Scripture and better arguments than they have done up to now. For I say to them in advance, they will have watchmen, and if I live and God helps me, I shall tell them forthrightly where they miss the mark.

77. The first sentence of the Apostles' Creed.

[Christ's Ascension: Seeking Christ's Glory]

Now Oecolampadius wants it known how greatly he seeks Christ's glory[78] when he vents his sarcasm against Pirkheimer, saying that it must truly be a fine King of glory who would permit his body to be tossed to and fro upon the altar even by

78. When referring to God, *Ehre* is translated as "glory," but it also means "honor." This section contrasts *Ehre* with shame, and so the secondary meaning of "honor" should be kept in mind. In sixteenth-century Germany, honor was a major factor affecting one's social status and reputation, and to attack a person's honor was a deadly insult.

y Zwingli, *Ad Bvgenhagii epistolam responsio*, Z 4:575–76; Oecolampadius, *Ad Pyrkaimerum responsio*, fol. a4v; *Apologetica*, fol. B8v; Bucer, *Common Places*, 337.

ungodly knaves, etc.[79] The purpose which these and similar words serve is that if a saint of Müntzer's stripe[80] should read it, he would say that he would do a mess on the King of glory and show him his backside: "What kind of glory of Christ is it, that his body is in the Supper?" Here I answer: According to Oecolampadius's cleverness, it is true, Christ has no other glory than to sit at the right hand of God on a velvet cushion and let the angels sing and fiddle and ring bells and play before him, and to be unconcerned with the efforts of the Supper. But according to the faith of us poor sinners and fools, his glory is manifold, when his body and blood are present in the Supper. The first way is that he makes fools of the learned and clever fanatics and permits them to become offended and hardened over his words and works, which he so foolishly speaks and performs that they cannot bring themselves to believe, as St. Paul says in 1 Cor. 1[:23], "We preach Christ, an offense to Jews and folly to the Gentiles," and again [1:25], "God's foolishness is wiser than human wisdom." Now, this is surely a great glory of the divine wisdom, and in the midst of us fools God is a glorious, praiseworthy God, who can catch the wise with mere folly and make their wisdom foolish so that they must be blind where they would like to be most wise. Such wisdom and glory no other king can wield, as St. Paul says in 1 Cor. 2 [1:20], "Has not God made foolish the wisdom of the world?" To reduce wisdom to folly and shame is no mean glory and virtue!

In the second place, it is a glory and praise of Christ's inexpressible grace and mercy that he concerns himself so profoundly with us poor sinners and shows us such gracious love and goodness,[z] not content to be everywhere in and around, above and beside us, but even giving us his own body as nourishment, in order that with such a pledge he may assure and promise us that our body too shall live forever, because it partakes here on earth of an everlasting and living food. Now, we poor fools hold that glory appears when someone shows his virtue, mercy, and goodness to others. For anyone to permit himself to be glorified and served by others is a mean sort of glory, not a divine glory. Therefore one might do well to take the fanatics to school to learn what glory means.

z An allusion to Eph. 1:5-6.

79. Luther refers specifically to Oecolampadius, *Ad Pyrkaimerum responsio*, fol. d1r, but Karlstadt used the deliberately offensive description of priests tossing Christ to and fro; *Pamphlets*, 200–201.

80. Thomas Müntzer was an early supporter of the Reformation, but under the influence of mystical writings he moved away from Luther and upheld the direct inspiration of the Spirit in contrast to the "dead letter" of Scripture. He advocated the use of violence against those he condemned as godless and became the leader of a peasant band during the Peasants' War. He was captured and executed after the defeat of his supporters in 1525. See n. 17, p. 174.

Here the fanatics really come out into the open and show what kind of spirit they have. Knowing that they do not have Scripture on their side, they pounce upon this idea and try to confirm their error through the glory of Christ, get all excited in vain, and argue: "It is not glorious but shameful for Christ to be in the Supper, therefore he surely is not there and cannot be there, for Christ must be glorious."[a] Now if I ask them, "Who says it is not glorious?" they answer, "We do!" If I ask further, "Who are you? How do you know this, and how do you prove it?" "Ho!" they retort, "isn't it enough that we say so? You always have to be answered with Scripture!"

Ha! You ought to be ashamed of yourselves to the bottom of your hearts that you have made such a display of this subject, and yet have failed to prove a single bit of it! Meanwhile, you do not see that if your conclusion were good and convincing, I also would brag and boast that the Son of God was not born of a woman, as the heathens bragged against Saints Cyprian[81] and Augustine.[b] Why? Because it is not glorious for God to be born from the frail body of a human. Again, it is not glorious for Christ to be led by the devil out of the wilderness to the temple and the high mountain,[c] therefore it did not happen. Again, it is not glorious that he was crucified, therefore it did not take place! [. . .][d]

But since we poor sinners must be abused as having profaned and blasphemed Christ with our belief and teaching that Christ's body is in the Supper, let us now hear how they glorify and praise him. First they take from him and deny to him the love, grace, and goodness that he wishes his body to be our food bodily in the Supper. In place of this they allot to him a seat at a special, single location, like a bird in its bower.[82] Isn't this to regard Christ as a child or a fool, from whom one can take a gulden[83] and give him back a false penny or aspen leaves, persuading him that it is more valuable than the gulden? In short, our belief is that all the works of God are glorious, as the 111th

a Oecolampadius, *Genvina expositione*, fol. E3v-E4r; *Apologetica*, fol. C4v-C5r, H8r-v; *Ad Pyrkaimerum responsio*, fol. d1r.

b Augustine, *A Treatise on Faith and the Creed* IV.9 (MPL 38:106; NPNF1, 3:325).

c Matt. 4:5-9.

d Text omitted (see LW 37:72–73).

81. Cyprian (d. 258) was the bishop of Carthage and one of the earliest church fathers to write in Latin. He was martyred during the persecution of Emperor Valerian (r. 253–260). It is unclear to which of his works Luther refers. Augustine (354–430) was writing against the Manichaeans, followers of a dualistic religion with roots in ancient Persia that rivaled Christianity in popularity in the third and fourth centuries. Augustine belonged to the Manichaeans as a young man, before his conversion to Christianity.

82. This was the logical conclusion Luther drew from Oecolampadius's argument that a body can be in only one place at a time; *Genvina expositione*, fol. K7v; *Ad Pyrkaimerum responsio*, fol. f7r; cf. Zwingli, *Responsio ad Billicani,* Z 4:904, 907.

83. A coin whose German name, meaning "golden," derived ultimately from the Latin *aureus nummus*, the "golden pfennig." When international trade began to demand a gold coin, many princes and city-states in medieval Germany (the Holy Roman Empire) began to mint coins of this name around 1500, on the model of the florin.

Psalm says [v. 3], *Confessio et decor opus eius*, i.e., whatever God does is praiseworthy and excellent.[e] God can do nothing dishonorable or hateful. But this excellence is not everyone's knowledge; it is spiritual.

[Christ's Ascension: Defense of Miracle in the Sacrament]

Out of exactly the same lofty spirit they also lay their foundation upon such a firm rock as this: "Yes," they say, "since this work is so great a miracle—that Christ's body is at the same time in heaven and in the Supper—why don't the apostles and evangelists praise it as a miraculous work, as they do with other miracles?"[f] Answer: What do you expect? Those who do not have Scripture must have their own ideas; those who have no mortar must build their wall with mud. Now who can answer this choice objection? One might say: "Perhaps the apostles and evangelists were so poor that they could not grow enough cinnabar or brazil wood with which to make a little pointer[g] in the margin with the caption, 'Here is a miracle.'"[84] Our fanatics would like Christ and his disciples to be summarily obliged, whenever describing a miraculous work of Christ, to add a caption that it is a miraculous work. Otherwise, they would contend that it is neither a work wrought, nor miraculous, but simply nothing. Now since Christ says, "This is my body," and does not add, "This is a great miracle," it is nothing when he says, "This is my body." This is almost as nasty a little trick as Dr. Karlstadt trotted in with his period and his capital letters,[85] but this too was supposed to become a rock upon which Christendom would stand or else fall and sink to the bottom altogether.[h]

Reasonable and conscientious people see clearly here that it is a shame to spread such drivel among the people, and it does not deserve an answer. Nonetheless, the people pounce upon it,

84. Sixteenth-century readers often drew in the margins of books a small hand with an extended index finger pointing to a significant passage. Red ink, made with cinnabar or brazil wood, was also used to highlight important passages.

85. Karlstadt argued that because "This is my body" began with a capital letter, signaling the beginning of a new sentence, it was a new thought and so separate from the preceding "take, eat." He used this to justify his argument that "this" referred not to the bread but to Christ's physical body.

e The Vulgate text (Ps. 110:3) is *confessio et magnificentia opus eius*.

f Oecolampadius introduced this argument, *Genvina expositione*, fol. B1r-v; cf. *Ad Pyrkaimerum responsio*, fol. e5r; *Zwingli and Bullinger*, 227.

g *Hendlin*, "little hand."

h Karlstadt, *Pamphlets*, 172; cf. Luther's response in *Against the Heavenly Prophets*, LW 40:158–61.

cling to it, and treat it as pure Scripture and truth in opposition to these words that are so clear, simple, and lucid: "This is my body." Not that they can regard it as truth in their conscience, but they dearly wish it were the truth. But we should give thanks to God the merciful Father for so reducing the fanatics to shame in their own cleverness that they themselves must announce how they traffic in lies and dreams.[86] Thus God warns us that it is sheer devil's delusion and mockery, in order that all persons may guard themselves[i] from such fanatics; but that if any refuse to heed the warning, they will be so much the more grievously damned. So we believe, now, that all the words and works of Christ are sheer wonders, and thus Isa. 9[:6] calls his name "Wonderful."[87] But we accord the evangelists and the apostles the freedom which events they wish to describe as miraculous works and which they do not.

They have one argument, however, which I regard as the strongest of all; they are in earnest about it too, and I believe it is true. It is this: such articles, they say, are burdensome to people. For it is difficult to believe that a body is at the same time in heaven and in the Supper.[j] So I praise my fanatics that for once they candidly confess the real reason that impels them. They might well have kept quiet about the other reasons and dispensed with so much writing long ago. This single one by itself most assuredly would have sufficed to demonstrate their faith. For out of this argument spring all their other arguments, and they would not have labored so much with the others if this one had not constrained them.

Now you have it! If anything is difficult for a person to believe, let that one believe and declare, "it is not true," and then it certainly is not true, as this argument proves and demonstrates! On these grounds it certainly is not true that Christ is God and man. For it is difficult, yes, impossible to believe—with the exception of the saints, to whom it is not only easy but also pleasure and joy, and even life and salvation—to believe all the words and works of God; but these do not concern us.

Here we have caught the fanatics in their own confession that they are enemies of the sacrament and feel spite, aversion,

i Singular in the original.

j Oecolampadius, *Genvina expositione*, fol. D5r; *Ad Pyrkaimerum responsio*, fol. e5v, f5r; Zwingli, *Subsidiary Essay*, HZW 2:217–18; *Responsio brevis*, Z 5:355.

86. Both Valentin Crautwald, CS 2:194–209, and Zwingli, *Subsidiary Essay*, HZW 2:209-10, described dreams that provided or confirmed their respective understandings of "This is my body." To Luther, this placed them with the "new prophets" such as Thomas Müntzer, who claimed direct inspiration from God.

87. Luther is making a play on words, since the German *Wunder* can be translated as both "miracle" and "wonder."

88. The statement came from Quintilian, *Institutio oratorica*, IV.2.91, who did not cite a Greek source. Erasmus included it in his *Adages* II.iii.74, *Collected Works of Erasmus* 33:175.

repugnance, and loathing in their hearts toward it; and this is why they rave so against it. Ah, they ought to be a bit more cautious, leaving such notions in their pens, but God does not will it. The Greeks say, "A liar should have a good memory."[88] So says Hilary, "An ungodly man cannot be prudent."[k] The devil always sets his seal on his works in this way and leaves his stench behind. Why? Ah, there's no fighting against God's wisdom; God is bound to win.

They have still more arguments: Since we do not read that the apostles did reverence to the sacrament or adored it, but sat at table as for other meals, it is concluded that the apostles did not believe that Christ's body was present; therefore it is certainly nothing but bread.[l] A very precious and strong argument is this! From it I shall also draw some further conclusions: the apostles sat at table during the Supper, and did not adore Christ whom they saw sitting there bodily, and did him no reverence, therefore I conclude that they did not believe that he sat there; therefore it is certainly not true that Christ sat at the table during the Supper. Mary and Joseph did not adore Christ when he was born; so it is certain that Christ was not there, but Mary bore a monstrosity.[m]

Such faith must have such proofs; on such pillars such a church must stand! Should the apostles adore the sacrament, which they did not see, and not adore Christ, whom they did see? "But they should have shown reverence."[n] Yes, if they had been fanatics! But they cling to Christ with unreserved love, believing his Word without any dread at all. This is what love is accustomed to do, as St. Paul says in 1 Cor. 13[:7], that it believes all things and regards nothing impossible, especially what it hears from its beloved. It clings more to his words than to that which the words say. Mary Magdalene at the grave thought she would take Jesus away by herself, so ardent was the love in her heart [John 20:15]. My foolish little fanatics, however, measure the

k Hilary, *On the Trinity* V.26 (MPL 10:146; NPFN2, 9:93, "blasphemy is incompatible with wisdom").

l Oecolampadius, *Genvina expositione*, fol. B3v; *Ad Pyrkaimerum responsio*, fol. e5r; Zwingli, *Responsio ad Billicani*, Z 4:898; *Zwingli and Bullinger*, 227–28.

m German *Monkind*, a misformed miscarriage.

n Oecolampadius, *Genvina expositione*, fol. B3v.

apostles' hearts by their own hearts, which are full of loathing and hatred against the sacrament, thinking, "We despise and loathe the sacrament, and we cannot believe in it or honor it. Therefore the apostles also had just as little desire and love for Christ's Word, and would have dreaded it if Christ's body had been present." Well, I can put up with it when the devil mocks us with such nonsense, for I believe that he mocks himself more than us.

One thing more. "Yes," they say, "the works and wonders that Christ did were visible, such as when he made wine out of water, made the blind see and the deaf hear, and so forth. But since the miracle here is not visible, surely Christ's body is not present. [. . .][o] Now I hold it to be true that whatever miraculous sign is not visible is nothing at all, and never took place."[89]

Christ, the Son of God, was conceived by the Holy Spirit in the womb of Mary, the greatest of all God's miracles. But this was not visible to human eyes, therefore it certainly is not true! The Godhead dwells in Christ on earth and to all eternity; but this is not plainly visible, therefore it is not true! What will they do here to their chief argument and cornerstone: Christ sits at the right hand of God? This is not plainly visible; is it therefore not true? But perhaps it is no miracle to them that Christ sits at the right hand of God, but an ordinary thing, as when a teacher sits in his chair!

If these are to pass for good arguments and reasons that ought to teach us certain truth, prove our beliefs, and assure consciences, then we are in a bad way indeed. If someone brought me such books with no title or name and I did not know that they were such learned and excellent men, I would certainly have thought they had been done by some gypsy or vagabond in order to mock us Christians. There is no evidence, at any rate, that despite good intentions and a devout spirit they were misled through spiritual blindness, as happened with the heretics, but it appears to be sheer willfulness which wants to play the buffoon with God's Word. It ought not be possible, of course, that such rotten, feeble, insipid drivel should seriously influence a person of sound mind, even if a Turk or a Jew, let alone a Christian. But the great spite and aversion they bear against the holy sacrament, and the passionate fondness that they have for their

89. Cornelis Hoen first argued that miracles must be perceptible to the senses, *Christian Letter,* 275–76. This argument was taken up by Karlstadt, *Pamphlets,* 122; Oecolampadius, *Genvina expositione,* fol. A8v-B1r; and Zwingli, *Zwingli and Bullinger,* 190, 195.

o Text omitted (see LW 37:78).

own ideas, make them so rash as to think that everything they may take hold of, even a straw, is a spear and a sword. And they delude themselves into thinking that they strike a thousand dead with every stroke. Their own ideas bring grief to us all; may God ward it off. Amen!

[John 6:63: "My flesh" vs. "the flesh"]

Hence our rock—our simple, clear text—still stands firm: "This is my body." It has submitted to storming by stubble and chaff, but these have been scattered and routed by a little breeze. Now we shall attack their second cornerstone and their other chief argument. For although they have, along with the first argument which we have now overthrown, many other flimsy arguments besides those we have mentioned, I shall pass over these now, and in connection with the second cornerstone I shall treat some of them, lest I too become a fanatic over such flimsy, rotten buffoonery. For I certainly hate this drivel, because these are not passages of Scripture by which one might usefully treat some aspects of spiritual doctrine, but I am forced to enter my objections, and meanwhile waste time and neglect better things. But this is the way Satan must act, always causing misfortune and obstruction.

Now their second chief argument is the saying of John 6[:63], "Flesh is of no avail,"[p] which Oecolampadius boasts of as his iron wall.[90] In truth, he needs a good one! But if all which is difficult to believe is false, as they say, it is certainly false also that this is his wall of iron. For I believe it with great difficulty; it appears to me to be of paper, though it may perhaps have an iron color.

In the first place, when they should prove with Scripture that "flesh" in this passage must mean Christ's body (for this above all is the heart of the matter and is what we are asking them about), they behave according to form: they glide over it, assert and declare it as if it were certain, like knights who had won a valiant victory, and say, "Oh, we regard it as sure truth." [. . .][q]

Here also, when you ought to prove that "flesh" necessarily means Christ's body in this passage, you are altogether speech-

90. Oecolampadius compared John 6:63 to the "angel armed with a fiery sword"; *Genvina expositione,* fol. K4v. This argument was even more central to Zwingli, who called the verse "a wall of bronze" and "an indestructible adamant" (*Commentary*, 212, 248), and cited Erasmus's authority in applying it to Christ's flesh (*Ad Bvgenhagii epistolam responsio,* Z 4:562).

p "The flesh is useless."

q Text omitted (see LW 37:79).

less; but when you are obligated to speak and tell us it must mean Christ's body, then you gush and gabble. Indeed, it might also mean a pork roast, if assigning meaning is up to me and gabble and gush are the rule. For one can irrefutably testify against you that as often as Christ speaks in Scripture of his flesh or body, he adds the word "my," saying, "my flesh," "my body," as he says in the same chapter, John 6, "My flesh is food indeed." Again, "The one who eats my flesh," etc. Again, "Unless you eat the flesh of the Son of man," etc. [vv. 55, 56, 53].

Now, however, since he does not say here, "My flesh is of no avail," but simply, "Flesh is of no avail," you really find yourself in trouble and distress because you must prove it means Christ's flesh here. There is a very great difference between Christ's flesh and ordinary flesh. When we ask you point-blank and challenge you, "Who commanded you to alter and emend this text, and make 'my flesh' out of 'flesh'?" you must become speechless. Likewise, you are unable to prove it, yet you assume it and insist on it as if it were proved with absolute certainty. So the argument lies prostrate; it is unproved and it will remain forever unproved. This is Oecolampadius's iron wall.

"Yes," they say, "the context of the saying shows that 'flesh' here means Christ's body." Where? "Oh, the word which Christ speaks, 'Flesh is of no avail'; he does not say, 'the fleshly mind or understanding is of no avail,' as you cannibals say.[r] Besides, the word 'of no avail,' in Greek ὠφελεῖ (*ōphelei*), [or Latin] *conducit, prodest*, means properly that which is of no use, of no good, or which profits nothing. If by 'flesh' Christ meant a fleshly mind, and not his own flesh, he would have had to say, 'Flesh perceives or understands nothing.' But since he actually says, 'Flesh does not help,' of course he must be speaking of his own flesh which indeed understands a great deal, but does not help anyone by being eaten."[91]

You see, I was perfectly certain that you would answer something different from what you were being asked, and pass by when you were hailed. You ought to prove that "flesh" here means Christ's body; so you prove and teach us that *percipere* and

91. Luther combines the arguments of Zwingli, *Ad Bvgenhagii epistolam responsio*, Z 4:561–65; and Bucer, *Common Places*, 331–32.

r Lit. *Fleischfresser* or flesh-eater; see n. 23, p. 177. The word *cannibal* for those who ate human flesh does not occur before the mid-sixteenth century. Zwingli used the Greek word *anthropophagi* ("man-eater"); *Commentary*, 216.

conducere, to perceive and to avail or be useful, are two different words. But who requested or asked you for that? All this we know perfectly well, and the *Vocabularius ex quo* or the *Gemma*[92] would also have taught it to us without the aid of these great spirits and experts.

92. These are the titles of two Latin-German dictionaries.

It still remains unproven that "flesh" here means Christ's flesh. Leaving aside that it is not the word *percipere* (to perceive) but rather *conducere* (to avail) that stands here, how does this help you? Couldn't Christ say, "Flesh is of no avail," i.e., all that flesh understands, perceives, wishes, says, does, leaves undone, has, experiences—in short, flesh and all that flesh is—this is of no avail? And if I wish to condemn the fleshly mind, I am not obliged to say, "The fleshly mind perceives nothing"; indeed, it is a much stronger condemnation if I say, "The fleshly mind is of no avail." Now it doesn't matter very much to us whether "flesh" here means precisely fleshly mind; we are satisfied that it means flesh. But flesh embraces all that is in the flesh: mind, reason, will, words, works, etc., as has just been said. All this is of no avail. And this word ὠφελεῖ (*ōphelei*), "is useful" or "avails," comes nowhere near requiring or proving that "flesh" here must be understood of Christ's body, since it can perfectly well be understood of ordinary flesh, as I have here proved. Now what has become of the iron wall? Where is the certain truth?

Thus the iron wall has been blown down by one little word: "my." For since it does not read, "My flesh is of no avail," but simply, "Flesh is of no avail," we have in the first place established that it may not be understood of Christ's body. Since he himself does not further say, "My flesh," it is forbidden to emend his words and add anything to them; and their meaning is certain and sure, if we do not understand them as referring to his flesh.

Secondly, they cannot prove with a single letter that "flesh" here means Christ's flesh. For if we conceded to them without proof that "flesh" here is the equivalent of "my flesh," who would thereafter prevent it from meaning "Christ's flesh" at every point where simply "flesh" occurs in the Scriptures? There would immediately come swarming in droves all the ancient heresies, who say that Christ did not have natural flesh and blood and was not real man (such as the Manichaeans, Valentinians,[93] et al.), because they saw that such evil things were said about the flesh in Scripture. Indeed, such bumblebees also are buzzing around Zwingli's head and stinging him when he writes against Dr. Eck

93. Valentinus (c. 100–c. 155) was a Gnostic Christian of the second century whose teachings were attacked by early Christian authors, especially Irenaeus of Lyons (d. c. 202). The Valentinians continued to exist into the fourth century. On the Manichaeans, see n. 81, p. 217.

at Baden,[94] "If Christ's flesh is eaten, nothing but flesh comes of it, because all that is born of the flesh is flesh [John 3:6], as we shall hear."[s]

[. . .][t]

We too would like to rave like fanatics and concede that "flesh" here means Christ's flesh, as they jabber. Not that it is really so—but we would like to play the fool and go along with this carnival mummery, so that all may see what comes of it. Let us assume now that the iron wall stands firm, that Christ's flesh is of no avail. Now I ask: When the Virgin Mary was bodily pregnant with the Son of God and carried Jesus Christ our Lord nine months in her womb, and then as a mother brought him bodily into the world, as our Creed and the Gospels say, did she also carry and bear Christ's flesh bodily in and through her flesh? As a fanatic I simply do not believe it. Why? Because Christ's flesh, bodily conceived, borne, and handled, is of no avail. If it is of no avail, then nothing took place, as our argument declares, "Christ's flesh is of no avail." Therefore nothing is there. For if his flesh is not present in the sacrament for the reason that flesh is of no avail, neither is it in his mother's womb, precisely for the same reason that it is of no avail. The reasoning is the same in both instances.

Again, the angels announced to the shepherds, and the shepherds found it so, that Christ lay in the manger in bodily form and present with his flesh [Luke 2:8ff.]. But who wants to believe that that is true? Even if Christ, and all the angels with him, said, "There lies my body in the manger," nonetheless we say, "No, for flesh is of no avail, therefore your body cannot be present physically, but the swaddling cloths and the manger signify your body, because for flesh to be of no avail and to be absent are one and the same thing." Again, Simeon took him up in his arms bodily when his parents brought him bodily into the temple [Luke 2:22ff.]. But all this is a big pack of lies and contrary to the glory of Christ, because flesh is of no avail, i.e., it cannot be bodily present. This is our position, with it we remain, and further, it is our iron wall! [. . .][95]

s Zwingli, *Die erste kurze Antwort über Ecks sieben Schlußreden*, Z 5:182.

t Text omitted (see LW 37:81–82).

94. The Catholic theologian Johann Eck (1486–1543) proposed seven theses for a disputation with the Swiss reformers in Baden that began on 17 May 1526. Zwingli did not trust the promise of a safe conduct, and so he did not attend the disputation, but he published a refutation of Eck's theses. The first thesis asserted that "the true body of Christ and his blood are present in the sacrament of the altar."

95. In the paragraph omitted (see LW 37:87), Luther cites several more examples: Christ's baptism in the Jordan, his earthly ministry, his walking on the Sea of Galilee, and his washing of the disciples' feet at the Last Supper; cf. Luke 5:16; 9:6; Matt. 14:25; John 13:1-11.

You say: "Stop, for God's sake, you will buzz[u] yourself to death. In this way you would even buzz Christ right out of the garden, the cross, and his whole passion, saying that none of these things happened bodily, because of course he had to be bodily present in them all and yet his flesh is of no avail if it is bodily there."

Yes, my friend, I shall also buzz him away about the right hand of God, on which our entire interest focuses, and prove that he is not there. For flesh is of no avail. Now although his flesh is seated at the right hand of God, it is still the same flesh of Christ, for it did not become a different flesh at the right hand of God. If it is the same flesh, it is of no avail there either. If it is of no avail, then it is not there either, but is nothing at all, and its fate is the same in this passage as in the Supper.

Indeed, what is more, I shall prove that Christ's body is not spiritually in their hearts either, which however is the height of their prattle. For, as I have said, flesh is of no avail; but flesh is and remains flesh whether in the stomach, bread, the cross, heaven, spirit, and wherever you will. The places do not change it: wine, grain, money, cloth remain exactly what they are, even if they change places a thousand times a day. Should not Christ's flesh also remain the same flesh whether in heaven, spirit, manger, mother, or wherever you will? If it is present there bodily, as it must be, it is of no avail. If it is of no avail, it is not there but is nothing at all.

Now you see what a mighty swarm of fanatics the saying can stir up: "Flesh is of no avail." It makes heaven and earth too narrow for Christ's body and hounds him straight out of heaven and out of the Spirit, though the fanatics had spirited him away as to a mighty fortress secured with genuine iron walls, to keep him well protected from dishonorable handling by knaves at the altar. Actually, this passage is the strongest argument of all, and a real iron wall—yes, for us to use against them! They could have brought forth nothing more strongly opposed to themselves than just this saying, of which they boast most of all. So it goes with us poor sinners and thoughtless, defenseless ministers of the baked and bready God;[v] those who wish to slay us bring us

u *Schwermerst*, "to swarm"; the verb from which Luther derived *Schwermer,* translated as "fanatic"; see n. 17, p. 174.

v See n. 23, p. 177.

plenty of weapons with which to slay them and defend ourselves.

Here perhaps they will answer: "We do not say that Christ's flesh is of no avail whatsoever, but only when one eats it bodily. Otherwise, if one eats it spiritually, i.e., if one believes that it was delivered into death for us, etc., it avails according to the word of Christ, John 6[:55], 'My flesh is food indeed.'"[w] I thank them for the good instruction; but the fact still remains, it is not thereby proved that Christ speaks of the bodily eating of his body. For he says not, "To eat my flesh bodily is of no avail," but simply, "Flesh is of no avail." Therefore such instruction does not help the matter at all; it shall and must be proved that he speaks of bodily eating. This you will never do.

Even if you proved it—which you cannot do—I would like to hear exactly why Christ's flesh is of no avail when it is bodily eaten, and not also when it is bodily conceived and born, laid in the manger, taken up in one's arms, seated at table at the Supper, hanging upon the cross, etc. All these are outward modes and uses of his flesh as truly as when he is bodily eaten. How is it better when it is in his mother's womb than when it is in the bread and in the mouth? If it is of no avail in the latter, it can be of no avail in the former either; if it avails in the former, it must also avail in the latter. For nothing more can be made out of this than that Christ's body is dealt with bodily and outwardly, whether it is eaten or conceived, born or carried, seen or heard. Nowhere in sight is the spiritual eating which avails, but only the bodily using or handling, to speak in your terms. Who will instruct me here? Is no one at home? Oh, well, then the previous instruction also is of no avail and does not help me at all. And I must continue to maintain what I have said, that Christ's flesh either must avail in the Supper or must be of no avail whatsoever, whether in heaven or in the spirit.

Once again I ask: What if I eat Christ's flesh bodily in the Supper in such a way that I also eat it spiritually at the same time; would you not concede then that Christ's flesh in the Supper avails very much? How can this be? In this way: I shall eat his body with the bread bodily, and yet at the same time believe in my heart that this is the body which was given for me for the forgiveness of sins, as the words read, "This is my body, which was

w Zwingli, *Letter to Alber*, HZW 2:133; *Commentary*, 209; Oecolampadius, *Genvina expositione*, fol. K4v-K5v; Bucer, *Common Places*, 327–28.

given for you"—which you yourselves call spiritual eating.[96] Now if the spiritual eating is there, the bodily eating cannot be harmful but must also be useful on account of the spiritual eating. Ho! Now answer me; I am in desperate need of instruction here.

"Yes," you say, "we separate the spiritual eating from the physical or bodily."[x] God's thanks to you for this! Are you such pious, upright people, that you thus defame and slander us poor, innocent sinners with shameless lies in so many books throughout the world? Is this your new talent and lofty spirit that the blinded Luther cannot grasp? When have you ever heard from us that we eat Christ's Supper, or teach that it should be eaten, in such a way that there is only an outward, bodily eating of the body of Christ? Have we not taught in many books that in the Supper two things are to be kept in mind? One, which is the supreme and most necessary point, consisting of the words, "Take, eat, this is my body," etc.; the other is the sacrament or bodily eating of the body of Christ.[97] Now, of course, no one can drive these words through the throat into the stomach, but through the ears they must be grasped in the heart. But what is grasped in the heart through these words? Nothing other than what they say—namely, "the body given for us," which is spiritual eating. We have said, further, that if anyone eats the sacrament bodily without these words or without this spiritual eating, it is not only of no avail to that person but even harmful, as Paul says [1 Cor. 11:27], "Whoever eats the bread in an unworthy manner will be guilty of the body of the Lord."[y]

Therefore you did not need to teach us that bodily eating is of no avail. We actually go further and say that physical eating is even poisonous and deadly. But this does not prove that Christ's body is not there; indeed, it proves instead that he is there. If he were not there, the bodily eating would be harmless and useful; but now since it is of no avail and even harmful, it must surely be present and be eaten. It also does not prove that Christ's saying, "flesh is of no avail," pertains to the Supper. Thus your dream consists entirely of sheer lies and slanders. The mouth, which eats Christ's flesh bodily, obviously does not know what it eats or what the heart eats in it, nor would this even be of any benefit

x Zwingli, *Letter to Alber*, HZW 2:132–35; Oecolampadius, *Genvina expositione*, fol. E3v, F4v-F5v.

y *Ain Sermon auf das Euangeli Johannis vj.*, WA 12:581.

96. The understanding of spiritual eating as faith went back to Augustine's sermons on John 6, while the distinction between sacramental eating, or reception of the consecrated elements, and spiritual eating, understood as mystical union with Christ and the elect, was made in Peter Lombard's *Sentences* IV, dist. VIII, c. 4, and dist. IX, c. 1 (MPL 192:857–58). Late-medieval preachers urged the laity to commune spiritually every time they attended Mass as an alternative to frequent physical reception of the sacrament; Burnett, *Karlstadt*, 41–42. In a sermon on John 6 for the feast of Corpus Christi published in 1523, Luther also emphasized the importance of spiritual eating, WA 12:580–84. In their early works, the Swiss used John 6 to emphasize the distinction between spiritual eating and reception of the sacrament, while the Strasbourgers used it to draw a somewhat closer connection between the two; see Amy Nelson Burnett, "Hermeneutics and Exegesis in the Early Eucharistic Controversy," in Bruce Gordon and Matthew McLean, eds., *Shaping the Bible in the Reformation: Books, Scholars and Readers in the Sixteenth Century* (Leiden: Brill, 2012), 85–105.

97. Although Scholastic theologians distinguished between spiritual and sacramental reception, they maintained that the highest form of communion combined the two. As he acknowledged in *The Sacrament of the Body and Blood of Christ—Against the Fanatics* (LW 36:335; TAL 2:39–126), Luther in his early works emphasized the centrality of faith for those wishing to receive the sacrament and did not discuss what one should believe about the consecrated elements. Only in 1523 did he begin to emphasize Christ's bodily presence in the elements,

to it, for it cannot grasp or comprehend the words. But the heart knows well what the mouth eats, for it grasps the words and eats spiritually what the mouth eats bodily. But since the mouth is the heart's member, it also must ultimately live in eternity on account of the heart, which lives eternally through the Word, because here it also eats bodily the same eternal food that its heart eats spiritually at the same time.

The Adoration of the Sacrament, LW 36:279–82.

So we request, dear sirs, that if you wish to rave against the Lutherans or new papists, as you slanderously call us,[98] you should at least refrain from lies, and preach or write about us nothing but what we really teach. For what you have falsely asserted about us in the past is not what we teach, as you have now heard. Or, if you wish indeed to write against us, then write and prove that the Lutherans are such idolaters that they teach there is no Word of God in the Supper, but only the body of Christ in the bread; again, that they have no heart or soul with which to grasp these words and eat, but only a mouth with which they eat the body of Christ. If you prove that, I shall concede that your writing is altogether right and firmly established. It is against such people and no one else that your fanaticism is directed—as if, for example, a mouse or pig ate the sacrament:[99] of course it would be of no avail to them.

But leave us the words in the Supper and grant that we have souls; and we shall quite frankly ask what devil commanded you to sever the Word from the body of Christ in the Supper, likewise to separate the heart from the mouth in us, and to push only the bodily eating in the Supper and rip the spiritual eating out of it. For although the ungodly divide and separate the two in the Supper to their own damnation and eat only the body of Christ without the Word, with the mouth but without the heart, only bodily and not spiritually, this is not the way Christ instituted the Supper. Instead, he joined both together, the Word and his body, to be eaten spiritually with the heart and bodily with the mouth. But misuse by the ungodly should not and cannot break or alter God's ordinance and institution.

From all this we conclude irrefutably that Oecolampadius's iron wall, or the saying, "Flesh is of no avail," cannot pertain to the Supper at all. As we have heard, a spiritual eating is instituted alongside the bodily eating in the Supper by Christ, for in it there is God's Word that says to the heart, "Take, this is my body," which the stomach or mouth cannot eat bodily or grasp.

98. Karlstadt was the first to accuse Luther and his followers of being "new papists"; *Pamphlets*, 110, 144. The insult was taken up especially by radical sacramentarians such as Eitelhans Langenmantel (c. 1480–1528) and Conrad Ryss.

99. The question of whether a mouse consumed Christ's body when it ate a consecrated host was debated by Scholastic theologians; Gary Macy, "Of Mice and Manna: Quid mus sumit as a Pastoral Question," *Recherches de théologie ancienne et médiévale* 58 (1991): 157–66.

Although the ungodly and the papists and fanatics disregard these words and so miss the spiritual eating, nevertheless Christians hit it right with their faith.

Consequently, less than nothing is expressed when they say, "Flesh is of no avail, therefore it is not there." In this way I too could easily prove that there is no God and no created thing, if only I set aside God's Word as they do in the case of the Supper. Set aside the word, "God created the heavens and the earth" [Gen. 1:1], and I would like to see who would have a God or of what use God would be. Set aside the word, "Christ, God's Son, is our Savior," and I would like to see who would have Christ, or to whom he would be of any use. Bodily, of course, we have him, for God and Christ would still be near at hand even if he did not cause a word of all this to be preached. But whom would this benefit? To whom would it be of any use? No one would be able to know that he was anything. If he is of no avail or use, well then, he certainly is nothing at all, as the iron wall that concludes that whatever is of no avail is nothing.

So too, if God's Word had not said that the heavens and the earth are his creation, to whom would they be of any use, or of what benefit would they be? To the stomach, of course, they are useful bodily, but not to the soul. If they are of no avail, then they are nothing under any circumstances. But if God's Word is added, the heart uses that same Word and partakes of it spiritually, in the Word that the body uses and partakes of outwardly and bodily. Ah, why should I say so much? The old rogue, the devil, has so blinded the fanatics that they do not know what they themselves say. They prattle a great deal about spiritual eating but do not know what either spiritual or bodily eating is. For that reason we intend to speak a little about this subject here for the instruction of those who need it, in order to expose the fanatics' foolishness still further and show up the sneering devil.

[John 6:63: Relationship between Spiritual and Corporeal]

In the first place, the term "spiritual eating, drinking, or acting" does not mean that what one eats, drinks, or does is spirit or a spiritual object.[100] For then Christ's flesh could not be spiritu-

100. The Swiss and South German reformers were all strongly influenced by Erasmus's understanding of flesh and spirit, which (in contrast to the position Luther describes here) identified flesh with what is material or corporeal and spirit with what is immaterial and invisible. This led to a downgrading of the spiritual value of external things, including the physical elements of the Lord's Supper. Erasmus expressed his position most strongly in his *Handbook of a Christian Soldier*, which was a bestseller on the eve of the Reformation.

ally eaten or drunk, since Christ's flesh, wherever it may be—in spiritual or bodily essence, visibly or invisibly—is by nature true, corporeal flesh that one can grasp, feel, see, and hear, that was born of a woman and died on the cross. Rather, it is called "spiritual" because it comes from the Spirit, and needs to be and must be partaken of by us in a spiritual way. *Obiectum non est semper spirituale, sed usus debet esse spiritualis.*[z] This we must prove with examples.

When the Virgin Mary conceived and gave birth, Christ was certainly a real, corporeal, visible person and not only a spiritual being; yet she received and bore him spiritually also.[101] How? In this way: She believed the word of the angel that she would become pregnant and give birth.[a] With the same faith in the angel's word, she received and gave birth to Christ spiritually in her heart[102] at the same time as she conceived and gave birth corporeally. If she had not received Christ spiritually in her heart, she would never have conceived him bodily. God could have made Christ's body from her body in her sleep, without her knowing it, as he made Eve from Adam, but then she would not have become his mother, just as Adam was not Eve's mother.

Now what did she receive in her heart? Nothing else than what the angel's words declare—namely, "You shall conceive the Son of God." Since she grasped the word and through faith became pregnant with it in her heart, she also became corporeally pregnant with that which the word in her heart said to her. Her body knows not what it receives, for it does not understand the angel's word, but her heart surely understands what the body receives. Thus she is doubly pregnant, spiritually and bodily, and yet with a single fruit. Becoming pregnant bodily would have been of no avail to her if it had taken place without the spiritual pregnancy. Here you see that the spiritual pregnancy does not require the fruit to be a spiritual object. Indeed, the fruit is corporeal, and yet there is a spiritual reception along with the corporeal.

Again, the shepherds saw the infant Lord bodily in the manger, as did the noble Simeon, also in the temple [Luke 2:8ff., 2:22ff.]. But the seeing would not have helped them at all had there not been also a spiritual seeing. Now who gave them this

z "The object is not always spiritual, but its use must be spiritual."

a Luke 1:26-38.

101. The German *empfangen* means both to conceive [a child] and to receive [communion], and so it has been translated using both words. Luther is able to make a stronger parallel between Mary's physical conception and her spiritual reception of Christ than is possible by using a single word in English.

102. By "heart" Luther meant the joining of intellectual understanding and emotions, and he could also use it for soul or will; Birgit Stolt, *"Laßt uns fröhlich springen!" Gefühlswelt und Gefühlsnavigierung in Luthers Reformationsarbeit: Eine kognitive Emotionalitätsanalyse auf philologischer Basis* (Berlin: Weidler, 2012), 33-39.

spiritual seeing? Without doubt it was not the sight of the baby but the word of the angel, which directed them to Bethlehem to behold the Savior, and the answer of the Holy Spirit who had inspired the noble Simeon, that he should see the Christ of the Lord before he died. By the same word there arose in their hearts a spiritual seeing, i.e., faith, with which they first saw the baby spiritually as the Savior, and then also with the corporeal eyes. Now, there is only one baby, a single Savior, and yet he is looked upon in two ways: spiritually through the Word, bodily through the act of sight. But the corporeal eyes do not know what they see. They see the Savior, of course, but cannot understand that he is the Savior; for they cannot comprehend the Word. But the heart knows well what the eyes see, for it understands the Word and knows that the eyes see the true Savior. Here the object is corporeal, and yet there is a spiritual seeing along with the corporeal.

Again, the woman with a hemorrhage certainly touched no spiritual thing when she touched the hem of Christ's garment, but the corporeal garment of Christ. Nevertheless, it was a spiritual touching of this garment in her heart when she said to herself, "If I only touch the hem of his garment, I shall be made well" [Matt. 9:21]. You see, these words and this faith in her heart are a spiritual touching. Of course, her hand could not grasp the word that her heart spoke, "Touch," and it did not know what it touched, but her heart knew well that her hand touched the Savior's garment. But where did this knowledge come from? Not from the touching but from the word, "This is the Savior." Now what did her heart touch spiritually here? Nothing other than this very same corporeal garment that the hand touched bodily. The corporeal garment is one, yet there are two ways of touching, spiritually and corporeally.

Abraham was given the land of Canaan by God. Now, the land is a corporeal thing, yet there is also a spiritual taking possession of this land. For Abraham took possession of it spiritually through his faith when his heart said, "I believe and accept it." But where did this possessing come from? Without doubt not from the land, of which he never possessed a single foot, but from the word that God spoke, "To you and your descendants I will give this land" [Gen. 12:7]. When his children took possession of it bodily, their bodies or hands of course did not know what they were taking, for the body does not understand God's Word, but Abraham's heart knew very well and saw what his children's bodies took. Now, they take possession bodily in no other way than Abraham had first taken it spiritually through faith in God's Word.

And when he begot his son Isaac of Sarah, his son was indeed a corporeal human, yet there were also two kinds of begetting, spiritual and corporeal. For Abraham first begot Isaac spiritually through his faith when his heart said, "I believe that I shall beget Isaac." But where did this begetting come from? Not from his body or from Sarah, but from the word, "Sarah shall bear you a son" [Gen. 18:10]. Now when he begot his son corporeally, his body certainly did not know what it did, for it could not understand the Word. But his heart knew very well what his body did, for the heart understood the Word very well and knew that his body had begotten Isaac, whom he had begotten first through God's Word in faith. Now there is only one corporeal Isaac, whom his heart begot spiritually through faith and his body begot bodily through the corporeal act, as St. Paul highly praises this faith of Abraham in Romans 4[:13ff.].

So it is with all that our body does outwardly and corporeally: when God's Word is added and it is done through faith, it is and is said to be done spiritually. Nothing can be so corporeal, fleshly, or outward, but that it becomes spiritual when it is done in the Word and in faith. "Spiritual" is nothing other than what happens in and through us through the Spirit and faith, whether the thing that concerns us is corporeal or spiritual, *scilicet in usu, non in obiecto spiritus est,*[b] whether seeing, hearing, speaking, touching, begetting, bearing, eating, drinking, or anything else. For if one serves one's neighbor and does it bodily, it is of no avail to that person, for flesh is of no avail. But if one does it spiritually, i.e., if that person's heart does it out of faith in God's Word, it is life and salvation. Now there is only one kind of corporeal neighbor with whom that person acts, but two kinds of action. The body does not know what it does and lets itself be directed like an animal, but the heart knows very well what the body does. Where does this come from? Not from the neighbor but from the Word of God, which says, "Love your neighbor" [Lev. 19:18].

For so God does with us when he sets before us two things: his work and his Word. The body should do the work; the soul

b "That is, Spirit consists in the use, not in the object."

should grasp the Word. If the work were presented without the Word, it would be of no avail to anyone. For example, if he had let Christ be born of Mary without the Word, the work would have been of no avail to her, for she would have known nothing of it and would not have recognized it. Again, if he had let Christ die and rise again, and had let this work remain hidden and not be proclaimed through the Word, whom would it help? How is it helpful even now for those before whose eyes he is carried bodily,[103] yet who do not accept the Word in their hearts? Now since our body must deal corporeally with such works and yet cannot understand the Word and, on the other hand, since the soul cannot come forth and deal bodily with the work, God divides the matter according to the two aspects and gives the Word for the soul and the work for the body, in order that they both may be saved and partake of the single grace under two modes, to each its proper part.

103. Consecrated hosts were carried in a procession on the feast of Corpus Christi and were taken to the homes of the sick. Bystanders were expected to remove their hats and kneel as a sign of reverence when the priest passed by with the hosts.

Now tell me who the real Capernaites are! Oecolampadius clamors that we are Capernaites because we eat Christ's flesh bodily in the Supper.[104] I say, however, that the fanatics are the real Capernaites, for the Capernaites also divided the work from the Word and fastened on the bodily eating of flesh, just as our fanatics do. They separate and set aside the words in which the spiritual eating consists, and meanwhile gape and gawk at the bodily eating, like fools who look someone in the face and stare with fixed eyes, so that they cannot perceive the words clearly confronting them, "Take, eat, this is my body." So the Capernaites would do.

104. Christ described the eating of his flesh to the Jews of Capernaum, who thought he was talking about physical eating; John 6:24-65. On the basis of this passage, Oecolampadius called Capernaites all those who believed Christ's body was contained in the consecrated host; *Genvina expositione*, fol. A5v-A6r. The term was one of many that offended Luther and his followers; see n. 23, p.177.

But we certainly cannot be Capernaites, for we maintain both the bodily and the spiritual eating. The mouth eats the body of Christ corporeally, for it cannot grasp or eat the words, nor does it know what it is eating. It tastes the same as if it were eating something other than Christ's body. But the heart grasps the words in faith and eats spiritually precisely the same thing that the mouth eats bodily, for the heart sees very well what the uncomprehending mouth eats bodily. But how does it see this? Not from the bread or from the mouth's eating, but from the Word which is there, "Eat, this is my body." Yet there is only one body of Christ, which both mouth and heart eat, each in its own mode and manner. The heart cannot eat it bodily nor can the mouth eat it spiritually. So God arranges that the mouth eats bodily for the heart and the heart eats spiritually for the mouth, and thus both are satisfied and saved by one food. Even the uncomprehending body does not know that it is eating a food by which it will live forever. For the body does not feel it, but dies and decays as if it had eaten some other kind of food, like an irrational animal. But the soul sees and clearly understands that the body must live eternally because it has partaken of an eternal food that will not leave it to decay in the grave and turn to dust.

"Yes," they say, "when Mary was pregnant and gave birth, she also saw her child corporeally, and the shepherds and Simeon saw him, and so with all the others, who saw everything that they believed."[105] What can one say? If I have heard you correctly, you soft, tender fruit, you would like to teach your God how [Christ] shall offer himself bodily to you.

Perhaps you would also like to become his mother Mary and Simeon, and not be content with the mode which he presents to you. As you will; go your way and make your own mode, and you will soon see what comes of it. But we trust our God, who has willed to be born of Mary spiritually and bodily but not to be eaten and drunk by her bodily or spiritually. By the shepherds and Simeon he wanted to be seen spiritually and bodily, but not born and not eaten. So, according to his good pleasure, by those whom he willed he was seen, heard, born, suckled, carried, touched, and the like, both bodily and spiritually. But here he wants to be neither born nor seen nor heard nor touched by us but only eaten and drunk, both bodily and spiritually. Accordingly, by this eating we obtain just as much and arrive at the same point as they with their bearing, seeing, hearing, carrying, etc.; and he is just as near to us bodily as he was to them, except that it had to be by another mode in order that he might be equally near everywhere in the world, which would not have been possible were he to appear visibly. Moreover, he has not denied the seeing, but promised it, except that it is deferred and reserved until the Last Day, in order that faith may have room and we may not obtain salvation here in this miserable life. What more should he do?

I hope now that all this has made it perfectly clear what "spiritual" means. Surely "spiritual" must mean what the Spirit does and what comes from the Spirit, just as "fleshly" is what flesh does and what comes from the flesh, as Paul says in Rom. 8[:5], "Those who are of the flesh are fleshly minded, but those who are of the Spirit are spiritually minded." Again [8:13], "If

105. Luther derives this from the argument that miracles must be perceptible to the senses; see n. 89, p. 221.

by the Spirit you put to death the deeds of the flesh you will live." Here, indeed, you find that even the fruit and works of the Spirit are called "spiritual" because they come from the Spirit, as he also says in Gal. 5[:22f.], "The fruit of the Spirit is love, joy, patience," etc. In short, he calls the entire life of Christians spiritual, and he calls them altogether spiritual, in 1 Corinthians 1 and 2. Thus without doubt the one who in faith bodily eats Christ's body in the Supper eats spiritually and lives and walks spiritually precisely in the bodily eating. Our fanatics, however, are full of fraud and humbug and think nothing spiritual can be present where there is anything corporeal, and assert that flesh is of no avail. Actually the opposite is true. The Spirit cannot be with us except in bodily things such as the Word, water, and Christ's body and in his saints on earth. Now have we properly overthrown the iron wall?

[John 6:63: Correct Interpretation]

Now we should like to consider the saying of Christ, "Flesh is of no avail" [John 6:63], and see whether we can handle it better than the fanatics. Our position is that where the two words, "flesh" and "spirit," are placed in opposition to each other in Scripture, flesh cannot mean Christ's body but always means the old flesh which is born of the flesh, John 3[:6]: "That which is born of the flesh is flesh." For why should Scripture contrast them if they are compatible with each other? Now Christ's body and flesh certainly are quite compatible with the Spirit; indeed, he is the Spirit's dwelling place bodily, and through him the Spirit comes into all others. The first witness is Moses, Gen. 6[:3]: "My Spirit shall not be judge among mortals forever, for they are flesh." Again, Isa. 40[:6f.], "All flesh is grass, but the Spirit blows upon the grass and it withers." And Christ in John 3[:6]: "That which is born of the flesh is flesh, and that which is born of the Spirit is spirit." But much more fully, St. Paul in Romans 8 contrasts spirit and flesh practically throughout the entire chapter; and Gal. 5[:17]: "These two, spirit and flesh, are opposed to each other," etc. I thought this was familiar to everyone who reads the New Testament. Let those who do not believe it just read, and they will find that where flesh and spirit are placed in opposition to each other, flesh is certainly condemned as something sinful, as the enemy and adversary of God, so it is not necessary to cite all the passages here.

Since, then, it is true and indisputable that where flesh is placed in opposition to spirit, it does not mean Christ's body but the old Adam born of the flesh, it is certain that this verse also, John 6[:63], "Flesh is of no avail," cannot be understood of Christ's body, because Christ in this passage contrasts flesh itself with spirit. For so his words clearly read, "It is the spirit that gives life, the flesh is of no avail; the words that I have spoken to you are spirit and life." Here you see manifestly that he distinguishes flesh from the Spirit and sets it in opposition to the Spirit. For he certainly teaches that life and spirit are in his words and not in the flesh; but in regard to the flesh he concedes that it is of no avail. How could it avail, if neither life nor spirit is in it? If no life or spirit is in it, then there must be nothing but death and sin in it. What heretic has ever been so utterly depraved, with the exception of the Jews, who maintain this of Christ's flesh? Now let the fanatics test themselves at this point, and let us see what they can do. They have boasted that it is an iron wall and the certain truth. If they can make good their boast, I shall pay attention.

We have seen now that in this passage "flesh" cannot mean Christ's body but surely means the old Adam. It is opposed to the Spirit, or at any rate is without spirit and is not spirit—which means the same thing as opposed to spirit. I hope, therefore, that we poor sinners have not too widely missed the mark when we have interpreted "flesh" to mean fleshly understanding. For in the flesh, which is not spirit, there are of course the highest and best of faculties: the intellect, senses, will, heart, and mind. If flesh is of no avail, then its senses, intellect, will, and all its actions and its powers are of no avail, and Christ's meaning in this passage must be: "My dear disciples, who murmur and become offended at my words, you do not understand me rightly. You seize upon the work—the bodily eating of flesh—and you interpret it as chewing it with the teeth and digesting it in the body, like meat from the butcher shop. That is a fleshly, deadly interpretation. I do not give such flesh to you to eat in that way. There must be spirit here, not flesh. My words must be understood spiritually, of the spiritual flesh. All my words are spirit; therefore both flesh and eating and everything that I tell you are spirit and are to be understood and used spiritually. For the spirit gives life, flesh is of no avail," etc.

The fanatics, then, stubbornly presume to take their stand upon this text, "Flesh is of no avail," and they insist loudly about it. The text in their hands must be altogether obscure and uncertain, but it is quite sure on our side, so that it is directly opposed to them. They must also pardon us if we take our stand firmly and steadfastly on the text, "This is my body," which is so completely lucid, certain, and clear that it cannot be made obscure and unsure by any ingenuity or force, and puts all fanaticism to shame. For we do not yet see any Scripture that—as they boast and claim—opposes this passage and on account of which we should not rely on it so steadfastly. What we do see is that their blind imagination sees through a painted glass and lets them imagine that Scripture contradicts this text at several places. On the contrary, they harmonize with it and resist this fanaticism.

[John 6:63: "Flesh" in John 3:6]

But Zwingli above all is a clumsy carpenter and hacks rough chips when he writes to Baden,[106] "'That which is born of the flesh is flesh,' John 3[:6]. If Christ's flesh is eaten, nothing but flesh comes of it. Fie and shame on him who says so! But it would follow from Eck's interpretation."[c] These are his words. I say that you fanatics are brazen, impudent fellows. To be sure, before others you display your great humility, meekness, and toleration; but before God and his Word you are both mad and foolish. Now see how fine this conclusion is: "That which is born of the flesh is flesh, therefore where Christ's flesh is eaten, nothing but flesh can come of it." The passage in John 3[:6] speaks of the birth and nature of the flesh, so he applies it to fleshly eating—so completely does this spirit hold Scripture in his power.

I maintain that Zwingli speaks here of becoming natural flesh, just as bread and meat when eaten become flesh and blood in the eater; and he holds that if Christ's flesh were eaten, it would have to be digested and become flesh and blood like other foods. He says that this is granted and asserted by the saying in John 3[:6], "That which is born of the flesh is flesh." Go harmonize yourself down the stairs! But if his meaning is that one who eats Christ's flesh becomes flesh or fleshly and not spiritual, it harmo-

106. A public disputation between Johannes Oecolampadius and the Catholic theologian Johannes Eck was held in the city of Baden in Switzerland from 19 May through 8 June 1526. Zwingli published a response to Eck's seven theses drawn up for the disputation (n. 94, p. 225).

c Zwingli, *Erste kurze Antwort*, Z 5:182.

nizes still more nicely, and may accordingly yield the conclusion: One who eats bread becomes bread, and one who eats sausage becomes a sausage, and one who drinks wine becomes wine. So it would be a miracle if wolves did not eventually make sheep or actually become sheep, because they eat so many of them. Well, such drivel we shall ignore.

We cannot tolerate the blasphemy, however, when these fanatics try to weave and merge Christ's flesh into this saying also: "That which is born of the flesh is flesh." Their meaning is simply that Christ's flesh is born of flesh. Thereby they show how nicely they read and understand the sixth chapter of John. Old Satan drives them to believe these things and to speak with such rashness and obstinacy. How would it be possible for them to think well at all of Christ's flesh when they insist that it is born of flesh and is flesh? For then they must surely continue on and say further that his flesh is of no avail; they cannot prevent it.

We poor sinners and ministers of the "baked God,"[d] however, say this: Christ's flesh belongs with the saying "That which is born of the Spirit is spirit." For his flesh was born not of flesh but of the Holy Spirit, as even children and the whole world confess in the Creed: "I believe in Jesus Christ our Lord, who was conceived by the Holy Spirit." And the angel said to Joseph in his sleep, Matt. 2 [1:20], "Do not fear to take Mary your wife, for that which is conceived in her is of the Holy Spirit."

And in Luke 1[:34-36], when Mary asks the angel how it could be that she would have a child, since she knew no man, Gabriel says, "The Holy Spirit will come upon you, and the power of the Most High will overshadow you; therefore the holy child which shall be born of you shall be called the Son of the Most High." Here you hear that Christ's body is born of the Spirit and is holy, therefore he must certainly be not flesh but spirit, according to the saying of Christ, "That which is born of the Spirit is spirit." Of no other man, however, does Scripture speak in this manner. Not that I present these passages for the sake of the fanatics—for they would scowl at them and skip right over them, as their virtue and lofty spirit are accustomed to do—but I wish by means of them to strengthen and comfort us poor Capernaites and cannibals[e] against their arrogant devil. For if

d See also n. 23, p. 177.

e Lit., flesh-eaters; see n. *r*, p. 223.

their fanaticism continues, that Christ's flesh is of no avail, soon Marcion, Mani, and Valentinus will come teaching that Christ had no real body but an apparition of a body, because it is not compatible for Christ's body to be of no avail and yet for him to have a real body.[107]

107. Marcion (c. 85–c. 160), like Valentinus, was a Gnostic of the second century who taught that Christ did not have a real human body. Mani was the founder of the Manichaeans; see n. 81, p. 217 and n. 93, p. 224.

From these passages now we learn what spirit or spiritual, flesh or fleshly means: we do not call "flesh" the fleshly eyes and fingers that may be seen and touched, as the fanatics do when they call Christ's body useless flesh; but, as I have said above, all is spirit, spiritual, and of the Spirit, in reality and in name, that comes from the Holy Spirit, however corporeal, outward, or visible it may be. On the other hand, all is flesh and fleshly that comes without spirit from the natural power of the flesh, however inward and invisible it may be. For St. Paul in Rom. 8[:5] calls the fleshly mind "flesh," and in Galatians 5[:19ff.] enumerates among the "works of the flesh" even "heresy, enmity, envy," etc., which, however, are entirely inward and entirely invisible.

Now if Christ's flesh is distinguished from all flesh and is solely a spiritual flesh for all, born not of the flesh but of the Spirit, then it is also a spiritual food. If it is a spiritual food, it is an eternal food that cannot perish, as Christ himself says in John 6[:27], "Labor for the food that does not perish, which the Son of man will give to you"; and again, "I am the living bread that comes down from heaven" [6:51]; again, "If anyone eats of me, he will live for ever" [6:51]. And so throughout the entire chapter he teaches that his flesh is the true, living, eternal food that gives life and sustains all who eat of it; and the one who does not eat of it must die, etc. Why? For this reason: His flesh is not of flesh, or fleshly, but spiritual; therefore it cannot be consumed, digested, and transformed, for it is imperishable, like all that is of the Spirit, and a food of an entirely different kind from perishable food. Perishable food is transformed into the body of the one who eats it; this food, however, transforms the one who eats it into what it is itself, and makes that person like itself, spiritual, alive, and eternal; as Christ says, "This is the bread from heaven, which gives life to the world" [6:33].

Whether Christ's flesh is eaten bodily or spiritually, then, it is the same body, the same spiritual flesh, the same imperishable food that in the Supper is eaten bodily with the mouth and spiritually with the heart, according to Christ's institution, or only eaten spiritually with the heart through the Word, as he teaches in John 6[:63]. Eating him bodily with the mouth in the Supper does not at all detract from the fact that he had to become flesh or a fleshly food. On the contrary, whether it enters the mouth or the heart, it is the same body; just as when he walked on earth, he remained the same Christ, whether he came into the hands of the faithful or of the wicked.

Therefore, Zwingli should not conclude, "If Christ's flesh is eaten, nothing but flesh comes of it." This would be quite true if we were speaking of beef or pork, and Capernaites talk this way. But he should conclude, "If Christ's flesh is eaten, nothing but spirit comes of it, for it is a spiritual flesh and does not let itself be transformed, but transforms and gives the Spirit to the one who eats it." Since this poor maggot sack, our body, also has the hope of the resurrection of the dead and of the life everlasting, it must also become spiritual, and digest and consume everything that is fleshly in it. And that is what this spiritual food does: when the body eats it corporeally, this food digests the body's flesh and transforms it so that it too becomes spiritual, i.e., forever alive and blessed, as Paul says in 1 Cor. 15[:44], "The body will rise spiritually."

To give a simple illustration of what takes place in this eating: it is as if a wolf devoured a sheep and the sheep were so powerful a food that it transformed the wolf and turned him into a sheep. So, when we eat Christ's flesh bodily and spiritually, the food is so powerful that it transforms us into itself and out of fleshly, sinful, mortal people makes spiritual, holy, living people.[108] This we are already, though in a hidden manner in faith and hope; this is not yet manifest, but we shall see it on the Last Day. And indeed, if they can eat and drink ordinary bread and wine without harm, because they spiritually eat Christ's body and blood along with it, they certainly ought to concede to us that it would be harmless to eat Christ's flesh bodily alongside the spiritual eating, since Christ's body is surely as good as bread and wine, as I have written against Dr. Karlstadt.[f] But this matter does not deserve to have such lofty spirits read and answer it, so I must let it pass here, too.

Here I shall drop the subject of the two cardinal points and cornerstones of the fanatics, as they put it: "Christ is seated at

108. The Eastern church fathers described a conversion or transformation of those who received the Eucharist; Jaroslav Pelikan, *The Christian Tradition: A History of the Development of Doctrine, Vol. 1: The Emergence of the Catholic Tradition (100–600)* (Chicago: University of Chicago Press, 1971), 233–38; J. N. D. Kelly, *Early Christian Doctrines*, 5th ed. (London: A. C. Black, 1977), 442–45.

f *Against the Heavenly Prophets*, LW 40:203–4. See also n. 18, p. 174.

the right hand of God, and flesh is of no avail, therefore his body cannot be in the Supper." If these two points are overthrown, they have utterly lost their case, as they themselves clearly sense and also confess. I hope, however, that they have been reduced to stubble and dust, and the truth has avenged itself on the devil. From now on there is nothing better he can do than come back with props of straw to shore up his case, but the One who has helped me has still more in reserve than they think. Peace I crave if possible, so I may publish the prophets,[109] but if it is not to be, then let come what may. I trust I shall accomplish more with one book than they will with ten. For lies require much babble and prattle; truth can be stated briefly.

109. At the time Luther wrote this treatise, he was also translating and commenting on the books of the prophets in the Hebrew Bible/Old Testament.

[Refutation of Other Arguments]

They lay pebbles for a foundation, however, and bring up Matt. 24[:23] just for show: "Then if anyone says to you, 'Lo, here, lo, there is the Christ!' do not believe them."[110] This I have answered sufficiently in my book *Against the Heavenly Prophets*, and my answer has not yet been refuted by them.[g] Similarly, when they say, "If the bread is Christ's body, then the bread was crucified for us," I have also answered this in the same book.[h] These two points come from Dr. Karlstadt, who brought them among others against me.[i] Again, their question, where Christ commanded the eating of his body in the Supper, also comes from Dr. Karlstadt,[j] and is easily answered thus: Put on your glasses, or have a boy spell out these words, "Take, eat, this is my body," and you will find out.

110. This verse was used against the doctrine of transubstantiation by the radical Hussites in the fifteenth century and introduced into the Reformation debate by Cornelis Hoen, *Christian Letter*, 276. It was adopted by Karlstadt and virtually all who wrote against Christ's bodily presence.

In short, if we conquer in these two principal points, that it is not a contradiction but perfectly congruous to say that Christ sits at the right hand and yet is in the Supper, secondly, that flesh is of no avail and yet that Christ's body is eaten in the Supper, then I shall gladly teach them where Christ commanded his body to be eaten, and where it is written that in the Supper there is forgiveness of sins, consolation of souls, and strengthening of

g LW 40:219–21.

h LW 40:193.

i Karlstadt, *Pamphlets*, 139, 197, 221.

j Ibid., 146–47, 151–54.

faith.[111] So too, with all their tatters of questions, with which like beggars they are trying to mend and patch themselves, and yet they can never cover their bad conscience or keep it warm with them. In this art I am bold enough to boast that by God's grace I am a master. For if Christ remains mine, everything remains and is found to be mine; I know this well.

Dr. Oecolampadius also pities us and seeks to help us poor people when he complains, "If Christ's body were in the bread, we would be so concerned and have so many thoughts about such a miracle, how Christ's body became bread, that we would surely forget his remembrance, which he earnestly commands. Therefore it is better to say there is nothing in it than to be burdened with such concerns."[k] Now really, this is a dangerous business, and it ought to make an inept, lazy schoolboy work hard, [like asking] how the cow walked through the door yet had to leave her tail in it, or how an ox could leave his dung on the beam above him.[112] Oh, it is tiresome business to waste time and words over such devil's buffoonery, just as if Christ had commanded us to investigate how his body is in the bread! In this way I could also say: Christ is not God, for if this were true, we would be saved so much thought about this great miracle—how the Godhead could become human—that we meanwhile have forgotten the faith. In order that this may not happen, it is better if Christ is not God!

Next the question begins to distress him greatly, whether the bread is nobler than the womb of the Virgin.[l] There is a superabundance of such prattle in their books. The very best part of all of them is that they testify how their hearts are unquiet, unsure, and uncertain in these matters, which cannot cease or desist from digging about and searching more and more because it feels that all it finds will not prove true and sound. Yet because they have seen that I am full of cheerful words, they would like to persuade us with lofty, defiant words that they too are altogether certain in these matters. But words won't do; there must be truth and a sure conscience. A sure conscience does not beg so.

To hold them now to their two principal points, I shall leave aside all their other prattle and be satisfied with these that I have

111. These ideas were all prominent in Luther's early discussions of the sacrament; see, for instance, *The Blessed Sacrament of the Holy and True Body of Christ* (1519), LW 35:45–731 TAL 1:225–56; *A Treatise on the New Testament* (1520), LW 35:79–111.

112. Luther describes practical jokes that might be played on a schoolboy.

k A polemical paraphrase and extrapolation of Oecolampadius, *Genvina expositione*, fol. E2v.

l Oecolampadius, *Ad Pyrkaimerum responsio*, fol. d1r.

mentioned. For I know these spirits well; I have had many of them to deal with. I know how slippery they are, how they flutter this way and that, just looking for an excuse for prattling even where there is none, if only to avoid having to stand still and answer the real main points about which they are being insistently asked. For they think an answer has been given if they produce a book and write on it the word *Answer*.[113]

113. Many of the works of Zwingli and Oecolampadius were written in response to challenges by others; see the introduction, above, pp. 165–68.

[The Church Fathers on the Sacrament]

Finally, we shall also deal with one or two of the fathers' sayings to see how Dr. Oecolampadius handles them.[114] To be sure, they regard St. Augustine as their own, for he often uses the words mystery, sacrament, sign, invisible, intelligible.[m] But Oecolampadius can deduce nothing certain from this, despite his boast that he has the sure truth. For although St. Augustine often says that the bread in the Supper is a sacrament and sign of the body of Christ, Oecolampadius has not yet established thereby that mere bread and not Christ's body is present, because one can say that Christ's body is invisibly present under a visible sign, as the same St. Augustine says, *sacramentum est invisibilis gratiae visibilis forma*, "the sacrament is a visible form of an invisible grace."[115]

114. The chief argument of Oecolampadius's *Genvina expositione* was that the church fathers did not teach that Christ was bodily present in the elements of the supper. He defended his interpretation of the fathers in two pamphlets responding to Willibald Pirckheimer; see n. 24, p. 178.

115. Luther gives the definition of a sacrament found in Peter Lombard's *Sentences* IV, dist. I, c. 2 (MPL 192:839), and derived from Augustine, although Augustine's wording differs slightly (MPL 34:712).

Here St. Augustine explains in his own words what he means by the terms *sacrament, sign, invisible, intelligible*—something altogether different from the way Oecolampadius interprets them. St. Augustine does not say that a sacrament is a figure or sign of a future or absent thing, like the stories of the Old Testament are, but a form of a present and yet invisible thing. Since we have Augustine himself here explaining his meaning in his own words, we need no other alien interpretation or explanation. Now, as often as St. Augustine uses these words, *sacramentum vel signum corporis et sanguinis domini*, "the sacrament of Christ's body and blood," and the like, he stands firmly on our side against the fanatics, for he means that bread and wine are a visible form of his present, invisible body and blood. [. . .][n]

m *Genvina expositione*, fol. G2r-G3r, H8r, K2v-K3r.

n In the paragraphs omitted Luther discusses passages from Augustine's *Epistle to Januarius* (MPL 33:203) and Augustine's preface to his exposition of Ps. 33 (MPL 36:306); see LW 37:105–6.

Holy Christendom has, in my judgment, no better teacher after the apostles than St. Augustine.[116] Should this dear and holy teacher be so reviled and defamed by the fanatics as to be regarded as the cloak and support of their poisonous, blasphemous, deceptive teaching? To this I shall answer "No" as long as I have breath; this does him an injustice. Indeed, it is a good thing to say "No" to this, because the fanatics interpret his words only according to their own understanding, and yet do not prove their interpretations; but they boast that they have the clear, pure truth with certainty. [. . .][o] Now surely Oecolampadius is doing nothing else with the sayings of the fathers than to wrench them out of the sense in which they have been held up to the present, and to render them uncertain. On the other hand, he does nothing to make them certain and firm for his position. He leaves them dangling and hanging between heaven and earth, with all his followers and adherents. But this is not teaching but foolery,[p] and to boast of this as sure truth is doubly to lie and deceive poor consciences.

116. Luther was a member of the Augustinian Eremite order, which combined the study of Scripture and Augustine's writings with an emphasis on higher education and care of souls. Luther had a thorough knowledge of Augustine's writing and quoted him often in his writings. It should be noted that everyone in the controversy—including Oecolampadius and Zwingli—cited Augustine frequently, and even Philip Melanchthon (1497–1560) admitted that Augustine seemed to support Zwingli.

Tertullian,[117] the most ancient writer of all after the time of the apostles, in the fourth book against the heretic Marcion, says:

117. Tertullian (c. 160–225) was a North African convert to Christianity who defended his faith against both pagans and Christian heretics. He was the first church father to write in Latin. In his later life he joined the Montanists, a rigorist Christian sect condemned as heretical for its advocacy of direct spiritual revelation. On Marcion, see n. 107, p. 240.

> The bread that Christ took and divided among his disciples, he made his body, when he said, "This is my body," which is the same as "form of my body." A form, however, there could not have been where there were no real body. An empty thing or void, such as a phantom, is incapable of form. Or did he make the bread an empty thing or a phantom of his body, because he did not have a real body? In that case he must have given bread for us.[q]

This saying is supposed to help Oecolampadius maintain that there is nothing but bread in the Supper, and he stands stubbornly upon the word *figura* since Tertullian explains the words of Christ thus: "This is my body, i.e., *figura* (or form) of my body." Thus Oecolampadius has his grounds for making Christ's words

o Text omitted (see LW 37:107].

p In the original German, this phrase rhymes: *nicht leren sondern nerren*.

q Tertullian, *Adversus Marcionem* IV.40; CSEL (Turnhout: Brepols, 1953), 1:656; ANF 3:418.

A sixteenth-century representation of church father and theologian Quintus Florens Tertullian.

in the Supper, "my body," into "sign of my body."[r] [. . .][s]

We are not now discussing whether Tertullian and other teachers teach rightly or wrongly, for we wish to build our faith not upon human words but upon God's Word, the one rock. Not that we despise them, for their intentions were as good as our intentions can ever be, and they have offered their work for our benefit. Instead, we are discussing whether the fanatics use the sayings of the fathers rightly, or whether they deal in lies, and we must see what the fathers believed. Now there is Tertullian who says that Christ made the bread in the Supper his body, according to the words, "This is my body." Here is no obscure or ambiguous word, for to make bread into body is distinct, clear, lucid speaking. This Oecolampadius ignores and overlooks, for it is on our side.

But that which follows, "This is the same as *figura* of my body," Oecolampadius claims as favoring him. But *figura* is an obscure and ambiguous word.[118] Of course, he would like to interpret it to mean a similitude, type, or interpretative sign, just as one describes the stories in the Old Testament as figures of the New, as Adam is called a figure or type of Christ, or as a bride is called a type or figure of the Church. But *figura* in the Latin language does not mean that kind of type; the word *figura* is misused in such an instance. Oecolampadius accepts this misuse most gladly, for it serves him well, but he ought to prove that his use is correct and he cannot do so. We say that Tertullian employs the word *figura* in accordance with proper usage in the Latin language, where it means a form or figure in the mathematical sense—describing something as long, thick, broad, round, white or black, which one can see, feel, and handle, as we Germans also say about the

118. On the various meanings of *figura* in Latin, see Erich Auerbach, "Figura," trans. R. Manheim, in Erich Auerbach, *Scenes from the Drama of European Literature: Six Essays* (Gloucester, MA: Peter Smith, 1973), 11–76. Luther's discussion of *figura* was strongly influenced by Pirckheimer's *Responsio*, WPBW 6:482–85.

r Oecolampadius, *Genvina expositione,* fol. C5v-C7r.

s Text omitted (see LW 37:108–9).

sacrament that Christ's body is present under the form of the bread and his blood under the form of the wine. Exactly that which we call *gestalt*, "form," Tertullian calls in Latin *figura*. [. . .][t]

Now to understand Tertullian's meaning, we must observe that the heretic Marcion, with many other heretics, taught that Christ had not assumed a real, natural body from Mary, but was only a shadow or phantom of a body that could be neither grasped, felt, nor held, just as the devils on occasion appear in various guises, although there is nothing, or a mere phantom, before one's eyes.

Against this Marcion Tertullian fights, maintaining that Christ had a real, natural body, and concluding that whatever is an empty thing, shadow, or phantom cannot have a form, for a phantom has neither color nor thickness nor length nor breadth; it is nothing but an apparition. If it had color, one could grasp it and identify the color. If it had thickness or length, one could break it, lift and carry it, put and lay it down. Again, one can apply no color, thickness, or length to it, upon it, around it, or above it. This is the first point. Now Marcion confesses that Christ's body, i.e., the shadow or phantom of his body, is in the bread. Thereupon Tertullian concludes: How could Christ's body be in the bread and assume the form of bread if it were not a real, genuine body, since it is impossible for a form to exist where no real body but only a phantom is present? [. . .][u]

What this conclusion of Tertullian establishes against Marcion, I leave open. It does not concern us here. But this much is perfectly clear: Tertullian's meaning is that Christ's real, natural body is present in the bread of the Supper in such a way that the form of the bread—its thickness, breadth, length, and color—has now become the form of Christ's body—in its thickness, length, and color—through his Word when he says, "This is my body." I certainly add no words of mine here, but instead refer to Tertullian's own words. And what kind of attack against Marcion would it have been if Tertullian had tried to prove from the Supper that Christ had a real body, while he himself did not believe that Christ's body was present in it? Now, however, he says that there cannot be the form without body; and yet the bread is the form of his body. Certainly, then, Christ's real body must be

t Text omitted (see LW 37:110).

u Text omitted (see LW 37:111).

truly present where its form is, which from the bread has become its form through the Word. This is Tertullian's meaning, I am perfectly sure, and his words are distinct and clear. [. . .][v]

From all this it is sufficiently clear, I think, that Tertullian does not understand *figura* here in Oecolampadius's manner as a similitude or sign, but as a form, and he calls it the form of Christ's body because Christ's body is in and under it. And he declares distinctly that if Christ's body were not present, it would remain bread and the form of bread that would be given for us. Let Oecolampadius prove his "figure" in this way too. [. . .][w]

What kind of spirits and people have we here, who play games with the good ancient teacher before the world, to mislead and confuse the common people's consciences with lies and deception, and then boast that it is the pure truth, and thereby blaspheme God the Holy Spirit besides? It would be much better for them frankly to repudiate the holy fathers than to try with such deception and fraud to lure them over to their side and seduce the world under the name of the fathers, to whom before God and the world they are doing an injustice.

Irenaeus also is one of the most ancient teachers.[119] He had to fight the Valentinian heretics who taught that Christ is not God's Son and that there was no resurrection of the flesh. They also held that the body would not be saved, but only the soul, because St. Paul says, "Flesh and blood cannot inherit the kingdom of God" [1 Cor. 15:50]. Against this Irenaeus writes that the body also will be saved, and that there is a resurrection of the flesh, as our Creed confesses.[120] Among other things he cites this proof against them: If the body is not to be saved also, why should it be fed with the body and blood of the Lord in the sacrament? If it eats an eternal food there, it will surely live eternally by means of it. But let us hear his own words. In the fourth book, chapter 5, he says, "Just as the bread which is produced from the earth, when it receives the naming of God is no longer mere bread but a sacrament, consisting of two things, an earthly and a heavenly, so also our bodies, when they receive the sacrament,

119. Irenaeus was born in Asia Minor but became bishop of Lyons in Gaul (France). He wrote a detailed treatise, *Against Heresies*, refuting Gnostic heretics, especially Valentinus and his followers; see 93, p. 224.

120. The Apostles' Creed affirms the resurrection of the body.

v Text omitted (see LW 37:111–12).

w In the section omitted, Luther discusses Tertullian's explanation of Jer. 11:19 from *Against the Jews*, 10 (MPL 2:629) and *Against Marcion*, III.19 (MPL 2:348), and a passage from his book *On the Resurrection of the Flesh*, 8 (MPL 2:806); LW 37:112–15.

are no longer corruptible, because they have the hope of the resurrection.[x]

What will the fanatics do here, who boast that Irenaeus is on their side, and claim to be sure about the matter besides? Oecolampadius, of course, wishes to use this saying like a knight against the papists and their transubstantiation, and against Valentinus.[y] But I should like to hear and see the person who could interpret this quotation to the effect that mere bread and wine are present in the Supper. There stands Irenaeus, saying that the bread is not simply common bread, after it has been named or called by God, but Eucharist (as the ancients called the sacrament). But what can this "naming" be, with which God names the bread? It can be nothing other than the word that he speaks, "This is my body." There, indeed, he names it, and gives it a new name which it did not have before when it was mere bread; and he says, "Let this bread, after this naming or word, consist of two things, the one earthly (i.e., bread, which is produced from the earth, as Irenaeus says here), the other heavenly," which must certainly be Christ's body, which is in heaven. What other sort of heavenly thing can be in the sacrament along with the earthly thing, which is there by God's naming or word?

161

THE LIFE OF

S. IRENÆUS

BISHOP of LYONS.

His Countrey enquired into. His Philosophical Studies. His institution by Papias. Papias *who. His education under S.* Polycarp. *His coming into* France, *and being made Presbyter of* Lyons. Pothinus *who; how and*

Y

St. Irenaeus of Lyons (the city in the background) as depicted in a seventeenth-century engraving by Michael Burghers. This appeared in a book by William Cave (1637–1713).

Oecolampadius here makes of the earthly and the heavenly a single thing—namely, the bread which is earthly, since as it comes from the earth, and also heavenly, because God is thanked and praised for it.[z] In this way Irenaeus is to be twisted and taught to buzz like a fanatic. If one asks: How do we become certain that this is Irenaeus's meaning, or who ever heard that our thanksgiving or words are a heavenly thing? The answer is, "I, Oecolampadius, say so. If this does not satisfy you, you have no spirit." In this way all bread on all tables, when the blessing is pronounced, may properly be called heavenly, for thanksgiving is there. Must we simply believe this and require no proof—but is it sure truth if the fanatics merely say so? Yes, indeed; despite

x Irenaeus, *Against Heresies* IV.18.5 (MPG 7:1028f.; ANF 1:486).

y Oecolampadius, *Genvina expositione*, fol. G3v-G4v.

z Ibid., fol. G4r.

anyone who demands further proof! Well, of course, this is simply to leap over Irenaeus and not to answer his words in the least. Yet this must be called not only an answer, but also the sure truth!

But Irenaeus will not tolerate this. For we know that mere common bread remains mere common bread even if Christ and all the apostles recite the blessing over it, and it does not thereby become a heavenly thing; just as Christ in John 6[:11] divided the bread among the people and thanked and praised God for it, yet it remained mere bread and did not become heavenly. But Irenaeus says here that on account of the Word of God it is no longer mere bread, but along with the earthly bread there is also something heavenly present. It would be shameless presumption if anyone tried to interpret God's naming as human thanksgiving, blessing, or praise.[121] Paul, indeed, teaches us in Rom. 4[:17] what God's naming or calling means when he says, "God names or calls into existence the things that do not exist." So too, Irenaeus speaks here of God's naming or calling, as Moses also testifies in Genesis 1 that God through naming or calling, i.e., through God's Word, created all things. Otherwise, you be the expert and tell me what else *vocatio Dei* may mean, when God calls, speaks, declares, names.[a] This is God's Word, when he says, "This is my body," just as he says in Genesis [1:3], "Let there be light," and there is light. My friend, it is God who names or calls, and what God names immediately comes into existence, as Ps. 33[:9] says, "God spoke, and it came to be." [. . .][b]

Again, in the fifth book, chapter 5, [Irenaeus] says, "The cup, which is a created thing, he acknowledges as his own body, by which he gives increase to our bodies."[c] Observe, again, that the body of Christ in the cup strengthens our bodies. This, of course, is said concerning bodily food beyond all doubt, yet it is the body of Christ, although at the same time the cup is a created thing. Again, shortly thereafter he says, "Now when God's word comes upon the cup that is mixed and the bread that is made, they become the sacrament of the body and blood of Christ, through

121. Influenced by Erasmus's annotation on 1 Cor. 10:16 (ASD VI/8: 214), Karlstadt argued that Christ's blessing of the bread and wine was not a consecration but, rather, a thanksgiving no different from other occasions when Christ gave thanks over food; *Pamphlets*, 118–20, 133–35.

a This phrase is in Latin in the original: *quando deus vocat, dicit, appellat, nominat.*

b Text omitted (see LW 37:117–19).

c Irenaeus, *Against Heresies* V.2.2 (MPG 7:1125; ANF 1:528). Oecolampadius quoted V.2.2-3 in *Genuine Exposition*, fol. G4v-G5r, to which Pirckheimer replied in *Responsio*, WPBW 6:492–93.

which the nature of our body grows and subsists. How dare they say, then, that the body is incapable of receiving the gift of God, which is eternal life, when this body is nourished with the body and blood of the Lord, and is his member?"[d] Here we learn that the Word of God comes upon the bread and wine. Above, Irenaeus called this "coming upon" the naming of God, and he clarifies himself by saying that the sacrament is not a sign of the absent body of Christ but is the body of Christ himself, as that by which not only is our body fed bodily, but also the nature and substance of our body is nourished, strengthened, and sustained unto eternal life and becomes a member of the body of Christ. I am eager to hear how the fanatics will try not only to counter these and similar sayings but also to harmonize them with their absurd interpretation, in such a way as to make it perfectly certain that Irenaeus agrees with them. We do not believe at all this wholly uncertain interpreting and word-torturing, such as Oecolampadius practices. There must be distinct, clear proof—stronger than ours. If they do this for me, I shall praise them as men who have the very heart of the Holy Spirit.

We should also like to hear St. Hilary,[e] who is another of the ancient teachers and an excellent interpreter of Scripture. He writes against the Arians in book 8, *On the Trinity*: "If the Word has truly become flesh, and we truly receive the Word that became flesh in the Lord's food, how are we to believe that he does not dwell in us by his nature, he who, when he became man, has assumed the nature of our flesh, never to lay it aside, and has mingled the nature of his flesh with his eternal nature in the sacrament of the flesh, of which we become partakers in common?"[f] Here, indeed, Hilary says that in the food of the Lord, that is, in the sacrament, we truly take the Word who became flesh, or as we might say more directly, the enfleshed Word; and for that reason Christ remains in us naturally, or with his nature and substance, not only spiritually as the fanatics dream. And he calls the sacrament *sacramentum carnis nobis communicande,* "a sacrament of the flesh divided among us in common," indicating that not only

d Irenaeus, *Against Heresies* V.2.3 (MPG 7:1125; ANF 1:528).

e See n. 68, p. 205.

f Hilary, *On the Trinity* VIII.13 (MPL 10:246; NPNF2, 9:141). A longer section of this passage was cited by Oecolampadius, *Genuine Exposition*, fol. H2v-H4r; cf. Pirckheimer, *Responsio secunda*, WPBW 7:548.

Head reliquary of Pope Cornelius in the St. Kornelius chapel of the abbey church of Kornelimünster Abbey in Germany.

bread is distributed among us but also flesh. He says further that in this sacrament Christ mingles together not only spiritually but also the nature of his flesh with his eternal nature. Now what is meant by "the nature of his flesh"? Does it mean bread and wine, or does it mean his natural, substantial body? Let them gloss and interpret as they will, just so they make their gloss certain and show good reason for interpreting Hilary's words differently from the way they sound. For as they stand, they give us in the sacrament not only Christ's natural flesh but also his eternal divinity. [. . .][g]

The holy martyr St. Cyprian[h] wrote to Pope Cornelius[122] how Christians should be strengthened by the sacrament for suffering in time of persecution:

> Now indeed the peace[123] is necessary not only for the sick but also for the strong; and communication—the sacrament—should be granted not only to the dying but also to the living, so that we do not leave naked and unarmed those whom we stir up and exhort to the battle, but fortify them with the protection of Christ's blood and body. For we use the sacrament so it may be a safeguard for recipients when we want them to be safe against the adversary, and thus we must equip them with the armor of the Lord's food. For how shall we teach or incite them to shed their blood in confession of his name, if we deny them Christ's blood when they are about to fight? Or how can we make them fit for the cup of martyrdom, if we do not first admit them to drink in the church the cup of the Lord, as is fitting in the sacrament?[i]

In this saying we see that for Cyprian *communicatio, eucharistia*, and *pax* are one and the same. He speaks of proffering the sacrament to strengthen those who are about to fight, and he states clearly that they receive the Lord's body and blood in this

122. St. Cornelius (d. 253 CE) became pope during a lull in the persecution of Christians under Roman emperor Decius. When the persecution of Christians resumed in 253, Cornelius was exiled to Centumcellae, where he likely died as a martyr.

123. The "peace" meant reconciliation of individuals with the church after a period of public penance.

g Text omitted (see LW 37:121–22)].

h See n. 81, p. 217.

i Cyprian, Letter 53.2 (MPL 3:856; ANF 5:337), cited by Pirckheimer, *Responsio secunda*, WPBW 7:544.

proffering. To be sure, a fanatic here can make of the blood, cup, and sacrament a sign of the blood and a signifying, so that Cyprian says what they want. But it is not necessary for them to prove this; it is enough when the spirit says so! [. . .][j]

Even the saying of Augustine on Psalm 98, which seems to have the greatest plausibility beyond all others, does not favor them: "You will not eat the body which you see, nor drink the blood which they who crucify me will shed. A mystery[124] have I given you; if you understand it spiritually, it will give you life";[k] and on John 6: "Why do you make ready your teeth and stomach? Believe, and you have already eaten."[125] Since Augustine speaks of teeth and stomach, his meaning is most certainly directed against the Capernaites[l] and our fanatics, who think that Christ's body is to be bitten and chewed by the teeth and digested by the stomach, like a piece of beef. But this is not what Christians teach, nor do we poor sinners teach so. This they know perfectly well, but they choose to ignore it.

So too, when Augustine says that one will not eat the flesh that one sees, he is also speaking of the manner in which one eats beef, as he himself explains earlier that he speaks against those who thought that Christ would carve his body into pieces and distribute it. Indeed, if they wish to hold fast this saying of Augustine, he will completely take away from us Christ's body and flesh, even spiritually. For so he says, "Not the flesh which you see, not the blood which is shed," just as if one should partake of a different blood and flesh than Christ's flesh and blood. Now, of course, we eat no other flesh and blood, even spiritually, than exactly that which was seen and crucified. So St. Augustine here does not deny or condemn the statement that Christ's body and blood are eaten, as his words say, but rather he condemns the fleshly eating as one eats sausage and bread, chews them with the teeth, and digests them with the stomach.

The fanatics fail completely in this: they do not discern the body of Christ from other flesh, as St. Paul says in 1 Cor. 11[:29].

j Text omitted (see LW 37:122–23).

k Augustine, *Exposition of Psalm 98.8* (Vulgate) (MPL 37:1265; NPNF1, 8:486). The citation was familiar through its inclusion in both Peter Lombard's *Sentences* IV, dist. X, c. 1 (MPL 192:860); and canon law, *Decretum* III, dist. II, *de Consecratione*, c. 44, CIC 1:1330.

l See n. 104, p. 234.

124. Luther translated Augustine's *sacramentum*, the usual Latin equivalent of the Greek *mysterion*, as *geheymnis*, or mystery.

125. Augustine, Gospel of John, Tract. 25.12 (MPL 35:1602; NPNF1, 7:164), cited in both the *Sentences* IV, dist. IX, c. 1 (MPL 192:858) and the *Decretum* III, dist. II, c. 47, CIC 1:1331. Luther cited this passage in his early writings on the sacrament (e.g., *Babylonian Captivity*, LW 36:8), and it was used by virtually everyone on both sides in support of their own position.

They speak of it no differently than if it were perishable, digestible meat to be chewed, such as one buys in the butcher shop and cooks in the kitchen. Such simpletons are they that they do not see that this flesh is an imperishable, immortal, incorruptible flesh, as the sixteenth Psalm [v. 10][m] sings of it, "Thou wilt not let thy holy one see corruption; my flesh also shall rest in hope." Death indeed tried once, wanting to devour and digest it; but it could not. This flesh tore its stomach and throat into more than a hundred thousand pieces, so that death's teeth fell to pieces and turned to dust, and this flesh remains alive. For this food was too strong for death, and has devoured and digested its devourer. God is in this flesh. It is God's flesh, a spiritual flesh. It is in God and God is in it. Therefore it lives and gives life to all who eat it, both to their bodies and to their souls.

If the fanatics had been able to see this little point, they would not have become so mad as to revile us as cannibals, but would have minded their own business.[126] For they are the real cannibals, because they act in this matter with such fleshly thoughts, believing that Christ's flesh is exactly like any other flesh, utterly useless and perishable. All their pride and boast is that when they twist and wrench the Scriptures and the sayings of the fathers to suit their own ideas, this is sufficient and the truth is surely established. But that is far from the case.

126. Luther uses a proverbial saying, "They would have grabbed themselves by the nose."

[The Benefit of Christ's Body: Against Claim of No Benefit]

I have written previously against the heavenly prophets,[127] too, asking how it happens that, in their view, bread and wine are of use[128] in the Supper and do not prevent people from remembering Christ's suffering, yet Christ's body and blood are not just as useful or good as bread and wine to enable us to remember his suffering.[n] Or why should this follow: "Christ's flesh is of no avail, therefore it is not present," and not this also: Bread and wine are of no avail, therefore they are not present?[o] But here one

127. See n. 18, p. 174.

128. *Nutz* is translated in this section as "use," "usefulness," "avail," or "benefit." This is Luther's response to the Swiss reformers' application of John 6:63, "[Christ's] flesh is of no avail/use [*Nutz*]" in the Lord's Supper.

m The original has Psalm 15, since Luther follows the Vulgate's numbering of the Psalms.

n LW 40:203–4.

o LW 40:202.

must rush past and not answer. Yet this is the sum of the matter: The fanatics direct all their teaching and writing and their persistent effort in order to render our text and our faith in this article uncertain and unsettled. If they were able to do this, they would imagine that they had won. But even if they could do this and made us uncertain and confused, they would still not have made their own belief certain. For they do not prove one letter of the glosses that they propose.

Now what kind of spirit is it that tries to make this side uncertain and confused but cannot make its own side certain or secure—indeed, does not even want to and does not try to make it certain? Surely it is no other spirit than the devil, who takes pleasure in jarring hearts everywhere, and does not allow them to be certain and sure about any part, but keeps them dangling and hovering whichever way his wind blows, like an aspen leaf. The Holy Spirit, however, is the sort of teacher who is sure and makes us sure, and does not let us toss and dangle, for "in Christ it is not yes and no, but yes and amen," 2 Cor. 1[:19]. And St. Paul teaches and boasts of a *plērophoria*[129] in Christ, a full, certain, sure understanding, upon which one can die and risk everything.

I should like to advise these fanatics, however, that they should buzz about completely, and not just partially, and since they have dared this, they should quickly go the whole way and remove these words, "This is my body, given for you," entirely and utterly from the Supper.[130] For the way they believe and celebrate the Supper, they do not need these words at all. It would be sufficient if they celebrated the Supper with these words: "Christ took bread, gave thanks, and broke it, and gave it to his disciples saying, 'Take, eat, do this in remembrance of me.'" For these words suggest well enough that one should eat this bread and thereby remember Christ. This is the fanatics' Supper, complete and entire. Why should the useless, unnecessary text remain, "This is my body, given for you," since this idea is sufficiently comprehended in the remembrance of the Lord when it is proclaimed that his body was given for us? For what else is to be remembered than that he was given for us, as St. Paul explains? [1 Cor. 11:26].

"O how gladly would we do this, if the words did not stand in all the Gospels!" Oh, here is good advice: you must boldly say, "They were inserted somehow from the margin into the text, but not written by the evangelists themselves." Because your reasoning is this: whatever appears to you useless and unnecessary is

129. "Assured understanding," Col. 2:2; "full conviction," 1 Thess. 1:5.

130. Karlstadt argued that the phrase "This is my body given for you," which referred to Christ's body, separated the two commands, "Take and eat," and "Do this in remembrance of me," both of which referred to the bread; *Pamphlets*, 147–49, 172. Luther sarcastically suggests that the intervening phrase should simply be eliminated.

not true, just as Oecolampadius says so cleverly, "There is no use or need for Christ's body to be in the bread, therefore it is not true."[p] So too, here: It is wholly useless and unnecessary prattle for the words to remain in the Supper, therefore they should not be there, since without them the Supper is quite completely described, instituted, and used, and no further need or use is shown why they must be there. If some need were shown, however, one can easily rave about something to respond to it. Still it is in your hearts that these words are superfluous and of no avail, and you dearly wish that they were not there, because they do you the greatest harm.

These are two of Dr. Oecolampadius's shameful, dreadful blasphemies: when he asks, "What use or need is there for Christ's body to be in the bread?" and if we do not show him, he concludes there is nothing to it. Now what shall I say of the outrageous audacity of this hellish Satan? Well then: even if we could not show how it is useful and necessary for Christ's body to be in the bread, should God's Word for that reason be false, or be twisted around according to our notion? A faithful, God-fearing heart does this: it asks first whether it is God's Word. When it hears that it is, it smothers with hands and feet the question why it is useful or necessary. For it says with fear and humility, "My dear God, I am blind. Truly I know not what is useful or necessary for me, nor do I wish to know, but I believe and trust that you know best and intend the best in your divine goodness and wisdom. I am satisfied and happy to hear your simple Word and perceive your will." But those who are possessed with devilish arrogance invert this procedure and, by asking why it is useful and necessary, try to smother God's Word. [. . .][q] If they had any understanding of faith, however, and ever felt a spark of it, they would know that faith's highest single virtue and quality and glory is that it does not want to know the benefit or necessity of what one believes. It refuses to circumscribe God or to demand why, for what purpose, from what necessity God commands or enjoins something, but is perfectly happy to be unwise, to give God the glory and believe God's simple Word. Shame on you, you leaders of the blind, that you still do not know this, yet spew so

p Oecolampadius, *Genvina expositione*, fol. D5r, F6r; *Apologetica,* fol. R4r; *Ad Pyrkaimerum responsio*, fol. d1r.

q Text omitted (see LW 37:128).

many books into the world with such great boasting, so that you expose before everyone your own folly and lack of understanding! [. . .][r]

Well, suppose I grant the possibility that Christ cut his flesh into pieces visibly and corporeally and gave it to us to eat, as the Capernaites understood it and the fanatics dream. It would not on that account be of no avail, and the saying, "Flesh is of no avail," would not apply. Why? Because we are confronted by the common article of our faith, that Christ's flesh is full of divinity, full of eternal good, life, and salvation, and one who takes a bite of it receives with it eternal good, life, full salvation, and all that is in this flesh. And if someone believed it, that person would also have life and salvation from it; but if someone did not believe it, this treasure would not help that person at all, but would rather cause harm.

Now, however, it is impossible that this flesh should be cut into pieces, divided, torn, corrupted, or destroyed. For it is a blessed, divine, incorruptible flesh, as Peter says in Acts 2[:24], "It was not possible that death should hold this flesh," because Psalm 15[131] says, "Thou wilt not let thy holy one see corruption" [16:10], and John 18 [19:36] quotes from Moses [Exod. 12:46], "Not a bone of him shall be broken." It could at one time suffer and die, but it is not possible to cut it into pieces, divide, break, chew, digest, consume, and destroy it. It must be entirely and all at once conceived, born, carried, eaten, and believed; and where it is, it must be of use. For there is pure usefulness and good in it, except where it is without faith. For without faith nothing is of any use, as St. Paul says [Titus 1:15], "To the impure all things are impure," and in Rom. 14[:23], "Whatever does not proceed from faith is sin."

Consequently, as has been said, it is one of the greatest blasphemies of our time and a truly abominable thing to hear, when Zwingli and Oecolampadius dare to say that Christ's flesh is of no avail if it is eaten bodily, even for believers.[s] Just as if the eternal good could not be good, and eternal life could not be life on account of our usage, and would have to change its essence, nature, and character according to whether it was eaten or not eaten by human beings; or as if it were just an empty flesh

131. Luther uses the numbering of the psalm in the Latin Vulgate. Luther's choice of words, too, reflects this translation.

r Text omitted (see LW 37:128–29).

s Zwingli, *Responsio ad Billicani*, Z 4:898; for Oecolampadius, see n. *p*, p. 256.

with no divinity in it. From this example we can judge with full certainty that the wicked Satan speaks through them, for the Holy Spirit is not so absent-minded as to blaspheme the flesh of Christ so shamefully and decry it as a useless flesh, when he himself indwells it and accomplishes perfect good and usefulness through it wherever it is, whether in the bread or in heaven or in the heart. Indeed, it cannot be of no avail; that is impossible.

Nor does it help them to boast that on other points they rightly teach and praise Christ.[t] For one who deliberately denies, blasphemes, and desecrates Christ in one subject or article cannot correctly teach or honor him at any other point; it is sheer hypocrisy and deception, however impressive its appearance. For this is the way it is: one either loses Christ completely, or has him completely. He does not divide himself into pieces; he desires to be loved and honored with the whole heart, with the whole soul. Through these fanatics, however, the devil prepares the way for other heretics who will come and say that Christ is nothing, and has neither flesh nor divinity, as happened in the early days of Christendom. Now if this point does not move and convert them, and if it does not help others to guard against them and to detect and avoid their devil, then there is no more help for them. They want to be lost, but it is not my fault; their blood be on their own heads.[u] I have warned them enough.

Although no Christian desires to know of what use it is to believe that Christ's body is present in the bread, but simply believes the words of God with fear and humility, we should like, nevertheless, to indicate certain benefits, not to instruct the fanatics—for they pay no attention, and are not even interested in learning—but because the devil mocks us through them. First, it is even a benefit that clever, arrogant spirits and reason be blinded and disgraced in order that the arrogant may stumble and fall and never partake of Christ's Supper; and on the other hand, that the humble may stumble but arise and alone partake of the Supper, as St. Simeon says [Luke 2:34], "This child is set for the fall and rising of many in Israel." It is useful and good that arrogant, godless blasphemers be cut off so that they should not join in partaking of the holy sacrament, for one should not

t Oecolampadius, *Billiche Antwortt*, W[2] 20:626; cf. Bucer, *Apologia*, 6v-7r, abridged in *Common Places*, 316–17.

u Acts 18:6.

"throw to the dogs what is holy, nor pearls before swine" [Matt. 7:6]. Now the fanatics believe that nothing but bread and wine are present, hence it is surely so. They have as they believe, and so they eat nothing but bread and wine, and partake of the Lord's body neither spiritually nor bodily. It is very good and useful that our possession should not be scattered among the unworthy but kept holy and pure among the humble alone.

In the second place, as we heard above,[v] Irenaeus and the ancient fathers pointed out the benefit that our body is fed with the body of Christ, in order that our faith and hope may abide and that our body also may live eternally from the same eternal food of the body of Christ which it eats bodily. This is a bodily benefit, nevertheless an extraordinarily great one, and it follows from the spiritual benefit. For Christ surely will make even our body eternal, alive, blessed, and glorious, which is a much greater thing than giving us his body to eat for a short time on earth. Therefore, as Hilary says, he wills to be in us by nature in both our soul and body, according to the word in John 6[:56], "Whoever eats me abides in me and I in him."[w] If we eat him spiritually through the Word, he abides in us spiritually in our soul; if one eats him bodily, he abides in us bodily and we in him. As we eat him, he abides in us and we in him. For he is not digested or transformed but ceaselessly he transforms us—our soul into righteousness, our body into immortality. So the ancient fathers spoke of the bodily eating.

The third benefit, I hope, will be convincingly proved. For they must grant us that in the Supper we have God's words, namely these: "This is my body, given for you; this is my blood, poured out for you for the forgiveness of sins." So I ask them again whether God's Word is of any avail? If it is of no avail, why does the prophet Isaiah say in chapter 55[:11], "God's Word shall not return empty, but shall accomplish that which avails"? Why does St. Paul call it in Rom. 1[:16] "the power of God for salvation to every one who believes in it"? Why does he call it "the word of life," "the word of grace," "the word of salvation," "the word of wisdom," etc.? Are life, grace, salvation, wisdom, strength, and power mere useless things? If so, what is useful?

v See above, pp. 248–49.

w Hilary, *On the Trinity* VIII.16 (MPL 10:246; NPNF2, 9:142).

Why do these great gentlemen rage so, and ask of what avail Christ's body is in the Supper, just as if it were nothing but a piece of beef, and remove the Word of God from their sight as if we had a Supper without God's Word? Who are the Capernaites and cannibals here? We have God's Word in the Supper: this they must concede to us. But God's Word accomplishes innumerable good things. Indeed, it does all things: it brings and strengthens faith, conquers sin, the devil, death, hell, and all evil; it makes us obedient to God, indeed, children and heirs; it glorifies God, it delights all angels and gladdens all creatures. But all this must also be in the Supper, because God's Word is in it.

"Yes," they say, "but we are not asking whether God's Word is of any avail, but what the body of Christ in itself avails in the bread; this, this, Luther—bite yourself with this!" When the lofty spirit asks this question, one might indeed lose heart. But if again I reply, "I will not let anyone separate the body of Christ from the Word," they would hiss and hoot at me. Well, suppose it is as they dream, that Christ's body is alone in the bread and no Word of God is there with it—though this is not possible. Let us see what they gain. Why, they will run out of the rain and fall into the water! For if Christ's body is present without the outward Word of God, it cannot be present there without the inner, eternal Word which is God himself, John 1[:1]. For this "Word became flesh" [John 1:14] and is in the flesh.

[The Benefit of Christ's Body: How Bodily Presence Is Useful]

Now I ask, in turn, whether God himself may also be of some avail? To be sure, when he walked on earth, he availed to the extent that whomever he touched with his flesh, he helped. Through his body, with his physical voice, he called Lazarus from the grave [John 11:43]. He touched the leper and made him clean [Matt. 8:3]. He walked upon the sea, and stretched forth his hand to the sinking Peter and drew him to the land [Matt. 14:31], and all his acts were miracles and good deeds. It is also his character and nature to do good wherever he is. How can it be that he is of no avail in the bread, when it is the same flesh, the same Word, and the same nature, and must be altogether good and useful?

They say, "Yes, but one does not see or feel the benefit."[x] My friend, is this the flaw? To the fanatics, of course, he is of no avail. They would like to grope and feel for something so they do not have to believe, like the cannibals and Capernaites who also would like to feel and bite into something. We who believe, however, know that the body does avail for us, wherever it is. If it is in the bread and is eaten bodily with faith, it strengthens the soul so that it believes it is Christ's body that the mouth eats, and so faith clings to the body that is in the bread. Now what raises, bears, and binds faith is not useless but salutary. Similarly, the mouth, the throat, the body, which eats Christ's body, will also have its benefit in that it will live forever and arise on the Last Day to eternal salvation. This is the secret power and benefit that flows from the body of Christ in the Supper into our body, for it must be useful and cannot be present in vain. Therefore it must bestow life and salvation upon our bodies, as is its nature.

Jesus reaches out to hold Peter's hand (Matt. 14:22-33). Illustration from a book by Henricus van den Leemputte (1588–1657). The illustration includes the monogram of woodcutter Christoffel van Sichem II (1577–1658), whose son, Christoffel van Sichem III (1618–1659), may have collaborated with him on the images in this book.

This I would want to say if it were possible that Christ's body alone were present in the Supper, without God's Word. This, however, is not the case, for there stand God's words, "This is my body," which grasp, comprehend, and give us bodily the body of Christ; therefore the body of Christ must be useful through the Word. Indeed, even if it were true that Christ's flesh were merely a piece of beef, and yet God's Word were there bidding us to eat of it, it would nevertheless be useful on account of the Word. For example, Abraham received the promise of his son Isaac, who, however, was only flesh and a child of the body. But Abraham was extolled as righteous by God because he believed he would have his son Isaac, Rom. 4[:22; Gen. 15:6]. Here the fanatics might also ask of what use Isaac was to Abraham's faith, and then they might say, "Isaac was nothing at all; the Spirit must be present, the flesh is of no avail."

x Zwingli, *Responsio ad Billicani,* Z 4:908; Oecolampadius, *Apologetica,* fol. T4v.

And what would be surprising if Isaac—or beef—were useful, if it were grasped and presented in God's Word? Even the devil, death, sin, hell, and all kinds of trouble would be nothing but benefit and advantage if they were presented and grasped in God's Word and were believed by us. Now, death can be of benefit to me, in body and soul, if I have Christ's word that says, "Whoever loses his life for my sake will find it" [Matt. 16:25]. Thus through the Word death must incite and strengthen my soul unto the righteousness and obedience of faith, and through it to chase my body into life. If this is so, should not Christ's body, which in itself is pure life and salvation, and full of God, be of such use to me through the Word as death, sin, and the devil? True, one does not feel and see it. But neither does one feel and see how the devil and death are of use through the Word. Faith feels it, however. My friend, come here and convince us that since death apart from the Word is of no use but is instead harmful, it must be nothing at all. For this is your argument, that whoever is of no use is nonexistent, so that Christ's body also must be of no use to you.

The result of this great and arrogant cleverness by which they scorn God's Word so shamefully, as Oecolampadius does in his blasphemous *Antisyngramma*,[132] is that they do not see the Word of God in the Supper, and simply gape and stare at the bodily eating, thinking that the divine Word must set forth nothing but spiritual things and have nothing to do with outward, bodily things. But this is the seed of Müntzer's and Karlstadt's spirit,[y] who also wanted to tolerate nothing outward, until they were utterly drowned in flesh. God inverts this order, however, and sets before us no word or commandment without its presenting and encompassing some bodily and outward thing. To Abraham God gave the word which encompassed his son Isaac [Gen. 15:4ff.], to Saul God gave the word which encompassed the slaying of the Amalekites [1 Sam. 15:2f.], to Noah God gave the word which encompassed the rainbow [Gen. 9:8-17], and so on.[133] You find no word of God in the entire Scriptures in which a bodily and outward thing is not encompassed and presented. If we followed the fanatical spirits, we would have to say that all these bodily, outward things were of no use and simply nothing. So too, here in the Supper, we have been given the word, which

132. In his response to the *Syngramma*, Oecolampadius sharply distinguished the external spoken word and the internal word spoken by God to the heart, *Apologetica*, fol. O1v-O3v.

133. Luther used these examples to explain the sacraments as the joining of promise and sign in *The Babylonian Captivity of the Church*, 9-129 above; also LW 36:39, 43-44.

y See nn. 17-18, p. 174; n. 80, p. 216.

encompasses Christ's body, crucified for us, in order to be eaten bodily. And this eating is of use for the forgiveness of sins, as the words state, just as Isaac had to come forth bodily and become Abraham's son, as the words state, and as the rainbow had to appear bodily, also as the words state.

But these fanatics must themselves concede that even in their spiritual eating a bodily thing is set forth. For Christ's body, even if it is at the right hand of God, is nevertheless a body, and an outward bodily thing having bone and flesh, which no spirit has—as he himself says in the last chapter of Luke [24:39], "A spirit has not flesh and bones as you see that I have." If they wish to be so much like Müntzer and not tolerate flesh and bone, then they must not eat Christ even spiritually, for they still are eating flesh and bone. What kind of distinction is that? Indeed, why is it any better for them to eat flesh and bone with their soul than to eat it with their mouth? If it is of no use in the mouth, how can it be of any use in the soul, since it is the same flesh and bone everywhere? But they want pure spirit; and indeed, this is what they do have: the devil, who has neither flesh nor bone.

I wrote diligently against Dr. Karlstadt concerning this point, that external things are of no use, and explained the proper distinction: outward things apart from God's Word, such as the pope's laws, are of no use.[z] But outward things connected with God's Word are salvation and blessedness, because they inhere in the Word and bind our faith, as I have just said concerning Isaac and the rainbow. Both of these are outward, bodily things, but since they are connected with the Word, Abraham had to attach his faith to the coming Isaac, who was encompassed in God's Word. The devil along with his fanatics, however, so hates the Word that he always seeks to sever it from outward things, but God seeks to keep these unsevered, and connects them to each other. What we say, that here we have something not merely outward but connected with the word, "This is my body," they do not hear, but rage past it like madmen, crying, "Outward things are of no use, outward things are of no use!" And they will not abandon this Müntzer-like spirit until they have caused such misfortune as Müntzer did.[134] For since they have the very same spirit, I am afraid they will bring forth the very same fruit; as the tree is, so it bears fruit [Matt. 7:16].

134. Müntzer had been a leader of the Peasants' War, which resulted in death and destruction in many German territories; see n. 80.

z *Against the Heavenly Prophets*, LW 40:146–49; TAL 2:104–8.

From such a spirit it must follow that civil government is of no use, being an outward thing, since people are unwilling to hear or see that it is encompassed in God's Word and must be believed to be God's ordinance, Rom. 13[:1-5]. This belief indeed is not of no use before God, and therefore this fanatical spirit must remain seditious and murderous. Now see, civil order is an outward thing, yet it binds our faith, and is also an article of faith on account of the word in which it is contained, Rom. 13[:1]: "All authorities that exist everywhere are of God." But this is of no help for those who are mad, until they knock their heads against it.[135]

I should like to know, however, where they get the idea that there is a God, that God's Son is man, that one must believe, and all the other articles of our faith, which of course have never occurred to reason. Did they get these ideas from the Spirit before they bodily and outwardly heard or read them? I know full well they must here say "no," for they got them through the bodily, outward Word and Scripture. Then how can this outward Word, through which the Holy Spirit is given with all his gifts, be of no use? Oh, in their blind arrogance they think they have Christ at the right hand of God, locked up in a closet, and do not believe that he is present in his Word and in the outward things of which his Word speaks. Therefore, as St. Paul says, "They themselves do not understand either what they are saying or the things about which they make assertions, but wishing to be masters of the Scriptures, they have become vain babblers," 1 Timothy 1.[a] On another occasion we shall deal with this better and more fully.

Further, they say, "But what is the need for Christ's body to be present in the sacrament? Faith can be strengthened perfectly well without it, through the gospel which is preached."[b] This is true—but again we are trying to summon God to trial and shove under his nose the question why he finds it necessary to proffer us this Word and work, or why we need him to do so.[136] Is he trying to make fools out of us—don't we ourselves know as well as he what we need and what he needs? Does he think, even though he is God, that he alone is wise, and is he trying to be the master of those who are spiritual? He may have flesh and blood, but we have the spirit; so, his flesh is of no use, but our spirit lives. We

135. Luther believed that all governments were established by God and that rebellion against even bad government was in most cases sinful. This was the reason for his harsh words against the peasants during the Peasants' War of 1525. Two years earlier, he had expounded his ideas of government and what Christians owe to government in his treatise *Temporal [Secular] Authority: To What Extent It Should Be Obeyed* (LW 45:75–130; see also TAL 5, forthcoming).

136. Luther uses the masculine pronoun in this paragraph for both God and Christ without making the change of referent clear, which reflects his belief that Father and Son were one God.

a A very loose paraphrase of 1 Tim. 1:6-7.

b Oecolampadius, *Billiche Antwort*, W^2 20:633.

intend to sing him another song so he will get busy and think over the matter, and speak to us words and show us works we can recognize as useful. If not, our verdict is that he is a Capernaite, an Atreus, a Thyestes, and a cannibal,[137] and we shall see how he defends himself from our charge! [. . .][c]

This is the second abominable blasphemy of Oecolampadius. For one who asks why something that God says and does is necessary is surely trying to set himself above God and be more clever and better than God. This is the real spirit of Müntzer, who also said he would do a mess on both Christ and the Scriptures if they would not be governed by his spirit. Immediately thereafter came Zwingli, and when he was confronted by the statement that in the Supper we eat Christ's body invisibly, in an ineffable manner, he went and screamed about Christ, "O what a fine light of the world Christ then turns out to be! How well he enlightens us, if we cannot know how his body is eaten there in the bread!"[d] Like Müntzer, he is not far from doing a mess on Christ.

A person's heart might burst at such insolent prattle of the hellish devil and his fanatics. They want to know how Christ's body is in the bread; otherwise, it is false to say that he is in it. Yet they also cannot know how it occurs that they can open their mouths, move their tongues, hold a pen in their hands, or even more trivial things, not to mention knowing how they see, hear, speak, and live in the body. All such things we feel, and we are daily involved in them, yet we do not know how they occur; nevertheless, we wish to know how Christ's body is present in the bread, otherwise we refuse to acknowledge Christ as our light and master!

Now even though it is not our obligation, we too would like to show for good measure why it is necessary for Christ's body to be present in the bread. Briefly, the first need is on account of God. For if it were not so, Christ would be a liar in his words, "Take, eat, this is my body, given for you." Here, you lovely devil, is the need! God is truthful; what he says, he can and does do [Ps. 33:4]. Since he says here, "This is my body," and refers with the word "this" to the bread, as the fanatics confess, his body must of necessity be present. The power of this necessity rests on this: that God maintains his glory, for he boasts that he is truthful

137. King Atreus of Mycenae slew the three sons of his brother Thyestes and served them to him at a banquet. Oecolampadius compared Pirckheimer's description of eating Christ's body to a "Thyestian banquet"; *Ad Pyrkaimerum responsio*, fol. c8v.

c Text omitted (see LW 37:138).

d Zwingli, *Responsio ad Billicani*, Z 4:901; *Zwingli and Bullinger*, 219–20.

and faithful. Meanwhile, we can readily believe that this need does not greatly concern the spiritual god of the fanatics, for he can easily assume that our fleshly and baked God is a liar, as he himself has been from the beginning, and that he does not keep or fulfill his words, as indeed is the case.

The second need is on account of our faith. Faith in God's Word is necessary for us, because it has been spoken in order that we should believe it, and God wills and demands of us to have faith where this Word is. Now, there stand God's words, which encompass and comprehend the body of Christ, saying that he is present. Therefore as the Word and faith are necessary, so also is the body comprehended in the Word necessary for us, in order that our faith may be correct and consistent with the Word, because the two, Word and body, are not to be separated. And even if the body were separate and apart from the Word, it still would be necessary, because life and salvation are in it.

Of course, it is true that this might well take place apart from the sacrament. It may also take place apart from the body of Christ, which is at the right hand of God. Should Christ therefore not be at the right hand of God? Again, it may take place apart from the gospel, for who could hinder God if God had actually willed to redeem us but not to have it preached or to become man? Just as God created heaven and earth, and accomplishes all things continuously even now without outward preaching, and does not on that account become man: would the gospel therefore be nothing? But if it is God's will to give it to you through the humanity of Christ, through the Word, through the bread in the Supper, who are you, arrogant, thankless devil, that you dare to ask why God does not do it in a different way and without these means? Will you prescribe and choose means and measures for God? You ought to leap for joy that God does it in whatever manner God chooses, if only you obtain it. Don't you think I also could ask: Since the gospel and the remembrance of Christ can be had in all preaching, what then is the need of celebrating a Supper in addition, and taking bread and wine in it? What is the need for anyone to read the Scriptures for himself? What is the need for anyone to admonish and comfort another individually, since all this can happen in regular public preaching? Aren't these childish, blind thoughts in such important matters? God means to fill the world and be present in many different ways, to help and strengthen us by God's Word and works;

shall we be so complacent and bored that we hinder God, and tolerate nothing but the way that happens to please us? You are a black, hopeless devil! Enough said for now.

[Benefits of Christ's Body: Lord's Supper Neither Mere Symbol nor Sacrifice]

Now that the fanatics think they have won their case, they go and make out of the Supper a *symbolon*, i.e., a sign of remembrance, by which Christians are recognized outwardly, as beggars and Jews are recognized by the yellow badge.[138] They regard it simply as a symbol of Christians among one another, without reference to God, whereby they practice and maintain love for one another.[e] Such things inevitably followed from this spirit,

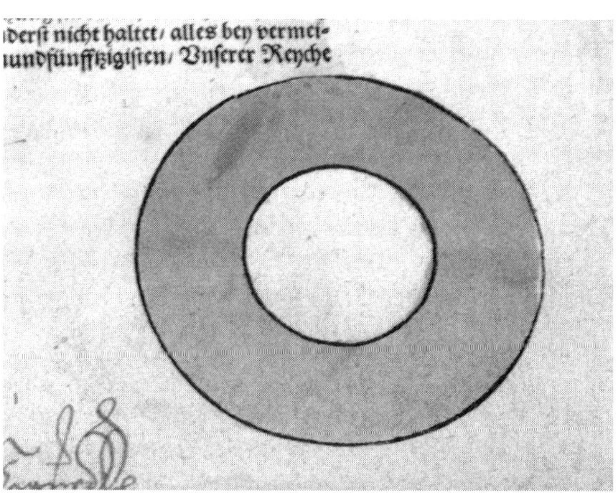

Detail from a decree of Ferdinand I, ruler in Austria and Germany, in which he orders Jews to wear yellow circles on their clothing (August 1, 1551). In 1558, Ferdinand succeeded his brother Charles as Holy Roman Emperor.

138. On *symbolon*, see n. 59, p. 197. In 1215 the Fourth Lateran Council required Jews to wear something that distinguished them from Christians; in Saxony, this was a yellow badge. In some cities, such as Nuremberg, resident beggars were given badges to distinguish them from vagrants and those able-bodied but unwilling to work; Carter Lindberg, *Beyond Charity: Reformation Initiatives for the Poor* (Minneapolis: Fortress Press, 1993), 46.

e Zwingli, *Commentary*, 237–38; Oecolampadius, *Genvina expositione*, fol. H7r.

for since they rip God's Word away from the bread and wine, and let nothing remain but eating and drinking, as in taverns, naturally God is not served by it at all, nor is our faith helped; but their observance makes gluttony and gourmandizing out of it. For what does God care about our eating and drinking, as the prophet says in Jeremiah?[f] What does it help our faith that the belly eats and drinks? It used to be said concerning parish fairs that they were held in order that friends might meet one another and friendships might be strengthened. So too, Christ's Supper here has been made into a parish fair.[139]

139. The parish fair was held yearly, on the feast day of the saint to whom the church was dedicated. It was a time for socialization and feasting, and reformers criticized it because of the overeating and drunkenness that often occurred.

If one asks how they prove this, however, the answer comes: "Oh, isn't it enough that we say so?" In truth, one who finds the words of God hard to believe in this article is relieved of a great vexation by such prattle. But if we maintain our position that his words are true and Christ's body and blood are present in the Supper, they must concede to us that the Supper is something more than a parish fair. But where his Word is torn away from the Supper and mere bread and wine are made of it, then I grant that they may make a parish fair or carnival of it. There is no difference. If they please, they may even make a dance or game of it. We don't care, just so long as we aren't involved with their blasphemous and hateful meal.

We know, however, that it is the Lord's Supper, in name and in reality, not the supper of Christians. For the Lord not only instituted it, but also prepares and gives it himself, and is himself cook, server, food, and drink, as we have demonstrated our belief above. Christ does not say, in commanding and instituting it, "Do this as your summons to mutual recognition and love," but, "Do this in remembrance of me" [Luke 22:19; 1 Cor. 11:24]. If we are to do it in remembrance of him, then surely it is instituted in his service and in his honor. But with what do we serve him? With eating and drinking? In my opinion, we do it by strengthening our faith and learning to know him, as we have often taught. And no doubt will remain if we insist that his body and blood are present, as the holy fathers also describe these fruits of the Supper.

I hear it said, too, that this error pleases some adherents of the papacy, and that certain persons now hope to prove above all that the Mass is a sacrifice, especially since some of the fathers

f Jer. 7:21-24.

call the sacrament a sacrifice, such as Irenaeus, Cyprian, and Augustine.[140] And since they feel it is un-Christian to sacrifice Christ daily, who sacrificed himself once and neither can nor will be sacrificed again, they seize upon the bread and wine, and since nothing but bread and wine are supposed to be in the sacrament, they think that there is no further danger in regarding the Mass as a sacrifice, and that now they may more easily earn their income, since they supposedly sacrifice only bread and wine.[141] If that were true, it would serve them just right, that God's judgment may remain truthful, of which St. Paul speaks [2 Thess. 2:10f.], "God sends upon them a strong delusion, to make them believe what is false, because they refused to love the truth and so be saved," and Christ in John 5[:43], "I have come in my Father's name, and you do not receive me; if another comes in his own name, him you will receive." Just so, these gentlemen also persecute and hate the gospel without end, hence they shall adopt fanaticism and falsehoods in its place.

But what if the Mass should now disappear precisely for the reason by which you thought to uphold it, and what if you thus lost both gospel and Mass through adopting this fanaticism, so that you retained neither faith for the soul nor income for the belly? For if the common people found out that you were offering nothing but bread and wine for their sins in the Mass, they would immediately pull back their hand and take back both offering and income. For who would be so crazy that he would have a piece of bread and a drink of wine given for his soul, especially in the New Testament, since we are redeemed by the precious blood of Christ, not by gold or silver, not by bread or wine?[g] For the fanatics also hope that through their teaching they can utterly overthrow the Mass along with the pope and all, and establish a great unity and equality among all Christians.[142]

Whoever wants to may regard the Mass as a sacrifice, and they may understand it as they want, whether merely bread or Christ's body, but they will have to answer this: It is quite certain that Christ cannot be sacrificed over and above the one single time he sacrificed himself.[143] For, praise God, the papists themselves now see that such daily sacrifices and the sale of such sacrifices for our sins, as used to be endowed and practiced, are the greatest blasphemy and abomination ever known on earth,

g 1 Pet. 1:18-19.

140. Early Christian authors discussed the idea of sacrifice in different ways. Irenaeus spoke of the offering of thanks and praise to God as a sacrifice, while Cyril of Jerusalem (c. 313–386) wrote of offering up Christ. Alasdair I. C. Heron, *Table and Tradition* (Philadelphia: Westminster, 1983), 75–79.

141. The belief that the sacrifice of the Mass could be offered for both the living and the dead led to the endowment of benefices (called chantries in England) held by priests whose sole function was to say Mass daily on behalf of the individuals and groups who had paid for them. These "Mass-priests," as the reformers called them, far outnumbered the parish clergy responsible for pastoral care.

142. Hoen was the first to claim that rejecting Christ's bodily presence would lead to the overthrow of the papacy, Oberman, *Forerunners*, 275.

143. Zwingli made this argument, based on Hebrews 9, in his 1523 *Exposition of the Conclusions* from the first Zurich disputation, HZW 1:92–98. Luther rejected the sacrifice of the Mass as a type of good work in *The Babylonian Captivity of the Church*, LW 36:35–36, 47–49; (this volume, pp. 38–39, 50–52), but he also objected to the words of the canon of the Mass on the basis of Hebrews 9 in his 1525 pamphlet *The Abomination of the Secret Mass*, LW 36:320.

and not one of the ancient teachers held, taught, or wrote about them. For Irenaeus calls it a sacrifice when one offers bread and wine, which through God's Word becomes the sacrament, solely for the purpose of giving thanks, in order that we may acknowledge thereby how God feeds us, just as it was done in the Old Testament, but never for our sins or to redeem our souls or to propitiate God, as is the case when the papists celebrate Mass.[h] Some call it a sacrifice because we remember thus the one sacrifice that Christ once made for us, just as every year we call Easter "the Resurrection" or "Day of Resurrection," and say, "Christ is risen today"; not that Christ rises every year, but that every year we commemorate the day of his resurrection. In this sense St. Augustine calls the sacrament a sacrifice.[144] But let those who refuse to believe go their way, sacrifice, and blaspheme until they stop; the truth on this topic has sufficiently come to light.

144. Augustine, Letter 98 to Boniface, 9 (MPL 33:363; NPNF1 1:409–10). In his 1523 *Exposition*, Zwingli also used this passage to argue against the Mass as a sacrifice; HZW 1:121.

[Conclusion]

With this I have asked and admonished my respected fanatics that they honor the truth so that we may soon end this matter and, avoiding unnecessary discussion, answer us concerning the genuine chief points solidly and firmly. I point them out again: it is not necessary in this matter for them to teach us that Christ is seated at the right hand of God, having left the earth and ascended into heaven, and that our hearts should cling to him there and not to earthly things—and a host of other such arguments; for by God's grace we know all these things perfectly well. Rather, what is necessary is to prove convincingly how these two points are contradictory: CHRIST'S BODY IS SEATED AT THE RIGHT HAND OF GOD, AND IS AT THE SAME TIME PRESENT IN THE SUPPER; how it may come to pass that God's power could become so weak that it is unable to accomplish this, and how all this may be proven by sound argument and clear Scripture. Here is where we should be instructed, here is the real need, to convince us that the words, "This is my body," are dark and obscure and need to be understood otherwise than the way they read. [. . .][i]

h Irenaeus, *Against Heresies* IV.17.5; 18.1.6 (MPG 7:1023, 1029; ANF 1:484, 486).

i Text omitted (see LW 37:144–45).

Similarly, you need not teach us that flesh is of no use, and that we must eat, live, and do all things spiritually, and that without the spirit nothing is of use. This we realize already. We should like to know more—namely, how the statement "FLESH IS OF NO USE" is contrary to the statement "CHRIST'S BODY IS IN THE BREAD." Again we should like to be assured that "FLESH IS OF NO USE" is said concerning Christ's body; again, that Christ's body is a perishable, useless, corruptible food, though he himself says in John 6[:27, 33] that it is an imperishable food which gives life; also, how in the Supper it is a perishable, useless flesh, although by nature and character it is an eternal food. Here, here, we cry; listen to us here! Explain, too, why the saying "If anyone says to you, 'Look, here is the Christ!' or 'Look, there he is!'" [Mark 13:21; cf. Matt. 24:23] must be referred to the sacrament. Make certain and clear to us these and all the other things that you regard as the grounds for your fancy. What you have worked out up to now is all in vain, and nothing is established by it; for you have said a great deal, indeed, but you have undertaken to prove nothing.

Zwingli, it is true, boasted that he would press and squeeze out of the words "This is my body" the sense "This is the sign of my body."[j] But there was one who stood by and watched how he worked the wine press, and observed that someone had played a trick on him and had filled the press with nothing but pebbles, painted the color of grapes. So the poor man pressed the pebbles with great effort, but nothing came out, until the whole press, stones and all, collapsed on his head and crushed him. Truly, Christ's words do not submit to much pressing and squeezing. They are pebbles, yes, real rocks, which dare not be handled by the godless with impunity, as he says in Matthew 22 [21:44], "He who falls on this stone will be broken to pieces; when it falls on any one, it will crush him."

If you wish to keep the fathers on your side, as you boast, and not completely disavow them, do not get into such a position that you simply gloss them at will, but press and squeeze their words well to see if they will yield such a meaning. You need not teach us that the sayings of the fathers may be twisted or turned this way or that, but show whether it is certain that they shall and

j Zwingli used the metaphor of a wine press in his *Responsio ad Billicani,* Z 4:899.

must be so turned. Surely you see that we are perfectly familiar with your skills and have not the slightest desire for your mastery in the topics that we already know. Yes, we acknowledge and praise you as the finest of all teachers, for you teach what one can easily understand without needing any faith. For anyone who cannot understand that bread is bread and wine is wine must surely be mad. But what is lacking is your proof that it is nothing but bread. St. Paul is not so fine a teacher, for he teaches what no one can understand; but his proof is so strong that he compels one to believe. This you do not do, but spend your time speaking about other subjects. But if you must flaunt your skill and if you imagine it helps the case, please do this: let the greater part of the talk deal with the main subject. Now I think I have given sufficient admonition as to what you ought to do. But what do you bet that it won't help? For I know this flighty, coy, slippery devil perfectly well.

You boast about your holy life and suffering, and you judge that the Spirit of God has forsaken me;[145] this we gladly allow. Indeed, we poor sinners wish you might be still better than your boast, because we are certain that it is not only harmless but even salutary to us when there are faithful, holy people on earth; of course we do not wish them harm, we appreciate them and, indeed, truly need them. But if in the future you wish to boast of your life even more, my request is that you prove your boast with deeds, and rebuke and correct your followers for their wickedness. [. . .][146]

Their faction also maligns me with the judgment that because I wrote against the peasants,[147] the Spirit has departed from me, and that having become hardened, I cannot understand the clear truth.[148] I ignore this and other talk about myself, of course, and I do not boast of my lofty spirit. Of great gifts and graces of my God and the Spirit, however, I do boast, I hope, quite justly and not without cause. And it seems to me to be not so profound to understand that mere bread and wine may be on a table, which even a child and a fool understand perfectly well. I too see them every day in front of me on my table. But you, dear councilors at Basel and Strasbourg,[149] and all you who have such sacramentarian sects in your midst—may this talk of theirs give you fair warning not to put bags over your eyes, but to pay close attention to the game. Müntzer is dead,[k] but his spirit is not yet eradicated.

145. See nn. 20, 21, and 25. Oecolampadius also complained about Luther's attacks, *Billiche Antwortt*, W[2] 20:583.

146. In the section omitted Luther criticizes Martin Bucer for inserting his own views into his Latin translation of Luther's collection of sermons and his German version of Bugenhagen's commentary on the Psalms; see LW 37:147–49. In recognition of the Wittenberg Concord, this passage was omitted from the 1548 Wittenberg edition of Luther's works, which generated some protest from Luther's followers. The passage was restored in the 1551 Wittenberg edition.

147. Luther wrote three pamphlets during the 1525 Peasants' War. In the first, *Admonition to Peace* (LW 46:3–43; TAL 5, forthcoming), he rebuked both princes and peasants. In the second, *Against the Robbing and Murdering Hordes of Peasants*, he condemned rebellion and urged the princes to deal harshly with the peasants, LW 46:45–55. In the third, he defended his stance against the peasants, *An Open Letter on the Harsh Book against the Peasants*, LW 46:57–85.

148. Conrad Ryss, *Antwort*, fol. B2r-B3r, accused Luther of contradicting his earlier statements about the Lord's Supper, condemned him for stating in a book against the peasants that what he had taught would remain right despite the criticism of others, and asserted that God had withdrawn the Spirit from him for the sin of pride.

149. The governments of the cities where Oecolampadius and Bucer lived. Luther apparently had no hope that the government of Zurich would heed him.

It is easy to see what we should make of this spirit who in a seditious way still comforts and exonerates the peasants and condemns me for writing against them. The devil does not sleep, but ever continues his sowing.[l] That is why I said above: This spirit is not good, and means no good through these fanatics, although I think the preachers against whom I write have no malice in mind. But dear God, they are not their own masters; the spirit has blinded and taken them prisoner. Therefore they are not to be trusted. For any spirit that does away with Christ's flesh is not of God, says St. John [1 John 4:2f.]. And he adds: Let there be a testing [4:1]. Now this spirit certainly does away with Christ's flesh, because he makes of it a useless, perishable, and altogether common flesh, like beef or veal, as we have heard. Therefore he cannot be honest. I warn, I counsel: Beware, watch out, Satan has come among the children of God!

Here I leave the matter for now, until they return. For the saying, "This is my body," still stands firm against all their fanaticism. This I have now upheld, praise God, with this book. God grant that they are converted to the truth; and if not, that all they write may become cords with which to entangle themselves and fall into my hands. Amen.

k See n. 80, p. 216.

l Matt. 13:25.

Concerning Rebaptism

1528

MARK D. TRANVIK

INTRODUCTION

Luther's teachings on baptism and the Lord's Supper have often been misunderstood. Early in his career he was concerned to attack the Roman church's emphasis on the objective power of the sacraments as long as they were properly administered and received. He believed this made baptism and the Lord's Supper into empty rituals that left little room for life-giving faith. He was faced with a different situation in the 1520s, however. Following his dramatic defense of his teachings at the Diet of Worms in 1521 and his confinement in the Wartburg castle, he returned to a Wittenberg engulfed in theological and social chaos. He would spend a good deal of time in the next decade sorting out issues related to sacramental understandings and practices. While the Lord's Supper received most of his attention,[a] he also had to explain his views on baptism. The immediate challenges on the latter came from within his own circle.

The main figure was Andreas Bodenstein von Karlstadt (1486–1541), Luther's senior colleague on the University of Wittenberg faculty. Karlstadt taught a theology that stressed a

a See, for example, the treatise *That These Words* . . . in this volume, above, pp. 162–273.

mystical union with Christ. He had become deeply suspicious of the value of anything external, such as sacraments and images, as being necessary for the life of faith. Bread, wine, and water at best pointed to the work Christ had done rather than being vehicles for the transmission of God's saving love and grace. In some ways, Karlstadt's views on the symbolic nature of the Lord's Supper would have much in common with the teaching of the Swiss reformer Ulrich Zwingli (1484–1531), whom Luther had debated in treatises and met face to face at Marburg in 1529.[1] In addition, Karlstadt also published treatises that denied infant baptism.[2]

But Karlstadt would not be Luther's only problem. Two other opponents also emerged in Saxony and took Luther's ideas in directions that astonished and angered him. Luther recommended a former student, Thomas Müntzer (c. 1489–1525), as pastor for the city of Zwickau, an important commercial center

The Marburg Colloquy is depicted in this anonymous woodcarving (1557). The Landgrave Philipp of Hesse invited Luther and Zwingli to Marburg in September 1529. They were accompanied by some of their followers, including Melanchthon. They hoped to settle their dispute about communion but were not successful.

1. In 1529 Luther and other reformers from Wittenberg met with Zwingli and Johannes Oecolampadius (1482–1531) and other theologians from Basel and Strassburg. See *The Marburg Colloquy and the Marburg Articles, 1529* (LW 38:3–89).

2. After leaving Wittenberg in 1523, Karlstadt was pastor of a parish in the town of Orlamünde where, among other things, he postponed the baptism of infants. He was expelled eventually from Saxony and moved to southern Germany where he began to publish treatises advocating a spiritual interpretation of the Lord's Supper as well as denying the validity of infant baptism. From 1525 to 1529 he actually came back to the Wittenberg area and worked as a common laborer. In his final years he returned to teaching as a professor at Basel. See Martin Brecht, *Martin Luther: Shaping and Defining the Reformation, 1521–1532*, trans. James L. Schaaf (Minneapolis: Fortress Press, 1990), 157–72; and Alejandro Zorzin, "Andreas Bodenstein von Karlstadt," in Carter Lindberg, ed., *The Reformation Theologians* (Oxford: Blackwell, 2002), 327–37.

south of Wittenberg. Müntzer was a firebrand who would go far beyond anything imagined by his former teacher. He eventually began to see himself as a prophet of God, appointed by the Holy Spirit in the last days to battle the godless—defined as anyone aligned with the authorities of church and state. Further, the sacraments could only be distractions that interfered with the work of the Spirit.[3] Müntzer ended up in a leadership role in the peasants' revolts of 1525 and was killed in a battle by forces loyal to the princes.

Also emerging from Zwickau, and probably under Müntzer's influence, was a group of "prophets" led by the weaver Nicholas Storch (d. 1525). Believing that God spoke directly to him by means of private revelations, Storch saw himself as the leader of a new church that would go far beyond the conservative reforms advocated by Luther. Because he thought the Holy Spirit communicated directly with him, Storch believed it was no longer necessary to rely on the Bible or on "outward ceremonies" such as baptism. The latter was little more than a "dog's bath." Of course, this meant the denial of infant baptism as well. Storch would also say that marriage vows were not permanent and that it was even permissible to practice polygamy. Luther and Storch did meet in 1522, but this self-styled prophet did not impress the Wittenberg reformer.[4]

In 1528, Luther took up his pen and wrote the treatise *Concerning Rebaptism*. The immediate occasion for this document was a request by two Roman Catholic pastors in a neighboring region to help them sort out the issues surrounding baptism, and infant baptism in particular. As Luther admits in the text, he had only a hazy knowledge of what is now known as Anabaptism, which literally means "rebaptism." His views were shaped by the context outlined above. As we know today, the teachings of Storch and Müntzer, in particular, were hardly representative of Anabaptism, which was actually only part of a wider and more complex movement now referred to as the Radical Reformation. But Luther did grasp well the core theological issues at stake. These concerned the nature of faith and the corresponding rationale for infant baptism. As one who upheld the centrality of justification by faith alone, he had to sort out why children should continue to be baptized. The treatise also provided an opportunity for him to explain in detail the relationship between the word and faith.

3. Luther addresses Karlstadt and Müntzer in his treatise *Against the Heavenly Prophets in the Matter of Images and Sacraments* (LW 40:79-223; TAL 2:38-125).

4. The conversation between Luther and Storch was brief. Luther felt like he was the object of a lecture by someone with a superficial knowledge of Scripture. See John Oyer, *Lutheran Reformers Against the Anabaptists* (The Hague: Martinus Nijhoff, 1964), 6-40; and Heinrich Bornkamm, *Luther in Mid-Career: 1521–1530*, trans. E. Theodore Bachmann (Philadelphia: Fortress Press, 1983), 77.

From the late 1520s to the end of his life, Luther had a growing appreciation of the power of baptism and its importance for creating and nourishing a relationship with God. Though he always upheld the inherited tradition regarding the baptism of infants, the emergence of the Anabaptist movement became a crucible for Luther where he deepened and refined his understanding of the sacrament. Baptism appeared with increasing frequency in his sermons. References to the sacrament also appear in unlikely places. As Jonathan Trigg has shown, Luther's commentary on Genesis (a project of the 1530s)—at first glance a peculiar choice for mention of baptism—is permeated by references to the sacrament.[b] In many ways, *Concerning Rebaptism* and the extended comments in *The Large Catechism*, which was written in the same year, represent the beginning of a new look at what Luther called "the greatest jewel" that can adorn our bodies and souls.[c]

Luther admits that he wrote *Concerning Rebaptism* in a hurried fashion.[d] And it is true that he repeats himself and, on occasion, seems to dwell too long on points that are not central to his main argument. As a result, section headings have been inserted to help the reader follow Luther's reasoning. As these captions indicate, Luther was basically replying to four questions that shape the entire treatise. First, if a teaching originates with the church of Rome, then does that mean it must be false? Second, is infant baptism false because it relies on human testimony? Third, does the truth of baptism depend on faith? And, fourth, does it make sense according to Scripture to baptize infants?

b Jonathan D. Trigg, *Baptism in the Theology of Martin Luther* (Boston: Brill, 2001).

c Martin Luther, *The Large Catechism*, BC, 462:46.

d See p. 315 below.

CONCERNING REBAPTISM[5]

A LETTER OF MARTIN LUTHER TO TWO PASTORS

MARTIN LUTHER, to the worthy and beloved pastors N. and N.,[6] my dear friends in Christ.

Grace and peace in Christ our Lord. Unfortunately, I know full well, dear sirs, that Balthasar Hubmaier[7] has included my name among others in his blasphemous booklet on rebaptism, as if I shared his perverted views. But I have comforted myself with the thought that no one, either friend or foe, would believe such a transparent lie as his. Not only is my conscience at rest in this, but my reputation is sufficiently safeguarded by the number of my sermons and especially by the latest postil [containing sermons for the Sundays] from Epiphany to Easter, where I have made known abundantly my faith concerning infant baptism.[8] Therefore I have deemed it unnecessary to answer his kind of book. For who can stop the mouths of all people, even of all devils? I have long ago found that if I stop one mouth of the devil, he opens ten others, and the lie grows constantly greater.[9] So, whether I wish it or not, I commit my cause to God, and if I have told the truth I depend on God as a true judge, who knows how to bring things to a right end. We can indeed grasp how God does this every day.

So far we have escaped the excrement of such preachers in the territory of our prince, God be thanked and praised in eternity.[10] We also have none of the foes of the sacrament,[11] but are at peace and in harmony in doctrine, faith, and life. May it be God's will graciously to keep us thus. Amen. Since there has not been much occasion here for it, I have not, for my part, given much thought to these baptizers. But it serves you right as papists[12] (I must call you such, as long as you are under your tyrants). Because you will not suffer the gospel, you will have to endure these devil's rebels, as Christ says in John 5[:43]: "I have come in my Father's name, and you do not accept me; if another comes in his own name, you will accept him." Still, it is not right, and I truly grieve, that these

5. The text is a revision of the one found in LW 40:229–62. The German version of *Concerning Rebaptism* is in WA 26:144–74.

6. Luther wrote this treatise in 1528 when the Lutheran movement was still in its early stages. Two anonymous pastors, who were in an area under control of Roman Catholics, wrote a letter to him with questions about baptism.

7. Balthasar Hubmaier (1485–1528) studied in Freiburg in southern Germany and became a professor of theology at Ingolstadt in 1512. In the early 1520s he was a pastor in Waldshut on the southern edge of the Black Forest when he became interested in the movements to reform the church. He was influenced by the Zurich reformer Ulrich Zwingli but soon thought the Swiss reform was moving too slowly. In particular, Hubmaier and his followers were convinced that baptism was only for those capable of making a confession of faith, thus ruling out infants. This was the beginning of the movement known as "Anabaptism," which literally means "rebaptizer." Hubmaier and other Anabaptists denied this name, claiming adult baptism was, in fact, the first baptism since the baptism of infants was without foundation in the Bible. In 1525 he wrote one of his most famous texts, *On the Baptism of Christian Believers*. (See Balthasar Hubmaier, *Theologian of Anabaptism*, trans. and ed. H. Wayne Pipkin and John H. Yoder [Scottdale, PA: Herald Press, 1989], 95–149.) Luther is not specifically cited in this work but he is quoted approvingly (and in a misleading way) in Hubmaier's 1526 tract, "Old and

New Teachers on Believers' Baptism" (see ibid., 256). Anabaptism became illegal in the Holy Roman Empire and in 1528 it was punishable by death (it was seen as a threat to the established order). Hubmaier eventually fled Zurich and ended up in Moravia. He was apprehended by imperial authorities and burned at the stake in Vienna in 1528.

8. In the Middle Ages a collection of sermons was known as a "postil." It comes from Latin and is shorthand for *Post illa verba textus*, which means "the words spoken after the text" or the message delivered in worship after the reading of the biblical texts. Luther published a number of postils or sermon collections. Here he is referring to his Lenten Postil of 1524–25 found in LW 76:257–66 and WA 17/2: 78–88.

9. A regular theme in Luther's writing is that he is not just contending against human foes but also against the devil. See Heiko Oberman, *Luther: Man Between God and the Devil*, trans. Eileen Walliser-Schwarzbart (New Haven: Yale University Press, 2006); and Robert Kolb, *Martin Luther: Confessor of the Faith* (Oxford: Oxford University Press, 2009), 163–71. With regard to the issue of this treatise, Luther had an intense belief that Satan opposed infant baptism and ultimately the teaching that we are saved by grace through faith and not through human effort.

10. Luther is speaking of his region in northern Germany, known as Electoral Saxony. Anabaptism by this time had spread rapidly but primarily in southern Germany. At least initially, areas in northern Germany were largely unaffected. See Martin Brecht, *Martin Luther: Shaping and Defining the*

Image of infant baptism from a 1545 Leipzig printing of Luther's *Small Catechism*.

miserable folk should be so lamentably murdered, burned, and tormented to death. We should allow all people to believe what they wish. If their faith is false, they will be sufficiently punished in eternal hell-fire. Why then should we martyr these people also in this world, if their error is in faith alone and they are not guilty of rebellion or opposition to the government?[13] Dear God, how quickly a person can become confused and fall into the trap of the devil! By the Scriptures and the word of God, we ought to guard against and withstand him. By fire we accomplish little.

I am not sure as to the ground and reason of their faith, since you do not tell me, and yet ask advice as to what to do in such cases. For this reason my answer cannot be very definite.

German Anabaptist Balthasar Hubmaier, from a seventeenth-century gravure screen print by Christoffel van Sichem.

Reformation, 1521–1532, trans. James L. Schaaf (Minneapolis: Fortress Press, 1990), 337.

11. By "sacrament" Luther is referring here to the Lord's Supper. His teaching on the presence of Christ in Holy Communion had been opposed by people within his own circle and also by Ulrich Zwingli in Zurich. By 1528 most of the opposition in the area of Wittenberg had disappeared.

12. He is responding to the inquiries of two pastors in a Roman Catholic area. Therefore, they are technically "papists" because they are under the rule of the pope in Rome. However, note at the beginning of the treatise that Luther refers to them as "worthy and beloved."

13. Luther opposed forcing anyone to believe a certain way. He thought God would take care of a faith that was false. By the middle of the 1530s, Luther changed his views on this matter and did not oppose capital punishment in matters of faith. See Egil Grislis, "Martin Luther and Menno Simons on Infant Baptism," *Journal of Mennonite Studies* 12 (1994): 8. As mentioned in the introduction above, there were some wings of the Radical Reformation that attempted to overthrow political authority by force of arms. Luther did not approve of insurrection and believed the death penalty would be appropriate in these cases.

In a sense you are yourselves Anabaptists. For many among you rebaptize in Latin when someone has been baptized in German, though your pope himself neither does this nor teaches it. For we know well enough that the pope recognizes it as a baptism when midwives administer emergency baptism, even though it be in German. Still you rebaptize persons whom we have baptized in German, as if our German baptism by pastors were not as good as German baptism by midwives.[14] So the bonehead of Leipzig recently did at Mühlhausen.[15] But the pope has never commanded that baptism should be only in Latin and not in another language. So you have your reward. You favor rebaptism, so you get plenty of Anabaptists, though you will not tolerate them, and yet you want to be rebaptizers in opposition to your own teacher and master, the pope.

[God Preserves the True Church—Even under the Pope]

But I pass by now what wrong your people do in their rebaptizing. Your shame is the greater since by your rebaptizing you at the same time contradict your idol, the pope. Teacher and pupil do not agree with each other. I will not speak further of this, but rather help you by appearing to be a papist again and flattering the pope. For my dear enthusiasts[16] will put no other interpretation on it (as they already have done) than that I flatter the pope and seek his favor. Anyone who does not follow their foolish enthusiasm ends up being called a new papist.

In the first place I hear and see that such rebaptism is undertaken by some in order to spite the pope and to be free of any taint of the Antichrist.[17] In the same way the foes of the sacrament want to believe only in bread and wine, in opposition to the pope, thinking thereby really to overthrow the papacy. It is indeed a shaky foundation on which they can build nothing good. On that basis we would have to disown the whole of Scripture and the office of the ministry, which of course we have received from the papacy. We would also have to make a new Bible. Furthermore, we would have to disavow the Old Testament, so that we would be under no obligation to the unbelieving Jews. And why the daily use of gold and goods that have been used by bad people, papists, Turks, and heretics? This, too,

14. The official position of the Roman Catholic Church held that baptism in the name of the triune God was valid. Up to this time, most baptisms were conducted in a church in Latin, the language of worship. However, in emergency circumstances where a priest was not available, it was permissible for a midwife (most likely a woman) to baptize in German. This was understood as a perfectly valid baptism. However, since Luther and his followers regularly baptized people in German, some opponents of the Lutheran movement (without official permission) were apparently denying the validity of these baptisms. Luther is pointing out the inconsistency.

15. A reference to Hieronymous Dungersheim (1465–1540), who was a professor of theology at the University of Leipzig.

16. A translation of the German word *Schwärmer*, which literally means "to swarm," as in the buzzing of bees. This became a way for Luther to describe some of his opponents that he believed were relying on their own subjective ideas rather than the authority of the Bible. See also *That These Words*, n. 17, p. 174.

17. Luther believed he was living in the last days, that is, he had an apocalyptic view of his own age. By the time he was excommunicated in 1521, he saw the pope as the "Antichrist" or the one foretold by Scripture to be coming at the end of time and setting up a false kingdom within the church. See Scott Hendrix, *Luther and the Papacy: Stages in a Reformation Conflict* (Philadelphia: Fortress Press, 1981), 97–120.

should be surrendered, if they are not to have anything good from evil persons.

The whole thing is nonsense. Christ himself came upon the errors of scribes and Pharisees among the Jewish people, but he did not on that account reject everything they had and thought, Matt. 23[:3]. We on our part confess that there is much that is Christian and good under the papacy; indeed everything that is Christian and good is to be found there and has come to us from this source.[18] For instance, we confess that in the papal church there are the true Holy Scriptures, true baptism, the true sacrament of the altar, the true keys to the forgiveness of sins, the true office of the ministry, the true catechism in the form of the Lord's Prayer, the Ten Commandments, and the articles of the Creed. Similarly, the pope admits that we too, though condemned by him as heretics, and likewise all heretics, have the Holy Scriptures, baptism, the keys, the catechism, etc. You think I am a hypocrite? You think, "O how you flatter the pope here!" How do I flatter him? I speak of what the pope and we have in common. He on his part acts in the same way toward heretics and us and plainly admits what he and we have in common. I will continue to be a so-called flatterer, though it does me no good. I contend that in the papacy there is true Christianity, even the right kind of Christianity and many great and devoted saints. Shall I cease to flatter in this way?

Listen to what St. Paul says to the Thessalonians [2 Thess. 2:4]: "The Antichrist takes his seat in the temple of God."[e] If now the pope is (and I cannot believe otherwise) the veritable Antichrist, he will not sit or reign in the devil's stall, but in the temple of God. No, he will not sit where there are only devils and unbelievers, or where no Christ or Christendom exist. For he is an Antichrist and must thus be among Christians. And since he is to sit and reign there it is necessary that there be Christians under him. God's temple is not the description for a pile of stones, but for the holy Christendom, 1 Cor. 3[:17], in which he is to reign. The Christendom that now is under the papacy is truly the body of Christ and a member of it. If it is his body, then it has

18. Some radical movements in the Reformation wanted to do more than reform the church. They advocated a "restoration" of New Testament Christianity according to the model in the book of Acts. They believed that everything added after the biblical period was a perversion of the true faith. Luther will argue that true Christianity remained even in the midst of the papacy and that the church needed to be *reformed* (cleansed of the false emphasis on works as a way to please God) rather than *restored*.

e The actual passage in the NRSV says: "He [the lawless one] opposes and exalts himself above every so-called god or object of worship, so that he takes his seat in the temple of God, declaring himself to be God." Luther assumes the reference is to the antichrist.

An arch-heretic stands in the center of this image, trampling a cross. A demon descends, almost whispering in his ear as he preaches. The Holy Spirit, in the form of a dove, ascends, fleeing the scene. This image appears in a 1603 publication by priest Jan David.

the true spirit, gospel, faith, baptism, sacrament, keys, the office of the ministry, prayer, Holy Scripture, and everything that pertains to Christendom. So we are all still under the papacy and from it we have received our Christian treasures.

As a veritable Antichrist must conduct himself against Christendom, so the pope acts toward us: he persecutes us, curses us, bans us, pursues us, burns us, puts us to death.[19] Christians need indeed to be truly baptized and right members of Christ if they are to win the victory in death over against the Antichrist. We do not rave as do the sectarian spirits,[f] so as to reject everything that is found in the papal church. For then we would cast out even Christendom from the temple of God, and all that it contained of Christ. But when we oppose and reject the pope it is because he does not keep to these treasures of Christendom which he has inherited from the apostles. Instead he makes additions from the devil and does not use these treasures for the improvement of the temple. Rather he works toward its destruction, by setting his commandments and ordinances above the ordinance of Christ. But Christ preserves his Christendom even in the midst of such destruction, just as he rescued Lot at Sodom, as St. Peter recounts, 1 Pet. 2 [2 Pet. 2:6].[g] In fact both remain, the Antichrist sits in the temple of God through the action of the devil, while the temple still is and remains the temple of God through Christ's preservation. If the pope will suffer and accept this "flattery" of mine, then I am and will be an obedient son and devoted papist, with a truly joyful heart, and take back everything that I have done to harm him.

So it is of no consequence when these Anabaptists and enthusiasts say, "Whatever is of the pope is wrong," or, "Whatever is in

f *Rotten geister.* A dismissive term Luther uses for the Anabaptists that might also be understood as "gangs of spirits."

g 2 Pet. 2:6-7.

the papacy we must have and do differently," thinking thereby to prove themselves the foremost enemy of the Antichrist. They do not see that in this way they greatly strengthen him, greatly weaken Christendom, and deceive themselves. For they should help us to reject abuse and false additions, but they would not get much credit for this because they realize they were not first to do this. So they attack what no one yet has attacked in the hope that here they might have the honor of being first. But the honor turns to disgrace, for they attack the temple of God and miss the Antichrist who sits within, just as the blind, who grope after water, take hold of fire.

In fact they remind us of what one brother in the forest of Thuringia did to the other. They were going through the woods with each other when they were set upon by a bear who threw one of them beneath him. The other brother sought to help and struck at the bear, but missed him and grievously wounded the brother under the bear.[20] So these enthusiasts. They ought to come to the aid of Christendom that the Antichrist has in his grip and tortures. They take a severe stand against the pope, but they miss their mark and murder the more terribly the Christendom under the pope. For if they would permit baptism and the sacrament of the altar to stand as they are, Christians under the pope might yet escape with their souls and be saved, as has been the case up to now.[21] But now when the sacraments are taken from them, they will most likely be lost, since even Christ himself is thereby taken away. Dear friend, this is not the way to blast the papacy while Christian saints are in his keeping. One needs a more cautious, discreet spirit, which attacks the addition that threatens the temple without destroying the temple of God itself.

[How Do I Know if I Have Been Baptized?]

Again, those who depend on such arguments say that they know nothing of their baptism, and exclaim, "How do you know you have been baptized? You believe people who say you have been baptized. But you should believe God and not people, and you must be sure of your baptism," and the like. This seems to me to be pretty a shaky argument. If I were to reject everything that I have not seen or heard, I would indeed not have much left, either

19. The Roman Catholic Church regarded false teachers as "heretics." They viewed the church as the body of Christ and false teaching could be seen as an infection that needed to be eliminated if the whole church was to avoid the disease. Early followers of Luther were burned at the stake in Holland in 1523. (See Martin Luther, *The Burning of Brother Henry*, in LW 32:265–86.) Luther himself was under the "ban," which meant he was denied protection of the law and forbidden to publish. He survived in part because the princes of Electoral Saxony protected him.

20. Thuringia is a region in Germany not far from Wittenberg. The source of the example is not clear.

21. At the Council of Florence in 1439, the Roman church affirmed the list of seven sacraments as it had been taught since about the twelfth century. Luther reduced the list of sacraments to baptism and the Lord's Supper. He held that in order for something to be a sacrament it must meet the following criteria: (1) it must be commanded by Christ in the Bible; (2) it must have some sort of material sign like bread, wine, or water; and (3) it must contain the promise of forgiveness. See his treatise *The Babylonian Captivity of the Church* in this volume, pp. 9–129.

of faith or of love, either of spiritual or of temporal things. I might reply, "My friend, how do you know that this man is your father, this woman is your mother? You cannot trust people, you must be sure of your own birth." In this manner all children would be free from obedience to the commandment of God, "Thou shalt honor thy father and thy mother." For I could respond, "How do I know who is my father and mother? I can't believe people. So I will have to be born again by them in order to see for myself, else I will not obey them." By acting in this way God's command would indeed be made altogether null and void.

Likewise I might refuse to recognize anyone as brother, sister, cousin, or relative, constantly repeating, "I did not know we were related, because I am uncertain who my parents were," etc. But (if I were ruler of the land) I would repay such spirits by forbidding them to retain, expect, or receive any inheritance, either house, land, or a single penny from their parents, and so play with them at their own game until their spirit takes on flesh again. For since they neither recognize nor trust their parents, they cannot know or hope for their possessions.[h] O, how well society would be ordered when no one would want to be related to another as child, brother, sister, cousin, relative, heir, or neighbor! To be among such Christians would be no better than being among wild wolves.

Then too I might refuse to be subject to any prince or lord, explaining that I am not sure he was born a prince, because I did not see it, but had to accept popular opinion. So I will be a free person, pay no attention to the command of God, have no authority above me, but run away from people to wolves, among whom there is no such commandment of God to honor parents and government. That the devil really desires this in these baptizers is apparent from the fact that these disciples of his are prepared (as it is said) to forsake wife and children, house and land, and go to heaven altogether alone.[22] More of this later.

Indeed I might then claim that Holy Scripture meant nothing, Christ meant nothing. The apostles, too, never preached. For I have not seen nor felt these things. I've only heard them from people. So I won't believe them unless they are reenacted anew and happen and are done again before my eyes. So I am above all a wholly free person, free also from the commands of

h The original text is singular here.

22. The Anabaptists were a complex movement and were certainly not unified in all their beliefs. Luther's first exposure to them occurred through the so-called Zwickau prophets, named for a city near Wittenberg. Some of the leaders of Zwickau began to teach that even marital vows were not permanent. See John Oyer, *Lutheran Reformers Against the Anabaptists* (The Hague: Martinus Nijhoff, 1964), 6–40.

God. That's the way I would have it, if I could, the devil declares. That would be a foundation for the Anabaptists on which nothing in heaven and earth could stand.

You reply: Have you not yourself taught that we should obey God and not human authority?[i] You think to slay me with my own sword, don't you? But since you are in such a fighting mood, I would ask you if we are to obey God when God commands us to honor parents and superiors? If you say, "Yes," I would ask, how then do you know who they are, since you don't want to believe any human authority? Where are you then? I see full well that your mistake is in not knowing what it means to believe other people, and so stumble into error as hopelessly as the Anabaptists do. Therefore listen to me.

When we teach that we are not to obey human authority, we mean of course that they are speaking entirely for themselves and God is not in their minds. In other words, they are using only human reasoning and are without reference to the word and work of God and cannot therefore prove anything either by the words or works of God. Why would you refer to something as a "human teaching" when it actually comes from God through humans? And who would say that faith in such teaching meant faith in humans and not in God? In Col. 2[:23], Paul chides the human teaching which has never proven what it proclaims. Put differently, it is imagined only and cannot be proved by a single word or work of God. So when you hear that human authority is not to be believed you are to understand that this applies only to what is purely human speculation and not to statements where a word or work of God is declared or affirmed. You are to distinguish simply (as the words indicate) between faith in God and faith in what is only of human origin.

When you were born, for example, it was no secret event, nor was it a human invention. Your birth was a work of God that became publicly known and could not be denied. And if anyone wants to contradict it as the Jews presumed to contradict the miracles and signs of Christ, it is of no importance. For those who see and witness to the divine public deed will nonetheless prevail and stop the mouths of the others in deed and truth. For the law of God holds here rigorously, that by the mouths of two

i Acts 5:29. See also Luther's treatise *On Secular Authority* ("Temporal Authority," in LW 45:51–74; TAL 5, forthcoming).

or three witnesses all things are to be confirmed.[j] You must truly believe people like that. For they bear witness to the work of God, namely, your birth. They prove that these were your parents. Besides, no one but they took care of you, and no one but they alone strove and labored for you. God's work progresses in public so that neither the devil nor human authority can invalidate it. But all people can know it and declare it, just as they declare that you are living.

When anyone bears witness to the work of God it does not mean believing human authority but in God. In sum, when anyone declares and bears witness to the work of God and which is not the figment of human imagination, and this can be denied neither by the devil nor any person, then you believe God and not human authority, for it is the work of God which is so publicly disclosed that even the devil cannot deny it.

This truth is in no way affected by the occasions when children are put or sent away and never know their true parents throughout their lifetime, for we are speaking here of ordinary divine public order.[23] Such children are dishonestly and secretly dealt with, against the will of God, so it is not surprising that theirs is a different lot. They are reared in secret, so that who their parents are remains a secret to them. Whatever the devil does is darkness: let it remain in darkness. But God's order functions in the light.

If now you ask why I believe this man and this woman to be my parents I reply: First, I am sure that I am a work of God and am a human being. Therefore I have to have a mother and father and am not sprung from a rock. God says in Gen. 1[:28] to the man and woman, "Be fruitful and multiply," from which it is clear that all people are born of man and woman, and have a father and mother. This is confirmed by the commandment to all, "Thou shalt honor father and mother."[k] (In both instances Christ as the Son of God is of course an exception.[24]) Since I am sure that I came from parents and am not grown on a tree, I am compelled, secondly, to believe, that it is from this man and this woman, who are represented to me by other people as being my parents, according to the word, "On the evidence of two or three

23. Luther might be making a reference here to the practice of parents committing their young children to monasteries and nunneries as a way of earning God's favor. See a similar comment in Philip Melanchthon's *Apology of the Augsburg Confession*, BC, 287:9.

24. Luther is speaking of the Christian belief in the virgin birth of Jesus.

j Deut. 19:15.

k Exod. 20:12.

witnesses all things shall be established."[l] So I am compelled by God to rely on such people. Thirdly, it is a work of God that no one other than these two in the entire world in their own name has taken me as a natural child, or in case of their death, those relatives or pious people who took me in their name. Such an indisputable fact is like any other of God's evident works before the devil and humanity. For neither the world nor the devil can doubt the evident works of God. They may try, but it will be to no avail. But the word of God—as long as the work is still hidden—*that* the devil can skillfully attack.

The reason that God speaks in Rom. 13[:1], "Let every person be subject to the governing authorities," is that I might believe the person who is my prince or lord. I conclude from this word that I must have a superior and I must be a subject. Secondly, since the entire world testifies and says this is my ruler and everyone recognizes him as such and no one denies that this is an evident work of God, I must believe such testimony. If anyone contradicts, this person does so in vain, for finally everyone admits that this person lies. Thirdly, it is an evident work of God, that no one else considers me as a subject. I live under this ruler's protection, law, and peace, as I should under government, and all other authorities leave me alone. They do not call my status into question or oppose it, provided I keep my place in the light of law and God's order. Robbers and murderers may well find their place under foreign rulers in secrecy and darkness, but these are rightly judged as not being their subjects.

Wait, you say, I will test you. Why do you no longer believe in the pope as your lord? Instead, you make him the Antichrist, though the entire world testifies that he is the head of Christendom, and they will prove easily that he has the rule. I answer, there you almost caught me! But let me tell you, that if you can convince me that the papacy meets the three requirements I have shown to hold in regard to parents and government, then I will consider the papacy as a work of God and happily be obedient and believe the work of God. But, dear friend, if you cannot do this, allow me to judge it as a human invention, without the word and work of God, and therefore in no circumstances is to be believed. I can forcefully prove that the papacy is a human invention.

l Deut. 19:15.

In the first place, the word of God clearly tells me that parents and government exist, and that I should and must have parents and government as I have said. But there is no word of God that says there is a pope, and that I must have a pope and be subject to him.[25] Since the Scriptures command nothing concerning the pope and his rule, there is no papacy that can be considered the work of God. For the Scriptures give testimony concerning what are the works of God. Therefore I said above, that we should believe in human witnesses, not when they invent things, but when they show and prove what they say by the word and work of God. For, before considering the question as to what a thing is, make sure that it exists.[26] Before you tell me what the pope is, you must convince me that there is a divinely appointed pope. If he cannot exist one does not ask who he is.

Secondly, though many bear witness to him, their testimony is not only in vain, since it cannot make a work of God out of the papacy, or prove it to be such, but is not unanimous and complete. For not only has the Eastern church borne testimony against the papacy and opposed it,[27] but also many subjects of the pope himself, who have been burned at the stake for their opposition and still are strangled daily. His rule thus has never been accepted, it has never been unopposed, nor has it been peacefully established as has the rule of parents or government, as we have related already.

Thirdly, it is not a work of God. The pope exercises no office for the welfare of his subjects. Indeed, he persecutes the gospel and Christians instead of being a teacher and guardian. He only teaches his filth and poison as human notions, leaves the gospel to lie under the bench, and even persecutes it, though it does not help him. He makes a sacrifice out of the sacrament, faith out of works, work out of faith.[28] He forbids marriage, [and issues prohibitions concerning] food, seasons, clothes, and places.[29] Furthermore, he corrupts and abuses Christian treasures so that souls are harmed, as we have sufficiently proved elsewhere.[30] Since on all three counts the papacy is deficient, we must judge it as a pure human invention, which is not worthy of belief and is in no way comparable to the institutions of parenthood and government.

Baptism, too, is a work of God, not invented by humans but commanded by God and witnessed to by the gospel. Secondly, there are people who can witness to the fact that you have been

25. The passage in dispute is Matt. 16:13-20. In this section Peter confesses that Jesus is the Messiah and in response Jesus says that Peter is a "rock" and that on this rock the church will be built. Roman Catholics believe this means that Peter functions as the first "pope" or leader of the church. Luther and his followers held that Jesus' designation of Peter as a rock was a reference to his confession of Christ as the Messiah and not the establishment of a church structure with Peter at its head.

26. Here Luther quotes a rule in medieval logic.

27. The Eastern Orthodox Church recognizes the importance of Peter's leadership in the early church but does not grant him a position of authority over all the churches.

28. This is a reference to Luther's earlier criticism of understanding the Mass as a sacrifice, that is, an offering made to God, rather than as a gift of God to those who receive it. See *The Babylonian Captivity of the Church*, p. 53 above.

29. Luther believed that clerical celibacy, as well as many other laws and rules issued by the church, was used to gain favor with God.

30. For Luther, the treasure of the church was not the supply of good works accumulated by Christ and the saints that could then be used to sell indulgences for the forgiveness of sin. The real treasure of the church is the preaching of the gospel so that people are freed from the power of sin and death. See theses 56–66 in *The Ninety-Five Theses*, LW 31:30–31; TAL 1:41–42.

baptized, and no one can contradict or prove the opposite. In the third place, there is the work, i.e., you are reckoned among Christians, admitted to the sacrament, and to the use of all Christian privileges. This would not be the case if you had not been baptized and all were not sure of it. So all of this is clear proof of your baptism. For all the world knows and sees that everyone is baptized as a child. Whoever refuses to believe this refuses to believe God, since God says, two witnesses are to be believed [Deut. 19:15; Matt. 18:16]. Such witnesses God does not punish, though God never leaves false witness unpunished or pure.

With this I have sufficiently proved that no persons ought to have doubts as to their baptism, as if they did not know that they are baptized. They sin against God who will not believe it. For they are much more certain of their baptism through the witness of Christians, than if they themselves had witnessed it. For the devil could easily have made them uncertain so that they imagined they had been dreaming or had a hallucination instead of being properly baptized. So they would have to fall back finally on the testimony of Christians to be at peace. This kind of testimony the devil cannot confuse or make dubious.[m]

In a woodcut from a 1543 publication, John baptizes Jesus in the Jordan River.

[Does Baptism Depend on Belief?]

In the third place, it is said, as I also have read, that they base their faith on this verse, "The one who believes and is baptized will be saved" [Mark 16:16]. This they interpret to mean that no persons should be baptized before they believe. I must say that they are guilty of a great presumption. For if they follow this principle, they cannot baptize before they are certain that the one to be baptized believes. How and when can they ever know that for certain? Have they now become gods so that they can discern people's hearts and know whether or not they believe? If they are not certain if they believe, why then do they baptize, since they contend so strenuously that faith must precede baptism? Are they not contradicting themselves when they baptize without being certain if faith is there or not? For whoever bases baptism on faith and baptizes on chance and not on the certainty that faith is present does nothing better than the one who

m The original uses the singular rather than the plural in this paragraph.

baptizes the person who has no faith. For unbelief and uncertain belief are one and the same thing, and both are contrary to the verse, "Whoever believes," which speaks of a sure faith which they who are to be baptized should have.

You say, I know, that they confess that they believe, etc.[n] But confession is neither here nor there. The text does not say, "The one who confesses," but "The one who believes." To have a person's confession is not to know his or her faith. With all your reasoning you cannot do justice to this verse unless you also know that a person has faith, since all people are liars and God alone knows the heart.[o] So whoever bases baptism on the faith of the one to be baptized can never baptize anyone. Even if you baptized a person a hundred times a day not once would you know whether that person believes. Why then do you carry on with your rebaptizing, since you contradict yourself and baptize when you are not sure that faith is present, and yet you teach that faith must most certainly be present. This verse, "Whoever believes," altogether opposes their rebaptizing, since the verse speaks of a certain faith. They base their rebaptizing on an uncertain faith, and in not a single letter do they follow the meaning of the verse.

I say the same thing about the baptized who receive or ground baptism on their faith. For none can be sure of their own faith. I would compare persons who let themselves be rebaptized with those who brood and have scruples because perhaps they did not believe as a child. So when next day the devil comes, the hearts of such persons are filled with scruples and they say, Ah, now for the first time I feel I have the right faith; yesterday I don't think I truly believed. So I need to be baptized a third time, the second baptism not being of any use. You think the devil can't do such things?[p] You had better get to know him better. He can do worse than that, dear friend. He can go on and cast doubt on the third, and the fourth, and so on incessantly (as he indeed has in mind to do), just as he has done with me and many others in the matter of confession. We never seemed able to confess sufficiently certain sins, and incessantly and restlessly sought one absolution after the other, one father confessor after the other.[31] Just because we sought to rely on our confession, as those to be bap-

31. Luther speaks here of his experiences as a young man in the monastery. He was taught that a confession must be complete. In other words, all known sins must be revealed and one remained accountable for any sins not confessed. This terrified him. Luther had a scrupulous conscience and he often felt unworthy before God, which led to his believing that perhaps God was not merciful or good. And those thoughts were blasphemous—the worst sin of all! As he says in his own words: "Though I lived as a monk without reproach, I felt that I was a sinner before God with an extremely disturbed conscience. I could not believe that God was pleased with my satisfaction. I did not love, yes, I hated the righteous God who punishes sinners, and secretly, if not blasphemously, certainly murmuring greatly, I was angry with God." See his *Preface to the Latin Works*, LW 34:336–38; TAL 4:489–503.

n The original here is singular.

o See Rom. 3:9-18 and Jer. 17:9-10.

p The original text of this section is singular.

tized now want to rely on their faith. What is the end result? Baptizing without end would result. All this is nonsense. Neither the baptizer nor the baptized can base baptism on a certain faith. This verse of Scripture is far more a judgment on them than on us. And these are the people who don't want to trust those who are witnesses of their baptism, but now are ready to trust themselves that they are baptized as if they were not human, or as if they were more certain of their faith than the witness of Christendom allows.

So I contend that if they want to do justice to this passage, "Whoever believes," according to their understanding, they must condemn rebaptism much more earnestly than the first baptism. Neither the baptizer nor the baptized can maintain this position, for both are uncertain of their faith, or at least are in constant peril and anxiety. For it happens, indeed it is so in this matter of faith, that often persons who claim to believe do not at all believe; and on the other hand, persons who do not think they believe, but are in despair, have the greatest faith.[q] So this verse, "Whoever believes," does not compel us to determine who has faith or not. Rather, it makes it a matter of every person's conscience to realize that if they are to be saved they must believe and not pretend that it is sufficient for a Christian to be baptized.[32] For the verse does not say, "Whoever knows that he believes, or, if you know that anyone believes," but it says, "Whoever believes." Who has it, has it. One must believe, but we neither should nor can know it for certain.[33]

[What about Children?]

Since our baptizing has been thus from the beginning of Christianity and the custom has been to baptize children, and since no one can prove with good reasons that they do not have faith, we should not make changes and build on such weak arguments. For if we are going to change or do away with something that has been done from ancient times until now, it is necessary to prove convincingly that these are contrary to the word of God. Otherwise (as Christ says), "For he that is not against us is for

q The original text here is singular.

32. Here Luther is not calling into question the certainty of God's action in baptism but rather condemning the understanding common in his day that relied on the sacrament of baptism apart from the faith it created.

33. Luther holds that a faith without doubt, struggle, and times of uncertainty would not be genuine. See Oswald Bayer, *Martin Luther's Theology: A Contemporary Interpretation*, trans. Thomas H. Trapp (Grand Rapids: Eerdmans, 2008), 35–37.

us" [Mark 9:40]. We have indeed overthrown monasteries, Mass-priests, and clerical celibacy, but only by showing the clear and certain scriptural arguments against them. Had we not done this, we should have let them stand as they previously existed.

When they say, "Children cannot believe," how can they be sure of that? Where in Scripture can they prove this and make an argument for their position? They imagine this, I suppose, because children do not speak or have understanding. But this position is deceiving and is false in every way. We cannot build [arguments] on what we imagine.

There are Scripture passages that tell us that children may and can believe, though they do not speak or understand. Psalm 72 [106:37-38] describes how the Jews offered their sons and daughters to idols, shedding innocent blood.[34] If, as the text says, it was innocent blood, then the children have to be considered pure and holy—this they could not be without spirit and faith. Likewise the innocent children whom Herod had murdered were not over two years of age.[35] Admittedly they could not speak or understand. Yet they were holy and blessed. Christ himself says in Matt. 18 [19:14], "For it is as such as these [children] that the kingdom of heaven belongs." And St. John was a child in his mother's womb but, as I believe, could have faith.[36]

Yes, you say, but John was an exception. This is not proof that all baptized children have faith. I answer, wait a minute! I am not yet at the point of proving that children believe. I am giving proof that your foundation for rebaptism is uncertain and false inasmuch as you cannot prove that there may not be faith in children. Because John had faith, though he could not speak or understand, your argument fails, that children are not able to believe. To hold that a child believes, as the example of St. John shows, is not contrary to Scripture. If it is not contrary to the Scripture to hold that children believe, but rather in accord with Scripture, then your argument, that children cannot believe, must be unscriptural. That is my first point.

Who has made you so sure that baptized children do not believe, given the evidence I have provided which suggests they can believe? But if you are not sure, why then are you so bold as to discard the first baptism, since you do not and cannot know that it is meaningless? What if all children in baptism not only were able to believe but believed as well as John in his mother's womb? We can hardly deny that the same Christ is present at

34. This psalm describes a dark period in Israel's history (the time of the judges) when they forgot God and adopted the religion and practices of the surrounding culture.

35. Matt. 22:16. This passage refers to Herod's murder of all children in and around Bethlehem that were two years old and younger. Though this verse does not describe them as innocent, the episode has long been known as the murder of the "holy innocents."

36. Luke 1:41 says, "When Elizabeth heard Mary's greeting, the child leaped in her womb." Luther infers from this that Elizabeth's child (John the Baptist) was able to have faith.

baptism and in baptism, in fact is himself the baptizer, who in those days came in his mother's womb to John. In baptism he can speak as well through the mouth of the priest, as when he spoke through his mother. Since then he is present, speaks, and baptizes, why should not his word and baptism call forth spirit and faith in the child as then it produced faith in John? He is the same one who speaks and acts then and now. Even before, he said through Isa. [55:11], "It [my word] shall not return to me empty."[37] Now it is up to you to bring forth a single Scripture verse that proves that children cannot believe in baptism. I have cited these many verses showing that they can believe, and that it is reasonable to hold that they do believe. I grant that we do not understand how they do believe, or how faith is created. But that is not the point here.

Furthermore, he commands us to bring the children to him. In Matt. 19[:14] he embraces them, kisses them, and says that theirs is the kingdom of heaven. The enthusiasts like to deny this by saying that Christ is not speaking of children, but of the humble. But this is false, for the text clearly says that they brought to him children, not the humble. And Christ does not say to let the humble come to him, but the children, and reprimanded the disciples, not because they kept the humble, but the children away. He neither embraced nor blessed the humble but the children, when he said, ". . . to such as these the kingdom of heaven belongs." So also Matt. 18[:10], "Their angels continually see the face of my Father in heaven," is to be understood as referring to such children, for he teaches us that we should also be like these children. If these children were not holy, then he would indeed have given us a bad example with which to compare ourselves. He would not have said, you must be like children, but rather, you must be otherwise than children. In sum, the swarming spirits[r] cannot make the humble out of the children in this text except by their own darkness, for the word stands too powerfully and clearly before our eyes.

Some want to take the force out of this text by saying that the Jewish children were circumcised. Therefore they were holy and could be brought to Christ, whereas our children are heathen, etc. I answer: But suppose there were also girls among these children who were brought to Jesus, and who were not circumcised?

r Der schwarm geist. Another way of referring to the enthusiasts.

37. Luther believed strongly in the power of God's word. He often used the example of creation, where God spoke and the entire world came into existence. Put differently, God's word is "performative." That means it actually does what it says. See Robert Kolb and Charles A. Arand, *The Genius of Luther's Theology* (Grand Rapids: Baker Academic, 2008), 131–59.

Jesus teaches his disciples about greatness through the example of children. From 1547 printing of *Hausspostil D. Martin Luther.*

For surely all kinds of children were among those brought to him, and since it does not expressly say that they were boys only we cannot exclude girls, but must let it mean children of both sexes.[38] They are not brought to him because of their circumcision, but that they might be blessed, coming to Christ out of the Old into the New Testament, according to his word, "Let the little children come to me and do not stop them; for it is to such as these that the kingdom of heaven belongs" [Matt. 19:14]. He says that those who come to him are of the kingdom of God. By their coming and being brought to Christ they are so holy that he embraces, blesses, and gives them the kingdom. So I let them swarm where they will.[s] But I maintain as I have written in the postil that the most certain form of baptism is child baptism.[39] For an adult might deceive and come to Christ as a Judas and be baptized. But a child cannot deceive. A child comes to Christ in baptism, as John came to him, and as the children were brought to him, that his word and work might be effective in them, move them, and make them holy, because his word and work cannot be without fruit. Yet it has this effect alone in the child. Were it to fail here it would fail everywhere and be in vain, which is impossible.

It cannot be denied that Psalm 77 [106:37] speaks of girls and uncircumcised when it says that they were offered to the idols of Canaan. Yet they were described as innocent blood. And surely Moses in Lev. 12[:5-6] included girls in the regulation of offerings for purification and atonement. Everybody knows that boys alone were subjected to circumcision, but that girls participated in its benefits as indicated in the saying spoken by God to Abraham, Gen. 17[:7]: "I will be the God of your descendants, and circumcision will be a covenant between me and you and your descendants. I will establish my covenant between me and you, and your offspring after you." Surely girls are the descendants of Abraham, and through this promise God is indeed their God, though they are not circumcised as are the boys.

If they now believe that through the covenant of circumcision God accepts both boys and girls and is their God, why should God not also accept our children through the covenant of bap-

38. The Jewish rite of circumcision, which engrafted the recipient into the people of Israel, was for males only.

39. Luther included a defense of infant baptism in a sermon he preached in 1525 on Matt. 8:1-13. See LW 76:257–66; also n. 7, p. 279.

s Another play on words related to the terms Luther uses to describe his opponents.

tism? God has in fact promised us that he wants to be the God not only of the Jews but also of the Gentiles, Rom. 3[:29], and especially of the Christians and those who believe. If the circumcision of boys benefits both boys and girls, so that they become the people of God because of the faith of Abraham from whom they are descended, how much more does baptism help each one to become a member of the people of God because of the merit of Christ—to whom the child is brought and by whom the child is blessed? Let everyone know the foundation of the Anabaptists is uncertain and they build on it absolutely impiously.

But, you say, he has not commanded the baptism of children; there is no reference to it in the writings or epistles of the apostles. I answer, neither has he commanded the baptism of adults, neither men nor women nor anybody in particular, so we had better not baptize anybody! But he has commanded us to baptize all Gentiles, none excluded, when he said in the last chapter of Matthew, "Go and baptize all heathen in my name," etc.[40] Now children constitute a great part of the heathen. We read in Acts and the epistles of St. Paul how whole households were baptized, and children are surely a good part of the household.[41] So it seems that just as Christ commanded us to teach and baptize all heathen, without exception, so the apostles did, and baptized all who were in the household. Had they not overlooked that the sectarian spirits[t] would seek to differentiate between young and old, they would have considered this more expressly, since otherwise in all the epistles they write so much about there being no respect or difference of persons among Christians. For St. John in 1 John 2[:14] writes to the little children, that they know the Father. And, as St. Augustine writes, child baptism has come from the apostles.[42] So the Anabaptists proceed dangerously in everything. Not only are they not sure of themselves but they also act contrary to the passages they cite and out of their own imaginings create differences between persons which God has not made. Even if they contended that their arguments had not been sufficiently refuted, they ought, however quarrelsome they are, to be concerned and frightened at their wrongdoing in rebaptizing on such uncertain grounds. They are already

t Rotten geister.

40. Matthew 28:19 reads: "Go therefore and make disciples of all nations, baptizing them." Luther used the word "heathen" (*Heiden*) for *nations* in his translation. In English the word has harsh connotations, but Luther simply meant those who had not yet heard of Christ.

41. Acts 10:48; 16:33; and 1 Cor. 1:16 speak of households undergoing baptism.

42. "But the custom of our mother the Church in the matter of infant baptism is by no means to be scorned, nor to be considered at all superfluous, nor to be believed except on the ground that it is the tradition of the apostles." Augustine, *The Literal Meaning of Genesis*, trans. J. H. Taylor, 2 vols. (New York: Paulist, 1982), 2:127. Luther most likely had access to this work through the 1506 printed edition of the complete works of Augustine by Bonifacius

convicted of doing wrong in being so uncertain. For in divine matters one should act on certain, not on dubious, grounds.[43]

Now let us say some Anabaptists hear (that is, if they do not want to be obstinate but teachable) that John believed and was made holy when Christ came and spoke through the mouth of his mother. Furthermore, in the same way a child becomes a believer if Christ in baptism speaks to him through the mouth of the one

AVRELII AVGVSTINI HIPONENSIS EPI LIBROR DECIVITATE DEI RETRACTATIO INCIPIT:
NTEREA CVM ROMA GOTHORV

A page from a 1470 printing of Augustine's *City of God (De Civitate Dei)*.

Amerbach (1495–1562). Another edition, this time by Erasmus (1466–1536), appeared in 1528, the same year that Luther published this treatise. St. Augustine (354–430) was a highly influential teacher in the early church. He was born in northern Africa and was converted to Christianity in 386. He was well known as a preacher and teacher. After a period in Milan and Rome he was called back to Africa to be a bishop in Hippo (present Algeria). His defense of infant baptism is rooted in his belief that original sin taints all of humanity, including babies. Therefore, infant baptism is necessary for their salvation. See the article on Augustine's views of baptism by William Harmless in Allan D. Fitzgerald, ed., *Augustine Through the Ages: An Encyclopedia* (Grand Rapids: Eerdmans, 1999), 89.

43. Luther's point here is that the Anabaptists are attempting to overthrow a teaching of the church that has stood for over a thousand years. If they are to be successful, then they must have arguments from the Bible that are absolutely clear and beyond dispute. He believes he has shown this is not the case.

who baptizes. For it is Christ's word and his commandment, and his word cannot be without fruit. Must not these same Anabaptists also admit that it may be so and that they cannot altogether and firmly deny it, nor cite any Scripture to the contrary? But if they cannot clearly and convincingly deny it, then they cannot firmly defend their rebaptisms. For they must first firmly prove that children are without faith when they are baptized, if they are to justify rebaptism. Consequently, I hold that it has been sufficiently proved that their reasoning is uncertain and arrogant throughout.[u]

Yet even if they could establish that children are without faith when they are baptized, it would make no difference to me. I would want to know their reason for rebaptizing when later on faith or the confession of faith is supposed to be present. For it is not enough to claim they were baptized without faith, therefore they should be rebaptized. Some reason is needed. You say it is not proper baptism. What does it matter, if it is still a baptism? It was a correct baptism in itself, regardless of whether it was received rightly. The words were spoken and everything that pertains to baptism was done as fully as when faith is present. If a thing is in itself correct you do not have to repeat it even though it was not correctly received. You correct what was wrong and do not have to do the entire thing over. Abuse does not change the nature of a substance; indeed it proves the substance.[44] There can be no abuse unless the substance exists.

When ten years after baptism faith appears, what then is the need of a second baptism, if baptism was correctly administered in all respects? For now a person believes, as baptism requires. Faith doesn't exist for the sake of baptism, but baptism for the sake of faith. When faith comes, baptism is complete. A second baptism is not necessary.

It is as if a woman married a man reluctantly and completely lacked affection for her husband. She is before God hardly to be considered his true wife. But after two years she gains affection for him. Would then a second engagement be required, a second wedding be celebrated, as if she had not previously been a wife, so that the earlier betrothal and wedding were in vain? Of course you would be considered a fool, if you believed that,

u The original of this paragraph is singular; i.e., Anabaptist rather than Anabaptists.

44. Luther writes this sentence first in Latin: "*Abusus non tollit substantiam, imo confirmat substantiam.*" He then gives a German translation. It is a maxim or saying from the legal world of his day meaning that just because something can be abused does not mean it cannot be used. It is more common in this form: "*Abusus non tollit usum.*"

especially since everything is in order now because she has affection for him and properly keeps to the man she had not properly accepted. So also if some adults falsely allowed themselves to be baptized but after a year came to faith, do you mean that they should be rebaptized? They received the correct baptism incorrectly, I hear you say. Their impropriety makes baptism improper.[v] Should then human error and wickedness be stronger than God's good and invincible order? God made a covenant with the people of Israel on Mt. Sinai.[w] Some did not receive that covenant rightly and in faith. If now these later came to faith, should the covenant be considered invalid, and must God come again to each one on Mt. Sinai in order to renew the covenant?

Likewise God provides for the preaching of the Ten Commandments. But since some people only grasp them with their ears, indeed improperly, [that does not mean] they are not Ten Commandments, are not virtuous, and God ought hence to issue ten new commandments in place of the former. It would be enough that people let themselves be rightly converted and give heed to the original Ten Commandments. It would be a curious situation when the word of God, which abides forever,[x] has to be changed and be renewed as often as people change and want something new. Yet it does remain firm and unique, so that they who do not now cleave to it or have fallen from it, may still have an immovable rock to which to return and to hold. If subjects paid homage to their ruler with the intention of putting him to death, but after three days repented and gave sincere obedience to him, would it be necessary here to set up anew the conditions of homage? Of course not, considering that their homage is sincere which formerly was treacherous.

Were we to follow their reasoning we would have to be baptizing all of the time. For I would take the verse "Whoever believes" with me and whenever I find a Christian who has fallen or is without faith, I would say that this person is without faith, so the baptism is fruitless; this person must be baptized again. If the same one falls a second time, I would again say, see there is no faith, there must be something wrong about the first baptism. This person will have to be baptized a third time, and so on

v The original of these sentences is singular.

w Exodus 19–20 records the giving of the covenant.

x Isa. 40:6-8.

and on. As often as a person falls or there is doubt about faith, I will say, this person doesn't believe and therefore the baptism is defective. In short, one will have to be baptized over again so often that one never again falls or is without faith. It must be this way if justice is to be done to the verse "Whoever believes." Tell me, what Christians will then ever be sufficiently baptized or consider that their baptisms are complete? But baptism can be truly correct and sufficient even if the Christian falls from faith or sins a thousand times a year. It is enough for people to right themselves and become faithful, without having to be rebaptized each time.[y] Then why should not the first baptism be sufficient and proper if a person truly becomes a believing Christian? Since there is no difference in baptism whether lack of faith precedes or follows, baptism doesn't depend on faith. But if faith is lacking, the Anabaptists would have us believe we must alter the nature of baptism to accord with the verse "Whoever believes."

I claim therefore that even if the Anabaptists could prove their thesis that children are without faith (which they cannot do), they would not have proved more than that the correct baptism, instituted by God, has been wrongly and not properly received. But whoever proves only an abuse, only proves that the abuse should be corrected and not that the thing should be changed. For abuse does not alter the nature of a thing.[z] Gold does not become straw because a thief steals and misuses it. Silver doesn't turn into paper if a usurer dishonestly obtains it.[45] Since then the Anabaptists demonstrate only the abuse of baptism, they fly in the face of God, nature, and reason, when they want to alter and make anew baptism itself in treating the abuse. All heretics do the same with regard to the gospel. They perceive it wrongly and so hear it wrongly in connection with an abuse, and then hasten to change and make a new gospel out of it. So no matter which way you look at it the Anabaptists are in error. They blaspheme and dishonor the order of God, calling baptism wrong on account of the wrongs and abuses of humanity, though even their claim of human wrongs and abuses is unconvincing.

There is, however, a devil that promotes confidence in works[46] among them. He feigns faith, but he really has a work in mind.[47]

y The original of these sentences is singular.

z See n. 44, p. 299.

45. A usurer is someone who lends money at extremely high rates of interest.

46. *Werck teuffel.* Literally, a "work-devil."

47. This is an important point for Luther about the nature of faith. Faith, or the ability to trust God, always remained a gift of the Holy Spirit. As he says in *The Small Catechism*, in the explanation to the Third Article of the Apostles' Creed, "I believe that by my own understanding or strength I cannot believe in Jesus Christ my Lord or come to him, but instead the Holy Spirit has called me through the gospel" (BC, 355:6). He felt the Anabaptists, though they supposedly emphasized faith, were really stressing human works because they saw faith as an act of the human will and not a gift of God. For more on Anabaptist beliefs, see James M. Strayer, "Anabaptists," OER 1:31–35.

He uses the name and guise of faith to lead the poor people to rely on a work. In the same way it happened to us under the papacy, when we were driven to the sacrament as a work of obedience. For no one went in order to nourish his faith, but everything was finished and the work accomplished when we had received the sacrament. So here again the Anabaptists are urging the performance of a work, so that when the people are baptized they may have confidence that everything is right and complete. In reality they pay little attention to faith, but only seem to praise it. For, as we have already said, were they to be sure beforehand of faith, they would never again baptize anyone. If they did not rely on works but earnestly sought for faith, they would not dare to rebaptize. The unchanging word of God, once spoken in the first baptism, ever remains standing, so that afterwards they can come to faith in it, if they will, and the water with which they were baptized they can afterwards receive in faith, if they will. Even if they contradict the word a hundred times, it still remains the word spoken in the first baptism. Its power does not derive from the fact that it is repeated many times or is spoken anew, but from the fact that it was commanded once to be spoken.

It is the devil's masterpiece when he can compel the Christian to leave the righteousness of faith for a righteousness of works, as he forced the Galatians and Corinthians to rely on works even though (as St. Paul writes) they were doing well in their faith and running rightly in Christ.[48] Because the devil saw that through the Gospel the Germans properly recognized and rightly believed Christ, and that they were then also righteous before God, he now interferes and tears them away from such righteousness as if it were nothing and leads them into rebaptizing as if into a better righteousness. He causes them to reject their former righteousness as ineffectual and to fall prey to a false righteousness. What shall I say? We Germans are and remain true Galatians.[49] For persons who permit themselves to be rebaptized reject their former faith and righteousness, and are guilty of sin and condemnation. Of all things such behavior is most horrible. As St. Paul says, the Galatians have severed themselves from Christ [Gal. 5:4], even making Christ a servant of sin, when they circumcise themselves.

Satan does these things against us, in order to make our teaching seem contemptible, as if we could not have the right spirit or teaching because we had not been rightly baptized. But

48. A major issue in Paul's letters is whether Christians had to keep the law. Paul argues that Christians are justified before God without works of the law (Gal. 2:21). They are now freed in Christ to serve the neighbor (Gal. 5:13-26).

49. This was Luther's complaint about Andreas Karlstadt. The latter attempted to cleanse the church of all ritual and ceremony. But his insistence on a singular way to conduct worship threatened the church with a new legalism. Luther believed he lacked discernment. See *Against Heavenly Prophets*, LW 40:79–223.

we know the tree by its fruits.[a] For neither among the papists nor among these rebellious spirits do we find people who can handle and interpret Scripture as skillfully as do those on our side by the grace of God. This is not the least of the Spirit's gifts, 1 Cor. 12[:10]. We see among them the natural fruit of the devil, namely, that some of them on account of rebaptism desert wife and child, house and land, and will recognize no authority and so forth.[b] Yet St. Paul teaches that persons who do not provide for their own have disowned their faith and are worse than unbelievers, 1 Tim. 6 [5:8].[c] And in 1 Cor. 7[:13] he expresses as his desire that a wife who believes should not divorce an unbelieving husband. Nor does Christ want a marriage broken, except where adultery becomes a reason for it. Our spirit allows—indeed commands—that every estate should remain and be held in honor,[50] and that faith should exercise itself peacefully in love so that no uprising or complaint could fairly be charged to our teaching. The papists of course by their lies blame us for all manner of ills, but even their own consciences are here in many instances their own judges.

This refutes too their position that baptism is nothing if the priest or baptizer had not believed. For if even St. Peter baptized someone, nevertheless no one could know whether St. Peter believed or doubted at that time. For indeed people cannot see their own hearts.[d] In brief, such arguments once led the Donatists[51] to separate themselves and to rebaptize, when they saw how unholy some were who preached and baptized. They began to base baptism on the holiness of humanity, though Christ had based it on his word and commandment. That is also the attempt of our enthusiasts, the foes of the sacrament.[e] They maintain, of course, that the truth and Scripture compel them, but they lie nevertheless. They are offended (as they sometimes experience) that any rogue may bring Christ into the bread of the sacrament, as if the entire world were sure that they themselves have faith and are completely holy. They act as though they were not great rogues in the eyes of God, just as much as they who

a See Matt. 7:16-20.

b See n. 13, p. 281.

c The original of this sentence is singular.

d See Ps. 19:12.

e See the treatise *That These Words* . . . in this volume, pp. 163-273 above.

50. Luther held that there were three "estates" or realms within the world by which God exercises care for creation: the church, the family, and the state. Christians are called to participate in all three of these areas through loving service to the neighbor. Luther was strongly opposed to any "spirituality" that attempted to flee from the world. This was why he felt monasticism was false for most people. And he believed that some Anabaptists also have a false understanding of what it means to be a Christian. See Bayer, *Martin Luther's Theology*, 120–53.

51. The Donatists were a movement in the fourth and fifth centuries that sought a "pure" church, untainted by collaboration with those Christians who, among other things, had compromised their faith and handed over the Scriptures in times of persecution by the Roman Empire. The Donatists claimed that sacraments distributed by "traitor" priests were not valid. In other words, the worth or value of the sacrament was dependent on the character of the person who distributed them. Augustine, who held that Christ is the real power who acts through ministers to distribute the sacraments, opposed them. See Eugene TeSelle, "Donatism," in Daniel Patte, ed., *The Cambridge Dictionary of Christianity* (Cambridge: Cambridge University Press, 2010), 333.

sharply condemn wickedness and call others rascals, forgetting the beam in their own eye.[f]

We recall that St. John was not averse to hearing the word of God from Caiaphas and pays attention to his prophecy [John 11:49f.]. Moses and the people of Israel received the prophecy of the godless Balaam as a word from God [Num. 24:17]. So also St. Paul recognized the heathen poets Aratus and Epimenides and honored their saying (as a word of God).[52] And Christ bids us hear the godless Pharisees in the seat of Moses, though they are godless teachers.[g] We should stop being so sensitive about these matters! Let God judge their evil lives. We can still listen to their godly words. If they are evil, it is to their own harm. If they teach correctly, we can be correctly instructed. Consider the pious Magi in Matt. 2[:4ff.]. They heard the word of God from the book of Micah through the mouth of Herod, the cruel king, who in turn had heard it from the godless high priests and scribes. Still on that word they set out for Bethlehem and found Christ. It was no great hindrance that they heard the word of God only through Herod the murderer of Christ.[53]

Still we must admit that the enthusiasts have the Scriptures and the word of God in other doctrines. Whoever hears it from them and believes will be saved, even though they [the enthusiasts] are unholy heretics and blasphemers of Christ. It is not a small mercy that God gives the word even through evil rogues and the godless. In fact it is in some respects more perilous when God proclaims it through holy than through unholy folk. For the thoughtless are tempted to attach themselves to the holiness of the people rather than to the word of God. Greater honor is then given to the person than to God and the word. This danger does not exist when Judas, Caiaphas, and Herod preach, though no one can make this an excuse for an evil life that God can make some use of it. Now if a godless people can have and teach the word of God correctly, much more can they baptize and give the sacrament properly.[h] For it is a greater thing to teach the word of God than to baptize, as St. Paul boasts in 1 Cor. 1[:17]. As we have said, whoever makes baptism dependent on the faith of the one who baptizes will never receive baptism from anyone. For if

52. In Acts 17, Paul is preaching to the citizens of Athens. In the middle of his speech (v. 28) he quotes two sayings: "For 'In him we live and move and have our being'; as even some of your own poets have said, 'For we too are his offspring.'" The first is a quote attributed to the ancient Greek philosopher Epimenides (c. seventh–sixth centuries BCE), while the second saying comes from *Phaenomena* by the Greek poet Aratus (flourished c. 315–c. 245 BCE). See the note on Acts 17:28 in *The New Oxford Annotated Bible* (NRSV) (New York: Oxford University Press, 1994).

53. Luther means that Herod tried to murder Christ when he slaughtered the baby boys of Bethlehem. See n. 35, p. 294.

f See Matt. 7:3-5.

g See Matt. 23:1-3.

h The original of this sentence is singular.

I ask you if you have been rebaptized, and you say, yes, I again ask, how do you know that you now are rightly baptized? Were you to reply, because the one who baptized me has faith, I would ask, how do you know that? Have you looked into that person's heart? So there you are, like butter in sunshine.[54]

54. That is, in an impossible position.

Our baptism is the strongest and surest of all foundations, affirming that God has made a covenant with all the world to be a God of the heathen in all the world, as the gospel says. Also, that Christ has commanded the gospel to be preached in the entire world, as also the prophets have declared in many ways. As a sign of this covenant he has instituted baptism, commanded and enjoined upon all heathen, as the last chapter of Matt. [28:19] declares: "Go therefore and make disciples of all nations, baptizing them in the name of the Father," etc.[i] In the same manner God had made a covenant with Abraham and his descendants to be their God, and made circumcision a sign of this covenant. Here in baptism stands our sure and firm foundation, namely, that we let ourselves be baptized not because we are certain of our faith but because God wishes it and has commanded it. For even if I were never certain any more of faith, I still am certain of the command of God. For God has commanded baptism and made it known throughout the world. In this I cannot be wrong, for God's command cannot deceive. But of my faith God has never said anything to anyone, nor issued an order or command concerning it.

True, one should add faith to baptism. But we are not to base baptism on faith. There is quite a difference between having faith, on the one hand, and depending on one's faith and making baptism depend on faith, on the other. Those who would allow themselves to be baptized on the strength of their faith are not only uncertain, but also idolators who deny Christ. For they trust in and build on something of their own, namely, on a gift that they have from God, and not on God's word alone. So others may build on and trust in their strength, wealth, power, wisdom, holiness, which also are gifts given by God.[j] But a baptism on the word and command of God even when faith is not present is still a correct and certain baptism because it takes place as

i See n. 40, p. 297.

j The original of this section is singular.

God commanded. Granted, it does not benefit the baptized who are without faith because of their lack of faith, but the baptism is not, for that reason, incorrect, uncertain, or of no meaning. If we were to consider everything wrong or ineffectual that is of no value to the unbeliever, then nothing would be right or remain good. It has been commanded that the gospel should be preached to all the world. The unbeliever hears it but it is useless. Are we therefore to look on the gospel as not being a gospel or as being a false gospel? The godless see no value in God. Does that mean God is not God?

If an adult wants to be baptized and says, "Sir, I want to be baptized," you ask, "Do you believe?" in the same way that Philip asked the chamberlain in Acts 4 [8:37] and as we daily ask those to be baptized. Then this person will not blurt out and say, "Yes, I intend to move mountains by my faith." Instead the person will say, "Yes, Sir, I do believe, but I do not build on this my faith. It might be too weak or uncertain. I want to be baptized because it is God's command that I should be, and on the strength of this command I dare to be baptized. In time my faith may become what it may. If I am baptized on his command I know for certain that I am baptized. Were I to be baptized on my own faith, I might tomorrow find myself unbaptized, if faith failed me, or I became worried that I might not yesterday have believed rightly. But now that doesn't affect me. God and God's command may be attacked, but upon this command I have been baptized and that is enough certainty for me. My faith and I make this venture. If I believe, this baptism is of value to me. If I do not believe, it is not of value. But baptism in itself is not therefore wrong or uncertain, is not a matter of speculation, but is as sure as are the word and command of God."

As Paul writes his epistle to the Galatians with the tablets of the Ten Commandments nearby, Jesus (above Paul) writes on new tablets the law of Christ.

Of baptism as a child someone would say, "I thank God and am happy that I was baptized as a child, for thus I have done what God commanded. Whether I have believed or not, I have followed the command of God and been baptized and my baptism was correct and certain. God grant that whether my faith today be certain or uncertain, or I think that I believe and am certain, nothing is lacking in baptism." Faith always lacks something. We have enough to learn regarding our faith to last our whole life.[55] It can happen that faith fails, so that it is said, "See, this person had faith but has it no more." But one cannot say about baptism, "See, baptism was there but now there is no more baptism." No, it still stands, for God's command still stands, and what is done according to his command also stands and will also remain.

[Shall Children Be Baptized?]

Up to this point we have clearly and sufficiently proved, in my opinion, that the Anabaptists are wrong in denying the first baptism. They act as if they were sure that children were baptized without faith, though of this they cannot be certain. On the other hand we cannot prove that children do believe with any Scripture verse that clearly and expressly declares in so many words, "You are to baptize children because they also believe." Whoever compels us to produce such a statement has the upper hand and wins, for we cannot find such words. But sincere and sensible Christians do not require such proof. These quarrelsome, obstinate, and rebellious spirits do in order to seem to be clever. But on their side they can produce no statement that says, "You are to baptize adults but no children." We are however persuaded by many good reasons to hold that child baptism is right and that children do believe.

First, because child baptism derives from the apostles and has been practiced since the days of the apostles. We cannot oppose it, but must let it continue, since no one has yet been able to prove that in baptism children do not believe or that such baptism is wrong. For even if I were not sure that they believed, yet for my conscience's sake I would have to let them be baptized. For it is much better that baptism be extended to children than that I abolish the practice. For if, as we believe, baptism is right and useful and brings the children to salvation, and I did away with it, then I would be responsible for all the children who were lost because they were unbaptized—a cruel and terrible thing. If baptism is not right, that is, without value or help to the children, then I would be guilty of no greater sin than the word of God had been spoken and God's sign given in vain. I would not be responsible for the loss of any soul, but only of an ineffectual use of the word and sign of God.

55. In the early 1530s, Luther wrote a commentary on Paul's letter to the Galatians. In his preface to the book he makes the following observation: "[A]s I often warn you, there is a clear and present danger that the devil may take away from us the pure doctrine of faith and may substitute for it the doctrines of works and of human traditions. It is very necessary, therefore, that this doctrine of faith be continually read and heard in public. No matter how well known it may be or how carefully learned, the devil, our adversary, who prowls around and seeks to devour us (1 Pet. 5:8), is not dead. Our flesh also goes on living. Besides, temptations of every sort attack and oppress us on every side. Therefore this doctrine can never be discussed and taught enough." *Lectures on Galatians* (1535), LW 26:3.

But this God would easily forgive me, since it was done in ignorance and, even more, out of fear. I did not invent it. It came to me by tradition and I was persuaded by no word of Scripture that it was wrong. I would have been unwilling to do it, had I been convinced otherwise. Indeed, it would be just like when I preach God's word—and I also must preach according to his command—in vain to unbelievers. This is the same as casting pearls before swine, or holy things to the dogs.[k] What could I do? Here, too, I would rather sin in preaching fruitlessly than in refusing to preach at all. For in fruitless preaching I would not be guilty of a soul [being lost] while in refusing to preach I might be held accountable for many souls. That would be too much for any individual. This I say even if there were uncertainty about the faith of children in baptism, for we cannot set aside baptism that is certain, on account of faith which is uncertain. Baptism did not originate with us, but with the apostles and we should not discard or alter what apart from a clear word of Scripture cannot be discarded or altered. Wondrous is God and the works of God. What God does not will, God clearly witnesses to in Scripture. What is not so witnessed to there, we can accept as God's work. We are guiltless and God will not mislead us. If we knew or believed that child baptism was useless, it would be a wicked thing to still baptize as the Waldensians[56] do. But that is to despise God and God's word.

In the second place, this is an important consideration: No heresy endures to the end, but always, as St. Peter says, soon comes to light and is revealed as disgraceful.[l] So St. Paul mentions Jannes and Jambres and their like, whose folly is finally plain to all.[57] If child baptism were wrong, God would certainly not have permitted it to continue so long, nor let it become so universally and thoroughly established in all Christendom. Instead, it would have gone down in disgrace. The fact that the Anabaptists now dishonor it does not mean anything final or injurious to it. Just as God has established that Christians in all the world have accepted the Bible as Bible, the Lord's Prayer as Lord's Prayer, and the faith of a child as faith, so also God has established child baptism and not allowed it to disappear while

k Matt. 7:6.

l 2 Peter 2.

56. The Waldensians originated in the twelfth century. Their founder, Valdes (also known as Peter Waldo) [d. c. 1218], was a layperson from Lyons who protested the worldly excesses of the church. A persecuted sect, they did not deny infant baptism but they did delay the sacrament when one of their own ministers was not available. They persisted in rural and isolated areas in Europe up to the time of the Reformation. In a 1525 sermon, Luther referred to the Waldensians as believing that the faith required for baptism was not that of church or sponsors but the future faith of the child once the age of reason had been reached (WA 17:81). Luther also often referred to the Bohemian Brethren, one of many Hussite groups, as "Waldensians." He seems to have conflated the two groups. See his *To the Councilmen of All Cities in Germany That They Establish and Maintain Christian Schools* (1524), LW 45:311-38; TAL 5, forthcoming. See also Euan Cameron, "Waldenses," in Patte, ed., *Cambridge Dictionary of Christianity*, 1297.

57. 2 Tim. 3:8-9. Jannes and Jambres are not mentioned in the Old Testament. According to Jewish tradition, they were the magicians at Pharaoh's court who opposed Moses.

all kinds of heresies have disappeared which are much more recent and later than child baptism. This miracle of God shows that child baptism must be right. God has not so upheld the papacy, which also is an innovation and has never been accepted by all Christians of the world as has child baptism, the Bible, faith, or the Lord's Prayer, etc.

You say this does not prove that child baptism is certain because there is no passage in Scripture for it. I agree—what you say is true. From Scripture we cannot clearly conclude that you could establish child baptism as a practice among the first Christians after the apostles. But you can well conclude that in our day no one with a good conscience may reject or neglect the practice of child baptism, which has such a long tradition. God has not only tolerated it in the course of history but also guided events from the beginning in such a way that it did not disappear.

For where we see the work of God we should yield and believe in the same way as when we hear God's word, unless the plain Scripture tells us otherwise. I indeed am ready to let the papacy be considered as a work of God. But since Scripture is against it, I consider it as a work of God but not as a work of grace. It is a work of wrath from which to flee, as other plagues also are works of God, but works of wrath and displeasure.[58]

In the third place, it is likewise the work of God that during all the time children were being baptized, God has given great and holy gifts to many of them, enlightened and strengthened them with the Holy Spirit and understanding of the Scripture, and accomplished great things in Christendom through them. Jan Hus and his colleagues are examples from that time, and many other holy men and women before him.[59] God does the same to many of his people in our day. God has not driven them to the Anabaptists, which God undoubtedly would have done if he had judged the commandment concerning baptism being improperly observed. God does not contradict himself, nor would God favor with gifts those who disobey divine commands. Since God thus gives such gifts—which we must admit to be holy gifts of God—this confirms the first baptism and means we are rightly baptized. By these works we thus prove the first baptism to be proper and rebaptism to be wrong, just as St. Peter and St. Paul [Acts 15:8f.] proved from the miracle of the gift of the Holy Spirit to the Gentiles that it was the will of God that Gentiles need not heed the law of Moses.

58. Consistent with his view that he is living in the last days, Luther believes the papacy represents part of the demonic forces doing God's work by punishing the wicked.

59. Jan Hus (1369–1415) was a Czech priest who protested against the extravagant lifestyles of the popes and higher clergy. He also attacked the abuses surrounding the sale of indulgences. In general, Hus and his followers embraced many of the teachings of the Oxford theologian John Wycliffe (1320–1384), who advocated a greater role for Scripture and a bigger responsibility for church councils as a check against papal authority. Hus was condemned a heretic by the Council of Constance in 1415 and burned at the stake. Luther often said that he agreed with many of Hus's teachings—particularly his views on the papacy. In the *Large Catechism*, Luther named Bernard of Clairvaux (1090–1153), Jean Gerson (1363–1429), and Jan Hus as examples of those who were baptized as infants and had that baptism confirmed by God's bestowal of the Holy Spirit on them. This is the same argument that Luther saw Peter and Paul employing in Acts 15. See BC, 462–63.

The burning of Jan Hus at the stake, as depicted in the Spiezer Chronicle, by Diebold Schilling the Elder (c. 1485).

In the fourth place, if the first, or child, baptism were not right, it would follow that for more than a thousand years there was no baptism or any Christendom, which is impossible. In that case the article of the Creed, "I believe in one holy Christian church," would be false. For over a thousand years there were hardly any other but child baptisms. If this baptism were wrong then for that long period Christendom would have been without baptism, and if it were without baptism it would not be Christendom. For the Christian church is the bride of Christ, subject and obedient to him. It has his Spirit, his word, his baptism, his sacrament, and all that Christ has. If, indeed, child baptism were not common throughout the world, but (like the papacy) were accepted only by some, then the Anabaptists might seem to have a case and might attack those who receive it. It would be similar to how we oppose the clergy who have made a sacrifice out of the sacrament though among the laity it still remains a sacrament.[60] But the fact that child baptism has spread throughout the entire Christian world to this day gives rise to no probability that it is wrong, but rather to a strong indication that it is right.

In the fifth place, the words of St. Paul in 2 Thess. 2[:4] concerning the Antichrist, that he shall sit in the temple of God, of which we have already spoken,[m] accord with our position. If it is the temple of God it is not a haunt of heretics, but true Christendom, which must have the true baptism and there can be no doubt about it. We see and hear of no other than child baptism, whether under the pope, among the Turks, or in the entire world.[61] Christ commands the children to come and to

60. In his *The Babylonian Captivity of the Church* (1520), Luther complained about Roman abuses in worship. His biggest criticism was reserved for the idea that the Mass (church service) was seen as a sacrifice. In other words, people were taught to think of worship as something they do for God (and earn merit) rather than the place where God (through preaching and the sacraments) comes to them with a word of law and gospel. See LW 36:35–57; also pp. 43–46 above.

61. Here Luther does not mean that the Turks practiced baptism. He is referring to Christians living under Turkish rule.

m See n. 17, p. 282.

be brought to him and in Matt. 19[:14] says that theirs is the kingdom of God. The apostles baptized entire households.[n] John writes to little children.[62] St. John had faith even in his mother's womb, as we have heard.[63] If all of these passages do not suffice for the enthusiasts, I shall not be concerned. They are enough for me to stop the mouth of anyone from saying that child baptism does not mean anything. If they are still uncertain, I am satisfied if they do not do away with it but let it be in doubt among them. We, however, are certain enough, because it is nowhere contrary to Scripture, but is rather in accord with Scripture.

In the sixth place, since God has made a covenant with all heathen through the gospel and ordained baptism as a sign of this covenant, who can exclude the children? If the old covenant and the sign of circumcision made believers out of Abraham's children, so that they were called and truly were God's people, as God said, "I will be the God of your descendants,"[o] then this new covenant and sign must be much more effectual and make those who receive it part of the people of God. Now God commands that the entire world shall receive it. On the strength of that command (since none is excluded) we confidently and freely baptize everyone, excluding no one except those who oppose it and refuse to receive this covenant. If we follow God's command and baptize everyone, we leave it to God to be concerned about how those who are baptized believe. We have done our best when we have preached and baptized. If now we have no particular passage of Scripture on the baptism of children, they on their side have just as little of Scripture that bids us baptize adults. But we have the command to offer the common gospel and the common baptism to everyone, and therefore the children must be included. We plant and water and leave the growth to God.[p]

[Conclusion]

In summary, the Anabaptists are too frivolous and insolent. For they consider baptism, not as a God-given ordinance or command, but as a human trifle, like many other customs under the

62. 1 John 2:12. Luther takes John's address, "little children," literally here. In his 1527 lecture on this verse Luther explains: "John means that young people have a more fervid inclination to sin" (LW 30:244).

63. Luke 1:41. See. See n. 36, p. 294.

n Acts 16:15.

o Luther's paraphrase of Gen. 17:7.

p 1 Cor. 3:6.

papacy relating to the consecration of salt, water, or herbs.[64] For if they looked on it as a God-given ordinance and command they would not speak so disgracefully and shamefully about it even if it were not rightly used. But now they have the insane idea that baptism is something like the consecration of water and salt or the wearing of cowl and tonsure.[65] So they carry on and call it a dog's bath, or a handful of water, and other such vile things. Those who hold the gospel to be the right word of God do not speak lightly of it even though there are many who do not believe or accept it, or who falsely use it. The person who does not hold it as the word of God is the one who treats it lightly, blasphemes, and says it is fable, fairy story, or a counsel of fools, and the like. It ought to be easy for such a one to acquire disciples who believe such blasphemy.

Observe this well, that if the Anabaptists at first had presented their idea with good arguments, they would not have misled or won many persons. For they have no substantial or certain arguments. But they attract a great many people by using great, high-sounding words of slander against baptism. For the devil well knows that if the mad mob hears high-sounding words of slander, it falls for and readily believes them, asking for neither reason nor proof. So they hear it said, baptism is a dog's bath and those who baptize are false and foolish servants of bathkeepers. So they conclude, aha, so the devil baptizes, and God shames the false servants of bathkeepers. That is the position they take and have nothing else with which to attack baptism. When I have discussed this with them I have listened to them use high-sounding words of slander (dog's bath, servant of a bathkeeper, handful of water, etc.) and then stood there as shorn monks,[66] having nothing more with which to defend their errors.

In the same way the devil deceives those who blaspheme the sacrament. When he realizes that his lies do not produce much effect, he sallies forth and fills the ears of the mad mob with high-sounding irreverence. For example, some claim our sacrament is an eating of flesh and guzzling of blood and the like.[67] When they have exhausted those same high-sounding words their art is soon exhausted, and they begin to talk about the ascension of Christ.[68] The Jews do the same to this day. In order to keep their children in their faith they blaspheme Christ shamelessly, refer to him as "the hanged one," and confidently lie about him.[q] This frightens an innocent, simple heart and misleads it, as

64. Luther often criticized the Roman Catholics for what he considered to be an excessive reliance on ceremonies that became superstitious and infected with works righteousness. In *The Babylonian Capitivity of the Church* (1520), Luther complains that the power of baptism has been obscured by an endless number of works connected with penance. See LW 36:58, pp. 84-94 above.

65. The cowl was the hooded garment typically worn by priests. For "tonsure," see n. 66 below.

66. Many medieval monks would shave the hair from their scalp while leaving a ring of growth above their ears. This practice was known as "tonsure" and seen as a demonstration of humility.

67. In the sixteenth century, opponents often lampooned the Lutheran teaching on the real presence of Christ in the Lord's Supper as "cannibalism." Lutherans were careful to refute this charge, as can be seen in Article VII of *The Formula of Concord*, BC, 604, 63-65.

68. Luther's great opponent on the Lord's Supper was the Swiss reformer Ulrich Zwingli. A key part of Zwingli's

St. Paul observes in Rom. 16[:18]. For this reason they always have an easy time of it, for their high-sounding sacrilege has enabled them to lead the people wherever they wanted, all the while not establishing a firm ground for their error. If they had first formulated a good and solid foundation for their case then it would be sufficient to give the lie a good blow and set it forth in its true light.

We who know that baptism is a God-given thing, instituted and commanded by God, look not at its abuse by godless persons, but simply at God's ordinance. We find baptism in itself to be a holy, blessed, glorious, and heavenly thing, to be held in honor with fear and trembling, just as it is reasonable and right to hold any other ordinance and command of God. It is not the fault of baptism that many people abuse it. It would be just as wrong to call the gospel an empty babbling because there are many who abuse it. As far as I have been able to see and hear, the Anabaptists have no argument but high-sounding words of sacrilege. Therefore, everyone ought properly to shun and avoid them as messengers of none other than the devil, sent out into the world to blaspheme the word and ordinance of God so that people might not believe it and be saved. For they are the birds that eat the seed sown by the wayside, Matt. 13[:4].

Finally I claim that if some persons had not been baptized, but did not know it and firmly believed that they had been rightly baptized, that faith would be sufficient for them. Before God these people have what they believe. All things (Christ says) are possible to the one who believes.[r] To rebaptize such people would be to imperil their faith.[s] How much less, then, should we rebaptize those who are sure they have been baptized! God grant they then believed, but it makes no difference if they did not. The Anabaptists cannot be sure their baptism is a right one, since they base their rebaptizing on a faith of which they cannot be sure. Hence they play a gambling game with those they rebaptize. To be uncertain and dubious in godly things is to

argument was that Christ's body could not be present in the bread and wine because, after Jesus' ascension to heaven, he was at the right hand of God and therefore unable to be present physically on an altar. See Zwingli's *On the Lord's Supper*, in *Zwingli and Bucer*, The Library of Christian Classics, trans. and ed. G. W. Bromily (Philadelphia: Westminster, 1953), 185–238. Luther's extended response is found in his *Confession Concerning Christ's Supper*, LW 37:161–372.

A pastor baptizes an infant.

q Luther's complicated view of the Jews is explained well in Mark U. Edwards Jr., *Luther's Last Battles: Politics and Polemics, 1531–46* (Ithaca: Cornell University Press, 1983), 115–42. See also Brooks Schramm and Kirsi I. Stjerna, eds., *Martin Luther, the Bible, and the Jewish People: A Reader* (Minneapolis: Fortress Press, 2012).

r Mark 9:23.

s These sentences are singular in the original.

sin and tempt God. Whoever teaches deceit for uncertainty in place of sure truth lies in the same way as the one who speaks openly against the truth. For such people speak of something they themselves are not sure and yet they want it to be taken as truth.[t] But whoever would base baptism on the commandment and ordinance of God would soon realize that rebaptism is neither necessary nor useful. The first baptism sufficiently meets the requirement of God.

They are guilty also of blaspheming and denying the commandment and work of God. For while the first baptism is in accord with the commandment of God and justice is done to it by its very performance, they still insist it is wrong and only a dog's bath. What else are they saying but that God's command and work are wrong and amount to a dog's bath? This they say for no other reason than that they demand a certainty of faith in baptism though it is impossible to have this certainty. This is to deny and blaspheme a sure command and work of God for an uncertain delusion.

Assume that the first baptism is without faith. Tell me which is greater and more important in the second baptism, the word of God or faith? Is it not true that the word of God is greater and more important than faith, since faith builds and is founded on the word of God rather than God's word on faith? Furthermore faith may waver and change, but God's word remains forever.[u] Then too, tell me, if one of these two should be otherwise, which should it rather be: the immutable word or the changeable faith? Would it not more reasonably be the faith that should be subject to change rather than the word of God? It is fairer to assume that the word of God would change faith, if a right one were lacking, than that faith would change the word of God. So they must confess that in the first baptism it was not the word of God that was defective, but faith, and that what is needed is another faith and not another word. Why then do they not concern themselves rather with a change of faith and let the word remain unaltered? Shall we call God's word and ordinance false because we do not truly believe it? In that case a true word would be rare thing. If they were to act rightly according to their own dim reason, they should be urging a "re-believing," not a rebaptizing. For baptism

t This sentence is singular in the original.

u Isa. 40:6-9.

is by the word and ordinance of God and dare not be different from or anything other than it is, while faith may be otherwise than it is (if it is not present). So really they should be "Anabelievers" and not Anabaptists, if they were right, which, of course, they are not.

Therefore, these baptizers are altogether unsure of themselves, and simply reveal that they are lying. They deny and blaspheme the ordinance of God through their deceitful uncertainty, making the last first, basing the word and ordinance of God on human work and faith, urging baptism when they should be urging faith. Accordingly, all devout Christians ought to be convinced that they are misleading, uncertain, and perverted spirits, and should avoid them at the peril of their souls' salvation.[v] May Christ, our Lord, grant this and help us. Amen.

This is as much as I can undertake now, briefly and hastily.[w] For at this time I am not able to go into this matter more thoroughly. As mentioned I am not sure what they do believe. For the devil is mad and exaggerates so much and stirs up so much confusion that absolutely no one knows what he or she believes. The Anabaptists agree with the foes of the sacrament that only bread and wine are in the Lord's Supper. Yet the sacramentarians disagree with the Anabaptists on baptism. Also, the sacramentarians are not agreed among themselves nor the Anabaptists among themselves.[69] They are at one only in regard to and in opposition to us. Likewise the papacy is divided into innumerable factions of priests and monks who once devoured one another among themselves. But now, because they are opposed to us, they are united. It is the same among temporal princes and lords. Pilate and Herod become one over against Christ, though previously they were mortal enemies. But in this particular case, the error of the Anabaptists is more tolerable than that of the sacramentarians. For the sacramentarians altogether destroy baptism, while the Anabaptists give it another character. Still there is reason to hope that they will right themselves. It is enough to have demonstrated that the Anabaptists' faith is uncertain and deceptive and that they cannot prove their case. For Satan needs do no more through the enthusiasts than always to produce doubt. He thinks it is enough to speak haughtily and contemptuously

69. The Anabaptists and the followers of Zwingli both agreed that the sacraments only *point* to Christ. Bread, wine, and water are signs but there is no real presence of Christ. However, Zwingli affirmed infant baptism in opposition to the Anabaptists. He saw baptism as the New Testament equivalent of circumcision and asserted that as such it should be applied to infants. See his "Of Baptism," in *Zwingli and Bullinger*, ed. by G. W. Bromily (Philadelphia: Westminster, 1953) 129–75.

v This sentence is singular in the original.

w See the introduction to this work, p. 278.

about us, as the rebel sacramentarians do. None of them take pains to make clear and to prove their arrogance, but their concern is to make our interpretation contemptible and uncertain. They teach doubt, not faith,[x] calling this Scripture and the word of God. The devil knows he can accomplish nothing in the bright light of truth, so he stirs up the dust, hoping to raise a cloud before our eyes so that we cannot see the light. In the cloud he dazzles us with false and ghostly images in order to mislead us. Having made up their minds concerning their peculiar notions, they attempt to make the Scriptures agree with them by dragging passages in by the hair. But Christ has faithfully stood by our side up to this point and will continue to tread Satan under our foot. He will protect you all against the seductions of your tyrant and Antichrist and mercifully help us to gain his freedom. Amen.

x 1 Tim. 6:3-5.

On the Councils and the Church

1539

PAUL W. ROBINSON

INTRODUCTION

Martin Luther dressed carefully on the morning of 7 November 1535. He had been shaved and now put on his best clothes, including a fur-lined coat.[a] He added to the ensemble a heavy gold chain and several rings. He wished to look as young and healthy as possible, though he was neither, for his meeting with the papal nuncio, Pietro Paulo Vergerio (c. 1497–1565).[1] He had come to Wittenberg to announce the pope's call for a general council of the church to meet in 1536. When Vergerio and Luther met that morning, the discussion quickly reached an impasse on the very point that had brought them together. Luther was convinced that the Evangelicals did not need a council, though clearly Rome did. Vergerio was sure that such a council would condemn Luther and his movement. Nevertheless, Luther assured the nuncio that he would attend the council even if it were sure to condemn him—in his own words, that he would come "with head and neck," that is, prepared to die a martyr's death.

1. Vergerio began his career in Italy as a lawyer. The early death of his wife led him to a career in the church, and he became papal nuncio to Germany in 1533. Afterward, he received two bishoprics, but returned to papal diplomacy in Rome in 1540. Vergerio, who was later suspected of Protestant leanings and convicted of heresy (see below, p. 323), escaped to Swiss territory. In his later life he published polemical writings and was a voice for reform.

a Unless otherwise noted, this account is based on Martin Brecht, *Martin Luther: The Preservation of the Church 1532–1546*, trans. James L. Schaff (Minneapolis: Fortress Press, 1993), 173–98 (hereafter Brecht 3), where more detail concerning these events can be found.

Papal nuncio Pietro Paulo Vergerio.

Many on both sides of the Reformation had previously expressed their desire for a council. General councils had dominated the landscape of church government in the first half of the fifteenth century—especially the Council of Constance (1414–1418), which dealt with the papal schism, heresy, and reform. Constance had settled the schism by removing all three claimants to the papal throne by deposition or forced resignation and then electing a new pope. The council had dealt with heresy most famously by condemning Jan Hus (1369–1415) to be burned as a heretic. It had promulgated several reform decrees, though the new pope, Martin V (1368–1431), diminished the time devoted to reform. Constance did attempt, through its decree *Frequens*, to limit papal power in the church by requiring the participation of a council in church government. The decree, however, proved difficult to implement, since it was left to the pope to summon the council, and the popes did so reluctantly, if at all. Finally, the Council of Basel (1431–1445) overreached when it provoked a new schism by electing an anti-pope, which allowed the papacy to assert its authority once again. By the end of the century, conciliarism, as this movement that elevated the authority of the council over that of the pope was known, had been condemned by the papacy. Yet conciliar ideology remained strong, particularly in the territory of the Holy Roman Empire, because conciliarism had seen the emperor's influence trump the pope's.[b]

Luther's opponents, in the first stirrings of controversy, identified him as a conciliarist because he questioned the papacy and its government of the church. When Cardinal Cajetan (1469–1534) met with Luther following the indulgence controversy,[2] he asserted the pope's superiority to a council, reminding the

2. Tommaso de Vio (Cardinal Cajetan), the papal legate, met with Luther at Augsburg in October 1518 in order to explain Rome's case against Luther. See Luther's own account of the meeting in *The Proceedings at Augsburg*, LW 31:253–92; TAL 1:121–65.

b Francis Oakley, "Conciliariasm," OER 1:394–97.

would-be reformer that conciliarism had been condemned.[c] As a result, Luther first appealed Cajetan's decision to Pope Leo X (1475–1521). When Leo reaffirmed the teaching on indulgences, Luther went on to appeal from the pope's judgment to that of a council[d] and then to call for a free and universal council to deal with questions fundamental to the reform of the church. His *To the Christian Nobility of the German Nation* of 1520 listed twenty-eight points that such a council should consider.[e] Luther's appeal resonated in Germany, in part because of the empire's history with conciliarism and in part because many Germans resented the pope, and the call for a council became part of the rhetoric and strategy of the Evangelical movement.

Emperor Charles V,[3] though he was no supporter of the Reformation, also pressed the pope for a council to settle the issues that divided the church, since he had agreed in 1532 to coexist with the Lutheran princes in the empire until such a council could meet. For that reason, Pope Paul III's (b. 1468; pope from 1534 to 1549) announcement that a council would be convened in Mantua in 1536 provoked a flurry of activity from the Lutherans. This was, of course, not to be the free council to be held in Germany that the Evangelical party had promoted, so there was debate over whether they should attend. Luther was convinced that they should in order to call the pope's bluff, since he was convinced the pope did not really wish any sort of council to meet. Others, like Elector John Frederick of Saxony (1503–1554), maintained that they should not attend a papal council, and some even proposed holding their own council to counter the pope's, while inviting the pope to attend. The elector asked Luther to draft articles of faith, which became the *Smalcald Articles*,[f] for the meeting of the Smalcald League to consider the question of the council. Though the league did not adopt the articles, its members did agree on a confessional position. Yet in the end the political leaders decided against attending a council that would be stacked against them.

Meanwhile, the question of a council had provoked numerous publications, in addition to the articles, from Luther's pen.

3. Also known as Charles I of Spain (1500–1558), he was Holy Roman Emperor from 1519 to 1556.

c WA 2:8; LW 31:262.

d WA 2:34–40.

e WA 6:427–69; LW 31:156–217; TAL 1:369–466.

f *The Smalcald Articles*, BC, 295–328; TAL 2:417–77.

He had already addressed in print the failure of previous councils to meet and, following Vergerio's visit to Wittenberg, had arranged a disputation, "On the Power of the Council." Luther also immersed himself in the history of the Council of Constance—not surprising, given the obvious parallels between his position in the church and that of Jan Hus, as well as the references made to Hus in the course of the Leipzig Disputation of 1519. After the meeting of the Smalcald League in 1537, Luther, in the words of Martin Brecht, "escalated his public controversy with the papacy into what was virtually a new pamphlet war."[g] Increasingly, Luther addressed historical topics in his attacks on papal primacy and the idolatrous piety of indulgences. One such treatise consisted of a German translation of the spurious *Donation of Constantine* with comments. Although the *Donation* was probably an eighth-century document and had been recognized as a forgery already in the late Middle Ages, it had become part of canon law, and papal apologists frequently appealed to it for justification of the primacy of Rome. The text purports to tell how Constantine ceded control of the Western empire to the bishop of Rome and gave him the imperial regalia to wear. Luther pointed out just how spurious this claim was and suggested that the coming council should deal with papal authority in the church. The pope, however, had postponed the council yet again, and in April 1538 the postponement became indefinite. At that point, Luther published the articles he had written for Smalcald, which provoked replies from his opponents, including Johannes Cochlaeus (1479–1552) and Georg Witzel (1501–1573).[4]

Finally, in 1539 Luther delivered on his promise to deal at length with the history of the councils by publishing *On the Councils and the Church*.[5] The treatise, the mostly deeply investigated and well written of his later career, consists of three parts. In the first, Luther addresses the papal abuse of general councils. He begins by saying the pope offers a council to the emperor the way someone tricks a dog by offering a morsel on the tip of a knife and then hitting the dog on the snout with the hilt for trying to snatch the treat. Moreover, the papacy wants no part of a reform council but only the kind of council where a favorable outcome for the pope can be determined in advance. The second part of the treatise deals with the nature of a council and the

4. Cochlaeus was a German humanist who was ordained a priest while in Rome (1517–19). He was a relentless critic of Luther and attended assemblies that tried to mend the growing split in the church, including the Diet of Worms (1521). Georg Witzel was ordained a priest in 1520 and studied under Luther at Wittenberg. He abandoned the priesthood in 1524 and married. However, later he became convinced that Luther's view of the church was not the true church.

5. Philip Melanchthon (1497–1560), who had also been considering the question, published his *De ecclesia autoritate et de veterum scriptis libellus* in the same year. Luther announced the completion of his treatise to Melanchthon in a letter of 14 March 1539 (WA Br 8:391). See also Timothy J. Wengert, "Melanchthon and Luther," in *Lutherjahrbuch* 66 (Göttingen: Vandenhoeck & Ruprecht, 1999), 55–56.

g Brecht 3:188, and following pages for examples of his publications.

Johannes Cochlaeus

Georg Witzel

authority of councils by examining the four principal councils—Nicaea, Constantinople, Ephesus, and Chalcedon—along with the Jerusalem council of Acts 15. Luther concludes that where the councils pronounced on the great christological issues they faced, their success resulted from affirming what Scripture says. On other issues, much that they did was unnecessary and even harmful for the church. So councils could not be relied upon as the solution to the church's ills.

Much of what Luther had to say about the papacy and the piety and practices of the Roman church he had said before, but his radical critique of even the four great councils went beyond his previous rejections of conciliar authority. His deep and serious engagement with the history of the church fueled this critique. Luther's treatment of the councils in 1539 relied on a number of texts that had only recently become available. He used recent editions of Eusebius's *Ecclesiastical History*, Rufinus's (b. c. 340–410) translation and continuation of Eusebius (c. 265–c. 340), and the *Historia tripartita* of Cassiodorus Senator (c. 485–c. 583). In addition, he relied heavily on the work of the Franciscan

Peter Crabbe (1470–1553) on the councils, *Concilia omnia*, which had just been published in 1538,[6] along with Platina's *Lives of the Popes* from the last quarter of the fifteenth century.

In light of this understanding of councils, Luther addresses the nature of the church, which is the third part of the treatise. Throughout the Reformation, Luther had been quite clear about what the church was *not*, for example, the pope and cardinals. He had also, of course, written about what the church *was* and how it could be identified in the world. Here he lays out once again some signs by which the true church could be identified.[7] The clear articulation of "signs" of the church in theological debate occurred for the first time in the fifteenth century. John of Ragusa (c. 1395–1443) defined five signs of the church—an idea he attributed to Augustine—in a treatise he composed against the Hussites.[h] The relatively recent origin of this approach reflects the novelty of the late medieval debate over the nature of the church.[8] Though Luther was probably unaware of Ragusa's argument, he developed the idea of signs of the church along his own theological lines and for his own uses. He had discussed the signs of the church long before *On the Councils and the Church* in the course of a controversy with Ambrose Catharinus[9] in 1521. In replying to Catharinus, Luther identified baptism, the Lord's Supper, and the gospel as "symbols, tokens, and characteristics of Christians," adding that "where you see baptism and the bread and the gospel—in any place whatsoever, with any person whatsoever—you may have no doubts that the church exists there."[i] Luther continued to use the idea, often expanding the number of marks well beyond three, as he does in this treatise.[j]

Though history informed Luther's understanding of the councils, his definition of the church owed much to current events. The pope was still, of course, the principal adversary as far as calling for a council was concerned. But when it came to thinking about the church, Luther had other reformers and their movements very much in mind. He was still engaged in the Antinomian controversy with his former pupil, Johann Agricola

6. Peter (Petrus) Crabbe was a Belgian Franciscan theologian and important editor of church documents.

7. These signs are commonly referred to as "marks of the church" (*notae ecclesiae*, the language used in *Apology of the Augsburg Confession* VII, and perhaps coined by Melanchthon); Luther himself rarely used this phrase.

8. Treatises that dealt exclusively with the nature of the church began to appear only after 1300, at first in the context of the debate between Pope Boniface VIII and King Philip IV of France. See Scott H. Hendrix, "In Quest of the *Vera Ecclesia*: The Crises of Late Medieval Ecclesiology," *Viator* 7 (1976): 348.

9. Ambrose Cartharinus (also Lancelotto Politi) (1483–1553) was an Italian Dominican canon lawyer.

h Gordon W. Lathrop and Timothy J. Wengert, *Christian Assembly: Marks of the Church in a Pluralistic Age* (Minneapolis: Fortress Press, 2004), 20.

i WA 7:720; trans. in Lathrop and Wengert, *Christian Assembly*, 27.

j See "The Marks of the Church in the Later Luther," ch. 5 in ibid., 81–112.

(1494–1566), and it was still fresh in his memory as he penned *On the Councils*. Throughout the treatise he refers to Anabaptists, Antinomians, and others as having departed from the genuine Evangelical faith.

After more delay, Pope Paul III finally convened a council at Trent in December 1545. Luther would die two months later. As he predicted, Trent was a papal council that served only to confirm Rome's teaching.[k] The assembly at Trent was also missing a key figure in the story recounted here. Vergerio, the nuncio who visited Wittenberg, had turned against Rome, and heresy proceedings against him began in 1545. He had become an adherent of the Reformation and spent the rest of his life writing Protestant propaganda.[l]

The Council of Trent painted by Pasquale Cati (1588). The woman in the foreground dressed in papal garb is the Church Triumphant, robed in the splendor of doctrinal clarity.

k Giuseppe Alberigo, "Trent, Council of," OER 4:173–77.

l Anne Jacobson Schutte, "Vergerio," OER 4:228–29. See n. 1, above.

ON THE COUNCILS AND THE CHURCH[10, m]

I OFTEN JOINED IN THE GENERAL LAUGHTER when I saw someone offer a morsel of bread on the tip of a knife to dogs and then, as they snapped at it, slap their snouts with the knife handle, so that the poor dogs not only lost the bread but also had to suffer pain. That is a good joke. It never occurred to me at that time that the devil could also play his jokes on us and consider us such wretched dogs, until I learned how the most holy father, the pope, with his bulls,[11] books, and daily practices plays the same kind of a dog's joke on Christendom. But, Lord God, with what great harm to the soul and with what mockery of divine majesty! It is just what he is doing with the council now: the whole world has been waiting and clamoring for it; the good emperor and his whole empire have been working to attain it for nearly twenty years;[12] and the pope has always made vain promises and put it off, offering the morsel of bread to the emperor, as to a dog, until, at the opportune moment, he slaps him on the snout while mocking him as his fool and dupe.

Now he is summoning the council for the third time;[13] but he first sends his apostles[14] into all lands to have kings and princes pledge their allegiance to the pope's doctrines. The bishops and their clergy concur in this strategy and absolutely refuse either to yield or to permit a reform, thus the course of the council is already determined, before it even convenes, namely, not to undertake any reforms, but to observe everything in accord with what has come to be present practice. Isn't that a splendid council? It has not yet convened, and already it has done what it was to do when it met, that is, to slap the emperor on the snout, and even more, to overtake the Holy Spirit and outstrip him by far![15] Yet I have feared, and often written and said, that they would not and could not hold a council unless they had first captured and

m The word *Kirchen* in the original title (*Von den Konziliis und Kirchen*) could be either singular or plural. The singular is retained here because Luther himself called this a treatise *on the church* (*de ecclesia*) in a letter to Philip Melanchthon and because sixteenth-century editions and translations used the singular.

10. The edition presented here revises the translation found in *Luther's Works* by Charles Jacobs and Eric Gritsch (LW 41:3–178) and has been compared with the editions in *Luthers Werke: Kritische Gesamtausgabe* and *Martin Luther: Studienausgabe* (WA 50:509–653; MLStA 5:456–617). Many of the notes in this edition rely on the outstanding work of these previous editors.

11. A bull is a papal decree named for the lead seal (*bulla*) affixed to the document announcing it.

12. On 28 November 1518, Luther made his first appeal to a general council (cf. WA 2:34 and Martin Brecht, *Martin Luther: His Road to Reformation, 1483–1521*, trans. James L. Schaff (Philadelphia: Fortress Press, 1985), 263–64; hereafter Brecht 1). In 1520, he included a section on matters to be considered by a general council in *To the Christian Nobility of the German Nation*, LW 44:156ff.; TAL 1:407ff. The emperor and various diets (meetings of the empire) had been demanding a council since 1523. Thus, approximately twenty years had elapsed between these demands and the time Luther wrote this statement.

13. On 2 June 1536, Pope Paul III called for a council to begin meeting at Mantua on 23 May 1537. On 20 April 1537, he delayed the opening of the council to 1 November 1537. On 8 October 1537, he changed the meeting place for the council to Vicenza and its assembly date to May 1538, and in April 1538 he postponed it indefinitely.

controlled the emperor, kings, and princes, so as to have total freedom to decree whatever they pleased, to buttress their tyranny, and to oppress Christendom with far greater burdens than ever before.[16]

In God's name, if you lords—emperor, kings, princes—like the way in which these accursed, damned people trample on your muzzles and rap your snouts, we have to let it happen and remember that they acted much worse in the past: they deposed

Title page of a 1539 publication of *On the Councils and the Church*. The intricate border features the seals of Martin Luther, Philip Melanchthon, Johann Bugenhagen, Casper Cruciger, and Justus Jonas, all arranged around an image of Jesus as the Good Shepherd.

14. Between 1533 and 1538 six nuncios (papal ambassadors) appeared in Germany to prepare for a general council: Ugo Rangoni in 1533; Pietro Paolo Vergerio in 1535 (see n. 1, p. 317); Peter van der Vorst in 1537; Giovanni Morone, Jerome Aleander, and Fabio Mignanelli in 1538. Aleander had previously served as nuncio in 1520 and 1521, proclaiming the bull *Exsurge domine* that threatened Luther with excommunication and participating in the negotiations leading up to Luther's appearance at the Diet of Worms. Vergerio visited Luther in Wittenberg to announce the summoning of a council; see Martin Brecht, *Martin Luther: The Preservation of the Church, 1532–1546*, trans. James L. Schaff (Minneapolis: Fortress Press, 1993), 173–98; hereafter Brecht 3.

15. A general council was believed to be directly inspired by the Holy Spirit, and the first session usually opened with the singing of the hymn "Come, Creator Spirit" (*Veni Creator Spiritus*).

16. The Council of Constance (1414–1418) succeeded because it had the support of the Holy Roman Emperor, who was the ruler of Germany, and other monarchs. It was Constance that decreed the superiority of a general council to the pope, and this idea still had many adherents in Germany in Luther's day. Luther believes that the pope will not risk calling a council until he has neutralized the secular rulers.

kings and emperors, anathematized them, drove them out, betrayed them, murdered them, and vented their devilish malice on them, as history testifies; and they intend to go on doing that. Despite this, Christ will know how to find and preserve his Christendom, even against the gates of hell [Matt. 16:18], though emperors and kings neither would nor could help in any way. He can dispense with their help much better than they can do without his. How did he get along before kings and emperors were born? And how would he get along now if no emperor or king existed, even though a whole world of devils raged against him? He is not unused to bitter fare, and he, in turn, can cook up even bitterer fare. Woe to them who must eat it!

But we poor, weak Christians, who must endure being dubbed heretics by such saints, ought to be happy and of good cheer. We ought to praise and thank God the Father of all mercy with great joy for taking such good care of us and for smiting our murderers and bloodhounds with such Egyptian blindness and such Jewish madness that they are determined to yield on no point and to let Christendom perish rather than to allow the most trifling idolatry (with which they are stuffed full and overfull) to be reformed. Of this they boast, and this they do. Cheerful (I say) we ought to be; for thus they make our case better than we could ever have desired, and make theirs worse than they now might think. They know and admit that they are wrong on many points and on top of it have Scripture and God against them, and yet they want to butt their heads against God, and knowingly defend wrong as right. Thus consoled, poor Christians should indeed be able to take the sacrament even without going to confession, and risk a hundred necks if they had them, when they see, indeed, when they feel so palpably, that God rules on our side and the devil on theirs.[n]

Thus we now have the final decree of the future council at Vicenza, and the severe verdict of the latest (so estimable) council: the entire world is to despair of a reformation of the church, and there is to be no hearing.[17] Instead (as they boast), they would let Christendom perish,[18] that is, they would have the devil himself as god and lord, rather than have Christ and abandon even a small fraction of their idolatry. Not satisfied with that, they want to coerce us poor Christians with the sword to consciously

n The original of this sentence is singular.

17. The fifteenth-century conciliar movement coupled the idea of church reform with general councils, most notably in the decree *Frequens*, in which the Council of Constance called for the routine summoning of general councils to govern the church. See Philip H. Stump, *The Reforms of the Councils of Constance (1414–1418)* (Leiden: Brill, 1994).

18. In this section, the terms *die, perish, go to ruin*, etc. all translate two German phrases—*zu grund gehen* or *untergehen*. Luther uses these phrases relentlessly in describing the true church as opposed to "the abiding lords" (*die bleibende Herrn*), that is, the pope and his followers who wish to remain rather than perish.

worship the devil with them and to blaspheme Christ. Such defiance has neither been recorded nor heard of in all of history. Other tyrants at least have the dubious honor of crucifying the Lord of majesty unknowingly, as do the Turks, heathen, and Jews.[19] But here they are, who in Christ's name and as Christians, indeed, as the most select Christians, boast and arm themselves against Christ, saying, "We know that Christ's words and deeds are against us; nevertheless, we refuse to tolerate or yield to his word. Indeed, he must yield to us and tolerate our idolatry; even so we want to be Christians and to be known as such."

19. Luther's language here is similar to the way medieval theologians used the phrase "pagans, Jews, and heretics" to define those outside the church.

So, since the pope, with his following, simply refuses to convoke a council and reform the church, or offer any advice or assistance toward that end, but boastfully defends his tyranny with crimes, preferring to let the church go to ruin, we, so shamefully forsaken by the pope, cannot go on and must seek counsel and help elsewhere and first of all seek and ask our Lord Jesus Christ for a reformation. These desperate tyrants, whose evil forces us to despair of a council and of a reformation, must not drive us also to despair of Christ or to leave the church without counsel and help; we must instead do what we can, and let them go to the devil as they wish.

In this way they testify and cry, to their own perdition, that they are the true Antichrists and "autocatacrites"[o] who condemn themselves and obstinately insist on their own damnation. They thereby exclude themselves from the church and boast publicly that they want to be and to remain the church's most bitter foes. For he who says that he would rather let the church perish than mend his ways or yield on any point confesses clearly and publicly that he is not only no Christian desirous of being in the church (which he would rather allow to founder so that he might survive and not sink with the church), but that he is also willing to contribute to the church's destruction—as they prove so horribly with their deeds over and above their words, permitting hundreds of parishes to lie waste and churches to die without shepherd, sermon, and sacrament.[20]

20. Reformers throughout the late Middle Ages complained about such absenteeism, meaning that the cleric who received the income from a parish was not himself present to serve the congregation.

In times past the bishops, and indeed every Christian (even as at present), let themselves be tortured and went to their deaths gratefully and cheerfully for the dear church. Christ himself died for his church, to preserve and sustain it. But the pope and

o From the Greek *autokatakritos*, "self-condemned." See Titus 3:11.

his following now boast that the church must die for them, so that they may be preserved in their tyranny, idolatry, knavery, and every villainy. What do you think of these fellows? They want to remain, so the church must go. How are we to know what's what? But if the church is to perish, then Christ, upon whom it is built as upon a rock against the gates of hell [Matt. 16:18], must perish first. If Christ is to perish, then God, who has established this rock and foundation, must perish first. Who could have suspected these lords to have such great power that the church, together with Christ and even God, should perish so easily before their threats? They must be far, far mightier than the gates of hell and all devils, against whom the church has prevailed and must now prevail.

Thus they scream (I say) about themselves that they neither want to be the church nor be in the church, but that they want to be the church's worst enemies and help it go to ruin. Yet until now they have pestered and harassed us with the word, "Church! Church!" There has been no limit or end to their shouting and spitting that they should be regarded as the church; and they charged us miserably with heresy, they cursed us and murdered us because we refused to hear them as the church.[21] Now, I am sure, we are honestly and mightily absolved so that they will not and cannot call us heretics any longer, for they no longer wish to be glorified as the church, but as enemies of the church want to let it be destroyed, even lending a hand in its suppression. It is incongruous for them to be the church and, simultaneously, to let the church perish rather than perish themselves, indeed, to have a hairsbreadth of themselves perish. This is what the passage means, "I will judge you by your own words, you wicked slave" [Luke 19:22].

If the Last Day were not close at hand, it would be no wonder if heaven and earth were to crumble because of such blasphemy. However, since God is able to endure this, this day cannot be far off.[22] But they laugh about all that, forgetting that God has made them blind, mad, raving, and foolish, esteeming it as great wisdom and courage. I, too, would feel as secure as they feel, if only their innocent blindness spoke in their actions; but the great wrath of God, revealed in them, terrifies me profoundly. It is high time for all of us to weep and to pray earnestly, as Christ wept over Jerusalem and commanded the women not to weep over him but to weep over themselves and their children [Luke

21. Luther had been declared a heretic in 1521, and the Reformation movement produced many martyrs. Luther had addressed the real possibility that the delegation to the 1530 Diet of Augsburg might be among them. See his *Sermon at Coburg on Cross and Suffering* (1530), LW 51:193–208; WA 32:28–39. See also Brad S. Gregory, *Salvation at Stake: Christian Martyrdom in Early Modern Europe* (Cambridge: Harvard University Press, 1999).

22. Luther believed throughout the years of the Reformation that God's final judgment must be coming soon. He saw papal opposition to the gospel and persecution of the church as a key sign, but events such as the Turkish invasion of Austria in 1529 also confirmed his apocalyptic mindset.

23:28]. For they do not believe that the time of their affliction is at hand, and they do not want to believe it, even though they can see it, hear it, smell it, taste it, touch it, and feel it.

How should one act in the future, now that the pope will neither accord us a genuine council nor tolerate any reform, but, together with his followers, is willing to let the church perish? He put himself out of the church to save himself and not perish in and with the church. He is gone and has bidden the church farewell! So what (I say) should one do or undertake now that we are to be without a pope? For we are the church, or in the church, which the papists are willing to let go to ruin so that they might survive. We too would like to survive, and are resolved, together with our Lord Jesus and his Father, the God of us all, not to go under miserably before the defiance of the papists. We see the necessity for a council or a reformation in the church, for we see such gross abuses that even if we were oxen or asses—not to speak of human beings or Christians—and could not perceive these abuses with our eyes or ears, we would still have to feel them with our paws and hoofs and stumble over them. What if we ourselves, the church destined to perish, were to hold a council against the abiding lords, without the pope and without their consent, and undertook a reformation which would appear quite transitory to these abiding squires, but which they nonetheless would have to put up with?[23] But we want to come to the point of our discussion, since we have now lost the most holy head, the pope, and have to take as much counsel with ourselves as our Lord may grant.

23. John Frederick of Saxony (1532–1547) had suggested such a plan in December 1536, CR 3:141.

Part I

[The Pope and the Councils][p]

Many of the papists occupied themselves for years with the councils and the fathers, until they finally gathered all councils into one book, which appeals to me, since I never before found all the councils together.[24] Now there are (in my opinion) several good, pious souls who would have liked to see the church reformed

24. A reference to the work of Peter Crabbe, a Franciscan monk, who published his two-volume *Concilia omnia* with Peter Quentel (d. c. 1548) in Cologne in 1538. Crabbe collected the decisions of all the councils. See also n. 6 above.

p Headings in brackets are additions to guide the reader and did not appear in the original text.

on the pattern of these same councils or fathers, as they too are aware that the present position of the church in the papacy is woefully at variance (as is evident) with the ways of the councils and the fathers. But in this case their good opinion is of no avail, for they undoubtedly have the idea that the pope, with his following, would or should participate in such a reformation.[25] That, however, is fruitless, for here stands the pope, with his abiding lords, declaring obstinately to them as well as to us that they would rather let the church perish than yield on one single point; that is, they would sooner let councils and fathers perish too than give in to them in any way. If councils and fathers were to be obeyed—for God's sake!—what would become of the pope and the present-day bishops? Indeed, they would have to become the church destined to perish, and would no longer be the abiding lords.

I shall pass over the ancient years, the period encompassing a thousand or fourteen hundred years after the birth of Christ, in silence. It is not more than one hundred years ago that the pope adopted the holy practice of bestowing two benefices,[26] such as canonries or parishes, on one priest,[27] about which the Parisian theologians and their associates grumbled and wrote many terrible things.[28] I am not yet sixty years old; nevertheless, I know that within my time it has become customary for a bishop to have more than one diocese.[29] But meanwhile the pope has devoured everything, stolen annates[30] and everything else, distributed dioceses by threes, abbeys and prebends[31] by tens and twenties. How can he regurgitate all this and dissolve his chancellery[32] for the sake of the fathers and the councils? Yes, you say, it is an abuse. Very well, then, take your ancient councils and fathers to heart and reform all this; for it was not like this a hundred years ago, indeed, not even sixty years ago, before you were born.[33]

Now of what use is your reformation according to the fathers and councils? You hear that the pope and the bishops will not tolerate it. And if they cannot tolerate the condition of the church as it existed fifty years ago, when you and I were children, dear reader, how will or can they tolerate our proposal to reform the church by restoring it to its condition of six hundred or a thousand or fourteen hundred years ago? Such a proposal is simply impossible, since the pope is in control and wants to remain unreformed. Therefore we must admit that councils and fathers are powerless in these matters, and so is anything we can

25. The papacy became the driving force behind reform in the eleventh century, but by the later Middle Ages it had come to be seen as an obstacle to reform. After 1300, the phrase "reform in head and members"—meaning the pope along with the church—became common. Yet the papacy was still considered essential to the church, and only a few considered dispensing with it entirely.

26. A benefice (*beneficium*) referred most often to the income from a position in the church.

27. Luther had listed such abuses in *To the Christian Nobility* (1520), LW 44:150–51; TAL 1:407–422.

28. The University of Paris was the center of activity for notable conciliarists like Henry of Langenstein (c. 1325–1397), Pierre d'Ailly (1350–c. 1420), and Jean Gerson (1363–1429). Luther was clearly familiar with some of Gerson's works and based his own appeal from the pope to a general council on an earlier appeal filed by the University of Paris. On conciliarism in general, see the introduction.

29. Cardinal Albrecht of Mainz (1490–1545) held two archbishoprics and one bishopric at the same time. He had promoted the sale of indulgences that Luther protested as part of a plan to pay back money owed to the pope for the office of Archbishop of Mainz, which included a fee for a dispensation for pluralism, i.e., permission to hold more than one office at a time. Cf. LW

say or think about them; for the pope is above councils, above fathers, above kings, above God, above angels. Let me see you depose him and make the fathers and councils his masters! If you do that, I shall gladly join you and assist you. But as long as that does not happen, what is the use of your talking or writing much about councils and fathers? There is no one to take this matter to heart. If the pope, together with his imperishable lords, cardinals, bishops, etc., is unwilling to participate in the reformation or to submit to the councils and the fathers with us, there is no use for a council, nor can we hope for a reformation from him, because he will knock down everything anyway and bid us to keep silent.

But do they desire that we, together with them, let ourselves be reformed according to the councils and fathers, and thus help the church, even though the pope with his followers would neither do it nor permit it? To this I give a double answer. Either they are hateful, poisonous, and evil, and do this with bad intent; or they are goodhearted and mean well (as far as this is possible for them). Let the former be told to first take themselves by the nose and remove the log from their own eye [Matt. 7:3-5], then, together with pope and cardinals, or without the pope and cardinals, etc., to grow fond of the councils and fathers and hold to them. When that happens we shall instantly be on hand to emulate such a holy example, and be much better than they are. We are not such accursed people (praise and thank God!) that we would let the church perish rather than yield even on major points, as long as they are not against God; on the contrary, if it depends on our knowledge and ability, we are prepared to perish, leaving neither hide nor hair behind, rather than to see the church suffer harm or loss.[34]

But when they themselves pay the fathers and councils no heed and yet would force us to do so, they go too far, and we have to say, "Doctor, cure yourself!" [Luke 4:23], and, as Christ says, "They tie up heavy burdens, hard to bear, and lay them on the shoulders of others; but they themselves are unwilling to lift a finger to move them" [Matt. 23:4]. That leads to nothing, and we have ample reason for refusal, especially since they make such great claims for the sanctity of the fathers and councils, which we do not uphold; nor do they, except with words they speak and write only to flaunt before us. Yet we confess, and must confess, that we are very poor, weak Christians on many points.

31:21; Brecht 1:179; see also Luther's *Letter to Albrecht*, TAL 1:47–56.

30. The first year's income of a church office owed to the pope.

31. A prebend was the portion of revenues from a cathedral or collegiate church granted to a canon, that is, a cleric serving there, as his income. The language of the medieval church focused on the income to be derived from ecclesiastical appointment rather than on the duties to be performed. See Francis Oakley, *The Western Church in the Later Middle Ages* (Ithaca: Cornell University Press, 1979), 25–31.

32. A reference to the papal administration that both lived off of these fees and made it possible for the pope to collect them.

33. Luther seems to exaggerate here, since complaints like this about abuses in the church were common throughout the Middle Ages. See Oakley, *Western Church*, 213–19.

34. Luther notes here a major difference between his reform and that of his opponents. Church abuses were a common target for reformers, and in that case legislation or observing existing legislation became the solution. Thus the councils and fathers were presented as the solution to problems with practice. Because Luther's focus was faith and the gospel, he can say that he is willing to accept such reform, as long as it does not contradict faith and the gospel, but he also does not believe it solves the church's real problems.

First, we have so much to do in our faith, day and night, what with reading, thinking, writing, teaching, exhorting, and comforting both ourselves and others that there is indeed neither time nor space left even to wonder whether there ever were councils or fathers, much less to concern ourselves with such sublime things as tonsures, chasubles, long robes,[35] etc., and with the profound sanctity of these things. If they have risen so far that they have even become angels, and have so much faith that the devil must leave them alone and cannot let an error loose among them, or terrify a timid conscience, we weak Christians have not yet attained this, and fear that we never shall attain it on earth. That is why they should be gracious and merciful with us and not condemn us because we cannot match their holiness yet. If we should leave our work in matters of faith and, weak as we are, dare their great holiness in dress and food, we might forsake our weak holiness and still not attain their high and splendid holiness, thus sitting down between two chairs.[q]

35. A reference to the regulations regarding the appearance of the clergy. The tonsure results from shaving part of the head as a sign of religious humility and was one of the marks of a monk in the Middle Ages. The chasuble was worn to celebrate the Mass and became the sign of a priest. The clergy in general typically wore long robes.

But if they decline to be gracious and merciful with us, we shall have to let them be angels and dance among the flowers in Paradise as those who have long since mastered faith and no longer experience any temptation from devil, flesh, or world in their celestial sanctity. But we must plague ourselves and wallow in mire and filth, as poor abecedarians[36] and beginners, unable to be such great doctors and masters in faith. For if we had as much faith as they imagine they have, we would bear and hold to tonsures, chasubles, councils, and fathers more easily than they do. But this is not so; they bear them easily (for to bear nothing is to bear very easily), meanwhile boasting that we do not want to bear them.[37]

36. Students first learning the alphabet. The original is *fibelisten*. The word *fibel* referred to a primer based on the Bible—*fibel* being the childish pronunciation of the German word *Bibel*.

37. Luther accuses his opponents of paying only lip service to the reform measures they advocate. In 1538, he had commented on a report issued by a committee of cardinals about what needed to be reformed in the church (*Counsel of a Committee of Several Cardinals with Luther's Preface*, LW 34:235–67; WA 50:288–308) and made similar accusations.

Likewise, the Ten Commandments occupy us poor Christians so much that we are unable to attend to other exalted works that they praise as spiritual, conciliar, and patristic. With utmost diligence we urge and discipline both ourselves and our followers to love God above all things and our neighbor as ourselves, to be humble and patient, merciful and kind, chaste and sober, neither covetous nor envious, and whatever else God's commandments enjoin. We should be happy if there were no pride, avarice, usury, envy, drunkenness, gluttony, adultery, or wantonness among our people. But there is so much weakness

q A German proverb that means, roughly, "to fall on one's face."

and imperfection among us that we induce but a few to do these good works. The masses remain unchanged and grow worse day by day. Now figure it out: if we are so unsuccessful in doing these necessary works commanded by God, how can we abandon these and devote ourselves to those sublime, splendid, unnecessary works of which they tell us? If we had done these divine, insignificant, contemptible, or, as they disdainfully call them, "civil" works, then, God willing, we would also begin to do their spiritual, ecclesiastical works having to do with eating meat, dress, certain days, etc.[38]

But it is easy for them because they keep all of God's commandments, love God above all things, are neither avaricious nor usurious, neither adulterers nor whoremongers, neither boozers nor drunkards, neither proud nor envious, etc.;[39] but they perform all these insignificant, good, divine works so easily they are downright idle. Therefore it is only right that they undertake, over and above our "civil" works, stronger and greater works in obedience to the church or the fathers, for they are far too strong to practice such insignificant, good works with us, having outstripped and outdistanced us by far. But according to their profound, great compassion and St. Paul's doctrine, they should nevertheless pity us weak, poor Christians and not condemn or mock us because we, like infants, learn to walk by toddling along holding on to chairs; indeed, we crawl in the mud and cannot skip and dance so nimbly over and around God's commandments as they do—these strong heroes and giants who can tackle greater and sublimer tasks than that of loving God above all things and one's neighbor as oneself, which St. Paul calls the fulfillment of the law in Rom. 13[:10], as Christ also does in Matt. 5[:19].

But if they will not have pity on us, we nevertheless ask for a time of grace until we have carried out God's commandments and the unimportant children's works. After that we will be glad to switch to their sublime, spiritual, knightly, and manly works. For what good would it do to force a child to work and keep pace with a strong man? It wouldn't work—a child is unable to do it. So we poor, weak Christians, who with regard to God's commandments and his insignificant good works totter along the chairs like children and at times can hardly crawl on all fours, indeed, even slide along the ground, and must be held by Christ on leading-strings[40] as a mother or nurse holds a child—

38. "Civil works" refers to basic obedience to the Ten Commandments. Though medieval theologians considered this sufficient for the laity, the works commanded by the church were thought to be far superior—the reason for Luther's ironic treatment of obedience to the commandments here and his reference to them as "children's works" below. Among the superior works commanded by the church, Luther names dress (perhaps a reference to monastic robes), observing certain fast days, and attending church or abstaining from work on certain festivals.

39. Luther's irony is obvious. The 1514 dialog *Julius Excluded from Heaven*, most likely the work of Erasmus, describes Pope Julius II (b. 1443), pope from 1503 to 1513, in precisely these terms. The dialog relates how Saint Peter fails to recognize Julius when he appears at the gates of heaven because, among other things, he is drunk and trying to break the door down with the key to the papal money chest. Such criticism of the pope was common in the years prior to Luther's reform efforts.

40. The long bands that were sown to the clothing of toddlers to keep them close as they learned to walk.

Heralds of Pope Julius II with a blessed sword and hat (sixteenth century).

we simply cannot keep pace with their strong, manly gait and performance, and may God preserve us from it! Therefore we shall save the ecclesiastical and conciliar holiness (as they call it) until we have no more work to do on God's commandments and divine works, and not bear a reformation we cannot bear. May this be a sufficient answer to the former class of people who with bad intentions ask this reformation of us.

To the others, who mean well and hope, albeit vainly, that a fine reformation such as they have in mind might perhaps still be achieved on the basis of the councils and fathers, even despite an unwilling pope's attempt to thwart it, I reply, also with good intent, that I regard this as an impossible undertaking, and indeed do not know how to go about it. I, too, read the fathers, even before I opposed the pope so decisively. I also read them with greater diligence than those who now quote them so defiantly and haughtily against me; for I know that none of them attempted to read a book of Holy Scripture in school, or to use the writings of the fathers[41] as an aid, as I did. Let them take a book of Holy Scripture and seek out the glosses[42] of the fathers; then they will share the experience I had when I worked on the

41. A reference to the theologians and church leaders of the earliest centuries of the church whose writings were considered authoritative throughout the Middle Ages. Luther does not accuse his opponents of not using the fathers at all, but he does indicate that they did not use the writings of the fathers appropriately, that is, as an aid to understanding Scripture itself.

42. A gloss is a comment on a word or phrase in a text placed either in the margin or between the lines of the text itself. Commentaries on Scripture took this form in the Middle Ages and came to be referred to generally as glosses. The substance of a gloss usually came from the writings of the church fathers or other authoritative commentators. The standard set of glosses on the Bible, called the *Ordinary Gloss*, was assembled in the twelfth century.

letter to the Hebrews with St. Chrysostom's glosses, the letter to Titus and the letter to the Galatians with the help of St. Jerome, Genesis with the help of St. Ambrose and St. Augustine, the Psalter with all the writers available, and so on.[43] I have read more than they think, and have worked my way through all the books; this makes them appear impudent indeed who imagine that I did not read the fathers and who want to recommend them to me as something precious, the very thing that I was forced to devaluate twenty years ago when I read the Scriptures.[44]

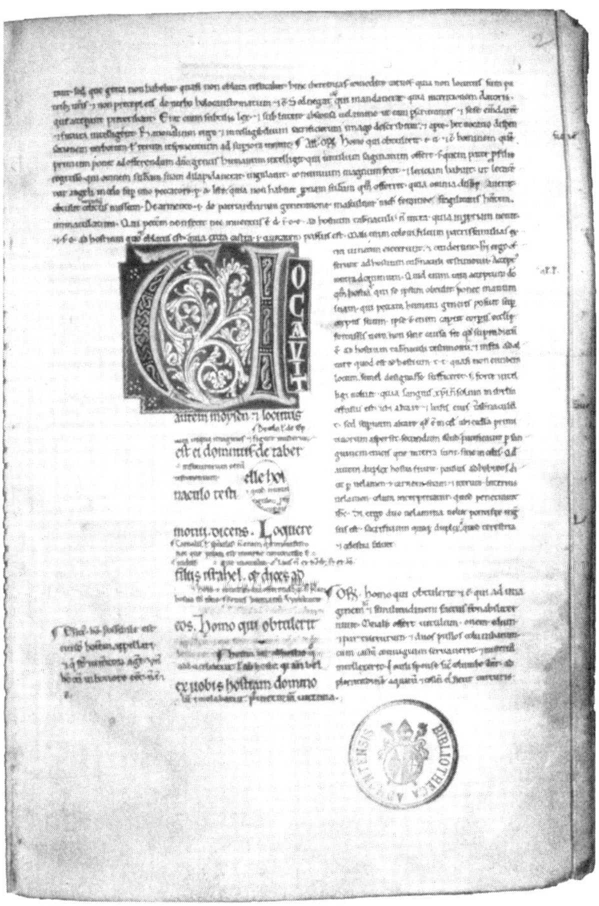

The biblical text in this manuscript from the latter half of the twelfth century is surrounded by the "Ordinary Gloss," explanatory notes by the church fathers and later medieval commentators.

43. Luther refers here to the period between 1513 and 1517 when he was engaged in an intensive study of biblical and patristic literature. See Brecht 1:128–50.

44. Luther approached the fathers and their writings as aids rather than absolute authorities. So, for example, his *Preface to the Latin Writings* of 1545 describes how he first found confirmation in Augustine for his understanding of the word *righteousness*, but then also discovered that Augustine did not speak about justification clearly; LW 34:337.

[Scripture Over Councils]

St. Bernard[45] declares that he learned his wisdom from the trees, such as oaks and pines, which were his teachers; that is, he conceived his ideas from Scripture and pondered them under the trees. He adds that he regards the holy fathers highly, but does not heed all their sayings, explaining why in the following parable: he would rather drink from the spring itself than from the brook, as do all people, who once they have a chance to drink from the spring forget about the brook, unless they use the brook to lead them to the spring. Thus Scripture, too, must remain master and judge,[46] for when we follow the brooks too far, they lead us too far away from the spring, and lose both their taste and nourishment, until they lose themselves in the salty sea, as happened under the papacy.

But enough of that! We want to cite reasons such an undertaking is impossible. First, it is obvious that the councils are not only unequal, but also contradictory. The same is true of the fathers.[47] If we should try to bring them into accord with one another, far greater discord and disputes would ensue than we have at present, and we would never get out of it. Since (in these matters) they are very unlike and often contradictory, we should first have to figure a way to cull out the best and let the rest drop. That would provoke an uproar. The one would say, "If we are going to keep them, then we must keep them in their entirety or not at all." The other would say, "Well, you pick out what you like and leave what you dislike." Who would be the judge here?

Look at the decree with which Gratian[48] had proposed to do this very thing—the book thus becoming known as *Concordantia discordantiarum*—that is, he had wanted to compare the discordant statements of the fathers and the councils, to reconcile the contradictions, and to cull out the best. He succeeded, like a crab walks; he often cast aside the best and kept the worst, and yet he neither compared nor harmonized. As the jurists themselves say, it stinks of ambition and avarice, and a canonist is nothing but an ass.[49] How much worse then would we fare if we tried to harmonize all the words and deeds of fathers and councils! All our labor and trouble would be futile, and the evil would only be aggravated.[r] And I do not wish to become involved in such a

r A German proverb.

45. Bernard of Clairvaux (1090–1153), Benedictine abbot and famed mystic. Luther is probably referring to Bernard's biography as reflected in the standard medieval collection of saints' lives, *The Golden Legend.* "He confessed that whatever he knew about the Scriptures he had learned while meditating and praying in the woods and the fields, and he sometimes said that among his friends he had no teachers except the oaks and beeches." Jacobus de Voragine, *The Golden Legend*, trans. William Granger Ryan, 2 vols. (Princeton: Princeton University Press, 1993), 2:101. Bernard himself expressed similar thoughts in a letter to a friend (Letter 107): "Believe me who have experience, you will find much more labouring amongst the woods than you ever will amongst books. Woods and stones will teach you what you can never hear from any master." *The Letters of St. Bernard of Clairvaux*, trans. Bruno Scott James (Kalamazoo, MI: Cistercian Publications, 1998), 156. The letter does not, however, contain any reference to the analogy of the spring and the brook.

46. A theme Luther turned to often in his writings. Teachings of the church should find their proper basis in Scripture.

47. Peter Abelard (1079–1142), a Scholastic theologian, had addressed the subject of discrepancies in the fathers in his work *Sic et non* ("Yes and No").

dispute because I am well aware that it would be interminable and in the end we would be stuck with a vain, uncertain thing, at the expense of wasted time and labor. These young scribblers[s] are much too untried when they think that whatever they read and imagine must be so, and all the world must worship it, although they neither know the *a b c* of Scripture, nor are they versed in the councils and fathers. They shout and sputter without knowing what they are saying or writing.

Frontispiece from Gratian's *Decretum* (*Decretum Gratiani or Concordia Discordantium Canonum*), twelfth century.

s *Papirklicker*, i.e., "paper-clippers."

48. Gratian composed the text commonly known as the *Decretum* around 1140, and it became the first part of canon law in the Roman church. Gratian himself gave his work the title *Concordia discordantium canonum* ("Harmony of Discordant Canons"). Little else is known about Gratian, who was probably a canon lawyer from Bologna rather than a monk as was traditionally thought. See Anders Winroth, *The Making of Gratian's Decretum* (New York: Cambridge University Press, 2000).

49. Although this particular saying cannot be documented, similar sayings were common in the Middle Ages. For example, "Jurists are bad Christians."

I shall say no more of Gratian. St. Augustine writes to Januarius[50] that the church in his day, three hundred years after the birth of Christ (for in this year 1539 he has been dead for eleven hundred and two years),[51] was already so encumbered on all sides with the ordinances of the bishops that even the Jewish political system was more tolerable. And he continues clearly and plainly with the words, "*Innumerabilibus servilibus oneribus premunt ecclesiam*,"[t] that is, "They oppress the church with innumerable burdens," while the Jews are burdened only by God and not by human ordinances, etc. He also states that Christ desired to have only a few easy ceremonies imposed on his church, namely, baptism and the Sacrament;[52] he mentions no more than these two, as everyone may read. The books are available, so no one can accuse me of inventing this.

But he also weakens this, saying in the same place, "*Hoc genus habet liberas observationes*,"[u] that is, "No one is obligated to keep all of these, but may ignore them without sin." If St. Augustine is not a heretic here, I never will be one. He who takes the statements of many bishops and many churches and throws the whole pile into the fire, pointing solely to baptism and sacrament, makes certain that Christ did not wish to impose any other burdens on the church—if that which is nothing but comfort and grace could be called a burden—when he says, "My yoke is easy, and my burden is light" [Matt. 11:30], that is, my yoke is peace and my burden is joy.

Yet this fine, sensible man does the great, or (as they are called) universal or principal, councils the honor of differentiating them from the other councils and the ordinances of all bishops, saying that one should esteem them, and he writes in the same place that one should reasonably obey the decrees of these great principal councils, since much depends on them; if I may use his own words, *saluberrima autoritas*, that is, it is very useful to regard them as authoritative.[v] But he neither saw any of these great principal councils nor attended any of them, otherwise he would perhaps have written differently, or more, about them. For not more than four great principal councils are famous and

50. Augustine (354–430), bishop of Hippo, whose writings Luther esteemed. He often cites this letter to Januarius, an otherwise unknown notary who was disturbed by the differences among churches in dating the celebration of Easter. *Epistola* 82, MPL 33:221=CSEL 34/II:209ff.; NPNF1 1:315. The letter was also quoted in canon law, for example, *Decreti prima pars*, dist. XII, C. XI. (CIC 1:29–30).

51. Here Luther follows the medieval chronology that recorded Augustine's death year as 436 rather than 430.

52. Luther frequently refers to the Lord's Supper as "the Sacrament."

53. A decretal is an authoritative decision by the pope on a point of doctrine or church law. The canon law reads: "Just as there are four books of the holy Gospels, so there are four councils that ought to be received and venerated." *Decreti prima pars*, dist. XV, C. II (CIC 1:35). The Western church accorded particular authority to the first four ecumenical councils, since the remainder met in the East after the fall of the empire in the West.

t Luther has added *innumerabilibus* and *ecclesiam* to the original text.

u MPL 33:200=CSEL 34/II:160, 9f.; NPNF1 1:300.

v MPL 33:200=CSEL 34/II:159, 18; NPNF1 1:300.

well known in all the books. The Roman bishops compare these to the four Gospels, as they loudly proclaim in their decretals.[53] The first is the Nicene council, held in Nicaea, in Asia, in the fifteenth year of the reign of Constantine the Great,[54] almost thirty-five years before Augustine's birth.[55] The second was held in Constantinople, in the third year of the emperors Gratian and Theodosius I, who ruled jointly.[56] St. Augustine was still a pagan and no Christian at that time, a man approximately twenty-six years old, so he could not concern himself with these matters. He did not live to see the third council held at Ephesus, still less the fourth one at Chalcedon.[57] All of this is reliable; it is based on history and a computation of the years.[58]

[The Pope Takes Over the Councils]

I had to say these things in order to make sure that the meaning of St. Augustine's statement that the great principal councils must be regarded as authoritative by reason of their importance is understood properly; namely, that he was speaking of only the two councils, held at Nicaea and Constantinople, which he had not attended, but about which he later learned from writings.[59] At that time no bishop was superior to any other, for neither the Roman nor the other bishops could ever have brought such councils about if the emperor had not convoked them, as is well evidenced by the particular, or small, councils held now and then in the different countries by the bishops themselves, without a summons from the emperor. I judge, in my foolishness, that the great principal councils derive their name from the fact that the bishops were summoned from all the countries by the monarch, the great chief or universal ruler.[60]

History will have to bear me out, even though all the papists get mad, that if Emperor Constantine had not convoked the first council at Nicaea, the Roman bishop Sylvester[61] would have been obliged to leave it unconvoked. And what could the wretched bishop of Rome do, since the bishops in Asia and Greece were not subject to him? And even if he could have done it without the power of the emperor Constantine, he would not have had it meet in Nicaea, in Asia, so far across the sea, where no one respected his authority (as he well knew and had experienced), but in Italy, near Rome, or somewhere else nearby; and he would have forced the emperor to come there. I say the same about the

54. The year 325. Constantine the Great (c. 280–337) ruled from 306 to 337.

55. Augustine was born in 361 according to medieval chronology.

56. Constantinople was held in 381. Gratian (359–383) ruled from 375 to 383, Theodosius I (347–395) from 379 to 395.

57. Ephesus was held in 431, Chalcedon in 451. Here, in contrast to his earlier statement (see note 51), Luther seems to use the modern dating for Augustine's death (430) in placing it prior to the Council of Ephesus. This is the date he later followed in his *Suppatatio annorum mundi* (see n. 58).

58. Luther's chronological computations are based upon the work of John Carion, a mathematician, who published a chronology of world history with the help of Philip Melanchthon in 1532 in Wittenberg. In 1541 Luther published his own chronology, *Supputatio annorum mundi*, WA 53:22–172. See John Headley, *Luther's View of Church History* (New Haven: Yale University Press, 1963), 109–111.

59. Only these first two councils had met prior to Augustine's death in 430.

60. In *Treatise on the Power and Primacy of the Pope* (BC, 339), Melanchthon exhorted "the most eminent members of the church, the kings and princes, to attend to the church and take care that errors are removed and consciences restored to health."

61. Sylvester I (r. 314–335) was also the supposed recipient of the western empire from Constantine. This purported gift of the western part of the empire to Pope Sylvester by Constantine

other three councils (named above). If the emperors Gratian, Theodosius, Theodosius II, and Marcian[62] had not assembled these three great councils, they would never have been held for the sake of the bishop of Rome or all the other bishops; for the bishops in other countries valued the Roman bishop just as little as the bishops of Mainz, Trier, and Cologne at present value each other in the matter of authority—indeed much less![63]

Yet one sees in the histories that the Roman bishops have from the first sickened, ailed, wheezed, and gasped for sovereignty over all the bishops, but could not achieve it because of the monarchs. For even before the Nicene council they wrote many letters,[64] sometimes to Asia, sometimes to Africa, and so on, demanding that nothing should be publicly decreed without the Roman See. But no one paid any attention to this at the time, and the bishops in Africa, Asia, and Egypt proceeded as though they had not heard it, although they addressed him with many fine words and humbled themselves, without, however, conceding anything. This is what you will find when you read the histories[65] and compare them diligently. But you must pay no heed to their clamor or that of their adulators; rather, keep eyes and mind fixed on the story and the text.

Since the word *council* now enjoyed the profound respect of Christians throughout the world—partly because of the above-mentioned letter of Augustine—and since these fine monarchs or emperors had died, the Roman bishops constantly strove to associate the name "council" with themselves so that all Christendom would have to believe what they said, and so that they themselves might secretly become monarchs with the help of this fine name (I wager that I am here hitting the truth and also their own conscience, if they could have a conscience). And it has come to pass; they have brought it about with their ailing and gasping, so that they have now become Constantine, Gratian, Theodosius, Marcian, and much more than these four monarchs and their four great principal councils. For now the pope's councils mean, "I will it; I command it; my will is the reason for it."[66] But this is not the case in the entire world, nor in all of Christendom; it is the case only in that part of the Roman Empire over which Charles the Great[67] ruled, through whom they attained and accomplished very much, until possessed by all the devils they shamefully murdered, kicked, and in many ways betrayed several emperors—as they still do wherever they can.[68]

is recorded in the *Donation of Constantine*, a medieval forgery. The text made its way into canon law and was used to support papal claims to political power. Part of the *Donation* relates how Constantine gave the pope the imperial regalia to wear. Luther had published a German translation of the *Donation of Constantine* with notes (WA 50:72) in 1537.

62. Theodosius II (408–450); Marcian (450–458). Theodosius II and Marcian ruled over the eastern half of the Roman Empire.

63. The Archbishops of Mainz, Trier, and Cologne also served as electors and were the most important bishops in the empire.

64. This is specifically mentioned in Peter Crabbe's work on the councils (see n. 24, p. 329).

65. The histories used by Luther. See the introduction.

66. *Sic volo, sic iubeo, sit pro ratione voluntas*. A satirical proverb by Juvenal (c. 60–c. 135), a Roman poet. Cf. *Satura* VI, 223, in *Juvenal and Persius*, trans. G. G. Ramsey, Loeb Classical Library (New York: Putman, 1918), 101. Luther refers to the fact that by his day the popes claimed sweeping temporal power in addition to power over the other bishops and the entire church.

67. Charlemagne (768–814). Charlemagne and his predecessors had protected the popes from their enemies. The pope crowned Charlemagne emperor on Christmas day, in 800. Charlemagne's empire, as Luther notes, formed the core of Western Christendom, which accepted the authority of the pope.

A woodcut showing Pope Celestine III (not IV) humiliating Emperor Henry VI. From the 1570 edition of John Foxe's *Actes and Monuments* (Book of Martyrs).

68. A reference to the humiliations of various Holy Roman emperors by the popes. For example, a fresco in the Palazzo Publico in Siena, Italy, shows Emperor Frederick I (c. 1123–1190), as a result of his defeat in 1176, kneeling in submission before Pope Alexander III (r. 1159–81). Similarly, a woodcut in John Foxe's *Actes and Monuments* of 1570 shows Pope Celestine III (r. 1191–98) kicking the crown from the head of Emperor Henry VI (1165–1197). The incident is based on a report of his coronation in 1191. (The woodcut erroneously identifies the pope as "Celestine IV.")

But this is enough for now about St. Augustine's comment on the councils. We also want to show what he thought of the fathers. In his letter to St. Jerome, also quoted by Gratian in dist. IX, he says about them: "I have learned to hold the Scriptures alone inerrant. Therefore I read all the others, as holy and learned as they may be, with the reservation that I regard their teaching true only if they can prove their statements through Scripture or reason."[69] Furthermore, in the same section of the *Decretum* is St. Augustine's statement from the preface to his book *On the Trinity:* "My dear man, do not follow my writing as you do Holy Scripture. Instead, whatever you find in Holy Scripture that you would not have believed before, believe without doubt. But in my writings you should regard nothing as certain that you were uncertain about before, unless I have proved its truth."[w]

69. Jerome (c. 345–420), translator of the Vulgate and renowned church father. The quotation is found in MPL 33:277=CSEL 34/II:354; NPNF1 1:350. Luther is quoting it from canon law, *Decreti prima pars*, dist. IX, C. V. (CIC 1:17). Luther had required proof from Scripture or reason in his answer to Emperor Charles V (1500–1558) at Worms in 1521.

w *Decreti prima pars*, dist. IX, C. III. (CIC 1:17). Quoting *On the Trinity* (*De Trinitate*), III, 2. MPL 42:869=CCSL 10:128, 38–41; NPNF1 3:56.

Many more such statements are found in his other writings; as when he says, "As I read the books of others, so I wish mine read," etc.[x] I shall let the other sayings wait for now; the papists know very well that many similar passages appear here and there in Augustine's writings, and that several of these are contained in the *Decretum*. Yet against their conscience they ignore or suppress these sayings and set the fathers, the councils, indeed, even the bishops of Rome, who by and large were very unlearned men, above all of this. St. Augustine must have felt many a shortcoming in the fathers who preceded him, because he wants to be free, and have all of them, including himself, subjected to the Holy Scriptures. Why should he have needed to disparage his forefathers, saying, ". . . as holy and learned as they may be"? He surely could have said, "Indeed, everything they write I put on a level with Holy Scripture because they are so holy and learned." However, he says no, as he also says in the other letter to St. Jerome, who was furious because St. Augustine disapproved of one point in his commentary on Galatians, "Dear brother" (for he was such a fine, friendly man), "I hope that you do not expect your books to be regarded as equal to those of the apostles and prophets," etc.[70] May a pious and good man never write letters to me like those St. Augustine addressed to St. Jerome, asking me not to regard my books as the equal of those of the apostles and prophets! I would be ashamed to death. But it is this with which we are dealing now, and which St. Augustine dearly observed: the fathers were occasionally very human and had not overcome what is written in the seventh chapter of Romans. Therefore he does not want to trust either his predecessors the holy and learned fathers or himself, and undoubtedly his successors much less, who very likely would be less trustworthy; but instead he wants to have Scripture as master and judge, just as it was related earlier of St. Bernard,[71] that oaks and pines were his masters and that he would rather drink from the spring than from the brook. He would not have spoken like this if he had regarded the books of the fathers the equals of Holy Scripture and had found no flaw in them. Then he would have said instead, "It is the same whether I drink from the Scriptures or from the fathers." He does not do that, but rather lets the brooks flow and drinks from the spring.

x Another portion of the same source, see n. 45, p. 336.

70. MPL 33:277=CSEL 34/II:354; NPNF1 1:350. Cf. Luther's statement: "I would have been quite content to see my books, one and all, remain in obscurity and go by the board." *Preface to the Wittenberg Edition of Luther's German Writings* (1539), LW 34:285.

71. St. Bernard (1090–1153). See also n. 45, p. 336.

What should we do now? If we should take the church back to the teaching and ways of the fathers and the councils, there stands St. Augustine to lead us astray and thwart our plan because under no circumstances does he want reliance placed on the fathers, bishops, councils, as learned and holy as they may be, or on himself. Instead, he directs us to Holy Scripture. Outside of that, so he says, all is uncertain, lost, and in vain. But if we exclude St. Augustine, then it conflicts with our purpose, namely, to have a church according to the teachings of the fathers. For when St. Augustine is eliminated from the ranks of the fathers, the others are not worth much.[72] Moreover, it would be senseless and intolerable not to consider St. Augustine one of the best fathers, since he is revered as the best by all of Christendom, and both schools and churches have preserved his memory above that of all others, as is clearly seen. And yet you force on us the endless trouble and labor of holding up councils and fathers against Scripture and living accordingly. Before that is done we shall all be dead and the Last Day will have long since come!

72. A generally accurate summary of Luther's attitude toward the fathers.

[The First Council at Jerusalem]

Well, we shall set aside St. Augustine, St. Bernard, and all others who write in the same vein, and take up the fathers and councils ourselves to see whether we can make our lives conform to them. But we shall take up the very best ones, lest we draw this out too long, particularly the first two principal councils praised by St. Augustine, namely, those of Nicaea and Constantinople, although he did not attend them, as we said above. Indeed, to play absolutely safe, and so that we cannot fail or worry, we shall take up the very first council of the apostles,[73] held in Jerusalem, of which St. Luke writes in Acts, chapters 15[:1-29] and 16[:4]. It is written there that the apostles boasted that the Holy Spirit had arranged this through them: "*Visum est spiritui sancto et nobis*," etc., "It has seemed good to the Holy Spirit and to us to lay upon you no greater burden than these necessary things: that you abstain from what has been sacrificed to idols and from blood and from what is strangled and from unchastity. If you keep yourselves from these, you will do well" [Acts 15:28-29].

73. This apostolic council took place c. 44 or 45.

There we hear that the Holy Spirit (as the preachers of councils boast)[74] commands that we eat nothing that has been sacrificed to idols, no blood, and nothing that is strangled. Now if

74. That is, those who uphold the authority of councils in general by appealing to the Acts 15 council.

we want to have a church that conforms to this council (as is right, since it is the first and foremost council, and was held by the apostles themselves), we must teach and insist that henceforth no prince, lord, burgher,[75] or peasant eat geese, doe, stag, or pork cooked in blood, and that they also abstain from carp jelly, for there is blood in them, or, as cooks call it, "color." And burghers and peasants must abstain especially from red sausage and blood sausage, for that is not only fluid blood, but also congealed and cooked blood, a very coarse-grained blood. Likewise we are forbidden to eat rabbits and birds, for these are all strangled (according to hunting customs),[76] even if they were only fried, not cooked in blood.

Should we, in obedience to this council, refrain from blood, then we shall let the Jews become our masters in our churches and kitchens; for they have an especially large book on the subject of eating blood,[77] so large that no one could vault over it with a pole. They look for blood so painstakingly that they will not eat meat with any heathen or Christian—even if it is not strangled, but butchered most meticulously (like oxen or calves), drained of blood, and washed—preferring to die. For God's sake, what harried Christians we would become because of that council, just with the two items of eating blood and the meat of strangled animals! Well then, begin, anyone who wants to or can, to bring Christendom into conformity with this council; I shall then be glad to follow. If not, I want to be spared the screams of "Councils! Councils! You neither heed the councils nor the fathers!" Or I will counter with the cry, "You yourselves do not heed the councils or the fathers, since you disdain even the supreme council and the supreme fathers, the apostles. Do you think I should or must heed councils and fathers you yourself do not as much as touch with one finger?" I would only say, as I said to the Sabbatarians,[78] that they should keep their Mosaic law first, and then we would keep it too. But now that they neither keep it nor are able to keep it, it is ridiculous that they expect us to keep it.

If you say it is impossible to carry out the decrees of such a council now because the contrary has spread too far, it is of no help, since we resolved to conform to the councils, and it says here that the Holy Spirit has so commanded it. Against the Holy Spirit no spreading or entrenching counts, and no conscience is safe with such a subterfuge. If we wish to be conciliar, we will have to keep this council above all others. If not, we need not

75. A citizen of a village or town, from the middle to upper class.

76. Rabbits for food would have been taken by snares rather than hunted with dogs. Birds caught in nets or snares would have been strangled.

77. Luther probably read the Babylonian Talmud, which had been available since 1523 in an edition printed by Daniel Bomburg (d. 1549) in Venice. Cf. *The Babylonian Talmud*, trans. I. Epstein, 34 vols. (London, 1935–1948). Examples of the subject are in *Hullin*, ch. 2. (*Hullin* means "mundane things." It is the part of the Babylonian Talmud that deals with the nonsacrificial slaughter and consumption of meat.)

78. The name comes from the word *sabbath*, and was used to refer to either Jews or Christians obeying only Jewish laws. Cf. *Against the Sabbatarians* (1538), LW 47:57–98.

keep any of the other councils either, and thus we are rid of all the councils. For in this council there were no ordinary bishops and fathers (as in the others), but the apostles themselves, assured of the Holy Spirit and the most exalted of the fathers. Furthermore, it is not so impossible for us not to eat blood and strangled animals. How would it be if we had to live solely on grain, cabbages, beets, apples, and all the other fruits of the earth and the trees, as our ancestors did before the Flood, when the eating of meat was not yet permitted?[79] We would still not starve, even though we did not eat meat or fish. How many people have to live today on a diet rare in meat and fish! So the impossibility does not help us at all to strengthen our conscience against the Holy Spirit because we could quite well revert, without harm to body or soul, to a fare not only free of blood or strangled animals, in accordance with the teaching of Moses, but also fishless and meatless, as before the Flood. I am very surprised anyway that the devil did not bring to light among so many quarrelsome spirits of today these beautiful ideas that have so many fine examples from Scripture on their side!

If we were to say that all these things are not only impossible, but also that they have fallen of themselves, either through disuse or nonuse, or, as I am wont to call the canons no longer applicable, dead,[y] it would not stand the test either. I know very well that the pope and his followers look for excuses like this to justify themselves, claiming that the church had the authority to alter such a council of the apostles. Yet they lie, for they cannot produce proof of any church that has done this or ordered any change. Therefore it is not appropriate for the church to alter the ordinances of the Holy Spirit, and it no longer does so.

Besides, these "blind leaders" [Matt. 15:14] do not see that they invite a switch for their own hide with such talk. For if we concede that man has the power to change the Holy Spirit's ordinance and commandment, we shall on the same day swiftly kick the pope with all his encyclicals and bulls, saying, "If the first decree of the apostles is not valid, though we are convinced that it was issued by the Holy Spirit, as they themselves boast, 'it is clear,'[80] how much less valid are the power and the decrees of the pope, since we are nowhere near as certain that the Holy Spirit is with them as he was with the apostles." For we will nevertheless

y *Mortuos.*

79. Gen. 7:11-24. Luther assumed that all animals were prohibited as food before the Flood.

80. *Visum est.* Luther's opponents often summed up their arguments against him by saying, "It is clear, it is clear." The phrase also echoes the language of Acts 15:28: "It seems good to the Holy Spirit and to us."

have to grant the apostles some status too; and if they were not above the popes (as the heretic, Dr. Luther, believes), they should at least be assigned a seat next to the popes. And the popes often were truly vile scoundrels, repeatedly repudiating one another's decrees.[81] As the Holy Spirit cannot contradict himself like this, and as the apostles could not have been such popes or scoundrels, it follows that we have to argue differently. Such rotten obscenities will not do it, unless one wished to say that the church is built upon a reed that the wind blows to and fro, depending on the whim of the pope or of other men. The church must not sway on a reed, but should stand on a rock and be firmly founded—Matt. 7[:25] and 16[:18].

81. Brian Tierney locates the origin of the idea of papal infallibility in just such a situation involving the Franciscans and apostolic poverty. The Franciscans argued for infallibility so that earlier papal pronouncements in their favor would stand. Tierney, *Origins of Papal Infallibility, 1150–1350: A Study on the Concepts of Infallibility, Sovereignty and Tradition in the Middle Ages* (Leiden: E. J. Brill, 1972).

But as we started to say, it fell of itself, with no changes by the church; that is why we don't have to keep it anymore. Well, dear friend, *Wrong*,[z] says the jurist—should one not keep a law or should it become invalid simply because it is no longer observed or because it has fallen into disuse? Then let us enjoy ourselves and disregard all laws! Let a whore say that she is right because the sixth commandment has fallen and is no longer in use among adulterers and adulteresses. Yes, we children of Adam shall, with the devils, convene and decree a council against God. Do you hear, God, all your commandments have fallen and are no longer in use among us human beings and devils, so we should no longer keep them but must oppose them. You must approve this and not damn us, since there is no sin where the law has fallen. So robbers and arsonists may work out their own salvation too, saying, "We no longer owe you princes and lords obedience, but do right in fighting and robbing you; for your law has fallen into disuse among us," etc.

Now advise us here, what should we do? It does not help that the apostolic council has fallen (which is the truth) or that it has been changed by the church (which is a lie). What harm would it do to scratch out the word "Holy Spirit" and attribute the council's work solely to the apostles, without the Holy Spirit—would this help the matter? Is it ridiculous? Well then think of something better! For if the Holy Spirit is not scratched out of the council, one of two things must happen; either both we and the papists must study and obey such a council, or, if it is to be a

z "*Male.*" This might be a pun on the Latin *male* in terms of a German proverb, "*Mal dir was!*" meaning approximately, "Fooled again!"

matter of freedom and not obeyed, then we poor heretics should be spared the screams of "Councils! Councils! Councils!" For as already stated, if this council is not to be kept, then none of the others is to be kept either. Otherwise, they, in return, will have to hear the cry, "Doctor, cure yourself" [Luke 4:23], "Hans, take hold of your own nose!"[a] Let those who scream like that obey the council first, and we shall be glad to follow in their footsteps. If not, it will be found that they do not cry and spew the word "Council! Council!" sincerely, but slap people's snouts with it to treacherously and maliciously terrify poor consciences, and to destroy simple souls.

I am pointing out all this about this council because it was the first and foremost, and so that we might reflect on these matters before we permit the church to live or govern according to the councils. If this council confuses us so much, what would happen if we were to take up all the others? It is true, I admit, that the word "council" is easily spoken, and the sermon "one should keep the councils" is easily preached. But what should be our attitude on the question of reinstating their authority? What about that, dear friend? The pope, with his followers, is clever indeed; he extricates himself easily, and says that he is above all councils and may keep what he will and allow others to keep what he wills. Yes, if the problem can be solved in that way, then let us stop using the word "council" and stop preaching (that the councils should be observed) and, instead, scream, "Pope! Pope!" and, "One must obey the pope's doctrine!" Thus we too will all extricate ourselves easily and become as fine Christians as they are. What does the council matter to us if we cannot or will not keep it, but boast only of the name or the letter?

Or what seems even better to me (since we have thus gotten into this conversation, and must also jest a little in this Carnival season)[82]—since the letters in the word "council" are after all the main concern, not deeds or results—is to make the professional penmen[b] popes, cardinals, bishops, and preachers; for they could write such letters beautifully, large, small, black, red, green, yellow, and in any way desired. Then the church would be nicely governed in accordance with the councils, and there would be

82. *Fastnacht*. In 1539 this day before Ash Wednesday was on 19 February.

a I.e., simply a proverbial way of repeating, "Doctor, cure yourself." Cf. WA 30/III:378.

b *Stulschreiber*.

no need to obey what these councils had decreed; instead, the church would be content with the letters *c-o-u-n-c-i-l, c-o-u-n-c-i-l.* But if the penmen do not please us, then let us take painters, carvers, and printers, who will paint, carve, and print beautiful councils for us. Then the church will be excellently governed! And let us make the painters, carvers, and printers popes, cardinals, and bishops too. Why ask further how to keep the decrees of the council? Letters and pictures are enough!

A penman (*Stulschreiber*) at work (1438). Notice the pen knives on the desk and the bottle glass window. The pen case and ink pot hanging from the hook on the wall could also be worn on the belt.

But think a little further. What if all men were blind and could not see these written, painted, carved, or printed councils? How could the church then be governed through the councils? My advice is to take the choristers in Halberstadt and Magdeburg[83] and, instead of singing the *Quicunque*,[84] let them shout, "*Concilium! Concilium!*" until the church shakes to its rafters! We could hear them, even far across the Elbe,[85] though we were all blind. Then the church would be well governed, and these choristers would promptly be made vain popes, cardinals, and bishops, who could easily govern the church, which would otherwise have become impossible for the most holy fathers in Rome. But I shall

83. The episcopal residences nearest to Wittenberg.

84. The Athanasian Creed. The first words of the creed in Latin are *quicunque vult salvus esse* ("whosoever wishes to be saved"). In the Roman liturgy of Luther's day this creed was to be sung by the choir in the afternoon service on Sundays that were not associated with a particular festival or saint. The creed can be found in BC, 23–25.

85. Magdeburg on the Elbe River was about forty miles from Halberstadt.

say more about this council a little later; it is getting too much for me. I must not forget the Council of Nicaea either, which is the best and the first principal council after that of the apostles.

[The Decrees of the Council of Nicaea]

This council decreed, among other things,[86] that apostate Christians shall be readmitted, for seven years of penance.[c] If they died in the meantime, they were to be absolved and not denied the sacrament; today's council-screamers do not keep this, but transgress it and consign the dying Christians to purgatory, thus giving them more penance. If the pope were to observe this decree—the devil!—what poor beggars he and all the monasteries would become if this mine, treasure-trove, and trade, namely, purgatory, Masses, pilgrimages, endowments, confraternities,[87] indulgences, bulls, etc.,[88] would have to go to ruin. May the devil preserve the pope and all cardinals, bishops, monks, and nuns from having the church ruled according to this council. What would become of them? But since this decree pertains only to me, a man who has until now been agitating against the pope and who can well imagine how they would like to twist the council's words to direct them against me, I shall now drop this subject. I must now deal with matters that affect both parties, to the praise and honor of the council-screamers.

The same council decreed that those who give up warfare for the sake of religion and later go to war again are to spend five years among the catechumens and are then to be admitted to the sacrament after two more years. I am now taking the word "religion"[89] to mean the common Christian faith—but more about that later. In order not to get derailed or interrupted, I shall not argue about such incidental questions as whether the council forbade warfare, or whether it had the power and fight to forbid or condemn war (so long as the soldiers do not otherwise deny the faith, to which the preceding statement refers).[d]

We want rather to investigate whether this article, that no soldier can be saved or be a Christian, had been kept before, or

c Canon XII in Rufinus's version. MPL 21:474; CH, 15.

d The "preceding statement" is Canon XII.

86. Luther could find the decrees of Nicaea in several different versions. Besides the edition of Crabbe (see the introduction and WA 50:531, n. *c*), Luther probably used the text preserved by Rufinus (MPL 21:473–475; CH, 14–16). Luther's citations are not always accurate. On Luther's judgment concerning the Council of Nicaea, see Headley, *Luther's View*, 164–70.

87. *Bruderschafft*. A community of clergymen and laymen committed to works of charity often for the sake of their "merits." See Christopher F. Black, "Confraternities," OER 1:406–8. See also TAL 1:249–55.

88. All these were ways of gaining grace or performing penance and were closely connected to the belief in purgatory. Luther is pointing out that the funding for many church institutions was based on the fear of purgatory engendered among the laity. He had done this, of course, in the indulgence theses. Here he alludes to other examples, such as monastery endowments that paid for Masses for the dead in order to speed their exit from purgatory. Similarly, good works like pilgrimage were undertaken as penance or to gain merit over against time in purgatory. In a similar vein, he referred to priests who relied on endowed Masses for the dead as *Totenfresser*, those who feed on the dead.

89. Canon XIII in Rufinus (MPL 21:474; CH, 15). Luther confuses the number of years: Canon XIII states "thirteen

whether it can be kept on and on as a matter of law.[90] The pope himself and all his followers will have to testify that this article has fallen and can moreover never possibly be re-established, even less than the apostles' decree about blood sausage, black jelly, and the like, of which we spoke earlier. The council does not speak of murderers, robbers, enemies, but *de militia*,[91] that is, "of regular wars," in which a prince, king, or emperor may under his banner take to the field, to whom God commanded us in Rom. 13[:1-7] to be subject and obedient (like St. Maurice[92] and many others), even if they are unbelievers, so long as they do not compel us to fight against God.

Well then, let us govern the church according to this council. First of all, we shall unbuckle the emperor's sword and then command the whole world to keep the peace, allowing no one to wage war or to tolerate it, for war is forbidden on pain of seven years' penance, in the Nicene council. What more do we want! The church is well ruled now; one needs no soldiers; the devil is dead; and all the years since the time of this council have been golden years,[93] indeed, they have been life eternal in profound peace, that is, if the council's statute is legal and enforcible.

But we would have to have unusually good painters here who could portray such churches for us so that we could see them; or if we were blind, we would have to have far greater criers than the choristers of Halberstadt so that we could at least hear it. Perhaps the professional penmen could also write the letters in the word *concilium* because they have more colors available and can make better letters than we poor Christians. And yet, since the work itself is no longer there, we cannot attain salvation through letters, pictures, and shouts. We must speak differently about these things, and leave letters, pictures, and shouts to the papists. As long as we want to be Christians it might behoove us to live according to the councils and not merely to glorify the letters in the word "council."

You may say that the council's decree applies to those Christians who voluntarily run after war for the sake of money,[e] and that one should rightly condemn them. Otherwise, it would be utterly ridiculous for a council to denounce a regular war or obedience to government. For heaven's sake! I am willing to be a senseless fool and an ass, I who certainly also esteem councils

e Cf. Canon XIII. MPL 21:474; CH, 15.

years." Luther could easily have made the error by looking up Canon XII instead of Canon XIII. Moreover, Canon XIII does not contain the term *religion*. The Latin, *religio*, appears only in canon law, which lists the decrees of Nicaea in various sections. Thus Luther might have used the text of Rufinus (MPL 21:474) and that of *Decreti secunda pars, De penitencia*, dist. V, C. IV (CIC 1:1,240–41), where the term appears in C. V. The editors of WA assume that Luther confused the canons in Rufinus and looked up C. V instead of C. IV in canon law. See WA 50:531 n. c.

90. Luther had argued for military service as a legitimate Christian vocation in *Whether Soldiers, Too, Can Be Saved* (1526), LW 46:87–137; TAL 5, forthcoming.

91. *De militia* literally means "on warfare." In the Middle Ages, *militia* could also mean a feudal army like those Luther gives as examples. J. F. Niermeyer, *Mediae Latinitatis Lexicon Minus* (Leiden: E. J. Brill, 1976), 681, No. 9.

92. The commander of an Egyptian legion (Theban) said to have been exterminated under the Roman emperor Maximian (286–305) because it would not participate in the persecutions of Christians; thus, 6,600 died. The story of Maurice and the Theban legion is one of the most famous legends of the Middle Ages. Ironically, Luther knows of Maurice because of his disobedience. Luther's point here, however, is that Maurice had been a soldier and a Christian. Cf. ODCC, 1,066.

93. "Golden" or "jubilee" years were instituted by Pope Boniface VIII (r. 1294–1303) in 1300 for the purpose of granting special penance to pilgrims

very highly. Interpret it as well as you can, and I will be content with it. Only tell me, were you present at the Nicene council when this article was adopted, since you can repeat this interpretation with such certainty? If not, where else did you read this? The article simply says *militia*, "of war"; it says nothing of unjust wars, which did not need to be condemned by councils since they are also thoroughly condemned, according to reason, by all the heathen, who were neither Christians nor councils.[94]

If a king or a prince must fight and defend himself in a just war, he has to take whatever he can get. If, however, mercenaries are to be condemned, how are emperors, kings, and princes going to survive, since there are now only mercenaries available? Tell me, are those lords to fight alone, or are they to weave scarecrows to oppose the foe? Ask the council's advice on whether this could be done! Yes, my dear friend, it is easily said that the council has decreed this, if one looks at the letters like a cow stares at the gate, without reflecting on the implications and on how one should act and comply. And why didn't the popes and bishops later keep this decree themselves—they who have waged so many wars and shed so much blood throughout the world, and still do this unceasingly,[95] meanwhile constantly screaming, "Councils! Councils! Fathers! Fathers!" while reserving the freedom to act contrary to them and culling from them whatever they want us to do?

This 1530 etching by Daniel Hofer depicts a group of mercenary soldiers (*Landsknechte*).

worshiping at the shrines in Rome. Though only every hundredth year was to be a jubilee year, the interval between such years was fixed at fifty in 1343, at thirty-three in 1389, and at twenty-five in 1473.

94. In some ways, the differentiation between "just" and "unjust" wars preceded Christianity, but it developed more fully in the context of Christian attitudes toward war and peace. Though the distinction for Christians had its roots in the thought of Augustine, the Scholastic theologian Thomas Aquinas (1225–1274) was responsible for the fullest and most definitive articulation of the just-war theory. According to Aquinas, for a war to be just it had to be carried out by a legitimate authority, serve a just purpose, and have peace as its ultimate goal. Luther's reference to condemnation of unjust war among non-Christians may be a reference to the Roman law as codified by Emperor Justinian (483–565) [*Corpus iuris civilis*]. This collection of Roman laws included many that predated the Christian emperors, and it addressed the just conduct of war as part of the natural law (*jus naturale*) and the law of nations (*jus gentium*).

95. Luther may have been thinking of the Catholic military league (*Bund*) formed at Nuremberg in 1538 against the Protestant Smalcald League.

See here, Luther, this way you will cast the suspicion of sedition upon the Council of Nicaea. If we were now to teach that the emperor and his soldiers (even though they had a just cause) were condemned, we should rightly be regarded as seditious on the basis of our own writings. I am now (I declare) and must be a good conciliarist; later I shall say more about it and explain myself. Now I repeat that the council cannot be speaking of anything but regular warfare, as it was being conducted at the time throughout the Roman Empire, under the same Emperor Constantine,[96] as well as previously under the heathen. The foot soldiers, called *milites*[97] at the time, were resident citizens then who drew permanent pay, so that whenever the father died or grew too old, his son was compelled to become a soldier in his stead, a custom the Turks still follow today. I am told that the king of France does practically the same thing in Switzerland and gives pay even to children.[98] If this is true, then, it is no lie.[f]

The horsemen, too, were professional and hereditary soldiers and served on salary, being called *equites*.[99] These horsemen were not unlike our noblemen, who must be equipped with mounts and armor, for which they have their fiefs. That the Roman Empire thus always had a certain number both of infantrymen and of cavalrymen receiving permanent pay, etc., I am mentioning to convey a proper understanding of the council, namely, that it cannot have referred to anything but regular warfare, since it had to speak about the Roman soldiery. According to St. Paul's teaching,[g] many Christians were duty-bound to obey orders therein—like St. Maurice[100] with his comrades—also Jovian, Gratian, Valentinian, Theodosius, etc., before they became emperors.[101] But if it was right to serve the pagan emperors in war before baptism, why should it have been wrong to serve Christian emperors in the same way after baptism?

Could it be that *religio* here does not refer to the Christian faith, but to monasticism?[102] Then I would be trapped and would, according to this council, have to crawl back into my cowl, even if I wanted to do something else. Furthermore, I should not be able to find St. Peter in heaven, because he was a fisherman before he became an apostle, and after his apostolic

96. Constantine's reign was a time of almost constant warfare. Just prior to the Council of Nicaea, he had gone to war against his co-ruler and brother-in-law, Licinius (d. 325).

97. The technical term for the Roman infantry. Although there were generations of soldiers among the imperial Praetorian guard, Rome's imperial armies had been secured by conscription and voluntary enlistment ever since Marius (120–70 BCE).

98. It was common practice in the late Middle Ages to hire Swiss citizens as soldiers. The Swiss relied heavily on this mercenary trade for income, and Ulrich Zwingli (1484–1531) bitterly assailed the entire system (LWZ 1:68–69). The pope's Swiss Guard is a modern remnant of this practice.

99. The technical term for the Roman cavalry.

100. See n. 92, p. 350. Maurice, of course, did not obey his emperor. Luther probably means that as a soldier he was prepared to obey lawful orders but not those that contradicted God's command.

101. Jovian (r. 363–364); Gratian was regent of the western half of Constantine's empire; he was preceded by Valentinian I (r. 364–375). Theodosius I, who succeeded Valens (r. 364–378) in the East, united the empire in 394. These rulers all distinguished themselves as military leaders.

102. *Religio* was frequently used this way in the Middle Ages.

f A proverbial German expression, "*Ists war, so sey es nicht erlogen.*" The origin of this proverb is not known.

g Rom. 13:1-7.

office he again plied his trade as a fisherman, although he had left it for Christ's sake.

But even if *religio* now would mean monasticism, the fact remains that neither religious orders nor monasteries or monks existed at that time, although they arose very soon thereafter. St. Anthony and his companions lived about that time; he is called the father of all monks.[103] But at that time a monk was what we today call a recluse or hermit, according to the Greek word *monachos*, and the Latin *solitarius*, that is, a solitary person who lives alone, apart from others, in a forest or wilderness or otherwise alone. I know of no such monks today, nor have there been any like that for more than a thousand years,[104] unless we were to call the poor prisoners in towers and dungeons monks, who unfortunately are true monks, for they sit alone, separated from their fellows. The monks of the papacy are more among people and less alone than anyone else; for what class or vocation in the world is more with and among people and less separated from people than these monks? Unless it be claimed that the monasteries located in the cities and in the country are built neither near nor among people.

But let us forget about grammar, we want to talk about the matter at issue. Does *religio* here mean the monasticism existing at that time? Then why does this council condemn the military, that is, obedience to temporal government, and say that monks who show this obedience cannot be saved? We could still put up with praise of monasticism, but that the regular army is damned, as though St. Anthony could not in good conscience serve the emperor in war, is going too far. Where then would the emperor finally get his soldiers if everybody wanted to become a monk preaching that he was forbidden to serve in war? Tell me, my dear man, how close do you suppose this teaching comes to rebellion, especially if we were to teach it?—particularly since we know that this self-chosen monasticism is not commanded by God, but obedience is commanded.[105] If the monks really wanted to escape from people, they should be honorable and honestly flee, not leave a stench behind them; that is, they should not by their fleeing give other vocations and offices a stench as though these were utterly damned and their own self-chosen monasticism were pure balsam. When a person flees from human society and becomes a monk it sounds as though he were saying, "Shame on you! How these people stink! How accursed is their vocation. I

103. Luther regarded the origin of monasticism as the end of apostolic times and the beginning of postapostolic times. Anthony (d. 356) took up the life of a hermit c. 270.

104. This is correct insofar as the Western tradition followed the communal model of monastic life. Occasionally, however, some monks lived a life of complete seclusion, and the members of the Carthusian Order founded in 1084 in France led solitary lives in their cells under the same roof.

105. Luther's criticism of the monastic life as a self-chosen and humanly created good work is common, as is his insistence that governments have been established by God.

want to be saved and let them go to the devil!" If Christ had fled like this too and had become such a holy monk, who would have died for our sin or atoned for us poor sinners? Do you suppose it would have been the monks with their unsociable and austere mode of life?

True, John the Baptist was also in the wilderness, but he did not withdraw entirely from mankind, for he returned to be among people and preached after he had attained manhood. Christ dwelt (like Moses on Mount Sinai) for forty days in complete solitude among the beasts in the wilderness, and neither ate nor drank. But he too returned to the midst of people. Well then, if we like, let us regard them as hermits and monks. Still, neither condemns the vocation of mercenaries, even though they themselves were not soldiers.[106] On the contrary, John addresses them, saying, "Do not extort money from anyone by threats or false accusation, and be satisfied with your wages" [Luke 3:14]. Christ went to the centurion at Capernaum, who undoubtedly also served for wages, to help his servant. Yet Jesus did not bid him to forsake his vocation, but instead praised his faith above all Israel [Matt. 8:10]. And St. Peter allowed Cornelius of Caesarea to remain a centurion after his baptism, together with his troops, who were there in the pay of the Romans [Acts 10]. How much less, then, should St. Anthony and his monks have cast a stench on this order of God with his new and self-appointed holiness, simple layman that he was, wholly unlearned in the vocation of preacher and administrator in the church. To be sure, I do believe that he was a great man in the sight of God, as were many of his disciples; but his undertaking was offensive and dangerous, though he was preserved in it as the elect are preserved amid sin and other offenses.[107] But the example and teaching of Christ and John is to be praised, not the example of Anthony's existence.

Now whether *religio* refers to faith or to monasticism, it follows from this council that military service, which at that time represented obedience to temporal government, is to be viewed either as disobedience to God or as stinking obedience to humanly chosen monasticism. But the legend of St. Martin[108] indicates that *religio* meant Christian faith; for when he desired to become a Christian, he gave up his hereditary military service, in which his father had been and when his father became too old, had had his son enrolled in his stead—in conformity with the

106. Here Luther calls any soldier who receives pay a mercenary. Usually mercenaries are distinguished from other soldiers not by the fact that they are paid but by their willingness to serve *anyone* who will pay them.

107. This is Luther's usual attitude toward the great monks, including Bernard of Clairvaux, since he rejected the monastic undertaking, at least insofar as it promised salvation as a result of adopting a particular way of life. Yet Luther was also sensitive to historical context and recognized that for many centuries monasticism was practically the only way for pious men and women to express their devotion. Cf. *The Judgment of Martin Luther on Monastic Vows* (1521), LW 44:289–90.

108. Martin of Tours (d. c. 400), one of the most celebrated monks of the West. Luther's source is the legendary account *The Life of St. Martin, Bishop of Tours* (*Vita S. Martini Episcopi Turonensis*), by Sulpicius Severus (c. 340–410), a well-known early chronicler. MPL 20:159–76=CSEL 1:107–137, NPNF2 11:3–17.

law and custom of the Roman Empire. This act was construed as cowardice and flight from the enemy, as though fear had moved him to become a Christian. We can read this in the legends about him. Thus it is apparent that the illusion had already taken root among the people at that time (not without the exhortations of several bishops) that soldiering was an accursed vocation dangerous to the soul, to be avoided by all who would serve God, for St. Martin lived not long after the Council of Nicaea, since he was a soldier under Julian.[109]

109. Julian the Apostate (r. 361–363), so called because he rejected Christianity. He was a nephew of Constantine the Great.

This fresco by Simone Martini (1285–1344) depicts St. Martin of Tours leaving his life as a soldier and renouncing the army.

Now if we wish to obey this council or to reinstate it, we have to emulate St. Anthony and flee into the wilderness and make monks of emperors and kings, or say that they can be neither Christians nor saved, or else proclaim that they live in a dangerous and stinking obedience and do not serve God. But if we choose to disobey this council, then we need obey none, for one is as good as another because the same Holy Spirit rules them all in equal measure. Moreover, we want to have councils in fact and consequences, not painted councils or the mere letters of the word "council." But I cannot escape the suspicion that a fraud was committed and that the dear holy fathers never did set up such an article. Surely they would have spared the emperor Constantine this, he who had liberated them from the tyrants, not with St. Anthony's monkery, but with war and sword. It looks as though the other loose bishops pasted it in or smuggled it into the records later.[110]

The same council likewise decreed that the Roman bishop should, in accordance with an old custom, take charge of the suburbicarian churches,[111] just as the bishop in Alexandria had charge of those in Egypt.[112] I cannot and will not explain the word *suburbicariae* because it is not my word, but it seems to mean the churches located up to that time in Italy around the Roman churches, just as the churches in Egypt were adjacent to the churches in Alexandria. Let whoever wants to interpret it do so, but I still understand it to mean that this council gave the bishop of Rome no dominion over his surrounding churches, but entrusted them to his care; and it did not do it as though it had to be done "by divine right,"[h] but because of an old custom. Custom, however, does not mean *scriptura sancta* or God's word. Furthermore, it took the churches of Egypt (also in keeping with an old custom) away from the bishop of Rome and entrusted them to the bishop of Alexandria. Likewise, it is to be assumed that the churches in Syria were entrusted to the bishop of Antioch or Jerusalem, since they are farther away from Rome than Alexandria or Egypt.[113]

Now if this council is to be valid in our churches and go into effect, we must first condemn the bishop of Rome as a tyrant and burn all his bulls and decretals.[114] There is no bull or decretal in which he does not boast vociferously and menacingly that he is the supreme head and lord of all the churches on earth, to whom everyone on earth must be subject, if they wish to be saved.[115] This is exactly as much as saying, "The Council of Nicaea is false, accursed, and damned for taking from me domination over all things and for making the bishop of Alexandria my peer." Any-

h *Iure divino.*

110. Having concluded that *religio* must mean the Christian faith, Luther finds that none of the possible interpretations save the council from having decreed against the teaching of the New Testament that government and the military are legitimate vocations for Christians. He is left to wonder whether this canon is authentic. The acts of the Council of Nicaea, as of the ancient councils in general, had been handed down in various forms, into some of which forgeries had been inserted; there was no authentic text available in Luther's day. Today's modern texts have been established by methods of literary criticism of the kind Luther here employs. For an account of the history of these texts, see NPNF2 14, XVI–XXI.

111. The dioceses nearest Rome headed by cardinal bishops. The term *suburbicarius* in Roman public law refers to the districts adjacent to Rome. By Luther's day, the term embraced all the provinces of Italy. Cf. *Treatise on the Power and Primacy of the Pope*, in BC, 332 and note.

112. Cf. Canon VI. MPL 21:473; CH, 14.

113. Luther points out that not all churches were placed under Roman jurisdiction. In fact, many were explicitly placed under the jurisdiction of other bishops. This undermined the traditional papal claim to a universal jurisdiction.

114. A bull is a papal decree named for the lead seal (*bulla*) affixed to the document announcing it. A decretal is an authoritative decision by the pope on a point of doctrine or church law. Some decretals became part of canon law.

115. This is a reference to the bull *Unam sanctam*, issued in 1302 by Pope

way, the Turk and the sultan long ago so interpreted and invalidated this article by destroying Alexandria[116] that neither we nor the pope need concern ourselves with it. Thus we learn that the articles of the councils are not all to be kept forever, like articles of faith.

The council likewise decreed that those who emasculate themselves because of the great and unbearable lust of their flesh shall not be admitted to the clergy or to any other office in the church.[i] Furthermore, it decreed that the bishops are to have no women about them or living with them, except mother, sister, aunts (that is, a father's or mother's sister), or other near relative.[117] Here I do not understand the Holy Spirit in this council at all. If those who emasculate themselves because of unbearable passion are not qualified for ecclesiastical office, and those who have a wife or take a wife to ward off such lust, according to St. Paul's suggestion in 1 Cor. 7[:2] are not qualified either, what will be the outcome? Should a bishop or a preacher be stuck in this unbearable passion, and be forbidden to rescue himself from this perilous state by either marriage or emasculation? Why should it be necessary to command a man who has a wife not to have any other women about him, which is, of course, unseemly even for laymen and husbands? Thus the matter of mother, sister, or aunt would take care of itself; if the bishop had a wife, there would be no need for a prohibition. Or does the Holy Spirit have nothing better to do in the councils than to bind and burden his servants with impossible, dangerous, and unnecessary laws?

The histories relate that St. Paphnutius, that excellent man, opposed the bishops in this council who proposed to forbid marriage even to those who had married before their ordination and who wanted to forbid them to discharge their conjugal duties with their own wives. He, however, advised against it, saying that discharging one's conjugal duties was also a mark of chastity.[118] It is recorded that he won out, but these two decrees sound as though the bishops had proceeded to forbid wives anyway, for there were also many incompetent, false bishops in the pious crowd and holy council, such as the Arians[119] and their gang (history clearly shows that), who perhaps contributed to this too.[120] But more of that later. Let us stop talking about the councils for a while and take a look at the fathers—although

i Cf. Canon I. MPL 21:473; CH, 14.

Boniface VIII, whose language Luther here imitates. *Readings in the Early and Medieval Church*, ed. Ray C. Petry, *A History of Christianity*, vol. 1 (Englewood Cliffs, NJ: Prentice Hall, 1962), 505–6.

116. Alexandria was destroyed by an Arab Muslim army in 641. Luther, as usual, uses the word *Turk* loosely for the Muslim world.

117. Canon III. MPL 21:473; CH, 14. Luther misinterprets this canon. It does not refer to clerical marriage, but to the presence of women who were neither wives nor relatives. They were called "associates" (*subintroductae*) because they lived in spiritual marriage. See ODCC, 1563.

118. *Historia tripartita*, II, 14. MPL 69:933=CSEL 71:107–8; NPNF2 2:256. Little is known of Paphnutius (d. 360) save that he was an Egyptian bishop and a member of the Nicene council, and that he opposed the prohibition of clerical marriage.

119. The Arians derived their name from Arius (d. 336), a presbyter in Alexandria condemned for his Christology. He asserted that Christ was not of the same substance with the Father. The language of the Nicene Creed ("of the same substance with the Father") was meant to refute his teaching.

120. Ernst Schäfer points out that there were only seventeen Arian bishops out of more than 250 (the numbers vary) gathered at Nicaea. Schäfer concludes from this that Luther's suggestion has more to do with his aversion to monasticism and celibacy and his desire not to implicate the orthodox fathers in this legislation at Nicaea than with historical fact. Schäfer, *Luther als*

St. Augustine confuses us because he wants none of them (as was said above) believed, but wants them all held captive and subject to Scripture. We shall nevertheless take a look at them too.

St. Cyprian,[121] one of the earliest fathers, since he lived long before the Council of Nicaea at the time of the martyrs, and was himself one of the outstanding martyrs, taught and staunchly insisted that those who were baptized by heretics had to be rebaptized.[j] He stuck to this until his martyrdom, although he was strongly admonished by other bishops, and St. Cornelius, bishop of Rome,[122] who was martyred at the same time, refused to support him. St. Augustine afterward had great difficulty in excusing him, and finally had to resort to saying that such an error had been washed away by his blood, shed for the love of Christ. Thus spoke St. Augustine, condemning St. Cyprian's doctrine of rebaptism, which has since been condemned again and again (and rightfully so). But we are well content with St. Cyprian, for in him Christ comforts us poor sinners mightily, showing that his great saints are after all still human—like St. Cyprian, this excellent man and dear martyr, who blundered in more serious matters, about which we lack the time to speak now.

But what will we do with the fathers who transmitted this doctrine to St. Cyprian? In the *Ecclesiastical History*, Book VII, pages 1 and 2,[123] you may read what that fine Bishop Dionysius of Alexandria[124] wrote about it to Bishop Sixtus of Rome,[125] saying that this policy had been followed by other great and prominent bishops before the bishops in Africa followed it, that it had been decided upon by the Council of Iconium,[126] and that therefore such important facts should be considered before condemning the practice. But in the Council of Nicaea is clearly written the article that one should rebaptize the heretics, the Paulianists or Photinians.[127] And if this article offends St. Augustine in his *On Heresies*[128] because he had plagued himself for a long time with the Anabaptist Donatists,[129] he nevertheless extricates himself for the sake of the Nicene council's decree by saying it must be assumed that the Photinians did not employ the baptismal formula, which other heretics did. If only one could believe it, since there is no proof. For the Photinians did not have, nor did

j See for example his letter to Jubaianus, MPL 3:1153–74=CSEL 3II:778–99; ANF 5:379–86.

Kirchenhistoriker (Gütersloh: C. Bertelsmann, 1897), 299 n. 4.

121. Cyprian (b. c. 210) became bishop of Carthage in 248 and was put to death in 258 because of his faith.

122. Cornelius I (r. 251–253).

123. *Historia ecclesiastica* 7, 4–6. MPG 20:642=GCS 9/II:639; NPNF2 1:294.

124. Dionysius (d. c. 264) was involved in many controversies over rebaptizing schismatics.

125. Sixtus II (r. 257–258).

126. Held in Phrygia, an ancient country of Asia Minor, c. 235.

127. Cf. Canon XIX. MPL 21:475=GCS 9/II:968, 19-22; NPNF2 14:40. This canon is not genuine, but is a later addition to the acts of the council. The Paulianists and Photinians are the followers of the heretical bishops Paul of Samosata (d. 269) and Photinus of Sirmium (d. 376). Both rejected Nicene Christology. Cf. ODCC, 1250, 1292.

128. MPL 42:34=CCSL 46:306; for an English translation see *The De Haeresibus of Saint Augustine: A Translation with an Introduction and Commentary*, trans. Liguori G. Müller (Washington, DC: Catholic University of America Press, 1956), 85.

129. A schismatic group named after Donatus (d. c. 355), under whose leadership they established their own church in Carthage. This schism still existed when Augustine became bishop of Hippo, and he exerted tremendous energy against the Donatists. They also

they create, a gospel different from that possessed by the whole church; it thus seems more plausible to assume that they used the common formula, for heretics always like to boast of possessing Scripture. Thus Anabaptism tries to justify itself against St. Augustine and us all, because the Nicene council and other earlier councils and fathers agreed with Cyprian.[130]

Furthermore, the *Constitutions of the Holy Apostles*,[131] the ordinances of the apostles, have now been printed in many editions so that the church may again be properly governed. Among them is this canon: "One should count the heretics' sacrament and baptism as nothing, but should instead rebaptize them."[132] And it can readily be inferred that if the apostles ordained this, it was transmitted (as Dionysius states)[133] by the earlier fathers and councils to St. Cyprian, and by him to the Council of Nicaea, for Cyprian preceded this council. If the apostles actually decreed this, then St. Cyprian is right, and St. Augustine with all of Christendom and with us who share his view are defeated. For who would teach contrary to the apostles? If the apostles did not decree this, then one should drown and hang all such authors and teachers for circulating, printing, and advertising such books under the apostles' names. They also deserve not to be believed with regard to other books or utterances of theirs henceforth, because they are constantly producing books that they themselves do not believe but nevertheless foist on us, with the letters *c-o-u-n-c-i-l, f-a-t-h-e-r-s*. If it is only a matter of letters—and their one concern is to fool us with them—a chorister in Halberstadt could cry them out far better than they.

[Testing the Councils and Fathers]

Now if St. Cyprian had such apostles' rules on his side, as well as the Nicene and other councils, how shall we compare the fathers? The apostles and St. Cyprian demand rebaptism; St. Augustine and the whole later church declare this to be wrong. Who is going to preach to Christians in the meantime until this dispute is adjusted and settled? Yes, it is fun to fool around with councils and fathers if one juggles with the letters or constantly postpones the council, as has now been done for twenty years, and does not think of what happens meanwhile to the souls who must be fed with conscientious teaching, as Christ says, "Tend my sheep" [John 21:16].

became known as Anabaptists (from the Greek "rebaptizers") because they rebaptized converts from the Roman church. Even though the imperial authorities made the Donatists liable to punishment as heretics in 405, an imperial conference of 411 failed to settle the schism. The Donatist church still existed when the Vandals conquered northern Africa in the years after 430. Cf. W. H. C. Frend, *The Donatist Church: A Movement of Protest in Roman North Africa* (Oxford: Oxford University Press, 1985).

130. Luther interprets these early heresies in light of his own battle against Anabaptism and assumes here that the Council of Nicaea settled the question of Anabaptism in favor of Cyprian's position. Yet the council simply acknowledged the Roman practice (with the exception of Paulianism).

131. *Canones apostolorum*. A collection of alleged decrees of synods, claiming apostolic origin. The collection stems from the late fourth or early fifth century and is closely related to the *Apostolic Constitution*. MPG 1:555–91; ANF 7:387–505. In 1524 a new edition was published in Paris by Jacques Merlin. Cf. WA 50:540, n. *d*. Luther could find them in Crabbe's work on the councils.

132. Canon XXXVIII.

133. Bishop of Alexandria, see n. 124, p. 358.

I excuse St. Cyprian first to the extent that he was not an Anabaptist such as ours are today, for he held that the heretics had no sacrament at all and that therefore they had to be baptized like other heathen. He was honestly mistaken in believing that he was not rebaptizing, but baptizing an unbaptized heathen; for he knows and holds not a rebaptism, but only one single baptism. But our Anabaptists admit that our baptism and that of the papacy is a true baptism, but since it is administered or received by unworthy people, it is no baptism at all. St. Cyprian would never have concurred in this, much less practiced it.[k]

I have a high regard for St. Cyprian's person and faith, and that is why I said the foregoing in his behalf; for doctrine is subject to the words of St. Paul, "Test everything," etc. [1 Thess. 5:21]. But we are not interested here in what I may say, but in bringing the fathers into agreement with one another, so that we may become certain of what and how to preach to the poor Christians. Here the apostles and Cyprian are at odds with St. Augustine and the church over baptism. If we obey St. Augustine, then we have to condemn the apostles with their rules and the Nicene council with the earlier fathers and councils, including St. Cyprian. And on the other hand, if St. Cyprian and the apostles are right, then St. Augustine and the church are wrong. Meanwhile, who is going to preach and baptize until we reach an agreement? The papists boastfully quote the canons of the apostles and the councils together with the fathers against us. Some of these, for example, are incorporated in Gratian's canon law.[134] Now if the dam should break and some of these canons and councils were found to be heretical, as the one about rebaptism is, who could prevent the flood from bursting forth irresistibly and proclaiming with a roar, "You lie in everything you write, say, print, vomit, and shout. Not a word of yours can be believed, even though you quote councils, fathers, and apostles"?

134. Several distinctions in canon law, for example, *Decreti prima pars*, dist. XXXV, C. I, dist. LXXXVIII, C. III (CIC 1:131, 307), quote the apostolic canons.

However, while we both thus cull from the councils and the fathers, they what they like, and we what we like, and cannot reach an agreement—because the fathers themselves disagree as much as do the councils—who, dear reader, is going to preach to the poor souls who know nothing of such culling and quarreling? Is that tending the sheep of Christ, when we ourselves do not know whether what we are feeding them is grass or poison,

k Cf. Luther's Concerning Rebaptism, pp. 275–316 in this volume.

hay or dung? And are they to dangle and hang until it is settled and the council arrives at a decision?[135] Oh, how poorly Christ would have provided for the church if this is how things have to go on! No, there must be another way than proving things by means of councils and fathers, or there could have been no church since the days of the apostles—which is impossible, for it is written, "I believe in one holy, Christian church,"[l] and, "I am with you always, to the end of the age" [Matt. 28:20]. These words must be the truth, even if all the fathers and councils were wrong! The Man must be called "I am the truth" [John 14:6]; fathers and councils should on the other hand be called "Everyone is a liar" [Rom. 3:4] whenever they contradict each other.

I am not saying this for the sake of our people, to whom I will later show what councils, fathers, and church are, if they do not know it (from which God has protected them!), but I am saying this for the sake of the screamers who think that we have never read the fathers and the councils. Although I have not read all the councils—I do not intend to read them all; this would be too great a waste of time since I did read the four principal councils very thoroughly, much more so than any of them did I am sure—I shall also make bold to say that I hold, after the four principal councils, all the others to be of lesser value, even though I would regard several (understand me rightly), I say several, as equally good. I am more familiar with the fathers, I hope, than these screamers who tear out of context whatever they choose and discard the rest if it annoys them. Therefore we must approach the matter differently.[136]

But why should we get excited? If we wish to harmonize the sayings of the fathers let us consult the master of the *Sentences*,[137] who is diligent beyond measure in this task and was way ahead of us, for he too felt this anguish over the disagreement of the fathers and wanted to remedy these things. In my opinion, he did it better than we would, and you will find in no one council, nor in all of the councils, and in none of the fathers, as much as in the book *Sentences*. The councils and fathers deal with several points of Christian doctrine, but none of them deals with them all as this man does; at least, he deals with most of them. And yet, about the real articles, such as faith and justification,[138] he speaks too undecidedly and weakly, even though he gives high

l The Nicene Creed.

135. Many in the Roman hierarchy expected Christians to forgo reforming activities until a council could meet. For example, this was the position represented by the representative of the bishop of Constance in his debate with Zwingli in 1523.

136. Luther insisted on interpreting texts in their context, including the historical context. In this, he shows the influence of Renaissance humanism.

137. Peter Lombard (c. 1095/1100–1160). His *Four Books of Sentences* (*Sententiarum libri quatuor*) was a collation of the sayings of the church fathers and was the standard theological textbook of the Middle Ages. To receive a doctorate in theology, late medieval candidates had to lecture on Lombard's *Sentences*. The marginal notes that Luther made in his own copy of the *Sentences* are printed in WA 9:28–94.

138. Neither faith nor justification on its own was a significant topic in pre-Reformation dogmatics.

enough praise to the grace of God.[139] Also, as was said above, we might as well have let Gratian do the work of harmonizing the councils for us, something to which he gave much effort, but in which he is not as pure as the master of *Sentences*, for he concedes too much to the Roman bishop, and applies everything to him. Otherwise, he would perhaps have done a better job in harmonizing the councils than we could do now.

If any one wishes further proof that the dear, holy fathers were human beings, he should read the booklet of Dr. Pomer, our pastor,[140] on the four chapters to the Corinthians. He will indeed have to learn from this that St. Augustine was right when he wrote, "My dear man, do not," etc., as was quoted above,[m] namely, that he will believe none of the fathers unless he has Scripture on his side. Dear God, if the Christian faith depended on men or were based on the words of men, what need would there be then for Holy Scripture? Or why should God have given it? Then let us shove it under the bench and, in its stead, lay only the fathers and councils on the desk.[141] Or if the fathers were not

Portrait of Johannes Bugenhagen (1537) by Lucas Cranach the Elder (1472–1553).

m See p. 341.

139. Lombard asserted in *Sentences*, book 1, distinction 17, that the love by which humans are saved was a gift of God and resulted entirely from the internal working of the Holy Spirit and not from any human effort. Luther agreed with this in his 1509/10 commentary on the *Sentences*. See Steven Ozment, *The Age of Reform, 1250–1550* (New Haven: Yale University Press, 1980).

140. Johannes Bugenhagen (1485–1528) was also known as Pomeranus from the place of his birth (Pommern), and Dr. Pomer was Luther's nickname for him. Bugenhagen had been pastor at the town church in Wittenberg since 1523 and thus Luther's own pastor. His *Commentary on Four Chapters of the First Epistle to the Corinthians* (*Ioannis Bugenhagii Pomerani commentarius, in quatuor capita prioris epistolae ad Corinthios*) was published in 1530. For the text, see Georg Geisenhof, ed., *Bibliotheca Bugenhagia* (Leipzig, 1908), No. 266.

141. The medieval church had assumed that Scripture, councils, and fathers were all authoritative, though in varying degrees. In his debate with Johann Eck (1486–1543) at Leipzig in 1519, Luther had publicly rejected any authority in the church other than Scripture.

human beings, how then shall we human beings attain salvation? If they were human they would also at times have thought, spoken, and acted just as we think, speak, and act, but afterward they would speak (like us) the beloved prayer, "Forgive us our trespasses," etc., especially since they did not have the same promise of the Holy Spirit that the apostles had, but had to be the apostles' disciples.

If the Holy Spirit had been so foolish as to expect or trust that the councils or fathers would do everything well and make no mistakes there would have been no need for him to warn the church against them, saying in 1 Cor. 4 [3:12] that one should examine all things and be on one's guard wherever men build with straw, hay, and wood on the foundation. In that way he foretold, not privately and feebly, but openly and mightily, that in the holy church there would be those who build with wood, straw, and hay, namely, teachers who would remain on the foundation and be saved, even though harmed by fire, which cannot be said of the heretics, for they lay a different foundation. The others, however, remain on the foundation, that is, in the faith in Christ, attain salvation, and are called God's saints, even though they too have hay, straw, and wood which must be consumed by the fire of Holy Scripture, albeit without injuring their salvation. As St. Augustine says of himself, "*Errare potero, hereticus non ero*," "I may err, but I shall not become a heretic."[142] Reason: heretics not only err, but do not want to be corrected; they defend their error as though it were right, and fight against the recognized truth and their own conscience.

St. Paul says of them in Titus 3[:10-11], "After a first and second admonition, have nothing more to do with anyone who causes divisions, since you know that such a person is perverted and sinful, being *autokatakritos*,"[n] that is, the person willfully and wittingly wishes to remain in error and be condemned. But St. Augustine willingly confesses his error, and lets it be pointed out to him, so he cannot be a heretic even though he has erred. All the other saints do the same and gladly consign their hay, straw, and wood to the fire so that they may remain on the foundation of salvation, as we did too, and still do.[143]

142. This quotation was used frequently in theological literature of the medieval and Reformation eras but without a citation. It cannot be found in Augustine's works.

143. Luther had always expressed a willingness to have his teaching judged by Scripture. In his famous answer at the Diet of Worms, he said he would continue to teach as he had unless he was convinced by Scripture or clear reason.

n "Self-condemned"; see n. *o*, p. 327.

Therefore, because it cannot be otherwise with the fathers (I am speaking of the holy and good ones)—when they build without Scripture, that is, without gold, silver, and precious stones, then they will build with wood, straw, or hay—we must, according to St. Paul's verdict, know how to differentiate between gold and wood, between silver and straw, between precious stones and hay; and we must not be compelled by those obnoxious screamers to believe that wood and silver are the same, that silver and straw are the same, and that emeralds and hay are the same. Or we ought to ask them (if this could be done) first to become so clever themselves as to take wood for gold, straw for silver, and hay for pearls. Otherwise, they should justly spare us, and not expect such foolishness or childishness of us.

And all of us should also take note of this miracle of the Holy Spirit, namely, that the Spirit wanted to give the world all the books of Holy Scripture, of both the Old and the New Testaments, solely through Abraham's people and seed, and that we Gentiles did not compose a single book, just as prophets and apostles were not chosen from among the Gentiles, as St. Paul says in Rom. 3[:2], the Jews enjoy a great advantage, since they "are entrusted with the oracles of God," and according to Ps. 147[:19], "He declares his word to Jacob, his statutes and ordinances to Israel." And Christ himself says in John 4[:22], "We worship what we know, for salvation is from the Jews," and Rom. 9[:4-5] says, "To them belong the covenants, the giving of the law, the patriarchs, and Christ."[144]

Therefore we Gentiles must not value the writings of our fathers as highly as Holy Scripture, but as worth a little less; for they are the children and heirs, while we are the guests and strangers who have come to the children's table by grace and without any promise. We should, indeed, humbly thank God and, like the Gentile woman, have no higher wish than to be the little dogs that gather the crumbs falling from their masters' table [Matt. 15:27]. As it is, we proceed arrogantly and put our fathers and ourselves on a level with the apostles, never thinking that God could break us to pieces more easily, since he did not spare the natural branches and Abraham's seed or heirs for their unbelief, Rom. 11[:21]. And yet, that accursed abomination in Rome usurps the authority to change Scripture arbitrarily solely to suit himself, without any regard for apostles and prophets.[145] That is why St. Augustine is right when he writes to St. Jerome

144. Luke might be considered an exception to this statement, since early tradition held that he was a physician from Antioch in Syria. Modern scholars are divided over whether he was a Gentile or a Hellenic Jew. In Luther's day, Luke was often identified as one of the seventy disciples Jesus sent out (Luke 10) or as the unnamed disciple who, along with Cleopas, met Jesus on the road to Emmaus (Luke 24). *Reformation Commentary on Scripture, New Testament III: Luke*, ed. Beth Kreitzer (Downers Grove, IL: IVP Academic, 2015), 3, 481–83.

145. In the Middle Ages, popes had claimed that they alone could interpret

(as related above), "Dear brother, I hope that you do not expect your books to be regarded as equal to those of the apostles and prophets. God forbid that you should desire such a thing."[o]

Moreover, there is neither a council nor a father in which one could find, or from whom one could learn, the whole of Christian doctrine. For example, the Nicene council deals only with the doctrine that Christ is truly God; the one at Constantinople, that the Holy Spirit is God; the one at Ephesus, that Christ is not two but one person; the one at Chalcedon, that Christ has not one but two natures, the human and the divine. These are the four great principal councils; they deal with no more than these four articles, as we shall hear. But this is still not the complete teaching of the Christian faith. St. Cyprian deals with how one must suffer and die in a firm faith; he rebaptizes heretics; and he also rebukes bad morals and women.[p] St. Hilary defends the Nicene council,[146] states that Christ is true God, and deals with a few psalms. St. Jerome extols virginity and the hermits.[q] St. Chrysostom teaches prayer, fasting, almsgiving, patience, etc.,[147] and St. Ambrose deals with many subjects;[148] but St. Augustine treats the greatest number, and that is why the master of the *Sentences*[r] has taken most of his material from him.

In summary, put them all together, both fathers and councils, and you still will not be able to cull from them all the teachings of the Christian faith, even if you culled forever. If it had not been for Holy Scripture, the church, had it depended on the councils and fathers, would not have lasted long. And in proof of this: where do the fathers and councils get what they teach or deal with? Do you think that they first invented it in their own day, or that the Holy Spirit always inspired them with something new? How was the church preserved prior to these councils and fathers? Or were there no Christians before councils and fathers

Scripture authoritatively. This claim was one of "three walls" Luther set out to demolish in his *To the Christian Nobility of the German Nation*, LW 44:133–36; TAL 1:369–466.

146. Hilary of Poitiers (c. 315–367) was famous for his defense of the Nicene council in his *Against the Emperor Constantius* (*Contra Constantium Imperatorem*). MPL 10:577–606=CSEL 65:41–177.

147. John of Constantinople (c. 354–407), known since the sixth century as Chrysostom ("gold mouth") because of his preaching. See, for example, his *Six Books on the Priesthood*. MPG 26:623–692=*De sacerdotio of St. John Chrysostom*, ed. J. Arbuthnot Nairn, Cambridge Patristic Texts (Cambridge: University Press, 1906); NPNF1 9:33–83.

148. Ambrose (c. 340–397) was bishop of Milan. His writings are in MPL 15–17; CSEL 32; NPNF2 10.

o See n. 70, p. 342.

p See, for example, *Exhortation to Martyrdom, Addressed to Fortunatus* (MPL 4:678–702=CSEL 3/I:315–47; ANF 5:496–506), and *On the Dress of Virgins* (MPL 4:451–478=CSEL 3/I:183–205; ANF 5:430–36).

q In *Epistola 22 Ad Eustochium*. MPL 22:394–425=CSEL 54:143–211; NPNF2 6:22–41.

r Lombard, see n. 137, p. 361.

came up? That is why we must speak differently about the councils and fathers and look not at the letters but at the meaning. May that suffice for the first part of this book, so that we can catch our breath too.

Part II

[The History of the Four Principal Councils]

First, concerning the councils, for the letters *c-o-u-n-c-i-l* afford us stupid people endless difficulty, even more than *f-a-t-h-e-r-s* and *c-h-u-r-c-h*. Yet I do not wish to set myself up as judge or master in this matter; I only wish to express my ideas. Grace and luck is wished to anyone who can do better. Amen.

I shall take to heart what St. Hilary says in *On the Trinity: "ex causis dicendis summenda est intelligentia dictorum*,"[s] that is, "He who wants to understand what is said must see why or for what reason it was spoken." In the same manner, actions are best understood by understanding that which motivates them.[t] Natural reason also teaches this. I shall illustrate it to make it simpler: if one peasant brings suit against another, saying, "Dear judge, this man calls me a rogue and a rascal," these words and letters, by themselves, convey the idea that the plaintiff has suffered a great wrong, and that they are false and sheer lies. But if the defendant appears and gives reasons for such words, saying, "Dear judge, he is a rascal and a rogue for he was flogged out of the city of N.[u] for his rascality, and he was saved from hanging only through the great efforts and pleading of pious people, and now he wants to do violence to me in my own home," the judge will understand these letters differently than he had before—as daily experience in government shows. For before one learns the

s Cf. *On the Trinity* IX, 2. MPL 10:282=CCSL 62A:373, 33–35; NPNF1 9:156. Luther was apparently quoting from memory since his quotation differs from the text: "*Cum dictorum intelligentia, aut ex praepositis aut ex consequentibus expectatur.*"

t Luther switches into Latin here: *Sic ex causis agendi cognoscuntur acta*.

u The abbreviation *N.* stands for the Latin *nomen*, indicating where a proper name would be inserted in a formula.

reason and the motive for what a man says, it is only letters, the shouts of choristers, or the songs of nuns.[149]

Likewise, Christ says to Peter, "Whatever you bind on earth shall be bound in heaven, and whatever you loose on earth shall be loosed in heaven" [Matt. 16:19]. The pope takes the letters, rides into Never Never Land[150] with them, and interprets them as, "Whatever I do in heaven and on earth is right. I have the keys to bind and to loose everything and all." And if wishes were horses, beggars would ride![v] But if one looks at the sense, one finds that Christ talks about binding and loosing sin, because these are keys[151] to the kingdom of heaven, into which no one can enter unless his sins are forgiven, and from which no one is excluded except him around whom they have been tied because of his impenitent life. Thus these words have nothing to do with St. Peter's power, but apply to the needs of despondent or proud sinners. But the pope converts these keys into two skeleton keys to all the kings' crowns and treasures, to the purse strings, the life, the honor, and the goods of the entire world.[152] For he, like a fool, looks at the letters and pays no heed to the sense.

There are many passages in Holy Scripture that are contradictory according to the letters; but when that which motivates them is pointed out, everything is all right. I should think that all jurists and medical men find a great deal of this in their books too, as I said earlier about the judge. And what is the entire being of humanity other than sheer antilogies and contradictions, until one hears the facts? That is why my antilogists[153] are admirable, fine, pious sows and asses, who collect my antilogies and discard that which motivates them, indeed, even diligently obscure them; just as though I, too, could not point out antilogies in their books, which cannot even be reconciled by any reason! But enough of this, for they do not deserve that many words.

[The Council of Nicaea: Constantine and Arius]

We shall now take up the Council of Nicaea, which was undertaken for the following reasons: the praiseworthy Emperor Constantine had become a Christian and had given the Christians

v The original says literally, "Indeed, if we had eaten beets, etc."

149. Here Luther reflects a criticism of medieval scholarship that was common in his day, namely, that interpretation of texts was done without regard to the historical or literary context.

150. *Schlauraffenland*, from a German fairy tale.

151. The authority of priests and bishops to forgive or retain sins was called the office of the keys, because of Jesus' words to the disciple Peter in Matt. 16:19: "I will give you the keys of the kingdom of heaven, and whatever you bind on earth will be bound in heaven, and whatever you loose on earth will be loosed in heaven."

152. Popes had often used excommunication for political purposes, thus turning the keys of confession and absolution into keys to the money chests of rulers and cities.

153. A reference to opponents like Johann Eck or Sylvester Prierias (c. 1456–1523) who had written treatises against Luther pointing out what they considered his errors and inconsistencies.

In this painting representing the ecumenical council of Nicaea in 325, Emperor Constantine sits in the middle, enthroned, while the condemned Arius is shown crouching at the bottom of the icon. Icon from the Mégalo Metéoron Monastery in Greece.

peace from tyrants and persecutors.[w] He was so filled with strong, earnest faith and sincerity that he warred even against his brother-in-law Licinius,[154] to whom he had given his sister Constantia in marriage, and whom he had made co-emperor, and pushed him out of the empire because he would not stop shamefully persecuting Christians, even after several warnings. Now when the good emperor had established this peace for the Christians and done everything for their good, promoting the church in every way he could, all was secure, so he planned a war outside his empire, against the Persians. Into such a fair and peaceful paradise and into such happy days did the old serpent come and arouse Arius, a priest in Alexandria, against his bishop. He wanted to bring up something new against the old faith, and because he coveted fame, he assailed his bishop's doctrine, declaring that Christ was not God. Many priests and great and learned bishops rallied about him, and the malady grew rapidly in many lands, until Arius dared to boast that he was a martyr, having to suffer for the truth's sake at the hands of his bishop Alexander,[155] who did not let him get away with these things and wrote terrible letters against him to all the lands.

When this came to the ears of the good emperor, he acted like a very wise prince; he wanted to douse the flames before the fire grew any bigger. He wrote a letter to both bishop Alexander and priest Arius, admonishing them so kindly and so earnestly that it could not have been better written. He explained to them with what difficulty he had effected peace for the Christians in the empire and if they should now war among themselves it would be a great irrita-

154. Licinius ruled the eastern half of the Roman Empire from 314 to 324.

155. Alexander, bishop of Alexandria (c. 313–328), who excommunicated Arius.

w Eusebius, *Ecclesiastical History*, IX, 10. MPG 20:830–38=GCS 9/II:838–49; NPNF2 1:332–33. The subsequent account is based on *Historia tripartita*, beginning in I, 12. MPL 69:901=CSEL 71:43–46; NPNF2 2:251–53.

tion to the heathen who would perhaps fall from the faith again (which then did happen and he himself complained), and he would thus be hindered from marching against the Persians. To sum up, it was a humble, Christian letter, written by this great emperor to these two men. To me it seems much too humble, for I know my own rough pen so that I could not have drawn such a humble missive from my inkwell, especially if I had been emperor, and an emperor like that!

But the letter did not help. Arius had now gained a large following, and wanted to butt his head against his bishop. The pious emperor did not give up either. He sent a personal ambassador, an excellent, world-renowned bishop named Hosius of Cordova, from Spain,[156] to the two in Alexandria, and throughout Egypt, to settle the dispute. This did not help either, and meanwhile the fire kept spreading as though a forest burned. Then the good emperor Constantine made his final move and collected the best and most renowned bishops in every land, ordered that they be brought to Nicaea on the imperial asses, horses, and mules, and asked them to find a satisfactory solution to the matter. Many fine bishops and fathers really did come, especially the famous Jacob of Nisibis and Paphnutius of Ptolemais,[157] bishops who had suffered severe persecution under Licinius and who had performed miracles. But there were also several Arian bishops among them, like mouse-droppings in the pepper.[158]

The emperor was now in good spirits, and hoped for the good ending of the matter; he honored them all. Then several of them came along and handed the emperor a bill of complaint for what one bishop had against the other, and asked for the emperor's judgment. He declined to have anything to do with them, for he was not interested in the bishops' squabbles, but wanted to have this article about Christ judged, and he had not convoked the council for the sake of their bickering. But since they persisted, he bade them to bring him all the bills, and then he cast them, unread, into the fire. However, he sent them away with the kind words that he could not be their judge, they whom God had set as judges over him; and he exhorted them to deal with the main issue.[x] Now then! That is my idea of a wise, gentle, and patient

156. Hosius of Cordova (257–c. 357) was Constantine's ecclesiastical adviser.

157. Jacob was a celebrated opponent of Arianism (d. 338); Nisibis is in Mesopotamia. Paphnutius is also known as Paphnutius of Thebes. See n. 118, p. 357.

158. A German proverb meaning that you have to look carefully to tell the difference between the good and the bad.

x Here Luther used, besides the *Historia tripartita*, II, 2 (MPL 69:922–23=CSEL 71:85–87), Rufinus's translation of Eusebius's *Ecclesiastical History*, I, 2 (MPL 21:468).

prince. Someone else would have been so irritated by these bishops that he would have knocked the cask to pieces.[y] And yet he did express his opinion clearly when he burned their complaints, without any regard for their episcopal dignity, thus reproving them for their childish conduct because they had been summoned for a far more important purpose.

Now when the council met, he sat down among the bishops, on a chair lower than theirs. The bishop of Rome, Sylvester, was not present, but (as some say) he had sent two priests.[159] After the bishop of Antioch, Eustathius[160] (who chaired this council), had thanked and praised the emperor for his kindness, Arius's doctrine was publicly read (for it appears that Arius himself was not present, being neither a bishop nor a delegate);[161] it stated that Christ was not God, but was created and made by God, as the histories record at length. At this the holy fathers and bishops arose from their seats in indignation, tore the document to pieces, and declared it was not true; and so Arius was openly condemned by the furious council, so deeply did it hurt the fathers and so unbearable was it for them to hear this blasphemy of Arius. All the bishops signed this condemnation, the Arian bishops too, albeit hypocritically, as the future showed, except two bishops from Egypt who did not sign. So the emperor dissolved the council on the same day, and he himself, and the council too, sent out a written report of this event throughout the world.[162] And the emperor Constantine, very happy that the matter was settled and disposed of, treated the bishops very kindly, especially those who had been persecuted.

This explains why the council met and what they had to do, namely, to preserve this ancient article of faith that Christ is true God against the new cleverness of Arius, who, on the basis of reason, wanted to falsify this article, indeed, to change it and condemn it; because of this he was himself condemned. The council did not invent this doctrine or establish it as something new as though it had not previously existed in the churches, but rather defended it against the new heresy of Arius. This was demonstrated by the fact that the fathers became upset and tore up the document, thus confessing that since the days of the apostles

159. *Historia tripartita*, II, 1. MPL 69:920=CSEL 71:82, 8; NPNF2 2:253. In the *Tripartita*, Julius (r. 337–352), not Sylvester (r. 314–335), is mentioned as bishop of Rome. On the basis of Crabbe's *Concilia omnia*, Luther named Sylvester. Later scholarship confirmed Luther's historical judgment.

160. Eustathius (b. c. 270) was bishop of Antioch from c. 324 to c. 330.

161. A peculiar error by Luther. Both the *Historia tripartita*, II, 5 (MPL 69:924=CSEL 71:89, 1–3; NPNF2 3:43), and Rufinus, I, 5 (MPL 21:472=GCS 9/II:964, 22–23), record that Arius was present.

162. The two who did not sign were Secundus of Ptolemais and Theonas of Marmarica. *Historia tripartita*, II, 15, 16. MPL 69:934–35=CSEL 71:108–111; NPNF2 2:14, 16. For Constantine's report see *Historia tripartita*, II, 12. MPL 69:931–32=CSEL 71:102–6; NPNF2 2:12–13.

y *Das fas in einen hauffen gestossen*, an intensification of the German proverb, "*Dem fas den boden ausstossen*." The meaning is that Constantine could have destroyed the entire undertaking at this point had he not been patient with the bishops.

they had learned and taught differently in their churches. Otherwise, what would have happened to the Christians who for over three hundred years prior to this council, ever since the days of the apostles, had believed in and worshiped the name of Jesus in prayer as true God, who had died in this faith, and had suffered cruel persecution because of it?

I have to point this out in passing, for the pope's hypocrites have lapsed into such gross folly that they think that councils have the power and the right to set up new articles of faith and to alter the old ones. That is not true, and we Christians have to tear up documents like this too. No council ever did it or can do it; the articles of faith must not grow on earth through the councils, as from a new, secret inspiration, but must be issued from heaven through the Holy Spirit and revealed openly; otherwise, as we shall hear later, they are not articles of faith. Thus the Council of Nicaea (as was said) did not invent this doctrine or establish it as something new, namely, that Christ is God; rather, it was done by the Holy Spirit, who came openly from heaven to the apostles on the day of Pentecost, and through Scripture glorified Christ as true God, as he had promised the apostles. It remained unchanged since the days of the apostles until this council, and so on until our own day—it will remain until the end of the world, as he says, "And remember, I am with you always, to the end of the age" [Matt. 28:20].

If we had nothing with which to defend this article except this council, we would be in a bad way. Then I myself would not believe the council either, but say, "They were human beings." But St. John, St. Paul, St. Peter, and the other apostles are reliable and offer us a firm foundation and defense; for it was revealed to them and through the Holy Spirit given to them openly from heaven. The churches prior to this council derived it from them and this council has it from them too. For before the council, when Arius first began, as well as in the council and after the council, they defended themselves vigorously with Scripture, especially with St. John's Gospel, and disputed sharply, as the books of Athanasius[163] and Hilary testify. The *Historia tripartita* also says in Book V, chapter 29, "At Nicaea the faith was grounded on the writings of the apostles."[z] Otherwise, if there

z "*Hanc solam fidem, quae Nicaeae apostolorum auctoritate fundata est.*" MPL 69:1007=CSEL 71:258, 42–44; NPNF2 3:83.

163. Athanasius (c. 296–373), bishop of Alexandria and the most vigorous defender of Nicene theology. As a result of this defense, he was strongly opposed by the Arian party. He wrote a series of theological works against Arianism but also at times resorted to violence and intimidation against his opponents. Under his direction, the Council of Alexandria (362) worked to reconcile the Semi-Arian party with orthodoxy by clearing up misconceptions about the term *homoousios*. He was deposed and exiled (335–336) under Emperor Constantine but recalled when Constantine died in 337. Athanasius was driven from his see and exiled several more times during the reigns of the Arian emperor Constantius II (r. 317–361, the pagan emperor Julian (r. 361–363), and even the generally tolerant emperor Valentinian I (r. 364–375).

were no Holy Scripture of the prophets and apostles, the mere words of the council would be meaningless, and its decisions would accomplish nothing. Therefore this article on the deity of Christ was the chief business of this council; indeed, it was the whole council, for that is why it was called and (as I said before) why it was adjourned on the same day on which it was adopted.

But on another day, when the emperor Constantine is not reported to have been present, they met again and dealt with other matters pertaining to the temporal, external rule of the church; among these were undoubtedly also the papers Constantine had previously thrown into the fire when he refused to judge. That is why they had to meet alone to settle these things without the emperor. Most of this was sheer clerical squabbling: there were not to be two bishops in one city; no bishop of a small church was to covet a larger one; clerics or servants of a church were not to leave their own church to wander aimlessly about from one church to another; no one was to consecrate the people of another bishop without his knowledge or consent; no bishop was to accept a person who had been expelled by another bishop; the bishop of Jerusalem should retain his ancient prerogative of preeminence before others; and more of such silly prattle.[a] Who could regard such things as articles of faith? And what can one preach about these things to the people in the church? What does all this have to do with the church or the people—unless one wanted to learn from this, as from a history book, that at this time there were everywhere in the church self-willed, base, disorderly bishops, priests, clerics, and people who were more concerned with honor, power, and wealth than with God or his kingdom, and who in this way had to be held in check!

It is easy to figure out that Constantine did not summon the council for these matters; otherwise, he probably would have done it before Arius ushered in this misery. Why should he have bothered about how these things would be kept? The bishops themselves, each in his own diocese, had to govern his own church and had done so before, as the articles themselves report. Moreover, it would have been a sin and a shame to call such a great council into session for such trivial matters, since

a Luther's source here is Rufinus I, 6. MPL 21:473–75=GCS 9/II:966–68. Luther lists the following canons of Nicaea: X, XVI, XVII, XVIII, V, VIII. On the difference in numbering, see NPNF2 14:43.

God-given reason is quite sufficient to regulate these external matters, and the Holy Spirit, whose mission is to reveal Christ and not to dabble in such matters as are subject to reason, is not needed for this—unless, of course, one would call every act of pious Christians, even their eating and drinking, the work of the Holy Spirit. But the Holy Spirit must have better things to do for the sake of doctrine than these works that are subject to reason.

Not all who were present at this council were pious men; not all were Paphnutiuses, Jacobs, and Eustathiuses, etc. One can count seventeen Arian bishops who were prominent men, although they had to bow and scrape before the others. The history of Theodoret[164] reports that there were twenty articles; Rufinus speaks of twenty-three. Now I cannot say whether the Arians or others afterward added to or subtracted from this number, or whether they substituted others (for the article which St. Paphnutius is said to have had adopted, concerning the wives of priests, is not among them).[b] But I do know well that nearly all of them have long been dead, buried in the books and fallen into decay, never able to rise again, as Constantine indicated and foretold by his act of throwing them into the fire and burning them. They are not kept and cannot be kept. They were hay, straw, and wood (as St. Paul puts it)[c] built on the ground; that is why fire consumed them in time, just as other transitory things disappear. But if they had been articles of faith or commandments of God they would have survived, like the article concerning the divinity of Christ.

164. Theodoret was bishop of Cyprus from 423 to 457. Although Luther did not read Theodoret's account in his *Ecclesiatical History*, Luther found it quoted in the *Historia tripartita* (II, 10–30), which usually quotes its sources. MPL 69:927=CSEL 71:96, 71–72.

[The Council of Nicaea: Debate over the Date of Easter]

However, one ember from these wooden articles has kept on glowing, namely, the one about the date of Easter.[d] We do not observe this article quite correctly either (as the mathematicians and astronomers point out to us) because the equinox in our time is far different than in that time, and our Easter is often cel-

b See n. 118, p. 357.

c 1 Cor. 3:12.

d Rufinus, I, 5 (MPL 21:475) and *Historia tripartita*, II, 12 (MPL 69:931–32=CSEL 71:102–6; NPNF2 2:13); IX, 38 (MPL 69:1153–56=CSEL 71:557–64; NPNF2 2:130–34).

ebrated too late in the year.[165] Long ago, shortly after the days of the apostles, the quarrel about the date of Easter broke out; and over this trifling and unnecessary matter the bishops accused one another of heresy and excommunicated one another, which was a sin and a shame. Several advocated observing it on the same day as the Jews, according to the law of Moses; others, lest they be regarded as Jewish, wanted to observe it on the following Sunday.[166] The bishop of Rome, Victor,[167] who also became a martyr, excommunicated all the bishops and churches in Asia approximately one hundred and eighty years before this council for not adhering to the same Easter date as he did. So early did the Roman bishops make a grab for majesty and power! But Irenaeus,[168] bishop of Lyons, in France, who had known Polycarp,[169] a disciple of St. John the Evangelist, reprimanded him and settled the quarrel so that Victor had to leave the churches in peace.

That is why Constantine also had to take up this matter and help to settle it in the council. He decreed that the same Easter date should be observed throughout the world; read the *Tripartita*, Book IX, chapter 38.[e] I suppose that the present again calls for a reform and correction of the calendar in order to assign Easter its proper place. But no one should undertake that except the exalted majesties, emperors and kings, who would have to unanimously and simultaneously issue an order to all the world saying when Easter is henceforth to be celebrated. Otherwise, if one country were to start without the others, and worldly events, such as markets, fairs, and other business, were governed by the present date, the people of the country would appear at the markets of another country at the wrong time, which would result in wild disorder and confusion in everything. It would be very nice, and easy to do, if the high majesties would want to do it, since all the preparatory work has been done by the astronomers[170] and all that is needed is a decree or command. In the meantime we hold to the flickering ember from the Nicene council that Easter is to be kept on a Sunday; meanwhile the date may wobble back and forth, for they are called "movable festivals."[f] I call them wobbling festivals[g] since the Easter day, with its associated festi-

e MPL 69:1153-56=CSEL 71:557-64; NPNF2 2:130-34.

f *Festa mobilia.*

g *Schückelfest.*

165. Luther is aware of the difference between the Julian calendar (adopted in 46 BCE) and the solar year. By 325 CE the equinox had moved from 25 March to 21 March, the date on which Easter was celebrated. Until the introduction of the Gregorian calendar the equinox was moving forward at the rate of one day in 129 years. Pope Gregory XIII (r. 1572–1585) omitted ten days (5 to 14 October) in 1582 and introduced the leap year to balance the Christian calendar with the solar year. The Greek church did not accept the Gregorian calendar, and thus its calendar differs from the Gregorian calendar by thirteen days. For an account of the chronological calculations in the history of the Christian calendar, see ODCC, 266–67; on the history of the date of Easter see Bonnie Blackburn and Leofranc Holford-Strevens, *The Oxford Companion to the Year* (Oxford: Oxford University Press, 1999), 791–800.

166. This quarrel took place in 190–191 between the churches of Asia Minor, favoring the Jewish date (the 17th of Nisan), and Rome, advocating the Sunday following.

167. Victor was bishop from 189 to 198.

168. An ancient church father, Irenaeus (c. 130–c. 200) was bishop of Lyons. He is most famous for his opposition to the teachings of Gnosticism, which was a serious threat to the church of his day.

169. Polycarp, bishop of Smyrna, died as a martyr in 155.

170. Pierre d'Ailly and Nicholas of Cusa (1401–1464) had suggested striking a few days from the Julian calendar. Pope Sixtus IV (r. 1471–1484) then asked the astronomer Regiomontanus (1436–1476) to undertake a calendar reform

vals, changes every year, coming early in one year, late in another, and not on a certain date like the other festivals.

This wobbling of the festivals is due to the fact that the ancient fathers (as was said) in the very beginning wanted to have Easter at the time established by Moses, namely, in the full moon of March, nearest the equinox; and yet they were unwilling to Judaize entirely, or to keep Easter with the Jews on the day of the full moon, so as Christians they dropped the law of Moses and took the Sunday after the March full moon. Thus it happened last year, 1538, that the Jews observed their Easter on the Saturday after Invocavit—as our church calls it—that is, about five weeks before we observed our Easter.[171] Now the Jews laugh about that and ridicule us Christians, saying that we do not keep Easter right and that we do not even know how to keep it right, thus hardening their unbelief. This then irritates our people, and they would gladly see the calendar corrected by the exalted majesties, for without their cooperation this is impossible to do and still less advisable.

In my opinion this experience with Easter is nicely described by Christ in Matt. 9[:16-17], "No one sews a piece of unshrunk cloth on an old cloak, for the patch pulls away from the cloak, and a worse tear is made. Neither is new wine put into old wineskins; otherwise, the skins burst, and the wine is spilled, and the skins are destroyed." They want to retain a part of the old law of Moses, namely, to pay heed to the full moon of March—that is the old garment. Then (as Christians delivered from the law of Moses by Christ) they do not wish to be subject to that same day of the full moon, but, instead want to take the following Sunday—that is the new patch on the old garment. That is why the everlasting squabble and the constant wobbling have to date caused much mischief in the church, and it will have to, until the end of the world, with books appearing without measure or end on this subject. Christ has permitted this to go on for a special reason, as he always proves his strength in weakness and teaches us to recognize our own weakness.

How much better it would have been if they had let Moses' law regarding Easter die altogether and had retained nothing of the old garment.[172] For Christ, to whom this law applied, has annulled it completely, killed it, and buried it forever through his passion and resurrection. He rent the veil of the temple and subsequently broke up and destroyed Jerusalem with its priesthood,

that was completed and went into effect under Pope Gregory XIII in 1582.

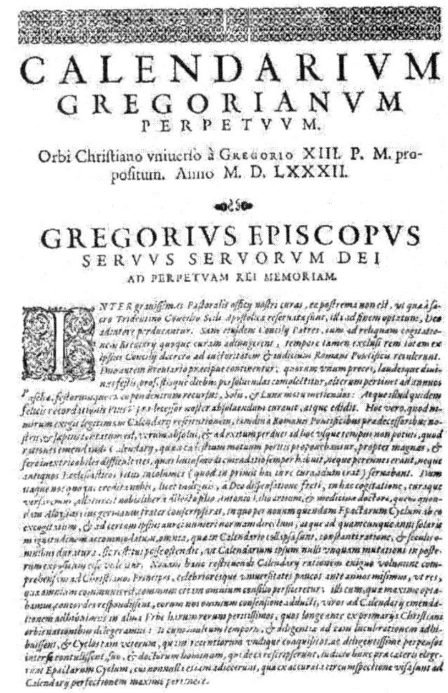
CALENDARIVM GREGORIANVM PERPETVVM.

Orbi Christiano vniuerso à GREGORIO XIII. P. M. propositum. Anno M. D. LXXXII.

GREGORIVS EPISCOPVS SERVVS SERVORVM DEI AD PERPETVAM REI MEMORIAM.

The first page of the papal bull *Inter gravissimas*, by which Pope Gregory XIII introduced his calendar in 1582.

171. In 1538 Easter was celebrated on 21 April. The Saturday after Invocavit Sunday, the first Sunday in Lent, was 16 March.

172. Luther had already addressed the question of whether or not the Old Testament law was binding on Christians. He concluded that it was not, but that the church retained the Ten Commandments as the best expression of natural law. *How Christians Should Regard Moses* (1525), LW 35:155–74; WA 16:363–93; TAL 2:127–52.

principality, law, and everything. They should instead have reckoned and noted the days of the passion, the burial, and the resurrection by the course of the sun and set a fixed date for these, as they did with Christmas, New Year's, the day of the Magi,[173] Candlemas,[174] the Annunciation of Mary, the Feast of St. John, and other festivals, which they call fixed, not wobbling festivals. Then one would know every year for certain when the day of Easter and its associated festivals must come, without such great difficulty and disputation.

173. Epiphany, 6 January.

174. The Purification of Mary (or the Presentation of Our Lord), 2 February.

Well, you say, Sunday should be held in reverence for the sake of Christ's resurrection—it is therefore called *dies Dominica*[h]—and Easter is assigned to that day, since Christ rose on the day after the Sabbath (which we now call Saturday). This is certainly an argument that moved them, but since *dies Dominica* does not mean Sunday, but the Lord's day, why shouldn't any day on which Easter had fallen be called *dies Dominica*, the Lord's day? Is not Christmas also *dies Dominica*, the Lord's day, that is, the day on which the Lord's special event, his birth, is celebrated, which does not fall on a Sunday every year? Yet it is still called Christ's day,[i] that is, the Lord's day, even if it falls on a Friday, because it has a fixed letter[175] in the calendar calculated by the course of the sun. Just so could Easter have a fixed letter in the calendar, whether it came on Friday or Wednesday, as happens with Christmas. That way we would be well rid of the law of Moses with its full moon of March, just as no one asks today whether the moon is full or not at Christmas, but we adhere to the days as calculated by the sun's course and ignore the moon.

175. In the calendar of Luther's time, as well as in ancient Christian calendars, each day was signified by a letter, enabling them to be used as perpetual calendars. The letters from *a* to *g* signified each day of the week. The correspondence between days and letters depended on the year.

One might argue that since the equinox (as the astronomers point out) is movable, and the years in the calendar move too slowly and so do not keep pace with it, and the more years go by the worse it is, after a while the equinox would move further and further from a fixed Easter day, as it would also move further and further from the day of St. Philip and St. James, and from other festivals. What does it matter to us Christians? Even if our Easter should coincide with the day of St. Philip and St. James[176] (which, I hope, will not happen before the end of the world) and move still further, we still celebrate Easter daily with our proclamation of Christ and our faith in him. It is enough to

176. In the Middle Ages, the festival of Saints Philip and James was celebrated on 1 May.

h "The Lord's day."

i *Christag.*

The labors of the months depicted by various artists in this medieval calendar from *Très Riches Heures du Duc de Berry* (c. 1412–1416).

celebrate Easter once annually on a special day as an obvious, public, and perceptible reminder, not only because it affords an opportunity to discuss more thoroughly the history of the resurrection before the common people, but also because it represents a definite season according to which people may arrange their various business affairs, such as the seasons of St. Michael, St. Martin, St. Catherine, St. John, SS. Peter and Paul, etc.[177]

177. Agricultural activities, markets, fairs, and the like were all tied to the church's calendar. Luther was given the name Martin because he was baptized on St. Martin's Day, 11 November.

But this has been neglected from the very beginning; we cannot make any changes because the fathers did not initiate a change. The old garment with its great tear has stayed on and on, and now it may as well stay until the Last Day, which is imminent anyhow. Since the old garment has endured being patched and torn for approximately fourteen hundred years, it may as well let itself be patched and torn for another hundred years; for I hope that everything will soon come to an end.[178] And if the Easters have wobbled back and forth for about fourteen hundred years now, they may as well continue to wobble for the short time still remaining, since no one will do anything about it anyway, and those who would like to do something cannot.

178. Luther's view is based upon the idea that the world would last for six thousand years, of which only a few were left at his time. He seems to have arrived at the number 1,400 on the basis of his estimate for the beginning of the Easter controversies c. 190 until 1539.

I am entering into this lengthy and needless chatter solely for the purpose of expressing my opinion, in case several sects[j] in the course of time dare arbitrarily to move the Easter festival to another date than that which we now observe. And I believe if the Anabaptists had been sufficiently versed in astronomy to understand these things, they would have rushed in headlong, and (as is characteristic of the sect) introduced something entirely new and observed Easter on a different day than the whole world. But since they were unlearned in the sciences, the devil was unable to employ them as that kind of instrument or tool. Therefore, I advise that one let Easter come as it now comes, and keep it as it is kept now, and let the old garment be patched and torn (as was said); and let Easter wobble back and forth until the Last Day, or until the monarchs, in view of these facts, unanimously and simultaneously change it.

For this is not going to kill us,[k] nor will St. Peter's ship[179] suffer distress because of it, since it is neither heresy nor sin (though

179. The ship is an ancient image of the church.

j *Rotten*, a term Luther used frequently to designate the Anabaptists and other opponents of his position. For a survey of the various religious movements opposing the major reformers see George H. Williams, "Radical Reformation," OER 3:375–84.

k A German expression, literally, "It doesn't break our leg."

the ancient fathers in their ignorance regarded it as such and dubbed one another heretics and excommunicated one another over it), but only an error or solecism in astronomy, which serves temporal government rather than the church. If the Jews mock us, as though we were doing it out of ignorance, then we, in turn, mock them far more because they adhere so rigidly and vainly to their Easter, and do not know that Christ fulfilled, annulled, and destroyed all that fifteen hundred years ago. For we do it willingly, knowingly, not out of ignorance. We would know quite well how to keep Easter according to the law of Moses—far better than they know it. But we will not and must not do it, for we have the Lord over Moses and over all things, who says, "The Son of Man is lord of the sabbath" [Matt. 12:8]. How much more is he the Lord over Easter and Pentecost, which, in the law of Moses, are less than the sabbath, which is on the tables of Moses,[180] while Easter and Pentecost are outside the tables of Moses? Furthermore, we have St. Paul, who flatly forbids anyone to be bound to holidays, feasts, and anniversaries of Moses, Gal. 4[:10] and Col. 2[:16].

We therefore have and must have the power and the freedom to observe Easter when we choose; and even if we made Friday into Sunday, or vice versa, it would still be right, as long as it were done unanimously by the rulers and the Christians (as I said before). Moses is dead and buried by Christ, and days or seasons are not to be lords over Christians, but rather Christians are lords over days and seasons, free to fix them as they will or as seems convenient to them.[181] For Christ made all things free when he abolished Moses. However, we will let things remain as they now are, since no peril, error, sin, or heresy is involved, and we are averse to changing anything needlessly or at our own personal whim, out of consideration for others who observe Easter at the same time as we do. We know we shall attain salvation without Easter and Pentecost, without Friday and Sunday, and we know that we cannot be damned—as St. Paul teaches us—because of Easter, Pentecost, Sunday, or Friday.

But to get back to the council, I say that we make too much of this ember from the Nicene council. The pope and his church subsequently made of this not only gold, silver, and precious stones, but also a foundation, that is, an article of faith, without which we could not be saved; and they all call it a commandment of, and an act of, obedience to the church. That makes them far

180. The Ten Commandments.

181. Luther maintained that in Christ, all Christians are lords of the sabbath (Mark 2:27-28) and could fulfill God's command to hear his word on any day of the week. Cf. *Sermon at the Dedication of Castle Church, Torgau* (1544), LW 51:333-54; WA 49:588-615.

worse than the Jews, for the Jews do have the Mosaic text commanded by God at that time in their favor, while these have nothing but their own fancy on their side; they come along and want to make a new garment out of the old rags of Moses. They claim that they are obeying Moses, though their doctrine is sheer fantasy, a dream about Moses who has long been dead and, as Scripture declares, buried by the Lord himself [Deut. 34:6] (that is, by Christ), so no one has ever found his grave. They want to reproduce the living Moses by magic before our eyes, but they fail to see, as St. Paul says in Gal. 6 [5:3], that if they wish to keep one part of Moses they must keep all of Moses. Consequently, if they regard it a part of Mosaic law to set the date of Easter according to the full moon in March, they must also keep the whole law concerning the paschal lamb and forthwith become Jews, keeping a bodily paschal lamb with them. If not, they must discard it all, the full moon too, with all the rest of Moses; or in any case not regard this as necessary for salvation like an article of faith, which is what I believe the fathers in this council (especially the best ones) did.

Thus we see that this council dealt primarily with the article that Christ was truly God, for which it was convoked and for which it is and is called a council. They also dealt with several nonessential, physical, external, temporal matters on the side, rightfully to be viewed as temporal and not to be compared with articles of faith; nor are they to be regarded as eternal law (for they are past and expired). But the council found it necessary to attend to such physical matters as were pertinent and needful in their time, which no longer concern us today, and which are neither possible nor profitable for us to observe. And in proof of this, the article prescribing the rebaptism of heretics is false and wrong, even if it was formulated by the true fathers themselves and not patched together by the Arians or the other loose bishops.

[The Apostolic Council in Jerusalem]

Thus the apostolic council in Jerusalem also found it necessary for their day to settle, after it had disposed of the important business, several nonessential, external articles, such as that dealing with blood, strangled animals, and the sacrifice to idols; but not with the intention of making this an eternal law in the church, to be kept as an article of faith, for it has fallen into disuse. And why should we not also examine how this council can be understood within the context of the reasons that made it necessary?[182]

182. Although it is not numbered among the ecumenical councils, this gathering of the apostles in Jerusalem is often referred to as the first church council.

This is how it came into being: Gentiles, who had been converted by Barnabas and Paul, had received the Holy Spirit through the gospel just as well as the Jews, and yet they were not under the law like the Jews. Then the Jews insisted very strongly that the Gentiles be circumcised and commanded to keep the law of Moses; otherwise they could not be saved. These were hard, harsh, and heavy words—no salvation without the law of Moses and circumcision. The Pharisees who had become believers in Christ were especially insistent on this, according to Acts 15[:5]. Thereupon the apostles and elders met to discuss this matter, and after they had quarreled at length and sharply, St. Peter arose and delivered the powerful and beautiful sermon in Acts 15[:7-11], "My brothers, you know that in the early days God made a choice among you, that I should be the one through whom the Gentiles would hear the message of the good news and become believers. And God, who knows the human heart, testified to them by giving them the Holy Spirit, just as he did to us; and in cleansing their hearts by faith he has made no distinction between them and us. Now therefore why are you putting God to the test by placing on the neck of the disciples a yoke that neither our ancestors nor we have been able to bear? On the contrary, we believe that we will be saved through the grace of the Lord Jesus, just as they will."

This sermon sounds as though St. Peter were really angry and disgusted about the harsh words of the Pharisees, who said that those who did not circumcise themselves and keep the law of Moses could not attain salvation, as was said above. He counters with hard, decisive words and says, "You are well aware that the Gentiles heard the Word and were saved through me, like Cornelius and his family; in proof of this, you grumbled against me and chided me because I had gone to the Gentiles, had converted and baptized them"—Acts 10 and 11.[l] "Is it possible that you have forgotten this and are determined to impose burdens on the Gentiles that neither our fathers nor we could bear? What

l Luther here paraphrases Acts 10:1—11:18.

is it but tempting God if we impose impossible burdens on others which we ourselves can carry as little as they can, especially since you know that God has given them the Spirit without this burden, and made them equal to us, since we, together with our fathers, did not receive the same Spirit due to the merit of the burden, but by grace. For because we were unable to bear the burden, we merited wrath far more than grace, since we were obligated to bear it as we had pledged to do."

This is the substance and the main concern of this council, namely, that the Pharisees wished to establish works or merits of the law, over against the word of grace, as necessary for salvation; that would have nullified the word of grace, including Christ and the Holy Spirit. That is why St. Peter argued so determinedly against it, asserting that one is saved solely by the grace of Jesus Christ, without any works at all. Not satisfied with that, he also dared to say that all their previous fathers—the patriarchs, the prophets, and the entire holy church in Israel—had been saved by nothing but the grace of Jesus Christ, and he condemned as tempters of God everyone who had wanted or still wanted to attain salvation in any other way. I think this is real preaching, and knocks the bottom out of the cask.[m] Shouldn't one burn this heretic who forbids all good works and holds grace and faith alone to be sufficient for salvation—and this for all the saints and all ancestors since the beginning of the world? We must now hear ourselves dubbed heretics and devils, though we simply teach this sermon of St. Peter and the decree of this council, as all the world now knows better than the Pharisees did, whom St. Peter is here chiding.

But St. Peter is far beyond us; and it is weird that he not only preaches the grace of God unto salvation, which everyone is surely glad to hear, but that he also declares that neither they themselves nor their ancestors were able to bear such a burden. In plain German this means, "We apostles and whoever we might be, including our ancestors, patriarchs, prophets, and the whole of God's people, have not kept God's commandments; we are sinners and are damned." He is not just speaking of blood sausage and black jelly here, but of the law of Moses, saying that no one has obeyed it or wanted to obey it. As Christ says in John 7[:19], "None of you keeps the law." That (it seems to me) is

m See n. *y*, p. 370.

really preaching the law unto damnation and making a damned sinner of oneself too. How then does that self-styled heir to St. Peter's throne dare to call himself "most holy"[183] and to elevate whatever saints he wants, by virtue of their works and not by the grace of Christ? And where are the monks who can bear a much heavier burden than that of the law so that they also sell their surplus holiness?[184] We do not have this strange Peter's mind, for we do not dare to regard the patriarchs, prophets, apostles, and holy church as sinners, but must also call the pope the "most holy," meaning "the saint of saints, that is, Christ"![n]

But St. Peter deserves a very gracious and honest absolution, and is no longer to be considered strange, for he preaches in this very great article: first, the law, that we are all sinners. Second, that solely the grace of Christ gives us salvation, including the patriarchs, prophets, apostles, and the entire holy church from its beginning, all of whom he makes and damns as sinners with himself. Third, long before the Nicene council comes into being he teaches that Christ is true God, for he says that all the saints must be damned if they are not saved by the grace of our Lord Jesus Christ. To bestow grace and salvation like a lord, one must be true God, who can remove sin by grace, and death and hell by salvation. No creature can do that, unless it be the "most holy" in Rome—but without harming St. Peter's sermon! Fourth, he who holds otherwise and teaches Christians to attain salvation or obtain mercy through the law or their own works is a tempter of God.

Anyone who will may interpret this burden only in terms of the law of Moses and of circumcision, and not the Ten Commandments or good works. I am satisfied with that; if you can keep the Ten Commandments more easily than the Mosaic ceremonies, go ahead and be holier than St. Peter and St. Paul! I am so weak in keeping the Ten Commandments that it seems to me all Mosaic ceremonies would be far easier for me to observe, if the Ten Commandments would not press me so hard. But there is no time to argue that now; it has been amply discussed in other ways and in other places.[185] But even reason will have to decide and admit that the Ten Commandments or the works of the Ten Commandments neither are nor can be called the grace of Jesus Christ, but are and must be called something entirely

n *Sanctum Sanctorum id est Christum.*

183. The original uses the Latin word *sanctissimum. Sanctissimum dominum nostrum papam* ("our most holy lord the pope") is still used as a formula for popes, particularly those who have been declared saints.

184. A reference to the idea that Christians who lived exceptionally holy lives, such as monks, did good works beyond what was necessary for their own salvation. The rationale for the sale of indulgences was that the excess good works of the saints were stored in a "treasury of merits" (*thesaurum meriti*). On the basis of this treasury the pope could remit works that had been assigned in the sacrament of penance to those who purchased indulgences. See Thomas Aquinas, *Summa Theologicae Pars III[a] et Supplementum,* Q. 25, Article 1 (Turin: Marietti, 1953), 723–25; *The "Summa Theologica" of Saint Thomas Aquinas* (London: Burns Oates & Washbourne, 1928), 307–310. Cf. Luther's *Explanations of the Ninety-five Theses* (1518), LW 31:83–252.

185. Probably a reference to the controversy with the Antinomians in 1537. This group, whose spokesman was Luther's old friend John Agricola (c. 1499–1566) of Eisleben, taught that sorrow for sin and repentance resulted only from the gospel rather than from the law. Although Agricola had already expressed such views in reaction to the articles composed in 1527 for the Saxon visitation, the controversy with Luther began only after Agricola had returned to Wittenberg in 1536 and began to preach his understanding of repentance there. This led to a break and subsequent reconciliation with Luther.

different. Now St. Peter asserts here that we must be saved solely by the grace of Jesus Christ; but that grace cannot be received or kept with one's hands, much less with the works of one's hands, but with faith in one's heart, is most certainly true.

It is also strange to see that St. Peter, who as an apostle had the authority and the power, together with the other apostles, to reformulate this article—which is why they are called the cornerstone of the church—nevertheless falls back on the holy church of God in former times, that church of all the patriarchs and prophets from the beginning, and says in effect, "This is not a new doctrine; for this is what our ancestors and all the saints taught and believed. Then how dare we teach a different or a better one, without tempting God and confusing and burdening our brethren's conscience?" That, I say, is the substance or main concern of this council, for which it was convened or convoked; and with which it was settled and adjourned. But the papal ass does not see this main item, and disregards it; instead, he gapes at the other four items added by James,[o] about blood, strangled meat, sacrifices to idols, and fornication, for they want to strengthen their tyranny thereby and claim that since the church has changed such articles, they want to have the power to change the articles of faith and the councils; that is, "We are the church and can decree and do what we like."[186] Listen, papal ass, you are a particularly crass ass, indeed, you are a filthy sow!

The article of this council has neither fallen nor been altered, but, as St. Peter says, has been and will remain in force until the end of the world, for there have always been godly people who were saved solely by the grace of Christ and not by the law. The text and the faith of the gospel, baptism, the sacrament, the office of the keys, the name of Jesus Christ, etc.,[187] have survived even under the devil of the papacy, although the pope ranted against them with his accursed lies and shamefully misled the world; just as has been said of the Nicene council, that its decree existed before it and remained after it. For the true conciliar decrees must always remain—as they indeed always have—especially the chief articles, for the sake of which the councils came into being and are called councils.

o Acts 15:13-21.

p *Natura petit exitum*. See Eduard Margalits, *Supplementum ad opus Florilegium proverbiorum universae latinitatis* (Budapest: L. Kókai, 1910), 178.

When Agricola continued to publish his views, Luther participated in three debates on the topic of Antinomianism, after which another reconciliation with Agricola was brokered by Melanchthon. At this point, Agricola asked Luther to write on the subject, and he responded with *Against the Antinomians* (1539), LW 47:99-119; WA 50:461-77. When the controversy flared again, Agricola filed a formal complaint with the elector. Proceedings against Agricola himself began in the Wittenberg Consistory in 1540, and as a result he fled to Berlin. See Timothy J. Wengert, "Antinomianism," OER 1:51-53.

186. The first twenty distinctions of medieval canon law, also known as the *Treatise on Laws*, claimed sweeping powers for popes and councils. See especially distinctions 17-20 that, among other things, emphasize that only the pope can call a general council and that papal decretals have an authority equal to the canons of councils. *CIC Decreti prima pars*, dist. XVII-XX. (CIC 1:50-66).

187. See Luther's signs of the church in Part III of this treatise.

But what are we to say here about this apostolic council in which James singles out four items—blood, what is strangled, sacrifices to idols, and fornication? Doesn't the council contradict itself, and isn't the Holy Spirit at variance with himself? For these two speeches are plainly and palpably contradictory—not to impose the burden of the Mosaic law, and simultaneously to impose it. Play the sophist, if you will, and say that the council did not speak of the whole law of Moses, but only of portions, several of which might be imposed and others not imposed. But that will not do; for in Gal. 6 [5:3] St. Paul concludes, "He who keeps one part of the law is bound to keep it in its entirety." This is equivalent to acknowledging one's duty to keep the whole law—otherwise, one wouldn't need a part of it either. Here, too, the new patch would be found on an old garment, creating a worse tear [Luke 5:36]. Thus it is quite evident that these items are contained in the law of Moses and nowhere else in the law of the Gentiles, for what need would there be to impose these things on the Gentiles if they were already familiar with them from their native law?[188] How then do we reconcile these two—no law and the whole law?

Well then, if we cannot make them agree, we must dismiss St. James with his article and retain St. Peter with his chief article, for the sake of which the council was held; for without St. Peter's article no one can attain salvation. But, as St. Peter preached in this council, Cornelius and the Gentiles whom St. Peter had baptized along with him in his house were sanctified and saved before St. James came along with his article, etc. I also touched on the question above of whether one may conscientiously let these items go, since the Holy Spirit rules this council and sets all this up. But the dispute[189] on whether the council contradicted itself and disagreed with itself is much sharper. And so, just when they want to relieve us of one impossible burden, they impose a still more impossible one on us, that we do simultaneously nothing and everything. To be sure, now that this has been invalidated we do well to adhere to that one part, namely, to St. Peter's article, that is, to the genuine Christian faith.

Only the fourth item mentioned by St. James, the one regarding fornication, has not been invalidated. To be sure, about twenty years ago courtesans[190] and accursed lords were already beginning to consider fornication not a mortal sin but a venial sin, and advocated the saying, "Nature should have its way,"[p]

188. Luther uses the word *Landrechtes*, which is a technical term for the local or regional laws of Germany as opposed to imperial law, Roman law, or canon law.

189. *Disputatio*. Luther's use of the Latin term suggests that he means something more formal than a simple disagreement.

190. Members of the papal court. The *Gravamina*, a list of grievances against the Roman church, presented at the Diet of Worms of 1521, also used this term, complaining about how the pope redistributed church offices to his "courtesans" (*cordisanen*). DRTA. JR 2, 673.

to which the holiest people in Rome still hold. And, I suppose, those blind leaders were led to this conclusion because St. James set fornication alongside the other three items that have fallen: if the prohibition of blood, strangled meat, and sacrifices to idols is no longer valid, the prohibition of fornication is no longer valid either, since it is listed with these three items, and is furthermore a natural and human act. Let them go their way, they do not deserve anything better.

I shall give my opinion about this; may someone else improve on it. It has now often been said that one should view and also keep the councils according to the chief article which has given the council its purpose; for that is, and in that consists, the real essence of the council, the true body of the council, to which everything else must be adjusted and fitted, like a garment is fitted to the person who wears it or is dressed in it. If the garment doesn't fit, one takes it off and throws it away; then it is no longer a garment. Nor can there be a council (or for that matter an assembly, even a diet or a chapter) after the main business is settled, unless one or two items of secondary importance are found needing to be patched up or settled, as in the Nicene council, when, after it was settled that Christ is true God, the external matters pertaining to the Easter date and the squabbles of the priests came up—so here St. James's articles come up after the chief article of St. Peter.

Thus the final opinion and verdict of all the apostles and the council was that men must be saved, without the law or the burden of the law, solely by the grace of Jesus Christ. When St. Peter, St. Paul, and their followers had reached this verdict, they were happy and quite satisfied, for they had worked and striven for such a decision against the Pharisees and Jews who had become believers, but still wanted to keep the law. Now when St. James submitted his article, they could put up with it, since it was not imposed as law or a burden of the law, as the council's letter also reports, "To impose on you no further burden than these essentials: that you abstain from blood," etc. [Acts 15:28–29]. They might even have liked St. James to add more items, such as the rule about leprosy or the like, even though they do not affect the Ten Commandments. But these things should not be law or a burden (they say), but items otherwise necessary. Yet when a burden is no longer a burden, it is good to bear; and when a law is no longer law, it is good to keep, like the Ten Commandments. How much more is that true of ceremonies, especially if they are abolished or if very few are retained. But more about this later. For if the pope would relieve us of his burden, so that it need no longer be law, we should readily obey him, especially if he were to retain but a few of his ordinances and drop most of them. Thus St. James and his article must now be interpreted without prejudice to St. Peter's article concerning grace without law, which must remain pure and constant and must rule alone without the law.

However, to understand this council fully we want to take a look at the causes of these secondary issues of St. James. The law of Moses was (so to say) ingrained, born into, suckled into, worked into, and lived into the Jews from their youth, so that it had become almost a part of their nature, as St. Paul says in Gal. 2[:15], "We are Jews by birth," that is, we are born Mosaic. He is here speaking of the law and not merely of birth; this is why they could not tolerate the nature of the Gentiles or be equated with them when they were dispersed among Gentiles in other lands and saw these Gentiles eat blood, strangled meat, and meat sacrifices to idols and still boast that they were God's people or Christians.[191] This moved St. James to guard against such offense, so that the Gentiles did not abuse their freedom too willfully just to spite the Jews, but acted decently, so that the Jews, rooted so deeply in the law, would not be offended and spurn the gospel. For, dear God, one should have patience with sick and erring men. We drunken Germans[192] too are wise at times and say, "A load of hay must give a wide berth to a drunken man; for no one can win his spurs against sick people, and no one can become an expert among ignoramuses."[193]

Now St. James nevertheless does it very moderately; he disregards the whole Mosaic law concerning sacrifice and all the other items that had to be observed in Jerusalem and in the country and takes up only the four items which offend the Jews dispersed among the Gentiles. These dispersed Jews could not but see the Gentiles' ways, live among them, and at times eat with them; so it was vexing, and also wrong, to place blood sausage, rabbits cooked in blood, blood jellies, and meat sacrifices to idols before a Jew, especially if one knew that he abhorred it and took it as an insult. It would be the same as if I said, "Listen, Jew! Even if I could bring you to Christ by refraining from eating blood sausage or from serving it to you, I would not do it. I would rather scare you away from accepting Christ and chase you to hell with

191. Luther takes Paul's "we" as applying to all people and suggests that Galatians 2 refers to more than literal Jewish descent but, rather, means being subject to God's law.

192. Luther used this phrase rather frequently. See his *To the Christian Nobility*, LW 44:141; TAL 1:394. Cf. also his *Sermon on Soberness and Moderation* (1539), LW 51:291–99.

193. Three German proverbs: "*Einem truncken Man soll ein fuder hau weichen,*" Wander 3:403, No. 942; "*an krancken Leuten kan niemand kein Ritter werden,*" Wander, 3:53, No. 94; "*an unverstendigen kann niemand kein meister werden,*" Wander 3:54, No. 97. Luther's point is that the Jews could not recognize the legitimacy of freedom in the gospel, just as ignorant people could not recognize an expert, etc. "Win his spurs" is a reference to becoming a knight.

blood sausage."[194] Would that be kind, not to mention Christian? Must not everyone at times keep silent and refrain from an action for the benefit of another human being, when he sees and knows that words and deeds would work his neighbor's harm, especially if this silence does not offend God? Now, at that time, the Gentiles were very antagonistic to the Jews, and very proud because they were their masters. The Jews, on the other hand, were intolerant, believing that they alone were God's people—as many histories clearly testify.

Therefore this good advice of St. James was the very best means to peace, indeed, even to the salvation of many; since the Gentiles had attained Christ's grace without law and merit, they should now, on their part, show themselves helpful in a few matters so that the Jews, as the sick and erring folk, might attain the same grace. For it did not harm the Gentiles before God to avoid the external custom of eating blood, strangled meat, and meat sacrifices to idols in public (since grace had liberated their conscience from all that) and to desist, for the benefit and salvation of the Jews, from giving willful offense; besides, in the absence of the Jews they could eat and drink what they wished, without jeopardy to their conscience. And the Jews, too, would be equally free in their conscience, but could not change the old external customs so suddenly—"Custom is second nature,"[195] especially when it has grown from God's law. Thus fairness and reason also teach that one should not spite nor hinder, but rather serve and help them in accord with the command, "You shall love your neighbor," etc. [Matt. 22:39].

So these two articles, that of St. Peter and that of St. James, are contradictory and yet they are not. St. Peter's deals with faith, St. James's with love.[196] St. Peter's article tolerates no law; it eats blood, strangled meat, meat sacrifices to idols, and the devil in the bargain, without paying much attention, for it feels responsible to God alone and not to man, and does nothing but believe in the gracious God. But St. James's article lives and eats with humanity; it also directs everything to St. Peter's article, carefully warding off any obstacle that might obstruct the way. Now the office of love is so constituted on earth that since whatever is loved and helped is changeable and transient, love cannot have the same object forever; the one passes away and is replaced by another which it must also love, until the end of the world. Now when the Jews had become upset or stiff-necked and the

194. Here Luther shifts the discussion from the Acts 15 consideration of Jewish and Gentile believers to how the "Gentiles" of his day deal with Jews. He had been very critical of the behavior of the papal church with regard to its witness to the Jews. See his *That Jesus Christ Was Born a Jew* (1523), LW 45:200; TAL 5, forthcoming.

195. *Consuetudo est altera natura.* A proverb preserved by Cicero (106–43 BCE), famous Roman philosopher and orator, in *De finibus*, V, 25, 74. See *Cicero: De finibus bonorum et malorum*, trans. H. Rackham, Loeb Classical Library (New York: Putman, 1921), 476.

196. In *The German Mass*, Luther advocated a simple way to interpret Scripture that involved imagining one pocket labeled *faith* and one labeled *love* in which to place verses of the Bible. See this volume, above, p. 145.

Gentiles no longer had so much love to give them, everything lapsed—not changed by the power of the church, as the papists lie, but because the cause was removed. So the Christians freely ate blood and black jelly, from which they had abstained for a time out of consideration for the Jews, even though they had not been bound to abstain before God in accordance with their faith. For if St. James had intended to impose these items as law he would have had to impose the entire law, as St. Paul says in Gal. 5[:3], "He who keeps one law must keep them all"; that would flatly contradict St. Peter's article, which St. James confirms.

But this, I believe, was the reason St. James added fornication, which has always been forbidden in the Ten Commandments, to the other items: fornication was regarded by the Gentiles as a light, indeed, as no sin at all, as one can read in the Gentiles' books and as I pointed out above, which twenty years ago the courtesans and worthless priests also began to say publicly and to believe. Thus among the Gentiles fornication was as great a sin as eating blood sausage, rabbits cooked in blood, blood jellies, or meat sacrifices to idols.[197] Just read in Roman history how unwilling they were to take wives, so that the emperor Augustus had to compel them to marry; for they thought fornication was right, and to be forced to marry was to suffer violence and injustice.[198] That is why St. James wants to teach the Gentiles that they should gladly abstain from fornication without being forced to by the authorities, and live purely and chastely in the state of marriage, as the Jews did, who were greatly offended by such license in fornication and who could not believe, because of this disparity in food and conduct, etc., that these Gentiles should attain God's grace and become God's people.

The apostles, therefore, did not impose the law on the Gentiles, and yet they permitted the Jews to retain it for some time, meanwhile vigorously preaching grace—as we note in St. Paul when he became a Jew among the Jews and a Gentile among the Gentiles, so that he might win them all, 1 Cor. 12 [9:20], and when he circumcised his disciple Timothy, who was already a believer, not because this was prescribed, but, as St. Luke says, "because of the Jews that were in those places" [Acts 16:3], because he did not want to offend them. Later, in Acts 21[:26], he let himself be purified in the temple with the Jews and he sacrificed according to the law of Moses, which he did as St. Augustine expressed it in that fine and now famous saying, "*Oportuit synagogam cum honore*

197. That is to say, no sin at all.

198. Augustus (30 BCE–14 CE) issued this marriage law in 9 CE for the third time after two previous attempts (in 28 and 18 BCE) had failed. Part of the problem was that the upper classes made no distinction between natural and adopted heirs, often preferring the latter.

sepelire," "One must give Moses or his church and law an honorable burial."[199]

[Arianism after the Council of Nicaea]

But how this council and both St. Peter's and St. James's articles were subsequently kept, you can gather amply from St. Paul's epistles,[q] wherein he complains everywhere about the false apostles who insisted on the necessity of the law to the detriment of grace, and who seduced whole clans and countries away from Christ and back to the law, albeit in the name of Christ—just as things became much worse after the Council of Nicaea. After that knave Arius had humbled himself and had even pledged allegiance to the council before Emperor Constantine,[r] for which the emperor reinstated him, he fanned the flames even more. And the bishops of his party pursued the game so abominably, especially after Constantine's death, through his son the emperor Constantius[200] (whom they had won over), that Constantius expelled all true bishops throughout the world except two, Gregory and Basil.[201] Some say that Constantine, the father, had also become an Arian[202] before he died and had in his will commended an Arian priest, strongly recommended by his sister Constantia on her deathbed, to his son Constantius, and that it was through him that the Arians later became so powerful.

Such examples from the histories remind us to pray faithfully for great lords, for the devil seeks them out more than others since he can do the greatest damage through them. And they are also a warning to us to be careful and not readily believe the sectarian spirits,[s] even when they humble themselves deeply, as this knave Arius did, and as Saul did with David [1 Sam. 24:16ff.]. "Sometimes even the wicked are defeated" (one says).[203] But they keep in the background until they have enough air and room; then they, like Arius, go ahead and do anyway what they had in mind, so that it really does not surprise me very much that the fathers imposed such severe and long penances on apostate Christians. They must have discovered how false their humility

q See, for example, 1 Cor. 1:10ff.; 2 Cor. 10:2ff.; Gal. 5:12.

r *Historia tripartita*, III, 6. MPL 69:950=CSEL 71:142, 4–6; NPNF2 2:277. Arius presented a "confession of faith" (*expositio*) to the emperor.

s *Rottengeister*. See n. *j*, p. 378.

199. This passage is not in Augustine's works, but it is frequently attributed to him by theologians in the Middle Ages and beyond. The following section from Augustine's letter to Jerome (*Epistola* 82, 16), which is often quoted alongside the spurious epigram, expresses the same thought: "But just as it is seemly that the bodies of the deceased be carried honourably to the grave by their kindred, so it was fitting that these [Old Testament] rites should be removed in a manner worthy of their origin and history." NPNF1 1:355.

200. Constantius was regent in the Orient (337–350) and then emperor (350–361). He supported the Arian party.

201. *Historia tripartita*, VII, 22. MPL 69:1086=CSEL 71:419, 23; NPNF2 2:99. Gregory of Nazianzus (c. 329–390), bishop of Constantinople, and Basil the Great, bishop of Caesarea (r. 370–379). Together with Gregory of Nyssa (d. c. 394) they defended the Nicene Creed against Arianism.

202. This was recorded in the *Chronology* (*Chronicon*) of St. Jerome. See MPL 27:499–500=GCS 47:234; *A Translation of Jerome's Chronicon with Historical Commentary*, trans. Malcolm Drew Donalson (Lewiston, NY: Mellen University Press, 1996), 42. The nature of Constantine's Christianity is much debated.

203. "*Aliquando compunguntur et mali.*" A Latin proverb of unknown origin. Luther used this same phrase with reference to Pharaoh in a 1524 Christmas Day sermon; WA 16:126.

was, and how rarely they sincerely and from the bottom of their hearts humbled themselves or repented—just as Sirach [Ecclus. 12:10] says, "Never trust your reconciled enemy," etc.

To sum up, I let anyone who does not know what *osculum Judae*, "Judas kiss" [Matt. 26:49], means read with me the story of Arius under Constantine, and he will have to say that Arius far outdid Judas. He deceived the good emperor Constantine with these nice words: "We believe in one God, the Father almighty, and in the Lord Jesus Christ, his Son, born of the Father before the whole world, one God, one Word, by whom everything was made," etc.[204] My dear man, what Christian could regard these words as heretical, or think that Arius still viewed Christ as a creature? And yet that he did became quite evident during the hearing. Auxentius,[205] the bishop of Milan, the immediate predecessor of Ambrose, later similarly fooled the people with such beautiful words that at first I really grew angry at St. Hilary when I read the words "Blasphemy of Auxentius" on the title page of Auxentius's *Confessions*.[206] I would have staked my body and soul on Auxentius's oath that he regarded Christ as true God. I also hope that despite such deceptive and crafty words many pious simple people retained their former belief and were preserved in it, not understanding these words in any way other than that of the faith, as no one could understand them differently who is not informed of the hidden meaning given them by the Arians.

And because it is necessary for Christians to know such an illustration, and since the ordinary reader does not study history so closely and does not realize how useful it is as a warning against all other sectarian spirits whom the devil their god makes so slippery that one cannot catch or grasp them anywhere, I will relate this affair briefly in several items.

First, Arius had taught that Christ is not God, but a creature.[t] Then the good bishops exacted from him the confession that Christ is God; but this he did in a false sense, meaning that Christ was God just like St. Paul, St. Peter, and the angels, who are called "gods and sons of God" in Scripture.[u]

Second, when the fathers became aware of this they again pressed him and his adherents to admit that Christ was true and

t *Historia tripartita*, I, 12. MPL 69:902=CSEL 71:44f., 41–43; NPNF2 3:34.

u See, for example, Job 38:7; Ps. 82:6; John 10:34; 1 Cor. 8:5.

204. Quoted from Arius's *Confession of Faith* (*Expositio*). See n. *r* on facing page.

205. Deposed in 370 by Damasus I, the bishop of Rome (r. 366–384), Auxentius kept his bishopric until his death (374).

206. Auxentius stated his position in a letter to the emperor. Hilary of Poitiers added his *Book Against the Arians or Auxentius of Milano* (*Liber contra Arianos vel Auxentium Mediolanensem*) and entitled the whole *An Example of Auxentius' Blasphemy* (*Exemplum blasphemiae Auxentii*). See MPL 10:617–18; *Historia tripartita*, V, 29. MPL 69:1006=CSEL 71:257; NPNF2 3:83.

very God; he used these words for the sake of appearance because it had theretofore been taught like this in all the churches. But among themselves they, particularly Eusebius,[207] bishop of Nicomedia and Arius's highest patron, interpreted these words like this: "*Omne factum dei est verum*,"[208] "Whatever God creates or makes is true and real; for whatever is false God did not make. Therefore we are willing to confess that Christ is a real, true God (but according to us a created god, like Moses and all the saints)," etc. Here they conceded everything that we still confess in our hymns in church on Sunday and have ever since the Nicene council: "God of God, light of light, very God of very God."[209]

Third, when the trickery that they with these words still called Christ a creature became known, the dispute became sharper, so that they had to confess that Christ had existed prior to the whole world. Who could here believe otherwise than that Arius and his bishops were genuine Christians and had been unjustly condemned by the Nicene council? For they were playing these tricks soon after the Nicene council (which had made short work of them and formulated the creed as it still exists) because they wanted to ruin the Nicene council and assailed one after another of its points.[v]

Fourth, when this dodge was discovered too, that Christ was still to be and to be called a creature, with the understanding that he had indeed existed before the whole world—that is, that he had been created and made before the whole world or any other creature [Col. 1:15]—they were forced to acknowledge that the whole world, all things, were made by him, as John 1[:3] declares. However, among their own people they interpreted this to mean that Christ was made first and then all things were made by him.[w]

Fifth, it was now easy for them to confess, "Begotten, not made," born of God, not made, born as all Christians, born of God, are children of God, John 1[:12-13]; not made among other creatures, but before all creatures.

Sixth, when it came to the core of the matter, that Christ is *homousius*[x] with the Father, that is, that Christ is of one and

v *Historia tripartita*, IV, 10. MPL 69:961=CSEL 71:166, 1; NPNF2 2:38.

w *Historia tripartita*, V, 7. MPL 69:988-90=CSEL 71:221, 1; NPNF2 2:56-57.

x A Latin transliteration of the Greek "of one substance."

207. Eusebius (c. 260-c. 340) was the leader of the middle party (over against orthodoxy and radical Arianism) at the Council of Nicaea. He granted Arius asylum, but did not change his position.

208. This quotation is not found in the *Historia tripartita*. Luther probably coined a phrase which may summarize the contents of a letter of Eusebius to Paul, bishop of Tyre, and the statements in a document ascribed to Athanasius; cf. *Historia tripartita*, I, 16; II, 7. MPL 69:915-16, 926-27=CSEL 71:70-72, 93-96; NPNF2 3:42-43, 44-46.

209. The Nicene Creed was sung every Sunday following the reading of the Gospel.

the same divinity with the Father and has one and the same power with him, they could find no more subterfuges, loopholes, detours, or evasions. *Homousius* means "of one essence or nature" or "of the same and not of a second essence," as the fathers had decreed in the council and as is sung in Latin, *consubstantialis*, and as some afterward called it, *coexistentialis, coessentialis*. This they had accepted in the council at Nicaea, and this they still accepted when they had to speak before the emperor and the fathers; but they fought it bitterly before their own people and asserted that such words were not used in Holy Scripture.[y] They held many councils, even during Constantine's lifetime, in order to weaken the Nicene council; they stirred up much trouble, and later frightened our people so much that St. Jerome, dismayed by it, wrote a distressing letter to Damasus, bishop of Rome, suggesting that the word *homousius* be stricken. "For," (he says) "I do not know what sort of poison there is in these letters that the Arians get so upset by them."[210]

A dialogue is still extant in which Athanasius and Arius argue about this word *homousius* before an officer called Probus.[211] When Arius pressed the point that no such word was to be found in Scripture and Athanasius countered in kind, saying that the words "*innascibilis, ingenitus Deus*," that is, "God is unborn"—which the Arians had employed to prove that Christ could not be God since he was born, while God was unborn, etc.—were not to be found in the Bible either, the official Probus decided against Arius. It is certainly true that one should teach nothing outside of Scripture pertaining to divine matters, as St. Hilary writes in *On the Trinity*, Book I,[z] which means only that one should teach nothing that is at variance with Scripture. But that one should not use more or other words than those contained in Scripture—this cannot be adhered to, especially in a controversy and when heretics want to falsify things with trickery and distort the words of Scripture. It thus became necessary to condense the meaning of Scripture, comprised of so many passages, into a short and comprehensive word, and to ask whether they regarded Christ as *homousius*, which was the meaning of all the words of Scripture that they had distorted with

210. *Epistola* 15. MPL 22:355–58; NPNF2 6:18–20. Jerome did not turn against the *homousius* but against the language of three hypostases, which Arians could agree to if it were not strictly interpreted as three persons.

211. *Dialogue Against the Arians* (*Contra Arianos dialogus*). MPL 62:155–79. This dialogue passed in the sixteenth century as a work of Athanasius. The author, however, was Vigilius of Thapsus (d. c. 500), whose exact role in the Arian controversy is unknown. Luther already knew of the dialogue during his stay in Erfurt. Cf. WA 30/III:530.

y *Historia tripartita*, V, 8. MPL 69:990–92=CSEL 71:226–27; NPNF2 2:57–58.

z Chapter 18. MPL 10:49; NPNF2 9:50–51.

false interpretations among their own people, but had freely confessed before the emperor and the council. It is just as if the Pelagians[212] were to try to embarrass us with the term "original sin" or "Adam's plague" because these words do not occur in Scripture, though Scripture clearly teaches the meaning of these words, that we are "conceived in sin," Ps. 51[:5], that we are "by nature children of wrath," Eph. 2[:3], and that we must all be accounted sinners "because of the sin of one man," Rom. [5:12].

Now tell me, if Arius would still today come before you and confess to you the entire creed of the Nicene council, as we sing it today in our churches, could you regard him as heretical? I myself would say that he was right. And if he nevertheless would, like a knave, believe otherwise and subsequently interpret and teach these words differently, wouldn't I have been nicely duped? That is why I do not believe that Constantine became an Arian, but that he adhered to the Nicene council. What happened to him was that he was deceived and believed that Arius agreed with the Nicene council. He also had him take an oath (as was said above) and then demanded that Arius again be received in Alexandria. But as Athanasius refused to do this because he knew the false Arius better than Constantine did, he had to be expelled.[a] It probably occurred to Constantine, as a human being, that Arius, this pious Christian, had been condemned in Nicaea out of envy or jealousy, especially since the Arians, particularly Eusebius of Nicomedia, won the emperor over, filled his ears with gossip, and eulogized Arius. For great kings and lords, though they may be pious, are not always surrounded at court by angels and St. John the Baptist, but often by Satan, Judas, and Doeg, as the book of Kings clearly testifies [1 Kgs. 22:22; 1 Sam. 22:9]. It is a good sign that Constantine, before his death, recalled Athanasius, no matter how hard the Arians tried to prevent it, *Tripartita*, III, 11,[b] whereby he indicated that he did not want to have the Nicene council and its doctrines rejected, but that he would have liked to establish unity.

That is just what some of our false papist scribblers are doing now; they pretend to teach faith and good works in order to

212. The followers of Pelagius (d. c. 418), who opposed Augustine's doctrine of original sin, teaching that sin is not a natural state, but an act of free will. Luther refers here not to the original Pelagians but to those Roman theologians who believed human beings could produce good works without help from God. They were often referred to by their opponents as Pelagians.

a *Historia tripartita*, III, 6. MPL 69:950=CSEL 71:142–43, 1–7; NPNF2 2:277.

b Actually *Historia tripartita*, IV, 1–3. MPL 69:957–58=CSEL 71:159, 1; NPNF2 2:283–84, 301.

embellish themselves and to besmirch us, as though they had always taught thus and we had unjustly accused them of teaching otherwise, so that, adorned in this sheep's clothing [Matt. 7:15] as though they were exactly like us, they may nicely bring their wolf into the sheep pen again. They do not seriously mean to teach faith and good works; but since they (like the Arians) cannot retain their poison and wolfishness or re-establish it except in this sheepskin of faith and good works, they decorate and hide their wolfskin until they get back into the sheep pen. But one should do to them as they do to our people and demand that they recant their abominations and prove it by casting off all the abuses that have prevailed against faith and good works in their churches among their people, so that one could know them by their fruits [Matt. 7:16]. Otherwise, one cannot believe their mere words and gestures, that is, their sheepskins. Arius, too, should have recanted in the same way, confessed his error, and actually attacked his former doctrine and conduct, as St. Augustine did his Manichaeism,[213] as many people are now doing with their former popery and monkery, among whom, by the grace of God, I can number myself. But they deny that they erred and cannot give God the honor of confessing it, just as the Arians wanted to have their lies defended and did not want people to think that they had been expelled by the council.

213. Named after Mani, a Persian religious philosopher who was executed in Persia c. 275. It was a syncretistic cult teaching the incompatibility of spirit and matter. Until 384 Augustine was a Manichaean.

We should remember such historical examples well, especially those of us who must be preachers and have the order to feed the flock of Christ, so that we may exercise care and be good bishops, as St. Peter says in 1 Pet. 5[:2]; for to be an *episcopus*, or bishop, means to be careful, to be alert, to watch diligently, so that the devil does not take us by surprise. Here we see that he is such a master of dissimulation, disguise, and pretense that he becomes far fairer than the "angels of light" [2 Cor. 11:14]; and false bishops are holier than true bishops, and the wolf more pious than any sheep. We are not dealing now with the crude, black, papal poltergeists[c] outside of Scripture. They are now to be found in Scripture and in our doctrine; they want to be like us and yet tear us to pieces. But here only the Holy Spirit can help, and we must pray diligently; otherwise, we shall be badly beaten.

c *Polter Bapst geister.* Luther believes that his opponents have become more subtle and no longer show themselves simply as malicious, evil men.

All of this explains quite clearly why the council was held, namely, not for the sake of outward ceremonies, but for the sake of the important article about the divinity of Christ. That was why the dispute arose and was dealt with in the council; afterward it was assailed by the unspeakable raging of the devil, while the other articles were ignored. And this misery lasted for approximately three hundred years among Christians,[214] so that St. Augustine believes that Arius's pain in hell grows worse from day to day as long as that error endures, for Mohammed has come out of this sect.[215] And from what I have presented above one can see clearly that this council neither thought up nor established anything new, but only condemned Arius's new error against the old faith on the basis of Scripture—from which may be inferred that no council (much less the pope in Rome) is authorized to think up or establish new articles concerning faith or good works, as they so falsely boast. This should be enough for the time being about the first principal council of Nicaea.

[Here we omit Luther's discussion of the other three principal councils—Constantinople (381), Ephesus (431), and Chalcedon (451).][216]

[What Is a Council?]

These then are the four principal councils and the reasons they were held. The first, in Nicaea, defended the divinity of Christ against Arius; the second, in Constantinople, defended the divinity of the Holy Spirit against Macedonius; the third, in Ephesus, defended the one person of Christ against Nestorius; the fourth, in Chalcedon, defended the two natures in Christ against Eutyches.[217] But no new articles of faith were thereby established, for these four doctrines are formulated far more abundantly and powerfully in St. John's Gospel alone, even if the other evangelists and St. Paul and St. Peter had written nothing about it, although they, together with the prophets, also teach and bear convincing witness to all of that. Since these four principal councils (which the bishops of Rome, according to their decretals,[218] put on a level with the four Gospels, as though these matters together with all articles of faith were not contained far more richly in the Gospels, or as if the councils had not taken them from there—so nicely do these episcopal asses understand

214. The last Arian kings in Europe were Grimoald, king of the Lombards (d. 671), and his son, Garibald, who was deposed three months after his father's death.

215. Cf. WA TR 5:695, 18–696, 2. John Damascene (c. 676–c. 749) considered Islam a Christian heresy, and the idea was perpetuated throughout the Middle Ages and into the sixteenth century. The identification with Arianism results from Islam's denial of the divinity of Jesus. See Headley, *Luther's View*, 185; and Rudolf Pfister, "Reformation, Türken und Islam," *Zwingliana* 10 (1956): 356–60.

216. LW 41:86 (para. 3) through 121 (para 1) are omitted.

217. Luther's language echoes that of his source, Crabbe's history of the councils: "There were four principal councils that convened to authenticate, authorize, and defend the faith preached by Sacred Scripture." Crabbe, *Concilia omnia* (Cologne, 1538), 1:393r. A similar description of the councils can be found in canon law, *Decreti prima pars*, dist. XV. C. II. (CIC 1:35).

218. See n. 114, p. 356.

the essence of the Gospels and of the councils) neither intended nor were able to create and establish anything new in matters of faith, as they themselves confess, how much less then can one assign such power to the other councils, which are to be regarded as lower, if these four are and are to be called principal councils.

All the other councils too must be viewed in this way, be they large or small. Even though there were many thousands of them, they do not introduce anything new either in matters of faith or of good works; but they defend, as the highest judges and greatest bishops under Christ, the ancient faith and the ancient good works in conformity with Scripture. To be sure, they may also deal with temporal, transient, and changeable things in order to meet the need of their particular time; this, however, must also be done outside the councils in every parish and school. But if they establish anything new with regard to faith or good works, you may rest assured that the Holy Spirit was not there, but only the unholy spirit with his angels. For in that instance they must act without and outside of Holy Scripture, indeed, in opposition to it, as Christ says, "Whoever is not with me is against me" [Matt. 12:30]. The Holy Spirit can neither know nor do anything more than St. Paul when he says in 1 Cor. 2[:2], "I decided to know nothing among you except Jesus Christ, and him crucified." The Holy Spirit has not been given to teach or instill in us anything except Christ, but he is to teach and remind us of all that is in Christ "in whom are hidden all the treasures of wisdom and knowledge" [Col. 2:3]. He is to make him clear to us, as Christ says [John 16:13], and not exalt our reason and notions or make an idol of these.

This is why these councils are outside Scripture and are councils of Caiaphas, Pilate, and Herod; as the apostles say in Acts 4[:26], "They have gathered together against the Lord." They take counsel, or hold councils, against God and his Christ [Ps. 2:2]. And all the evangelists relate[d] that the chief priests and Pharisees conferred, or assembled councils, deliberating how they might kill Christ—as David had foretold in Ps. 2[:2-3] that they would take counsel together against God and his anointed, calling Christ's preaching "bonds" and "cords" which they would burst asunder and cast from them. Such are the majority of the pope's councils, in which he sets himself up in Christ's stead as

d Matt. 26:4; Mark 14:1-2; Luke 22:2; John 11:47-53.

head of the church, makes Holy Scripture subject to himself, and tears it asunder. His decretals show how he condemned the sacrament in both kinds at Constance[219] after he had already rent marriage asunder,[220] forbidden it and condemned it, and virtually crucified and buried Christ.

This brings us to the main question prompting me to write this booklet: what, then, is a council? Or, what is its task? If it is not the function of a council to establish new articles of faith, then all the world has to date been fooled terribly because it neither knows nor believes anything other than that a decision of a council is an article of faith or at least a work necessary for salvation, so that he who does not keep the decree of a council cannot be saved because he does not obey the Holy Spirit, the council's master. Well then, I think that my conscience is clear when I say that no council (as I said before) is authorized to initiate new articles of faith, because the four principal councils did not do that. Consequently, I will state my opinion here and reply to this main question as follows.

First, a council has no power to establish new articles of faith, even though the Holy Spirit is present. Even the apostolic council in Jerusalem introduced nothing new in matters of faith, but rather held that which St. Peter concludes in Acts 16 [15:11], and which all their predecessors believed, namely, the article that one is to be saved without the laws, solely through the grace of Christ.

Second, a council has the power—and is also duty-bound to exercise it—to suppress and to condemn new articles of faith, in accordance with Scripture and the ancient faith, just as the Council of Nicaea condemned the new doctrine of Arius, that of Constantinople the new doctrine of Macedonius, that of Ephesus the new doctrine of Nestorius, and that of Chalcedon the new doctrine of Eutyches.[221]

Third, a council has no power to command new good works; it cannot do so, for Holy Scripture has already abundantly commanded all good works. What good works can one think of that the Holy Spirit does not teach in Scripture, such as humility, patience, gentleness, mercy, faithfulness, faith, kindness, peaceableness, obedience, self-discipline, chastity, generosity, readiness to serve, etc., and in summary, love? [Gal. 5:22-23]. What good work could one imagine that is not included in the commandment of love? What sort of a good work would it be if it were not motivated by love? For love, according to St. Paul's teaching,

219. The Council of Constance condemned communion in both kinds, that is, distributing both bread and wine to the laity. Its decree on the subject, *Cum in nonnullis*, was adopted in 1415, after Hus's final trial and before his condemnation. Hus's followers made communion in both kinds emblematic of their battle with Rome, often adopting the chalice as a symbol. The text of the decree can be found in Heinreich Denzinger, *Compendium of Creeds, Definitions, and Declarations on Matters of Faith and Morals*, 43rd ed. (San Francisco: Ignatius, 2012), 325-26. Luther had composed a set of theses against this decree for a disputation in 1535 (WA 39/I:13-39).

220. The prohibition of clerical marriage had been one of the reforms introduced by the papacy in the eleventh century, and the church had continued to legislate against the practice throughout the Middle Ages.

221. On the heresy of Arius, see n. 119, p. 357. Macedonius became bishop of Constantinople c. 339 by usurping the office with the help of a faction of Arian supporters. He was deposed and exiled by the council in 360. Nestorius (d. 451) became bishop of Constantinople in 428. He opposed Arianism but taught that Christ was not one unified person (God and human) but that he was really two different persons who had merged.

This sculpture by Charles-Antoine Bridan (1787) depicts the condemnation of Nestorius at the Council of Ephesus in 431. It is located in the Cathedral of Our Lady of Chartres.

is the fulfillment of the whole law [Gal. 5:14]—as Christ himself says in Matthew 5.

Fourth, a council has the power—and is also duty-bound to exercise it—to condemn evil works that oppose love, according to all of Scripture and the ancient practice of the church, and to punish persons guilty of such works, as the Nicene council's decree rebuked the ambition and other vices of bishops and deacons. But here one should speak of two kinds of evil works: some that are, and are called clearly wicked, such as greed, murder, adultery, ambition, and the like. These we find condemned by the councils, as they are also condemned, outside the councils, in Holy Scripture and are, moreover, also punished by civil law. But besides these there are other, new good works which are not called evil but are seemingly good, refined vices, holy idolatries invented by strange saints, or even mad saints; in summary, they

He had several supporters who kept this controversy alive and created Nestorian churches that exist even today. Pope Celestine I commissioned Cyril, patriarch of Alexandria, to conduct proceedings against Nestorius at the Council of Ephesus in 431. Eutyches (c. 375–454) opposed Nestorius at Ephesus but later was accused of monophysitism, meaning the belief that Christ has only one nature, in which humanity and divinity are combined. The Council of Chalcedon in 451 held that Christ has two natures, one divine and one human. Eutyches was removed from his position as a monastic leader and banished.

are the white devil and a glittering Satan.[222] Such evil—I should say new, good works—should be condemned by the councils most sharply and severely, for they pose a danger to the Christian faith and an offense to Christian life and are a caricature or mockery of both.

For instance, when a weak Christian hears or sees a holy hermit or monk leading a special kind of life, more austere than that of the ancient, ordinary Christian way and vocation, he stumbles over this and supposes that the life of all the ancient Christians was nothing, or even worldly and dangerous, in comparison with that of this new saint. That gave rise to the following abomination throughout the Christian world. A burgher or peasant believes in Christ with a true and pure faith and practices the genuine, ancient good works commanded by God in Holy Scripture, such as humility, gentleness, patience, chastity, charity, and faithfulness toward his neighbor, industry, and application to his work, office, calling, and station. But then this burgher or peasant, thinking that such a new saint is a true old saint and Christian, considers himself as a stench and a cipher compared to the new saint with his special garb, food, fasting, bed, expression, and other similar new good works, when, in fact, this new saint is a conceited, ambitious, angry, impatient, hateful, lustful, presumptuous, and false Christian. St. Paul himself calls such people arrogant and egotistic saints who choose a new mode of life for themselves and a new way of serving God not commanded by God, over and above the Christian church's old, true, common way of life and service to God, ordained and commanded by God.

The elect may have been preserved amid these offensive new works, but they had to shed this new skin and be saved in the old Christian skins, just as happened to St. Anthony when he had to learn that a cobbler or tanner in Alexandria was a better Christian than he was with his monkery.[223] He also conceded that he had not advanced as far as this cobbler had. So it was with the great St. John too, the "first hermit,"[224] who was also a prophet for the emperor Theodosius and highly lauded by St. Augustine.[225] When the people, among them St. Jerome, admired the severity of his life, he replied, "Why do you look for anything extraordinary among us? After all, you are more fortunate in your parishes, where the writings and the precepts of apostles and prophets are preached to you." That is what I call taking

222. That is, evil disguised as good. "Even Satan disguised himself as an angel of light"; 2 Cor. 11:14.

223. This story is recorded in the *Lives of the Fathers* (*Vitae patrum*), III, 130, which passed as the work of Jerome, but is now ascribed to Rufinus. See MPL 73:785.

224. *Primus eremita*, known as John the Hermit. See Rufinus, II, 20, 32. MPL 21:526=GCS 9/II:1024, 1–3, MPL 21:538=GCS 9/II:1036, 13–18.

225. Augustine's praise is found in *The City of God* (*De civitate Dei*), V, 26. MPL 41:172=CCSL 47:161; NPNF1 2:105.

off the cowl and subjecting oneself to Holy Scripture, praising solely the ordinary Christian way of life. Paphnutius[226] too had to learn that he was on the same level with a fiddler who had been a murderer, and with two wives who had lain with their husbands that same night. Thus he was constrained to remark, "Alas! One must not despise any estate." The same thing also happened to St. Bernard, to Bonaventure,[227] and undoubtedly to many other pious men. In the end, when they realized that their new holiness and monkery could not stand the test against sin and death, they crawled and were saved in the ancient Christian faith, without such new holiness—as the words of St. Bernard testify in many places.[228]

In none of the councils, especially not in the four principal councils, do we find these new good works condemned, except that one or two small councils—for instance, the one that met at Gangra and was composed of twenty bishops (the proceedings of which recently appeared in print)[229]—did do something about it. On the contrary, they let the new holiness get the upper hand until the Christian church was hardly recognizable any longer. They acted like lazy gardeners who permit the vines to grow so rampant that the old true tree has to suffer or perish. Even before St. Anthony's day monasticism had made such headway that by the time of the fourth council there was an abbey near Constantinople, of which the aforementioned Eutyches was abbot—although the monasteries of that day were not such imperial castles of stone as they afterward became. For they called him *Archimandrita. Mandrae*[e] is said to mean a fence or hedge, made of bushes, shrubs, and boughs, used as an enclosure for animals or as a fold for sheep. And Eutyches, as the head of it, lived with his followers in such an enclosure and led a secluded life. From this one can gather what a monastery was like at the time, before it was enclosed with walls.

But just as happens in a garden, where the weeds grow much higher than the true fruit-bearing shoots, so it also happens in the garden of the church: these new saints, who sprout and grow out from the side and yet want to be Christians, nourished by the sap of the tree, grow far better than the true old saints of

e *Archimandrita* probably means "sheep tender." As Luther notes, it is derived from *mandra* ("sheepfold"). See *A Greek-English Lexicon of the New Testament and Other Early Christian Literature*, 3d ed. (Chicago: University of Chicago Press, 2000), 615.

226. Paphnutius (see n. 118, p. 357) was a disciple of Anthony (d. 356). See also n. 103, p. 353. See Rufinus, *History of the Monks* (*Historia monachorum*), XVI. MPL 21:436=*Historia monachorum sive de vita santorum patrum*, ed. Eva Schulz-Flügel (Berlin: De Gruyter, 1990), 340–47. This chapter is one of the excerpts in the English translation by Helen Waddell, *The Desert Fathers* (Ann Arbor: University of Michigan Press, 1957), 46–52.

227. Bonaventure (1221–1274), a Franciscan theologian known as "the seraphic doctor" because of his mysticism. He taught at the University of Paris, served as minister general of the Franciscan order, and wrote the official life of Francis.

228. Throughout his career, Luther expressed great appreciation for Bernard, often quoting him and citing him as an example, even though this appreciation was frequently mixed with criticism of Bernard's monasticism. See Franz Posset, *Pater Bernhardus: Martin Luther and Bernard of Clairvaux* (Kalamazoo, MI: Cistercian Publications, 1999).

229. The little synod of Gangra, in Paphlagonia, held in 343, adopted a series of canons directed against extreme asceticism. Johann Kymaeus (1498–1552), pastor in Homberg, used these canons in 1530 in an attack on the Anabaptists. The book was published in 1537 with a preface by Luther (WA 50:46–47). The canons to which Luther here refers are noted in WA 50:609, n. *c*.

the Christian faith and life. And since I have touched on the subject, I must relate what I noticed in the histories. St. Bernard was an abbot for thirty-six years, during which time he founded one hundred and sixty monasteries of his order.[230] Now, one knows what kind of monasteries the Cistercians have. At that time, perhaps, they may have been smaller, but today they are regular principalities. And I will say even more: at that time, that is, under the reign of the emperors Henry III, IV, and V,[231] within the span of twenty years, four different princely monastic orders came into being—the Grandmontines, the Reformed Regular Canons, the Carthusians, and the Cistercians.[232] And what do you suppose happened in the four hundred years since then? I truly believe that one could well say it rained and snowed monks—and it would be no wonder if there were no city or village today without a monastery or two, or at least a terminary or stationary.[233] The histories chide Emperor Valentinian[234] because he used the monks for service in war. Alas, my dear man, these idle folks were multiplying too fast. One also reads that several kings of France forbade men, especially serfs, to become monks, for everybody flocked to the monasteries in search of freedom under the cowl.

A view of the Eberbach Abbey (1638). Bernard of Clairvaux founded this Cistercian monastery in 1136 on the east bank of the Rhine River.

230. Based on the *World Chronicle* of Johannes Nauclerus (c. 1426–1510) published in 1516, Luther incorrectly gives the first year of Bernard's abbacy as 1122 when it was 1115. Cf. Luther's *Supputatio annorum mundi*, WA 53:156. Cf. also the analysis of his sources in WA 53:9–15.

231. Emperors of the Holy Roman Empire: Henry III (r. 1039–1056), Henry IV (r. 1084–1106), and Henry V (r. 1111–1125).

232. The Order of Grandmont, originally located in Normandy, was formed in 1073. It disappeared after the French Revolution in 1789. The Augustinian Canons, founded after 1059, are to be distinguished from the Augustinian Eremites, the order Luther joined in 1505. The Carthusians were founded by Bruno of Cologne (1030–1101) in 1084 in the mountainous region near Grenoble in France. They were known for their almost total seclusion from the world. The Cistercians were founded at Cîteaux in 1098 by Robert of Molesme (c. 1029–1111). A stricter form of Benedictine monasticism, the Cistercian Order became famous through Bernard of Clairvaux. All of these orders express the yearning for renewed forms of religious life that found its fullest expression in what has been called the Reformation of the twelfth century.

233. Terms originally used to designate the houses of mendicant orders and later applied to other monasteries.

234. Luther confuses Valentinian I with his brother Valens, the Roman emperor from 364 to 378. It was Valens who, according to Platina (1421–1481), compelled Egyptian monks to enter the army and to return to the civic duties

The world wants to be fooled. If you wish to catch many robins and other birds, you must place an owl or a screech owl on the trap or lime-rod,[235] and you will succeed. Similarly, when the devil wants to trap Christians, he must put on a cowl, or (as Christ calls it) a sour, hypocritical expression [Matt. 6:16]. Thus we stand in greater awe of such owls and screech owls than of the true suffering, blood, wounds, death, and resurrection, which we see and hear that Christ, our Lord, endured because of our sin. So we fall, in throngs and with all our might, away from our Christian faith and into the new holiness, that is, into the devil's trap and lime-rod. For we always must have something new. Christ's death and resurrection, faith and love, are old and just ordinary things; that is why they must count for nothing, and so we must have new flatterers (as St. Paul says). And this serves us right since our ears itch so much for something new that we can no longer endure the old and genuine truth, "that we accumulate,"[f] that we weigh ourselves down with big piles of new teachings. That is just what has happened and will continue to happen. For the subsequent councils, especially the papal ones (for afterward they are almost all papal), did not merely refrain from condemning these new good works, but exalted them throughout the world far above the good old works, so that the pope canonized or elevated many saints from the monastic orders.

At first it was rather nice to look at—and still is—but in the end it becomes an abominable, monstrous thing, since everyone adds to it from day to day. Thus, the beginning of St. Francis's order[236] looked fine, but now it has become so crude that they even put cowls on the dead so that the dead might be saved in them.[237] Isn't it terrible to hear that? Well, that is the way it goes: if one starts to fall away from Christ and gets into the habit of falling, one can no longer stop. That has happened in our own time in the Netherlands, when Madame Margaret[238] ordered that she be made a nun after her death. It was done; she was dressed in a nun's garb, placed at a table, and offered food and drink served as for a true princess. Thus she atoned for her sin and became a holy nun. But after this had lasted a few days, the pious Emperor Charles heard of it, and he had it stopped. Had he not done that, I believe such an example would have flooded

f *Ut acervemus*, 2 Tim. 4:3. Luther's reference to flatterers also derives from this verse.

they had abandoned through their decision to become monks.

235. A lime-rod is a stick coated with an adhesive substance; it is used to catch birds. Because owls are predators, other birds will attack them. If they attack the owl attached to the lime-rod, they will be trapped by it.

236. Francis of Assisi (c. 1182–1226) and his original companions were itinerant preachers who scrupulously avoided having money and possessions. Shortly after his Order of Friars Minor (commonly known as the Franciscans) was founded, the order began to accumulate wealth. The debate about this wealth led to schism within the order in 1250 and to charges of heresy against those who insisted on absolute poverty.

237. This practice was not confined to Franciscans and was normally associated with a contribution to the monastery.

238. Margaret of Austria (1507–1530), aunt of Holy Roman Emperor Charles V and regent of the Netherlands.

the whole world. That is what the new holiness does and must do because it wants to do better than the true, old Christian holiness, which does not fool like this, but remains constant and always exercises itself in faith, love, humility, discipline, patience, etc.; one sees in it nothing abominable, but only lovely, charming, peaceful, kind, and useful examples that please God and all people. But the new holiness blusters with a peculiar, new demeanor to entice unsteady souls to itself. It makes a great ado, but there is nothing to it,[g] as St. Peter writes [2 Pet. 2:14-22].

Likewise, Gerson writes that the Carthusians are right when they apply their rule so rigorously that they eat no meat even if they should have to die.[239] Well then, if a pious physician here notices that the sick man could be helped by nothing but chicken broth or a bite of meat, then one does not obey the physician, but rather the sick man must die. There I praise St. Augustine, who writes in his *Rule*[h] that one should ask the physician's advice saying, "Not all people have the same capability, hence one should not regard all as equal." This is a true and beautiful "equity";[240] moreover, it does not force them to remain forever, for the monastery was not a prison but a voluntary association of a few priests. Dr. Staupitz[241] once told me that he had heard from the bishop of Worms, who was a Dahlberg,[242] that if St. Augustine had written nothing but the *Rule*, one would still have to say that he was an excellent, wise man. This is certainly true, for he would have utterly condemned those Carthusians as murderers, and their monasteries as veritable, physical dens of murderers (which in truth they are). I myself saw a sick man, who was still young, walking with a crutch in the Carthusian monastery in Erfurt;[243] I asked him whether he was excused from the choir and the watch. "No," he replied sadly, "I must perish."

But we got our just desserts. God sent us his Son to be our teacher and savior. Not satisfied with that, God preaches from his high, heavenly throne to us all, saying, "*Hunc audite*," "Listen to him" [Matt. 17:5]. Thus we should drop to our knees with the apostles and believe that we hear nothing else in the whole world. But instead we let the Father and the Son preach in vain,

g A German proverb, "*Ist doch nichts dahinden*."

h *The Rule of St. Aurelius Augustine* (*Regula S. Aurelii Augustini*), IX. MPL 32:1383=*La règle de saint Augustin*, ed. Luc Verheijen, O.S.A., Etudes Augustiniennes (Paris, 1967); *The Monastic Rules*, trans. Agatha Mary and Gerald Bonner (Hyde Park, NY: New City Press, 2004).

239. Jean Gerson, chancellor of the University of Paris. He asserted the authority of the general council over the pope at the various "reform councils" held in the beginning of the fifteenth century and wrote widely on topics related to reform of the church. See *Concerning the Carthusians' Abstention from Meat* (*De non esu carnium Carthusiensium*), *Œuvres complètes*, ed. P. Glorieux (Paris: Desclée & Cie, 1962), 3:77–95.

240. *Epiekeia*. Luther gives a transliteration of the Greek word usually translated as *equity* that Aristotle used to describe moderation in applying the law. Aristotle, *The Nicomachean Ethics*, trans. H. Rackham, Loeb Classical Library (Cambridge: Harvard University Press, 1934), Book 5, Ch. 10, 313–17.

241. Johann von Staupitz (c. 1460–1524) was Luther's superior in the Augustinian order and also his confessor and spiritual advisor. As such, Staupitz emphasized God's grace in his dealings with Luther. Staupitz arranged for Luther to begin teaching at Wittenberg and stood by him in the early years of the Reformation. When Staupitz saw that the dispute would not be resolved, he released Luther from his monastic vows. Staupitz remained in the Roman church but left the Augustinian order in 1521 and became a Benedictine abbot. See David C. Steinmetz, "Staupitz, Johann von," OER 4:109–111.

242. Johann von Dahlberg, bishop of Worms (1482–1503).

243. Luther stayed in Erfurt as a student and as a monk in the Augustinian monastery there from 1501 until 1508 and was undoubtedly familiar with the nearby Carthusian monastery.

do things on our own, and invent our own sermon. This then is the way it goes, as Ps. 81[:11-12] says, "My people did not listen to my voice; so I gave them over to their stubborn hearts." From this come such fine *etelothreskiae* and *apheidiae*—Col. 2[:23], "self-chosen spirituality" and "merciless severity to the body"—that we kill ourselves despite God's command that one should care for, not kill, the body. Don't you think that, if in accordance with St. Augustine's *Rule* and St. Paul's teaching, one had let the physicians give advice about the bodies of those in the religious orders, especially the women, many a fine person would have been helped who otherwise has had to go mad or has died—as daily experiences have indeed taught us? However, this was the time of wrath, when the new and mad holiness had to reign for the punishment of the world.

Fifth, a council has no power to impose new ceremonies on Christians, to be observed on pain of mortal sin or at the peril of conscience—such as fast days, feast days, food, drink, garb. But if they do this, St. Augustine confronts them with the words addressed to Januarius, "Observance of these things is free. Christ instituted few ceremonies."[i] Because they have the power to command them, we have the power to ignore them; indeed, we are forbidden to observe them by St. Paul in Col. 2[:16], "Let not your conscience be troubled over certain days, over fasting, food, or drink," etc.

Sixth, a council has the power and is bound to condemn such ceremonies in accordance with Scripture; for they are un-Christian and constitute a new idolatry or worship, which is not commanded by God, but forbidden.

Seventh, a council has no power to interfere in worldly law and government, etc.; for St. Paul says, "He who wants to serve God in spiritual warfare should refrain from engaging in civilian pursuits" [2 Tim. 2:4].[244]

Eighth, a council has the power and is bound to condemn such arbitrary ways or new laws, in accordance with Holy Scripture, that is, to throw the pope's decretals[j] into the fire.

Ninth, a council has no power to create statutes or decretals that seek nothing but tyranny, that is, statutes on how the bishops should have the power and authority to command what they

i *Epistola 54*. MPL 33:200=CSEL 34/II:160, 9–10; NPNF1 1:300.

j See n. 186, p. 384.

244. Many of the decrees of popes and councils touched on issues that the reformers considered to be the province of secular government. The NRSV of the verse Luther quotes reads, "No one serving in the army gets entangled in everyday affairs; the soldier's aim is to please the enlisting officer." Luther's wording of the verse is influenced by the Vulgate translation, with *militans* being understood as spiritual warfare.

will and everybody should tremble and obey; but it has the power and is bound to condemn this in accordance with Holy Scripture, 1 Pet. 5[:3], "Do not lord it over those in your charge," and as Christ says, "But not so with you; rather let the leader become as one who serves" [Luke 22:26].

Tenth, a council has the power to institute some ceremonies, provided, first, that they do not strengthen the bishops' tyranny; second, that they are useful and profitable to the people and show fine, orderly discipline and conduct. Thus it is necessary, for example, to have certain days, and also places where one can assemble; also certain hours for preaching and for the public administration of the sacraments, for praying, singing, praising and thanking God, etc.—as St. Paul says, 1 Cor. 14[:40], "All things should be done decently and in order." Such items do not serve the bishops' tyranny, but only the people's need, profit, and order. In summary, these must and cannot be dispensed with if the church is to survive.

But if someone is occasionally hindered by some emergency, sickness, or whatever it may be from observing this, it need not be sin. For it is done for his benefit and not for the benefit of the bishops. Christians will not harm themselves as a result.[k] What difference does it make to God if someone does not want to belong to such a group or participate in this way? All will find out for themselves. In summary, Christians are not bound to such order; they would rather do it than let it go if they are not forced into it. Here, therefore, no law can be laid down for them; they would want to do and would prefer to do more than such a law demands. But they who haughtily, proudly, and willfully despise it—let them go their way, for such people will also despise a higher law, be it divine or human.

Perhaps you might say here, "What do you finally want to make of the councils if you clip them so close? At that rate a pastor, indeed a schoolteacher (to say nothing of parents), would have greater power over his pupils than a council has over the church." I answer: Do you think then that the offices of the pastor and the schoolteacher are so low that they cannot be compared with the councils? How could one assemble a council if there were no pastors or bishops? How could we get pastors if

k This and the following sentences in this paragraph are singular in the original.

there were no schools? I am speaking of those schoolteachers who instruct the children and the youth not only in the arts,[245] but also train them in Christian doctrine and faithfully impress it upon them; I also speak in the same manner of pastors who teach God's word in faithfulness and purity. For I can easily prove that the poor, insignificant pastor at Hippo, St. Augustine, taught more than all the councils (to say nothing of the most holy popes in Rome, whom I fear to mention). I will go further than that: there is more in the Children's Creed[246] than in all the councils. The Lord's Prayer and the Ten Commandments also teach more than all the councils. Moreover, they not only teach, but also guard against anything new that opposes the ancient doctrine. For heaven's sake! How the papists will pluck these words of mine from their context, shout them to bits, torture them to death, and prove them illogical; but meanwhile they will not mention the reasons I have spoken in this manner. For they are pious and honest people, who cannot do anything but calumniate[l] and lie, something I should indeed be afraid of! But may God forgive me, I really cannot do it; I would rather let them go on with their slander and their lies.

But let us, you and me, discuss this subject together. What then can a council do, or what is its task? Listen yourself to their own words. *Anathematizamus* is the name of their office—"We condemn." Indeed, they speak even more humbly and do not say, "We condemn," but *anathematizat ecclesia*, "The holy Christian church condemns." The council's condemnation would not terrify me, but the holy church's condemnation would slay me in an instant because of the Man who says, "I am with you always, to the close of the age" [Matt. 28:20]. Oh, this Man's condemnation is not to be endured. But the councils, since they appeal to the holy Christian church as to the true and supreme judge on earth, testify that they cannot judge according to their own discretion, but that the church, which preaches, believes, and confesses Holy Scripture, is the judge—as we shall hear. Just as a thief or a murderer would be secure from the judge as a private person, but law and country are united in the judge, their servant, and of these two he must be afraid.

A council, then, is nothing but a consistory, a royal court, a supreme court,[247] or the like, in which the judges, after hearing

245. A reference to the liberal arts, that is, basic education.

246. The Apostles' Creed.

247. *Consistorium, Hofegericht, Camergericht*. These terms represent names for courts in sixteenth-century Germany. The first Protestant *Consistorium*, not unlike a modern denominational synod, was formed in Saxony in 1539. The *Consistorium* was originally the supreme court in ancient Rome, and later the highest ecclesiastical court within the medieval church.

l Ger.: *Calumnirn*.

the parties, pronounce sentence, but with this humility, "For the sake of the law," that is, "Our office is *anathematizare*, 'to condemn'; but not according to our whim or will, or newly invented law, but according to the ancient law, which is acknowledged as the law throughout the entire empire." Thus a council condemns a heretic, not according to its own discretion, but according to the law of the empire, that is, according to Holy Scripture, which they confess to be the law of the holy church. Such law, empire, and judge must surely be feared on pain of eternal damnation, for such law is God's word, the empire is God's church, and the judge is the official or servant of both.[248]

248. By saying the law is God's word and the empire is God's church, Luther emphasizes the divine origins of civil government.

Not only the council, but every pastor and schoolteacher is also the servant or judge of this law and empire. Moreover, a council cannot administer this judicial office forever without intermission; for the bishops cannot forever remain assembled together, but must gather only in times of certain emergencies and then anathematize, or be judges. Thus, if an Arius in Alexandria grows too strong for his pastor or bishop, attracts the people, and also urges other pastors and people in the country to join him, so that the pastor in Alexandria is defeated and his judicial office can no longer defend the law of the empire, that is, the true Christian faith—in such an emergency and at such a time the other pastors and bishops should rally with all their might around the pastor of Alexandria and help him defend the true faith against Arius and condemn Arius to save the others, so that this misery does not get the upper hand. And if the pastors are unable to come, the pious Emperor Constantine should add his power to help assemble the bishops. It is just like when a fire breaks out; if the man of the house cannot extinguish it alone, all the neighbors should hurry over and help quench it. And if they do not hurry over, the government should help and command that they must gather to anathematize or condemn the fire, in order to save the other houses.[249]

249. Melanchthon, in "Treatise on the Power and Primacy of the Pope," wrote: "It is especially necessary for the most eminent members of the church, the kings and princes, to attend to the church and take care that errors are removed and consciences restored to health." BC, 339.

Thus the council is the great servant or judge in this empire and law. Yet when the emergency has passed, it has done its duty—just as, in temporal government, the supreme, great judges have to help when the lower, secondary courts prove too weak to cope with an evil, until the case is at last brought before the highest, greatest court, the diet, which cannot meet forever either, but must adjourn after the emergency is over and again leave matters to the lower courts. At the diet, however, it happens that occasionally new or additional laws have to be enacted, or that old laws have to be amended, improved, or even abolished; justice cannot forever be administered according to an eternal law, for this is a temporal government which rules over temporal, changeable, and variable things. Therefore the laws that are made for these changeable things must also change. If that for which the law was made no longer exists, then the law no longer represents anything, just as the city of Rome no longer has the institutions and ways of life that it had before; and therefore the laws that were passed for these are also dead and invalid. Transient things have transient laws.

But in this empire of the church the rule is, "The word of our God will stand for ever" [Isa. 40:8]. One has to live according to it and refrain from creating new or different words of God and from establishing new and different articles of faith. That is why pastors and schoolteachers are the lowly, but daily, permanent, eternal judges who anathematize without interruption, that is, fend off the devil and his raging. A council, being a great judge, must make old, great rascals[250] pious or kill them, but it cannot produce any others. A pastor and a schoolteacher deal with small, young rascals and constantly train new people to become bishops and councils, whenever it is necessary. A council prunes the large limbs from the tree or pulls up evil trees. But a pastor and a schoolteacher plant and cultivate young trees and useful shrubs in the garden. Oh, they have a precious office and task, and they are the church's richest jewels; they preserve the church. Therefore all the lords should do their part to preserve pastors and schools. For if indeed we cannot have councils, the parishes and schools, small though they are, are eternal and useful councils.

One can see quite well how earnestly the ancient emperors regarded parishes and schools,[251] since they endowed the monasteries so richly. That they were primarily schools is evidenced by these names: provost, dean, *scholasticus*, cantor, *canonici*, vicars, custodians, etc.[252] But what has become of these? O Lord God! If they were at least willing to do something, remain what they were, keep what they had, were princes and lords, and again introduced hours of study and compelled the canons, vicars, and choir pupils to listen to a daily lesson from Holy Scripture so that they would again, in some sense, look like a school, and so that one could have pastors and bishops and thus help to

250. That is, those judged heretical and condemned by the councils.

251. Charlemagne set the example for subsequent emperors of looking to the monasteries for aid in educating the Christian empire he ruled. Luther had already expressed the idea that monasteries were originally schools in *The Smalcald Articles*, Part II, Art. III. BC, 306; TAL 2:437-38.

252. Monastic offices whose titles no longer necessarily corresponded to the duties the office holder performed in the monastery.

rule the church. O Lord God, what immeasurable benefit they could be to the church! And God would not begrudge them their wealth or power, but let them have them, if they but amended their shameful lives. But all our sighs and complaints are in vain. They neither hear nor see; they allow the parishes to lie waste and the people to become rude and wild without the word of God. I have heard it from people whom I must believe that in many dioceses there are two, three, and four hundred good parishes vacant. Isn't it dreadful and terrible to hear of such conditions among Christians? May God in heaven have mercy and give ear to our pitiable sighs and lamentations. Amen.

And to finish this matter of the councils at last, I hold that one should now be able to understand what a council is, its rights, power, office, and task; also, which councils are genuine and which false: namely, that they should confess and defend the ancient faith, and not institute new articles of faith against the ancient faith, nor institute new good works against the old good works, but defend the old good works against the new good works—because he who defends the old faith against the new faith also defends the old good works against the new good works. For as the faith is, so are also the fruits or good works, though the two councils[253] did not see this conclusion. Otherwise, they would have condemned the archimandrite[254] Eutyches not only because of the faith he professed (which they did in earnest), but also because of his monkery (which they did not condemn); on the contrary, they affirmed it, thereby proving that they were poor dialecticians,[255] stating a premise but not drawing the conclusion—a common evil throughout the world. They just made the error with regard to good works that Nestorius and Eutyches[256] made with regard to faith. That is to say: God not only wants to make us children in the faith, but also wants to show us up as fools in dialectic and regards us as simple Nestoriuses and Eutycheses, in order to humble us. For even if the theology of Nestorius and Eutyches is condemned, their rotten dialectic still remains in the world for all time, as it was there from the beginning, namely, that one states the premise, but does not draw the conclusion. How much can one say about it? If you have all the councils you are still no Christian because of them; they give you too little. If you also have all the fathers, they too give you too little. You must still go to Holy Scripture, where you find everything in abundance, or to the catechism,[257]

253. Ephesus (431) and Chalcedon (451).

254. The head of a monastery. See p. 401.

255. *Dialectici*. In the medieval university, dialectic, or logic, was the most important part of the trivium, that is, the three liberal arts dealing with language—grammar, rhetoric, and dialectic.

256. For Nestorius and Eutyches, see n. 221, p. 398–99.

257. By *catechism*, Luther means not only his printed catechisms but any basic instruction in the Christian faith centered in the Ten Commandments, the Apostles' Creed, and the Lord's Prayer.

where it is summarized, and where far more is found than in all the councils and fathers.

Finally, a council should occupy itself only with matters of faith, and then only when faith is in jeopardy. For public evil works can be condemned and the good ones maintained at home by the temporal government and by pastors and parents. But the false good works also belong to matters of faith, since they corrupt the true faith. Therefore they too are part of the business of a council, if the pastors are too weak to deal with them. The councils (as was already said) did not pay any attention to them, with the exception of one or two small councils, such as that of Gangra mentioned above. Ceremonies ought to be completely disregarded by the councils and should be left at home in the parishes, indeed, in the schools so that the schoolmaster, along with the pastor, would be "master of ceremonies."[m] All others will learn these from the students, without any effort or difficulty. For instance, the common people will learn from the pupils what, when, and how to sing or pray in church; they will also learn what to sing by the bier or at the grave. When the pupils kneel and fold their hands as the schoolmaster beats time with his baton during the singing of "And was made man,"[n] the common people will imitate them. When they doff their little hats or bend their knees whenever the name of Jesus Christ is mentioned, or whatever other Christian discipline and gestures they may exercise, the common people will do afterward without instruction, moved by the living example. Even under the pope all the ceremonies originated in the schools and the parishes, except where the pope was bent on exercising his tyranny with measures regarding food, fasts, feasts, etc. However, here too moderation must be applied, so that there do not get to be too many ceremonies in the end. Above all, one must see to it that they will not be considered necessary for salvation, but only serve external discipline and order, which can be changed any time and which must not be commanded as eternal laws in the church (as the papal ass does) and embodied in books with tyrannical threats, for this is something entirely external, bodily, transitory, and changeable.

m *Magister ceremontarum.*

n "*Et homo factus est.*" From the Nicene Creed.

Accordingly, we would have enough matters today that are sufficiently important and weighty to warrant the summoning of a council. For we poor, wretched Christians of small faith and, unfortunately, real *Misergi*,[o] that is, Christians who hate work—those of us who are still left—would have to put the pope on trial, together with his followers, because of the aforementioned article of St. Peter which says that it is tempting God if one encumbers the faithful with unbearable burdens "that neither our ancestors nor we have been able to bear" [Acts 15:10] (and which especially the pope and his ilk will not touch with one finger). St. Peter indeed speaks of the law of Moses, which God commanded; but the papal ass oppressed us with his own filthy, foul, and stinking burdens, so that the holy church was forced to be his toilet—and whatever issued from him above and below, we had to worship as God. Furthermore, he set fire to and burned down not one or two churches, as Arius and his kind did,[258] but the whole Christian church when he destroyed, as far as he could, St. Peter's ancient, true article of faith; for that we must be saved by the grace of God alone (as St. Peter testifies [Acts 15:11]), as all of Christendom since the beginning of the world was saved, all the patriarchs, prophets, kings, saints, etc.—this he calls heresy, and he has consistently condemned this same article from the beginning, and cannot desist from doing so.

258. Arius himself never burned down a church. Luther is probably referring to destruction caused by the Vandals, who were Arians, in fifth-century North Africa.

At this point we ask and cry for a council, requesting advice and help from all of Christendom against this arch-arsonist of churches and slayer of Christians, so that we can again have this article of St. Peter. But we also demand that no Nestorian or Eutychian logic be employed in it, which states or confesses one point but denies the conclusion or other point. We demand the whole article, full and pure, as it was instituted by St. Peter and taught by St. Paul, namely, that everything be condemned whose condemnation follows from this article—or, as St. Peter calls it, "the unbearable, impossible burden," and St. Augustine, "the countless burdens imposed on the church by the bishops."[259] What good does it do to admit the truth of the first part, that we are to be truly justified and saved solely by the grace of Christ, and still not let the second part, its necessary conclusion, follow? Thus St. Paul says, "But if it is by grace, it is no longer on the basis of works; otherwise, grace would no longer be grace"

259. In the frequently quoted letter to Januarius. *Epistola 54*. MPL 33:201=CSEL 34/II:160; NPNF1 1:300.

o A Latin term meaning "those who feel miserable about work."

[Rom. 11:6], and St. Peter, "If it is grace, it is not the intolerable burden; if it is the intolerable burden, then it is not the grace of Christ, and it is tempting God."[260] St. Augustine, too, says, "Since Christ did not wish to burden the church with many ceremonies—indeed, wanted it to be free—it was not his will to have it oppressed by the innumerable burdens of the bishops, making the lot of the church worse than that of the Jews, who were burdened with God's laws and not (like the church) with human, presumptuous, arbitrary ordinances."[p]

This dialectic of St. Peter, St. Paul, and St. Augustine is what we want to have, for it is the dialectic of the Holy Spirit that treats matters in their entirety rather than breaking them up in Nestorian fashion, allowing one thing alone to be true, but not the other that must also be true because it follows from the first. Otherwise, it would be like the stories recorded about several kings of Israel and Judah, who, to be sure, re-established the worship of God, but failed to do away with the high places or other altars and worship. This the prophet Elijah called "limping with two different opinions" [1 Kgs. 18:21]. We Germans call it "trying to make two brothers-in-law with one sister."[261] Thus they tried to give one nation two different gods—or, even if they did institute any reforms at all, they still permitted a strange, different god to remain alongside the true one. They too were stupid Nestorian dialecticians who confessed that only one God should be worshiped and yet did not see and did not permit the logical conclusion that all other gods had to be removed; otherwise, they could not have the one God either. That is why, in the council we demand, we will not tolerate a Nestorius, who gives us one thing, yet takes another from us, with whom we cannot even keep the one thing given to us, and the pope is just the sort who does that.[q] If the council grants us that the grace of Christ alone saves us and does not also grant us the conclusion and deduction that works do not save us, but maintains that works are necessary for satisfaction or for righteousness, then the first that was granted to us is thereby again taken from us, namely, that grace alone, without works, saves us.[262] Thus we keep nothing, and the evil is made worse.

p *Epistola 54*. MPL 33:200=CSEL 34/II:160, 9–10; NPNF1 1:300.

q *Und ist ein rechter Gebers Nemers.*

260. Luther's paraphrase of Acts 15:10-11.

261. That is, offering the same woman in marriage to two men at the same time.

262. The significance of this position can be seen in the subsequent official conversations between Protestants and Roman Catholics. Such colloquies, held in the years following this treatise, found agreement on some significant theological points, including a statement on justification adopted at the Colloquy of Regensburg (1541). Luther accepted this formula on justification, but considered it problematic unless the opposition also abandoned certain other positions concerning the relationship between faith and works. See Vinzenz Pfnür, "Colloquies," OER 1:375–83. Today, the ongoing dialogue between the Lutheran World Federation and the Roman Catholic Church has reached numerous agreements, including one on justification similar to that of Regensburg. Regional dialogue in the United States is in the process of considering doctrines and practices that flow out of the understanding of justification.

I will speak German:[r] the pope should not only abolish all his tyranny of human ordinances in the council, but also believe with us that even the good works performed in accordance with God's commandments cannot help to achieve righteousness, to blot out sin, to attain God's grace—only faith can do this, faith in Christ, who is a king of righteousness in us through his precious blood, death, and resurrection, with which he blotted out our sin for us, made satisfaction, reconciled God, and redeemed us from death, wrath, and hell. Therefore he should condemn and burn all his bulls, decretals, books on indulgences, purgatory, monasteries, saint worship, and pilgrimages, together with all his countless lies and idolatries, since they rant directly against this article of St. Peter. He should also return everything he bought, stole, robbed, plundered, or acquired through it, especially his false primacy, which he extols as being so necessary that no one can be saved who is not subject to him.[263] The pope's hat[264] did not die for my sin, nor is its name Christ—and all Christians before and under him were sanctified and saved without his hat.

This, I think, is indeed an important enough matter about which to hold an impressive, decisive, and mighty council. The emperor and kings should lend a hand here and force the pope into it, if he is unwilling, as the emperors did in the four principal councils. But not all the bishops, abbots, monks, doctors, and worthless riffraff, or the large number of hangers-on, should come to it. Otherwise, it will be a council that spends its first year in arriving and in quarreling over who shall sit at the head, and who is to walk ahead of whom; the second year in reveling, banqueting, racing, and fencing; the third year in other matters and also in burning, perhaps a Jan Hus[265] or two—and meanwhile incurring expenses so vast that one could indeed finance a campaign against the Turks.[266] On the contrary, it would be necessary to summon from all lands people who are thoroughly versed in Holy Scripture and who are also seriously and sincerely concerned with God's honor, the Christian faith, the church, the salvation of souls, and the peace of the world. Among them there should also be a few intelligent and reliable members of the temporal estate (for this is also a matter that concerns them).[267] For instance, if Sir Hans von Schwarzenberg[268] were living, he and

r I.e., frankly.

263. A reference to the last line of the bull *Unam sanctam* issued by Pope Boniface VIII in 1302: "Furthermore, we declare, we proclaim, we define that it is absolutely necessary for salvation that every human creature be subject to the Roman Pontiff." Petry, ed., *Readings in the Early and Medieval Church* (Baker, 1981), 506.

264. The hat, whether of bishop, cardinal, or pope, symbolized the power of the office. See the image of Pope Julius II's heralds, p. 334.

265. Jan Hus (c. 1369–1415), reformer of Bohemia who was burned at the stake after being condemned by the Council of Constance. Eck had compared Luther to Hus during the Leipzig debate (1519), which led Luther to defend Hus in the debate against the condemnation of Constance. There were many similarities between Luther and Hus, including their criticism of indulgences, but they also differed on many key points, including the nature of the church. See Scott H. Hendrix, "'We Are All Hussites': Hus and Luther Revisited," *Archiv für Reformationsgeschichte* 65 (1974): 134–61.

266. Pope Paul III (r. 1534–1549) issued a bull on 15 June 1537, *De indulgentiis contra Turcam*, asking for assistance against the Turks. Cf. Luther's comments on the bull in *The Bull of Paul III* (*Bulla Papae Pauli III*). WA 50:113–16.

267. Luther's willingness to include lay representatives reflects his conviction that all Christians should be "people taught by God" (*theodidacti*).

268. Johann Freiherr zu Schwarzenberg (1463–1528), a supporter of the Reformation, was imperial chamberlain in 1521 and an influential adviser to the emperor during the diets in Nuremberg

men like him could be trusted. And it would suffice if there were a total of three hundred select men to whom the fate of the country and the people could be entrusted—just as the first council[269] had only three hundred and eighteen members, summoned from all the lands the Turks and our monarchs now rule, and seventeen of them were false and Arians anyway. The second at Constantinople had one hundred and fifty; the third at Ephesus, two hundred; the fourth at Chalcedon, six hundred and thirty, almost as many as the others combined, and yet these men were quite unlike the fathers in Nicaea and Constantinople.[270]

Moreover, the affairs of all countries that no one else can or cares to judge, as well as old, out-of-date, and bad quarrels should not be unearthed and dumped into the lap of the council. A Constantine should be there to rake up all these matters and cast them into the fire, ordering that they be judged and decided at home in the respective countries; he should order them to attack instead the questions at issue and dispose of these as quickly as possible. Then the pope's heresies, indeed, abominations, would be read in public, one by one, and all would be found in opposition to St. Peter's article and to the ancient, true Christian faith of the church, which has adhered to St. Peter's doctrine from the beginning of the world; and they would be promptly condemned, etc.

"Well," you say, "it is futile to hope for such a council." I myself think so too. But if one wants to talk about it and asks and wishes for a council, one would have to wish for a council like that, or forget about it completely, desire none, and say nothing at all. For the first council in Nicaea, and the second one in Constantinople were councils like that—whose examples could indeed be easily followed. And I point this out to show that it would be the duty of emperors and kings,[271] since they are Christians, to summon such a council for the salvation of the many thousands of souls that the pope, with his tyranny and avoidance of a council (as far as he is concerned), allows to perish, even though they all could be restored to St. Peter's article and to the true, ancient Christian faith. Otherwise, they would have to be lost, for they cannot obtain this doctrine of St. Peter's because they neither hear nor see anything of it.

And even if other monarchs declined to do anything toward a principal council, Emperor Charles[272] and the German princes could still hold a provincial council in Germany. Some think

in 1522 and 1524. *Lexikon der deutschen Geschichte*, ed. Gerhard Taddey (Stuttgart: Alfred Kröner, 1977), 1103.

269. Nicaea (325).

270. Luther derived this information from the work of Crabbe. Cf. WA 50:605, n. *b*.

An etching of Johann von Schwarzenberg by Albrecht Dürer (1471–1528).

271. Luther had made the point that the secular rulers had the right to reform the church if the bishops refused to do it already in his *To the Christian Nobility of the German Nation* (1520), TAL 1:369–466.

272. Emperor Charles V ruled the Holy Roman Empire from 1519 to 1556.

that this would result in a schism, but who knows?[273] If we did our part in it and sincerely sought God's honor and the salvation of souls, God might yet touch and turn the hearts of the other monarchs so that they would, in time, approve and accept the judgment of this council. It could not happen suddenly; but if Germany were to accept it, it would also have an echo in other countries, whither it cannot or can hardly reach without a great preacher such as the council is, and without a strong voice heard from afar.

Well then, if we must despair of a council let us commend the matter to the true judge, our merciful God. Meanwhile we shall promote the small and the young councils, that is, parishes and schools, and propagate St. Peter's article in every way possible, preserving it against all the accursed new articles of the faith and of the new good works with which the pope has flooded the world. I shall comfort myself when I see the children wearing bishop's masks,[274] thinking that God makes and will make genuine bishops of these play-bishops; on the other hand, I shall regard as play-bishops and mockers of God's majesty those who, according to their title, ought to be real bishops—as Moses says, "They made me jealous with what is no god. . . . So I will make them jealous with what is no people, provoke them with a foolish nation" [Deut. 32:21]. It will not be the first time that he repudiates bishops. In Hosea he threatened, "Because you have rejected knowledge, I reject you from being a priest to me" [Hos. 4:6]. And so it came, and so it comes to pass.[s]

May that suffice regarding the councils. In conclusion, we shall now also speak about the church.

Part III

[The Church]

Just as they scream about the fathers and the councils, without knowing what fathers and councils are, only to drown out our voices with mere letters, so they also scream about the church. But as for saying what, who, and where the church is, they do not render either the church or God even the service of asking

s *Et factum est ita, et fit ita.*

273. This was the reason the Lutheran princes rejected the idea of holding their own council to counter the papal council. See the introduction, pp. 319–20.

274. Boys sometimes took the place of bishops as part of festival celebrations, usually during the Christmas season or on the Feast of St. Gregory the Great (12 March). ODCC, s.v. "boy bishop," 231; "Fools, Feast of," 625.

the question or thinking about it. They like very much to be regarded as the church, as pope, cardinals, bishops, and yet to be allowed, under this glorious name, to be nothing but pupils of the devil, desiring nothing more than to practice sheer knavery and villainy.

Well then, setting aside various writings and analyses of the word "church," we shall this time confine ourselves simply to the Children's Creed,[275] which says, "I believe in one holy Christian church, the communion of saints." Here the creed clearly indicates what the church is, namely, a communion of saints, that is, a crowd[276] or assembly of people who are Christians and holy, which is called a Christian holy crowd, or church. Yet this word "church"[t] is not a truly German word[u] and does not convey the sense or meaning that should be taken from this article.[277]

In Acts 19[:39] the town clerk uses the word *ecclesia* for the assembly or the people who had hurried together to the market place, saying, "It shall be settled in the regular assembly." Further, "When he said this, he dismissed the assembly" [v. 41]. In these and other passages the *ecclesia* or church is nothing but an assembly of people, though they probably were heathens and not Christians. It is the same term used by town councilmen for their assembly that they summon to the city hall. Now there are many peoples in the world; the Christians, however, are a specially called people and are therefore called not just *ecclesia*, "church," or "people," but *sancta catholica Christiana*, that is, "a Christian holy people" who believe in Christ. That is why they are called a Christian people and have the Holy Spirit, who sanctifies them daily, not only through the forgiveness of sin acquired for them by Christ (as the Antinomians foolishly believe),[v] but also through the abolition, the purging, and the mortification of sins, on the basis of which they are called a holy people. Thus the "holy Christian church" is synonymous with a Christian and holy people or, as one is also wont to express it, with "holy Christendom," or "whole Christendom." The Old Testament uses the term "God's people."

If the words "I believe that there is a holy Christian people" had been used in the Children's Creed, all the misery connected

t *Kirche.*

u *Undeudsch.*

v See n. 185, pp. 383–84.

275. The Apostles' Creed.

276. Luther uses this word, *hauffe* (*Haufen*), to describe both the true church as an assembly and the pope with his followers who claim the title *church* for themselves.

277. The German word *Kirche* and the English word *church* are both derived from the Greek word *kyriakon*, meaning "of the Lord." A church was a "building of the Lord" (*kyriakon doma*).

with this meaningless and obscure word ("church") might easily have been avoided. For the words "Christian holy people" would have brought with them, clearly and powerfully, the proper understanding and judgment of what is, and what is not, church. Whoever would have heard the words "Christian holy people" could have promptly concluded that the pope is no people, much less a holy Christian people. So too the bishops, priests, and monks are not holy, Christian people, for they do not believe in Christ, nor do they lead a holy life, but are rather the wicked and shameful people of the devil. He who does not truly believe in Christ is not Christian or a Christian. He who does not have the Holy Spirit against sin is not holy. Consequently, they cannot be "a Christian holy people," that is, *sancta et catholica ecclesia*.

But since we use this meaningless word "church" in the Children's Creed, the common man thinks of the stone house called a church, as painted by the artists; or, at best, they paint the apostles, disciples, and the mother of God, as on Pentecost, with the Holy Spirit hovering over them. This is still bearable; but they are the holy Christian people of a specific time, in this case, the beginning. *Ecclesia*, however, should mean the holy Christian people, not only of the days of the apostles, who are long since dead, but to the end of the world, so that there is always a holy Christian people on earth, in whom Christ lives, works, and rules, *per redemptionem*, "through grace and the remission of sin," and the Holy Spirit, *per vivificationem et sanctificationem*, "through daily purging of sin and renewal of life," so that we do not remain in sin but are enabled and obliged to lead a new life, abounding in all kinds of good works, as the Ten Commandments or the two tables of Moses' law command, and not in old, evil works. That is St. Paul's teaching. But the pope, with his followers, has applied both the name and the image of the church to himself and to his vile, accursed crowd,[w] under the meaningless word *ecclesia*, "church," etc.

Nevertheless, they give themselves the right name when they call themselves *ecclesia* (that is, if we interpret this term to agree with their way of life), either *Romana* or *sancta*, but do not add (as, indeed, they cannot) *catholica*. For *ecclesia* means "a people"; that they are, just as the Turks too, are *ecclesia*, "a people." *Ecclesia Romana* means "a Roman people"; that they are too, and indeed

w *Hauffe*. See n. 276, p. 417.

much more Roman than the heathen of ancient times were. *Ecclesia Romana sancta* means "a holy Roman people"; that they are too, for they have invented a holiness far greater than the holiness of Christians, or than the holy Christian people possess. Their holiness is a Roman holiness, *Romanae ecclesiae*, a holiness "of the Roman people," and they are now even called *sanctissimi, sacrosancti*, "the most holy," as Virgil speaks of a "holy thirst for gold,"[278] and Plautus of "the most holy one of all";[279] for they cannot stand Christian holiness. Therefore they are not entitled to the name "Christian church" or "Christian people," if for no other reason than that "Christian church" is a name and "Christian holiness" an entity common to all churches and all Christians in the world; therefore it is called "catholic." But they have little, if any, regard for this common name and holiness; instead, they invented a special, higher, different, better holiness than that of others. This is to be known as *sanctitas Romana et ecclesiae Romanae sanctitas*, that is, "Roman holiness and the holiness of the Roman people."

For Christian holiness, or the holiness common to Christendom, is found where the Holy Spirit gives people faith in Christ and thus sanctifies them, Acts 15[:9], that is, he renews heart, soul, body, work, and conduct, inscribing the commandments of God not on tables of stone, but in hearts of flesh, 2 Cor. 3[:3]. Or, if I may speak plainly, the Holy Spirit imparts true knowledge of God, according to the first table, so that those whom the Spirit enlightens with true faith can resist all heresies, overcome all false ideas and errors, and thus remain pure in faith in opposition to the devil. The Holy Spirit also bestows strength, and comforts timid, despondent, weak consciences against the accusation and turmoil of sin, so that the souls do not succumb or despair, and also do not become terrified of torment, pain, death, and the wrath and judgment of God, but rather, comforted and strengthened in hope, they cheerfully, boldly, and joyfully overcome the devil. The Holy Spirit also imparts true fear and love of God, so that we do not despise God and become irritated and angry with his wondrous judgments, but love, praise, thank, and honor him for all that occurs, good or evil. That is called new holy life in the soul, in accordance with the first table of Moses. It is also called *tres virtutes theologicas*, "the three principal virtues of Christians,"[280] namely, faith, hope, and love; and the Holy Spirit, who imparts, does, and effects this (gained for us by Christ) is

278. *Sacra fames, sacra hostia*. Virgil (70–19 BCE), a Roman poet, in *Aeneid*, III, 57. See *Virgil: Eclogues, Georgics, Aeneid I–III*, trans. H. Rushton Fairclough, Loeb Classical Library, 2d rev. ed. (Cambridge: Harvard University Press, 1956), 352. Luther, quoting from memory, leaves out the term "gold" (*auri*). Luther points out through these quotes from pagan Roman authors that the word *holy* in and of itself is not Christian.

279. *Omnium sacerrumus*. Plautus (d. 184 BCE), another Roman poet, in *Mostellaria*, IV, 2, 67, in *The Comedies of Plautus*, trans. Henry T. Riley, 2 vols. (London, 1884), 2:500.

280. Literally, "the three theological virtues." Added to the four cardinal virtues of classical antiquity—prudence, justice, fortitude, and temperance—they became the seven virtues of medieval theology. Frequently the subject of preaching, the virtues were also depicted in art. In both sermons and art, they were usually pitted against their opposite, the seven vices, or deadly sins—lust, gluttony, greed, sloth, wrath, envy, and pride.

therefore called "sanctifier" or "life-giver."[x] For the old Adam[281] is dead and cannot do it, and in addition has to learn from the law that he is unable to do it and that he is dead; he would not know this of himself.

In accordance with the second table of the Law, the Holy Spirit also sanctifies Christians in the body and induces them willingly to obey parents and rulers, to conduct themselves peacefully and humbly, to be not wrathful, vindictive, or malicious, but patient, friendly, obliging, brotherly, and loving, not

The Seven Virtues (c. 1465–1470), painted by Anton Francesco dello Scheggia (1441–1476).

unchaste, not adulterous or lewd, but chaste and pure with wife, child, and servants, or without wife and child. And on and on: they do not steal, are not usurious, avaricious, do not defraud, etc., but work honorably, support themselves honestly, lend willingly, and give and help wherever they can. Thus they do not lie, deceive, and backbite, but are kind, truthful, faithful, and trustworthy, and do whatever else the commandments of God prescribe. That is the work of the Holy Spirit, who sanctifies and also awakens the body to such a new life until it is perfected in the life beyond. That is what is called "Christian holiness." And there must always be such people on earth, even though it may be but two or three, or only children. Unfortunately, only a few of them are old folks. And those who are not such new people

x *Sanctificator* or *vivificator.*

281. In *The Large Catechism*, Luther describes the "old Adam " (old creature) in this way: "What is the old creature? It is what is born in us from Adam, irascible, spiteful, envious, unchaste, greedy, lazy, proud—yes—and unbelieving; it is beset with all vices and nature has nothing good in it" (BC, 465).

should not count themselves as Christians; nor should they be comforted with much babbling about the forgiveness of sins and the grace of Christ, as though they were Christians—like the Antinomians do.[282]

For they, having rejected and being unable to understand the Ten Commandments, preach much about the grace of Christ, yet they only strengthen and comfort those who remain in their sins, telling them not to fear and be terrified by sins, since they are all removed by Christ. They see and yet they let the people go on in their public sins, without any renewal or improvement of their lives. Thus it becomes quite evident that they truly fail to understand the faith and Christ, and thereby abrogate both when they preach about it. How can someone speak lightly about the works of the Holy Spirit in the first table—about comfort, grace, forgiveness of sins—if that person does not heed or practice the works of the Holy Spirit in the second table, which can be understood and experienced, while that same person has never attempted or experienced those of the first table? Therefore it is certain that they neither have nor understand Christ or the Holy Spirit, and their talk is nothing but froth on the tongue, and they are, as already said, true Nestoriuses and Eutycheses, who confess or teach Christ in the premise, in the substance, and yet deny him in the conclusion or *idiomata*;[283] that is, they teach Christ and yet destroy him through their teaching.

All this then has been said about Christian holiness, which the pope does not want. He has to have a special holiness that is much holier, namely, that found in the prescription of chasubles, tonsures, cowls, garb, food, festivals, days, monkery, nunnery, Masses, saint-worship, and countless other items of an external, bodily, transitory nature. If one lives under it without faith, fear of God, hope, love, and whatever the Holy Spirit accomplishes according to the first table, if one lives in misbelief, uncertainty of heart, doubts, contempt of God, impatience with God, and false trust in works (that is, idolatry), if one lives not in the grace of Christ and his merit, but in the atonement by works, even selling the surplus ones to others and taking in exchange all the goods and wealth of the world as well earned—all that is of no consequence because such a person may be holier than Christian holiness itself.

Thus, in the second table it matters not that they teach disobedience toward parents and rulers, that they even murder,

282. See n. 185, p. 383–84.

283. A Greek word that means what is distinctive to or characteristic of something. The Antinomians wished to preach Christ to the exclusion of all else. Because they excluded even God's work in the law, they failed, according to Luther, to bring the message of salvation to their hearers, with the result that precisely that which Christ came to do was left undone.

Pope Cornelius (r. 251-253) is depicted in full papal regalia, including tiara (crown), in a sixteenth-century painting by Meister von Meskirch (1500-1543). He holds a sword rather than the more common shepherd's staff. The sword is here as an attribute—a pictorial reference to the common story that he was martyred by beheading. In his other hand he holds a palm frond, which is a reference to martyrdom. Cornelius was sent into exile during the persecution under Emperor Trebonianus Gallus and died in 253.

make war, set people against on another, envy, hate, avenge, are unchaste, lie, steal, are usurious, defraud, and indulge in every villainy to the utmost. Just throw a surplice over your head and you are holy in accordance with the Roman church's holiness, and you can indeed be saved without the Christian holiness. But we will pay no attention to these filthy people, for any effort expended on them will be futile. "God's wrath has overtaken them at last," as St. Paul says [1 Thess. 2:16]. Instead, we shall discuss the church among ourselves.

[The Marks of the Church]

Well then, the Children's Creed teaches us (as was said) that a Christian holy people is to be and to remain on earth until the end of the world. This is an article of faith that cannot be terminated until that which it believes comes, as Christ promises, "I am with you always, to the end of the age" [Matt. 28:20]. But how will or how can a poor confused person tell where such Christian holy people are to be found in this world? Indeed, they are supposed to be in this life and on earth, for they of course believe that a heavenly nature and an eternal life are to come, but as yet they do not possess them. Therefore they must still be in this life and remain in this life and in this world until the end of the world. For they profess, "I believe in another life"; thereby they confess that they have not yet arrived in the other life, but believe in it, hope for it, and love it as their true fatherland and life, while they must yet remain and linger here in exile—as we sing in the hymn about the Holy Spirit, "As homeward we journey from this exile. Lord, have mercy."[284] We shall now speak of this.

First, the holy Christian people are recognized by their possession of the holy word of God.[285] To be sure, not all have it in equal measure, as St. Paul says [1 Cor. 3:12-14]. Some possess the word in its complete purity; others do not. Those who have the pure word are called those who "build on the foundation with gold, silver, and precious stones"; those who do not have it in its purity are the ones who "build on the foundation with wood, hay, and straw," and yet will be saved through fire. More than enough was said about this above. This is the principal item, and the holiest of holy possessions,[286] by reason of which the Christian people are called holy; for God's word is holy and sanctifies everything it touches; it is indeed the very holiness of God, Rom. 1[:16], "It is the power of God for salvation to everyone who has faith," and 1 Tim. 4[:5], "For it is sanctified by God's word and by prayer." For the Holy Spirit himself administers it and anoints or sanctifies the Christian church with it rather than with the pope's chrism,[287] with which he anoints or consecrates fingers, garb, cloaks, chalices, and stones. These objects will never teach one to love God, to believe, to praise, to be pious. They may adorn the bag of maggots,[y] but afterward they fall apart and decay with the chrism and whatever holiness it contains, and with the bag of maggots itself.

Yet this holy possession is the true holy possession, the true ointment that anoints unto life eternal, even though you cannot have a papal crown or a bishop's hat, but must die bare and naked, just like children (in fact, all of us), who are baptized naked and without any adornment. But we are speaking of the external word, preached orally by men like you and me, for this is what Christ left behind as an external sign, by which his church, or his Christian people in the world, should be recognized. We also speak of this external word as it is sincerely believed and openly professed before the world, as Christ says, "Everyone therefore who acknowledges me before others, I also will acknowledge before my Father and his angels"[z] [Matt. 10:32]. There are many who know it in their hearts, but will not profess it openly. Many possess it, but do not believe in it or act by it, for the number of those who believe in and act by it is small—as the parable of the seed in Matt. 13[:4-8] says that three sections of the field receive and contain the seed, but only the fourth section, the fine and good soil, bears fruit with patience.

Now, wherever you hear or see this word preached, believed, professed, and lived, do not doubt that the true *ecclesia sancta catholica*, "a Christian holy people" must be there, even though their number is very small. For God's word "shall not return empty," Isa. 55[:11], but must have at least a fourth or a fraction of the field. And even if there were no other sign than this alone, it would still suffice to prove that a Christian, holy people must exist there, for God's word cannot be without God's people, and

284. The fourth line of a pre-Reformation hymn adapted by Luther in 1524, "Now Let Us Pray to the Holy Ghost." LW 53:263–64.

285. As Luther enumerates how the church can be recognized in the world, he uses the language of "sign" (*Zeichen*). Though the idea of marks of the church (*notae ecclesiae*) had been used in the fifteenth century, its purpose was to exclude from the church. Here Luther speaks of how the church can be recognized by these signs or marks, which became the tradition of using the marks in the sixteenth century. Note that even those who do not have the word in its purity are understood to be God's people. See Gordon W. Lathrop and Timothy J. Wengert, *Christian Assembly: Marks of the Church in a Pluralistic Age* (Minneapolis: Fortress Press, 2004), 17–36.

286. *Heiligthum* or *Heilthum*. These words recur continually in the following section. The term "holy possession" conveys both the meaning of "sanctuary" and "relic." Luther plays constantly on the idea of wonder-working objects of reverence when he speaks of the marks of the church.

287. Holy oil used to anoint, or bless, objects and people.

y *Madensack*, i.e., the body that goes to decay.

z NRSV, "Father in heaven."

conversely, God's people cannot be without God's word. Otherwise, who would preach or hear it preached, if there were no people of God? And what could or would God's people believe, if there were no word of God?

This is the thing that performs all miracles, effects, sustains, carries out, and does everything, exorcises all devils, like pilgrimage-devils, indulgence-devils, bull-devils, brotherhood-devils, saint-devils, Mass-devils, purgatory-devils, monastery-devils, priest-devils, mob-devils, insurrection-devils, heresy-devils, all pope-devils, also Antinomian-devils, but not without raving and rampaging, as is seen in the poor men mentioned in Mark 1[:23-26] and 9[:17-29]. No, the devil must depart with raving and rampaging as is evidenced by Emser,[288] Eck,[289] Snot-nose,[290] Schmid,[291] Wetzel,[292] Bumpkin, Boor, Churl, Brute, Sow, Ass,[a] and the rest of his screamers and scribes. They all are the devil's mouths and members, through whom he raves and rampages. But it does them no good. He must take his leave; he is unable to endure the power of the word. They themselves confess that it is God's word and Holy Scripture, claiming, however, that one fares better with the fathers and the councils. Let them go their way. It is enough for us to know how this chief holy possession purges, sustains, nourishes, strengthens, and protects the church, as St. Augustine also says, "The church is begotten, cared for, nourished, and strengthened by the word of God."[293] But those who persecute and condemn it identify themselves by their own fruits.

Second, God's people or the Christian holy people are recognized by the holy sacrament of baptism, wherever it is taught, believed, and administered correctly according to Christ's ordinance. That too is a public sign and a precious, holy possession by which God's people are sanctified. It is the holy bath of regeneration through the Holy Spirit [Titus 3:5], in which we bathe and with which we are washed of sin and death by the Holy Spirit, as in the innocent holy blood of the Lamb of God. Wherever you see this sign you may know that the church, or the holy Christian people, must surely be present, even if the pope does not baptize you or even if you know nothing of his holiness and power—just as the little children know nothing of it, although when they are grown, they are, sad to say, estranged from their baptism,[294] as

a Probably names suggested by the sound of "Wetzel," which lose their force in translation.

288. Jerome Emser (1478–1527), a humanist who became an adviser to Duke George of Saxony (1471–1539), Catholic ruler of Saxony and an enemy of Luther. Cf. Luther's polemic tract *To the Leipzig Goat* (1521), LW 39:105–115.

289. Johann Eck (1486–1543), known for his debate with Luther at Leipzig in 1519. Cf. LW 31:309–325.

290. *Rotzleffel*, a German term for "impudent young rascal" and Luther's name for Johann Cochlaeus (1479–1552), a Catholic theologian who was a fanatic opponent of the Reformation and the author of *Memoirs on the Actions and Writings of Martin Luther* (*Commentaria de actis et scriptis M. Lutheri*) (1549), a polemic biography of Luther. See Ralph Keen, "Cochlaeus," OER 1:369–71.

291. John Faber (1478–1541), the son of a smith (*faber* in Latin, *Schmid* in German) and bishop in Vienna. He had been writing polemic tracts against Luther since 1521.

292. Used as a name for dogs and as a pun on Georg Witzel (1501–1573), who was originally a follower of Luther but since 1533 had been an opponent of the Reformation and a protégé of Duke George of Saxony.

293. *Ecclesia verbo dei generatur, alitur nutritur, roboratur.* The saying could not be located in Augustine's writings.

294. Luther contended that Christians in his day had not been taught to turn to their baptism for the assurance of forgiveness in Christ but had been instructed to rely on the sacrament of penance. As a result, they did not value baptism.

St. Peter laments in 2 Pet. 2[:18], "They entice with licentious passions of the flesh men who have barely escaped from those who live in error," etc. Indeed, you should not even pay attention to who baptizes, for baptism does not belong to the baptizer, nor is it given to the baptizer, but it belongs to the baptized. It was ordained for them by God, and given to them by God, just as the word of God is not the preacher's (except insofar as the preacher too hears and believes it) but belongs to the disciples who hear and believe it; to them is it given.[b]

Third, God's people, or Christian holy people, are recognized by the holy Sacrament of the Altar, wherever it is rightly administered, believed, and received, according to Christ's institution. This too is a public sign and a precious, holy possession left behind by Christ, by which his people are sanctified so that they also exercise themselves in faith and openly confess that they are Christian, just as they do with the word and with baptism. And here too you need not be disturbed if the pope does not say Mass for you, does not consecrate, anoint, or vest you with a chasuble. Indeed, you may, like a patient in bed, receive this sacrament without wearing any garb, except that outward decency obliges you to be properly covered. Moreover, you need not ask whether you have a tonsure or are anointed. In addition, the question of whether you are male or female, young or old, need not be argued—just as little as it matters in baptism and the preached word. It is enough that you are consecrated and anointed with the sublime and holy chrism of God, with the word of God, with baptism, and also this sacrament; then you are anointed highly and gloriously enough and sufficiently vested with priestly garments.

Moreover, don't be led astray by the question of whether the man who administers the sacrament is holy, or whether or not he has two wives. The sacrament belongs to the one who receives it, not to him who administers it, unless the one who administers also receives it. In that case he is one of those who receives it, and thus it is also given to him.[295] Wherever you see this sacrament properly administered, there you may be assured of the presence of God's people. For, as was said above of the word, wherever God's word is, there the church must be; likewise, wherever baptism and the sacrament are, God's people must be, and vice

295. Luther speaks here about receiving the Sacrament, as opposed to hearing Mass. The average person received communion only once a year in the Roman church of his day, more frequent communion being generally practiced only by priests, in monastic communities, and by a few laypeople. The laity communed more frequently in the Lutheran churches.

b The original text here is singular rather than plural.

versa. No others have, give, practice, use, and confess these holy possessions save God's people alone, even though some false and unbelieving Christians are secretly among them. They, however, do not profane the people of God because they are not known; the church, or God's people, does not tolerate known sinners in its midst, but reproves them and also makes them holy. Or, if they refuse, it casts them out from the sanctuary by means of the ban and regards them as heathen, Matt. 18[:17].

Fourth, God's people, or holy Christians, are recognized by the office of the keys exercised publicly.[296] That is, as Christ decrees in Matt. 18[:15-20], if Christians sin, they[297] should be reproved; and if they do not mend their ways, they should be bound in their sins and cast out. If they do mend their ways, they should be absolved. That is the office of the keys.[298] Now the use of the keys is twofold, public and private. There are some people with consciences so tender and despairing that even if they have not been publicly condemned, they cannot find comfort until they have been individually absolved by the pastor. On the other hand, there are also some who are so obdurate that they neither recant in their heart and want their sins forgiven individually by the pastor, nor desist from their sins. Therefore the keys must be used differently, publicly and privately. Now where you see sins forgiven or reproved

Johannes Bugenhagen is pictured holding the keys (see above) on the Wittenberg Church altarpiece (1547) in this painting by Lucas Cranach the Elder and Lucas Cranach the Younger.

296. In 1530, Luther had written at length on the proper practice of confession and absolution over against the papal misuse of confession and misunderstanding of the power (i.e., the keys of the kingdom) Christ had conferred on the church. *The Keys* (1530), LW 40:321-77.

297. This sentence and the one following use singular pronouns in the original.

298. See n. 151, p. 367.

in some persons, be it publicly or privately, you may know that God's people are there. If God's people are not there, the keys are not there; and if the keys are not there, God's people are not there. Christ bequeathed them as a public sign and a holy possession, whereby the Holy Spirit again sanctifies the fallen sinners redeemed by Christ's death, and whereby the Christians confess that they are a holy people in this world under Christ. And those who refuse to be converted or sanctified again shall be cast out from this holy people, that is, bound and excluded by means of the keys, as happened to the unrepentant Antinomians.

You must pay no heed here to the two keys of the pope, which he converted into two skeleton keys to the treasure chests and crowns of all kings.[299] If he does not want to bind or reprove sin, whether it be publicly or privately (as he really does not), let it be reproved and bound in your parish. If he will not loose, or forgive it, let it be loosed and forgiven in your parish, for his retaining or binding, his remitting or releasing, makes you neither holy nor unholy, since he can only have skeleton keys, not the true keys. The keys belong not to the pope (as he lies) but to the church, that is, to God's people, or to the holy Christian people throughout the entire world, or wherever there are Christians. They cannot all be in Rome, unless it be that the whole world is there first—which will not happen in a long time. The keys are the pope's as little as baptism, the sacrament, and the word of God are, for they belong to the people of Christ and are called "the church's keys"[c] not "the pope's keys."[d]

Fifth, the church is recognized externally by the fact that it consecrates or calls ministers, or has offices that it is to administer. There must be bishops, pastors, or preachers, who publicly and privately give, administer, and use the aforementioned four things or holy possessions in behalf of and in the name of the church, or rather by reason of their institution by Christ, as St. Paul states in Eph. 4[:8], "He received gifts among men . . ."[e]—his

299. In the 1530 treatise, Luther had criticized the papal idea that one key pertained to power (*clavis potestatis*) and the other to knowledge (*clavis scientiae*). This understanding of the keys asserted papal power to issue commands and prohibitions and to judge all laws, doctrines, and human affairs. LW 40:353–56.

The keys of heaven insignia of Pope Paul III (r. 1534–1549), who was pope when Luther wrote this treatise.

c *Claves ecclesiae.*

d *Claves papae.*

e Here Luther quotes the wording of Psalm 68, from which the wording of Ephesians 4 is derived. In the quotation of the psalm in Ephesians, the word *received* is changed to *gave*. Paul's authority as an apostle was traditionally cited as justification for this change. The fact that these two verses were always kept closely together perhaps explains Luther's imprecise reference.

gifts were that some should be apostles, some prophets, some evangelists, some teachers and governors, etc.[f] The people as a whole cannot do these things, but must entrust or have them entrusted to one person. Otherwise, what would happen if everyone wanted to speak or administer, and no one wanted to give way to the other? It must be entrusted to one person, and he alone should be allowed to preach, to baptize, to absolve, and to administer the sacraments. The others should be content with this arrangement and agree to it. Wherever you see this done, be assured that God's people, the holy Christian people, are present.

It is, however, true that the Holy Spirit has excepted women, children, and incompetent people from this function, but chooses (except in emergencies) only competent males to fill this office, as one reads here and there in the epistles of St. Paul that a bishop must be pious, able to teach, and the husband of one wife[g]—and in 1 Cor. 14[:34] he says, "Women should be silent in the churches." In summary, it must be a competent and chosen man. Children, women, and other persons are not qualified for this office, even though they are able to hear God's word, to receive baptism, the sacrament, absolution, and are also true, holy Christians, as St. Peter says [1 Pet. 3:7].[300] Even nature and God's creation makes this distinction, implying that women (much less children or fools) cannot and shall not occupy positions of sovereignty, as experience also suggests and as Moses says in Gen. 3[:16], "You shall be subject to man." The gospel, however, does not abrogate this natural law, but confirms it as the ordinance and creation of God.

Here the pope will object through his loudmouths and brawlers of the devil, saying, "St. Paul does not speak only of pastors and preachers, but also of apostles, evangelists, prophets, and other high spiritual vocations; that is why there must be higher vocations in the church than those of pastors and preachers. What, Sir Luther, do you have to say now?" What do I have to say now? This is what I have to say: if they themselves would become apostles, evangelists, prophets, or would show me at least one among them—oh, what nonsense I am talking!—who is worth as much as a schoolboy or who is as well versed in Holy Scripture and in Christian doctrine as a seven-year-old girl,[301]

f Similar to language in Eph. 4:11.

g For example, 1 Tim. 3:2; Titus 1:6.

300. Although this statement seems obvious and sounds almost condescending today, it contrasted vividly with the clericalism of the Roman church. The church was frequently defined in the Middle Ages in terms of its hierarchy, meaning that all laypeople only received the actions of the clergy, and many among the clergy doubted whether any layperson could truly be a good Christian. That Luther particularly elevated women and children is significant in terms of redefining what it means to be Christian, and thus part of the church, as a matter of faith, since they could not hope to be elevated to the ranks of the clergy.

301. In *The Smalcald Articles* (Article XII), Luther had asserted that even a seven-year-old child knew what the church was. BC, 324; TAL 2:463.

I shall declare myself caught. Now I know for certain that an apostle, an evangelist, [or] a prophet knows more, or indeed as much, as a seven-year-old girl. (I am speaking about Holy Scripture and about faith.) For I thoroughly believe, more firmly than I believe in God, that they are acquainted with more human doctrine, and also with more villainy, because they are proving it before my very eyes by the things they are doing, and so they are apostles, evangelists, and prophets just as little as they are the church; that is to say, they are the devil's apostles, evangelists, and prophets. The true apostles, evangelists, and prophets preach God's word, not against God's word.

Now, if the apostles, evangelists, and prophets are no longer living, others must have replaced them and will replace them until the end of the world, for the church shall last until the end of the world [Matt. 28:20]. Apostles, evangelists, and prophets must therefore remain, no matter what their name, to promote God's word and work. The pope and his followers, who persecute God's word while admitting that it is true, must be very poor apostles, evangelists, and prophets, just like the devil and his angels. But why do I keep coming back to these shameful, filthy folk of the pope? Let them go again, and bid them not to return, or etc.

Just as was said earlier about the other four parts of the great, divine, holy possession by which the holy church is sanctified, that you need not care who or how those from whom you receive it are, so again you should not ask who and how he is who gives it to you or has the office. For all of it is given, not to him who has the office, but to those who are to receive it through this office, except that he can receive it together with you if he so desires. Let him be what he will. Because he is in office and is tolerated by the assembly, you put up with him too. His person will make God's word and sacraments neither worse nor better for you. What he says or does is not his, but Christ, your Lord, and the Holy Spirit say and do everything, insofar as he adheres to correct doctrine and practice. The church, of course, cannot and should not tolerate open vices; but you yourself be content and tolerant, since you, an individual, cannot be the whole assembly or the Christian holy people.

[Here we omit Luther's discussion of the prohibition of married priests in terms very similar to a sermon he preached on 2 March 1539 (WA 47:671–78).][302]

302. The omitted section can be found in LW 41:156–64.

Sixth, the holy Christian people are externally recognized by prayer, public praise, and thanksgiving to God. Where you see and hear the Lord's Prayer prayed and taught; or psalms or other spiritual songs sung, in accordance with the word of God and the true faith; also the Creed, the Ten Commandments, and the catechism used in public, you may rest assured that a holy Christian people of God are present. For prayer, too, is one of the precious holy possessions whereby everything is sanctified, as St. Paul says [1 Tim. 4:5]. The psalms too are nothing but prayers in which we praise, thank, and glorify God. The Creed and the Ten Commandments are also God's word and belong to the holy possession, whereby the Holy Spirit sanctifies the holy people of Christ.[303] However, we are now speaking of prayers and songs that are intelligible and from which we can learn and by means of which we can mend our ways. The clamor of monks and nuns and priests is not prayer, nor is it praise to God; for they do not understand it, nor do they learn anything from it; they do it like a donkey, only for the sake of the belly and not at all in quest of any reform or sanctification or of the will of God.

Seventh, the holy Christian people are externally recognized by the holy possession of the sacred cross. They must endure every misfortune and persecution, all kinds of trials and evil from the devil, the world, and the flesh (as the Lord's Prayer indicates) by inward sadness, timidity, fear, outward poverty, contempt, illness, and weakness, in order to become like their head, Christ. And the only reason they must suffer is that they steadfastly adhere to Christ and God's word, enduring this for the sake of Christ, Matt. 5[:11], "Blessed are you when people persecute you on my account." They must be pious, quiet, obedient, and prepared to serve the government and everybody with life and goods, doing no one any harm. No people on earth have to endure such bitter hate; they must be accounted worse than Jews, heathen, and Turks.[304] In summary, they must be called heretics, knaves, and devils, the most pernicious people on earth, to the point where those who hang, drown, murder, torture, banish, and plague them to death are rendering God a service. No one has compassion on them; they are given myrrh and gall to drink when they thirst. And all of this is done not because they are adulterers, murderers, thieves, or rogues, but because they want to have none but Christ, and no other God. Wherever you see or hear this, you may know that the holy Christian church

303. Luther demonstrated how to pray the catechism in *A Simple Way to Pray* (1535), LW 43:187–211; WA 38:358–75; TAL 4:253–81.

304. Medieval theologians used the phrase "pagans, Jews, and heretics" to define those outside the church. Luther uses "Jews, heathens, and Turks" in a similar way to account for all who are not Christians.

is there, as Christ says in Matt. 5[:11-12], "Blessed are you when people revile you and utter all kinds of evil against you on my account. Rejoice and be glad, for your reward is great in heaven." This too is a holy possession whereby the Holy Spirit not only sanctifies his people, but also blesses them.[305]

Meanwhile, pay no heed to the papists' holy possessions from dead saints, from the wood of the holy cross.[306] For these are just as often bones taken from a carrion pit as bones of saints, and just as often wood taken from gallows as wood from the holy cross. There is nothing but fraud in this. The pope thus tricks people out of their money and alienates them from Christ. Even if it were a genuine holy possession, it would nonetheless not sanctify anyone. But when you are condemned, cursed, reviled, slandered, and plagued because of Christ, you are sanctified. It mortifies the old Adam and teaches him patience, humility, gentleness, praise and thanks, and good cheer in suffering. That is what it means to be sanctified by the Holy Spirit and to be renewed to a new life in Christ; in that way we learn to believe in God, to trust him, to love him, and to place our hope in him, as Rom. 5[:1-5] says, "Suffering produces hope," etc.

These are the true seven principal parts[307] of the great holy possession whereby the Holy Spirit effects in us a daily sanctification and vivification in Christ, according to the first table of Moses. By this we obey it, albeit never as perfectly as Christ. But we constantly strive to attain the goal, under his redemption or remission of sin, until we too shall one day become perfectly holy and no longer stand in need of forgiveness. Everything is directed toward that goal. I would even call these seven parts the seven sacraments, but since that term has been misused by the papists and is used in a different sense in Scripture, I shall let them stand as the seven principal parts of Christian sanctification or the seven holy possessions of the church.[308]

[Other Outward Signs of the Church]

In addition to these seven principal parts there are other outward signs that identify the Christian church, namely, those signs whereby the Holy Spirit sanctifies us according to the second table of Moses; when he assists us in sincerely honoring our father and mother, and conversely, when he helps them to raise their children in a Christian way and to lead honorable lives;

305. See n. 307.

306. Bones of saints and pieces of the true cross were common relics in the Middle Ages. As Luther observes, their source and background were often questionable.

307. In summary, Luther's seven principal parts, or marks, of belonging to God's people are: the word of God; baptism; sacrament of the altar; office of the keys; consecrated ministers; prayer, praise, and thanksgiving to God; and possession of the holy cross (suffering).

308. The idea that there should be seven sacraments was of great antiquity, but *which* seven were the chief sacraments, along with the recognition that these were the only sacraments, became standard only in the twelfth century. The "different sense" in which Luther says the word is used in Scripture refers to the fact that the Greek word *mysterion* (mystery) was translated into Latin as *sacramentum*.

when we faithfully serve our princes and lords and are obedient and subject to them, and conversely, when they love their subjects and protect and guard them;[309] also when we bear no one a grudge, entertain no anger, hatred, envy, or vengefulness toward our neighbors, but gladly forgive them, lend to them, help them, and counsel them; when we are not lewd, not drunkards, not proud, arrogant, overbearing, but chaste, self-controlled, sober, friendly, kind, gentle, and humble; when we do not steal, rob, are not usurious, greedy, do not overcharge, but are mild, kind, content, charitable; when we are not false, mendacious, perjurers, but truthful, trustworthy, and do whatever else is taught in these commandments—all of which St. Paul teaches abundantly in more than one place. We need the Decalogue[310] not only to apprise us of our lawful obligations, but we also need it to discern how far the Holy Spirit has worked sanctification in us and by how much we still fall short of the goal, lest we become secure and imagine that we have now done all that is required.[311] Thus we must constantly grow in sanctification and always become new creatures in Christ. This means "grow" and "do so more and more" [2 Pet. 3:18].

However, these signs cannot be regarded as being as reliable as those noted before since some heathen too practice these works and indeed at times appear holier than Christians; yet their actions do not issue from the heart purely and simply, for the sake of God, but they search for some other end because they lack a real faith in and a true knowledge of God. But here is the Holy Spirit, who sanctifies the heart and produces these fruits from "an honest and good heart," as Christ says in the parable recorded in Matt. 13 [Luke 8:15]. Since the first table is greater and must be a holier possession, I have summarized everything in the second table. Otherwise, I could have divided it too into seven holy possessions or seven principal parts, according to the seven commandments.

Now we know for certain what, where, and who the holy Christian church is, that is, the holy Christian people of God; and we are quite certain that it cannot fail us. Everything else may fail and surely does, as we shall hear in part. Representatives should be selected from this people to form a council; that might be a council ruled by the Holy Spirit. Thus Lyra, too, writes that the church is not to be assessed by the high or spiritual vocations in it, but by the people who truly believe.[312] I am surprised that

309. Luther had given precisely this advice to Christian princes in the third section of *Temporal Authority: To What Extent It Should Be Obeyed* (1523), LW 45:118–29; WA 11:271–81; TAL 5, forthcoming.

310. The Ten Commandments.

311. Luther refers here to the civil and theological uses of the law.

312. Nicholas of Lyra (1270–1340), a Franciscan theologian and famous interpreter of the Bible. Luther frequently quotes him, as does Melanchthon, who quoted this statement of Lyra's in the *Apology of the Augsburg Confession*, Arts. VII, VIII; BC, 174–83. The quotation Luther cites is found in *Comments on Matthew XVI (Annotationes in Matth. XVI)*. See WA 50:644, n. *a*. Five volumes of Lyra's works were published in 1471–72 in Rome. ODCC, 1158.

he was not burned at the stake for these words, for denying that popes, cardinals, bishops, and prelates compose the church; this amounts to abominable heresy, intolerable and offensive to the holy Roman church. More about this elsewhere.[h]

Now when the devil saw that God built such a holy church, he was not idle, and erected his chapel beside it, larger than God's church. This is how he did it: he noticed that God utilized outward things, such as baptism, word, sacrament, keys, etc., whereby God sanctified his church. And since the devil is always God's ape, trying to imitate all God's things and to improve on them, he also tried his luck with external things purported to make people holy—just as he tries with rain-makers, sorcerers, exorcists of devils, etc. He even has the Lord's Prayer recited and the gospel read over them to make it appear a great holy possession. Thus he had popes and papists consecrate or sanctify water, salt, herbs, candles, bells, images, *Agnus Dei*, pallia,[313] altars, chasubles, tonsures, fingers, hands—who can tell it all?—finally the monks' cowls to a degree that many people died and were buried in them, believing that thereby they would be saved. Now it would have been fine indeed if God's word or a blessing or a prayer were spoken over these created things, as children do over their food or over themselves when they go to bed and when they arise. St. Paul says of this, "Everything created by God is good, for it is sanctified by God's word and prayer" [1 Tim. 4:4-5]. The creature derives no new power from such a practice, but is strengthened in its former power.

But the devil has a different purpose in mind. He wants the creature to derive new strength and power from his aping tomfoolery. Just as water becomes baptism by the power of God, a bath unto eternal life, washing away sin and bringing salvation, a power which is not inherent in water; just as bread and wine become the body and blood of Christ; just as sins are remitted by the laying on of hands in accordance with God's institution—so the devil too wants his mummery and aping tomfoolery to be strong and imbued with supernatural power. Holy water is to blot out sin, exorcise devils, fend off evil spirits, protect women in childbed, as the pope teaches us in the *Aquam sale, de pe*;[314] they say consecrated salt does the same thing. An *Agnus*

h Cf. *The Smalcald Articles*, Art. IV; BC, 307–310; TAL 2:438–43.

313. *Agnus Dei*, as used here, were amulets usually made of wax and stamped with the image of a lamb. The *pallium* (pl.: *pallia*) was a band made of white wool and decorated with black crosses that marked the bishop of an important see, or *metropolitan* bishop. It became controversial in the Middle Ages when the popes began to charge a "pallium fee" for its bestowal.

314. *Aquam sale*, a section in canon law dealing with consecration, according to which holy salt is used in rites of purification. *De pe* is either a slip of the pen for *de co* (*de consecratione*) or Luther's abbreviation for *de poenitentia*, the title of the chapter on penitence. Cf. *Decreti tertia pars: De consecratione*, dist. III, C. XX (CIC 1:1358).

A depiction of Anselm assuming the pallium signifying his office as Archbishop of Canterbury. He held the office from 1093 to 1109.

Dei consecrated by the pope is to do even more than God can do, as this is described in verses that I should some day publish with marginal notes.[i] Bells are to drive away devils in thunderstorms. St. Anthony's knives stab the devil;[315] consecrated herbs expel venomous worms; some blessings heal cows, keep off milk thieves,[316] and quench fire; certain letters give security in war and at other times against iron, fire, water, wild beasts, etc.;[317] monasticism, Masses, and the like are said to confer more than ordinary salvation. Who can tell it all? There was no need so small that the devil did not institute a sacrament or holy possession for it, whereby one could receive advice and help. In addition, he had prophetesses, soothsayers, and sages able to reveal hidden things and to retrieve stolen goods.

Oh, he is far better equipped with sacraments, prophets, apostles, and evangelists than God, and his chapels are much larger than God's church; and he has far more people in his holiness than God. One is also more inclined to believe his promises, his sacraments, and his prophets than Christ. He is the great god of the world. Christ calls him "ruler of the world" [John 12:31; 14:30; 16:11] and Paul "the god of this world" [2 Cor. 4:4]. With this aping tomfoolery he estranges people from faith in Christ and causes the word and the sacraments of Christ to be despised and almost unrecognizable because it is easier to perceive such things than to blot out sin, help in time of need, receive salvation through the devil's sacraments rather than through Christ's. For it is Christ's will to make people holy and pious in body and soul through his Holy Spirit and not let them remain in unbelief and sin. This is too hard for those who do not wish to be pious or to desist from sin. They can readily dispense with this work of the Holy Spirit after they learn how they can be saved more easily without him—for example, by holy water, *Agnus Dei*, bulls and breves,[318] Masses and cowls—thus making it unnecessary to seek or heed anything else.

But not only that! The devil has armed himself with these things in order to abolish God's word and sacraments with them. This is the devil's line of thought: if someone arises to attack my church, sacraments, and bishops, saying that exter-

315. Although the story of St. Anthony's life makes it obvious that he should be invoked against demonic temptation, no reference to knives related to the saint could be found.

316. I.e., witches who make cows go dry.

317. In 1518 Luther dealt with these ecclesiastical customs more favorably. Cf., for example, *The Decalog, Preached to the People of Wittenberg* (1518) (*Decem praecepta, Wittenbergensi praedicata populo*), WA 1:401.

318. A breve is a writ of law issued by the papal court.

i Cf. Luther's notes *On the Blessed Water and the Agnus Dei of the Pope* (1539) (*Von dem Geweihtem Wasser und des Papstes Agnus Dei*), WA 50:668–73.

nal things do not save, then God's word and sacraments shall perish with them, for these too are external signs and his church and bishops are also human beings. If mine do not stand approved, God's will stand approved even less, especially because my church, bishops, and sacraments work promptly and help now and in this life, visibly and tangibly, for I am present in them and help quickly, as soon as it is desired. Christ's sacraments, however, work spiritually and invisibly and for the future so that his church and bishops can only be smelled, as it were, faintly and from afar, and the Holy Spirit behaves as though he were absent, permitting people to endure every misfortune and making them appear as heretics in the eyes of my church. Meanwhile, my church is not only so close that one can actually grasp it, but also my works follow very quickly; so everyone assumes that it is the true church of God. This is the advantage I have.

Lampoon of the papal seal (1538). Woodcut made according to Luther's directions by the monogramist BP.

And that is what happened. When we began to teach, on the basis of the gospel, that these external things do not save, since they are merely physical and creatural and are often used by the devil for the purpose of sorcery, people, even great and learned people, concluded that baptism, being external water, that the word, being outward human speech, that Scripture, being physical letters made with ink, that the bread, being baked by the baker, and the wine were nothing more than outward, perishable things. So they devised the slogan, "Spirit! Spirit! The Spirit must do it! The letter kills!" So Müntzer[319] called us Wittenberg theologians scribes of Scripture and himself the scribe of the Holy Spirit, and many others followed his example. There you see how the devil had armed himself and built up his barricades. If anyone were to attack his outward doctrine and sacraments (which afford quick, visible, and mighty aid), then the outward words and sacraments of Christ (attended by tardy or, at least, by invisible and feeble help) must go down to far worse destruction along with them.

319. Thomas Müntzer (1489–1525), labeled the "restless spirit of Allstedt" by Luther, became a leader of the rebellious peasants in the Peasants' War of 1525. The passage is found in Hans J. Hillerbrand, "Thomas Müntzer's Last Tract Against Martin Luther," *The Mennonite Quarterly Review* 38 (1964): 26; see also TAL 2:39–126.

Therefore the *ecclesia*, "the holy Christian people," does not have mere external words, sacraments, or offices, like God's ape Satan has, and in far greater numbers, but it has these as commanded, instituted, and ordained by God, so that he himself and not any angel will work through them with the Holy Spirit. They are called word, baptism, sacrament, and office of forgiveness, not of angels, human beings, or any other creature, but of God; only God does not choose to do it through his unveiled, brilliant, and glorious majesty, out of consideration for us poor, weak, and timid mortals and for our comfort, for who could bear such majesty for an instant in this poor and sinful flesh? As Moses says, "No one shall see me and live" [Exod. 33:20]. If the Jews could not endure even the shoes of God's feet on Mount Sinai, that is, the thunder and the clouds, how could they, with their feeble eyes, have endured the sight of the sun of his divine majesty and the clear light of his countenance? No, God wants to work through tolerable, kind, and pleasant means, which we ourselves could not have chosen better. God has, for instance, a godly and kind man speak to us, preach, lay his hands on us, remit sin, baptize, give us bread and wine to eat and to drink. Who can be terrified by these pleasing methods, and wouldn't rather delight in them with all his heart?

Well then, that is just what is done for us feeble human beings, and in it we see how God deals with us as with beloved children and not, as would surely be God's right, in his majesty. And yet, in this guise God performs majestic, divine works and exercises might and power, such as forgiving sin, cleansing from sin, removing death, bestowing grace and eternal life. Indeed, these things are missing in the devil's sacraments and churches. No one can say there, "God commanded it, ordered it, instituted it, and ordained it; God is certainly present and will do everything"; but one must say, "God did not command, but forbade it. Man, or rather that ape of God, invented it and misled the people with it." For he effects nothing except that which is temporal, or, if it purports to be spiritual, it is sheer fraud. He cannot forgive sin eternally and save, as he lyingly claims, by means of holy water, Masses, and monkery, even though he may restore a cow's milk that he had first stolen from her by his prophetesses and priestesses. Among Christians these are called the devil's harlots and, when apprehended, are rightfully burned at the stake, not because of the theft of milk, but because of the blasphemy with which they fortify the devil, his sacraments, and his churches against Christ.[j]

In summary, if God were to bid you to pick up a straw or to pluck out a feather with the command, order, and promise that thereby you would have forgiveness of all sin, grace, and eternal life, should you not accept this joyfully and gratefully, and cherish, praise, prize, and esteem that straw and that feather as a higher and holier possession than heaven and earth? No matter how insignificant the straw and the feather may be, you would nonetheless acquire through them something more valuable than heaven and earth, indeed, than all the angels, are able to bestow on you. Why then are we such disgraceful people that we do not regard the water of baptism, the bread and wine, that is, Christ's body and blood, the spoken word, and the laying on of man's hands for the forgiveness of sin as such holy possessions, as we would the straw and feather, though in the former, as we hear and know, God wishes to be effective and wants them to be his water, word, hand, bread, and wine, by means of which he wishes to sanctify and save you in Christ, who acquired this for us and who gave us the Holy Spirit from the Father for this work?

On the other hand, what good would it do you even if you went to St. James,[320] clad in armor, or let yourself be killed by the severe life of the Carthusians, Franciscans, or Dominicans in order to be saved, and God had neither commanded nor instituted it? God still knows nothing about all this, but you and the devil invented them, as special sacraments or classes of priests. And even if you were able to bear heaven and earth in order to be saved, it would still all be lost; and the one who would pick up the straw (if this were commanded) would do more than you, even if you could carry ten worlds. Why is that? It is God's will that we obey his word, use his sacraments, and honor his church. Then God will act graciously and gently enough, even more graciously and gently than we could desire; for it is written, "I am the Lord your God; you shall have no other gods before

320. A reference to the shrine of St. James of Compostela in Spain, where according to Spanish tradition the apostle's remains were brought after he was martyred in 44 (see Acts 12:2). Christians pilgrimages to this shrine and other sites were common in late medieval Europe, but Luther criticized such pilgrimages as self-centered, providing an illusion of doing good works, thereby escaping the demands of living faith in daily life.

j See Edward Peters, *The Magician, the Witch, and the Law* (Philadelphia: University of Pennsylvania Press, 1978), esp. ch. 6; Richard Kieckhefer, *Magic in the Middle Ages* (Cambridge: Cambridge University Press, 1990), 80–85; Karen Jolly, Catharina Raudvere, and Edward Peters, *Witchcraft and Magic in Europe: The Middle Ages* (Philadelphia: University of Pennsylvania Press, 2002), 238–45.

me" [Exod. 20:23]. And, "Listen to him and to no other" [Matt. 17:5]. May that suffice on the church. More cannot be said unless each point is elaborated further. The rest must deal with different ideas, about which we want to speak too.

Besides these external signs and holy possessions the church has other externals that do not sanctify it either in body or soul, nor were they instituted or commanded by God; but, as we said at length above, they are outwardly necessary or useful, proper and good—for instance, certain holidays and certain hours—forenoon or afternoon—set aside for preaching or praying, or the use of a church building or house, altar, pulpit, baptismal font, candlesticks, candles, bells, priestly vestments, and the like. These things have no more than their natural effects, just as food and drink accomplish no more because of the childrens' *Benedicite* or *Gratias*,[321] for the ungodly or rude folk who don't say it, that is, who neither pray to nor thank God, grow just as fat and strong from food and drink as Christians do. To be sure, Christians could be and remain sanctified even without these items, even if they were to preach on the street, outside a building, without a pulpit, if absolution were pronounced and the sacrament administered without an altar, and if baptism were performed without a font—as happens daily that for special reasons sermons are preached and baptisms and sacraments administered in the home. But for the sake of children and simple folk, it is a fine thing and conducive to good order to have a definite time, place, and hour to which people can adapt themselves and where they may assemble, as St. Paul says in 1 Cor. 14[:40], "All things should be done decently and in order." And no one should (as no Christian does) ignore such order without cause, out of mere pride or just to create disorder, but one should join in observing such order for the sake of the multitude, or at least should not disrupt or hinder it, for that would be acting contrary to love and friendliness.

321. I.e., table prayers.

Nevertheless, there should be freedom here: for instance, if we are unable, because of an emergency or another significant reason, to preach at six or seven, at twelve or one o'clock, on Sunday or Monday, in the choir or at St. Peter's, one may preach at a different hour, day, or place, just as long as one does not confuse the people, but properly apprises them of such a change. These matters are purely external (as far as time, place, and persons are concerned) and may be regulated entirely by reason, to which they are altogether subject. God, Christ, and the Holy Spirit are not interested in them—just as little as they are interested in what we wish to eat, drink, wear, and whom we marry, or where we want to dwell, walk, or stand; except that (as was said) no one should, without reason, adopt a way that confuses or hinders the people.[322] Just as at a wedding or other social event no one should offend the bride or the company by doing something special or something that interferes, but one should join the rest, and sit, walk, stand, dance, eat, and drink with them. For it is impossible to order a special table for each individual, and also a special kitchen, cellar, and servant. If the guests want anything, let them get up from the table and leave the others to sit in peace.[k] Thus here too everything must be conducted peacefully and in order, and yet there must be freedom if time, person, or other reasons demand a change; then the masses will also follow harmoniously, since (as was said) no Christian is thereby made any more or less holy.

The pope, to be sure, has scribbled the whole world full of books about these things and fashioned them into bonds, laws, rights, articles of faith, sin, and holiness so that his decretal really deserves, once again, to be consigned to the fire.[323] For we

322. Luther criticized the people of Wittenberg on precisely this point as a result of the way they implemented reform while he was in hiding in the Wartburg castle. See *The Eight Sermons at Wittenberg* (*The Invocavit Sermons*, 1522), LW 51:67–100; WA 10/III:1–64; TAL 4:7–45.

323. On 10 December 1520, in Wittenberg, Luther burned copies of the canon law along with the bull *Exsurge domine*, which threatened him with excommunication. "This book" in the next sentence is a reference to canon law.

Martin Luther burning the papal bull threatening him with excommunication (1520).

k The original here is singular.

could do well without this book that has caused so much great harm. It has pushed Holy Scripture aside and practically suppressed Christian doctrine; it has also subjected the jurists, with their imperial law, to it. Thus it has trodden both church and emperor underfoot; in their stead it presented us with these stupid asses, the canonists, these will-o'-the-wisps who rule the church with it and, still more deplorable, left the best parts in it and took the worst out, foisting them on the church. Whatever good there is in it, one can find much better and more richly in Holy Scripture, indeed, also in St. Augustine alone, as far as teaching Christendom is concerned; and then, as far as temporal government is concerned, also in the books of the jurists. For the jurists themselves once contemplated throwing this book out of jurisprudence and leaving it to the theologians. However, it would have been far better to throw it into the fire and reduce it to ashes, although there is something good in it, for how could sheer evil exist unless there was some good with it? But there is too much evil, so much that it crowds out the good, and (as was said) a greater measure of good is to be found in Scripture and also in the fathers and among the jurists. Of course, it might be kept in the libraries as evidence of the folly and the mistakes of the popes, some of the councils, and other teachers. That is why I am keeping it.

We will regard these externals as we do a christening robe[324] or swaddling clothes in which a child is clad for baptism. The child is not baptized or sanctified either by the christening robe or by the swaddling clothes, but only by the baptism. And yet reason dictates that a child be thus clothed. If this garment is soiled or torn, it is replaced by another, and the child grows up without any help from swaddling clothes or christening robe. Here too one must exercise moderation and not use too many of these garments, lest the child be smothered. Similarly, moderation should also be observed in the use of ceremonies, lest they become a burden and a chore. They must remain so light that they are not felt, just as at a wedding no one thinks it a chore or a burden to conform his actions to those of the other people present. I shall write on the special fasts when I write about the plague of the Germans, gluttony and drunkenness, for that properly belongs in the sphere of temporal government.[325]

Above and elsewhere[326] I have written much about the schools, urging firmness and diligence in caring for them. Although they

324. *Westerhemd* (from the Latin *vestis*, meaning "garment"). The robe was usually white (in accordance with Rev. 6:11) and was used in the early church to dress those to be baptized. Cf. WA 50:651, n. *a*.

325. Luther wrote about this in 1518 in his *Explanations of the Ninety-five Theses*, LW 31:86–88. See also his *Sermon on Soberness and Moderation* (1539), LW 51:289–99; WA 47:757–71.

326. See Luther's *To the Councilmen of All Cities in Germany That They Establish and Maintain Christian Schools* (1524), LW 45:339–78; WA 15:27–53; TAL 5, forthcoming; and *A Sermon on Keeping Children in School* (1530), LW 46:207–258; WA 30/II:517–88.

may be viewed as something external and pagan, in as much as they instruct boys in languages and the arts, they are nevertheless extremely necessary. For if we fail to train pupils we will not have pastors and preachers very long—as we are finding out. The school must supply the church with persons who can be made apostles, evangelists, and prophets, that is, preachers, pastors, and rulers, in addition to other people needed throughout the world, such as chancellors, councilors, secretaries, and the like, men who can also lend a hand with the temporal government. In addition, if the schoolteacher is a godly man and teaches the boys[327] to understand, to sing, and to practice God's word and the true faith and holds them to Christian discipline, then, as we said earlier, the schools are truly young and eternal councils, which perhaps do more good than many other great councils. Therefore the former emperors, kings, and princes did well when they showed such diligence in building many schools, high and low, monastic schools and convents, to provide the church with a rich and ample supply of people; but their successors shamefully perverted their use. Thus today princes and lords should do the same, and use the possessions of the cloisters for the maintenance of schools and provide many persons with the means for study.[328] If our descendants misuse these, we at least have done our duty in our day.

In summary, the schools must be second in importance only to the church, for in them young preachers and pastors are trained, and from them emerge those who replace the ones who die. Next, then, to the school comes the burgher's house, for it supplies the pupils; then the city hall and the castle, which must protect the schools so that they may train children to become pastors, and so that these, in turn, may create churches and children of God (whether they be burghers, princes, or emperors). But God must be over all and nearest to all, to preserve this ring or circle against the devil, and to do everything in all of life's vocations, indeed, in all creatures. Thus Ps. 127[:1] says that there are only two temporal governments on earth, that of the city and that of the home, "Unless the Lord builds the house; unless the Lord guards the city." The first government is that of the home, from which the people come; the second is that of the city, meaning the country, the people, princes and lords, which we call the secular government. These embrace everything—children, property, money, animals, etc. The home must produce,

327. In Luther's day, few children attended school, and those that did were boys. Luther himself advocated education for all children, both boys and girls. *To the Councilmen of All Cities in Germany That They Establish and Maintain Christian Schools* (1524), LW 45:339–78; WA 15:27–53; TAL 5, forthcoming.

328. Cf. *The Smalcald Articles*, Art. III; BC, 306.

whereas the city must guard, protect, and defend. Then follows the third, God's own home and city, that is, the church, which must obtain people from the home and protection and defense from the city.

These are the three hierarchies ordained by God, and we need no more; indeed, we have enough and more than enough to do in living aright and resisting the devil in these three. Just look only at the home and at the duties it alone imposes: parents and landlords must be obeyed; children and servants must be nourished, trained, ruled, and provided for in a godly spirit. The rule of the home alone would give us enough to do, even if there were nothing else. Then the city, that is, the secular government, also gives us enough to do if we show ourselves really obedient, and conversely, if we are to judge, protect, and promote land and people. The devil keeps us busy enough, and with him God gave us the sweat of our brow, thorns and thistles in abundance [Gen. 3:18-19], so that we have more than enough to learn, to live, to do, and to suffer in these two governments. Then there is the third rule and government. If the Holy Spirit reigns there, Christ calls it a comforting, sweet, and light burden [Matt. 11:30]; if not, it is not only a heavy, severe, and terrible task, but also an impossible one, as St. Paul says in Rom. 8[:3], "What the law could not do," and elsewhere, "The letter kills" [2 Cor. 3:6].

Now why should we have the blasphemous, bogus law or government of the pope over and above these three high divine governments, these three divine, natural, and temporal laws of God? It presumes to be everything, yet is in reality nothing. It leads us astray and tears us from these blessed, divine estates and laws. Instead, it dresses us in a mask or cowl, thereby making us the devil's fools and playthings, who are slothful and no longer know these three divine hierarchies or realms. That is why we no longer want to put up with it, but, acting in conformity with St. Peter's, St. Paul's, and St. Augustine's teaching, want to be rid of it and turn the words of Ps. 2[:3] against them, "Let us burst their bonds asunder, and cast their cords from us." Indeed, we shall sing with St. Paul, "Even if an angel from heaven should preach a gospel contrary to that, let him be accursed" [Gal. 1:8]; and we shall say with St. Peter, "Why do you put God to the test by putting such a yoke upon the neck?" [Acts 15:10]. Thus we shall again be the pope's masters and tread him underfoot, as Ps. 91[:13] says, "You will tread on the lion and the adder, the young lion and the serpent you will trample under foot." And that we shall do by the power and with the help of the woman's seed, who has crushed and still crushes the serpent's head, although we must run the risk that he, in turn, will bite us in the heel [Gen. 3:15]. To this blessed seed[329] of the woman be praise and honor, together with the Father and the Holy Spirit, to the one true God and Lord in eternity. Amen.

329. Jesus Christ.

Image Credits

xiii, xiv (maps): © 2006 Lucidity Information Design, LLC. Used by permission.

4, 249, 261,284, 306: Courtesy of Pitts Theological Library, Candler School of Theology, Emory University.

60, 95, 97, 111, 130, 136, 203, 280, 291, 295, 313, 321 (both), 325: Courtesy of the Richard C. Kessler Reformation Collection, Pitts Theological Library, Candler School of Theology, Emory University.

7, 12, 14, 16, 19, 31, 34, 39, 55, 70, 85, 93, 121, 143, 165, 167 (both), 175, 179, 183, 187, 213, 246, 252, 267, 276, 281, 298, 310, 318, 323, 334, 348, 351, 355, 362, 368, 375, 377, 399, 402, 415, 420, 422, 426, 427, 433: Wikimedia Commons.

8, 162: The Lutheran School of Theology at Chicago (Gruber Rare Books Collection). Used by permission.

188, 193: Zentralbibliothek Zürich. Used by permission.

335: "Leviticus with the ordinary gloss" (MS Typ 204) courtesy of Houghton Library, Harvard University.

337: Universal Images Group / Art Resource, NY.

341: Thompson Library Special Collections. The Ohio State University. Rare Books and Manuscripts Library. John Foxe's *Actes and Monuments* (*Book of Martyrs*). 1570 Edition. Used by permission.

345: Public domain.

Index of Scriptural References

OLD TESTAMENT
HEBREW BIBLE

NEW TESTAMENT

Index of Names

Index of Works by Martin Luther and Others

Index of Subjects